D1458397

Studies in Historical Archaeoethnology

Volume 4

THE VISIGOTHS
FROM THE MIGRATION PERIOD TO THE SEVENTH CENTURY

AN ETHNOGRAPHIC PERSPECTIVE

Studies in Historical Archaeoethnology

SERIES EDITOR: GIORGIO AUSENDA

Already published:

After Empire: Towards an Ethnology of Europe's Barbarians

The Anglo-Saxons from the Migration Period to the Eighth Century: An Ethnographic Perspective

Franks and Alamanni in the Merovingian Period: An Ethnographic Perspective

Forthcoming:

The Scandinavians from the Vendel Period to the Tenth Century: An Ethnographic Perspective

The Continental Saxons to the Carolingian Period

Forthcoming conferences:

The Ostrogoths from the Migration Period to the Sixth Century

The Langobards from the Migration Period to the Eighth Century

THE VISIGOTHS

FROM THE MIGRATION PERIOD TO THE SEVENTH CENTURY

AN ETHNOGRAPHIC PERSPECTIVE

Edited by

Peter Heather

THE BOYDELL PRESS

Center for Interdisciplinary Research on Social Stress
San Marino (R.S.M.)

First published 1999
The Boydell Press, Woodbridge

ISBN 0 85115 762 9

The Boydell Press is an imprint of Boydell & Brewer Ltd
PO Box 9, Woodbridge, Suffolk IP12 3DF, UK
and of Boydell & Brewer Inc.
PO Box 41026, Rochester, NY 14604-4126, USA
website http://www. boydell.co.uk

*This volume contains the papers presented
at the fourth conference on 'Studies in Historical Archaeoethnology'
organized by the Center for Interdisciplinary Research on Social Stress,
which was held in San Marino from 5th to 9th September 1996.*

A catalogue record for this book is available
from the British Library

Library of Congress Catalog Card Number 99-045402

Printed in the Republic of San Marino

CONTENTS

LIST OF MAPS

INTRODUCTION

PETER HEATHER

Dept. of History, University College, London University, Gower St., GB-London WC1E 6BT

The Visigoths in the Migration Period is the fourth volume to appear in a series produced under the auspices of CIROSS, the San Marino Center for Interdisciplinary Research on Social Stress (Ausenda 1995, Hines 1997, Wood 1998). Each volume contains revised versions of the papers originally produced by participants for discussion in the course of an intense three-day conference, together with written versions of the discussions themselves. As with the previous conferences and volumes in this series, the conference on the Visigoths presented in this book was driven forward by the idea that anthropological and other comparative materials are necessary to explicate the fragmentary and generically formal materials available for the study of the fall of the Roman Empire and its aftermath, and particularly of the groups of outsiders whose military power played a major role in its dismemberment. The topics of the papers were also set with an anthropologically analytical agenda in mind, the range of skills assembled included historians, philologists, and archaeologists, as well as a 'proper' anthropologist in the form of our host, Doctor Ausenda himself, and the discussions do, I think, reflect the commitment we all shared to think very broadly in methodological terms.

The history of the Visigothic kingdom and of the Visigoths themselves is inextricably linked to the fall of the Roman Empire. The Visigoths as such were actually a socio-political/military unit constructed out of a number of previously separate Gothic and other groups in the period *ca* 376-410. The Gothic elements had been occupying lands in south-eastern Europe, particularly the northern hinterland of the Black Sea, many spending a further generation or so in a semi-tolerated occupation of some of the provinces of the Roman Balkans (382-408), before moving west into Italy. Having united, the Visigoths were finally settled by the Roman state as autonomous subordinates in the south-west corner of what is now France in 418. After *ca* 455, as Roman power in the west slipped away, they were able both to redefine their political position as one of total independence from the now rump Empire, and extend their power all the way from the Loire to the straits of Gibraltar. The Visigothic kingdom established in this era, particularly in the reign of Euric (466-84), then went through a period of major crisis in the early part of the sixth century which eventually both broke dynastic continuity and restricted its boundaries largely to the Hispanic peninsula, its previously substantial Gallic possessions falling to the Franks. The reconstructed and eventually monolithically Catholic state which eventually emerged in the second half of the century (especially under Liuvigild and his son Reccared: 569-601)

1

then survived down to the second decade of the eighth century when it was overthrown by invading Islamic forces from North Africa. The history of the Visigoths thus starts in the era of Roman collapse, but stretches well beyond it, falling naturally, in fact, into three phases: a highly volatile period in the late fourth and early fifth centuries of movement and group creation, the expansions of the later fifth century, and the largely Hispanic state of the later sixth and seventh centuries. Each of these phases has its own sources and historical questions, and each is addressed by different papers in this collection.

It begins, both chronologically and physically, with the paper of Dennis Green which reaches back into Visigothic and perhaps even Gothic pre-history, using philological evidence to explore the nature of cultural contacts between the Baltic and the Black Sea in the centuries before the Christian era. This clear-headed and highly critical study assaults many of the sacred cows of supposed early Germanic history, and sets the scene by placing the presence of Goths in south-eastern Europe in the fourth century AD in a very broad context of trading links and population movements which stretched back into the very distant past. My own paper then takes up the story of how the Visigoths as such emerged out of that reservoir of different population groups which had established itself north of the Black Sea by the second half of the fourth century. The term Visigoth is one of modern scholarly convention, but, using it—as is normally done—to designate that group of immigrants into the Empire who were settled in Aquitaine in late 410s, it is becoming increasingly widely recognized that this group had no ancient history (as is still commonly believed, at least by the writers of text books), but was itself a creation of new circumstances which prevailed between *ca* 376 and 418, particularly Hunnic attack and the need to survive in the face of Roman power and hostility.[1] The scholarly agenda has now moved on from this basic point to consider what links, if any, with the past made the group itself and Roman outsiders view it as Gothic. Recent studies have tended to minimize the importance of such links, but this paper presents an opposite point of view, essentially arguing that, given the state of the evidence, such visions have narrowed down the range of possibilities being considered with unwarranted haste. Also dealing with the earliest phase, indeed stretching back before the creation of the Visigoths as such, is the paper of Andreas Schwarcz, which reconsiders the religious life of the *Tervingi*, one of the fourth-century Gothic groups which seem to have contributed large numbers of people to the new Visigoths. This paper explores in highly illuminating fashion what can be reconstructed from very fragmentary evidence, both literary and archaeological, of the non-Christian beliefs of the fourth-century Goths, before taking another look at the conversion of the *Tervingi* to Christianity. One extremely important aspect of the paper is its vision of Gothic religion—both pagan and Christian—as a dynamic phenomenon subject to considerable change

---

[1]   Different recent treatments which would agree on this basic point are Wolfram 1988, Liebeschuetz 1990, Heather 1996.

over time, in the face of new conditions and different contacts. Older visions of a monolithic primitive Germanic paganism must be entirely overthrown.

The second phase of Visigothic history is in many ways the least documented of the three. Many different types of record of Roman reaction to the creation and expansion of an autonomous Visigothic kingdom, particularly among élite landowners, survive (letter collections: Anderson 1936; chronicles: Burgess 1993 amongst many others), but information pertaining to the Goths themselves is scant indeed, both in literary sources, and in archaeological remains, where the Gothic settlement in Aquitaine is famous for its invisibility. Ana Jiménez's paper bravely confronts these difficulties head on, and to good effect. In the absence of better information, details can and will continue to be argued over, but her paper incorporates one fundamental and highly convincing alteration to received accounts of the settlement, namely that it should not be viewed as a monolithic, regimentally enforced set of arrangements which affected all Goths in the same way. She convincingly argues that the prevailing social structures of the Goths themselves, combined with the fact that the Roman state authorities were themselves improvising as they went along, means that we should expect arrangements which varied very widely, in other words a wide diversity of experience for different members of the overall Visigothic group which moved, was moved into the Garonne valley at the end of the second decade of the fifth century.

The third phase of Visigothic history—the Hispanic kingdom as reconstructed by Liuvigild and converted to Catholicism by his son Reccared—is, in contrast, by far the best documented, a wide range of both literary and archaeological sources illustrating many aspects of its development. Many specific aspects of this material are addressed in the rest of the collection. These begin with the paper of Giorgio Ausenda. The first half of this study comprises an illuminating history of the modern attempts to analyse and understand kinship systems starting in the nineteenth century. It then moves on to consider the available evidence for the construction and operation of such systems among the later Visigoths, drawing mainly on materials preserved in the law codes. Using the comparative perspectives established in the first part of the paper, and material from the in some ways better documented Lombards, the paper lays out what can be constructed of the operation of kinship among the Visigoths, and also makes clear where crucial information is missing. The studies which follow Ausenda's in order through the book in many ways serve to set these initial findings in an ever broader context, moving 'outwards' and 'upwards', as it were, from the family, through locally hierarchic social relations, to the operation of different macro-level institutions of the Visigothic state. Ian Wood's paper is in particular worth reading as pair with that of Ausenda, since it focusses on the wider range of social relations which formed the immediate context for the operation of kinship ties. Legal materials and hagiographic-cum-narrative sources, above all *The Lives of the Fathers of Merida*, are drawn upon to generate Wood's central conclusion that vertical ties of patronage had come to replace horizontal ties of kinship as the central organizing bond of Visigothic society by the late sixth and early seventh centuries at the absolute latest.

Great insight into the general cultural context in which both kinship and social patronage operated is provided by the paper of Isabel Velázquez. On one level, the paper is important for its highly useful general introduction to the evolution of modern Spanish historiography in the field of Visigothic legal materials. More specifically, it provides a methodologically exemplary case study into a highly characteristic element of the Visigothic inheritance system: 'La mejora', or the reservation of one third of an individual's property for their immediate descendents. This has for a long time been a battleground between those arguing that its origins must be sought in Germanic custom, and those who would look to Roman law. As Velázquez shows, however, in a careful review of the evidence and previous scholarship, the institution had its origins fundamentally in the dynamic processes of evolution specific to the Visigothic kingdom itself, making any 'Roman' or 'Germanic' label highly misleading. It also emerges very strikingly from this paper that the Visigothic state legislated fully and coherently on the subject of inheritance; this contrasts markedly with the pattern of evidence surviving from some of the other successor states to the Roman Empire (notably the Franks and the Anglo-Saxons).

Velázquez' paper also marks the transition to the four remaining papers in the collection which, between them, deal with the Visigothic kingdom on a much more macro, state-wide, level. To take them in the order of the book, Felix Retamero's study makes use of literary and archaeological evidence, combined with perspectives derived from broad comparative reading in the subject, to construct a basic model of the operation of Visigothic taxation, concentrating in particular upon the role of coins and coinage, and the fundamental questions of who actually had coins and at what point in the Visigothic fiscal cycle. In toto, it makes a striking and powerful case in favour of the view that peasant producers had little access to and were probably largely unaffected in their activities by the operation of the Visigothic monetary economy, which was simply a fiscal rather than any kind of redistributive market mechanism. Mayke de Jong's study focusses on another aspect of the operation of the kingdom on the macro level: relations between Church and State. Basing herself on one of the very few surviving narrative—or purportedly narrative—sources from the seventh century, Julian of Toledo's *History of King Wamba*, de Jong explores the fundamental role played by right religion, indeed more specifically right religious ritual, in the self-identification of the kingdom's élite. On the basis of the *History* and related texts, she constructs a clear and convincing vision of the kingdom, understood in its own terms, as a ritual community, where right religion had to be properly pursued in order that Divine favour might bring overall prosperity and success. As she herself comments, this strikingly prefigures the set of normative ideas which later operated in the Carolingian world. Her paper also sheds much incidental light upon an important cluster of late seventh-century political texts.

The last two papers in the collection—those of Pablo Díaz and Gisela Ripoll—between them sketch in a still broader context for the rest of the volume. The former takes as its subject matter the evolution of Visigothic political institutions.

The central theme running through it is a concentration upon how changing patterns of association among the immigrant Goths, as they participated over time in a profound mutual transformation by interaction with Roman élites and institutions, profoundly altered the political structures of the kingdom. As such, it charts the evolving redefinition of the Visigoths over the full history of the kingdom, and analyses transformation in the institutions of rule. Gisela Ripoll's paper, based on her own very extensive research into the available archaeological evidence, presents a quite different perspective on the same processes, by focussing on the transformation of the symbolic life of the kingdom as expressed in its material culture. As she explores in her introduction, this is a formidably difficult task, but, using her first-hand knowledge of the famous 'Reihengräber' of northern Spain, particularly the Meseta, she presents and then seeks to explain a fascinating transformation in burial clothing and personal adornments, which her own work has done much to demonstrate. Before the mid-sixth century, obviously Germanicizing norms prevailed in these cemeteries, harking back to the so-called 'Danubian Culture' which originally emerged in the fifth century under the auspices of the Hunnic Empire. After *ca* 550, however, these gave way to alternative dress norms which corresponded to an evolving Mediterranean *koiné*. As such, this transformation seems to echo some of the themes explored by Díaz, namely the evolution whereby the structures of the kingdom came much more into line with post-Roman norms which prevailed right across the Mediterranean. Ripoll then goes on to reconsider traditional interpretations of prevailing traditions of sculptural decoration, the other main corpus of material surviving from the Visigothic kingdom. Here she effectively brings out the methodological problems which vitiate the traditional interpretations, and begins to sketch in some alternatives.

As will have become obvious even from these brief summaries, the papers collected in this volume are all on specific subjects, which vary very widely in time and space. On a series of levels, however, the whole is greater than the sum of its parts. First, there is a strong initial design behind the choice of topics covered. And, particularly in the case of the run of papers relating to the sixth- and seventh-century Visigothic kingdom, these very much do work methodically through topics which increase in scale from the familial and local, to the state as a whole, and its legal, institutional, economic, and indeed symbolic expressions. In their entirety, all these papers do indeed shed light from different angles on what is clearly the same human edifice. Second, between them, the papers in this collection consider, or at least touch on, all the major types of source material available for reconstructing the history of the Visigothic kingdom in Spain, and the opportunities and problems associated with some particular clusters of material come in for very extensive treatment. Anyone reading this book, therefore, will come away with a strong sense of the major types of Visigothic source material, both literary and archaeological, and the main methodological issues involved in their use. Third, the book has the additonal merit, of particular interest to the world of Anglophone scholarship, of making available in English, in many cases for the first time, work representative of a new generation of Spanish scholarship.

Because the centre of the Visigothic kingdom had switched by *ca* 500 AD largely to the Hispanic peninsula, the Spanish tradition in Visigothic studies is naturally long-standing and powerful. It is no exaggeration to say that one of the legacies of the Franco era, a relative cultural isolation from the rest of Europe, has been dynamically overturned in recent years, as the range and quality of Hispanic scholarship both directly illustrated and incidentally drawn upon in this book powerfully exemplifies.[2]

Finally, but not least important, the discussions, on which Giorgio Ausenda has laboured so long and hard to turn into print, provide a further binding force, adding to the coherence and coverage of the book as a whole. In terms of wordage, the record of our discussions take up a substantial number of the pages of this book. They provide, moreover, the main memory of the conference for all its participants. In contents, they range as widely as the knowledge and interests of the people gathered in that room in San Marino, and we all reserved the scholar's right (occasionally, or often) to think creatively in a lateral direction, otherwise known as going off in only partially related tangents. Which is which, of course, it is up to the reader to decide: beauty being firmly in the eye of the beholder. In at least two major ways, however, the records of the discussions work to supplement and unite the papers gathered in this collection. First, many important issues, covered only relatively briefly in the papers themselves, received a much fuller airing, as the different participants sought to understand each other, seeking out the meanings which sometimes got lost behind the words chosen to express them in the original versions of our texts. In the discussion of my own paper, for instance, in between detailed questions of historical reconstruction for the period 376-418, much was said by many different participants about the central question of ethnicity. Amongst many other things, the discussion of Ausenda's paper brought out the full potential significance of the concept of preferential marriage. The overall size of the Visigothic coinage came in for illuminating discussion after Felix Retamero's paper, and Gisella Ripoll's paper led us to consider how such global changes in burial dress and personal ornamentation could actually have happened. How were such items manufactured and distributed? These are isolated examples, picked essentially at random, but there are many nuggets of gold dotted liberally throughout the discussions.

Second, the discussions especially of the bulk of the papers dealing with the sixth- and seventh-century kingdom kept bringing us back to what is essentially the 'big' question in Visigothic historiography. Why did the kingdom come to an end in the early eighth century? On the most obvious, narratival level, its history was terminated by Islamic conquest, organized from adjacent North African territories which had themselves fallen under the rule of the Caliphate in the late seventh century. In the historiography of the subject, however, the assumption runs

---

[2]   An interesting comparison is provided by the table of contents of the last volume of essays published in English on the Visigothic kingdom (James 1980), where, of ten participants, only one scholar was of Spanish origin.

very deep that this was only a final coup de grace, that the Arab conquest was only possible because the coherence of the kingdom had already been lost for entirely internal reasons. In the discussions of various papers, the reader will find comment on most of the major different culprits identified in this internalist historiography. Mayke de Jong's paper, for instance, provoked us to think about the vicious persecution of Jews which was such a marked feature of the seventh-century kingdom, and which has been seen by many scholars as a sign of dislocation in high places. The question of whether the state had fallen prey to an overly powerful Church also received comment. Felix Retamero's paper confronted us with the Visigothic taxation system and whether the collapse of the kingdom should be blamed upon an increasing inability to recoup sufficient revenues. Isabel Velázquez's paper raised the question of the whether, in the case of inherited wealth, the state was capable of preserving a balance between its own interests and those of élite landowners, and, in a similar way, some of the discussion of Ian Wood's paper turned to the related questions of Church wealth and the degree to which town and country were successfully integrated. Last but not least, Pablo Díaz' analyses prompted comparisons with the equivalent institutions of the Frankish world, and whether differences between the two are perceptible which might explain the survival of one and disappearance of the other. Most of the major planks of the traditional, internalist historiography were given a thorough airing in our discussions, many of them being picked up again in the final day's consideration of possible future directions for research into Visigothic history. The results, I am confident, will prove extremely useful for anyone seeking to understand the issues which have to be faced when attempting to develop an overarching interpretation of the history of the Visigothic kingdom as a whole.

On a whole series of levels, then, this volume will, the contributors all firmly hope, inform and stimulate its readers: through the papers themselves as individual pieces of scholarship, through groups of papers dealing with interrelated topics, and through the unfolding themes of several days of concentrated discussion. It is perhaps worth finishing by attempting to set the Visigothic kingdom and its history in a still wider context. In many ways, it seems to me, the dominant model for the development of post-Roman early medieval Europe has been built on the back of evidence from the Frankish kingdom, not least for reasons of hindsight, since the Frankish world eventually begat Charlemagne, who is often seen as picking up where the Roman Empire left off. As a model of post-Roman development, however, the Visigothic kingdom is just as 'relevant' as the Frankish. Indeed, a different range of evidence tends to survive from the Visigothic kingdom than from the Frankish—much less narrative history and more legal and ecclesiastical materials—so that the evidence from Spain not only fills out, by adding further variations to, the Frankish version of the 'post-Roman experience', but also positively complements it. It is to be hoped that this volume will help to make the Visigothic evidence much better known in all its details, and hence facillitate its integration into general understandings of the end of Roman Europe. The Frankish post-Roman model is one variation in a spectrum of experience running from maximum disruption (the Anglo-Saxon take-over of Roman Britain perhaps) to maximum continuity (Visigothic Spain or Ostrogothic Italy). There is very good reason to read the three latest CIROSS volumes in conjuction, therefore, as fully illustrative of this possible range. Beyond such exhortations to the reader to read yet more widely, it is my final and very pleasurable duty to thank Giorgio Ausenda, as the director of CIROSS, on behalf of all the participants. We thank him for the original invitation to attend, for the congenial but demanding conditions under which he led us through our discussions, and for all his efforts underlying the preparation of this volume. My name will appear on the front cover, but the vast majority of the editing work was done by Giorgio Ausenda himself.

References

Anderson, W. B. (ed.)
 1936   *Sidonius Poems and Letters.* London: Loeb.
Ausenda, G. (ed.)
 1995   *After Empire: Towards an Ethnology of Europe's Barbarians.*
             Woodbridge: The Boydell Press.
Burgess, R. (ed.)
 1993   *The Chronicle of Hydatius and the Consularia Constantinopolitana: Two
             contemporary accounts of the final years of the Roman Empire.* Oxford:
             Oxford University Press.
Heather, P. J.
 1996   *The Goths.* Oxford: Blackwells.
Hines, J. (ed.)
 1997   *The Anglo-Saxons from the Migration Period to the Eighth Century: An
             Ethnographic Perspective.* Woodbridge: The Boydell Press.
James, E.
 1980   *Visigothic Spain: New Approaches.* Oxford: Oxford University Press.
Liebeschuetz , J. H. W. G.
 1990   *Barbarians and Bishops.* Oxford: Oxford University Press.
Wolfram, H.
 1988   *History of the Goths.* Berkeley, CA: California University Press.
Wood, I. N. (ed.)
 1998   *Franks and Alamanni in the Merovingian Period: An Ethnographic
             Perspective.* Woodbridge: The Boydell Press.

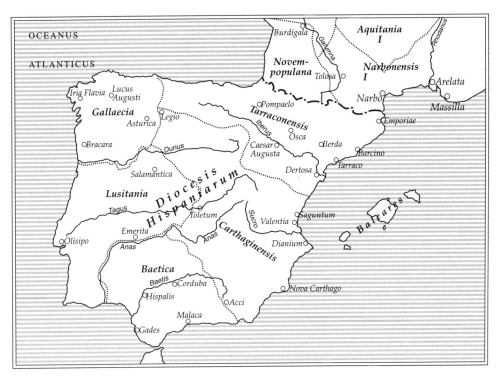

OCEANUS
ATLANTICUS

Aquitania I

Burdigala

Novem-
populana

Narbonensis I

Tolosa

Arelata

Narbo

Massilla

Iria Flavia   Lucus
               Augusti

Gallaecia

Asturica   Legio

Pompaelo

Tarraconensis

Emporiae

Osca

Bracara

Durius

Caesar
Augusta

Ilerda

Barcino

Salamantica

Dertosa

Tarraco

Diocesis
Hispaniarum

Lusitania

Tagus

Toletum

Sucro

Valentia   Saguntum

Baleares

Emerita

Carthaginensis

Anas

Anas

Dianium

Olisipo

Baetica

Baetis   Corduba

Hispalis

Acci

Nova Carthago

Malaca

Gades

Map of late Roman south-western continental Europe

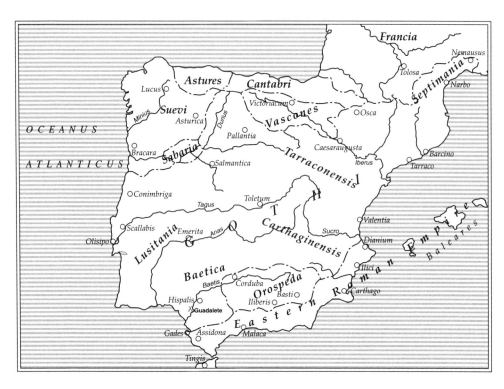

Map of sixth-century *Hispania* and Gothic territories in Gaul

LINGUISTIC EVIDENCE FOR THE EARLY MIGRATIONS OF THE GOTHS

DENNIS H. GREEN

Trinity College, Cambridge CB2 1TQ

In this contribution I am concerned with the migration of the Goths in a southeasterly direction from the southern shores of the Baltic to the northern shores of the Black Sea. By starting with their departure from northern Poland I deliberately leave out of account the still debated question whether the Goths' homeland was on the continent or whether they had come across the Baltic from Scandinavia (and, if so, from what part of Sweden). By contrast, their settlement for some time on the Polish coastline between the Oder and the Vistula commands general assent nowadays, which provides us with a firm starting-point in following their footsteps down to the Pontic region. About this early stage of the Gothic migrations there is remarkably little evidence that has been accepted as reliable, which is borne out by the fact that Herwig Wolfram devotes little over a page to the Goths' trek to the Black Sea, whilst Peter Heather's study (1991) is concerned with their relations with the Romans in southeastern Europe and therefore begins as late as 332. This shortage of evidence may justify my concentration as a philologist on what language may have to tell us, even though this confronts us with the question how far the linguistic testimony may be reconcilable with the conclusions of historians and archaeologists.

The Goths were not the first East Germanic tribe to move in this direction from the same initial area. It is commonly accepted that various tribes were settled in the Lower Vistula area several centuries BC and that the *Bastarnae* (accompanied or followed by others like the *Sciri* and the Vandals) reached as far as the Upper Vistula, from where they migrated further, reaching the Black Sea at the close of the third century BC, centuries before the Goths followed in their wake. Their presence is attested at the mouth of the Danube about 200 BC (they are mentioned alongside the Thracians), but a stage on their route may be reflected in the name *Alpes Bastarnicae* given to the Carpathians in the *Tabula Peutingeriana*. If the later migration of the Goths over much the same route is anything to go by (the archaeological evidence suggests that it took them about 100 years, with intermediate halts and in the face of local resistance, to reach the southernmost parts of the northern Pontic area) the *Bastarnae* must have set out from the Lower Vistula at about the beginning of the third century BC.

This dating is important for philology, since amongst the words designating objects or places of their new colonial area which the *Bastarnae* are thought to have passed back to the rest of *Germania* are two which were early enough to undergo the effects of the First (or Germanic) Sound Shift. The first of these is the designation for the Carpathians (Ptolemy: *Karpátēs óros*) where the *Bastarnae* must have settled for some time. In Old Norse this mountain range is known as

THE VISIGOTHS FROM THE MIGRATION PERIOD TO THE SEVENTH CENTURY:
AN ETHNOGRAPHIC PERSPECTIVE

© C.I.R.O.S.S.
San Marino (R.S.M.)

Harfaðafiöll, where the second element refers to mountains (as in the Viking loanword *fell* in northern English), whilst the first shows a triple effect of the Sound Shift ($k > h$, $p > f$, $t > ð$). For these changes to have been possible we may assume that the Shift (spread over some length of time) had not been concluded by the third century, but had at least begun at the time when the *Bastarnae* separated geographically from the rest of *Germania*.

A similar conclusion can be drawn from the second word which, because it also undergoes the Sound Shift, must have been loaned into Germanic early enough to associate it with the *Bastarnae* (or perhaps *Sciri*). The word is attested in a number of Germanic languages (e.g. Old English *hænep* 'hemp') and corresponds to Greek *kánnabis* with the same meaning, showing this time two results of the shift ($k > h$, $b > p$). This correspondence does not mean that we are dealing with an extremely early loan from Greek into Germanic (for which there would be no linguistic parallel or historical explanation), but rather with a loan into both these languages from a common source. Where we may seek this source is suggested by the comment of Herodotus that hemp was especially cultivated in the east by the Scythians and the Thracians. The conjunction of such an early dating and the Thracians suggests the same setting for this loanword as for the Carpathians (where Thracians were also settled). Even though our evidence suggesting the Thracians as a source for both these words may be purely fortuitous, their origin in the South-East and adoption into Germanic long before the Goths reached this region seem unquestioned.

Whether the Goths, like other Germanic tribes settled in northern Poland before them, also came from Scandinavia has latterly been called into doubt, but these tribes were drawn in a southeastern direction in their further expansion, following the course of the rivers Oder and Vistula which permitted penetration far inland. In addition to this geographical consideration, the Baltic and Black Sea were linked by a prehistoric trade-route whose products may have held out the promise of wealth and agricultural benefits to tribes in search of land. Nor should we discount the precedent of the *Bastarnae* and *Sciri*, whose links with the North must have been maintained if their loanwords were spread throughout *Germania*, as a stimulus for subsequent waves of migration. The second and third centuries AD therefore see numerous Germanic tribes in the Pontic area (south Russian steppes and Lower Danube), amongst whom the Goths appeared in the early third century in Thrace, launching attacks by land and sea (across the Black Sea and into the Aegean) against Roman territory. The question which this migration of the Goths from a northern to a southeastern sea poses is how far the evidence permits us to follow their tracks in the approximately hundred years which it took them.

In talking of the Goths we must be aware that we are often making use of a blanket term. The Gothic settlement area in the Ukraine comprised a variegated and ethnically different substratum, of which the Slavs and such Iranian peoples as the Sarmatians and Alans are only the most obvious, whilst the polyethnic nature of Gothic kingship (not merely under Ermanaric) attracted or swallowed up a number of other Germanic tribes. Nor is it often possible to distinguish archaeologically or linguistically between the Goths and other East Germanic tribes attracted to this region (including *Heruli*, Burgundians, Vandals and Gepids), the more so since Gothic, known to us almost entirely from Wulfila's translation of the Bible, is the only language of which we have any direct knowledge. Gothic has, therefore, often to do duty linguistically for East Germanic at large.

Geographically it is likely that the course taken by the Gothic migration was largely that taken by the *Bastarnae* before them along the by now established trade-route. The first penetration inland would have been in general terms up the Vistula in the direction of the Carpathians and then, following their semi-circular course, into the south Russian steppes. Or, in more detailed terms, from the lower to the upper Vistula as far as its junction with the western Bug, from there to the southern Bug and then down to its estuary in the Black Sea (alternatively: up the Vistula as far as the San, then to the Dniester, thence to the Black Sea). Either of these routes would have avoided the major obstacle of the Pripet marshes which the Goths, if they were at all guided by migratory or trading predecessors, would have kept away from at all costs.

Although not based on him, this sketch of a possible route in the light of geographical possibilities largely agrees with the route given by Jordanes (*Getica* 16 f., 25 ff.). In view of doubts about his historical reliability, however, this agreement may raise more difficulties than it solves. His dependence on Gothic oral tradition may tell us how the Goths later imagined their trek, but not how it actually took place. His Amal genealogy bears some of the marks of a mythical, legitimizing genealogy, serving later political purposes rather than accurately reflecting the distant past. Jordanes after all was separated by centuries from the events he was reporting and it is a moot point how far his debt to classical historiography and attitude to the barbarians coloured his presentation. Nonetheless, with all these qualifications, he provides us with information otherwise lacking. He draws on earlier histories of the Goths and some of his material, even though exposed to the vagaries of oral transmission, stems from Gothic sources, a unique feature which heightens his value for us. Even in the case of the Amal genealogy we do not have to reject it in its entirety, but rather to decide where the dividing line is to be drawn between legend and history. His view that the Goths began their trek in northern Poland agrees with what we are told of their settlement by Tacitus and Pliny and their arrival in the Pontic area is likewise reported by classical sources, so that our task is to consider whether what Jordanes reports of their movement between these two regions can be confirmed by other sources, even if only in isolated details which may add up to a general line of direction.

We may do this, as the first step in the argument, by following through selectively some of the place-names and tribal names listed by Jordanes as points on the trek, relating them briefly to what is also known from other sources. He traces the Goths back to the northern island of Scandza which he significantly locates opposite the *Vistula*, representing for Jordanes the starting-point for the Goths' continental migration as much as for modern archaeology which has identified the Wielbark culture, situated between the Oder and the Vistula, with the Goths. Jordanes is then much more precise, saying that the place where they landed is still to-day called *Gothiscandza*. Whether or not this name is related to Scandza, it has been interpreted as a Gothic formation (*Gutisk andja* 'Gothic end, Gothic coast'), in which case Jordanes would conserve good native tradition. Next to be mentioned is a tribe already dwelling on the coast with whom the Goths had to fight for territory, namely the *Ulmerugi*, again a vernacular name for 'island *Rugii*', showing the characteristic Gothic -*u*- in the first part and paralleled by Old Norse *Holmrygir* and Old English *Holmrygas*. The next tribe to be subdued by the Goths seeking to establish themselves are the Vandals who, together with Burgundians, *Rugii* as well as Goths and Gepids, are regarded by archaeologists as the main bearers of the so-called Przeworsk culture of northern Poland, so much so that its eventual disappearance is correlated with the departure of the *Vandilii* for new territory.

After this focus on the lower and middle Vistula, Jordanes passes with too much of a jump to satisfy us to the Goths' arrival in Scythia which he says was called *Oium* in their language and was characterized by great (agricultural) wealth. For this reason and also because he also says that the furthest part of Scythia lies by the *Pontus,* the region now reached by the Goths is associated with the Ukraine. The agricultural quality of this terrain is not merely still true today, it is also borne out by the vernacular name *Oium* which corresponds (as a dative plural used for a place-name) to a word **aujō-* or **auwō-*, widespread in Germanic and ranging in meaning from 'island' to 'well watered meadow'. (The same word occurs later when Jordanes refers to the Gepids occupying an island surrounded by the shallows of the (lower) Vistula and quotes the name they give it: *Gepedoios* 'island of the Gepids'.) After his mention of Scythia and the sea of Pontus, Jordanes lists in quick succession three rivers (*Ister*, the classical name of the lower Danube, *Danaster* 'Dniester' and *Danaper* 'Dnieper') with all of which other classical historians and modern archaeological finds associate the Goths at this stage of their wanderings. There follow references to the *Taurus* (a mountain range in the Crimea), to lake *Maeotis* (the sea of Azov) and to the *Caucasus* and to *Persis* (Persia), but also, further to the north and the east, to peoples now identified as Slavs (*Venethi, Sclaveni, Antes*), to the river *Tanais* (the Don) and beyond that to the Huns. Also mentioned are *Thrace* and *Dacia*, where contact is made with the Roman Empire.

Such, in brief selective outline, is the course of the Gothic trek described by Jordanes who understandably provides richer detail about the Goths as they cross the horizon of classical historiography in the Pontic area, some information about their period in Poland (known to him from oral tradition and as a result of early Roman trading contacts with the Baltic), but relatively little in between. At the start of their migrations, while the Goths still formed geographically part of a solid Germanic block in the north, indirect contact had already been made between them and the Roman world in the shape of trading connections and a few loanwords from this context, but by the close of the trek whose course we have followed only up to the Roman frontier they were exposed to the full and immediate force of a superior civilization, which left its mark on the Gothic language in the shape of many more loanwords from Latin and, with their relatively early conversion to Christianity, of specifically religious loanwords from Greek, even though some of those may have entered Gothic through Roman transmission.

Between the Polish coastline and the Roman Danubian frontier, however, the Goths traversed a large-scale territory which, even before the irruption of the Huns, was a veritable ethnic melting-pot. In the course of this first stage of their migrations the Goths therefore came into contact with a wide variety of peoples: Balts, Finns and Slavs, but also with Thracians and Dacians and, after 375, with the Huns. Of particular importance, however, was their contact in southern Russia with a number of Iranian peoples who in succession had entered and settled in this area: the Scythians (to whose linguistic influence such river-names in this region as the Danube, the Dniester, the Dnieper and the Don are attributed), the Sarmatians and the Alans. These Iranian peoples incorporated a completely different culture, in large measure adapted to the geographical conditions of the steppes, so that the entry of the Goths into this region and their new contacts there resulted in a noticeable process of acculturation before the even more overwhelming contact with the Greco-Roman world. What I have termed an ethnic melting-pot is also for the philologist a linguistic melting-pot, which confronts him with impossible linguistic demands, for no one scholar can command specialist knowledge of such a wide range of disparate languages. Despite the need for much interdisciplinary work still to be done, the following attempt is made to suggest linguistic connections between East Germanic tribes (or the Goths in particular) and the different peoples whom they encounter in eastern Europe. By this means it may be possible to supply philological support for Jordanes' historical evidence and to fill in something of the gap which he left between the Baltic and the Pontus.

Before this linguistic review, however, a word must be devoted to the confirmatory evidence provided by archaeology, mainly the work of Russian, Romanian and Polish scholarship. The reliability of Jordanes is after all not so much above question that there is no need to buttress it from as many different angles as possible, especially since the archaeological evidence suggests an equation of a particular culture in northern Poland with the Goths and its gradual transposition in a southeasterly direction to the Ukraine and Romania.

The most recent attempt to follow this through is by Bierbrauer (1994) who proceeds by chronological stages (more accurately determined from archaeological finds than from linguistic evidence), each of which he concludes by correlating his archaeological conclusions with historical testimony. His starting-point is the Wielbark culture of northern Poland (at the mouth of the Vistula) between 0 and 220/230 AD, generally identified with the Goths or *Gutones* of written sources for this region and this period. Only gradually (between 80 and 160 AD) do the finds suggest this settlement spreading far enough eastwards (towards the river Passarge) to establish cultural contact with the Balts and influence them, a development which is carried further eastwards in the next 60 or 70 years. From about the middle of the second century until 215 another expansionary change begins to be detectable: a move of this Wielbark culture from this region towards the area of the middle Vistula and east of it (Mazovia and Polesia, including the bend in the river Bug). This move has been interpreted archaeologically not as a short-term one, but as a large-scale migration over more than two generations, which is reconcilable with what Jordanes reports of the migration under Filimer (*Getica* 26 f.). Whether, as is implied by his compressed account, this move also took them as far as Scythia (*Oium*) is more open to doubt in view of Bierbrauer's suggestion of a further expansionary stage, reaching as far as the Ukraine and northern Moldavia by 220-30 and the rest of Moldavia by 250, an archaeological conclusion in agreement with classical reports on the appearance of the Goths on the Black Sea coast from the beginning of the third century.

This Pontic settlement area of the Goths has been well investigated by archaeologists, who refer to it as the Sîntana de Mureş/Černjahov culture (the first part named after finds in Transylvania, the second after a site in the Ukraine near Kiev). Finds from this culture date it from the later third and fourth centuries, a period when a variety of literary sources attest the dominance of the Goths in this area adjoining the Roman Empire, lasting until the Hunnic invasions from 375. These chronological considerations, together with the Germanic nature of the finds from this culture and their similarity to the Wielbark culture, suggest the predominantly Gothic nature of this culture, however many other factors may have been at work in what was a highly polyethnic region. Underlying the uniformity of this culture, stretching from the Danube to the Ukraine and the steppes are elements associated with earlier local inhabitants such as the Dacians or, especially, betraying Sarmatian (Iranian) influence, for these nomads were at home on the steppes to which the Černjahov culture extended. It is important not to underestimate the influence on the Goths of such non-Germanic peoples, especially those at home in and long since adjusted to the geographical necessities of a region to which the Goths were newcomers. Nonetheless, the Goths must have established themselves as predominant amongst the many peoples north of the Black Sea in this period if only because literary sources refer primarily to them as the military and political power. Finally, the identification of this culture with the Goths is borne out not merely chronologically, but also geographically, for its extent (from the lower Danube northeastwards across the rivers Pruth and Dniester, beyond the Dnieper out into the steppes) coincides with what Ammianus Marcellinus reports of their power, spreading from the Danube even as far as the Tanais (Don), since the Alans who are their neighbours there are termed *Tanaites* or 'people of the Don'. It needs hardly to be added in conclusion that many of the place-names mentioned here (or included in their sweep) take up those listed by Jordanes and serve to corroborate him.

If archaeology can be used to throw light on Jordanes in this way, can the same be said of linguistic evidence, given the notorious inability of philology to come up with precise absolute datings and in view of the difficulties of coping with the range of languages involved? In dealing with this problem I propose to look at two classes of evidence: first that of names (of places or of people), then that of words.

As a first onomastic example I take a negative case, i.e. one where the Gothic background to a group of names is not so certain as has been suggested. Although the Gothic origin of Jordanes' *Gothiscandza* (< *Gutisk andja*) may be acceptable, the same does not hold of the further proposal that from this word for the Gothic coastline derives the name for a particular place on that coast, namely *Danzig*, Polish *Gdańsk*. It may be the case that the palatalization of the Polish *-n-* implies that it once preceded *-i-*, whilst lack of palatalization of *G-* suggests that it preceded *-u-*, thereby leading to an earlier **Gudanisk*, but this form still differs from the *Gutisk* presupposed by Jordanes' form. Moreover, Prussian (i.e. the westernmost member of the Baltic language-family and adjacent to the Gothic settlement in northern Poland) has place-names with *gudde* to which this term could belong. A further difficulty with the Gothic explanation lies in the presence of *-d-* whereas Gothic regularly had *-t-* (e.g. *Gutones*, *Gutþiuda*). This is a difficulty shared with other terms at home in this same region for which a Gothic origin has been put forward: the place-name *Gdingen*, Polish *Gdynia*, but also a Baltic term for a 'White Russian' (Lithuanian *gudas*, Latvian *guds*) which is supposed to have derived from a term denoting a Gothic trader, then a foreign trader at large. For all these forms with *-d-* where we might expect *-t-* it has been suggested that they were borrowed from Germanic into Baltic before the First Sound Shift. In theory there need be no objection to this, for if words like 'hemp' and 'Carpathians' betray contact between non-Germanic and Germanic peoples as early as this there is no reason why an early influence could not have operated in the opposite direction. But the difficulty with Gdańsk, Gdynia and *gudas* lies in the fact that they are supposed to betray Gothic influence on Baltic speakers in the Polish coastal area centuries before the Goths are known to have occupied this region. This by no means solves the problems posed by these names (are they of Baltic or even Slavonic origin?), but it casts doubt on the theory of Gothic origin.

The same is true of another place-name with *-d-* in the Lower Vistula area, *Graudenz*, Polish *Grudziądz*. Difficulties of another kind are found here insofar as this name has been associated with *Greutungi*, the name given to one branch of the Goths by contrast with the *Tervingi*, which opens up the whole question of when and where the Goths were seen as forming two branches with these names (Specht 1939). For those who derive Graudenz from *Greutungi* the answer is clear: at least this branch of the Goths must have been termed thus already in northern Poland, but the attempt to take this nomenclature further back to Scandinavia is not merely uncertain philologically, it also rests on the by no means certain assumption that the Goths came from Scandinavia. Opposed to this is the view that *Greutungi* arose as a term in the Pontic area (and cannot therefore be used to explain Graudenz in the north), although even this southern theory has been put forward on a number of different grounds (Altheim 1956). Some see the twofold division of the Goths which it presupposes as the result of different reactions to a specific historical event, the Hunnic onslaught (375), whilst for others it stems from more general geographical features of the Pontic area which the Goths now inhabited. A number of different cultures and languages suggest that the nature of the south Russian terrain repeatedly occasioned a twofold naming of those who occupied its two types of ground: the cattle-raising nomads of the open steppe and the sedentary agriculturalists of the woodland steppe. The Gothic distinction (*Greutungi* deriving from a Germanic root for 'sand, sandy soil' of the steppe and *Tervingi* from a root for 'tree') would thus be echoed in Slavonic for this same region (*poljane* 'field-dwellers' and *drevljane* 'wood-dwellers'), but also in Hunnic and Turkish. The genesis of this distinction of the Goths as late as their settlement in southern Russia is borne out by the fact that the name *Greutungi* is attested only from the fourth century. These considerations, together with the phonological difficulty of -*d*- in Graudenz, make it unlikely or at least uncertain that this place-name is a trace of earlier Gothic occupation.

Other place-names provide rather more certainty about Gothic traces. The Old English *Widsith* (Malone 1935), which betrays an astonishing familiarity with early Germanic history and geography in however distorted a form, mentions the Goths and the Huns in close association (v. 57), but also claims that the Goths fought the Huns ('the people of Attila') for their homeland by the Vistula wood (v. 121: *ymb Wistla wudu*). We shall soon turn to the evidence for another battle between the Goths and the Huns, but neither in this case nor in historical tradition is any such battle known to have taken place in the vicinity of the Vistula. It is more likely that we have here a conflation of repeated conflicts between the two peoples, situated near the Vistula because in retrospect this could be regarded as a Gothic homeland, if not their earliest. This location is confirmed by the naming of the Goths in this poem as *Hrēðgotan*, a term also attested for them in Old Norse and etymologically suggesting 'nest Goths', i.e. those of the original homeland or those who had not joined the trek southeastwards. In this connection it is significant that the Gepids, seen by Jordanes as belonging to the Goths even if they were the last to settle in northern Poland, remained for some time in that region (east of the Vistula) after the main body of the Goths had moved on, certainly as late as the fourth century. However bowdlerized, the details given in *Widsith* are not totally irreconcilable with linguistic and archaeological surmises.

Pointers which can be geographically located in rather more detail are given in another literary source, the Old Norse *Battle of the Goths and Huns* (Heusler & Ranisch 1903:1-12). It is commonly regarded as one of the oldest Germanic heroic lays, a genre which is held to have originated amongst the Goths in the South-East (its focus on such figures as Ermanaric, Attila and Theoderic, even if it unhistorically makes contemporaries of them, points in that direction). From the Goths the heroic lay spread to other Germanic tribes, incorporating Gothic persons and Gothic experiences into a common Germanic repertoire. A group of early lays in Old Norse, including the *Battle of the Goths and Huns*, testifies to this radiation of Gothic themes and it is even possible, on the basis of fossilized linguistic forms, to venture suggestions as to the route taken in their transmission from the south-east to the north. What concerns us now, however, is not the route taken to

Scandinavia, but the original location in the South-East. Here this particular heroic lay is informative about much more than the battle which it treats, for it includes linguistic fossils which would have meant little in the North, but which point to the area of Gothic settlement at the time of the Huns' invasions. The holy graves of the Goths (perhaps a reference to royal burial mounds?) are said to lie on the banks of the Dnieper (7, 6: *á stöðum Danpar*) and the battle itself is located on the plain of the Don (23, 2: *á Dúnheiði*). In this latter context reference is also made to mountains called the *Iassarfiöll* (23, 4), where the first element is identified with a term for the Alans, also known as the *Assi*, whose language possessed an epenthetic *j-*, which would explain the form in the lay. *Iassarfiöll* thus corresponds to what Ptolemy calls the *Alanà órē*, 'the Alan mountains' and the Alans, settled in our period between the Don and the Caucasus, were in close contact with the Goths and were the first to suffer the onslaught of the Huns. Although it has been suggested that *Dún-* may refer to the Danube rather than the Don, the other references speak against this and in favour of a location further to the east.

A last piece of onomastic evidence is provided by the name of the Hunnic leader, Attila himself. Of the three possible explanations of the name (Hunnic, either pure or assimilated to Germanic, or genuine Gothic) the third has most to be said in its favour. First linguistically, because the meaning 'little father' creates no problems at all if one proceeds from Gothic *atta* 'father' + diminutive *-ila* (cf. *Wulfila* 'little wolf'). Secondly, if we consider Attila's name in conjunction with his brother's (*Bleda*) the Germanic origin of the latter (meaning 'renown' or 'good fortune' and used in Germanic name-formation) would speak in favour of a Germanic origin for Attila's, too. Thirdly, there are also significant pointers to onomastic interchange between the two peoples, with Huns adopting Germanic names and conversely *Germani* bearing Hunnic names (attested explicitly by Jordanes, *Getica* 58). Mutual naming practice of this kind and particularly a name like 'little father' may seem to fit badly with a traditional negative view of the ferocity and destructiveness of the Huns which, even if largely Christian (Attila as a *flagellum Dei*), must have been shared by the tribes who were their first victims. Although this negative view is also reflected in Germanic heroic poetry, it is accompanied by a positive view which is anomalously at home with the East Germanic tribes who, after the Alans, felt the earliest onslaught of the Huns. This favourable attitude was the result of a symbiosis established after the Hunnic occupation of Gothic territory, for the nomads were dependent on what the sedentary Goths could provide (agricultural products), whilst the prospect of booty enticed Goths to take part in Hunnic campaigns. Most of the Germanic tribes still dwelling in the steppes became Attila's vassals so that, according to both Jordanes and Priscus, their leaders were loyal to Attila, shared his plans and occupied high places in his empire. Under such conditions onomastic interchange between Gothic and Hunnic and the nature of the name Attila need occasion less surprise.

Greater prospects of information, but also greater difficulties of interpretation are opened up when we pass from names to words pointing to cultural contacts between the Goths and other peoples encountered on their trek. We may follow these contacts through in considering Gothic loanwords into Baltic languages (Old Prussian, Lithuanian, Latvian), into Slavonic and into the Finnic group, concluding this section of the argument with a look at what is known as Crimean Gothic.

The name given to the Balts by Tacitus and Jordanes is *Aesti(i)*, situated in the first century AD along the Baltic coastline east of the Vistula and engaged in the amber-trade. (We do not know under what circumstances their tribal name was later passed on to their non-Indo-European neighbours, the Estonians.) Two difficulties face us in considering their linguistic connections with the Germanic tribes. Since the area of first contact was the lower Vistula any loanwords from Germanic must first have been adopted by the Prussians, the westernmost of the Baltic tribes. However, Old Prussian died out later, leaving us only a few sources on which to work, whilst any loanwords which it may have passed on to other Baltic languages are more difficult to retrieve. The other difficulty has to do with the particular Germanic language from which the Baltic languages drew their loanwords. For example, it is uncertain whether Prussian *sarwis* 'weapons' derives from Gothic *sarwa* 'weapons' or from Germanic at large (or, if the latter, whether this may not simply represent 'pre-Gothic', a stage in the development of the language earlier than that represented by Wulfila's Bible). Equally, we cannot tell whether Prussian *asilis* 'ass' was taken over from Gothic *asilus* or Old High German *esil*, or whether Lithuanian *mũĩtas* 'customs duty' came from Gothic *mōta* or Old High German *mūta*. We also have to reckon with the possibility that the origin of a loanword may have been West Germanic at large, as seems to be the case with Lithuanian *kùnigas* 'king' (a corresponding form is not attested, nor to be assumed, for Gothic). Related to this difficulty is the question, not always answerable, whether a Gothic loanword entered Baltic directly or *via* Slavonic.

This last point suggests that, despite these difficulties, it is possible to suggest some specifically Gothic loans into Baltic. This is the case, for example, with Gothic *hláifs* 'loaf' and Lithuanian *kliẽpas*, with Gothic *hilms* 'helmet' and Prussian *ilmis* (with a variation of meaning), with Gothic *katils* 'cauldron' and Prussian *catils*, with Gothic *stikls* 'goblet' and Prussian *sticlo* 'glass'. If we divide the very restricted number of these loanwords into cultural categories two main fields stand out where the Baltic languages were exposed to this influence. The first is military, represented by examples such as Prussian *brunyos* 'armour', Lithuanian *šálmas* 'helmet' (if we can accept this as a 'pre-Gothic' loan, earlier than Prussian *ilmis*) and Prussian *sarwis* 'weapons'. To this group could be added Prussian *wumpnis* 'oven, furnace' if, as is the case with the earlier loan of this same word from Celtic into Germanic, we regard it as originally designating a furnace for metal-working and the manufacture of weapons (and only later as an oven for baking). The second category is made up of trading terms, two of which ultimately derive from Latin, so that we are dealing with a linguistic trade-route from Latin into Germanic, then from Gothic into Baltic: Prussian *asilis* 'ass' (ultimately from Latin *asinus/asellus*, a beast of burden for Roman merchants in *Germania*) and Prussian *catils* 'cauldron' (going back finally to Latin *catinus/catillus*). Another trading term possibly exemplifies a shorter linguistic

route, from Germanic into Baltic: Lithuanian *muĩtas* 'customs duty'. That two
categories such as warfare and trade should stand out need not surprise in the least,
since these are historically two sides of the same coin and also dominate the much
richer loanword traffic between Latin and Germanic (in both directions).

In considering the historical and geographical aspects of these cultural loans
into the Baltic languages we may see them as effected directly by the Goths or
through the Slavs as intermediaries. Direct contact was first established in the
earliest period of Gothic occupation of northern Poland as the Wielbark culture
spread eastwards of the Vistula where the *Aestii* were settled and where, amongst
the Goths, the Gepids were present in particular. In this area we can best assume
contact between Goths and the Prussians who in this period represent the entrance
for these loanwords. We need not regard this area east of the lower Vistula as the
only possibility of direct contact, however, for work on Baltic-language
hydronymy has made it likely that the boundaries of this linguistic area reached
much further south, into White Russia and the northern Ukraine, an area which the
Goths later passed through on their gradual trek southeastwards. The other
possibility (indirect influence *via* the Slavs) is suggested by archaeological
evidence for trade-routes extending northwards from the Černjahov culture through
Slav territory and as far as the Dnieper-Dvina culture associated with the Balts.
The purpose behind this radiation, which could have been carried to the Balts by
Goths and/or Slavs, was not expansion and occupation over such improbable
distances as such, but rather military control at first and then exploitation of a
valuable trade with the North. If so, this might explain the two categories of
warfare and trade implied by the linguistic evidence.

This last point (Slavs as possible intermediaries between Goths and Balts) opens
up the question of Gothic influence on Slavonic. Jordanes, looking northwards
from the Pontic area and just before saying that Ermanaric's influence reached as
far as the Balts, mentions first the Slavs (*Getica* 119), associating them more
closely than the Balts with the centre of Gothic power. He says that they have three
names: *Venethi* (also mentioned by other classical sources and still surviving in
German 'Wenden' as a general term for the Slavs), *Antes* (located by Jordanes
between the Dniester and the Dnieper, *Getica* 35, and attacked by the Gothic king
Vinitharius, *Getica* 247) and *Sclaveni* (at home between the Upper Dniester and
Vistula). This location of the primitive Slavs partly at least within the area covered
by the Černjahov culture together with their contacts (warlike or otherwise) with
the Goths under Ermanaric—and almost certainly before—explains their openness
to Gothic loanword influence. That this must for the most part have come early,
before the expansion of the Slavs, is implied by the presence of these loanwords in
a number of Slavonic languages.

As with the loanwords into Baltic, light is thrown on the nature of these contacts
between Goths and Slavs by dividing the loanwords into various cultural
categories (in listing these I give only the Gothic starting-point). Foremost
amongst these categories is once more trade, with examples such as *kaupōn* 'to
trade', *mōta* 'customs duty', *katils* 'cauldron', *sakkus* 'sack', *stikls* 'goblet', *akeit*

'vinegar', *wein* 'wine', *asilus* 'ass', including two coins: *skilliggs* 'shilling' and *kintus* 'penny'. Political authority is represented by *gastfaþs* 'lord', *gards* 'house' (but cf. *þiudangardi* 'kingdom') and *dōms* 'judgment'; agriculture by *haírda* 'herd' and *aúrtigards* 'garden' (perhaps also here *hláifs* 'loaf'); warfare by *brunjō* 'breastplate', *wargs* 'enemy' and *mēki* 'sword'; skills by *lēkeis* 'doctor' and *bōka* 'letter' (plural *bōkōs* 'book'). Merely from this selection it is clear that Gothic loanwords into Slavonic are much more frequent than into Baltic and cover a much wider and varied range.

The chronology of these loans falls into three distinct stages. An early stage (Primitive Germanic or, if we draw a parallel with what we saw with Baltic, 'pre-Gothic') is represented by an example belonging to the category of warfare: Primitive Slavonic *šelmj* 'helmet', presumably from the Goths in the Upper Vistula area whilst they still retained -*e*- as distinct from Wulfila's *hilms*. By contrast, the bulk of the loanwords must come later, from the time when the Černjahov culture saw the Goths in closer and more protracted relationship with the Slavs. Examples under this heading include *biuþs* 'table' (producing Slavonic forms meaning 'eating-board') and *hansa* 'cohort' (leading significantly to Slavonic words to do with theft and booty). Finally, some loans from Gothic into Slavonic may come even later, from a period when the Goths had penetrated into the Balkans and the expansion of the Slavs had brought their southern branch into contact with them in this region. Examples from this later stage include *ausahriggs* 'ear-ring' (the fate of Gothic -*h*- in Slavonic shows that this loan must be later than that of *hláifs*) and *weinagards* 'vineyard' (unlike the mobile trade-word *wein* 'wine' the word for vineyard was taken over only in a wine-growing district further south).

The richest category in this loanword traffic is represented by trade-words, but it is possible to extend the course it followed in two directions, backwards as well as forwards. By 'backwards' I mean that, as was the case with Gothic loanwords into Baltic, some of those into Slavonic are ultimately Latin in origin (*kaupōn, katils, sakkus, akeit, wein, asilus, kintus*). From this it has been concluded that such words can only have been transmitted to the Slavs after the Latin originals had been adopted into Gothic (from the third century on, after the Goths' arrival in the orbit of the Empire), but this ignores the fact that a number of Latin trade-words entered *Germania* considerably earlier, reaching the Goths at a time when they were still in northern Poland. Significantly, the seven trade-words just listed are all, for phonological and other reasons into which I cannot go here, candidates for inclusion in this early group. Equally, it is possible that the loanword traffic from Gothic to Slavonic was taken further, namely into the Baltic languages. Although we cannot always tell whether a Gothic word entered Baltic directly or *via* the Slavs it is of interest that some of the trade-words are common to both loan-processes (*kaupōn, mōta, katils, stikls, asilus*) and that two apparently military terms (*brunjō, hilms*) may have accompanied the objects as trading-goods. These loanwords indicate a linguistic trade-route from Latin to Gothic to Slavonic and then perhaps to Baltic.

More than one historical-geographical contact has to be taken into account to explain these loans. The earliest possibility was provided by the Goths' trek towards the area of the Černjahov culture, for their expansion towards the Upper Dniester and the Upper (southern) Bug brought them into territory inhabited by Slavs (*Antes* and *Sclaveni*?) still at a stage of Common Slavonic. As for the Černjahov culture itself, its northern boundary adjoined the area of Slav ethnogenesis where contacts, both in trade and in warfare, are especially attested for the fourth century. This is the period of Ermanaric, whose war against the *Venethi* must presumably have been waged in southern Russia, but whose conquest of profitable sources of trade in the North had brought the Goths into closer touch with the Slavs of the Upper Dnieper-Volga region. Here, too, loanword traffic has to be seen against a background of trade (and warfare) much of which can be substantiated from archaeological finds.

The background to Germanic and possibly Gothic influence on Finnish seemed reasonably clear a few decades ago, but recent work has introduced new prospects which leave us more uncertain than ever before. Some have explained this influence by postulating immediate contiguity of Goths and Finns along the coastline of the southeastern Baltic, but this is no longer accepted (there is no evidence that the Finns extended as far as the Prussians, whilst it is improbable that Baltic, with a very restricted number of Gothic loanwords, transmitted the considerably larger number of Germanic loanwords found in Finnish). This lack of geographical contiguity, however, does not render contact between the Goths at the mouth of the Vistula and Finnic speakers in southwestern Finland and Estonia impossible, for greater importance is now attached to the connecting as well as separating function of water (across the Baltic as much as the North Sea), especially where trade is involved. That the Goths on the Vistula could be involved in this was made likely (forty years ago!) by a phonological examination (from both linguistic directions) of early Germanic loanwords in Finnish, which showed that the earliest date for this loan-traffic was about the birth of Christ, when the Goths were settled in northern Poland (Fromm 1957-8). This in itself did not establish that the Germanic starting-point for this traffic was necessarily Gothic, but this was then suggested on non-linguistic grounds by adducing archaeological evidence for Gothic settlements at about this time in southwestern Finland and Estonia, particularly in the form of trading centres.

As with the other language-groups it is possible to divide the Finnish material into several cultural categories, but in what follows I can give only a brief selection in which, because of still remaining doubts as to their point of origin within Germanic, the words in question are given in their Finnish form. Political authority is exemplified by *kuningas* 'king', *ruhtinas* 'lord', *valta* 'power', *tuomita* 'to judge'; warfare by *keihäs* 'spear' and *miekka* 'sword'; agriculture by *lammas* 'sheep', *kaura* 'oats', *ruis* 'rye', *pelto* 'field'; the household by *lattia* 'floor', *paita* 'shirt', *patja* 'cushion', *laipio/laupio* 'ceiling'; minerals by *kulta* 'gold', *rauta* 'iron'; trade by *kauppa* 'trade'. The range of terms for political authority and agriculture suggests that we may be dealing here with more than trading-centres, rather with settlements from which political control was exercised.

Contact between the Goths and the Finnic peoples was possible by more routes than the maritime one from the mouth of the Vistula across the eastern Baltic Sea. Ermanaric's trade-routes to the north in the Dnieper-Volga area also reached as far as the Volga/Oka Finnic peoples with whom the names given by Jordanes (*Getica* 116: *Merens, Mordens, Imniscaris*) have been associated. Even though linguistic traces have been claimed for this trade-route, too, the difficulty in making use of this lies in the fact that by this time linguistic contact between these eastern Finnic peoples and those settled round the Baltic Sea had been lost, so that Gothic loanwords could not have reached the latter from this direction. Ermanaric's trade-routes also ran northwestwards, however, where they possibly reached the Baltic peoples, so that we may ask whether conceivably the loanword traffic they carried also penetrated to the neighbouring Finns. If it did, this was unlikely to have been, as we have seen, *via* the Balts, so that the remaining possibility would be transmission by the Slavs. Here it is significant that amongst the Gothic loanwords into Slavonic which could be regarded as trading terms several are also attested in Finnish (and/or Baltic). Even here we are uncertain whether these terms were borrowed separately into each of the three recipient languages or whether we face a consecutive loan-process running by stages from south to north.

The whole question of Germanic loans into Finnish has been radically affected by recent suggestions which transfer their beginning back to the Bronze Age, thus dating them at least a thousand years earlier. However, it remains uncertain how far this rethinking affects the Goths in particular, since it concerns only the *earliest* loans, so that the duration of linguistic contact need not exclude later loans, in a period such as that traditionally proposed when the Goths could come into question. With such a revolutionary redating, affecting the internal chronology of Primitive Germanic as much as the relationship of Germanic to Finnish, the last word has not yet been spoken. We still need clarification on the dating of such later loanwords (could they indeed have come from the Vistula Goths?) and on the cultural categories into which they fall.

After extending his sway to the north, Ermanaric, Jordanes tells us, subdued the Germanic *Heruli*, dwelling near lake *Maeotis* or the Sea of Azov. We are taken in this same direction by the next stage in our argument, the existence of so-called 'Crimean Gothic' (Stearns 1978). Goths were present in the Crimea from the last quarter of the fourth century, where their peninsular semi-isolation protected them to some extent from the fate which the Hunnic irruption brought upon the Goths of the Pontic mainland, at least to judge by later references to them. (A ninth-century *Vita* of St Cyril refers to them praising God in their own tongue and in the thirteenth century Wilhelm Ruysbroek who visited the Crimea talks of their Germanic language.) This remained a spoken idiom at least until the sixteenth century when a Flemish ambassador Busbecq recorded a number of Crimean Gothic words. Despite a bowdlerized transmission most of them are recognizably Germanic, but some even explicitly Gothic, since although some features differ from Wulfila's Gothic others are more significantly in agreement with it, especially on points which distinguish it from North or West Germanic. (The list also happens to contain two words, for 'hundred' and 'thousand', from the Iranian languages, the first of which has also reached as far as Finnish.) However restricted the material, it is an important linguistic confirmation of the southeasternmost point to which the Gothic migrations took them.

Up to this point (with the exception of Crimean Gothic) we have been dealing with the Goths' contacts with peoples who, to judge by the line drawn by Tacitus (*Germania* 46) between the *Germani* and those dwelling beyond them, lived in a state of abject and impoverished barbarism. Even if we take into account any exaggeration by Tacitus something of this must be true, for it is an attitude shared by the *Germani* themselves if we accept the etymological derivation of 'Finn' (a people placed by Tacitus on the bottom rung of civilization) from the verb *finþan* 'to find', referring to their status as no more than hunter-gatherers. On the boundaries of the civilized world Germanic must have possessed prestige amongst these other peoples, since the loanword traffic we have been considering is significantly one-way traffic (with one exception only, Gothic *plinsjan* 'to dance' from Slavonic, presumably because it denoted a particular form of dancing). From now on, however, the position changes radically: the Goths are now the recipients of cultural loanwords, first in their contacts with the Iranian nomadic horse-peoples of the steppes and in their need to adjust to these novel surroundings and then, beyond the self-imposed limits of this essay, in the even more fundamental changes brought about by their encounter with the Greco-Roman world on the Danubian frontier.

Not merely the Goths, but all the Germanic tribes that reached the extreme southeast confronted new geographical conditions in the open steppes to which they had to adjust, mainly by learning from the nomadic peoples largely dominant there, above all by adapting to the use of the horse as a means of overcoming the problem of distance. It was in the treeless steppes, as opposed to the woodland of the North, that the wild horse had been domesticated and stronger or faster varieties bred. How novel the use of the horse in warfare was for the *Germani* is suggested by Tacitus: they may use them, but they lack speed, so that the real strength of their armies lies with foot-soldiers (*Germania* 6). By contrast, the horse was the focus of the military tactics of the nomadic peoples of the steppes and it is from their example that the *Germani* learned to make greater use of the horse. Our earliest evidence of this adaptation concerns, not surprisingly because of their earlier migration to the southeast, the *Bastarnae*, but these are followed by the Goths and other East Germanic tribes whose model was provided by the Sarmatians and the Alans. In addition to this adoption of mounted warfare other features such as the short sword or a form of armour as body-protection were taken over. By contrast with these changes in the East the Germanic tribes in the West remained largely true to traditional Germanic modes of warfare.

The question which this acculturation of the Goths and their predecessors to the world of the steppes raises for us is whether it left any reflection in the Germanic languages. In considering this I divide my examples into two groups: words which were borrowed so early from the south-east that they reached the Goths while they were still in northern Poland and words which were adopted only in the new surroundings of the Pontic world. This distinction corresponds to what can also be shown for Latin loanwords in Gothic: some (mainly trade-words) are likewise early (before the Goths began their trek), whilst most derive only from the Danubian border-zone. This parallel suggests that the Germanic tribes, while still in northern Europe, were exposed to cultural influence from the south from two sources: from Rome (whose main trade-routes were from the North Sea to the Baltic and from *Carnuntum* along the amber road to the Baltic) and from the Black Sea (along the trade-route to the Baltic).

We have already looked at one example of an early loan from the south-east: the word for 'hemp' was probably passed from the Thracians to the *Bastarnae* before the First Sound Shift and spread throughout *Germania* long before the Goths penetrated this far. Another word which was also borrowed early from the southeast is possibly connected with it: Gothic *páida,* 'jerkin, short coat' (also in other Germanic languages) (Frings 1955). It is cognate with Greek *baítē* 'leather coat' (of Illyrian or Thracian origin), but the change of *b-* to *p-* implies, as with the word 'hemp', an early loan before the First Sound Shift. This renders unlikely any direct contact with Greek at so early a date and suggests, again as with 'hemp', direct contact between the Thracians and the *Bastarnae*. What may have occasioned a loan of this kind is suggested by one of the uses to which Wulfila puts a verb formed from *páida* in translating the Bible: it is used in the phrase 'putting on the breastplate (*brunjö*) of 'righteousness'. That this was no chance translator's decision is confirmed by Old English *herepād* 'coat of mail' and other *here-* compounds where the second element equally suggests protective clothing. This particular meaning not merely suggests the context in which the word may have been borrowed, it also provides a further link with 'hemp', since this piece of clothing was made of wool, linen or hemp, the latter being a stout fabric used for protection in fighting as long as metal armour was relatively rare in *Germania*. Several considerations combine to suggest that *páida* and 'hemp' were loaned together at a very early stage.

An early loan has likewise been suggested for Gothic *mēki* 'sword', with parallels in other Germanic languages, but also in Slavonic and in Finnish (Szemerényi 1979). This word is regarded as an itinerant word, not inherited by Germanic and Slavonic from Indo-European, but adopted as a loanword from one of the Iranian languages where it denoted originally something attached to the waist-belt. The Gothic form of the word would account for the Germanic forms and also, as we have seen, possibly for its presence in Slavonic and Finnish. However, if we make the temptingly obvious assumption that the Goths acquired this word from one of the Iranian peoples in south Russia this places us chronologically in a tight corner, since the earliest North Germanic example of the word is from a runic inscription from Vimose, dated around 250 AD. This allows an improbably short timespan for the Goths to have adopted the word in the south, passing it back to the north, and for North Germanic to have adopted it in turn. If we take this difficulty seriously we must entertain the possibility that the word reached the Goths (as a trade-word or do we have to fall back on the *Bastarnae* yet again?) while they were still in the Vistula area, from which transmission to North Germanic by 250 is much more credible. This early loan would be confirmed if we can identify the *gladii breves*, mentioned by Tacitus (*Germania* 43) as characteristic of the East Germanic tribes without being restricted to them, with the *mēki*. It may be significant that the sword found at Vimose is a short two-bladed one. By contrast with this early spread from Gothic into North Germanic, the borrowing into Slavonic is dated later (because of Slavonic sound-changes), some time in the fifth century, but this does not contradict what we have seen above.

We turn now to some words for which there is reason to think that they were adopted by the Goths only in the new conditions they faced in south Russia. Unsurprisingly, given their need to adapt to the mode of life of mounted nomads, one of these is a word for horse, even though it happens not to be attested in the restricted lexis of Wulfila's translation of the Bible, but rather in Old High German *(h)ros*, Old English *hors*, Old Norse *hors/hross*. To argue that the word is a loanword is not to suggest that Germanic possessed no word for 'horse', but rather that the new word competed with native ones (e.g. Old English *eoh*, Old Norse *jór*, cognate with Latin *equus*) because it denoted a new breed of horse, not just for horse-riding, but for fighting on horseback. This word has parallels in Finnic, both in the western and in the eastern branches, which in view of their later separation suggests an early loan into Common Finnic, which for that reason cannot have been from Gothic. The origin for both the Germanic and the Finnic forms has been traced to Sarmatian (attested in Ossetian and some Caucasian languages which borrowed the word from the Alans). That the mounted nomads of the steppes should have been the source of such a word need not surprise us, but it is difficult to imagine that the Goths who encountered them and adapted to their ways only in the empty expanses of the South East could have felt the need for this loanword before this encounter. In this respect the word for 'horse' differs from trading words like 'hemp' and *páida*.

Our next word refers to the living conditions of horsed nomads and for that reason is also likely to have been taken over in the steppes. Cognates of the English adjective 'sour' occur in West and North Germanic with that meaning, but also in Slavonic ('raw', but also as a noun in Old Slavonic meaning 'cheese') and in Lithuanian ('salted'). Despite this spread it has not been possible to establish an Indo-European descent for these forms, except to link them with Iranian terms from which they were probably borrowed and which mean 'fermented drink, beer' or 'koumis, mare's milk'. A word originally suggesting a fermented drink or food and in regular use with nomadic peoples spread from them to Germanic and Slavic tribes in eastern Europe (but also reaching the Baltic languages as well as the western and eastern branches of Finnic) in much the same way as modern 'yoghurt' (of Turkish origin). Just how characteristic of the Iranian peoples the use of mare's milk as a standard food was can be seen from the description of the Scythians in the *Iliad* as 'milk-eaters'.

If these two words conjure up a picture of nomads carrying their food with them on horseback the routes they followed are suggested by another term, however unlikely seeming: English 'path' (with parallels in West and North Germanic as well as Finnish). Germanic words beginning with *p-* are extremely rare and generally loanwords, but possible parallels like Greek *póntos* 'sea' and Latin *pons* are semantically too distant to be acceptable. Only in Iranian **paθ-* 'path' do we find a unique combination of semantic, phonological and morphological agreements which could explain the northern words. If we accept Iranian origin then the contact must have been with East Germanic (thence into the other Germanic languages and Finnish), but in this case the loan must have taken place *after* completion of the First Sound Shift (*p-* remains *p-*) and after the earliest possible contact between East Germanic and Iranian but, since the word is common West Germanic, some time *before* the Anglo-Saxon invasion of England. This gives us admittedly an uncomfortably long timespan (300 BC - 300 AD). There is no indication that the word was adopted into Gothic in particular, rather than East Germanic at large, but equally, especially given the dating after the Sound Shift, no pointer to an early spread northwards (as with 'hemp' and *páida*). Instead, it is probable that it was taken over in the region through which the Sarmatian or Alan nomads' paths passed over the steppes into which the *Germani*, too, had now penetrated (already with Aeschylus we find a reference to the 'Scythian path').

By contrast, a loan from Iranian into Gothic in particular has been established for a last example, the second element in four Gothic compound nouns: *brūþfaþs* 'bridegroom', *hundafaþs* 'centurion', *þūsundifaþs* 'chiliarch' and *swnagogafaþs* 'ruler of a synagogue'. Gothic is the only Germanic language to continue this Indo-European word for 'master' (as in Latin *potis* 'powerful', Greek *pósis* 'husband'), which is enough to make one suspect special factors at work. The first of these Gothic examples (*brūþfaþs*) stands apart as an archaism: it differs from all other Germanic languages (which employ another second element, e.g. Old High German *brūtigomo*) and it belongs to the same household context as other Indo-European compounds with the same element (e.g. Greek *despótēs* 'master of a slave'). The other three Gothic terms differ in referring either to a military formation or to a social group, where the last (*swnagogafaos*) stands apart likewise, this time as a late (Christian) formation, called into being in order to render Greek *archisynágōgos*.

Our problem therefore is reduced to accounting for the origin of the two words denoting leaders of a military formation made up of a hundred and a thousand combatants respectively. In using these forms Wulfila can have derived no impetus from Latin *tribunus* or *centurio* (derivatives, not compounds), but also no assistance from Greek compounds with *archi-* or *-archēs/-archos*, because his normal translations of these Greek models follow a quite different pattern. It is true that Gothic *hundafaþs* and *þūsundifaþs* correspond to Greek *hekatontárchēs* and *chilíarchos*, but the Gothic formations are unique in Wulfila's text as renderings for the Greek. Where the impetus in Gothic may have come from is suggested by the fact that the Greek forms themselves are based on Persian models. Their earliest occurrences in Greek are in regard to the organization of the Persian army and civil administration, based on a decimal grouping, running from ten to 10,000. Moreover, the original Persian terms for those in charge of these decimal groups are compounds made up of the relevant numeral and the word *pati* which is the Iranian equivalent of the Gothic *faþs* which was our starting-point. Greek may have followed the Persians in devising its own terms for their military formations, but the Goths were dependent not on the Persians themselves but on Iranians of the Pontic region for terms which followed the Iranian model more closely in using the cognate Gothic term for the second element of its compounds. (Gothic dependence on Iranian may have gone even further, affecting the numeral itself, if we recall that the two Iranian loanwords in Crimean Gothic are words for 'hundred' and 'thousand'.) A striking parallel with Gothic is also provided by another language which followed the Persian model in this group of words, for Armenian makes use of *pet* as its equivalent of *pati* not merely in its military titles, but also (in a Christian context) in its term for 'ruler of a synagogue', as in Gothic.

A last step in our linguistic survey following the footsteps of the Goths to the point where on the Danubian frontier they were finally exposed to the influence of the Greco-Roman world, from which they took over many more loanwords than from the peoples of the steppes, is to mention briefly their contact with the Latin speakers in the Sîntana de Mureş area, in other words the possible presence of Gothic (or Gepid) loanwords in Romanian. It is a subject which has been plagued by scholarly chauvinism, but which is rendered difficult in any case by the number of alternative languages which have to be taken into account before we can fall back on Gothic as the possible source of a Romanian word (Greek, Slavonic, Hungarian, Albanian, Turkish). In other words, this problem repeats in concentrated form the range of linguistic demands imposed upon us by the nature of the Goths' migration and by the movements of other peoples since then. It also repeats the twofold division established for Gothic loanwords into the languages of other peoples they encountered on their trek up to this point. On the one hand there are therefore Romanian place-names which, like *Gueux* in France, are taken to go back to their settlement in the region in question (e.g. *Goteşti* or *Munte Gotului*). On the other hand there are words which could have found their way directly from Gothic into Romanian or *via* another Balkan language. To the first category belongs, for example, Romanian *gard* 'fence, enclosure': this cannot be derived from the Slavonic forms of the same loanword **gordj/gradj*, for they mean 'town, castle' and do not show the meaning shared by Romanian and Germanic. To the second category we may attribute Romanian *tureci* 'gaiters', which has been shown to have entered Romanian *via* Albanian.

With this arrival of the Goths in the borderland of the Roman Empire and with their first contact with Latin speakers and the totally new cultural influence to which they were now subjected we break off our accompaniment of them from the Baltic to the Black Sea area. Up to now their migrations have taken them in a southeasterly direction, but after their sojourn in the Balkans their direction is pronouncedly westwards (Italy, Gaul, Spain). The point where we have broken off is of pivotal importance in more than just a geographical sense, for it is here that the Goths, whose earlier acculturation had been to the conditions of life on the steppes, come under influences which are, by contrast, pronouncedly western: the riches of Roman civilization (going far beyond what had earlier reached them by trade-routes to the north), writing in a Mediterranean script, Christianity. Wulfila is the focal point of all these influences, with him the Goths enter the realm of recorded history and leave behind the period of prehistory on which language, however contentious its findings, can throw some light which is not available to other disciplines.

References

Textual sources:

Battle of the Goths and the Huns: see Heusler and Ranisch 1903: 1-12.
Jordanes
        Getica: see Mommsen 1882.
Tacitus
        Germania: see Anderson 1938.
Widsith: see Malone 1935.

Bibliography:

Altheim, F.
  1943   *Die Krise der Alten Welt im 3. Jahrhundert n. Zw. und ihre Ursachen. Erster Band: Die außerrömische Welt.* Berlin: Ahnenerbe-Stiftung.
  1956   Greutungen. *Beiträge zur Namenforschung* 7: 81-93.
  1959   *Geschichte der Hunnen. I: Von den Anfängen bis zum Einbruch in Europa.* Berlin: de Gruyter.
Anderson, J. G. C.
  1938   *Cornelii Taciti de Origine et situ Germanorum.* Oxford: Clarendon Press.
Bailey, H. W., & A. S. C. Ross
  1961   Path. *Transactions of the Philological Society* [1961]: 107-142.
Benveniste, É.
  1963   Interférences lexicales entre le gotique et l'iranien. *Bulletin de la Société Linguistique de Paris* 58: 41-57.
Bierbrauer, V.
  1994   Archäologie und Geschichte der Goten vom 1.- 7. Jahrhundert. Versuch einer Bilanz. *Frühmittelalterliche Studien* 28: 51-171.
Brøndal, V.
  1928   Mots 'scythes' en nordique primitif. *Acta Philologica Scandinavica* 3: 1-31.
Frings, T.
  1955   Paida. *Beiträge zur Geschichte der deutschen Sprache und Literatur (Halle)* 77: 221-234.

Fromm, H.
 1957-8   Die ältesten germanischen Lehnwörter im Finnischen. *Zeitschrift für deutsches Altertum* 88: 81-101, 211-240, 299-324.

Gamillscheg, E.
 1935   *Romania Germanica. Sprach- und Siedlungsgeschichte der Germanen auf dem Boden des alten Römerreichs. Band II: Die Ostgoten. Die Langobarden. Die altgermanischen Bestandteile des Ostromanischen. Altgermanisches im Alpenromanischen.* Berlin: de Gruyter.

Heather, P. J.
 1991   *Goths and Romans 332-489.* Oxford: Clarendon Press.

Heusler, A., & W. Ranisch
 1903   *Eddica Minora. (Das Lied von der Hunnenschlacht).* Dortmund: Ruhfus.

Karsten, T. E.
 1928   *Die Germanen. Eine Einführung in die Geschichte ihrer Sprache und Kultur.* Berlin: de Gruyter.

Kazanski, M.
 1992   Les *arctoi gentes* et 'l'empire' d'Hermanaric. Commentaire archéologique d'une source écrite. *Germania* 70: 75-122.

Kiparsky, V.
 1934   Die gemeinslavischen Lehnwörter aus dem Germanischen. *Annales Academiae Scientiarum Fennicae,* B. 32 (2): 1-329.

Kluge, F.
 1913   *Urgermanisch. Vorgeschichte der altgermanischen Dialekte.* Strassburg: Trübner.

Koivulehto, J.
 1995   Finnland. Sprachliches. In *Reallexikon für Germanische Altertumskunde* (2. ed.). 9: 77-89.

Malone, K.
 1935   *Widsith.* London: Methuen

Mommsen, T.
 1882   *Iordanis Romana et Getica.* In *Monumenta Germaniae Historica. Auctores Antiquissimi,* 5, 1. Berlin: Weidmann.

Otrębski, J.
 1966   Die ältesten germanischen Lehnwörter im Baltischen und Slavischen. *Die Sprache* 12: 50-64.

Ritter, R.-P.
 1993   *Studien zu den ältesten germanischen Entlehnungen im Ostseefinnischen.* Frankfurt: Lang.

Specht, F.
 1939   Greutungi - Graudenz? *Zeitschrift für vergleichende Sprachforschung* 66: 224-226.

Stearns, M.
 1978   *Crimean Gothic. Analysis and etymology of the corpus.* Saratoga, CA: Anma Libri.

Struve, K. W.
 1991   Zur Ethnogenese der Slawen. In *Starigard/Oldenburg. Ein slawischer Herrschersitz des frühen Mittelalters in Ostholstein.* M. Müller-Wille (ed.), pp. 9-28. Neumünster: Wachholtz.

Szemerényi, O.
 1979   Goth. *meki* 'sword'. *Zeitschrift für vergleichende Sprachforschung* 95: 110-118.

Vernadsky, G.
   1951   Der sarmatische Hintergrund der germanischen Völkerwanderung.
                   Saeculum 2: 340-392.
Wagner, N.
   1967   *Getica. Untersuchungen zum Leben des Jordanes und zur frühen
                   Geschichte der Goten.* Berlin: de Gruyter.
Wolfram, H.
   1988   *History of the Goths.* Berkeley: University of California Press.

Discussion

SCHWARCZ: On page 11: Goths and Scandinavia. It's a question of Gothic prehistory, as you remarked, a lot of the Visigoths were stationed on the Vistula. You noted Bierbrauer's study (1994), but I am not quite convinced about the possible connections with Scandinavia, so I would like you to enlarge on this.

GREEN: I did not go into that question for three reasons. First because to deal with the question whether the Goths came from the continent or from Sweden (mainly Sweden as far as Scandinavia is concerned) would have taken up much too much space. Secondly, since I was basing my argument at that stage on the evidence provided by Jordanes, I thought it safer to start where Jordanes starts, namely with their settlement in the lower Vistula area. A third reason is that, as long as we talk about a 'Traditionskern' of tribal migrations with any number of scattered tribal elements or fragments joining and leaving in unending confusion, it seems to me that we have a very uncertain idea of what the actual Gothic constituent is. If that is so, I think it makes it largely irrelevant what the origin of the Goths may be.

SCHWARCZ: I occupied myself with this part of the early history of the Goths, especially when they were *Gotones*, and with the question of where they arrived on the Black Sea coast and where they were before. I think one of the biggest obstacles on the way to this is Jordanes because of his accounts of the sixth century. He is given too much attention in comparison to the sources which appear from the first and the third century AD. If you look at those, you must ask the question where is the name of the *Gotones* first mentioned. You find that it is around Christ's birth and it is mentioned in connection with Maroboduus and his realm in Bohemia. All early contemporary mentions of *Gotones* are on the continent. If you ask the historical question, contemporaries do not mention them in Scandinavia but on the continent. As to the first mention of Goths in Scandinavia, you find that it occurs in the second century and it concerns those people who are in Jordanes' *Getica* later, especially the Gauts. These are mentioned in Scandinavia by Ptolemy in the second century.

GREEN: Could I interject. Earlier this year I was in Sweden discussing this problem with a number of Swedish archaeologists. They, of course, are firmly convinced of the Swedish origin of the Goths. But even amongst the Swedes there is dissension as to where in Sweden the Goths may have come from. Four of the contestants being Västergötland, Östergötland, Åland and Gotland. So to take the problem back to Swedish origins would have opened up yet another hornets' nest of scholarly disagreement.

SCHWARCZ: I am personally convinced that late sixth-century Scandinavia is connected with the Baltic, and not through the *Gotones*. And concerning archaeology I think the *Gotones* developed in the Wielbark culture in the region of northern Poland. This is now quite clear and the Scandinavian connections of that culture are usually are seen in those things called 'Dummarringers', stone rings where there are a few graves or none at all, and the evidence for those started in 80 AD, and the earliest mention of the *Gotones* in the historiographical sources are before this. So the possible Scandinavian influence on the Wielbark culture has no connection with the ethnogenesis of that culture and of the Gotonic entity in this region.

GREEN: I hope I made it clear that I too have my doubts about the Scandinavian origin of that culture and therefore of the Goths. That's another reason for my not wanting even to touch that hornets' nest.

SCHWARCZ: You are quite right, I too think so. Only a correction on page 11 where you say where the southernmost parts of the Gothic tribe are. I think you meant 'northernmost'.

GREEN: I mean northern Pontic area. Even that does not exclude the possibility of Gothic sea raids into the south Pontic area.

AUSENDA: I agree with your coherent groups on this. I have another question on the same page, it is a very simple one: what was the timing of the First Sound Shift and what was its cause.

GREEN: Cause! Certainly to deal quickly with the latter, we don't know about the cause of the First Sound Shift. Even when we move into historical times and come to the Second Sound Shift, we still don't know the cause. So I'm not going to stick my neck out on what unfortunately for philologists is an understandable, but impossible question. When did it occur? There too there is a buzz of scholarly disagreement. I think the nearest consensus could be reached for about the third or fourth century BC. That I think would attract most support amongst philologists today.

AUSENDA: Yes, but I am sure there are some theories about the First Sound Shift. We are curious; could you say something about it?

GREEN: No, I cannot.

AUSENDA: Perhaps for acculturation reasons, in contact with another language and they tried to keep the difference. For instance Latin rhotacism seems to have occurred more or less at the beginning of the Second Punic War. It might have had to do with alliances and the expansion of the Latin-speaking world.

GREEN: Giorgio, if I were convinced that any of the arguments put forward for an explanation of either sound shift were acceptable, I would say something. This has attracted, not really disagreement, but some way-out suggestions. For example, it has been suggested, as regards the Second Sound Shift, that the shift of Germanic *p* to OHG *pf* came about in South Germany—I am stating the matter as hilariously as I can to show you my attitude towards such information—because the Bavarians and *Alamanni* were in a mountainous area at the time, lost breath and were panting and so instead of *p* they uttered *pf*. I am not going to waste our time by discussing theories of that nature.

AUSENDA: It is interesting to see that philologists are so far away from the truth that they put forth such theories.

GREEN: That situation is not confined to my discipline [laughter]. Another theory which has been put forward for the First Sound Shift has been to invoke the possibility of what's known as a substratum, the Germanic tribes coming in and imposing their language on non-Germanic people beneath them. The trouble with that to account for the First Sound Shift is that the evidence for Germanic occupation of northern Europe is centuries earlier than the First Sound Shift.

It is unfortunate that the type of question that the outsider asks the philologist in a place like this is precisely the type of question to which the philologist has no answer. We record linguistic changes, we can do something about dating and locating them but as to explaining them, only in the very rare case can we come up with an explanation, but indeed very rarely.

AUSENDA: Interestingly enough this is not true only about past events but of contemporary ones as well, I have detected a tendency toward nasalization in modern Italian and I have no idea why. It is difficult to explain sound shifts even while they are going on. Maybe it's a sociolinguistic effect of class differentiation.

WOOD: My question concerning page 12 is, can the philologists say anything about numbers or proportions of peoples needed to effect linguistic change?

GREEN: I don't think we can say anything about numbers. I think we might be able to say something about the position of people in a society who could possibly be influential in bringing about linguistic change. For example, the adoption of a different language by a tribe in its movement almost certainly was triggered by intermarriage and by the fact that in such cases it was the wife who spoke the new language and passed that language on to the children. In other cases where we are dealing with the import of terms, say Latin into Germanic, expressing luxury goods, then it's likely to be people in the higher ranks in that society who have an interest in these luxury goods, who are responsible for adopting the word. Where we have military terminology, then it could be a case of Germanic warriors adopting Roman military technique or Germanic warriors going into service in the Roman army. So that it is possible to come up with a number of suggestions, but they are no more than suggestions, as to the areas in society where one can imagine words first finding a hold within that language. But as to numbers I don't think that we can provide any information at all.

WOOD: Can I push the subject further on to gender. Would the point about the mother's language lead you to think that there was a greater tendency for migrating groups who ended up in the Roman Empire to marry Roman women than for Roman males to marry barbarian females?

GREEN: Yes, I would. I quote one example. It is the only clear and uncontested example of an East Germanic, I think myself Gothic, loanword into Latin in the

Balkans in the third century (one example in the early fourth) namely the word for a bride, or a young married woman. The Latin attested on inscriptions from this area is *brutis* and it is, of course, from Gothic (similar to the English word 'bride'), as attested by Wulfila *brūþs*. So that kind of evidence would point in that direction.

AUSENDA: But you can also trace the marriage of Germanic women to Roman soldiers to the names they gave them, Barbara and so on, which are popular to this day among German women. Those are very common names. On the contrary there are very few male Latin names in German.

GREEN: That is true of the period up to 400. The situation gets immediately different, however, once one comes to the occupation of Gaul by the Franks, where the converse takes place and it is an onomastic mode for even non-Germanic speakers in *Francia* to adopt Germanic names. I think that one must pose a chronological distinction in that area.

AUSENDA: At that point the Germanic population was dominant over the Roman population. That is the reason for this naming fashion.

GREEN: Yes, but not, of course, numerically dominant, although politically dominant.

DÍAZ: A question about the numbers and proportions of the linguistic changes. I am thinking of the situation where, in the process of migration, the groups were of different origin and then joined together. Therefore, we must think about one *lingua franca*, a language that is used by the groups; these elements possibly used one of these languages and that was the first one that was developed.

GREEN: Yes, certainly that's an important addition. One needs a term for that situation, a *lingua Gothica*.

DÍAZ: Yes, I understand that, but there should be a possibility to obtain other references confirming the use of that tongue.

GREEN: That would imply that the linguistically dominant 'Traditionskern' was itself Gothic.

DÍAZ: I think their feeling about their own language is important in the self-definition of the group.

GREEN: It's one of the ways of defining themselves, just one of them and an important one.

SCHWARCZ: Expansion and migration clear from Bierbrauer (page 15). I agree with most of what you wrote there and I want to make a remark about the scarcity of sources concerning the way south. It is fascinating that for two hundred years of history of Goths on the Pontic frontier we have such scarcity, and I think this must be connected with the fact that in the sources of the period we usually only find a common denomination for those barbarians outside the northeastern border. Especially Herodian does not give names for these groups north of the Carpathians. I think especially if we take the time of the family of Septimius Severus and Marcus Aurelius, we have indications of political upheavals in this northern region, and I think that this was demonstrated by Herodian, he saw evidence of strong political disturbance in the region north of the Carpathians. I personally think that we must take Herodian seriously in his indications of the group of northern barbarians. I found the name of the first Roman officer with a clear Gothic relation for the period of Caracalla on an inscription from Motha; there is a *praepositus Herminarius* and his son is Guththa (*Année Épigraphique* 1911:244; or Fiebiger 1944:19f. n° 20).

GREEN: What you say is in addition to or in confirmation of my argument, I take it. Could I ask you some time for bibliographical references to what you say, because I find it useful.

SCHWARCZ: Yes, I treated this in my dissertation (1984). I have a question concerning page 15 concerning Gothic contacts with the Scythians in the Ukraine. I take it that one should not confuse the inclination of the ancients to use Scythians as a term for all those peoples in the Pontic region. We could take the Scythians as a collective entity. I don't think of those Scythians continuing in the second and first century AD but only before. It's a fact that Alans, Goths, and Sarmatians, in the sources of the later Roman Empire over the third, fourth and fifth centuries, were also called all together Scythians and, therefore, the region was called Scythia.

GREEN: That difficulty and that confusion from the Roman point of view is a long-standing one. Classical ethnography knew of the Celts and the Scythians in the far North and, if they made contact with the *Germani* in the West, the *Germani* were confused with Celts and, if they contacted them in the East, then they were confused with Scythians.

RETAMERO: Page 15, about the criteria to distinguish a superior civilization. You made reference to an immediate force and what we should understand as a superior civilization. You refer to a more complex government apparatus or another type of thing that allows us to think of a superior civilization.

GREEN: That would be one consideration, but only one. Another consideration is when we have traces of a word being borrowed from Latin into Germanic to express an object of everyday use for which the *Germani* already had a parallel, but one which obviously was driven to the perimeter by the rapid ascendancy of the Latin loanword. This suggests that the original Germanic object was of less utility or perhaps even less fashionableness than the imported Roman one. So to that extent whether one calls the adoption of a fashion a necessary acknowledgement of a superior civilization or not is a moot point, but in certain cases it can be shown that what comes in is not really a fashion but a better fabricated or designed or more long-lasting object than what the *Germani* possessed already.

RETAMERO: But could you say then that this predominance of Latin over Germanic language is tied to the fact that Romans had a more complex state apparatus than *Germani*.

GREEN: What must be brought into consideration is the fact that we are dealing with a clash between two cultures and a clash between two languages, and if one looks at the linguistic interaction between the two there is a striking disparity between the number of Latin words which enter Germanic and on the other hand Germanic words which enter Latin. Germanic words which enter Latin number at the most 30 and occur generally with only one classical author. On the other hand when one looks at Latin words into Germanic languages, their number is about

600 and they are words which, for the most part, spread in one form or another throughout most of the Germanic languages. It's that disparity which underlies my argument.

AUSENDA: I believe that there is some written evidence that the Goths were overwhelmed by Constantinople with its monuments and wealth. Can you give some support to this idea?

SCHWARCZ: Even in the sixth century there is evidence that anybody occupying a post of importance in the Gothic world and could do it, was content to change it for a title and a villa near Constantinople.

GREEN: There is evidence, too, from Anglo-Saxon, where the ruins of the Roman city of Bath were regarded with such awe that they were described as the work of giants. Giants in the metaphorical sense, in the sense of cultural giants.

DÍAZ: A question about the changes in the linguistic usage and new reality. The Goths were using more and more the Latin language but when did they decide to change the use of the language? We have, for example the reference to Euric using an interpreter with the bishop of Pavia, and later we have a passage in the Third Council of Toledo that refers to *plurimae linguae* and the Reccared intervention. Perhaps the evolution of the Gothic language was related to the acceptance of the Romans and the acceptance of a new role by the Goths in the Empire. They considered that a self-definition was necessary in the period when they were fighting the Romans but not later when they took up the new civilization. What was the reason for abandoning the Gothic language? It is the usual question in order to understand the general process.

GREEN: The question is well beyond the limits of this paper.

DÍAZ: I know, but I would like to know whether you can shed some light on it.

GREEN: I don't know the answer. Similarly, in a field which I know slightly better there is clear evidence that the Franks in occupation of northern Gaul went on speaking their Germanic vernacular for some considerable time. There is also evidence that the linguistic frontier between Germanic and Romance in northern *Francia* was not a static one and reached only a roughly final definition towards the late Middle Ages. So that one must assume a lengthy period with a hither and thither of the linguistic frontier.

SCHWARCZ: I think there was one difference between the Franks and the Goths. The Goths actually in the fifth and also in the sixth century in southern *Francia* and in Spain were never settled exclusively here and there, but were settled among Romans and there was close interchange. The evidence for which is that the language of the Visigothic administration of Toulouse was Latin.

VELÁZQUEZ: There is a written tradition in Latin; both have a written language. The fact of being able to use a written language with a cultural base in administration seems very important to me.

GREEN: Another conjunction one has to take into account is the use of the vernacular primarily for oral communication and Latin primarily for writing. I'm convinced it played a part in linguistic differentiation and linguistic change.

JIMÉNEZ: I think that we have to assume that the notion of state that Visigoths have reached was a notion in Latin terms not in Germanic ones. Therefore, when Gothic kings established the Gothic state in *Hispania* they had to make use of the Latin language, because the law was in Latin and because more than two thirds of their subjects were Latin speakers.

GREEN: May I make just one comment about one word you used just then and which is used in some papers which could cause an immediate reaction from philologists and Germanists like myself. You said they did not use German but used Latin. Of course they didn't use German, what you mean is not German but Germanic. German is something quite distinct.

SCHWARCZ: Of course, they used Gothic.

AUSENDA: If I may add something: what you were saying is true for Spain, it is not true for Britain, because in Britain the Germanic population continued to speak Germanic, what's the difference?

SCHWARCZ: The difference is in the relative strength of the administration. The Visigothic realm was founded in a period of relative strength, also of the Western Roman Empire of the fifth century. As far as political administration is concerned, there was a civil administration changing from a lay urban to an ecclesiastical one, and the Visigothic one within the administration of the Roman Empire still existed.

RETAMERO: Page 15 about the pre-historic route between the Baltic and Black Sea. The Goths moved from their homeland and they followed a prehistoric trade route. Is it a mere coincidence that the Goths followed this prehistoric trade route or is there a causal link between the two facts?

GREEN: I do not think it is a coincidence because, as I said in my paper, before the Goths moved in that direction other Germanic tribes had moved in that same direction. Since there is evidence of words of south-east European origin reaching back to northern *Germania* as a result of these earlier tribes' movements, then clearly there was interaction between the *Bastarnae* who had moved to the South-East and the Germanic tribes who had remained up in the North. But, it's also been argued by the Swedish archaeologist Ellegård that, in this period, one must reckon with a nearly continuous Germanic stretch between the Baltic and the Black Sea, which would assist this two-way traffic. So that when the Goths set forth much later in their south-easterly trek, they would be following the precedent of earlier Germanic tribes. There is also—here I have to accept classical archaeologists' word for this—evidence for this early trade route from the Black Sea area northwestwards, and philologists like to assume that if the *Bastarnae* moved in this direction in search of wealth or land they had knowledge of greater wealth and the possibility of land in this direction. So that I would certainly not argue in terms of this being a coincidence.

RETAMERO: Why did they travel; why was it so common in ancient societies?

GREEN: Again, a variety of suggestions have been proposed, only suggestions: climatic change, overpopulation, flooding.

RETAMERO: We can pose the same question related to the Arabic migration westwards from Asia to North Africa, the case of the Berbers or the Vandals. Can we pose the same question?

SCHWARCZ: No, we cannot. I don't think it's the same set of circumstances. This of course cannot be compared because the southern movement of the Goths is essentially in the second century. If we take the development of the Wielbark culture, we find that it is in part an expansion from the first settlements near the coast of the sea. Then it is a slow expansion southwards, and in part in the second century some of the old seats are completely left, while others remain. On the whole it is a rather slow southwards expansion and what is important is that the new places of settlement remain for another hundred and fifty to two hundred years later and can be archaeologically shown. The Arab invasion makes us think of a sudden movement with a certain purpose and destiny.

GREEN: Can it be shown archaeologically why some areas, as you just said, were left vacant when migration took place beyond them and others remained occupied?

SCHWARCZ: This is a question of historically interpreting archaeology. Now we can say something about the reasons why there is a slow movement of settlement because of the way the people lived. We can show that there are fixed cemeteries, that the settlements moved around them in a circle, because of the way they lived. They lived in a kind of agrarian economy such that after about 20 years it was necessary to find new fields because the old ones were exhausted. And this is one of the problems of settlement archaeology of this barbarian period, because there are so few traces left.

GREEN: My second question is this: how far can these settlements which remained occupied after others had moved on be associated particularly with the Gepids in northern Poland?

SCHWARCZ: Well, that is a reasonable supposition.

GREEN: You would not pronounce against that.

SCHWARCZ: Not at all, because the written sources which state a certain feeling of togetherness are realistic because there were Gepids, as shown archaeologically, and they seem to have spoken the same language.

AUSENDA: On page 21, on war and trade being two sides of the same coin. This characterized not only the relation between Romans and barbarians, but also contemporary relations between states, e.g. the biggest trade partner of Russia is Germany.

GREEN: It did not only relate to the Goths, but to countless other Germanic tribes including the Vikings.

JIMÉNEZ: Still on page 21-2 and connected to my own paper, I find this idea that military and trade terms were the most important amongst Gothic loanwords quite interesting. Was that perhaps because during this period the Goths obtained their resources from both war and trade? I believe that the first Gothic chiefs, especially Athaulf, obtained their wealth from military life and from travel as well, and I find these similarities between two groups of Goths belonging to such distant periods very interesting.

GREEN: I don't mean these to be a total explanation of Gothic society. I would say trade, agriculture and war, but at this point I was merely dealing with those two aspects, but not to the exclusion of Gothic agriculture and its importance. What is interesting is the proportion of Gothic loanwords into Slavonic and Finnish which are concerned with agriculture. Agriculture is certainly of importance, that must be stressed.

JIMÉNEZ: Yes, who practiced this agriculture? Did every Goth do so? Were the chiefs peasants as well?

GREEN: We can't say from linguistic evidence. At least I can't.

DÍAZ: Can we detect in linguistic terms the change from nomadic peoples to sedentary ones?

SCHWARCZ: They are people who moved very slowly.

DÍAZ: In the Roman army they were mobile until their definitive settlement.

GREEN: I think one must make a distinction between the Goths and such more clearly nomadic people as the Sarmatians, Alans and Huns with whom they came into contact. If the Goths migrated it was not because they were nomads, but because they were forced by military, economic, agricultural pressure to do so and they settled whenever these pressures let up, and moved on when pressures started again. In that sense one must make a distinction between migratory tribes and nomadic tribes. The Goths I would see as migratory in contrast to nomadic.

SCHWARCZ: Every time that they moved, they left their settlements which they had occupied at least for two centuries, you cannot call that nomadic. Except in time of great pressure they acted not as a people but as an army in movement. You cannot call that nomadic.

AUSENDA: Concerning this trade and war question: we are talking about the fact that Prof. Green mentioned that there was also agriculture. I think that agriculture was at a subsistence level, whereas war and trade brought surplus. They needed it for greater cohesion and concentration of resources to support a chiefdom and later a state and they could obtain it through trade and war.

JIMÉNEZ: That is because military chiefs needed a lot of money to give to their *Gefolge*. Agriculture was not a sufficient resource.

AUSENDA: Agriculture at that stage satisfied only subsistence.

DÍAZ: I think it is the same as that on page 23, about this Gothic settlement in Estonia.

SCHWARCZ: Well, it is a different one.

VELÁZQUEZ: I would like to ask what *wadia* and other words of Germanic origin mean. I am very interested in Isidore of Seville and I have done some work on the *Etymologies*. There are some interesting words of Germanic origin in the *Etymologiae*. I recall the word *Guaranen* is of different origin but the sound is the same; it has become 'garañón', the name for 'horse' in Spanish. I think that it is quite necessary to study Gothic loanwords in Latin. I believe that the main problem, or at least one of the most difficult ones, is the chronology of the loan from Germanic to Latin and vice versa. It is quite interesting but difficult.

GREEN: The word you quote as an example also comes from Germanic into Old French but from the sound changes it is clear that that loan must have been effected before the big dividing line, before 400, while the unity of the Roman Empire still made it possible for a word to be adopted into Latin at one place on the imperial frontier and to be accepted throughout imperial Latin. In other words, this particular example comes across so early that either we need not invoke the Goths as the transmitters of this word into Spanish, or, if we do, then we have to reckon with a double loan process, one before 400 in northern Gaul and one after 400 in Spain. But certainly either possibility exists for this particular word.

VELÁZQUEZ: From Gothic into Latin and the evolution of Latin to Romano-Christian is less important to me, since I am especially interested in the evolution of Latin to Spanish. However, at present I consider loans from Gothic to Latin. Onomastic words and the source of the Gothic language in Latin is a really important research topic.

SCHWARCZ: On page 23 you mention archaeological evidence of Gothic settlements in southern Finland and Estonia. I am sceptical about that.

GREEN: I was basing myself on Kazanski. I refer you to the article of his in *Germania*.

SCHWARCZ: I must say I am very sceptical of that. If you want archaeologists, you are safer with Biebrauer than with Kazanski.

GREEN: Yes, but Bierbrauer doesn't go into this point, does he?

SCHWARCZ: There is no historical evidence of them having been so far off the road.

GREEN: I was not using Kazanski as an article about settlement. I was using it as an example of military raids to ensure trade or to protect the trade route. I am not suggesting settlement.

SCHWARCZ: Is it not related to settlement? Look on page 24, second paragraph.

GREEN: Ah, that is totally different, that is not connected with Finnish evidence for Gothic settlements in western Estonia and south-western Finland at that time.

SCHWARCZ: That's too late for Gothic. There is archaeology, that's the interesting point.

GREEN: There are archaeological links between the finds in these two areas and the Wielbark culture at the same time around the mouth of the Vistula.

SCHWARCZ: Well, I would like to see them.

AUSENDA: Page 24, you refer to "recent suggestions which transfer Germanic loans back into the Bronze Age". How can this be possible with Latin loanwords in Germanic such as *kaupa* 'trade'?

GREEN: The argument does not concern Latin loanwords into Germanic which then go into Finnish. That happened much later.

SCHWARCZ: On page 24 concerning the presence of Goths in Crimea. I don't think that there is much evidence of Gothic settlement in the Crimea in the last quarter of the third century.

GREEN: I don't think that undermines my argument, which rested on the presence of the Goths subsequently and their existence there well into the sixteenth century.

References in the discussion

Textual sources:

Herodian
  Historia see Whittaker (ed.) 1969.
Isidore of Seville
  Etymologiae: see Lindsay (ed.) 1911.

Bibliography:

Bierbrauer, V.
  1994   Archäologie und Geschichte der Goten von 1.-7. Jahrhundert. Versuch einer
          Bilanz. In *Frühmittelalterliche Studien* 28: 151-171.
Ellegård, A.
  1986   The ancient Goths and the concept of tribe and migration. In *Vetenskap och
          omvärdering. Till Curt Weibull på hundraårdagen 19 augusti 1986.*
          C. Dahlström, P. Hallberg, Å. Holmberg (eds.), pp.32-62. Göteborg:
          Göteborgs universitetsbibliotek.
Fiebiger, O.
  1944   *Inschriftensammlung zur Geschichte der Ostgermanen. Neue Folge.*
          (Denkschriften der Akademie der Wissenschaften in Wien. Philosophisch.
          historische Klasse 72/2). Vienna: Verlag der Österreichische Akademie der
          Wissenschaften.
Kazanski, M.
  1992   See References at end of paper.
Lindsay, W. H. (ed.)
  1911   *Isidori Hispalensis Episcopi Etymologiarum sive Originum Libri XX.*
          Oxford: Clarendon Press. [Repr. 1966].
Schwarcz, A.
  1984   Reichsangehörige Personen gotischer Herkunft. Prosopographische Studien.
          Philolosophische Dissertation, Universität Wien.
Whittaker, C. R. (ed.)
  1969   *Herodian, History of the Empire,* 2 vols. (Loeb Classical Library). London:
          Heinemann.

THE CREATION OF THE VISIGOTHS

PETER HEATHER

Dept. of History, University College, London University, Gower St., GB-London WC1E 6BT

Although they never called themselves such, 'Visigoth' is the modern designation for that Gothic group which, under the leadership of Alaric, sacked Rome in 410, and then went on to be settled in Aquitaine 418 or 419. In the course of the fifth century, this same group went on to establish a kingdom independent of the Roman Empire, and to spread its domination across large parts of southern Gaul and Spain. This paper is not concerned, directly at least, with the factual history of this group, but rather with its nature. How are we to understand the structure of a socio-political entity which, in a twenty year period from *ca* 395 to 418, could move from the Balkans to Aquitaine, stay there for another seventy to eighty years, and then move on to Spain? This is very much the kind of question currently being asked not just of Gothic, but of all the social groups involved in the history of the so-called Migration Period.

(Visi-)Gothic studies

The old answers to such questions were straightforward. Germanic and other groups of the Migration Period were understood as closed, biologically self-reproducing entities, which moved around the map of Europe in response to simple stimuli, whether overpopulation, or desires either for better land, or to share in the wealth of Rome. Billiard balls, I suppose, might provide a reasonable analogy. If, for whatever reason, something knocked into one of these entities in the Ukraine, it might keep on rolling, bouncing off one or two places in between, until it came to rest in Spain: the same ball in a different place. For the Goths in particular, this vision of historical action was supported above all by the account of the sixth-century Gothic historian Jordanes. In his view, Ostrogoths and Visigoths, around whose military power successor states to the Roman Empire coalesced in the fifth century, were social groupings which already existed in southern Russia in the fourth. In the meantime, they had simply been propelled westwards at different moments (*Getica* esp. 5. 42; 14. 82). One extra twist was always necessary to the argument, however, because while the late Roman historian Ammianus Marcellinus mentions two Gothic subgroups in the fourth century (his own day), he names them not Visigoth and Ostrogoth, but *Tervingi* and *Greutungi*. It thus became an associated dogma of the 'billiard ball' school of history that *Tervingi* was another name for Visigoth, and *Greutungi* for Ostrogoth (e.g. Demougeot 1979:325, 342; Musset 1975:36; Thompson, 1966:1 f.).

THE VISIGOTHS FROM THE MIGRATION PERIOD TO THE SEVENTH CENTURY: AN ETHNOGRAPHIC PERSPECTIVE

© C.I.R.O.S.S.
San Marino (R.S.M.)

Such a conception of Migration Period history was also supported more generally—before say World War II—by anthropological analysis and archaeological observation. Before this date, anthropologists understood group and particularly ethnic identity as an immutable fact transmitted unerringly between generations. In the same era, archaeological study tended to focus on so-called 'culture history': the detection of clearly bounded areas of similarity in ancient remains, often based largely on archaeologically-visible pottery. The basic idea was that each cultural area belonged to a different socio-political entity of the past, and the game thus became one of guessing which archaeological area corresponded to which of the groups mentioned in ancient literary sources.

By the 1960s, further investigation had cast doubt on both of these old, essentially late-nineteenth century certainties. Anthropologists had come to stress that identity is above all a subjective perception and claim on the part of individuals, who, in the right circumstances, could change their identity or choose from a variety of options. Likewise, English-speaking archaeologists in particular were showing that archaeological cultures could not easily be equated with socio-political units of the past.[1]

In the field of Gothic studies too, a closer examination of the sources raised great doubts about Jordanes' billiard-ball vision of Gothic history. First Reinhard Wenskus in the 1960s, and then Herwig Wolfram in the 1970s departed substantially from Jordanes' account. For these two scholars, the *Tervingi* are not simply the Visigoths by another name, nor the *Greutungi* the Ostrogoths (Wenskus 1961:471 ff.; Wolfram 1988: *passim*). Even so, for both, the Goths were permanently divided in two from the third century onwards, and both perceive a broad continuity between the two pairs. For Wolfram, the *Tervingi* and Visigoths are 'ethnically identical' (1988:24), and the two sets of names are alternative designations for the same groups. *Tervingi* and *Greutungi* are the names each gave the other, where Ostrogoth and Visigoth are self-chosen, boastful names (1988:25). Thus even though Ostrogoths and Visigoths are in certain respects new peoples,[2] Wenskus and Wolfram do perceive some continuity between them and the fourth-century *Tervingi* and *Greutungi*.

That said, Wenskus and Wolfram also argued that the real conduit of continuity in Gothic history comprised not the large-scale social aggregates who fought all the battles, but a relatively small 'Traditionskern' of noble or royal families. It was these families who really defined the groups they led as Gothic, not their followers. Wolfram in particular argued that Gothic groups of the Migration Period might better be viewed as armies than peoples, and that anyone who fought with the army could become a Goth, whatever their actual biological origins. How small or large such a 'Traditionskern' might have been, is a question never explicitly addressed. But, in practice, its importance has actually been discussed in relation to

[1] Reviews of the literature on identity: e.g. Bacal 1991; Barth 1969; Bentley 1987; Kivisto 1989; Roosens 1989. On 'Culture Archaeology', see e.g. the essays in Shennan 1989; Ucko 1995.

[2] E.g. Wolfram 1988:482 note 1 and the title of his fifth chapter: "The 'New' Ostrogoths".

just two royal families, the *Balthi* of the *Tervingi*/Visigoths and the *Amali* of the *Greutungi*/Ostrogoths. This is partly because the sources provide much more substantial information about these families than any other family group, and partly because both Wenskus and Wolfram see Amal and Balth family traditions as a key determinant of Gothicness (Wolfram 1988, esp. c.1, 164-70, 248-58, 300-302).[3]

In the 1990s, Wolf Liebeschuetz adopted a still more radical position, although his debt to Wenskus and Wolfram is clear and fully acknowledged by himself. In his view, the Visigoths, which he took to mean that group of Goths which grew up around Alaric between 395 and 411, bore little if any relation to preceeding Gothic groups. They had a Gothic 'ideology', but that was little more than a cover. They were much more an army of mercenaries than a biologically self-perpetuating entity. Of ethnically heterogeneous composition, their numbers ebbed and flowed over time; they had few women amongst them, preferred cash to land, and, above all, decidedly did *not* represent a general revolt of the Goths who had crossed the Danube in 376 and who were later settled in the Balkans by the emperor Theodosius I in 382. For Liebeschuetz, events after *ca* 376 had generated a flotsam and jetsam of assorted individuals and small groups who could be put together in new combinations by an able leader (Liebeschuetz 1990:48-85; 1986). In some respects, therefore, it is a view related to those of Wenskus and Wolfram, but encompassing even less continuity.

In the last thirty years or so, then, scholarship on the Visigoths has veered from one end of a spectrum of continuity to another. Argument continues, and no doubt will continue, essentially because the sources, while full of interesting and pertinent information, leave many questions open to doubt. It would be wrong to suggest, however, that all consensus has broken down. All are clear, first of all, that the old billiard-ball vision of total continuity between pre-Hunnic fourth-century Gothic groups (*Tervingi*/*Greutungi*) and late fifth-century ones (Visigoths/Ostrogoths) must be abandoned. There is also consensus, moreover, on the next set of issues that this throws up, even if, as yet, no widely accepted answers. What degree of continuity should we envisage between third- and fourth-century Gothic groups (*Tervingi*/*Greutungi*, etc.) and their late fifth-century successors (Visigoths/Ostrogoths, etc.)? And, very much the other side of the same coin, how was this continuity transmitted? Taken together, the answers to these first two questions start to imply an answer to a third, overall, question: how strong was the sense of Gothic identity operating within the different groups labelled Gothic in our sources? What I will try to do in this paper is present my own answer to these questions, taking the Visigoths as a case study, although, as will emerge, I

---

[3] Wenskus (1961:322-3, 472 ff.) is similar, but there is disagreement on precise points. E.g. Wolfram, even if accepting the *Tervingi*/Visigoth and *Greutungi*/Ostrogoth equations, stresses to a greater extent the ethnic heterogeneity of the kingdom-forming Visigoths and Ostrogoths. Likewise, Wolfram (1979) takes a much more suspicious view of some of the details of recorded dynastic history than does Wenskus (1973:246-9; 1975:13-4).

will on occasion have to use Ostrogothic evidence where parallel Visigothic material is lacking.

From *Tervingi* to Visigoths: cruxes of continuity

The basic pattern

The basic pattern of historical transformation underlying the formation of the Visigoths is, I think, beyond dispute and would be accepted by the vast majority of scholars. The sixth-century Jordanes portrays the Visigoths as a billiard ball knocked across the river Danube into the Roman Empire by the action of Huns in 376. Reality was more interesting. In 376, at least three separate Gothic groups (that we know about) crossed the Danube in reaction to the disruption created in the north Pontic region by the arrival of the Huns:

1. Some *Tervingi* led by Alaviv and Fritigern (Ammianus 31. 3. 8 ff.). Other *Tervingi*, however, remained outside the Empire under the former overall leader Athanaric. According to Ammianus, the "majority of the population" fled with Fritigern (31. 3. 8), but Athanaric's group was powerful enough to drive some Sarmatians out of its new refuge (31. 4. 13), and may have maintained its independence into the 380s.[4]
2. Some *Greutungi*, originally from the group of Ermenaric, now led by Alatheus and Saphrax (Ammianus 31. 4. 12).
3. A force, seemingly of more *Greutungi*, led by one Farnobius, which arrived at the Danube with Alatheus and Saphrax (Ammianus 31. 4. 12), but which later suffered a separate fate from no.2 (31. 9. 3-4).

The year 376 was a time of great chaos, and Ammianus' narrative probably picks out the more organized military groupings who would figure in the run up to the battle of Hadrianople. There may also have been other, smaller social units criss-crossing the landscape (cf. Ammianus 31. 4. 2). Jordanes is straightforwardly wrong, therefore, in supposing that an already well-defined group of Visigoths simply crossed the Danube in 376. Goths deriving from previously separate Gothic groups—*Tervingi* and *Greutungi*—came separately to the river, and were treated separately by the Roman state. The *Tervingi* of Alavivus and Fritigern were allowed across the frontier, while troops were posted to exclude the *Greutungi* by force (Ammianus 31. 4. 13; 31. 5. 3).

Indeed, the Huns had very generally disrupted prevailing patterns of socio-political organization among the Goths. The *Tervingi* explicitly split as a result of Hunnic pressure. Alavivus and Fritigern and their followers (no. 1 above) had rejected Athanaric's continued leadership, even if a minority continued to support

---

4   Achelis (1900:318-19) describes the remains of 26 Gothic martyrs being brought into the Roman Empire between 383 and 392. They had been martyred under Athanaric (Sozomen *HE* 6. 37. 13 f.) so the remains must have come from some *Tervingi* left north of the Danube after 376.

the latter. Likewise, although the *Greutungi* of Alatheus, Saphrax, and Farnobius arrived in one block, those of Farnobius soon operated independently (nos. 2 & 3). Other *Greutungi* led by one Odotheus also tried to cross the Danube about a decade later in 386, but were defeated, suffering heavy casualties.[5] It is not unlikely that all these different *Greutungi* had originally belonged to the one group led by Ermenaric before the arrival of the Huns (but see Heather, 1989 for doubts about Jordanes-derived visions of the extent of Ermenaric's power). If that is the case, both the Gothic groups known before 376 fragmented in the face of Hunnic pressure, their different constituent elements adopting different strategies for self-preservation in drastically changing circumstances. Thanks to Ammianus, one half of the equation is clear. The arrival of the Huns fragmented the pre-existing political order among the Goths. The various Goths who came to the Danube in 376 did not already belong to one clearly-defined, well-established social entity.

Let us now turn our attention to the formation of the 'Visigoths', defining this group as those Goths who were settled by the still existing Roman state in Aquitaine in the late 410s, some forty odd years after the Danube crossing. The pattern is what we might expect given the fragmentation of the Goths generated by the Huns in 376. The Visigoths of Aquitaine were a new political unit largely put together during the reign of Alaric I (*ca* 395-411). The sources document the following major stages of recruitment:

a) Balkan Goths who backed the revolt against the Roman state which first made visible Alaric's power in 395, after the death of the Emperor Theodosius I.

b) Zosimus, based on Olympiodorus, reports Alaric being joined in Italy in 408 by Athaulf who led a group of Goths and Huns from Pannonia (Zosimus 5. 37. 1 ff.).

c) On the murder of the Western generalissimo Stilicho, a large number of allied 'barbarian' soldiers whom Stilicho had recruited into the Roman army, deserted Roman service to join Alaric. Their families, quartered in Italian cities, had been massacred in a pogrom (Zosimus 5. 35. 6).

d) Outside Rome, in 409/10, a large number of slaves flocked to join Alaric's Goths (Zosimus 5. 42. 3).

e) By 411/12, a group of Alans also formed part of Alaric's force, now led by his brother-in-law Athaulf. These Alans detached themselves, for payment, to defend the city of Bazas (Paulinus of Pella *Euch.* 343 ff.).[6]

Alaric may have had other sources of recruits besides, but the basic pattern is clear enough. The Visigoths settled in Aquitaine in 418 were a new creation.

---

[5]   Zosimus 4. 35. 1; 38-9 (a doublet); *Cons Const s.a.* 386; *CM* 1 244; Claudian *IV cons Hon* 626 ff.

[6]   Theoretically, the Alans of group e) could be the descendants of the Alans of the mixed Hun/Alan force which crossed the Danube in autumn 377. After 30 odd years of cooperation, it seems unlikely, however, that they would suddenly have asserted their independence.

Three Issues

This much, I think, would command consensus, although it is certainly worth stressing. While specialists are well aware of the point, handbooks continue to talk about 'Visigoths' before 376. To see that the Visigoths were a new entity, however, does not fully answer the questions raised above. The Visigoths were clearly a new *political* entity, but how much continuity of Gothic identity was there between it and Gothic groups of the pre-Hunnic period? Likewise, how was that identity transmitted? Answers to these questions turn, in fact, on some very precise issues of interpretation within the basic pattern of development we have already established.

Whom did Alaric lead in 395?

The traditional answer to this question is that Alaric led a revolt of those Goths (and their descendants) who had crossed the Danube in 376 and subsequently made a peace agreement with the Roman state in 382.[7] If so, then we can obviously identify one major element of continuity, at least, since Alaric's first supporters were Goths who had survived as such from the pre-Hunnic era north of the Danube.

As Liebeschuetz has recently pointed out, however, the one narrative source to record the start of Alaric's revolt, the history of Zosimus, does not describe it as a rebellion of the 382 Goths. In 395, Zosimus reports, Alaric demanded 'command of an army' rather than just barbarians (Zosimus 5. 5. 4). This, Liebeschuetz suggested, better fits a man wanting a career in the Roman army rather than a would-be Gothic king: an alternative career path followed by a number of known Gothic nobles (Gainas, Fravittas, Munderic and Modares). For Liebeschuetz, Alaric was the commander of a mutinous regiment of Goths in the Roman army, around whom a large, but essentially disparate, following eventually gathered. Such a vision would obviously greatly undermine the idea that there was any substantial continuity between the pre-Hunnic Goths and the Visigoths later settled in Aquitaine (Liebeschuetz 1990:51 ff.).

Zosimus' account, however, is problematic. He was not independently knowledgable, but a later compiler working at least a hundred years after the events, putting together material from, amongst others, the more contemporary historians Eunapius and Olympiodorus. The latter sources do not independently survive. It is precisely with Alaric's revolt, moreover, that, in Gothic affairs at least, Zosimus made his join between these two sources. After revolting in 395, Alaric eventually moved on to Epirus in 397. The story of these years was originally told by Eunapius. The start of Olympiodorus' historical narrative also found Alaric's Goths revolting in Epirus, but this was actually a second period of

---

[7]   In my view, the treaty of 382 encompassed both the *Tervingi* and *Greutungi* of 376, together with some other groups, but this is a further sub-issue in itself: see below notes 10, 11, & 13.

revolt dating from *ca* 405. Zosimus, however, thought the two were one, hence didn't bother to say anything about Alaric in between, and in the process erased nearly a decade of Gothic history, about which one or both of Eunapius and Olympiodorus must originally have said something.[8]

Our other sources for the years 395 to 399 are very fragmentary, and give no real information about the composition of Alaric's force. The first available characterizations of Alaric's activities date from 399, and, as soon as they begin, contemporary Romans of both East (Synesius, *De regno* 19-21, of 399; cf. Heather, 1988) and West (Claudian *De bell. Get.* 166 ff.; 610 ff., of 402) explicitly describe Alaric as leading a general revolt of the 382 Goths. No source, it should be stressed, ever describes him as anything else. Likewise, Alaric already had sufficient followers to stand up to major Roman field armies commanded by Stilicho, the de facto ruler of the Western Empire, in both 395 and 397. Alaric's supporters clearly comprised, then, even in the beginning, far more than a mutinous regiment (in more detail, Heather 1991:193 ff.).

As to the demand for a military command reported by Zosimus, this probably did originate in Eunapius' account and does seem authentic. Alaric was to demand a Roman generalship at intervals throughout the rest of his career (Heather 1991:199-200). Even after 408, when he certainly commanded a large force of Goths, Alaric continued to make this demand, the concession of which probably involved large annual payments in gold for his followers. Such payments had certainly not been granted the Goths in the treaty of 382. Notionally, it was probably presented as pay, since under this kind of agreement Alaric's followers could be seen as Roman troops. By the 440s, this kind of arrangement was used to disguise tribute payments to Attila (Priscus fr. 11. 2; Blockley 1983:278, ll. 627-31), and was also applied to Goths in the Eastern Empire in the 470s and 480s (e.g. Malchus, frr. 2, 18. 4). Under the 382 treaty, Gothic military service en masse—for instance against western usurpers—had to be negotiated in each case, and presumably paid for. Hence this previously occasional service may have been the source of the idea of at least notionally putting Alaric and his Goths on a more regular military footing, via a generalship and annual pay.[9] Even if we do see Alaric as the leader of a general Gothic revolt—as other sources, much better informed than Zosimus, report—there is still no need to reject Zosimus' report.

In addition, and perhaps most important, recent events had given the Goths a reason to rebel. Mobilized en masse against the Western usurper Eugenius, the Goths had recently found themselves, in summer 393, in the front line at the battle of the river Frigidus. They suffered there heavy casualties in fierce fighting. Reportedly 10,000 Goths died, but this figure probably cannot be taken literally.

---

[8]   On Zosimus and his sources, see generally Paschoud (1975) or Matthews (1970). The join is made at Zosimus 5. 26. 1 causing the entire omission, amongst other matters, of Alaric's first invasion of Italy (401/2).

[9]   Heather (1991:160 ff.) cf. esp. the difficulties Theodosius encountered in mobilizing Gothic troops for the Eugenius campaign (Eunapius, fr. 59; Zosimus 4. 55. 3-56. 1; see Heather 1991:183-8).

On these events, the Roman historian Orosius commented that Theodosius had won two victories for the Roman state: the first over a usurper, the second over his Gothic 'allies' (7. 35. 19). Where such attitudes prevailed, the Goths had every reason to be suspicious of Roman motives in the longer term, and must have realized that casualties incurred in Roman civil wars threatened their continued independence.

The Roman state had tolerated Gothic autonomy in the peace of 382, in fact, only because it had no choice. Heavy Roman defeats at Hadrianople in 378, and in Macedonia in 380 had made it impossible militarily to dismantle Gothic autonomy in line with normal Roman practice towards immigrants. Thus a compromise was eventually negotiated, but this was not a spontaneously voluntary change in Roman policy, nor was it generally applied (cf., in more detail, Heather 1991:165-75 commenting esp. on Themistius *Or.* 14-16). A further group of Gothic *Greutungi* under Odotheus who came to the Danube in 386, for instance, were defeated with heavy casualties and had their political autonomy dismantled according to normal Roman policy towards migrant groups (cf. Heather 1988). The compromise extracted by the Goths in 382 was thus the product of a very particular military balance of power, and should their military manpower be whittled away, so would any need for the Romans to continue to tolerate Gothic autonomy.

In sum, sources much more contemporary and less problematic than Zosimus unanimously portray Alaric as leader of the 382 Goths in revolt, and there was a real reason, early in 395, why these Goths might have wanted to revise the terms of their treaty. In my view, therefore, we can retain the element of Gothic continuity which depends upon viewing Alaric's original support as stemming from the survivors of the 376 Danube crossing who had made the original peace treaty with the Roman state in 382. They may not all have revolted as one body, but, even in 395, they must have done so in sufficient numbers for Alaric to be able to fend off the immediate and hostile attentions of Stilicho.

Even this amount of continuity, however, represents an important restructuring of the pre-Hunnic Gothic world. Of the Gothic groups who came to the Danube in 376, the survivors of both the *Tervingi* of Fritigern and the *Greutungi* of Alatheus and Saphrax (nos. 1 & 2 above) were settled under the treaty of 382. These groups never subsequently reappear as such in our sources after 382, so that, even by 395, two originally separate Gothic groups had already merged.[10]

Whom did Alaric subsequently recruit?

Of Alaric's known subsequent moments of large-scale recruiting (see above), group b) is straightforwardly described as a mixed force of Huns and Goths. There is actually quite a good argument for seeing it as a group which was already an integral part of Alaric's force, and which had been detached only recently and

---

[10] This issue occasioned much debate in San Marino, as it is usually held that the *Greutungi* of Alatheus and Saphrax were settled separately by Gratian in Pannonia in 380. This is a side issue,

temporarily to cover the flanks and rear of Alaric's advance on Italy.[11] This does not, however, affect the degree of Gothic continuity involved. For group b), the answer is partly positive (the Gothic contingent) and partly negative (the Huns). There is no indication of its overall size, nor of the balance between Huns and Goths within it. Likewise, group e) was straightforwardly non-Gothic, although the nature of its attachment to Athaulf's force is potentially germane (see below). The problematic cases are groups c) and d). Who were Stilicho's former allies who joined Alaric in 408, and who the slaves of 409/10?

Exact proportions are beyond recovery, but there were substantial numbers of Goths among group c): Stilicho's former allies. In 405/6, a pagan, and, in contemporary sources, explicitly Gothic king called Radagaisus led a major invasion of Italy (refs. as *PLRE* 2, 934). Stilicho was able to defeat it, not least, it seems, by negotiating a deal with a large number of Radagaisus' followers which led them to abandon their leader to his fate. Radagaisus was subsequently executed outside Florence, but 12,000 of his followers are said to have been recruited as Roman allies at this point (Olympiodorus, ed. Blockley fr. 9: a passage to which we will return). There is every reason to think, therefore, that many members of group c) were indeed Goths: the former followers of Radagaisus. Some doubt is again sowed by Zosimus, who seems to imply that Radagaisus led a multi-ethnic force recruited from both Rhenish and Danubian tribes (5. 26. 3). But here too, our compiler has confused separate events: Radagaisus' invasion of Italy in 405/6 and

---

since all agree that this second Gothic group joined Alaric by 408 at the latest (see below note 11), but I will reiterate my reasons for rejecting this supposed second settlement. The case for it rests on a combination of 4. 34. 2-5 and Jordanes *Getica* 27. 140-28. 142. Zosimus 4. 34 is clearly a doublet account of the whole war, however, and shows no more than that the *Greutungi* were in Pannonia in *ca* 380, while Jordanes clearly thinks the peace agreement he records at *Getica* 27. 140 was made by Gratian with all the Goths (Heather 1991: App. B). These texts make it *possible* that there was an agreement between Gratian and the *Greutungi*, but do not provide proof positive, while the silence of Themistius *Or.* 15 (of Jan. 381) about such a development is, in context (Theodosius at this point required Gratian's assistance), very good evidence that no such agreement had occurred (see further Heather & Moncur 1999 forthcoming). The other texts (*Pan. Lat.* 12 (2). 32. 4; Ambrose *Ep.* 20; *ILCV* 1061; Zosimus 5. 37. 1: on which see note 11) usually taken to document the subsequent history of this settlement do no such thing (Heather 1991:340-4), and the attempts of Varady (1969) to adduce other texts have been rightly rejected by others (refs. as Heather 1991:344 n.31). To my mind, therefore, accepting that Gratian settled the *Greutungi* separately in Pannonia involves more hypothetical leaps of argument than rejecting it.

[11] Zosimus 5. 37. 1 ff. Athaulf's positive response to Alaric's summons is usually taken as the final act of the group of *Greutungi* settled separately in Pannonia by Gratian in 380, but, as we have seen, the texts taken to document the settlement and its subsequent history are highly problematic (note 10). Alaric had just advanced from Epirus to Noricum and then to Italy. Sending part of his forces to Pannonia to cover his flank as he moved would have been an entirely sensible move. Athaulf was *already* Alaric's brother-in-law at the moment of the summons (Zosimus 5. 37. 1). Given the lack of any documentation for a continuous Gothic occupation of Pannonia between 380 and 408, therefore, it is easier to see Alaric and Athaulf as two parts of an already integrated force.

the famous multi-ethnic Rhine crossing of December 31, 406 (cf. Demougeot 1979:422).

This does not mean that *all* of Alaric's new recruits in group c) must have been Goths. We know, for instance, that already in 402, before Radagaisus' arrival in Italy, Stilicho's army included numerous Alans, who played a major role in battles of Alaric's first invasion of Italy (Cameron 1970:374-6). These are not heard of again in Italy after Alaric's occupation (408-11), and it is quite possible that they, along with other non-Roman military elements also joined Alaric. Nonetheless, there are likely to have been large numbers of Goths in group c).

The same, it seems to me, is also very likely true of group d). Highly pertinent in this respect is Orosius' account of what happened after the suppression of Radagaisus. As we have seen, some of his followers were recruited by Stilicho, but many more suffered less favourable treatment. So many were sold into slavery, and at such cheap rates, that the bottom dropped out of the slave market (7. 37. 13 ff.). Again, no doubt, some Roman slaves saw joining Alaric as an opportunity for a better life, but many of these slave recruits were highly likely to have been former followers of Radagaisus, rather than of the normal Roman household variety.

Multi-ethnicity and number crunching

My answers—and they are indeed *my* answers rather than definitive ones—to the questions raised by the first two issues—begin to imply an understanding of the Visigoths as an historical phenomenon. Alaric's original followers were (and of this much, I am *very* confident) the Goths of 382 in general revolt. This provides us, of course, with a substantial element of continuity between pre- and post-Hunnic Gothic groupings. It was not only Goths, however, who had made peace with the Romans in 382.

In particular, a group of Huns and Alans had attached themselves to the Goths in the autumn of 377 (Ammianus 31. 8. 4 ff.), and some of these survived to treat with the Romans in 382. This being so, there is no reason why they should not also have been involved in the revolt led by Alaric in 395, especially since Huns from Thrace had participated in the campaign against Eugenius (John of Antioch, fr. 187), which had precipitated the revolt in the first place (see above). Likewise, Huns and Alans, as well as Goths, had also fought in Theodosius' campaign against a first Western usurper, Maximus, in 387 (*Pan. Lat.* 12 (2). 32. 4; cf. Heather 1991:341).[12] To my mind, this is even the likely source of the Huns led by Athaulf to Italy in 408 (see note 11), but there is no way to be certain. The

---

[12] Varady (1969:20-6, 31 ff.) argued that the *Greutungi* of Alatheus and Saphrax formed with the Huns and Alans mentioned by Ammianus a "Dreivolker Confederation", and that it was only in autumn 377 that any of these joined the *Tervingi* in revolt. This contention, despite the rejection of Varady's other hypotheses (note 10), has achieved some approbation (e.g. Wolfram 1988:120-2), but is equally ill-founded. Ammianus is quite explicit that the *Greutungi* were Goths and makes it clear that the Huns and Alans who joined the revolt in autumn 377 were quite separate: e.g. Ammianus 31. 12. 17, 31. 16. 3-4 with Heather (1991:144-5).

crucial point, however, is clear: alongside the Goths settled in the Balkans in 382, there were also Huns, and probably some Alans too, and there is every reason to suppose that some if not all of them participated in Alaric's revolt.[13]

The same is also true of Alaric's subsequent recruiting drives. Again, I am very confident that many of the allies of Stilicho—group c) above—were indeed Goths, former participants in Radagaisus' invasion of Italy. Likewise, many of the slaves of group d) were probably also less fortunate Goths from the same source. At the same time, however, both of these groups, like the settlement of 382 and Alaric's initial revolt in 395, will have encompassed non-Goths as well, and, as we have seen, group e) was straightforwardly composed of Alans.

Overall, then, the literary evidence suggests that the creation of the Visigoths brought together very substantial numbers of Goths. These Goths derived from a number of older Gothic socio-political units which had fragmented, directly or indirectly, under Hunnic pressure. At the same time, some non-Goths were involved at every stage of the process. In terms of continuity of Gothic manpower, we are dealing with a question of degree. Hence, relative numbers are (unfortunately), of straightforward importance in deciding how we should think of this new Gothic political unit. If the non-Goths from various sources represented a relatively small percentage of its manpower, then the Visigoths, despite encompassing some non-Goths, would still be essentially Gothic, in the sense that the vast majority of its manpower came from sources which were already 'Gothic' before the creation of the new group. In other words, the new group was Gothic because it mostly consisted of Goths. How large a percentage of outsiders we might allow in "an essentially Gothic" force is itself a moot point. In my view, even if something like 25 % of Visigothic manpower came from non-Gothic sources, it would still be perverse *not* to view it as an essentially Gothic unit.[14]

On the other hand, if non-Goths amounted to 25-50% (or even more) of Visigothic manpower, then we should clearly be thinking of some kind of Gothic dominated confederation. We know it was Gothic dominated, at least, from the fact that both outsiders and its own propaganda later understood it as a Gothic unit (cf. Wolfram 1967:77-8).

What, then, can we say about relative numbers? None of the figures are unproblematic, but, for what they are worth, the sources preserve the following indications:

Groups a) & b)
i)   The *Tervingi* of Fritigern may have consisted of *ca* 10,000 warriors. Valens was deceived into giving battle in 378 because he seems to have thought he was facing just Fritigern with a force of this size (Ammianus 31. 12. 3; 31. 12. 8).

---

[13] Cf. note 10, this holds true even if one accepts there was a separate Pannonian settlement of *Greutungi*, which collapsed only when Athaulf joined Alaric in 408.

[14] I make this point, because I do not believe that the 'fundamental polyethnic' character of the Visigoth and Ostrogoth groups can be established simply by noting that there were *some* non-Goths within them (cf. Wolfram 1988:7 ff., 92 ff., 301). Consideration of the terms on which any non-Goths were included might also be relevant: see below.

ii) We have no indication for the *Greutungi* of Alatheus and Saphrax, but they
were clearly substantial in number, perhaps of about the same size as
Fritigern's *Tervingi*.[15]

iii) The group of Huns and Alans who joined the Goths in autumn 377 probably
was not very numerous, since both of these nomadic groups tended to operate
in small, politically independent groups at this point, rather than large masses
(e.g. Ammianus 31. 2. 7, 17).

Group c)

Zosimus (5. 35. 5-6) reports that 30,000 auxiliaries joined Alaric on the death
of Stilicho in 408, but this is obviously too large.[16] According to Photius'
summary, Olympiodorus, Zosimus' source, said 12,000 of "the best of"
Radagaisus' followers had been drafted into the Roman army by Stilicho in
405/6 (Olympiodorus, fr. 9). If we can take this as an order of magnitude, then
perhaps *ca* 10,000 of Alaric's new recruits in 408—whatever their overall
numbers—may have been Gothic. It is possible, indeed, that Zosimus' 30,000
'recruits' is a confusion of the new *total* for Alaric's force after the recruitment
(see next paragraph).

Group d)

Zosimus reports that the runaway slaves of 409/10 brought the total of Alaric's
following to 40,000 (5. 42. 3). This is obviously not consistent with the same
historian's own report that 30,000 recruits had joined Alaric in 408, but the
figures do add up if Zosimus' earlier 30,000 is interpreted, like the 40,000, as
another *total* figure for the size of Alaric's force, which Zosimus misconstrued.
If so, then *ca* 10,000 slaves joined Alaric, but we have no way of knowing how
many of them were Goths.

Group e)

The Alans who deserted Athaulf to protect the town of Bazas were probably
not very numerous, since it was a contingent of the right kind of size to defend
one single and not very large urban centre.

If the question of numbers was avoidable, one would not want to rest anything of
importance on these indications. But the issue they address—the relative numbers
of Goths and non-Goths among the Visigoths—really is an important one, and I
am, in truth, fairly confident of some of those figures. In the cases of groups a) ii,
a) iii, and e), of course, we really know nothing. The figure for the *Tervingi,* group
a) i, is probably somewhere near the truth, however. More problematic are
numbers for groups c) and d), which involve detailed argument. None of the
individual steps in the arguments is too wild, however, and again I am reasonably

---

[15] Further discussion: Heather (1991:139 n 44), cf. note 12 on the myth of the "Dreivölker
Confederation".

[16] Like many other figures for Radagaisus' force. Zosimus says he led 400,000 (5. 26. 3 ff.),
Orosius 200,000 (7. 37. 4 ff.); Orosius is copied by Marcellinus Comes *sa* 406 *CM* 2. 68.

confident that the basic supposition underlying such efforts is well-placed. Olympiodorus, the original source, is likely to have provided accurate figures which have been corrupted in transmission by Zosimus.[17]

If we take these different indications as somewhere close to the mark, what, then, do they suggest? Of the different groups involved in the creation of the Visigoths, two contingents of *ca* 10,000 would appear to have been unambiguously Gothic in the sense that they derived from earlier fourth-century Gothic groups: the *Tervingi* of 376 and the followers of Radagaisus who joined Alaric in 408. In addition, the *Greutungi* of 376 were similarly Gothic, but we do not know how many of them there were. Likewise, a substantial proportion of the slaves who joined Alaric in 409/10 were probably also Goths. Compared to these contingents, the non-Gothic ones seem *relatively* small: the Huns and Alans of autumn 377, non-Gothic allies of Stilicho, and non-Gothic slaves. It is obviously not a matter for certainty, but, on the basis of the information available, I would conclude that there is a strong *probability* that people who were already Goths made up well over half of, and may very well have predominated within the newly-created Visigoths. This is a point well worth emphasising in the context of a modern historiography which seems to think it a point proved beyond dispute that the new Gothic groups created in the Migration Period were fundamentally polyethnic.

Overall, any account of the creation of the Visigoths must clearly balance continuities against discontinuities. The Visigoths were a new political unit, created in the period *ca* 376-410. They also included non-Goths. But a direct narrative line for some of their number does lead from the crossing of the Danube in 376 to Alaric's revolt in 395 and the sack of Rome in 410 (p. 50, this vol.), and a substantial majority both of those who crossed the Danube in 376 and of those subsequently recruited by Alaric probably were already Goths (p. 52 ff., this vol.). The Visigoths thus represent a major reshuffling of the Gothic pack, as it were, but most of the cards involved in the reshuffling were probably already Gothic, in the sense that they derived from pre-Hunnic groups which already thought of themselves as Gothic. How had these previously separate Goths come together?

Processes of amalgamation

The role of kings

Jordanes' *Getica* reports that, when the Goths were settled above the Black Sea, the two groups then in existence served two ruling families: the Visigoths the Balths, and the Ostrogoths the Amals (5. 42). Since these dynasties also ruled the successor states, it has often been supposed that each subdivision of the Gothic people had its own ruling family which maintained its position throughout the

---

[17] Maenchen-Helfen (1973:459) takes a gloomy view of Olympiodorus' likely accuracy, but, cf. Matthews (1970), what survives suggests to me that wild errors are more likely the result of the intermediaries by whom his text has been transmitted.

Migration Period (e.g. Musset 1975:42 ff.). The *Getica* also reports, however, that, before the arrival of the Huns, both Visigoths and Ostrogoths were ruled by an Amal called Ostrogotha (17. 98). And, apart from the one statement which puts the two dynasties on an equal footing, Jordanes consistently presents the Amals as much more important than the *Balthi* (explicitly: 29. 146, 33. 174-5; by implication: 14. 78-81).[18] Despite these inconsistencies, Jordanes' report that there were Gothic ruling houses who had a continuous history running across the divide represented by the Hunnic invasions has, in recent years, been given huge importance.

Having demonstrated that the Visigoths (and Ostrogoths for that matter) were essentially new political units, and that they contained some non-Goths, Wenskus and Wolfram went on to argue that a few—how many is an issue never explicitly addressed—noble clans, and particularly these two royal families, were the basic mechanism by which Gothic identity was transmitted over the historical gulf dividing the earlier fourth century from the later fifth. For them, the Visigoths and Ostrogoths were 'Gothic' because their royal families were 'Gothic', and the identity of the rank and file of these groups was not relevant. Many of them may already have belonged to Gothic groups, but that was not the point; anyone could become a Goth who served these two Gothic royal clans (Wolfram 1988:290-302; Wenskus 1961:322-3, 472 ff.; but see also note 3). This is a neat solution to a messy problem—as we have seen, the Visigoths certainly contained recruits from a mixture of backgrounds—and has won considerable acceptance (e.g. García Moreno 1992, who conveniently labelled this view the 'Neue Lehre').

In my view, however, it is also unsustainable. Jordanes' vision of two ruling families with a continuous history through the Migration Period (*ca 375-500*) bears as much resemblance to reality (in so far as it can be reconstructed from more contemporary sources) as his idea that Visigoths and Ostrogoths existed before the Hunnic invasions. As we have seen, three major pre-existing Gothic groups contributed to the Visigoths: the *Tervingi* and *Greutungi* who crossed the Danube in 376, and the fifth-century Goths led by Radagaisus. None of the leaders under whom these groups crossed the frontier maintained their control in the first shock of contact with the Roman Empire. Radagaisus was executed outside Florence, while Fritigern, and Alatheus and Saphrax (leaders respectively of the *Tervingi* and *Greutungi* in 376) are never heard of again after *ca* 380.[19] Fritigern's leadership of the *Tervingi* was in any case itself a break with established loyalties, since he ousted Athanaric, whose family had probably ruled the *Tervingi* throughout the fourth century (Ammianus 31. 3. 4-8; cf. Wolfram 1988:62 ff.).

---

[18] Thus, following Jordanes, Wolfram has both families established before the Hunnic invasions, but the Amals with the greater prestige, "demi-gods", where the Balths were mere mortals (1988:14 ff., 30 ff.). According to Wolfram, the Amals were already kings in the fourth century (1988:85 ff.), whereas the *Balthi* ruled the "Tervingian Visigoths" as Judges, wielding less than monarchical power, and only transformed themselves into kings in the course of subsequent migrations (1988:94 ff., 143 ff.).

[19] At San Marino, we likewise discussed *Cons. Const. ad a 382*, which reads "*ipso anno universa gens Gothorum cum rege suo in Romaniam se tradiderunt...*", where *cum rege suo* has sometimes

Within the Empire, another generation of Gothic leaders equally failed to establish any kind of dynastic control (this does not apply to Radagaisus' group, whose survivors joined Alaric without reforming as an independent political unit). From those who had crossed the Danube in 376 emerged Fravittas and Eriulf sometime before 392. Champions of alternative policies, they were also rivals attempting to fill the leadership vacuum which had existed since 382. There is no sign that they were related to any of the previous leaders of the *Tervingi* and *Greutungi*, and both failed to establish themselves. At a banquet, their rivalry erupted into violence; Eriulf was killed, and Fravittas forced to flee Gothic society (Eunapius ed. Blockley fr. 59; Zosimus 4. 55. 3-56.1; cf. Heather 1991:186-8, 190-1).

After 395, the situation began to stabilize under the rule of Alaric. It has been argued from the fact that his name alliterates with those of Ariaric and Athanaric, probably grandfather and grandson who ruled the *Tervingi* before the advent of the Huns, that Alaric came from the same ruling family (Wolfram 1988:64-5; cf. Wenskus 1975:13-4). There is no evidence in favour of this hypothesis except the alliteration, however, and the scholars who developed this methodology in relation to the much fuller evidence of the Carolingian period and after, have always stressed that the evidence of names alone can never constitute proof. Naming patterns can provide only supporting evidence for the identification of family lines based primarily on more circumstantial historical evidence (e.g. Schmid 1979:38 ff.; Werner 1979:149 ff.). In any case, it is far from certain that these names would have alliterated in their original Gothic forms. The original name behind Ariaric is either *Arjareiks or *Harjareiks. The latter would not alliterate with Alaric (*Alareiks) under old Germanic rules where *h* is a full consonant. Nor do we have any documented cases of Gothic ruling houses using alliteration as a naming practice. In the securely documented cases of the fifth-century Visigothic ruling house and later, more historical generations of the Amal family, variation on the father's name, reusing its leading element—rather than alliteration—would appear to have been the preferred naming principle (cf. Heather 1991:31). These observations combine, in this case, with the great political discontinuity which separates *Tervingi* from Visigoth to make it extremely unlikely that Alaric and Athanaric were in any way related.[20]

Alaric definitively united the Visigoths and handed on power to a designated and related successor: his brother-in-law Athaulf.[21] Between them Alaric and Athaulf ruled for twenty years, but there was yet another break before a Visigothic

---

been taken to refer to Fritigern, but there is no mention of him in Themistius' account of this event (*Or.* 16), and, under the previous year, the Chronicler had recorded the surrender of Athanaric to Theodosius calling him *Aithanaricus rex Gothorum*. I have no doubt that he is also the king meant in 382, and that the Chronicler mistakenly made a causal connection.

[20] Because of his persecution of Christians north of the Danube and later reception by Theodosius in January 381, Athanaric was a very well-known figure in Roman literary-cum-political circles. So too was Alaric for the sack of Rome. If the two were related, one might reasonably expect some report of it in the sources.

ruling dynasty finally established itself. When an assassination attempt mortally wounded Athaulf, he tried to transfer power to his brother, but it was usurped by an outsider, Sergeric, who slaughtered Athaulf's children—and probably also the brother who is not mentioned again. Sergeric was the brother of one Sarus who had consistently opposed Alaric, so that the coup against Athaulf probably represents a rival line's attempt to reassert itself (cf. Heather 1991:31-2, 197-8). As it was, Sergeric himself failed to hold on to power, being murdered after only seven days (refs. as *PLRE* 2, 987). He was succeeded by Valia for whom there is no record of family ties with previous leaders (refs. as *PLRE* 2, 1147-8). Sergeric and Valia thus interrupted nascent dynastic succession, and only in the thirty-three year reign of Valia's successor, Theoderic I, did a dynasty establish itself. Theoderic's family ruled the Visigoths for the rest of the century (*PLRE* 2, 1070-1; Stemma 40:1332 in *PLRE* 2). Theoderic does seem to have married Alaric's daughter, so that, to some extent, his dynasty was a continuation of Alaric's. But Sergeric and Valia had intervened, and nothing suggests that Theoderic was elected *because* he had married Alaric's daughter. We only hear of the marriage because a later panegyric portrays Theoderic's son Thorismud as Alaric's grandson (Sidonius Apollinaris *Carmina* 7. 505).[22]

There is thus no sign of dynastic continuity between fourth-century Gothic leaders and the rulers of the Visigoths. If Alaric was a Balth, as Jordanes maintains, it was nearly twenty years after the Danube crossing before a representative of the family first asserted himself. Alternative lines, particularly that of Sarus and Sergeric, still had to be defeated over another twenty year period before the family's position was secure. Even then, Theoderic I was probably related to Alaric only by marriage, and must again have owed his position primarily to his own ability. What we see is not one pre-eminent royal family, but a number of rival noble lines competing for the overall leadership of a new group. This, of course, makes perfect sense. As we have seen, the formation of the Visigoths represented a major socio-political reshuffle of pre-existing Gothic groups. It would hardly be surprising for this process to have occasioned a concomitant period of ferocious competition among ambitious Gothic royal 'wannabes'.

For present purposes, this point is of extreme importance because it means that we cannot use the idea of a single, pre-eminent royal dynasty as a convenient answer to the messy problem of the Gothic identity of the Visigoths. The Visigoths were not 'Gothic' because they gathered behind the rule of a Gothic dynast. It is quite clear, on the contrary that the extensive realignments in the Gothic world which created the Visigoths, also let loose an equally extensive struggle for power.

---

[21] *Getica* 30. 158 uses *consanguineus* of Athaulf and Alaric, implying that they were blood relatives (cf. Wolfram 1988:165), but this is probably a later misunderstanding of their well-documented relationship by marriage (Zosimus 5. 37. 2).

[22] Wenskus (1975:14) suggests that Theoderic I was Alaric's son, but the sources would surely say so had this been the case.

The new ruling house was as much a product of the struggles between 376 and *ca* 420 as the group itself, and could not have neatly defined the latter's identity. This, of course, does not necessarily mean that Wenskus and Wolfram were mistaken in thinking of identity being defined by a relatively restricted 'Traditionskern'. The evidence for dynastic turbulence could be accommodated within a historical vision which identified a 'Traditionskern' of no more than a dozen or a score of families of 'noble' say (for want of an alternative designation), rather than a single one of 'royal', status as the key factor in determining whether a larger group was seen and saw itself as Gothic or not. The literary evidence relevant to the Visigoths does not rule out such a view, but a slightly wider range of evidence makes me think that even such an expanded 'Traditionkern' is still too narrow a view of the spread, as it were, of Gothic identity.

Social status, enfranchisement, and identity

In the Romantic and nationalistic conceptions of the nineteenth century, the Goths and other Germanic groups of the Migration Period were seen as consisting of large numbers of free peasant warriors, meeting frequently to decide issues by largely democratic means. 'Gothicness' and other types of Germanic identity, in such conceptions, were naturally envisaged as equally the preserve of all. In more recent years, however, it has become clear that migrating groups of free peasant warriors is a wildly anachronistic vision of the fourth and fifth centuries. By *ca* 400 AD, social stratification was well established in the non-Roman world, the product of long-term processes of change with their roots in the Bronze Age (e.g. Hedeager 1992). And, in some ways, more recent views of group identity, stressing the role of a few royal or noble clans, have run in parallel with such revisions of the development of social stratification in Germanic society. Was group identity defined by relatively few, or relatively many members of the groups encountered in the Migration Period? *A priori*, of course, there is no reason why one answer to this question should be applicable in every case.

With regard to the Visigoths, my arguments have so far been veering away somewhat from the kind of orthodoxy which has come to prevail since the 1960s. I do not believe that the Visigothic royal dynasty was a phenomenon of sufficient permanence and strength to define the group as Gothic. It is more possible to view a somewhat larger group of noble clans as the essential bearers of Gothic identity, but I do actually think it significant that the majority of those forming the Visigoths were already Goths before they joined. In adopting this position, I hasten to add, I am not returning to a nineteenth-century view of a group consisting entirely of free peasant warriors, all of whom shared equally in political enfranchisement and group identity.

The full range of available evidence does indeed suggest to me that full political rights and ethnic participation were the preserve of an élite, but an élite of freemen,

significantly larger than the 'Traditionskern' envisaged by Wenskus and
Wolfram.[23]

The foundation of my thinking on this subject is provided by Procopius of
Caesarea in his *Gothic Wars*, which show that a defined and recognizable élite
existed among the Ostrogoths. To describe it, he uses three Greek terms: λόγιμος,
δόκιμος, ἄριστος ('worth mentioning' or 'remarkable'), ('esteemed' or 'notable'),
and ('the best'). These are clearly synonyms,[24] and, at different points, are attached
to Goths engaged in the same range of activities:

i)   Significant individual Goths (λόγιμος: *Wars* 5. 4. 13; δόκιμος: *Wars* 6. 1. 36,
     6. 20. 14, 7. 18. 26, 8. 26. 4; ἄριστος: *Wars* 7. 1. 46).

ii) Small numbers taking part, alongside (or in opposition to) Gothic kings, in
     important policy decisions (λόγιμος: *Wars* 5. 13. 26, 7. 24. 27, 8. 35. 33;
     δόκιμος: *Wars* 6. 28. 29; ἄριστος: *Wars* 6. 9. 8 (n.b. 7. 1. 46 again).

iii) To rather larger Gothic forces:

     λόγιμος: *Wars* 8. 23. 10 (these Goths man 47 ships).

     δόκιμος: *Wars* 3. 8. 12 (1,000 of them attend Theoderic's sister when she
     marries Thrasamund, king of the Vandals), 6. 23. 8 (they comprise the garrison
     of Auximus), 8. 26. 21 (they comprise Teias' force sent to Verona).

     ἄριστος: *Wars* 5. 13. 15 (they comprise the whole of Marcias' army sent to
     Dalmatia), 6. 20. 2 (garrison of Auximus, 6. 28. 29 ff. (many, πολλοί of them
     defend the Cottian Alps).

At different places, therefore, Procopius applied all three of these terms to very
substantial military forces: to garrisons, the complements of 47 ships, entire
military units (the forces of Marcias and Teias), and to losses in the range of four
figures. It clearly comprised, therefore, several thousands. At the same time, not
every adult male belonged to this social group. The terms are in themselves
exclusive, of course, implying the existence of other, lesser social groups.
Procopius' narrative confirms the point. When the élite among the Goths of
Dalmatia were killed, for instance, the rest of the Gothic population of the area
surrendered to the invading East Romans (*Wars* 5. 7. 3-10; 7. 7. 26-37). One
passage, indeed, gives some indication of the proportion of the élite to the rest of
the Gothic population. The bodyguard sent with Theoderic's sister to Vandal Africa
comprised 1,000 men from the élite, and a body of attendants amounting to a total
of 5,000 fighting men (*Wars* 3. 8. 12). The lesser social group or groups, just as
much as the élite, then, were Gothic fighting men, and the élite in this force, at
least, amounted to about one fifth of the total. As this makes clear, simply
belonging to a Gothic army was *not* enough to make one a fully-fledged Goth.

[23] The fact that neither attempts precisely to define a 'Traditionskern' can make it difficult to be
certain whether one is in agreement or disagreement. Both certainly have a very top-down model of
ethnicity, however, and both place great emphasis on the importance of royal families. This suggests
that they envisage only a very limited group of families as being critical to ethnicity.

[24] E.g. two are used to describe the garrison of Auximus: δόκιμος (*Wars* 6. 23. 8); ἄριστοι (*Wars*
6. 20. 2).

How should we conceptualize this élite, several thousand strong? A priori, one might be tempted to think of them as a nobility, but the numbers seem too large to use that term in its traditional, medieval sense. Only *ca* 2,500 Norman invaders divided England between themselves after 1066, for instance, and many of these would not have counted as noble. On further reflection, I would argue that this much larger élite should be equated with the so-called 'free' class which one encounters in many of the sixth- and seventh-century so-called 'barbarian' law codes, not least those of the later Visigothic kingdom in Spain. The pattern of the evidence here is a little problematic, and I would not want to hide that fact. For the Ostrogoths we have an extensive narrative source showing a numerous élite in action in the mid-sixth century, but no descriptive, normative legal sources to identify it in conceptual terms. For the Visigoths (and other groups) we have normative and descriptive legal sources from the sixth and seventh centuries, which do describe an élite of freemen, together with subordinate classes of freedmen and slaves. In these cases, however, there exists no detailed narrative to give a sense of relative numbers. In applying this perspective to the Visigoths, I am making, obviously enough, two methodological jumps: first in regarding the two types of later material as mutually illuminating, not perhaps too big a jump, and then, second, in retrospectively applying the model of Gothic society they suggest for the sixth century to the Visigoths of *ca* 420.

In support of the legitimacy of the second jump—surely the more problematic— a number of arguments can be made. First, social stratification is likely only to have become more entrenched over time, especially once the Goths were established on Roman territory and set about enjoying all the wealth that even a declining Roman economy could offer them. If anything, therefore, Gothic social stratification will probably have been less in *ca* 420 than *ca* 550, so that if a freeman class still existed at the latter point, it surely would have done a hundred or so years earlier.[25] Second, such a vision of the distribution of power in Gothic society makes sense of the pattern of politics among the nascent Visigoths, where would-be leaders clearly had to bid for support, while pursuing out their political rivalries, rather than just enjoying unchallenged pre-eminence. Such processes are demonstrated consistently in a variety of sources all the way from the Hadrianople campaign to the settlement in Aquitaine.[26]

Third, an interesting fragment of the lost history of Olympiodorus reports, as we have seen, that, after defeating Radagaisus, Stilicho recruited into the Roman army "12,000 of the leading men of the Goths who are called *optimatoi*" (τῶν Γότθων...

---

[25] Although this would not deny that there were also dominant ruling inner élites among the Gothic social formations of the pre-Hunnic period. The Hunnic revolution certainly threatened their power—the dynasty of the *Tervingi* judges, for instance, was overthrown—but it is unclear how far down the scale any social revolution went.

[26] On the pre-Hunnic *Tervingi* and nascent Visigoths of the Hadrianople campaign, see Heather (1991:103-7, 178-80). Such a model also better fits the evidence available for 395-418/9 than that of a fundamental leader/led division proposed by Thompson (1963).

ὁι κεφαλαιῶται ὀπτίματοι ἐκαλοῦντο): ed. Blockley fr. 9). This passage,
preserved only in the summary of Olympiodorus made by the Byzantine
bibliophile Photius, has usually been considered (by myself too, I hasten to add:
Heather 1991:213-4) a confusion, since *optimatoi* are usually equated with
'nobles', and 12,000 nobles seems far too many for a single force. In the light of
Procopius' evidence, however, the passage begins to look much less odd, and it
may well be that we should simply accept it as meaning that Stilicho recruited
12,000 of the freemen élite among Radagaisus' followers. If so, the social structure
of at least one of the contributing groups to the Visigoths was broadly comparable
to that described by Procopius for the Ostrogoths.

Fourth, evidence for a military élite attended by equally militarized servants is
quite generally available for this period. Thus allied barbarians (*foederati*) in the
Western Roman army of the fifth century were expected to have slaves (*C.Th.*
7.13.16), and a Lombard contingent for Justinian's wars in Italy was composed of
2,500 'good fighting men' and 3,000 fighting servants (*Wars* 8. 26. 12). Fifth, and
much more generally, a quite different range of diplomatic and legal evidence has
led a number of recent studies to the conclusion that a numerically substantial free
peasantry remained a powerful local political force in much of early medieval
western Europe. These groups had military and legal rights which marked them
out as a social élite, generating the broader suggestion that a medieval-type
nobility exercising powerful control over large tracts of land took longer to emerge
than is sometimes imagined (Wickham 1992; 1995). This is exactly the kind of
political pattern that would have been created by sharing out land grants and other
economic benefits fairly equally—at least in the first instance—among the
relatively numerous freeman military élite which would appear characteristic of
the Goths and other Migration Period groups.[27]

On the basis of Procopius and a substantial amount of supporting evidence,
therefore, I would argue that we can define a middle way between romantic
nineteenth-century visions of political participation, and very restricted modern
ones generated in reasonable reaction to this earlier view. The Gothic freemen
class was still a critical political player in the Migration Period, but was itself a
restricted, oligarchic élite of somewhere between, perhaps, one fifth and one half
of the Gothic population. The rights of full social, political, and legal participation
accorded this group in the law codes thus extended to only a minority, if a
substantial one, of the population. By extension, this also defines for us the social
group among the Goths making crucial political decisions, such as whether to join
a new political unit such as the Visigoths, or to find some other option.

Such a vision of political participation gives some insight into the range of
issues which would have required negotiation whenever outside groups attached
themselves to a Gothic socio-political unit. Decision-making not only centred on

---

[27] Land versus tax shares as a means of reward has been a major issue in recent years. I believe
that Theoderic, for instance, distributed both after the Ostrogothic conquest of Italy (Heather
1996:242 ff. with refs).

whether to join or not, but also on the social status(es) to be assigned to the new recruits. Who among them, if any, was to be accorded élite freeman status, and who apportioned to lesser categories? When non-Goths, and particularly non-Germanic speakers, such as Alans and Huns with very different social structures, were involved, comparisons must have been even more complicated.[28] To become fully a Goth, it was not sufficient merely to attach oneself to the military following of a Gothic king. Many who did so were clearly not accorded full freeman status. Unfortunately, no source describes an example of amalgamation in any detail. We can make more progress, however, in the area of causation. Why did a number of different Gothic groups, as we have already seen, decide to come together to create the Visigoths?

Causation

The press of circumstance

On one level, a picture of a pragmatic Gothicness can be built up from the narrative of political events in the Migration Period. Goths had to fight both Huns and the Roman state to preserve their autonomy, and uniting to survive, especially in the face of Roman power, was an extremely sensible policy. In the process, one Gothic political order was destroyed and a new one created. The Huns conquered or displaced the Gothic élites who had generated the fourth-century kingdoms, and some of the latter reformed themselves to create two new supergroups: the Visigoths, with whom we are concerned here, and the Ostrogoths. Everything suggests that these political formations were much larger than the predecessors out of whom they had been created (cf. Heather 1996: pt. ii).

Other options were available. At different moments in the fourth and fifth centuries, various Gothic individuals made their way in the world as Roman generals, and whole Gothic groups as bodies of allied Roman soldiery. Among the latter, the defeated supporters of Radagaisus drafted into the Roman army by Stilicho are an obvious example. For most Goths, however, a desire for independence eventually won out over the financial and other blandishments of serving the Roman Empire. Most of the individuals known to have become officers of the imperial army were defeated candidates for the overall leaderships of the new Gothic supergroups (or their associates). These men had been driven from Gothic society by the consequences of feud.[29] Likewise, Stilicho's allies eventually chose to attach themselves to the Visigoths in 408, because their families were attacked after their patron's overthrow and death (Zosimus 5. 35. 5-6). Hence the attachment of these Goths to Alaric was straightforwardly a negative response to Roman power, and the same may be well be true of the revolt which

---

[28] Cf. Ammianus 31. 2. 25 on the equally high status of all Alans, and the lack of slavery among them.

[29] True in the Visigothic case of Munderic, Modares, Fravittas, and Sarus.

started Alaric's career in 395. As we have seen, losses on the Eugenius campaign probably provided Alaric with an initial issue to exploit. In the same way, many Goths had fallen in their initial wars against the Romans between 376 and 382, not least the three whole Gothic sub-groups destroyed by the imperial commanders Frigeridus (Ammianus 31. 9), Sebastianus (Ammianus 31. 11) and the renegade Goth Modares (Zosimus 4. 25).

The need to survive in the face of Roman power, once the insecurity generated by the Huns had led them to enter Roman territory, thus played a major role in generating the realignment in Gothic society which created the Visigoths. The same is also true of the Ostrogoths, but that is another story (Heather 1991: pt. 3), and also of the Vandals led to Africa by Geiseric. The latter were not a long-established entity, but a new confederation, created in Spain, of Hasding Vandals, Siling Vandals, and numerous Alans; the official titulature of Geiseric and his successors remained, indeed, 'Kings of the Vandals and Alans'. As with the Visigoths, the new Vandal alliance was a defensive response to Roman power, created when the Siling Vandals and Alans had suffered heavy defeats at the hands of Roman forces (in alliance with the Visigoths) between 416 and 418 (Hydatius 22-24; cf. Wolfram 1967:79 ff.). Examples could be multiplied, but the general point is clear. Politically enfranchised Gothic freemen were ready to pool their sovereignty, and accept the leadership of new dynasts, because they were otherwise unlikely to survive (either physically or as an established social élite), as many found to their cost. The Visigoths were thus—like many of their Migration Period peers—in part created in negative reaction to the dangerous upheavals in which their constituent groups found themselves trapped. Many recent general studies of ethnicity have stressed the extent to which identity is often forged in conflict (e.g. Smith 1981, 1986).

The importance of being Gothic

Before concluding, however, I would like to ask one further question. On a level beyond the pragmatic, did a positive feeling of Gothic identity play any role in establishing the new political order? Once strong senses of identity exist, individuals can be forced to act in certain ways *because* they exist. They are too powerful to be easily manipulable even towards those ends which, by straightforward material calculation, would appear the most desirable. Indeed, even within the same society, inherited senses of identity can exercise a more or less powerful pull on individuals, and a given individual can be both emotionally dependent upon their inherited identity and simultaneously manipulate it. Is there any evidence of a 'Gothicness' in *ca* 400 AD exercising some kind of powerful hold?

With the sources available to us, this is an extremely difficult question to answer. Even in modern case studies, with access to detailed first-hand accounts of personal experience, the conclusions of anthropologists differ radically over what significance to accord any pre-existing ethnic identity as a force shaping individual action. Two points of reference are worth keeping in mind. First, there is no reason to suppose that Gothicness will have been expressed by the same means in every period where our sources report the existence of Goths. We do not have to find unchanging cultural constants to prove the existence of Goths as a historically continuous entity. Second—the reason why this is so—it is the reaction of individual consciousnesses to such peculiarities, not the items themselves, that are important. Identity is an internal attitude of mind which may express itself through objects, norms, or particular ways of doing things. These may be more or less consciously used as symbols of identity, and, as circumstances change, unconscious symbols can evolve into conscious ones. But, in all cases, symbols are the *result* and not the *cause* of any sense of separate identity. Particularities can symbolize and express identity, but identity cannot be reduced to a process of listing differences between groups.[30]

Taking now the specific case of the Goths, there is just about enough, and I would not want to press matters further, to suggest that, in certain instances, Gothicness may have been sufficiently powerful to have lain—at least for some— beyond the range of simple individual pragmatic manipulation. Again, I should signal that the emphasis of my argument differs in some ways from much recent work which has stressed the pragmatic manipulability of ethnicity in the Migration Period (e.g. Amory 1993, 1997; Geary 1983).

To start with, there is the general point that most of those recruited to create the Visigoths would seem to have been Goths from pre-existing, pre-Hunnic Gothic groups (see above). This point would not go undisputed, and the Visigoths were certainly not exclusively Gothic. As we have seen, non-Goths—Huns and Alans find particular mention—were recruited at different moments. What we do not know, of course, is exactly how these others were incorporated into the unit they joined. Did they play the role of allies, or participate fully in social processes and decision making? Unfortunately, there is no way to be sure, and, indeed, no reason to think that the mode of incorporation need have been the same in every case. The Alans who abandoned Athaulf to defend Bazas were clearly not very firmly attached to the Visigoths. On the other hand, the Huns who followed Alaric to Italy in 408, if indeed descended from those settled under the 382 treaty who had been operating with the Goths since 377, probably were. Among the Ostrogoths in Italy, likewise, there were *Rugi* who preserved their separate identity over fifty years, and, in Totila's campaigns, many former Roman allied troops joined him on a very temporary basis, returning to a Roman allegiance when Narses arrived, but only a relative few threw in their lot fully with the Goths (Heather 1996: App. 2).

Second, to judge by the *Tervingi*, at least, quite an aggressive sense of Gothicness had emerged before the Hunnic invasions. The *Tervingi* had a strong sense of their own territory, manifested in Athanaric's determination to make the Emperor Valens recognize the boundaries of his kingdom. When making peace in 369, Athanaric insisted that the two men meet on a boat in the middle of the river

---

[30] On all issues to do with ethnicity, see the literature cited at note 1.

Danube, an attitude which Valens accepted but found provocative. The *Tervingi*, or some of their leaders at least, likewise tried to assert a sense of religious solidarity around their own traditional cults. Public acts of conformity to the ways of traditional Gothic religion were demanded, and Christians were occasionally persecuted because their religion was identified with the Roman state. While in many senses a client state of the Empire, they resisted the more overt symbols of its domination, and, at times, even succeeded in asserting a less unequal relationship (e.g. Heather 1991:107-21)

A not dissimilar vision of a relatively powerful sense of Gothicness emerges when one looks at the religious history of the Goths even after they adopted the Christianity they had previously associated with the Roman Empire. The leaders of the *Tervingi* seem to have espoused Christianity as they crossed the Danube in 376, adopting the non-Nicene brand of Christianity—often misleadingly called Arianism—favoured by the then Emperor Valens. It was also consonant with the teachings of Ulfila, missionary to the Goths in the 340s, and translator of the Bible into Gothic. There was nothing specifically Gothic about Ulfila's teachings. Ulfila taught that the Son was 'like', rather than 'of one substance with', the Father, as the Council of Nicaea had defined it in 325. The latter eventually became the hallmark of Catholic orthodoxy, but 'likeness' was one of a number of old established positions, not some radical new Gothic heresy. In 376, then, the Goths adopted an established form of Roman Christianity as part of their attempt to persuade a Roman emperor to admit them into the Empire.[31]

Soon after 376, however, the eastern half of the Empire joined the West in definitively adopting the Nicene definition of faith. Although the Goths had become Christians, it seems, to please a Roman emperor, they did not follow suit. Instead, they held to Ulfila's teachings, which became, over time, increasingly a distinctive cultural feature of Goths (although Roman 'Arians' also continued to exist well into the fifth century). In the sixth century, Italian papyri refer to the Goths' non-Nicene Christianity as *lex Gothorum*, the law of the Goths, and the Visigothic king Amalaric seems to have caused a diplomatic incident in the 520s by demanding that his Catholic Frankish wife convert. The Goths' brand of religion was in origin an entirely Roman phenomenon, and, by its nature, could never separate itself completely from the Roman culture in which it had been born. Ulfila's Gothic translation was made from a standard Greek Bible of the fourth century. Later on, this translation was reworked, probably in the fifth century, against the Latin Biblical texts with which Goths had now come into contact. The effects of this are particularly evident in the Epistles, which were the battleground

[31] On the date of conversion (Heather 1986), I remain entirely convinced— despite much discussion at San Marino and publications over the last decade (e.g. Lenski 1995)—that it is methodologically correct to restructure Socrates' account of Gotho-Roman affairs on the basis of the more contemporary and better-informed Ammianus and Themistius, and not vice versa as those must, who would date the split between Athanaric and Fritigern and the latter's conversion to either 367-9 or the early 370s. Ulfilas' and the Goths' religious position was condemned by Nicenes primarily because it did not exclude more radical Arian positions (Heather & Matthews 1991: c. 5 with refs).

of theological argument (Friedrichsen 1926: pt. A; 1939: pt. 4). Likewise, the same writing office, attached to Theoderic's Arian cathedral of St Anastasius in Ravenna, which produced the great Gothic biblical masterpiece of the *Codex Argenteus*, also produced a beautiful Latin manuscript of the Christian Roman historian Orosius' account of the unfolding of God's providence in history (Tjäder 1972). Ulfila's brand of Christianity thus operated as a distinctive mark of Gothicness, but only in a context where Goths were living alongside Romans who generally held to Nicaea (cf. Heather 1996:312 ff.).

This process of development nicely illustrates two things. First, the way in which ethnic symbols are specific to particular contexts. And second, how an underlying sense of difference will find expression, even when profound cultural exchange—such as that necessary to improve one's text of the Bible and knowledge of Christian history—was unavoidable. This suggests to me that if the Goths had crossed the Danube slightly later, in the reign of Theodosius, and hence adopted Catholic Christianity, symbols of difference other than Arianism would have emerged to express the socio-political distinctiveness of, and conflict between, Roman and Goth.

Conclusions

The symbols and mechanisms of Gothic identity, and their transformation over time, are a subject worthy of study in their own right, and it is more than time to bring this paper to an end (cf. Heather 1996: c. 10 for one approach). Its subject has been the formation of an entirely new unit in Gothic society—the Visigoths— and the processes, mechanisms, and causes which underlay its appearance. At some points, the argument has dwelt on matters of quite intricate detail, but, as I hope has emerged, these details really do matter. Their interpretation does dictate our overall view of the Visigoths. Was a Gothic heritage in the form of manpower from pre-Hunnic Gothic groups of fundamental or merely incidental importance to the creation of this group? Did a substantial caste of Gothic freemen make the choices which generated this new unit, because of similarities between themselves as well as because there was safety in numbers? Was the Gothic designation of the Visigoths no more than a 'flag of convenience' for a multi-ethnic confederation, or did it reflect the affiliations of a the substantial majority of the participants?

At this level of enquiry, answers become elusive. Many of those constituting the Visigoths were already Goths before they joined. I am, in fact, ready to argue that detailed consideration of the evidence suggests that actually *most* of them were, although others would take a different view. Nor can the identities of royal families provide a simple solution to the question of how ethnic affiliations were decided. Leaders came and went for forty years, as would-be dynasts struggled to win the backing of a relatively large politically enfranchised class of freemen. To my mind, it is the pre-existing affiliations of this class which really decided Visigothic identity. The Visigoths were Gothic because the majority of politically enfranchised freemen within the group thought of themselves as Goths.

Whether the new group was created for purely pragmatic reasons, such as the need to survive in the face of hostile Roman power, or whether an emotionally powerful Gothicness was also an important factor, is much more difficult to say. I cannot prove that pre-existing Gothicness was important to the process, but I do hope to have shown that it is at least *possible* that it was. When sources are few and the questions complex, historical argument tends to come to rest at the point where matters are beyond dispute. This can generate a tendency to disregard the different possibilities the evidence leaves open. To my mind, this has happened with the historiography of the Migration Period since the 1960s: positions deeply reductive to the importance of ethnicity have become entrenched, not least in very reasonable response to the Nazi ideological excesses which started from nineteenth-century visions of free and equal Germanic-speakers sweeping across the map of Europe. The fact that you cannot *prove* that Gothic ethnicity constrained the individual choices among the élite freeman class which generated the Visigoths, is hardly surprising and essentially meaningless. Given the general lack of first-hand biographical information available, it could hardly be otherwise. The fact that some of the surviving information makes it *possible* that an inherited Gothic ethnicity might have been an operative factor is, in context, well worth pointing out. Argument must not be allowed to become too reductive. The lowest common denominator, the point at which no one disagrees, is the easiest point for an argument to come to rest, but can nevertheless be misleading. Human reality tends much more often to the complex than the simple.

References

Textual sources:

[Abb.: *CM = Chronica minora*; *IV cons. Hon* = Claudian; *CSEL = Corpus Scriptorum Ecclesiasticorum Latinorum*; *C.Th. = Codex Theodosianus*; *Ep. = Epistulae*; *GCS = Die Griechischen Christlichen Schriftsteller*; *HE = Historia ecclesiastica*; *ILCV = Inscriptiones Latinae Christianae veteres*; *Or.* = Themistius, *Orationes*; *Pan. Lat. = Panegyrici Latini*; PLRE = Prosopography of the Later Roman Empire].

Ambrose
        Epistulae: see Faller & Zelzer (eds.) 1968-90.
Ammianus Marcellinus
        Res gestae: see Rolfe (trans.) 1950-2.
Chronica Minora: see Mommsen (ed.) 1892 & 1894.
Claudian
        Poemata: see Platnauer (trans.) 1922.
Codex Theodosianus: see Pharr (trans.) 1952.
Consularia Constantinopolitana: see Burgess (ed.) 1993.
Eunapius
        Histories: see Blockley (ed. & trans.) 1983.
Hydatius
        Chronica: see Burgess (ed. & trans.) 1993.
Inscriptiones Latinae Christianae veteres: see E. Diehl (ed.) 1925-31.

John of Antioch
        Historiae: see C. Müller (ed.) 1868.
Jordanes
        Iordanis Romana et Getica: see Mommsen (ed.) 1882; Mierow (trans.) 1912.
Malchus
        Historiae: see Blockley (ed. & trans.) 1983.
Olympiodorus
        Historia ecclesiastica: see Blockley (ed. & trans.) 1983.
Paulus Orosius
        Historia adversus paganos: see Zangmeister (ed.).
Panegyrici Latini: see Gallétier (ed. & Fr. trans.) 1955.
Paulinus of Pella
        Eucharisticon: see Evelyn White (ed. & trans.).
Priscus
        Historia ecclesiastica: see Blockley (ed. & trans.) 1983.
Procopius
        Opera: see Dewing (trans.) 1914-1940.
Prosopography of the Later Roman Empire: see Martindale (ed.) 1980
Socrates
        Historia ecclesiastica: see Hansen (ed.) 1995.
Sozomen
        Historia ecclesiastica: see Bidez (ed.) 1995.
Synesius of Cyrene
        De regno: see Terzaghi (ed.) 1944; Fitzgerald (trans.) 1930.
Themistius
        Orationes: see Downey & Norman (eds.) 1965-74.
        Orationes 8 and 10: see Heather & Matthews (trans.) 1991.
        Orationes 14-16: see Heather & Moncur (trans.) 1999.
Zosimus
        Nea historia: see Paschoud (ed. & trans.) 1971-89; Ridley (trans.) 1982.

Bibliography:

Achelis, H.
    1900   Der älteste deutsche Kalender. *Zeitschrift für die neutestamentliche Wissenschaft* 1: 308-335.
Amory, P.
    1993   The Meaning and Purpose of Ethnic Terminology in the Burgundian Laws. *Early Medieval Europe* 2 (1): 1-28.
    1997   *People and Identity in Ostrogothic Italy 489-554*. Cambridge: Cambridge University Press.
Bacal, A.
    1991   *Ethnicity in the Social Sciences. A View and a Review of the Literature on Ethnicity*. Coventry: Sheffield University Press.
Barth, F.
    1969   Introduction. In *Ethnic Groups and Boundaries: The Social Organization of Culture Difference*. F. Barth (ed.), pp. 9-38. Boston: Little, Brown & Co.
Bentley, G. C.
    1987   Ethnicity and Practice. *Comparative Studies in Society and History* 29: 24-55.
Bidez, J. (ed.)
    1995   *Sozomenus Kirchengeschichte*. (GCS, NF, vol. 4). Berlin: Akademie Verlag. [2nd edition revised by G. C. Hansen].

Blockley, R. C.
1983   *The Fragmentary Classicising Historians of the Later Roman Empire: Eunapius, Olympiodorus, Priscus and Malchus*, vol. 2. Liverpool: Francis Cairns.
Burgess, R. (ed. & trans.)
1993   *The Chronicle of Hydatius and the Consularia Constantinopolitana: Two Contemporary Accounts of the Final Years of the Roman Empire*. Oxford: Oxford University Press.
Cameron, A. D. E.
1970   *Claudian: Poetry and Propaganda at the Court of Honorius*. Oxford: Oxford University Press.
Demougeot, E.
1979   *La formation de l'Europe et les invasions barbares: ii. De l'avènement de Dioclétien (284) à l'occupation germanique de l'Empire Romain d'Occident (début du VIe siècle)*, vol. 2. Paris: Aubier.
Dewing, H. B. (trans.)
1914-40   Procopius, *Works*. Loeb, 7 vols. London: Heinemann. [Repr. Cambridge, MA: Harvard University Press].
Diehl, E. (ed.)
1925-31   *Inscriptiones Latinae Christianae veteres*. Berlin: Weidmann.
Downey, G., & A. F. Norman (eds.)
1965-74   *Themistius: Orationes*, 3 vols. Berlin: Teubner.
Evelyn White, H. G. (ed. & trans.)
1921   *Paulinus of Pella: Eucharisticon*. [in vol. 2 of his Loeb Ausonius] London: Heinemann.
Faller, O., & M. Zelzer (eds.)
1968-90   *Sancti Ambrosi Opera*. CSEL 82: 1-3.
Fitzgerald, A. (trans.)
1930   *The Essays and Hymns of Synesius of Cyrene*. Oxford: Oxford Univ. Press.
Friedrichsen, G. W. S.
1926   *The Gothic Version of the Gospels: A Study of its Style and Textual History*. Oxford: Oxford University Press.
1939   *The Gothic Version of the Epistles: A Study of its Style and Textual History*. Oxford: Clarendon Press.
Gallétier, E.
1955   *Panegyrici Latini*, 3 vols. Paris: Budé.
García Moreno, L. A.
1994   Gothic survivals in the Visigothic Kingdoms of Toulouse and Toledo. *Francia* 21 (1): 1-15.
Geary, P.
1983   Ethnicity as a situational construct in the early Middle Ages. *Mitteilungen der anthropologischen Gesellschaft in Wien* 113: 15-26.
Hansen, G. C. (ed.)
1995   *Sokrates Kirchengeschichte*. (GCS, NF, vol.1). Berlin: Akademie Verlag.
Heather, P. J.
1986   The crossing of the Danube and the Gothic conversion. *Greek Roman and Byzantine Studies* 27: 89-318.
1988   The Anti-Scythian Tirade of Synesius' *De Regno*. *Phoenix* 42: 152-172.
1989   Cassiodorus and the rise of the Amals: Genealogy and the Goths under Hun domination. *Journal of the Royal Society* 79: 103-128.
1991   *Goths and Romans 332-489*. Oxford: Oxford University Press.
1996   *The Goths*. (Peoples of Europe Series). Oxford: Blackwell.

Heather, P. J., & J. F. Matthews
   1991   *The Goths in the Fourth Century*. Liverpool: Liverpool University Press.
Heather, P. J., & D. Moncur
   1999   *Themistius - Select Orations, Liverpool Translated Texts for Historians*. Liverpool: Liverpool University Press.

Hedeager, L.
   1992   *Iron Age Societies. From Tribe to State in Northern Europe 500 BC to AD 700*. [Trans. J. Hines]. Oxford: Oxford University Press.

Kivisto, P.
   1989   *The Ethnic Enigma: The Salience of Ethnicity for European Origin Groups*. Philadelphia: Bulch Institute Press/Associated University Press.

Lenski, N.
   1995   The Date of the Gothic Civil War and the Date of the Gothic Conversion. *Greek, Roman, and Byzantine Studies* 36: 51-87.

Liebeschuetz, J. H. W. G.
   1986   Generals, federates and *buccellarii* in Roman armies around AD 400. In *The Defence of the Roman and Byzantine East*. P. Freeman & D. Kennedy (eds.), pp. 463-473. (British Archaeological Reports, IS 297). Oxford: B.A.R.
   1990   *Barbarians and Bishops*. Oxford: Oxford University Press.
Maenchen-Helfen, O. J.
   1973   *The World of the Huns*. Berkeley: California University Press.
Martindale, J. R. (ed.)
   1980   *Prosopography of the Later Roman Empire*, vol 2, *AD 395-527*. Cambridge: Cambridge University Press.

Matthews, J. F.
   1970   Olympiodorus of Thebes and the history of the West (AD 407-425). *Journal of Roman Studies* 60: 79-97.

Mierow, C. C. (trans.)
   1912   *Getica*. New York: Barnes & Noble.
Mommsen, T.
   1882   *Iordanis Romana et Getica. Monumenta Germaniae Historica. Auctores antiquissimi*, 5, 1. Berlin: Weidmann.
   1892   *Chronica minora saec. IV. V. VI. VII. (I). Monumenta Germaniae Historica. Auctores antiquissimi*, 9. Berlin: Weidmann. [Repr. 1981].
   1894   *Chronica minora saec. IV. V. VI. VII. (II). Monumenta Germaniae Historica. Auctores antiquissimi*, 11. Berlin: Weidmann. [Repr. 1981].

Müller, C (ed.)
   1868   *Fragmenta Historicorum Graecorum*, vol. 4. Paris: Firmin Didot.
Musset, L.
   1975   *The Germanic Invasions: The Making of Europe AD 400-600*. London: Elektra.

Paschoud, F.
   1971-89   *Zosime: Histoire nouvelle*. Paris: Budé.
   1975   *Cinq études sur Zosime*. Paris: Budé.
Pharr, C. (trans.)
   1952   *The Theodosian Code*. New York: Greenwood Press.

Platnauer, M.
   1922   *Claudian, Poems*, 2 vols. Loeb. London: Heinemann. [Repr. Cambridge, MA: Harvard University Press].

Reuter, T. (ed.)
1979   *The Medieval Nobility.* Amsterdam: North Holland.
Ridley, R. T. (trans.)
1982   *Zosimus, New History: A Translation with Commentary.* Canberra: Australian Association for Byzantine Studies.
Rolfe, J. C. (ed.)
1950-52   *Ammianus Marcellinus: Res gestae.* Loeb, 3 vols. London: Heinemann. [Repr. Cambridge, MA: Harvard University Press].
Roosens, E. E.
1989   *Creating Ethnicity: The Process of Ethnogenesis.* Berkeley: Sage.
Schmid, K.
1979   The structure of the nobility in the earlier Middle Ages. In *The Medieval Nobility.* T. Reuter (ed.), pp. 37-59. Amsterdam: North Holland.
Shennan, S. J.
1989   *Archaeological Approaches to Cultural Identity.* London: Unwin Hyman.
Smith, A. D.
1981   War and ethnicity: The role of warfare in the formation, self-images and cohesion of ethnic communities. *Ethnic and Racial Studies* 4: 375-395.
1986   *The Ethnic Origins of Nations.* Oxford: Oxford University Press.
Terzaghi, N. (ed.)
1944   *Synesii Cyrenensis Opuscula.* Roma: Typis regiae Officinae Polygraphicae.
Thompson, E. A.
1963   The Visigoths from Fritigern to Euric. *Historia* 12: 105-126.
1966   *The Visigoths in the Time of Ulfila.* Oxford: Oxford University Press.
Tjäder, J.-O.
1972   Der Codex argenteus in Uppsala und der Buchmeister Viliaric in Ravenna. In *Studia Gotica.* U. E. Hagberg (ed.), pp. 144-164. Stockholm: Almqvist & Wiksel.
Ucko, P. J.
1995   *Theory in Archaeology: A World Perspective.* London: Routledge & Kegan Paul.
Varady, L.
1969   *Das letzte Jahrhundert Pannoniens: 376-476.* Amsterdam: A. M. Hakkert.
Wenskus, R.
1961   *Stammesbildung und Verfassung: Das Werden der frühmittelalterlichen Gentes.* Köln: Böhlau Verlag.
1973   'Amaler'. In *Reallexikon der germanischen Altertumskunde*, 2nd ed, vol. 1. Pp. 246-249. Berlin: W. de Gruyter.
1975   'Balthen'. In *Reallexikon der germanischen Altertumskunde*, 2nd ed, vol. 2. Pp. 13-14. Berlin: W. de Gruyter.
Werner, K. F.
1979   Important noble families in the kingdom of Charlemagne. In *The Medieval Nobility.* T. Reuter (ed.), pp. 137-202. Amsterdam: North-Holland.
Wickham, C. J.
1992   Problems of comparing rural communities in early medieval western Europe. *Transactions of the Royal Historical Society.* (6th series) 2: 221-246.
1996   Rural society in Carolingian Europe. In *The New Cambridge Medieval History*, vol. 2. R. McKitterick (ed.), pp. 510-537. Cambridge: Cambridge University Press.

Wolfram, H.
    1967   *Intitulatio I: Lateinische Königs- und Fürstentitel bis zum Ende des 8.*
                Jahrhunderts. (Mitteilungen des Instituts für österreichische
                Geschichtsforschung, Erganzungsband 21). Wien: Böhlau Verlag.
    1979   Theogonie, Ethnogenese und ein kompromittierter Grossvater im
                Stammbaum Theoderichs der Grossen. In *Festschrift für Helmut*
                Beumann. E. K. Jaschke & R. Wenskus (eds.), pp. 80-97. Sigmaringen:
                Jan Thorbecke.
    1988   *History of the Goths*. Berkeley: California University Press.
Zangmeister, C.
    1882   *Paulus Orosius Historiarum adversus paganos libri. CSEL*, 5. Wien:
                Gerold.

Discussion

WOOD: A general point, on the *gens* as it came to be understood in the light of Herwig Wolfram's work. This is an attempt to try and tease out what sorts of traditions might be transmitted within the 'Traditionskern'. The question in my mind is that if the *gens* had a relatively fluid centre, to what extent could something like ancient legal tradition be transmitted, and whose legal tradition would be involved?

HEATHER: I forgot to say what I thought I left out of the paper and your reflection leads into it, because what occurred to me subsequently is that this kind of picture, if one accepts it, brings up the question of what happens at the moment of negotiation when, for instance, Stilicho's former allies decide that a future in the Roman world offers them nothing and they approach Alaric. What happens then? How do they attach themselves? What precise range of issues have to be addressed? And obviously, if one accepts, as I am finding myself increasingly inclined to, the idea of a wide élite or what one might call freeman class or whatever, then you have to negotiate who is equivalent to whom and what is their status. And since I am locating social and political power in this wide élite, I would be expecting their norms to be dominating. There is a substantial reason to think that these social structures were actually created in the third and fourth century in the conquest and domination of the Pontic region by Goths. That's when an élite, making itself in charge, is likely really to have taken off, when a fundamentally non-egalitarian but stratified society was created.

WOOD: What, in a sense, worries me, and what I would want to be further clarified is, if this élite is so wide, is it going to have a homogenous set of norms?

HEATHER: Sorry, I didn't understand that was your question. The thought was in my mind that this very general classification of society into three groups—free, freed, slaves—is about the most substantial negotiable norm that they would share. Beyond that I really don't know. It's interesting, how much more would be passed down and how much more you would need to be passed down.

WOOD: Yes, I am sure it is an unaswerable question, it just struck me as a question that had to be posed in the light of the sort of model you were setting up.

GREEN: On page 44, Andreas [Schwarcz], you have a point which I have here as "Ethnic identification is not exclusively English" [laughter]. Can you tell us what you mean by that?

SCHWARCZ: This is just a comment on the sentence which was the criticism of ethnic identification exclusively of English archaeologists and this, I'm sure, by the knowledge of international archaeological discussions is not quite true.

HEATHER: Well, I did say "in particular", and I think that a certain drift of it has come from Anglo-Saxon—American and certain English— archaeologists in the 1950s and 60s. But, yes, I take your point on the general issue. Although, some of the discussion in my ESF [European Science Foundation] group would suggest that it has not been very generally taken on board.

SCHWARCZ: It's still one of the most central points of archaeological discussion. I think that we are now past the point that everything is attributed to ethnic identification, but also past the other point that there is no ethnic identification. The discussion now is "where is it possible to identify, where is it not?"

HEATHER: Yes, I couldn't agree more, I'm sure that's right.

GREEN: Page 44, two points. The first is taking up what was said this morning. You said that it was these families who defined the groups as Gothic, not their followers. I made the point this morning about the constant addition and subtraction of other tribal groups. What we call (or what the sources call) Gothic, must be seen as polyethnic, rather than individually Gothic. Ellegård (1986), a Swedish archaeologist makes a point that I used in reference to the question why I had not gone into the possible Scandinavian origin of the Goths. I hope I made it clear that I wasn't convinced of it anyhow and that I wanted to get it out of my survey for reasons of space, but I also made reference to the point made by Ellegård which I quote here: "The question of the origin of the tribe really only makes sense as long as one assumes that tribes are genetically homogeneous and that migrations generally do not disturb that fundamental homogeneity". And it's for that reason that I felt justified in leaving out the question of the origin of the Goths. Now I imagine that ties up with your statement that Gothic was perhaps the defining term for the leaders of a 'Traditionskern', but nothing much beyond that.

HEATHER: Well, this is the view of Wenskus and Wolfram; it is not my view.

GREEN: Well, could you expand on that?

HEATHER: Yes, my view is this. You can certainly show some bits and pieces of people, who are previously called Goths, coming and going, and this is the point of the number-crunching section. As far as I can see, the evidence doesn't necessarily add up to making them fundamentally polyethnic, as it were, or multi-ethnic. And certainly the royal families have too discontinuous a history to be the bearers of Gothicness. The Ostrogoths kill Theodahad when the Amal family doesn't provide a suitable leader, but they still remain the Ostrogoths in Italy. So, it certainly cannot be royal families. That being so, I would turn to the description of social structures. The locus of political power in Ostrogothic Italy that you find in Procopius suggests a kind of alternative view, that it's an élite, a rather large élite.

At the moment this is the view I am arguing for, but I can see that there is an intermediate position available as well which would be going for, rather than a few royal families or a few thousand freemen élite members, for something in the middle, tens or a few hundreds of families who might be the crucial ones. Although I don't believe the evidence suggests this is right.

SCHWARCZ: I would like to say something to this. I think the main problem in treating Wenskus is that this damned book of his is too hard to read and that nowhere does he give an explicit theory of 'Traditionskern'. It's only mentioned in passing and the effect of the term itself is not quite the same as that used by Chadwick (1912) fifty years before. The 'Traditionskern' as understood by Wolfram is not the exclusive bearer of ethnic identity of the tribe throughout its existence but it's crucial in the beginning; for the formation of this ethnic group it is necessary that the ethnic group crystallize around something. There is then the individual consciouness of the people which may change and add a double, a triple identity because of different traditions in every person. So I don't think that on this point there is so much difference between Wolfram's view and yours, Peter [Heather].

If I may make another note to page 44, I think that the question of *Tervingi* and Visigoths must be discussed, as I have the impression that, in regard to his [Wolfram's] first German edition, you got mixed up about the division he makes, because the term *Vesus* for the fourth century is something different from Visigoth in English for the fifth century, and he clearly distinguishes between the two. And, bearing in mind the sources at the turn of the fourth century, especially the eastern *auxilia palatina* list in the *Notitia dignitatum,* I am sure that he is right that *Vesus* was used as an alternative for the *Tervingi* in the fourth century.

HEATHER: Well, that's entirely arguable, but so is the opposite. And what really muddles the argument for anyone trying to read Wolfram, because I haven't had the benefit of your long exposure to him, is when he starts talking about things such as Greuthungian Ostrogoths or indeed the *Vesi-Tervingi*. That really messes things up, and you can find statements that, on the face of it, are mutually contradictory. I am not the only one to have found this one difficulty, see particularly Philippe Rousseau's interesting article in *Historia* (1992), where he devoted his footnotes to trying to reconcile different Wolframian statements from different editions of the book. I do accept your characterization as a very sensible and clear statement and position. That may be what Wolfram thinks, but it's not what he has ever said, and I will say that with some firmness.

SCHWARCZ: I would like to show you somewhere the fiddling.

HEATHER: I am not sure that you are not making your own more substantial intellectual pattern with the various things that he has tried out.

GREEN: You are trying to describe Andreas [Schwarcz] as post-Wolfram.

HEATHER: Yes, he may well be.

SCHWARCZ: Some of this is the outcome of 20 years of discussion.

HEATHER: Well, absolutely.

SCHWARCZ: But I think that also for the term Ostrogoth for the *Greutungi* there is some evidence in the fourth especially in those lines by Claudian (Claudian, *De IV consulatu Honorii,* 11. 626 ff.)

HEATHER: Well, that is one piece of evidence, but Claudian does talk about Ostrogoths mixed with *Greutungi* which, on the face of it, means they were different [laughter].

SCHWARCZ: I think that he says that because he also got mixed up.

HEATHER: There is also the question whether he has actually made the term up himself. Yes, it does seem to me awkward and I'm being difficult making the maximum possible case and there are perfectly reconcilable intermediate positions, between whatever view Wolfram holds, and Wenskus, and myself. But I am just currently interested and excited about that stuff found in Procopius.

SCHWARCZ: I would say something on this later in discussing your paper.

GREEN: Can I come back to my second point on page 45, where you go on to say that Gothic groups on the migration might better be viewed as armies than peoples. Here, I think you've got linguistic support in that the Germanic word *folk* meant originally and for some considerable time both 'army' and 'people'. I think that could be brought in to assist the argument here.

HEATHER: Again this is not really my view. I am sure that's reversible too, in the sense that you could regard peoples as armies: it works either way round.

GREEN: There is another point there which I should make in that connection. The traditional Germanic term for the ruler or a king, in Wulfila's Gothic *thiudans*, derives from the word *thiuda* which means 'people' in the ethnic sense of the word. The interesting thing is that this word declines in importance in the other Germanic (non-Gothic) languages and eventually disappears and is replaced by other terms for king. The philological argument has been to suggest that, with polyethnicity as a result of the migrations, the relevance of a term such as *thiudans*, meaning leader of an ethnic totality, became not really superflouous, but out of date, no longer relevant to the political position.

HEATHER: Sure, I'm not arguing with a kind of basic Thompsonian vision or Wolframian vision of the breaking up, by the Romans, through increasingly divisive social inequalities, of Gothic tribal communities. What I'm suggesting is that it may happen later, essentially. I think, in other words, that it is a creation of the successor states in the aftermath of the Migration Period, and probably of the land divisions and all the jumbling up that goes on, for instance, in Visigothic Spain, when that land division takes place.

WOOD: Dennis [Green], since you raised the question of words for leadership, can I get you to say something about your view on what Ammianus Marcellinus means by *iudex* (*Res gestae*, XXVII 5, 6)?

GREEN: Can I keep that for the moment because I want at a later stage, not in connection with this paper, to voice my misgivings about Wolfram's use of the word *iudex* and the way in which he, I think too readily, equates it with the Gothic word *reiks*. Could I leave it until then, because it would be more relevant if we discuss it in that context.

DÍAZ: On page 45, I have a point: the question of Gothic identity is central, I think, in different papers that we are going to discuss here. We do speak about a

Gothic identity and when we speak about the Visigoths, we speak about the idea of a completely new personality of the Visigoths in the fourth century. Evidently it is not necessarily a contradictory situation. However, there are several questions that we can consider to solve this apparent contradiction. The first question concerning page 48 is whether it is possible to identify elements of continuity or not. We have several references, e.g. the idea of a multi-ethnic force in general, not only on page 51, but in several cases. However, on page 53 we get the idea that the Visigoths are essentially Goths. Concerning the Visigothic royal dynasty we say that it was not a phenomenon of sufficient permanence to define the group as a Gothic one. In another instance we can think about the social composition of the Gothic population and perhaps we can speak about a group of Goths perhaps dominant over other groups. Finally, concerning the idea of the importance of being Gothic, the question is that when the Visigoths invented tradition, we think about them looking back and probably taking a central element of identity. In this case, the self definition of the Visigoths, taken in their totality, is not necessarily a new or a completely new personality. This, is a consideration that I better let you make.

HEATHER: Right, this is where the arguments on historical detail really matter. Because, the view that I hold depends on the answers to a few key questions. Whom did Alaric lead in revolt in 395? Whom did he subsequently have in his following? I take the view that the vast majority of these were actually and already Goths, though some were not, but real life is complicated. Nonetheless, my calculations and my best ability at reading the evidence suggest to me that the vast majority were actually already Goths and already talked about that way by the Romans, by outsiders. They all looked like Goths to a number of different Romans.

DE JONG: That is the same thing.

HEATHER: Not necessarily the same thing. But, the way I think of it is that you've got various interlocking layers of history. If this freeman class have one layer where they think of themselves all as Gothic and united in some way, then that goes back to the deep past and is more or less myth. Then they have a fourth-century history where they are divided, because there certainly isn't one Gothic kingdom before the arrival of the Huns. In the time of Alaric, some of these put to one side that history of separation and created another level of cooperation and unity. And that, I think, is a classic case where a sense of identity was generated in and through contact, because the one united group is a response to Roman imperial power. I think it's simply wrong to suppose that Valens let the Goths in voluntarily in 376, I think you can show he had no choice. If the Romans had a long history of accepting outsiders in small groups, they had no history at all of voluntarily accepting large politically independent militarized groups. And there are plenty indications that until the whole strategic situation changed, that there were many attempts to destroy the Goths inside Roman borders, and plenty of hostility towards them too. In other words, the new circumstance that renovated old ideas of commonality between Goths was the need to survive in the face of Roman power. Before that applies, I think these people had various potential ways they could go. They had their heritage, what they learned literally at their mothers' knees, which offered them a number of possibilities, not an infinite number, but more than one. And then life experience and other things decided which one of these choices they would activate, and I think what was critical here was Roman hostility. If you want to be an independent Goth on Roman soil, then you have to stick together in large numbers. It is possible to have alternative readings of these critical questions. If so, you end up with a substantially different account from mine.

DÍAZ: I think this point must be included in our discussion.

SCHWARCZ: On page 47, about Alaric's elevation to kingship. I'm not convinced that the elevation of Alaric to kingship was in 395 after the death of Theodosius I. Claudian indicates in different laudatory poems that the elevation to kingship was a thing of the early 90s of the fourth century, concerning the fights of 391/92, and then they ended with a *foedus* which was only made possible because there was someone with whom it could be made. This concerns also the relation between the *Balthi*. I agree that there is no contemporary source for the name of the leading group of fourth century *Tervingi*. But an elevation to the leadership in the rebellion of 391/92 could not be made only because of military personal prowess and was only made possible by family connections and prestige.

HEATHER: Yes, that's interesting. I have to think about that. I can think of some counterpoints, which would start from the fact that the treaty of 382 was not made with one person.

SCHWARCZ: That's also a matter of discussion. I thought about this; actually, the *Consularia constantinopolitana s.a. 382* have it this way: *Universa gens Gothorum cum rege suo se dediderunt.*

HEATHER: Yes, but that means Athanaric. It's been put in the wrong year.

SCHWARCZ: It cannot be Athanaric, because he is a fugitive when he arrives, and it is not a peace treaty which is signed with him in 380, but he got an honorary reception of some sort before he died.

HEATHER: Yes, but, you know, Theodosius makes a big deal of that treaty with Athanaric because he was losing the Gothic war, and he has to have some kind of propaganda claim in January 380, because his new army has just been beaten by Fritigern the year before. And to my mind absolutely decisive is Themistius. If Fritigern had been alive in 382, we would hear about it in Oration 16. Themistius is very explicit that this peace was made with a group of leading men.

SCHWARCZ: That's what held me back. There is the possibility, and I always thought that not mentioning Fritigern may be due to the fact of accepting someone with his group as a whole without distributing them in different places, and it is this newness of the *foedus* of 382 which makes its interpretation so difficult.

HEATHER: But this is a new thing presented in old clothing. And that's what makes it tricky. In other words the state has to present the agreement in old clothing to its taxpayers but it's really a new thing. There is no doubt about that. This is one objection. The other objection is, I am very attached to the thought of the quarrel between Fravittas and Eriulf which is absolutely dated to 392-3, the preparations for the Eugenius campaigns, as also being about the struggle for leadership. I would agree that when talking about Alaric, his pre-history is important too, but I think that's one part of him building up his prestige and rivals disappearing that enables him to state his claim to be the new Gothic leader when it comes to the revolt on Theodosius' death. But even if Alaric is related to Fritigern, that doesn't make him related to Athanaric who was part of the previous royal dynasty.

SCHWARCZ: I think he was related to Fritigern.

HEATHER: Fritigern is certainly an outsider. Already in that generation between 376 and 380 you have documented the fact that other people can emerge as leaders, and therefore I cannot see why you need, in the face of no positive evidence, to attach Alaric to Athanaric. What you are looking for is someone certainly from a fairly prominent family, with a good history of the right kind of politics, but the attachment to Athanaric seems very redundant.

SCHWARCZ: I agree there that it is more probable that Alaviv was related to Alaric. We know nothing of him after Marcianople and the banquet there, and he may have been killed then. We know by Claudian that Alaric lost his father as a boy.

HEATHER: Yes, that's possible.

SCHWARCZ: Marcianople. There is a dinner given by the Roman commander to the two leaders of the Goths who accepted his invitation, and this banquet ends with one of them dead, and this is Alaviv. He was the more prominent of the two.

HEATHER: So it seems from the one mention of the two together.

SCHWARCZ: Another point on the first revolt of Alaric. I don't see that Peter [Heather] is openly against this but he seems to keep an open mind about it.

HEATHER: Yes, the thing that interests me about Alaric is, here anyway, who he precisely is. I think that Andreas must be right. Obviously he was not a nobody. But the point I wanted to stress is that I think that Liebeschuetz (1990) mistakes a discontinuity in the narrative sources for a discontinuity in the actual historical sequence of events. Those things are not the same thing. There is nothing in Zosimus's mistaken joining of Olympiodorus and Eunapius which contradicts the view you get in 399 from Synesius (*De regno* 19-21) and Claudian (*De bello Getico*, 166 ff., 610 ff.) of 402 that Alaric led the Goths of 382 in revolt and very large numbers of them. And you know, they're contemporaries, very close to the action. I don't see that there was a big problem here, but Liebeschuetz made a lot of it.

SCHWARCZ: Anyway Zosimus' *Historia nea*, I'm always suspicious of him when he uses Eunapius. And one of the points which can't be correct concerns the quarrel between Eriulf and Fravittas. This might not have been a quarrel for leadership in the area of the settlements, but it's a quarrel that takes place after a banquet in Constantinople, and I would not make too much of it.

HEATHER: Yes, but there is more than one source which tells us that Theodosius had these Goths to dinner regularly, and that would make a lot of sense.

SCHWARCZ: Yes, if he has them regularly to dinner in the metropolis it's possible that all those people already were commanders of different groups of soldiers belonging to different regiments that were quartered in the city itself, and Fravittas, this is for the case in point quite exemplary, because he is not a tribal leader, but a career officer in the Roman army.

HEATHER: Ah, but there is no evidence that he was a career officer in the regular army before the fight, and Eunapius (see Blockley frg. 59; cf. Zosimus 4. 55. 3-56. 1) is very clear that he had to flee Gothic society because he killed Eriulf. And actually my feeling on the Eunapius-Zosimus question is that I think most of the real mess is made by Zosimus and not by Eunapius.

SCHWARCZ: An example of the point which made me suspicious and where there is a great difference between Wolfram's thoughts and mine, is this absolutely fantastic account about the end of Gainas going back across the Danube and turning once again to tribal pagan religion and then finally being killed. If you take the *Consularia constantinopolitana* and the ecclesiastical sources, you get a completely different picture and, what is more important, it is chronologically consistent but totally contradicts Eunapius. And according to this it is impossible that Gainas, after his final defeat, went north of the Danube, because within 14 days he was dead, and his head was placed on one of the main gates of Constantinople. And if this is not right I'm very suspicious of the other fantastic stories of Eunapius because he's not a historiographer, he is a sort of romancer.

GREEN: Can we move to page 51, eleven lines from the bottom. You say "in contemporary sources an explicitly Gothic king called Radagaisus". Your use of the word 'explicitly' there suggests to me the possibility of a slight doubt as to whether he was in fact Gothic. I should like to allay that doubt on linguistic grounds. The Germanic name 'Radagaisus' means literally an 'agile spear' and, if I may use a technical philological term, it is a so-called *bahuvrihi* compound, someone who has, who wields an agile spear. The first element is Germanic at large and we have no indication within that first element *rada* that it's Gothic. The second element *gaisus* has parallels throughout Germanic, but the form *gaiz-* can only be East Germanic and in this context surely Gothic is at issue, it cannot be anything else but Gothic.

HEATHER: That's interesting. Why I put 'explicitly' in there is because, it's our pal Zosimus again, he talks about Radagaisus and talks about him recruiting Germanic and Celtic tribes from above the Rhine. But Zosimus has no account of the Rhine crossing in 406 and it seems clear that he actually conflated the two things together again and stuck the Rhine crossing and Radagaisus together.

SCHWARCZ: And I think for the Gothicness there is the contemporary evidence in Augustine's *De civitate Dei* (5. 23) who states undoubtedly that Radagaisus was a Goth.

HEATHER: That's right and I think it's probably generally accepted now that Zosimus has messed up, but for a while, when multi-ethnicity was in vogue, we had Zosimus on Radagaisus as a substantial documentation of multi-ethnicity at work.

GREEN: You're implying that polyethnicity is not involved elsewhere.

SCHWARCZ: His followers were polyethnic because he took many groups from Pannonia with him. On page 52, concerning the peace with Huns and Alans, my own thought provides that there is a great difference in the interpretation of events of 376 to 382. Because Peter [Heather] doesn't believe in a separate *foedus* with a group of Goths, Huns and Alans who were settled in Pannonia by Gratian.

But I think in this point he is mistaken and you cannot explain the presence of Goths in the middle of the Roman Empire in the 80s and 90s without this settlement. In my opinion these are the main followers of Alatheus and Saphrax and later of Radagaisus and of Athaulf in 408.

HEATHER: Rather than rehearse all the arguments here, I would only say that this is a phantasy of modern scholarship and that actually they did not make a settlement with Gratian and there is not the slightest bit of evidence in favour of it.

SCHWARCZ: That is not true archaeologically and it is not true historically.

HEATHER: I'm not saying that there are not some Huns and Alans somewhere in Pannonia, but there is no statement that the Huns and Alans who joined the Goths in 377 and fought at Hadrianople settled in Pannonia.

SCHWARCZ: I have noted that we did discuss this in the evening and after that I looked it up once again in the book. You have to explain away all mentions of Goths also by Ambrose (*Ep.* 20) in Milan at the time of Valentinian II.

HEATHER: Ambrose talks much more about Huns and Alans, rather than Goths, and very clearly a body of Huns and Alans who were part of Gratian's military and then picked up by Valentinian II for his regime. The Goths are not talked of in the same way. There are some Gothic bodyguards and some Gothic troops probably in Milan, but that's not the same as Goths in Pannonia. The question is whether you need Goths in Pannonia to have Goths in the Roman army in Milan—and they are explicitly in the Roman army, they are not a separate body of federates.

SCHWARCZ: You don't have them only in Milan. You also have the Roman army which is composed of Goths in Poetovio, because there is a story of the Arian bishop of Poetovio who is accused by Ambrose of having produced himself before the soldiers dressed like a Visigothic heathen priest (*Ep.* 10).

HEATHER: And?

SCHWARCZ: And, of course, their settlement in Pannonia was a military one, they were part of the army, they had no king, the military settlement of these federates was integrated into the *limes* defence of Pannonia.

HEATHER: Well, Goths got as far as Pannonia in the war, there is no doubt about that. The question is whether they were settled there. Just because Julian Valens is actually accused in Poetovium it doesn't mean that that's where Goths were hanging around. I don't see how he proves their settlement. I am sorry.

SCHWARCZ: Really it is a problem, if you make a theory then you have to explain away all these sources, and in that case I have to think that the theory is wrong or the sources are wrong. If it's only one source it can be wrong, but if you have to explain away all the sources, I think the theory is a flop.

HEATHER: First I can say that part of this theory was invented by Lázló Varady (1969), who came up with the most extraordinary story I ever came across.

SCHWARCZ: I agree that you cannot trust Varady.

HEATHER: More generally, I wouldn't say in fact that I have to explain away anything. When you look at the sources, it seems to me it's the proponents of the supposed *foedus* of the 380s who have to explain away. There is no source that ever says that there was more than one peace treaty with Goths in the early 380s. Western sources do talk of a peace in 381 rather than 382 but they consistently misdate the treaty of 382 to 381, because they mistake Athanaric's arrival as the same event as the peace treaty with the rest of the Goths. This is in Jordanes and it is in Cassiodorus's chronicle. And if you then look for the supposed subsequent history of these Goths in Pannonia, there is one mention in Pacatus, which talks about Gothic members in the army of Theodosius occupying Pannonian cities. But that was obviously in a move which was a part of the campaign. There is no indication there that they had been in Pannonia since 380. After that, the next reference is 408 when you've got Athaulf there, and, of course, Alaric had just been next door in Noricum, having moved from Epirus, at the same time. So that it is again very unclear whether Athaulf was there through a permanent settlement or a temporary occupation which was part of Alaric's move to Italy. I don't think, therefore, it would be fair to say that I have to explain away more than the proponents of the theory.

SCHWARCZ: Of course, I have one last argument and then I'll close. In fact this varies not so much for the Visigoths, but it is material for the understanding of the constitution of those who followed Alaric in 408 into Italy. You also have to explain away the Alans and the predilection of Gratian for Alan troops which led to his death; his murder cannot be explained without a special treaty of Gratian with the Alans, Goths, and Huns in 380.

HEATHER: This is exactly the problem with all the arguments surrounding this question. This is Várady's line of argument, when we see Huns, Alans or Goths mentioned anywhere, in his view that must be a reference to the 'Dreivölker' confederation made up of the three of them, but when only one is mentioned, the other two—in his line of argument—must be supposed to be there, even if they are not mentioned. And what does Ammianus tell us about the Alans? That they operated in a number of independent units. So, there's absolutely no reason why the particular Alans that Gratian certainly recruited have to be the group who supported the Huns who joined the Goths in 377, none in the slightest.

RETAMERO: On the motives for the fragmentation in socio-political units, I would like to comment on one of the key questions posed on page 53. Why did a number of different Gothic rulers decide to come together to create the Visigoths? Why did the Goths fragment under the pressure of the Huns and, on the contrary, afterwards they came together to face the Roman threat.

HEATHER: That's an interesting question. I understand it this way, that it's the difference between a general threat creating a general instability versus a very direct and monolithic threat. The Roman state has certain instruments of power, notably its army, and, once you are inside the Roman territory, to survive you have to make some kind of demonstration to the Roman state that it's not worth their while to dismantle you. Because that's what they normally do, that's what they had done for five, six, seven hundred years. They will take people in, but they break them up, and they separate them geographically although specific terms vary; some groups they treat more favourably, some groups they treat less favourably.

But if you want to enter the Roman state and survive, you have to show them that it's not worth their while to dismantle you. Outside the Empire, I see the instability created by the Huns unfolding certainly in a number of stages between *ca* 370, when you first hear of Goths wondering what they are going to do, out across the Pontic litoral somewhere near Crimea, and the 420s, when you finally have secure references to Huns in Hungary. So, the Hunnic threat evolved over huge distances and a fifty year period. And within that geographical area and chronological time frame, different Goths had a range of options that they could take, a range of ways of trying to secure their lives in changed circumstances. You can try accommodation with the Roman Empire, the Roman option: we here are speaking of 376. If the Romans won't let you, as they don't let Athanaric, then you can try going for a geographically isolated one. Athanaric obviously clears off up into Transylvania somewhere, and other Goths, we know of later, moved into the Crimea, sheltering behind the mountains there. You can move westwards, you can move northwards, you can move southwards, or you can move into the Roman Empire, or indeed, I suppose, probably try to make accommodations with the Huns as well. Thus there are a variety of options open; and for their own particular reasons, different Goths took different options. That's what caused the fragmentation. And I even think one can document that with, for instance, the Alans too. Some are already attached to Huns by 377 and joined Goths, others are attached by Gratian in the 380s, others still remained north of the Danube at that point and take part in the Rhine invasion of 406. I think it's the variety of possible responses which causes fragmentation.

DE JONG: On page 53 ff. concerning 'number crunching'. Well, perhaps I can take together various questions of mine, also I feel that number crunching is the one issue. I very much enjoyed your paper it was wonderfully illuminating to have it all outlined, and it sounded all terribly sensible until I got to 'number crunching', because then I was aware of the importance you attach to what is in the mind, and I agree. So, given the importance of identity in the minds of people I thought "why does Peter need to do this 'number crunching'"? I can see why you would like to argue for a fairly substantial group of carriers of a tradition rather than only a small 'Traditionskern' connected to royal houses, that seems fine. But if you look at where the numbers come from, these are Roman sources talking about Goths, so there is an identity described for two groups of people not by themselves but by others. I think you should take that into account, before you decide to count noses. Furthermore, the one thing that interests me throughout the rest of your paper is that Gothicness apparently arises in opposition to Romanness quite consistently and in different ways, in very different historical contexts. And I think it's very hard to argue for any kind of continuity, real continuity. But in a state of flux like that, nothing is more important than a tradition which is perceived as ancient, ancient, and ancient. So I think you can profit from this paper much more if you throw the numbers out and concentrate more on thinking about what exactly this identity is, as a situational construct. By which I do not mean it was a figment of the imagination. Do you see my point?

HEATHER: Yes, I take your point and if one were to write in the margin the probability of being right, I wouldn't ascribe to this section a very high probability.

DE JONG: I can see you have reservations already, because I am not trying to say that you are trying to be exact.

HEATHER: No, but, in fact, it is important and it matters, I think, in this way. All identities are situational constructs, Barth's (1969) famous aphorism is to talk about identity as an "evanescent situational construct" and that I think posits a false dichotomy. All ethnicities are situational constructs, but some are more evanescent than others. All I'm interested in doing is this. It's quite clear that Visigothicness is a situational construct in conflict with Roman power. What I am then interested in doing is poking it a little bit further to see if anything suggests that Visigothicness is drawing not only on a straightforwardly pragmatic 'unite to survive', material calculation. I am wondering, in other words, whether there may also be a more positive motivation for unification underneath as well. In other words, were there things which were familiar already to the different groups coming together, on which they could also draw. And I suppose, in some ways, you have to explain why the hell did they want to be independent. Is it sufficient to say that the Romans, while accepting them in certain circumstances, were too unpredictable, they could turn around and massacre your women and children, as happened to Stilicho's allies who joined Alaric? In other words that Roman traditions about how to treat the 'other', the outsider, are sufficiently aggressive in themselves to make other people hang together. This has got a lot to do with it, obviously, but there is at least the possibility that there is something else underneath as well. You have to do some fairly extensive fiddling, as is quite clear, to make the numbers work. But none of the individual steps is totally outrageous in itself; it is more the agglomeration of steps which is problematic. And all I'm doing is trying to demonstrate the fact that the argument is possible.

DE JONG: Yes, OK, I can see that. But the only problem that remains is Romans who call Goths 'Goths', not Goths who call themselves 'Goths'.

HEATHER: Well, that's a potential problem, rather than necessarily a fundamental one.

GREEN: Could I come into a point that you just made, Mayke [de Jong], that it is the Romans who call the Goths 'Goths'. There is an exception to that in the Gothic calendar, where the Goths are described as *Gutthiuda*, the Gothic people.

DE JONG: OK.

SCHWARCZ: Yes, peoples without a main tradition, the sources speak about them and on their own, but if I may say so, I agree with one exception, that maybe they did not want to become independent, they wanted to become autonomous enough to get a good post individually and as a group in the Empire.

HEATHER: Well, their political agenda at this point doesn't foresee that the Empire is going to fall. So the agenda must be one of working within a framework of the continued existence of the Roman Empire. No one in 400 or in 410 could imagine that the Roman Empire was going to fall.

SCHWARCZ: Two points on page 57. We already discussed, one, the question of Alatheus and Saphrax; the other one concerns your note about the alliteration in Gothic. I think there you are completely wrong. And I can show this by some examples. I think, if you take the Tervingian leaders of the fourth century, the question about h and no h is a difficult one because for most of them, in the manuscripts we've got both variants. So, it is not really possible to say that Alaric and Ariaric do not alliterate, because you cannot be sure with any of these names that they are not spoken with an h but that they were spoken without an h. And for this group you must also take into account not only Euric, Athanaric and Alaric but Aoric, Ariaric and Alaviv which gives many more alliterations. Other alliterations among the houses of the fifth century are shown by the family of Theoderic himself. His father's name is Theudimir, you've got his two sons Theoderic and Theudimund, you've got his daughter Theudigotha, his nephew Theodahat, and his two children Theodegisels and Theodelinda. In the family of Sarus, his brother is Sigeric or Sergeric, and in the family of the *Balthi* from the fifth century you get Theoderic I, Theoderic II and his brother Thorismund.

HEATHER: And his other brother Euric, which does not particularly alliterate.

SCHWARCZ: I do not say that alliteration is the exclusive element of name building with Gothic ruling families, but it surely is one. And I think as well, if I may add, I haven't read it yet in any literature, but it can be shown by the examples with the suffix which is used in alliteration, for instance Valamir, Vidimir, Theodemir. And if you take the brothers of Theoderic II there you have either alliteration or variation of the suffix, Theoderic, Euric, Friedric.

HEATHER: Yes, but I think what we have here is a variation on the father's name, which is what many of your claimed alliterations actually are, and that clearly is a documented naming principle: Theodemir, Theoderic and so on. Whether that's alliteration or whether that's taking this element and varying it seems to be a matter of debate. What worries me is this idea that if you make Alaric alliterate with other names, then, 'bingo', 2 and 2 makes 4 and you have a family relationship. Never mind that you are making any number of assumptions about who is related to whom. No one actually tells us that they are related.

SCHWARCZ: No, but if they alliterate, I would tie Alaric with Athanaric.

HEATHER: Yes, but it's also got to work with other members of the same family, if the principle works.

SCHWARCZ: It is true that we cannot be sure, but it is at least a small indication.

HEATHER: Yes, but there are other principles at work too, as you made clear.

GREEN: You've anticipated what I was coming on to on page 57. So I'll be very brief and just make one point on what was just said by Andreas. I'm not convinced by your suggestion that *Harjareiks* and *Arjareiks* may all alliterate because we cannot be sure that the *h* was dropped. The *h* was dropped only in later Latin tradition, not in Germanic tradition. In Germanic an *h* word cannot alliterate with a non *h* word.

SCHWARCZ: Of course, but we have Latin transcriptions of Germanic names. For instance for Alaric we also have written variations with Halaricus.

GREEN: Yes, and we also have Latin transcription giving an *h* as a *c* or as a *ch*. So it is tricky to base the argument on a Latin form, when dealing with Germanic names.

SCHWARCZ: Of course, yes.

JIMÉNEZ: I think that you link two ideas (p. 58), the idea of the creation of the Visigoths as a people and the idea of the creation of the dynastic family with Euric. Are the two ideas connected?

HEATHER: They are connected in the sense that what I would really argue is that these are two parallel things going on at the same time, and that Alaric and Athaulf nearly create a dynasty, but the dynasty is really created by Theoderic I.

JIMÉNEZ: I think that maybe this question of a dynasty was in fact a Roman idea. I mean: I think that the Visigoths, especially Theoderic I, created the dynasty when the Roman Theodosian-Valentinian dynasty was in a crisis, that is at the end of the Theodosian dynasty, while the other emperors had been successful so quickly. So, maybe Euric feared for his kingdom and it was then that this idea of a dynasty came to him and he named his son Alaric as successor. This was a Roman idea, not primarily a Gothic one.

HEATHER: Hm, it's interesting.

JIMÉNEZ: Otherwise, why was Euric the first one to name his son Alaric? Why is there not another Alaric before, among all the other kings and princes of Toulouse. If Alaric I started the dynasty, why isn't there another Alaric until the end of the fifth century?

HEATHER: Yes, that's interesting. I suppose what you are doing is separating, as it were, the de facto transmission of power from Theoderic I to his sons from the idea that power can only be in this descent line.

JIMÉNEZ: Theoderic's sons were murdered one by the other between themselves. Therefore, it would seem that they did not have yet the idea of a dynasty. The elder son, Thorismund, was murdered by his brothers Theoderic and Friederic (*HG* XXX, XXXI); Theoderic II was murdered by his brother Euric "who succeeded him to the throne by a similar crime to that committed before by Theoderic II".

Jordanes' version, curiously omits partially these crimes, saying that Thorismund was murdered by his *cliens* Ascalcus (*Getica*, XLIII. 228), while he says nothing about the way Theoderic II died.

SCHWARCZ: You see, if someone kills his brother he has to obtain the acceptance of those he has got to rule and if they accept his being in power, they accept his being from the ruling family.

JIMÉNEZ: The last one who killed the others was the one who gave rise to the dynasty.

SCHWARCZ: No, the *stirps regia* is the basis for the creation of a people, that was the point I have to make to Peter [Heather]. His contention about the dynastic connection to Euric. You see, it's the same case as with Vitiges, his military prowess is enough to become king, but to ensure that he remains king it is necessary to get into the royal family, so he's got to find a wife who is the answer.

HEATHER: It sounds perfectly logical, except that the marriage is only ever mentioned in the context of Vitiges's propaganda to Justinian, and the point is to say that by marrying Amalasuentha's daughter and killing Theodahad, Vitiges has removed Justinian's cause for war. Now, I don't doubt that marrying an Amal helped. And Vitiges is obviously having to start again, so that he was drawing on every possible resource. Hence, he is drawing on dynastic tradition to some extent, but it is a kind of ancillary help, not fundamental. To say that it is necessary for him to marry an Amal to stay in power seems to me to be overstating the case. Indeed, Totila doesn't marry into the Amal dynasty when he comes to power.

SCHWARCZ: But Hildebad is a relative of the Visigothic king Theudis, and so is Totila. It's a different thing if you choose a king in time of war and so for necessity you take a promising general. This is the case with Vitiges, and he has the necessity, for political reasons, to find an alliance with the old ruling family within a short time. It's a different case with Theoderic I who is not the king chosen to fight a war, but he still finds it necessary, at least in the propaganda of his son Theoderic II, to connect his family with Alaric I.

HEATHER: We don't know whether he married.

SCHWARCZ: We don't know anything about the woman he married because we don't know that there was a marriage connection with the family of Alaric since that is impossible, and it can only be explained by his gaining prestige.

HEATHER: It all helps, every little helps. But my basic point is that you have to manufacture power, that power is being manufactured and that the formation of a tradition by Alaric and Athaulf was actually cut off by Sigeric. Theoderic, elected because there was no male heir, used Alaric's daughter as ancillary power. Besides, you should not just talk about Vitiges, you also should talk about the succession to Theoderic the Great himself. It is very clear that, as early as 526, one faction thought that Tuluin, a non-Amal, should be king.

SCHWARCZ: He was married to an Amal princess.

HEATHER: I know, but that's not why they thought he should succeed. They thought he should succeed because Theodahad as an Amal was useless. Athalaric was too young and Tuluin had beaten the crap out of the Burgundians just recently and had a long history of being militarily effective.

SCHWARCZ: I mean, it is a thousand years later, but if you take a look at some of those elected in the Holy Roman Empire of the Middle Ages you find all those changes of dynasty are made by promising military men but all are connected either directly or by marriage with the former dynasty.

AUSENDA: On page 59, concerning stratification. It is quite certain that Germanic groups were stratified as is also abundantly clear from the literature. However, it stands to reason that the relationship of clients to dominant individuals became less demanding when they settled in new territories within the Roman Empire, in that members of dominant clans obtained different sources of livelihood and furthermore clients reoriented their main activity from prevalently pastoralist to prevalently agricultural, where agricultural activity is much more difficult to control than pastoral. It would not be surprising if client status did disappear altogether after a couple of hundred years or shortly thereafter.

DE JONG: I thought we got rid of the pastoralists this morning.

SCHWARCZ: Because both Alans and Huns had with them many who had been previously pastoral, but at the moment they arrived they all became warriors.

AUSENDA: Even the clients?

SCHWARCZ: Yes. You see if you take Peter [Heather]'s argument with the stratification, if you take Procopius of Caesarea, it is clear you have two groups of clients, but not only with the Goths, but in the retinue also of Byzantine officers. That's the case in point, there are two layers of warriors, the better one and the one with a humble status, and those two types are not only found in Procopius for the Ostrogothic warriors, but were also in the retinue of Belisarius.

HEATHER: It's already there in that fifth-century law about *foederati*.

SCHWARCZ: Yes, and one thing I would like to say to your stratification is that I agree that there was a warrior class among the *Tervingi* and in the fourth century it is quite clear from the different texts, that there was one and it's known too. But it is not necessary to go for the sixth to find that this is part of the personal retinue of the sub-leaders, of the *reguli*.

HEATHER: Responding generally to the thought in Giorgio [Ausenda]'s mind, he is questioning, in a sense, the economic redistribution that followed from kingdom creation: whether one is talking of the Ostrogoths who just conquered a whole entity, or of the Visigoths who after 450 were able to extend their power into Spain, first of all on a kind of looting basis, but then permanently. A key question is how the loot was divided up subsequently. This, in a sense, was Edward Thompson's point (in all his works on the Goths, but esp. 1963). Those who were already dominant, who were already slightly dominant, got a bigger share and set up the conditions which would allow them to become really very dominant in subsequent times. This might explain how you get from what seems to be described by Procopius, where there is a lot of power distributed outside an élite, to something more like Carolingian situations of small and very dominant élites; and I suppose that's what Thompson had in mind. I would not claim to have any answers at this point, but the share out of loot is obviously crucial.

Just on these *reiks*, I'm sure too that there are vertical ties. I would imagine horizontal ties between members of the warrior class or freeman class whatever you want to call it. I use 'freemen' because it is in the sources. But there are obviously vertical ties too. What's not clear is how permanent those vertical ties are. Is *reiks* a distinction that is inherited, or is it something you gained in your own lifetime and that your heirs subsequently had to get for themselves, rather than something consistently passed down? That is a question that, at the moment, cannot really be answered.

SCHWARCZ: On a warrior élite on page 60, I just would like to say that if you take the evidence of those archaeological sources, I think the position is inherited in those chronicles.

HEATHER: I'm sorry, I'm not with your point.

SCHWARCZ: When you take those sources about the persecution of Christians among the *Tervingi*, it's clear that there is a family in power in the sub-groups.

HEATHER: Yes, I see what you mean. Well, it seems to me that the social pack of cards gets shuffled at various points. One major shuffle obviously comes when you get the land and booty distribution within the successor states. But historical narratives concerning the effects of the Huns show that moment to have been another shuffle. Whether those distinctions that had given power to the group of families in charge of the *Tervingi* would have survived the Hunnic reshuffle, seems to me very unclear.

SCHWARCZ: To me too.

WOOD: Yes, you raised the question (p. 61) of problems of normative and non-normative texts. Should comparisons be made with Franks for whom we do have normative and non-normative texts?

HEATHER: Yes, I believe this to be essential.

GREEN: Page 61, Ian [Wood] again on "Why does stratification have to be less in 420 than 550"?

HEATHER: Yes, I find the arguments that Guy Halsall has been making recently about prestige and power among the Franks in the sixth century having to be made in your own lifetime and only being turned into something heritable only in the seventh quite impressive. Although actually some of the evidence is so early seventh, that it is really late sixth in a sense. Overall, you can put together quite an interesting argument which might suggest that it is in the course of the sixth century that the kind of heritable distinctions which would create a real nobility, as opposed to some people being just a bit more important than others, actually emerge. My model for Gothic society would be that it takes a hundred plus years inside the successor states for these social distinctions to firm up.

WOOD: You wouldn't even need Guy [Halsall]'s argument. In a sense, the whole debate about whether there is Frankish nobility revolves around the issue of whether there is any documentation for it in the sixth century. In the narrative sources there is no major Frankish family other than Merovingians.

SCHWARCZ: Right in the passage, but you have to take into account that an emperor is elevated by the army. It is necessary also for the king to be elevated by the army. Everybody can rise in the army, there is no question of position in it.

HEATHER: Fair enough.

AUSENDA: On page 62, concerning numbers of élite individuals with respect to clients. The ratio you suggested of one to five is quite similar to that given by anthropologists for Beni Amer. Siegfried Nadel (1945) actually made a census of Beni Amer dominant individuals and clients and gave a ratio of one to nine in Eritrea, while Andrew Paul (1959) estimated the ratio in eastern Sudan for the same population as one to five.

SCHWARCZ: Another example: the Hungarian nobility was about 10% of the population. On page 63, Goths in the Roman army were defeated candidates for kingship. But Alaric studied soldiery in the Roman army from 394 to 410.

JIMÉNEZ: Why were there no external symbols of Gothicness in Gaul? Probably the Roman nobility which worked with the Goths from Euric's reign onwards would practice Gothicness, initially by speaking Gothic and later by using their Germanic names.

HEATHER: Entirely possible. Although I strongly believe that the reverse was true, in the sense that Goths were buying some *villae* in fifth-century Aquitaine.

JIMÉNEZ: But if there were no external symbols of Gothicness in fifth-century Gaul, how can we identify this attitude?

HEATHER: My vision of what happened is that the warrior-freeman class was destroyed by the rise of a nobility, which was in part due to the settlement itself. In the legislation, we see the free class divided by different wergilds, obviously reflecting an unequal distribution of landed wealth. Another process was surely the assimilation of Roman aristocrats into the new nobility. You can see this happening in the critical area of military service. Romans fight in the Gothic army at the battle of Vouillé. Likewise Dux Claudius at the time of Reccared, a Catholic, put down Gothic revolts after Toledo III. The only question is chronology, whether this happened from 418 or only later. There is not much evidence before 450; and the Roman state, alive in Gaul up to 450, maintained the council of seven provinces to keep Goths and Romans separate. After 450 you find that the rush of Romans to the Gothic court accelerates dramatically, and integration clearly happens quickly.

SCHWARCZ: Agreed, I showed in my article (Schwarcz 1995) that aristocrats fighting for Visigoths had fought before in the service of the emperor. In the fifth century religious division became more rigid, hence prohibition of intermarriage.

HEATHER: I believe the reign of Avitus to have been critical. The correspondence of Sidonius 455-470 shows various Romans jumping to Goths, as the Empire was breaking up.

AUSENDA: On page 65 your remark that in the final analysis those who coalesced with Gothic 'rulers' were Gothic to begin with makes sense. In fact we have many instances of populations splitting away from different ethnic groups, such as the Saxons from the Langobards after settling in Italy, because they were averse to a 'foreign' domination. We also have many instances of groups remaining with the larger dominant ethnic group; however, they were small splinters which would have fared badly if they had tried to make it on their own.

VELÁZQUEZ: Non-Nicene Christianity as *Lex Gothorum*. Difference between Arianism and Catholicism. A symbol of identity?

HEATHER: Goths were Homoeans who believed in 'likeness' between the Son and the Father. It became an heretical view, but was in origin traditional Catholicism. The Goths were left behind with an old fashioned Christianity which had been perfectly acceptable in the fourth century. Goths were not Arian because they followed Arius. Rather they were lumped together with Arians because Ulfila's theology did not deny Arius' position.

SCHWARCZ: Concerning the date of acceptance of Christianity, there is the question of perceiving the difference (see discussion of Schwarcz's paper). At the beginning of the fifth century the Roman Arians quarreled among themselves. Early around 410, one faction in Constantinople was led by a man who sold cakes in the street. This faction was called *Psathyriani* or *Gothi*.

GREEN: The Gothic word *reiks* is pronounced 'reeks'. Secondly when written the form with s is not a plural. The Gothic plural is *relkeis*.

References in the discussion

Textual sources:

[Abbr.: *HG = Historia Gothorum*].

Ambrose
　　　　　Epistulae: see Faller/Zelzer (eds.) 1978-1996.
Ammianus Marcellinus
　　　　　Res gestae: see Rolfe (ed.) 1964.
Augustinus
　　　　　De Civitate Dei: see Hoffmann (ed.) 1899.
Cassiodorus
　　　　　Chronica minora saec. IV. V. VI. VII. (II): see Mommsen (ed.) 1894.
Claudian
　　　　　De bello Getico: see Platnauer (ed. & trans.) 1922.
　　　　　De IV consulatu Honorii: see Platnauer (ed. & trans.) 1922.
Consularia Constantinopolitana: see References at end of paper.
Eunapius
　　　　　Histories: see References at end of paper.
Isidore of Seville
　　　　　Historia vel origo Gothorum Wandalorum Sueborum: see Mommsen (ed.)
　　　　　1894:267 ff.
Jordanes
　　　　　Romana et Getica: see References at end of paper.
Notitia dignitatum: see Seeck (ed.) 1876.
Procopius
　　　　　Wars: see References at end of paper.
Synesius
　　　　　De regno: see References at end of paper.
Themistius
　　　　　Orationes: see References at end of paper.
Zosimus
　　　　　Historia nea: see References at end of paper.

Bibliography:

Barth, F.
　　1969　　See References at end of paper
Blockley, R. C.
　　1983　　See References at end of paper.
Chadwick, H. M.
　　1912　　*The Heroic Age*. (Cambridge Archaeological and Ethnological Series, 4).
　　　　　Cambridge: Cambridge University Press.
Ellegård, A.
　　1986　　The ancient Goths and the concept of tribe and migration. In *Festschrift for
　　　　　C. Weibull*. C. Dahlström, P. Hallberg, Å. Holmberg (eds.), pp.32-62.
　　　　　Göteborg: Göteborgs universitets-bibliotek.
Faller, O., & H. Zelzer (eds.)
　　1968/1966 *Ambrosi epistulae*. *C.S.E.L.*, 82. Wien: Österreichischen Akademie der
　　　　　Wissenschaften.

Hoffmann, E. (ed.)
    1899   *Sancti Aureli Augustini De Civitate Dei. C.S.E.L.*, 40. Wien: F. Temsky.
Liebeschuetz, J. H. W. G.
    1990   See References at end of paper.
Mommsen, T. (ed.)
    1894   See References at end of paper.
Nadel, S.
    1945   Notes on Beni Amer society. *Sudan Notes and Records* 25 (1): 51-94.
Paul, A.
    1959   Notes on Beni Amer society. *Sudan Notes and Records* 31: 223-225.
Platnauer, M. (ed. & trans.)
    1922   See References at end of paper.
Rolfe, J. C.
    1964   See References at end of paper.
Rousseau, P.
    1992   Visigothic migration and settlement 376:418: some excluded hypotheses.
                Historia 41: 345-361.
Schwarcz, A.
    1995   Senatorische Heerführer im Westgotenreich im 5. Jh. In *La noblesse
                romaine et les barbares.* F. Vallet & M. Kazanski (eds.), pp. 49-54. Condé-
                sur-Noireau: Assiciaton Française d'Archéologie Mérovingienne.
Seeck, O. (ed.)
    1876   *Notitia Dignitatum: accedunt notitia urbis Constantinopolitanae et laterculi
                provinciarum.* Berlin: Weidmann.
Thompson, E.
    1963   The Visigoths from Fritigern to Euric. *Historia* 12: 105-126.
Várady, L.
    1969   *Das Letzte Jahrhundert Pannoniens*: 376-476. Amsterdam: A. M. Hakkert.
Wolfram, H.
    1979   *Geschichte der Goten.* Munich: Beck.

SETTLEMENT OF THE VISIGOTHS IN THE FIFTH CENTURY

ANA MARIA JIMÉNEZ GARNICA

Independent scholar, c\ General Pandiñas, 82 - c, E-28006 Madrid

The material history of the Goths in the last years of the fourth century and during the fifth century, raises a serious question due to the shortage of sites that can be attributed to them with certainty. Even without these and in order to set forth the part of the topic we are dealing with—the settlements—it is necessary to approach it from some other points of view apart from the archaeological evidence, since this consists mostly of burials. We also must not lose sight of who these Goths were, what their occupation was and what stage of social evolution they had reached. Nor should we ignore the fact that, being immigrant people urged by the need of being accepted, they gradually adopted the customs of the places they settled in (Rouche 1991:143). Hence they seem to have kept their particular habits to their own privacy. We should avoid as well treating them as a single monolithic entity, singling out instead the ideological and other developments to particular groups, which were largely dictated by their chiefs' personal disposition and interests.

As a former statement, we have to bear in mind that they came into the Empire hired as a substitute military force which could solve the lack of interest among Roman citizens in their own defence, which had been traditionally their right and duty. Thus, from the end of the fourth century, half of the Roman officers were of barbarian origin (Demandt 1989:268 ff.). So it seems logical to deny their incompetence in this area (Elton 1992:162) in comparison with the Roman army, though every individual chief used military life for a different purpose. For some it was an easy and stable way to make a living; while for others, among whom should be included those who were given to Rome as hostages when they were children, and that had been given a military upbringing (Bachrach 1994), entered a military career with the logical aim of achieving maximum distinction. There were others who were able to take advantage of independent local forces to recover their own situation previous to 376, and control some territory where a Roman presence, civil or ecclesiastical, was not strong. Finally, there were some who wanted to be equal to the Roman aristocracy and imitate their way of life, based on incomes from fiscal, country estate and/or trading interests. However, acquaintance with the Roman institution of the *comitatus*, made it possible for these chiefs to reinforce their domestic supremacy with military leadership, binding to themselves groups of warriors who had special obligations of loyalty, in exchange for personal gifts and wealth. On the other hand, the opinion and concerns of those Goths who were born with no regard for the concept of *res publica* could not be the same as those brought up in the bosom of Roman Christian civilization, whose historical memories ignored their parents' non-state system which had been linked to the practice of a non-Christian religion.

THE VISIGOTHS FROM THE MIGRATION PERIOD TO THE SEVENTH CENTURY:
AN ETHNOGRAPHIC PERSPECTIVE

Moreover, as generational change took place within the Empire, they all suffered from an unavoidable process of Roman military acculturation. All this makes it easier to understand the doings of Gothic chiefs whose actions, at first sight, might seem mutually contradictory and antagonistic. We will then turn to the Goths' mode of settlement.

As long as they were not ascribed to a certain *ciuitas* or *territorium*, Goths used to move in carts (probably military *carragines*) where they carried their families and goods. However, whenever they were given an official position, they lodged in local Roman headquarters or, else, in private houses, as established by the law of *hospitalitas* (*C.Th.* VII. 8. 5) as is documented by many textual references. Being soldiers who fought with Roman detachments and using Roman tactics, they wore Roman uniforms and kept their own leather clothing, which caused surprise among contemporary Romans, such as Claudian and Sidonius, for occasional private ceremonies. That is why they might not have been buried in a noticeably different way (James 1977:197), with the exception of some personal belongings limited to dress, bone combs (Kazanski 1985), or some ritual objects linked to the Cherniakhov culture (Kazanski 1991:15).

Alaric stood out among those who decided to make a military career in the Roman way. A man unknown to the sources until sometime between 391 and 394 (Liebeschuetz 1992:77-8), he saw in the army the possibility of achieving a hero's glory and fame—after the manner of mythical *Tervingi* warriors—which he could never have reached living a quiet and sedentary life in Thrace working in the fields. His military qualifications led him to try and follow a *cursus honorum* in the Roman army according to his skills shown in many occasions.[1] In the first place with Arcadius who appointed him *magister militum per Illiricum* (397 AD) and later with Honorius. Jordanes' reference (*Get.*, XXX.153) to the emperor's offer to give them Gaul and *Hispania* ("far away provinces almost lost as if they had always belonged to them...in case they were able to seize them"),[2] suggests that his plan was a response to Alaric's demand for "some places (*sedes*) to live" (Orosius, *Historia adv. pag.*, VII. 38. 2). Obtaining arable lands, contrary to the strategy of other chiefs who already had them, was not part of this demand.

When Stilicho died (August 408), Alaric incorporated the Vandal's imperial barbarians in his group of warriors and claimed for them the restoration of their recently rescinded rights over lands and serfs. Meanwhile, he still had no interest in sedentarization, so he offered his services once more to Honorius, who agreed to

---

[1] He had an outstanding position at the moment of Theodosius' victory over Eugenius at the river Frigidus, for which he only got some inaccurate *romanis dignitatibus* (Cassiodorus, *Historia triparti- ta*, IX. 9) instead of the desired position of *magister militum* for which he applied repeatedly. Being rejected, he broke with Rome in 395 (Zosimus, V. 5) and, not receiving regular pay, he had to make a living out of plunder.

[2] However, Stilicho retained them in *Illyricum* and let them conquer the area as a compensation for their pay, until the situation changed dramatically due to the break of the *limes* on the Rhine and the following usurpations that led to the occupation of Arles (407 AD) by Constantinus III.

pay him, but not to appoint him as *magister militum* (Zosimus, 5. 48. 4; Sozomenus, 9. 7). Even though he did not acquire the position of *magister utriusque militiae* he longed for, his demand for gold, silver, clothes and provisions, his legal share of the fiscal revenue as pay for his military services in the area (*C.Th.*, 11. 9. 1, 11. 9. 2), shows that he knew his rights as a Roman soldier. After the death of Eucherius, the prefect of Rome, Priscus Attalus, offered to Alaric the supreme command of the Western forces in exchange for his support so that the senate should proclaim him emperor. It seems that there might be a close relation between these facts and the fiscal exemptions given by Honorius to all provinces of middle and southern Italy in the four following years, while only the northern ones remained as a *regio annonaria* (Faure 1965:149-231). In opposition to the traditional view that saw in this action a sign of the emperor's benevolence with regard to the supposed catastrophic consequences of the Goths' presence, I consider it more likely that the aim was to deny pay to the new army in the area. This compelled Alaric to try to move into Africa against Attalus' will (Zosimus, 6. 12), and try their luck over there.

Once Alaric died, Athaulf exerted a different type of leadership, of which Galla Placidia was not completely unaware. He was in the service of Honorius and, under the command of the praetorian prefect of Gaul, Dardanus, the Visigoths defeated in 413 AD the Gallic usurper Iovinus, who was supported by the Burgundians. Athaulf was perhaps unhappy with the reward given him, which may explain why he went to Marseille. It was thought up to now that the Visigoths were seeking boats to move to Africa, but, if so, there is no explanation for the Roman general Bonifatius' resistance (Olympiodorus, *frag.* 21). After all, no one had forbidden this to Alaric when he tried the same thing in southern Italy. Athaulf might have wanted to take control of the *cataplus* of Marseille, a warehouse of luxury goods and state monopolies under imperial control and the place of payment of taxes coming from commercial transactions (Hendy 1993), involving the aristocracies of *Narbonensis*, *Tarraconensis*, Africa and Italy and their trade with the Eastern Roman Empire (Hitchner 1992:122-31). This action would have allowed him to recruit a greater group of followers than Sarus, the other famous Gothic chief left in the region after Radagaisus had been eliminated. His alleged purpose of being "the maker of Roman restoration" (Orosius, *Hist. adv. pag.*, VII. 43. 6) suggests that he had been taken under the influence of a part of the Aquitanian aristocracy—with which he had a way of life and ideas in common— whose purpose was to continue the Roman imperial order without Honorius. Orosius wrote that Galla Placidia's advice and counsel—whose relationship with her half brother was less than good—lay behind all Athaulf's policies. Thus, while some aristocrats loyal to Honorius were moving into areas faithful to that emperor (Mathisen 1984:161-4), Athaulf was giving military support to the creation of a local goverment conducted by aristocrats from Bordeaux, who had seen how the transfer of the diocesan capital to Arles (407 AD) had decreased their chances of personal promotion {this was the general unrest in which the Bagaudic movement also thrived (Drinkwater 1992)}.

As usual for soldiers, in accordance to *hospitalitas,* Athaulf and his army were lodged in barracks and in private homes. Nevertheless, at the same time, he insisted on his purpose of controlling a harbour and did so this time as Galla Placidia's husband, whom he married, in January 414, in the Roman way, near Narbonne supported by a part of the Gallic aristocracy. Constantius "especially blockaded him from all maritime trade and the importation of foreign products" (Orosius, *Hist. adv. pag.,* VII. 43. 1). This situation was made even more critical by the revolt of the *comes Africae* Heraclianus, because it cut off the supply of wheat for the *annona*. It was a time of civil war. Aquitanians had to do without the Goths' services who, in revenge, sacked the houses they were not lodged in. Athaulf and the Visigoths had to renew their pact with Constantius, who hired them as a regular army to support Honorius' cause in Spain, and fight against *Suevi* and Vandals, who had supported the usurper Maximus. Many desertions probably took place among his *Gefolge* troops, apart from the Alans who defended Bazas, and only a group of those loyal to him came with him (Jordanes, *Get.*, XXXI. 163: "*cum certis fidelibus derelictas plebesque inbelle*").

I believe that, from that moment onwards, the Ravenna goverment hired the Goths to try to solve the conflicts carried on by certain families related to the Theodosian dynasty which, established on both sides of the Pyrenees, exercised far-reaching economic and religious powers. It is possible that this was the reason why he established his headquarters in Barcelona, the most important coastal city of *Tarraconensis*, where the *Acilii* family, which was running the see along with six other bishoprics of the province, was being harassed (García Moreno 1988:166 ff.). The Goth's mysterious death and how happily the news was received in Constantinople (*Chron.Pasc.* 415) should be related not only to the fear on the part of the local aristocracy for his prevention of their trading business, but also to fear of another secession after Maximus' deposition in 411. This group would not have been favourable to a new infant from the Theodosian-Valentinian dynasty who, besides, had an enormous military support.[3] That is why they supported Everwulf, a Goth who belonged to the murdered Sarus' party, opposed to Athaulf's party, and who assassinated the latter, in accordance with the Germanic law of revenge (Mayer 1992). This feud was later carried on by Sigeric, of Sarus' group, who

---

[3]   I am talking about the *Anicii* from Rome, who practised an urban Catholicism and had a strong economic power (Zosimus, VI. 7. 4). This family—to which the future emperor Petronius Maximus, who averred being a descendant of the usurper Magnus Maximus (Mommaerts 1992:118), belonged—had not agreed to the proclamation of Attalus, because it was linked to a revival of traditional values (Sozomenos, IX. 8. 2). The year before, the Spanish Maximus had been proclaimed emperor in *Hispania*. We might have some hypothetical theories about his family relations with the other usurper. This is possible not only on the basis of the identity of name and origin, but also because the latter considered himself the real emperor of Gaul, *Hispania* and Britain—as shown on his coins (Marot 1994:60-3). This was another attempt to go back to the situation established by Magnus Maximus at the end of 382 or the beginning of 383 (Zosimus, IV. 37. 3). Bishop Hidatius' omission of the proclamation of Maximus in 409, because he was loyal to Honorius, may be understood as an agreement with his fellows of *Tarraconensis*, members of a branch of that family.

killed all of Athaulf's sons. Sigeric, himself subject to the same code, died a few days later.

Meanwhile, another group of Goths, wealthy enough to rent boats, was trying once more to cross to Africa. This failed because of the Roman naval blockade (Orosius, VII. 11). The patrician Constantius, determined to give back to Honorius control over Gaul and *Hispania*, took advantage of the moment and reoriented the military duty of those left (20.000 according to Liebeschuetz 1992:81; 25.000 according to Nixon 1992:62) and integrated them into the cavalry forces of the Roman army—as suggested by Consentius' letter to Saint Augustine (García Moreno 1988:162). These troops were under the command of the *comes Hispaniarum* Sabinianus and they fought against *Suevi* and Hasding Vandals (416 AD). Once the pacifying mission was carried out, only Roman troops remained in *Hispania*.

At an indefinite date between the spring of 416 (García Moreno 1988:159) and the summer of 418 (Scharf 1992:379), the Goths were settled as border auxiliary troops (Burns 1992) in Aquitania just in case their help was needed again. This was a region well connected by the Pyrenees' passes (Rouche 1981), whose cities were dismantled. Their retreat made possible a second reign of Maximus in 418, who was defeated by the Roman army of Castinus, briefly helped by a group of Goths in 421 (García Moreno 1988:161-2; 1989:51). The return of Galla Placidia and Attalus to Honorius meant the latter's formal recognition and the restoration of his rule in secessionist Gaul, on account of which Valia inherited from Athaulf the role of restorer of the "*Romani nominis causa*" (Hydatius, 63, *s.a.* 417).

One must underline the negotiating skills of Valia and Constantius, and their ability to agree on what seems to have been a complex settlement formula, in spite of the paucity of the sources. The formula must be related to the above commented internal diversity among the Goths. Some of them, probably those who preferred a military life, were quartered (*sedentes*) "*ad inhabitandum*" in well-served cities spread out along the provincial boundaries by the ocean (Prosperus, 1271, *s.a.* 419; Hydatius, 69, makes it clear that they chose "*Tolosa sibi sedem*"), where, as regular auxiliary troops, they were lodged in accordance with the system of *hospitalitas* and paid directly by the provincials with money, provisions and clothing. Meanwhile the others, more nostalgic for their old ways of life, probably veteran chiefs too old for such an unstable way of life (Liebeschuetz 1992:81), according to Philostorgius (*Historia ecclesiastica*, 12.4; *P.G.* LXV: col. 609-612), obtained a part of Gaul's territory to cultivate. Thus, each one settled there with his respective *Gefolge* (García Moreno 1993:298), and started to make joint plans with the provincials, the most immediate result of which appears to have been their swift romanization. All of this is reflected in the fact that the lexical reminiscences left by the Gothic language on the langue d'Oc in Aquitaine—an area between the Pyrenees and the Auvergne—in Provence and in Dauphiné (Billy 1992:115), refer to social and institutional military status (companion, band, troop).

It does not seem wise to infer from the brief notice of Philostorgius that the lands granted were part of the *tertia Romanorum*, as was done when calculating the beginning of the fifty-year period referred to in Euric's legislation related to this issue (*CE* 277. 1: "*Sortes Gothicas et tertiam Romanorum quae intra L annis non fuerint revocate nullo modo repetantur*"), because the same fifty-year period appears as well in Recceswinth's *Liber Iudiciorum* (654 AD) and in Erwig's one (681 AD). These soldiers lived off the incomes obtained by themselves and their servants from cultivating the land and from carrying out any military duties "as mercenaries, assistants and defenders" of private persons (Orosius, VII. 41. 4), for which they volunteered. They hired themselves as well for official campaigns (e.g. in 421 in the service of Castinus), not necessarily under the command of the king of *Tolosa*. In this case they received the *annona* and the five-year donative in money granted by the emperor to his soldiers. This system was not new in the area and it is identical to the one described by Orosius (VII. 40. 8) when he records that the usurper Constantine's barbarians expelled "the loyal and useful peasants' garrison" from the Pyrenees passes.

There are no Goths looked for additional income, from which they could distribute gifts among their soldiers and maintain an important *Gefolge*, by controlling the harbours and in individual initiatives. These same men must have had a leading role in the various military disasters suffered by the Goths between 418 and 439 (in 430 Aetius defeated a group of soldiers led by the *optimus* Anaolsus; in 436 certain Goths conquered Narbonne, as Hydatius recalls, who, nervertheless, specifies that Aetius besieged king Theoderic (I) in Toulouse in 439, with the consequence that "*inter Romanos et Gothos pax efficitur*"). Briefly stated, the peace agreement of 381 between Theodosius and Athanaric was renewed in 418 (Eunapius, *Frag.* 45. 3, related to what is said in Zosimus, IV. 34. 4-5) and the formulation of a border programme—where agricultural and military duties were combined—was repeated, though in that area of Gaul there was no formal *limes*. This decision was acclaimed by Prosper of Aquitaine (Muhlberger 1992:31) who probably thought, from the safety of Marseille, that this was the only valid way to destroy political opposition in the area. Prosper of Aquitaine had no religious prejudice against Arians. The Goths thus had little economic and ideological importance. However, it does not seem that their sedentarization altered the local order, because, "abandoning weapons, they dedicated themselves to agriculture and respected the Romans who remained there nearly like allies and friends" (Orosius, VII. 41. 7), and they let them live freely. Archeological surveys, that are being carried out systematically in Languedoc, show the continuity of clustered and open dwellings (Raynaud 1988:125) between the fourth and seventh century, and the continuity of architectural and building techniques. Usually, cities were established during the Middle Ages on the sites of these clusters.

There remains the still unanswered question of whether the lands granted belonged to the senatorial class (Burns 1992:63) or they were part of the *agri deserti* (Nixon 1992:64) of depopulated Aquitaine (Bonassie 1991:1-7). These would have been lands 'empty' in the sense of not paying tax (Goffart 1980:112) whose value had fallen as the result of a labour shortage due to previous events. This is corroborated by the pitiful description offered in *Carmen de providentia divina* (*P.L.*, LI: col. 617 vs. 8-90)—a poem probably written in southern Gaul between 415-420 (Roberts 1992:101)—about the ravaging of crops and progressive destruction of the *villae*, through abandonment and population decline. If these lands were granted to the Goths, thus, neither the owner lost his ordinary ownership, nor the holder had to pay *capitatio-iugatio* for them. Nonetheless, one must suppose that a long permanence in the same place would encourage the Goths to acquire ownership of the lands in the region.

Without good archaeological evidence about Visigothic settlements in southern Gaul, the study of place-names with Gothic elements has been used to try to define the area they occupied and exploited. However, after the first euphoric moments in which, as happened with other art materials, everything that looked Germanic was attributed to them, the list of 'Gothic' place-names has now seriously decreased after being subject to careful philological critique. This is shown by occupation maps with many blanks.

Out of three groups of place-name types that could have been left by the Visigoths, we have to be extremely cautious with the first one, the names of places derived from nicknames, in that many of them, still used in the langue d'Oc, might not be of Gothic origin (Billy 1992:102). It even seems that there is a tendency to exclude the place-name *Margastaud*—accepted until now as one of the most trustworthy (Rouche 1979:42, 534 n.26) on the basis of its translation as "person who has acquired a territory". As previously suspected by Soutou (1964:33-40), even though he finally was persuaded by the other option and believed it to be a Visigothic place-name, it has been shown to be a hydronym. The group of place-names that include a person's name plus the suffix *-ingus/-ingos* or *-inga/-ingas* which appear mostly in the department of Aude (fig. 4-1), whose meaning "the peoples of..." (Vincent 1937:137), or the "dominance of..." (Lapart 1985:I-310; cf. Billy 1992:104)) supports the idea that rural settlements consisted of small military units organized around the household authority of a military chief—has been reduced as well. This seems to show the oldest Visigothic presence. Those ending in *-ingos* would have changed into *-ens, -enx* (Gascogne), *-encs* (Gers), *-eins* (Lot-et-Garonne), *-an* (Gers), *-ans* (Charente). Those ending in *-ingas* have changed into forms usually finishing in *-enques* (Gamillscheg 1934). However, bearing in mind the generation of Germanic languages, it seems wise to accept as Gothic only those repeated in Aquitaine, Septimaine and Spain. Thus the number of names formed out of compound forenames is reduced to twenty nine (Wallace-Hadrill 1961:218), or seven according to other hypercritical positions (Billy 1992:103).[4] In Gaul they are found between Montauban and Carcassonne (département of Tarn) as well as in the place-names Caladroi (Pyrénées Orientales) and Montanou (Lot-et-Garonne). However, all these are only confirmed in documents from the eighth century onwards, so, as a last resort, they show evidence of the surviving anthroponymy of Visigothic origin, which was especially thick in Roussillon and

---

[4] Arlengs (<*Arilo*), Gatilens (<*Gattila*), Gogenchos (<*Gogius*), Scatalens (<*Skatila*), Ossilingus (<*Usila*), Wistrilingus (<*Wistrila*) and Guitalens (<*Vitila*).

Fig. 4-1: Probable regions where *sedes* settlements took place.

Catalonia, but does not allow us to imply a Gothic presence as long as the names are not supported by archaeological evidence.

Legal and documentary references referring to Visigothic *sortes* come after the sedentarization of 418. They are written down for the first time in the fragmentary *Codex Euricianus*, 276 and 277, 1-2, a clear antecedent of *LV* X, 3. 5 and X, 2. 1 *Antiquae*. Other relevant *Antiquae* are also *LV* X, 1. 8, 9 and 16 which, even though they do not have to go back necessarily to the fifth century, seem to confirm the financial dimension that *CE* 277 suggests, and so we would be talking about *tertiae professionum* granted by the emperor, (and after 476 AD by the Visigothic king), whose ordinary ownership in private law would still belong to the previous Roman owner. If so, at an uncertain date in the middle of the fifth century, barbarian military chiefs began to imitate the pattern proposed by the new local nobility from the fourth century onwards (Durliat 1994:15), who achieved a living without having to work thanks to the collection of rents and dues. Thus, to the old Germanic nobility of ancient origin and religious prestige, a new one was added. For the first time chronicles are a little more explicit concerning this new system, when Aetius applied it to the Alans of Goar in 440 AD and to those of Sambiba in 442, whom he settled in the *rura deserta* of Valentina (Valence) (*Chron. Gall. 452*, in *Gallia ulterior*). We know they had to fight the owners of these lands with weapons, an unreasonable reaction if it had not been for the novelty and if certain social groups had not felt that such proceedings were seriously damaging their interests.

Fig. 4-2: Alan settlements.

The chronicle's reference is complemented by the data given by place-names (fig. 4-2) (Bachrach 1969; 1973), which allow us to see Alans settling in Aude, Pyrenées-Orientales and Haute-Garonne, although I do not think this was possible as early as 414 AD (Bachrach 1969). According to guidelines which were quite similar to those used for the Visigoths of Aquitaine (García Gallo 1941), in 443 AD Burgundians were granted *sortes* as well. Therefore, it seems clear that from the 440s onwards, but not before, at the same time that Aetius had to turn his attention to Italy (Demougeot 1983:11 ff.; Zecchini 1983:239), the Roman state looked at the barbarians with an additional consideration beyond the merely military one, maybe with the aim of widening the landowning nobility supporting the reigning dynasty (fig. 4-3). From that moment on, barbarians did not cause

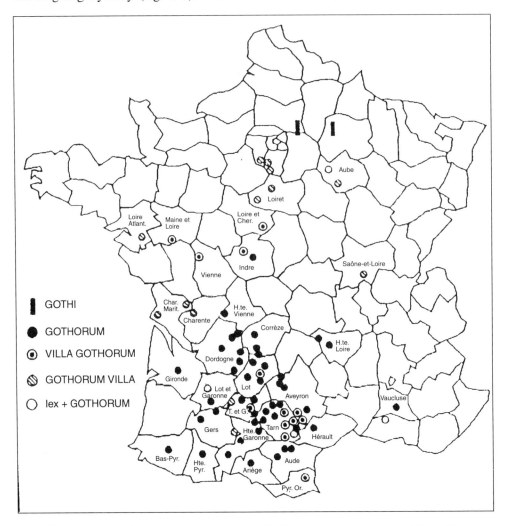

Fig. 4-3: Areas where the ethnic toponyms *Gothi* (or derived words) could recall the granting of *sortes* (map based on Billy, 1992:123).

trouble in Gaul any longer (Elton 1992:170). At the same time, a kind of military settlement was maintained, as it is inferred from the famous verses of the Panegyric II of Merobaudes, delivered in honour of Aetius (*MGH*, XIV, *Panegyricus II*, 14-15): "...*et quamvis Geticis sulcum confundat aratris/barbara vicinae refugit consortia gentis*".

We can infer from the Eurician laws that the Goths, at least from the time of Theoderic I onwards (therefore before 451 AD), had already been granted *sortes* (*CE* 277. 3), whose extension they would have tried to enlarge by moving the boundaries with their hosts' *tertiae* (*CE* 276. 3); and from the *Passio S. Vincenti* we can infer as well that, with time, they tried to take control over the *possessio* of their *sortes*.

During the time of Theoderic II the Goths collected incomes on their own initiative. We know that in the city of Saintes they made extortions from the provincials (*Vita S. Bibiani Sanctonensis*, Krusch 1885:96), though its nobles were protected directly by the king who, probably, was trying to avoid a revolt by aristocrats, such as the one that took place in Athaulf's time. In 475, Emperor Nepos allowed Euric to consolidate his presence in the Auvergne, in the Provence, and up to the Loire. In the same years, Sidonius, who was leading the defence of the first region, refers often to Gothic *sortes* (*Epist*. VII. 6. 10; VIII. 3. 3) and in II. 1. 3 he regrets the fact that vicar Seronatus was filling up the *villae* with *hospites;* that is to say, with Romans that had to transfer their incomes to a barbarian, which is confirmed by *CE* 276, where the possibility of establishing new *termini* to the *sortes* is allowed. From none of these references can we infer the proportion of the *tertiae* that was given to them, and the 'two thirds' mentioned in the *Antiquae* of the *Lex Visigothorum* might be later than the Eurician compilation. There is a vague allusion in Sidonius (*Epist*. VIII, 9. 2; 476 AD) where he complains to his friend Lampridius that Euric had not permitted him to receive anything of his stepmother's inheritance, not even the *usum tertiae*, but the word *sors* is not mentioned, thus making it difficult to know what exactly he was referring to.

The fact that Goths acceded to this new kind of ownership, clearly of country estates (fig. 4-4), does not mean, by a long shot, that all Gothic society had become agrarian. Let us hope that, in the future, archaeology will help us to alter the widespread opinion that during the early Middle Ages kings, nobles and bishops obtained all their wealth from land (Duby 1979) since other ways are proposed, such as trade. Such a hypothesis is the result of a prejudiced interpretation from part of the aristocracy, of intellectual as well as ascetic thought (Paulinus, *Eucharisticus*, 465), and also of a non-Christian one (Rutilius Namatianus), about the late Roman Empire, which minimized the importance of trade as an activity peculiar to aristocrats. Visigoths did not interfere with trading patterns in the area controlled by them {this is well proved by archaeology in Bordeaux (Sivan 1992)}, and took advantage of the possibilities provided by the Garonne River. Likewise, after the occupation of Africa by the Vandals, trade relations in the Mediterranean were maintained (cf. Hitchner 1992), or declined (cf. Fentress & Perkins 1987; Mattingly & Hitchner 1995:210-1).

In conclusion, it seems that sources were quite attentive in their use of terminology and accurately distinguished two concepts: (1) *sedes*, that means, rural settlements by small military units disposed under the household sovereignty of a military chief, that would integrate themselves with the natives of the country; and (2) *sortes*, part ownership over country estates bringing incomes from *villae* or a *locus*. All of this should not be linked to other laws mentioned in the *Lex Visigothorum* concerning pastures and the exploitation of common forests.

There is another group of place-names formed by a person's name plus the noun *villa* as a second part of the compound, or vice versa (fig. 4-5). It probably points to another kind of land ownership, more aristocratic and comparable to the rural estates of the late Roman Empire (Hubert 1959:529-58). This development would have started in 455 AD, the second evolutionary stage of Visigothic settlement in Gaul (Heather 1992:84), which began with the withdrawal of the Theodosian-Valentinian dinasty after the assassination of Valentinian III, for which Petronius

Fig. 4-4: Areas where Visigothic country estates were probably located.

Maximus from the *Anicii* family was responsible. Then, under the protection of emperors who had to buy the support of Goths and Burgundians, Gothic influence spread quickly throughout Aquitaine, while a higher participation of Gallo-Roman aristocracy in military and civil posts was taking place at the court of *Tolosa*. The first group of place-names, more plentiful in Aquitaine, is accepted as being a consequence of the Frankish colonization after 507 AD. On the contrary, the combination of late Latin term *villa* + person's name is more plentiful in *Septimania*, especially in the department of Aude,[5] and it seems compatible with the early romanization that the Visigothic language suffered at the same time in which the Latin language was undergoing a spontaneous evolution (Lot 1970:127-8). This evolution was the cause of the change of compound names which had

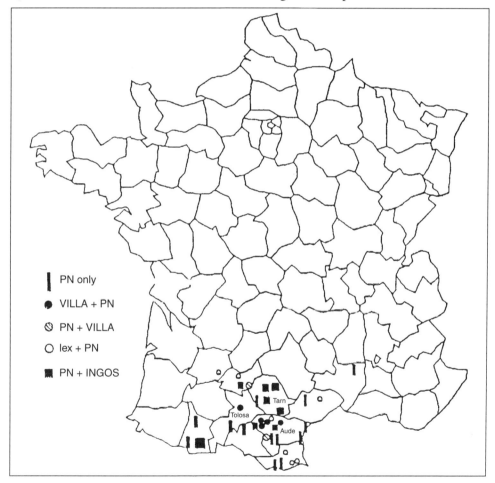

Fig. 4-5: Personal names of Visigothic origin current in the Middle Ages (map based on Billy 1992:123).

---

[5] *Vilaciscla <Adiscle; Villa Ranesindi <Ranesindus; Villa Lavigildo* and *Villa Vigildo <Vigildus;* and *Villa Wuitizani <Witiza.*

ended in *-acum* to end in *-villa* (Dauzat 1926:136-40). The increased frequency of the combination *villa* + person's name shows the change going on in social and property relationships and the reciprocity of interests between Gothic and Roman aristocracy, which might have been caused by a widening of Gothic authority and of the territory under Gothic rule.

The Goths had a greater influence on certain aspects, such as personal names, evident in the area of *Septimania* and Roussillon, more than in place-names. However, architecture retained Roman building techniques, and so a continuity similar to the one discussed in the case of the *sortes* is found. On the other hand, graves that might be called Visigothic are plentiful only in this area (fig. 4-6). According to the contents of these burials, it appears that the owner's metal crafts underwent an artistic evolution similar to that which occurred in the rest of

Fig. 4-6: Objects of Visigothic origin (map based on James 1977:197, 247; Kazanski 1985)

Hispania (Erlande-Brandenburg 1988:47 ff). This seems to confirm the close relation between these provinces and those of *Hispania*.

Finally, there is a last group of place-names formed by the ethnic name *gothic*, among which there are also some compounds with the noun *villa, sylva* and *mons.* The list has now been shortened (Billy 1992:108) in comparison to the list originally made by E. Gamillscheg (1934:301-2) and its documentary verification cannot be traced back further than the mid-Middle Ages. Its origin has been related to the presence of Visigothic garrisons (Rouche 1979:140), when the names display a Latin syntax, and to Frankish ones when the syntax is Germanic. Nevertheless, there are some who prefer to see a Roman model (Billy 1992:108) in the denomination of Gothic territory in those place-names found on the border areas where the extension of the kingdom of *Tolosa* reached the farthest border.

Fig. 4-7: Distribution of other ethnic toponyms.

In the territory controlled by the Visigoths there are also place-names formed by an ethnonym, such as *Taïfali, Vandali* or *Romani* (fig. 4-7). The first is more plentiful in Aquitaine, between the rivers Creuse, Loire and Charente, where, on the other hand, ethnic names made up containing the element *Gothi* are quite rare. The ethnic name *Vandali* appears all around the more densely gothicized area, in Agenais (Lot-et-Garonne) and to the east of Rouergue (Aveyron); whereas those referring to the country as *Vandalonia* are mostly found in Limousin. Finally the ethnic name *Romani* appears in Aquitaine, on the right side of the Garonne, from the Charente to the Atlantic; that is, on the northern border of the territory obtained by Valia. Although there is no convincing interpretation of who the authors of these place-names might have been, one cannot dismiss the fact that they were originally ethnic communities, in the light of the Visigothic example, where, once they abandoned the kingdom of *Tolosa*, they gave the name of *Gothia* to the province of Gaul they were able to keep around Narbonne. This shows that there was a meaningful enough relationship between people and place-names for its inhabitants to keep its memory alive over many generations (Percival 1992:164). The same is confirmed by the note in Gregory of Tours (*Vitae Patrum,* XV): "*Igitur, beatus Senoch, gente Theiphalus, Pictavi pagi quem Theiphaliam vocant oriundus fuit*".

Regarding *Hispania*, the situation is quite similar. The Visigoths reaffirmed their official military presence in 446 AD when they repressed the Bagaudic movement, and in 455 AD "by will and order" of the new imperial governor of Gaul, Avitus, who made a formal alliance with them. This was originally accepted by the conservative Hydatius, who stressed the loyalty to the Empire of the Goth Theoderic II (*C.C.H.,* 170) whilst he was acting in the *Tarraconensis* in 456. But then he changed his evaluation into an apocalyptical one when Theoderic moved into *Gallaecia* and *Lusitania*. Hydatius again used the word *sedes* for the Goths in 456 AD, "*qui in Spanias consedebant*" (*C.C.H.*, 174). Hydatius' chronicle provides information (*C.C.H.,* 180) about the defection of Aiolphus, who settled in *Gallaecia* to live, and it corroborates the strictly military character of that expedition.

The Gothic military presence in *Hispania* in the following years aimed at strengthening Majorianus' and Anthemius' authority. It also enabled Euric to consolidate his position here, in addition to Provence, and Auvergne, and up to the Loire. His interest in these lands and their resources was closely related to his eagerness to occupy the harbours of Arles and Marseille (*Chron. Caesarag.*; Mommsen 1894:473). Nevertheless, the response of certain aristocrats, such as Sidonius, was openly hostile. The bishop, doubting that the state had any strength or garrisons left (*Epist.,* II. 1) and condemning the Goths for breaking the agreements (*Epist.,* VI. 7), vainly headed the defence of Clermont in 471. His region, the Auvergne, was definitively granted by Nepos to the Gothic king in 475, at a time when his independence from Rome was nearly a fact, as proved in references to Euric's *regnum*. The new state organization caused a considerable migratory movement by Visigoths to the plateau area of *Hispania* (*Chron. Cesarag.*; Mommsen 1894:494, 497) where in former years there had been a strong tendency towards self-rule (Jiménez Garnica 1995:192-3). The arrival of the Goths apparently did not alter either social or property relations, because there is no mention of such changes in the *Chronica Caesaraugustana*, where it is only recorded that the Goths settled in *sedes*.

On the other hand, the mixed Germanic- and Roman-style grave-goods found in the rural cemeteries there, and the continuity of their occupation (Ripoll 1991) seem to prove that from the begining Goths lived with Hispano-Roman settlers, and that they took these provincials under their household sovereignty in accordance with an aristocratic social structure of military retainers. All this favoured continuity between late Antiquity and the early Middle Ages. This was not, therefore, a population migration (Abadal 1958:545; 1970:43 ff.) but a take-over by an army in charge of submitting the territory to the sovereignty of Alaric II and avoiding further separatist movements, such as that headed by Burdunellus in 496, or the one by Petrus in 506. At the same time, the new Visigothic state may have redefined the share of the *possessores* in the *tertiae professionum,* granting them now two portions of the land and one of the *servi*.

In these pages I have tried to show that the topic of Visigothic settlement must be understood in a different way from how it was interpreted until a few years ago. Initially, the Visigoths were given the usual treatment accorded soldiers of the late Empire established in border areas who carried out rural as much as military tasks, with a spontaneous character. Such settlements were made by groups under the authority of a leader and they agreed to integrate within their midst the region's provincials, in accord with an ethnogenetic practice which was familiar to them. At the same time, other groups were sent as military garrisons to some Gallic cities which were averse to the control of Theodosius' descendants. There the Goths were quickly romanized and this led them to imitate the patterns of the Roman aristocracy. They began to own property and to control taxation starting from the final years of the dynasty. All of this enabled them to take over the Empire's heritage, while not causing disruptions which were substantial enough for contemporaries to realize any major change.

References

Textual sources:

[Abbreviations: *AFAM* = Association Française d'Archéologie Mérovingienne; *C.C.H.* = *Continuatio chronicorum Hieronymianorum*; *CE* = *Codex Euricianus*; *C.Th.* = *Codex Theodosianus*; *C.S.E.L.*= *Corpus Scriptorum Ecclesiasticorum Latinorum*; *LV* = *Lex Visigothorum*; *P.G.* = Migne: *Patrologia Graeca*; *P.L.* = Migne: *Patrologia Latina*]

Carmen de providentia divina (or *Dei*): see Migne (ed.) 1861: 617-638; McHugh (ed.) 1964.
Cassiodorus
          Historia tripartita: see Hanslik (ed.) 1952.
Chronica Caesaraugustana: see Mommsen (ed.) 1894:221-223.
Codex Euricianus: see D'Ors (ed.) 1960.

Eunapius
>*Fragmenta*: see *Fragmenta Historicorum Graecorum* 1885:8-61.
Gregory of Tours
>*Vitae patrum*: see Krusch (ed.) 1896.
Hydatius
>*Continuatio chronicorum Hieronymianorum*: see Mommsen (ed.) 1894:13-36.
Jordanes
>*De origine actibusque Getarum*: see Mommsen (ed.) 1882:53-138.
Lex Visigothorum: see Zeumer (ed.) 1902.
Marcellinus comes
>*Chronicon paschale*: see Mommsen (ed.) 1894:37-108.
Merobaudes
>*Panegyricus*: see Vollmer (ed.) 1905:3-20.
Orosius
>*Historiarum adversus paganos libri VII*: see Zangemeister (ed.) 1889.
Passio sancti Vincenti: see Gaiffier (ed.) 1952.
Paulinus of Pella
>*Eucharisticos*: see Brandes (ed.) 1888:291-314.
Philostorgius
>*Historia ecclesiastica*: see Migne (ed.) 1864:col.453-col.624; Bidez & Winkelmann (eds.) 1972.
Prosperus
>*Epitoma Chronicon*: see Mommsen (ed.) 1892.
Sidonius Apollinaris
>*Carmina*: see Loyen (ed.) 1960.
>*Epistulae*: see Loyen (ed.) 1970.
Sozomenus
>*Historia ecclesiastica*: see Bidez & Hanson (eds.) 1960.
Vita sancti Bibiani Sanctonensis: see Krusch (ed.) 1885:92-100.
Zosimus
>*Historia nova*: see Paschoud (ed.) 1971-1989.

Bibliography:

d'Abadal, R.
  1958   À propos du legs wisigothique en Espagne. In *Caratteri del secolo VII in Occidente*. (Settimane di studio del Centro Italiano di Studi sull' Alto Medioevo, V). Pp. (II) 541-585. Spoleto: C.I.S.A.M.
  1970   *Dels Visigots als Catalans*, vol. I: *La Hispania visigótica i la Catalunya carolingia*. Barcelona: Edicions 62.
Bachrach, B. S.
  1969   Another Look at the Barbarian Settlement in Southern Gaul. *Traditio* 25: 354-358.
  1973   *A History of the Alans in the West*. Minneapolis: Minnesota Univ. Press.
  1994   The Education of the 'Officer Corps' in the Fifth and Sixth Centuries. In *La noblesse romaine et les chefs barbares du IIIe au VIIe siècle*. F. Vallet & M. Kazanski (eds.), pp. 7-13. Rouen: AFAM.
Bidez, J., & F. Winkelman [rev. ed.]
  1972   *Historia ecclesiastica, Die griechischen christlichen Schriftsteller der ersten Jahrhunderte*, 5. Berlin: Akademie Verlag.

Billy, P. H.
1992   Souvenirs wisigothiques dans la toponimie de la Gaule méridionale. In
        L'Europe héritière de l'Espagne wisigothique. J. Fontaine &
        C. Pellistrandi (eds.), pp. 101-124. (Colleccion de la Casa de Velázquez,
        35). Madrid: Casa de Velázquez.
Bonassie, P.
1991   L'Aquitaine et l'Espagne au Ve-VIIIe siècles. Pour une approche
        historique et archéologique des quelques grands problèmes. *Gallo-
        Romains, Wisigoths et Francs en Aquitaine, Septimaine et Espagne*.
        P. Périn (ed.), pp. 1-7. Actes des VIIes Journées Internationales
        d'Archéologie Mérovingienne (Toulouse, 1985). Rouen: AFAM.
Brandes, W. (ed.)
1888   *Eucharisticos. C.S.E.L.*, vol 16. Vienna: F. Tempsky & G. Freitag.
        [Repr.: Johnson Reprint Co., New York/London 1972).
Burns, T. S.
1992   The settlement of 418. *Fifth-century Gaul: A Crisis of Identity?*
        J. Drinkwater & H. Elton (eds.), pp. 53-63. Cambridge: Cambridge Univ.
        Press.
Dauzat, A.
1926   *Les noms de lieux. Origine et évolution*. Paris: Delagrave.
Demandt, A.
1989   *Die Spätantike. Handbuch der Altertumswissenschaft*, III, 6. München:
        Beck Verlag.
Demougeot, E.
1983   À propos des *solidi gallici* du Ve siècle aprés J.C. *Revue Historique*
        270: 3-30.
D'Ors, A. (ed.)
1960   *Codex Euricianus*. Estudios visigóticos II. Cuadernos del Instituto
        Jurídico Español, 12. Roma-Madrid: Consejo Superior de Investigaciones
        Científicas.
Drinkwater, J. F.
1992   The Bacaudae of fifth-century Gaul. In *Fifth-century Gaul: A Crisis of
        Identity?* J. Drinkwater & H. Elton (eds.), pp. 208-217. Cambridge:
        Cambridge University Press.
Duby, G.
1973   *Guerriers et paysans: 7e - 12e siècle. Premier essor de l'économie
        européenne*. Paris: Gallimard.
Durliat, J.
1994   Les nobles et l'impôt du IVe au VIe siècle. In *La noblesse romaine et les
        chefs barbares du IIIe au VIIe siècle*. F. Vallet & M. Kazanski (eds.),
        pp. 15-22. Rouen: AFAM.
Elton, H.
1992   Defence in fifth-century Gaul. *Fifth-century Gaul: A Crisis of Identity?*
        J. Drinkwater & H. Elton (eds.), pp. 167-176. Cambridge: Cambridge
        University Press.
Erlande-Brandenburg, A. B.
1988   La Septimaine et le royaume visigothique d'Espagne. Approche
        Archéologique. VIe-VIIe s. In *Gaule mérovingienne et monde
        méditerranéen*. C. Landes (ed.), pp. 47-62. Actes des IXes Journées
        d'Archéologie Mérovingienne. Lattes: AFAM.

Faure, E.
1965   *Italia annonaria*. Note sur la fiscalité du Bas-Empire et son application
               dans les différentes régions d'Italie. *Revue Internationale des Droits de
               l'Antiquité* 11: 149-231.
Fentress, E., & P. Perkins
1988   Counting African red slip ware. In *L'Africa Romana*. (Atti del V
               Convegno di Studi). A. Mastino (ed.), pp. 205-214. Sassari: Ed. Gallizi.
Fragmenta Historicorum Graecorum
1885   *Fragmenta Historicorum Graecorum*, vol. 4, book 7. Paris: ed. C. Müller.
Gaiffier, B.
1952   Passio S. Vincenti. *Analecta Bollandiana* 70: 140-181.
Gamillscheg, E.
1934   *Romania germanica. Sprach-und Siedlungsgeschichte der Germanen auf
               dem Bodem des alten Römerreich*, Band I. Berlin/Leipzig: de Gruyter
               Verlag.
García Gallo, A.
1941   Notas sobre el reparto de tierras entre visigodos y romanos. *Hispania*
               1: 40-63.
García Moreno, L. A.
1983   El término 'sors' y relacionados en el 'Liber Iudicum'. De nuevo el
               problema de la división de tierras entre godos y provinciales. *Anuario de
               Historia del Derecho Español* 53: 137-175.
1988   Nueva luz sobre la España de las invasiones de principios del s. V. La
               Epístola XI de Consencio a San Agustín. In *Verbo de Dios y Palabras
               Humanas*. M. Merino (ed.), pp. 153-174. Pamplona: Eunsa.
1989   *Historia de España visigoda*. Madrid: ed. Catedra.
1993   Dos capítulos sobre la administración y fiscalidad del reino de Toledo. In
               De la Antigüedad al Medioevo, s. IV-VIII. Pp. 293-314. III Congreso de
               Estudios Medievales. León: Fundación Sánchez Albornoz.
Goffart, W.
1980   *Barbarians   and   Romans.   A.D.418-584.   The   techniques   of
               accommodation*. Princeton, NJ: Princeton University Press.
Hanslik, R.
1952   *Historia ecclesiastica tripartita*. C.S.E.L., vol. 71. Vienna: Hoelder-
               Pichler-Tempsky.
Heather, P.
1992   The emergence of the Visigothic kingdom. In *Fifth-century Gaul: A
               Crisis of Identity?* J. Drinkwater & H. Elton (eds.), pp. 85-94.
               Cambridge: Cambridge University Press.
Hendy, M. F.
1993   From Antiquity to the Middle Ages: economic and monetary aspects of
               the transition. In *De la Antigüedad al medioevo, s. IV-VIII*. Pp. 325-360.
               III Congreso de Estudios Medievales. León: Fundación Sánchez
               Albornoz.
Hitchner, R. B.
1992   Meridional Gaul, trade and the Mediterranean economy in Late Antiquity.
               In *Fifth-century Gaul: A Crisis of Identity?* J. Drinkwater & H. Elton
               (eds.), pp. 122-131. Cambridge: Cambridge University Press.
Hubert, J.
1959   Evolution de la topographie et de l'aspect des villes de Gaule du Ve au Xe
               siècle. In *La città nell'Alto Medioevo*, pp. 529-558. (Settimane di studio
               del Centro Italiano di Studi sull'Alto Medioevo, VI). Spoleto: C.I.S.A.M.

James, E.
1977   *The Merovingian Archeology of South-West Gaul*, 2 vols. (British Archaeological Report, 25). Oxford: BAR.
Jiménez Garnica, A. M.
1995   Consideraciones sobre la trama social en la Hispania temprano visigoda. *Pyrenae* 26: 189-198.
Kazanski, M.
1985   Le peigne en os. In *La nécropole mérovingienne de la Turraque à Beaucaire-sur-Baïse (Gers)*. M. Larrieu, B. Marty, P. Périn & E. Crubezy (eds.), pp. 257-269. Toulouse: Société de Recherches Speleo-Archéologiques de Sorezois et Revelois.
1991   Contribution à l'étude des migrations des Goths à la fin du IVe et au Ve siècles: le témoignage de l'Archéologie. *Gallo-Romains, Wisigoths et Francs en Aquitaine, Septimaine et Espagne*. P. Périn (ed.), pp. 11-25. Actes des VIIes Journées Internationales d'Archéologie Mérovingienne, Toulouse, 1988. Rouen: AFAM.
Krusch, B.
1885   *Gregorii Turonensis Opera*. Teil 2. *Miracula et opera minora. Monumenta Germaniae Historica. Scriptores rerum Merovingicarum*, 1. Hannover: Hahn. [Repr. 1969].
1896   *Passiones vitaeque sanctorum aevi Merovingici et antiquiorum aliquot. Monumenta Germaniae Historica. Scriptores rerum Merovingicarum*, 3. Hannover: Hahn.
Lapart, J.
1985   Les cités d'Auch et d'Eauze de la conquête romaine à l'indépendance vasconne (56 avant JC-VIIe siècle après JC). Enquête archéologique et toponymique. Thèse, Université de Toulouse - Le Mirail [2 vols.].
Liebeschuetz, J. H. W. G.
1992   Alaric's Goths: nation or army? In *Fifth-century Gaul: A Crisis of Identity?* J. Drinkwater & H. Elton (eds.), pp. 75-83. Cambridge: Cambridge University Press.
Lot, F.
1970   *Naissance de la France*. Paris: Fayard.
Loyen, A. (ed.)
1960-70   *Sidonius Apollinaris, Poèmes, Lettres*, 3 vols. Paris: Budé.
McHugh, M. P.
1964   *Carmen de Providentia Dei*. Catholic University of America Patristic Studies. Washington, D.C.: Catholic University of America Press.
Marot, T.
1994   Máximo el usurpador: importancia política y monetaria de sus emisiones. *Bulletin de l'Association pour l'Antiquité Tardive* 3: 60-63.
Mathisen, R. W.
1984   Emigrants, exiles, and survivors: aristocratic options in Visigothic Aquitania. *Phoenix* 38: 159-170.
Mattingly, D. J., & R. B. Hitchner
1995   Roman Africa: An archaeological review. *Journal of Roman Studies* 85: 165-213
Mayer, M.
1992   El asesino de Ataúlfo. In *Humanitas in honorem Antonio Fontán*. Pp. 297-302. Madrid: Gredos.
Migne, J. P.
1861   *S. Prosper Aquitanus, Idatius Aquaeflaviensis episcopus, Marcellinus comes, et al. Patrologiae Latinae Tomus LI*. Paris: J.-P Migne in rue d'Amboise. [Repr.: Turnhout: Brepols].

Migne, J. P. (*cont.*)
1864   *S. P. N. Procli archiepiscopi Constantinopolitani Opera omnia, et al.*
                Patrologiae Graecae Tomus LXV. Paris: J.-P. Migne in rue d'Amboise.
                [Repr.: Turnhout: Brepols].
Mommaerts, T. S., & D. H. Kelley
1992   The Anicii of Gaul and Rome. In *Fifth-century Gaul: A Crisis of*
                Identity? J. Drinkwater & H. Elton (eds.), pp. 111-121. Cambridge:
                Cambridge University Press.
Mommsen, T. (ed.)
1882   *Iordanis Romana et Getica. Monumenta Germaniae Historica. Auctores*
                antiquissimi, 5, 1. Berlin: Weidmann.
1892   *Chronica minora saec. IV. V. VI. VII.* (I). *Monumenta Germaniae*
                Historica. Auctores antiquissimi, 9. Berlin: Weidmann.
1894   *Chronica minora saec. IV. V. VI. VII.* (II). *Monumenta Germaniae*
                Historica. Auctores antiquissimi, 11. Berlin: Weidmann.
Mühlberger, S.
1992   Looking back from mid-century: The Gallic Chronicler of 452 and the
                crisis of Honorius' reign. In *Fifth-century Gaul: A Crisis of Identity?* J.
                Drinkwater & H. Elton (eds.), pp. 28-37. Cambridge: Cambridge
                University Press.
Nixon, C. E. V.
1992   Relations between Visigoths and Romans in fifth-century Gaul. In *Fifth-*
                century Gaul: A Crisis of Identity? J. Drinkwater & H. Elton (eds.),
                pp. 64-74. Cambridge: Cambridge University Press.
Paschoud, F. (ed.)
1971-89   *Zosime. Histoire Nouvelle*, 3 vols. Paris: Les Belles Lettres.
Percival, J.
1992   The fifth-century villa: new life or death postponed? In *Fifth-century*
                Gaul: A Crisis of Identity? J. Drinkwater & H. Elton (eds.), pp. 136-164.
                Cambridge: Cambridge University Press.
Raynaud, C.
1988   Les campagnes du Languedoc oriental à la fin de l'Antiquité et au debut
                du Haut-Moyen Âge (IVe-VIIe s.); continuité, transition ou rupture? In
                Gaule Mérovingienne et monde méditerranéen. C. Landes (ed.), pp. 125-
                130. Actes des IXes Journées d'Archéologie Mérovingienne, Lattes, 24-
                27 septembre 1987. Lattes: AFAM.
Ripoll, G.
1991   Materiales funerarios de la Hispania visigoda: problemas de cronología y
                de tipología. In *Gallo-Romains, Wisigoths et Francs en Aquitaine,*
                Septimaine et Espagne. P. Périn (ed.), pp. 111-119. Actes des VIIes
                Journées Internationales d'Archéologie Mérovingienne, (Toulouse, 1985).
                Rouen: AFAM.
Roberts, M.
1992   Barbarians in Gaul: the response of the poets. In *Fifth-century Gaul: A*
                Crisis of Identity? J. Drinkwater & H. Elton (eds.), pp. 97-106.
                Cambridge: Cambridge University Press.
Rouche, M.
1979   *L'Aquitaine des Wisigoths aux Arabes (418-507). Naissance d'une région.*
                Paris: Jean Touzot.
1981   Les relations transpyrénéennes du Ve au VIIIe siècle. In *Les*
                comunications dans la Péninsule Ibérique au Moyen Âge. Pp. 13-20.
                Actes du colloque tenu à Pau (28 et 29 Mars 1980). Paris: Éditions du
                C.N.R.S.

1991   Wisigoths et francs en Aquitaine. In *Gallo-Romains, Wisigoths et Francs en Aquitaine, Septimaine et Espagne*. P. Périn (ed.), pp. 143-148. Actes des VIIes Journées Internationales d'Archéologie Mérovingienne (Toulouse, 1985). Rouen: AFAM.

Scharf, R.
1992   Der spanische Kaiser Maximus und die Ansiedlung der Westgoten in Aquitanien. *Historia* 41 (3): 374-384.

Sivan, H.
1992   Town and country in late antique Gaul: the example of Bordeaux. In *Fifth-century Gaul: A Crisis of Identity?* J. Drinkwater & H. Elton (eds.), pp. 132-143. Cambridge: Cambridge University Press.

Soutou, M.
1964   Le nom de lieu wisigothique 'Margastaud'. *Revue internationale d'onomastique* 16: 33-40.

Vollmer, F.
1905   *Fl. Merobaudis reliquiae. Monumenta Germaniae Historica. Auctores antiquissimi*, 14. Berlin: Weidmann.

Wallace-Hadrill, J. M.
1961   Gothia and Romania. *Bulletin of the John Rylands Library* 44: 213-237.

Zangemeister, K. (ed.)
1882   *Historiarum adversus paganos libri VII. (C.S.E.L., 5)*. Wien: Teubner.

Zecchini, G.
1983   *Aezio: l'ultima difesa dell'Occidente romano*. Roma: L'Erma di Bretschneider.

Zeumer, K.
1902   *Leges Visigothorum. Monumenta Germaniae Historica. Leges nationum Germanicarum*, 1. Hannover: Hahn.

Discussion

DÍAZ: About nomadic groups, page 1. It's the question that we have been talking about before: in what sense can we speak about a nomadic group or a group only in transfer? I think that the question is whether a settled people, which at a given moment decide to transfer over a period of 20 or 50 years, become nomadic or not.

SCHWARCZ: Nomadic life is a form of permanent economy, it is totally different from the way the Goths move in the Roman Empire because that was a military movement, a movement of armies. You cannot call an army nomadic.

DÍAZ: This is questionable and I have my doubts about it.

JIMÉNEZ: I think they were not a nomadic group, they were a sedentary group who were looking for a permanent settlement.

SCHWARCZ: This was a group in the military service of the Empire.

AUSENDA: I think Prof. Díaz has some ground to stand on when he says that these people moved very easily. At least a part of the population was used and equipped to move easily. From my knowledge of these populations, there must have been some parts of it which were nomadic, while other groups may have been sedentary and cultivated fields. It remains quite difficult for anyone to say how many were the sedentary ones and how many those who moved with flocks or herds. If a population can rely on a considerable moving capability, it means that it is part of their culture. There is a difference of opinion here. I have seen it in the field, where there are populations, e.g. the Beni Amer, with a dominant group which is more sedentary; they commute from the mountains to the sea shore according to the season: when it's cold they move to the seashore and when it's hot they move back to the plateau. They have fixed settlements in both places. The greatest part of the population, about 70% or 80%, are nomadic pastoralists who travel with their herds or flocks looking for pastures. They move around. So there is no difficulty in envisaging a population which is partly sedentary and partly nomadic, but I tend to agree with Prof. Diaz who speaks about these people probably moving with such ease that they must have practiced a nomadic way of life as a second nature.

SCHWARCZ: I think you are realizing the picture of a separate civilization of these people from their surroundings at the moment of migration into the Empire, and this is where we have to see that they were stationed as Roman soldiers. When they left they had the right to take from the cities which they left a *viaticum*, the means for transport from one city to the next one, where they could get their *annonae*, their pay and their bread to eat from the citizens. They had no need of flocks to support them and they had to march frequently because they belonged to the army. They only had to take their families with them, when they stayed longer at their new station. According to all the sources of the fifth century they demanded land to till as a part of self assistance. And there is in no source for this period any mention of nomadic forms of life.

AUSENDA: Of course you don't have any special mention of pastoral forms of life because they were taken for granted. There must have been a part of the population which was dedicated to a pastoral economy.

SCHWARCZ: You see, the point is that there is mention of ways of life, of tilling land, but we have no mention of nomadic ways of life and you have a lot of mentions of subsistence provided by the state and by the cities as in the case of regular Roman soldiers.

DÍAZ: Apart from the question of a nomadic movement, my opinion here is that a population in movement can take with them many small things; they may have their own manufactures and, when moving, they only have patrimonial traditions, perhaps, but not elements of material culture. This can be important, the stage at which they have come to a conquered place and are in the process of settlement. This is my question.

JIMÉNEZ: They did not have conquered places, they were granted these places.

SCHWARCZ: They were quartered like Roman soldiers.

DÍAZ: Yes, but at a given moment when, after many years in *Aquitania*, they started a sedentary way of life.

JIMÉNEZ: They were sedentary from the beginning.

DÍAZ: Perhaps.

JIMÉNEZ: It's the same as if you said that the people of the Far West were nomadic. Those people were not nomadic, they were people who were looking for a settlement, a permanent settlement. The main difference is that nearly all those people were peasants, while these Visigothic populations were above all military.

SCHWARCZ: Yes.

GREEN: On page 93, you refer to the Roman institution of the *comitatus*, and then you signal features such as military leadership that could provide for loyalty and personal presents. These are precisely the features of the Germanic *comitatus*, the Germanic war band, what you refer to later by the German word 'Gefolge' or 'Gefolgschaft'. Why do you call this a Roman institution when it has these Germanic features and a Germanic background to it?

JIMÉNEZ: I think the explanation of why the *Germani*, the Visigoths in this case, had blended so well as military soldiers into the Roman Empire, was precisely because of the similarity between the 'Gefolge' and the Roman *comitatus*.

GREEN: Yes, but then it is necessary to see how the two interfused with each other and I would still hesitate to call it simply a Roman institution when it is derived from two sources, a Roman and a Germanic one.

JIMÉNEZ: There are no direct sources from this period that explain what the 'Gefolge' was. It is just a working hypothesis. That is, we know what the 'Gefolge' was, we know it above all from epic songs, and we know what the military *comitatus* was and that there were similarities between them.

GREEN: Yes, but then, given the bi-polar state of this Visigothic or sub-Roman society, I think it is essential not to concentrate on one side, the Roman side, or on another, the Germanic, but to stress the intermingling of the two. And by using the word 'Roman institution' you place the emphasis too much on one side.

SCHWARCZ: I don't think you have any evidence for the Roman *comitatus* before 300 but the word *comitatus* is officially in existence only from the time of Constantine and at this point there was a massive change which was already underway because of the presence of the Germanic people. Before, I agree, with one Roman institution which is parallel and which had made this transition of *comitatus* also in the Roman institution possible was the institution of *clientes*. And I would talk of the Roman institution of *clientes* and the Germanic 'Gefolge' before the *comitatus*.

WOOD: Right. I think there is a further problem with the *comitatus* in that it is very much a military institution, and when you see the Roman *comitatus* really emerging it is actually when the Roman military starts to collapse. It evolves into a relatively private war band in the fifth century, as in Clermont. So I think that it's much safer to use the word *clientes*. I think that, in so far as there is a Roman *comitatus* which is similar to the Visigothic *comitatus*, it is a late fourth- to fifth-century development. In other words, it is contemporary with or later than the Gothic *comitatus*. If you want a Roman model which the Goths can be copying, it is that of *clientes*.

GREEN: One can take your point about the possible Gothic priority of this by pointing to the evidence in Wulfila's Biblical translation of the very word for a Germanic *comitatus*, **draúht*. So it's already there in the fourth century and must have been common Germanic.

SCHWARCZ: If you go by Roman law, at first the imperial law forbids private persons to have a *comitatus*. It's put under strict discipline and punishment, and gradually the fifth and sixth centuries it's accepted that private persons also may have their military retinue, which is new, as it was first officially forbidden.

GREEN: On page 94, you mentioned the Goths moving in carts, *carragines*. The word is attested in Latin by Ammianus Marcellinus, and the interesting thing there, is that he refers to this in the context of a Gothic battle, so we are clearly in a Germanic context. He also says that this is the word which the Goths themselves used and, of course, we have other evidence for a kind of barricade of carts and waggons being used to protect the women and children in the course of a Germanic battle. When Ammianus says that this is the word used by the Goths themselves, this creates a difficulty in that the first element of this word *carr-* has no native Germanic parallel, but there is for the second half. So what has happened here I frankly confess I do not know, it may be a fusion of a Latin word *carrus* with a Germanic word *hag*, which is used in the sense of a protective wall, in which case we have got a fusion of Latin with Gothic, which makes it uncertain when Ammianus says that this is the word used by the Goths. They could have taken over the Latin word, but there is no evidence anywhere in Germanic for that having been taken over anything like so early.

My other point is on page 94, the last line of your second paragraph, where I think you give a false impression when you refer to the Danubian culture of Cherniakhov. It stretched much further, from the Danube to way beyond the Dnieper in the direction of the Don. So to call it just a Danubian culture, I think, restricts it much too drastically.

SCHWARCZ: The Cherniakhov culture reached the Danube in the west. But then the Danube may be seen as a late frontier of this culture. In the fourth century this culture, we can say that Romania and Moldavia, the Romanian culture of Cherniakhov and Sîntana de Mureş you would be more correct.

I think that you should completely strike the term 'Danubian' because the archaeological colleagues use the term 'Danubian culture' for something completely different which is the fifth century AD.

JIMÉNEZ: This 'Danubian culture' is an expression used by Kazanski, that is the reference I have taken.

GREEN: Well, we know what he thinks about Kazanski.

SCHWARCZ: I know him personally, he is a very charming and likeable fellow, but he is not always exact in his terminology, so I would just strike out 'Danubian'.

One page 94, the career of Alaric, I don't agree with Liebeschuetz (1990:56), I don't think he was made king in 395, and I think you must take into account the remarks of Claudian (*Paneg. de VI con. Honorii*, 105-108; and in *De bello Getico*) about the early career of Alaric before 394-5, before Theodosius I and the battle of the Frigidus, and I think Alaric was made king already in 390-391. Because a lot of fighting is going on in the Balkans, and in this fight between Alaric and the Roman troops where the *magister militum* Promotus found his death and, according to Claudian, Theodosius I was nearly captured by the Goths, and Stilicho made his first steps in his military and political career. And this ended with a *foedus* in 392. I am sorry that Peter [Heather] isn't here because this is one of the main points of his interpretation.

AUSENDA: You stressed the fact that Gothic military units were housed in garrisons and private houses (page 96), that there was a continuity of dwellings (in the countryside) with the pre-migration types (page 98), that the Goths adopted the Roman building technique and that, therefore, there was continuity (page 106), giving the impression that traditional dwellings were immediately abandoned for more local forms.

On the other hand you state that Goths were given the right to "cultivate part of Gaul's territory" (page 97), that they were dedicated to agriculture (page 98), that in parallel with military tasks they were also dedicated to rural tasks (page 109). All these observations make excellent sense. However, is it possible that in a situation where they were given the possibility to exercise their own agricultural practices they would not rely, at least at the beginning of their settlement, on their traditional dwellings?

Could you give a brief summary of the archaeological finds in the various areas where the Goths mostly settled so as to let us understand what kind of evolution their dwellings had from arrival to complete acculturation?

In simple words, the understanding I received from your paper is that there were no Gothic traditional buildings used even by that part of the population addicted to agriculture, but that they went immediately over to Roman building techniques.

JIMÉNEZ: Because the archaeological finds are very few and this is a field of archaeological investigation that has not been pursued until recently; it remains an impression but there is little evidence to study.

SCHWARCZ: You see, if I may add something, the main difficulty we have with the Visigoths in the fifth century is that we can't find them using archaeology and there is only one explanation: there are no Visigothic settlements in the fifth century, but they live like Roman garrisons in houses and like Roman soldiers. In this period in peacetime they till the land as all the other people in the cities do, because the late-antique city is a city of citizens who live by agriculture. There were none in the countryside.

JIMÉNEZ: The main problem is that we have no remains of Visigoths in *Aquitania* in the fifth century. Hence we don't know how they were dressed nor how their dwellings were. Therefore, I think that they lived as the Romans did.

SCHWARCZ: They were Christians; they were regarded as Christian citizens of the Empire and usually they lived on other peoples' places.

JIMÉNEZ: I think that the Gothicness that Prof. Heather is speaking of in his paper, is a feature that appears later.

SCHWARCZ: Their Gothicness is in their private life, when they talk at home with their families, their Gothicness is in the army and service in church but it is not in their role in the late Roman public sphere.

JIMÉNEZ: Their public Gothicness is a question which appears later. It appears when the Visigoths decide that they have become a state and that's of course not before the reign of Euric, I think.

SCHWARCZ: Yes, the second thing which is one of the main points of the difficulty, in the archaeology there is the question of why we have traces of a distinct Gothic material culture in the sixth century and none in the fifth. I think this is because archaeologists have fallen into a trap, because any Gothic culture in the fifth century had the main characterstic that it could no longer be a Cherniakhov culture. In fact they had been in the Roman Empire and they used *terra sigillata* not Cherniakhov pottery; they used the products of cities, hence the material culture of the sixth century had strong symptoms of the so-called 'Völkerwanderungs' culture of the fifth century which came out of the *barbaricum*. And probably this *fibula* was of the sixth century where they were very similar to the Ostrogothic ones and I think that this material culture developed under Ostrogothic domination.

JIMÉNEZ: I agree with you, although I prefer to speak of 'infuence' rather than 'domination'. I think that those few remains from the Cherniakhov culture found in Gaul are some of the objects that the Visigoths had carried with them in their migration. So, their Gothicness is a feature that was born later and was born under an Ostrogothic influence, not under a Visigothic influence.

DÍAZ: On page 97, concerning *ad inhabitandum* I have a simple question: whether *ad inhabitandum* is always a technical expression. It is found in relation to a reference in Hydatius' chronicle (49, *s.a.* 411)[1] to the settlement of *Suebi*, Alans and Vandals in northwestern Spain. There has been a long lasting polemic whether *ad inhabitandum* means a special relationship with the Empire or refers to the distribution of settlements in different areas. I prefer this second interpretation.

JIMÉNEZ: I have used just this word because I think that *ad inhabitandum* is a very important expression. That means that the Visigoths were permanently settled in several cities as they were soldiers to be used in war and the defence of the towns.

DÍAZ: This is what I also believe, but sometimes we read that this means a special relationship within the Empire.

JIMÉNEZ: No I don't think so. I don't think there was a special meaning of *foedus* attached to this word. It is simply to express that the Goths were settled permanently in several cities in Gaul and one of these cities was Toulouse. I believe that it is very interesting that Hydatius outlined that the Visigoths chose Toulouse *sibi sedem*. In fact I have read that in the Cherniakhov culture the *Tervingi* had a central town of different *gentes*.

---

[1] The text is: "*provinciis barbari ad pacem ineundam, domino miserante conversi sorte ad inhabitandum sibi provinciarum regiones*".

SCHWARCZ: I don't think so. I think the *Tervingi* had no centre in the fourth century, whereas you might locate the central seat of the Greuthungian kingdom in a rather populous town, I think on the Dnieper or the Dniester.

But for the *Tervingi* in the fourth century there was nothing like a metropolis. Because of the oligarchic structure of the *Tervingi* you have regional seats of power but no central point.

JIMÉNEZ: If different Visigoths were distributed over Gallic territory, they must have had a central city as a point of reference.

SCHWARCZ: Of course, because the situation changed after Alaric and Athaulf. Now it was a structure with a king, Theoderic I, with a treaty with the Empire guaranteeing payments, and because he was part of the Roman structure of power he had to have a permanent seat like a Roman general.

VELÁZQUEZ: I think we can join two questions on page 98 about *sortes gothicae*, my question on Euric's code and the question of Pablo Díaz on *sortes*. What do you think about *sortes*?

JIMÉNEZ: I don't know whether the tax theory [of W. Goffart] is right or wrong, but I think that, if the Visigoths were soldiers it is ridiculous to think that Romans were paying them with land which was taken from its owners. It is simpler to think that they were paid with money, provided that in the previous year they were paid with money. When Alaric in Italy asked for his pay, he was paid in gold and silver and clothes. Thus, for the first few years in Aquitania, I think it is much more probable that they were paid with money than with land, almost for the whole population. It is for this that I distinguish two groups: one group who were granted land and which settled, and they were given charge to cultivate the land and to defend this territory, and another group, a more military one, who were given charge to defend the cities from the possible usurpation of the Aquitanian nobility, and they were paid with money.

VELÁZQUEZ: Perhaps a kind of usufruct over the land?

JIMÉNEZ: I don't think so.

VELÁZQUEZ: When do you believe that the *sortes* could mean land? Because *sortes* is a Latin word.

JIMÉNEZ: ...which means different things, but the problem is that historians think that *sortes* has only one meaning, and that is not correct.

VELÁZQUEZ: Related maybe to land? It is very difficult, for example, to distinguish between *proprietas* and *possessio*, between ownership and possession.

JIMÉNEZ: But which kind of *proprietas* over land, the real *proprietas* over land, or all the fiscal *proprietas* over land? I think it is much more probable that this means fiscal *proprietas* over the land; that is, the Roman nobility was allowed to have fiscal resources from many *sortes*. From the second half of the fourth century the Roman state gave to the Roman nobility the capability to obtain fiscal resources which were later used by local Roman administrators to pay the soldiers and for other expenses. This is the reason for which I believe that what the Roman state did was to transfer this capability of the Roman nobility to the Visigothic chiefs.

I refer to the end of the fourth and the fifth century while the situation in the sixth and seventh centuries could be quite different.

VELÁZQUEZ: Yes, but because of these *sortes*, that is only one meaning.

JIMÉNEZ: Where do *sortes* have only one meaning?

VELÁZQUEZ: No they haven't, I agree with you, if we are referring to the semantic evolution of the word and of its possible meanings throughout history. However, it seems that at each specific moment and in each text, *sortes* had a given meaning. Because of this I have mentioned the letter of Bishop Montanus (*a.* 531), in the minutes of the II Council of Toledo (ll. 202-39), where he says to his faithful in the region of Palentia that any presbyter may invite a bishop from other dioceses ("*alienae sortis*") to consecrate churches in his diocese (Martínez Díaz & Rodríguez 1984:361). Anyway my question refers in particular to the *Codex Eurici*.

JIMÉNEZ: The *Codex Eurici*? What does that have to do with *sortes*? For me the word means 'fiscal resources'.

SCHWARCZ: I quite agree.

RETAMERO: I would like to comment on this question, on the way by which ancient states established links with the different social organizations. Ancient states could establish links with these organizations by two ways, or better said, two sides of the same way, i.e., treaties implying the participation of notables or *principes*, whatever they were, in the fiscal administration or in the military organization of the state. This procedure is fairly and broadly documented in the Andalusian period and in North Africa when the Khalifa signed treaties with Berber notables. The structure of these treaties was always the same: *gentes* represented by these notables were more or less involved in fiscal administration and/or in the military administration, depending on the actual relation of forces.

JIMÉNEZ: And that is very clear and in this period even clearer, because the Roman emperor was facing a big crisis and so he needed considerable new support, apart from the provincial support which he had lost.

RETAMERO: I don't know whether we can talk about 'support' or not. Anyhow it was the only way to involve the social organizations in the fiscal military mechanism, especially in those twilight zones where the state's presence was weaker.

SCHWARCZ: But you know it's a question of the quality of relations. You see the Roman state had a lot of instruments to integrate ethnic groups into the Empire, it depended on the way that relations developed. If they were defeated they were integrated and distributed as *coloni* or *gentiles* to landowners, or taken as soldiers for the regular troops. If it was a process of treaty they were integrated as groups as the Franks were in the late fourth and fifth centuries. The chief was given a military command and his soldiers were paid as regular Roman soldiers. There is the difference of the quality of the way they came in: whether they were defeated or accepted.

WOOD: I think it is more complicated than that. That's why I like Ana [Jiménez]' emphasis on the question of land being given *ad inhabitandum*. It seems to me that the real problem with the fiscal Gothic model is that it is so single-minded. What is clear is that a whole series of transactions happen in the last quarter of the late fourth and early fifth centuries. And it is very rare that we can discern what type of transaction takes place at what moment. I think the attractive aspect to your interpretation is that it allows more than one of these models at once. And I think it is dangerous to be too precise about any one model being used at any one time, unless we know we have a particular *foedus*. The crucial thing, I think, is to say that there are there a series of possible ways of integrating peoples. And we can see that they are all being used in the course of the fifth century. And we can't be absolutely certain which one is used and which one is not.

SCHWARCZ: I think that in the fifth century we can be more certain that the fiscal is used in the beginning and also certain that it is used in Italy at the end of the fifth century and it depends on the way Romans and also their government thought in agrarian and fiscal terms. You see for the late Roman fiscal administration the term for the land and for the tax which was taken from the land were the same. So for the historian it is difficult to distinguish which one is meant. The other difficulty is that you can take two kinds of income from land at this time: you can take a land rent as owner and you get a tax income from the owner of the land.

If you get for a long time tax from a land, you tend to think of it as land of your own, and you think of the money you get as a land grant and no longer as taxes, especially when the state becomes weaker. So I think that is a gradual transition from the fiscal problem to the land grant problem. But that's why in the Burgundian law as well as in the Visigothic one you have the great difficulty to distinguish between its interpretation as referring to land or tax.

WOOD: Yes, I agree with you, but I would not see this transition as beginning from a totally fiscal model and leading to a totally landed model. I think that there must be instances of land allocation quite early on; this phrase *terra data eis ad inhabitandum*[2] is crucial, and it crops up in a number of cases.

JIMÉNEZ: There are two expressions in the sources, one which says *ad inhabitandum* and another one which says 'to cultivate the land'.

SCHWARCZ: Of course, you must take into account the treaty. In fact the king was integrated into the upper layers of Roman society, which means that, of course, he got also land because he was a great officer who was honoured by the Empire and also got a *villa* from the emperor; he must get signs of honour, of grace and, of course, they acquire land when they are there. For instance Paulinus of Pella (*Eucharisticos* ll. 292 ff.) gives us a report of a Visigoth paying the owner for land. So like normal soldiers they also own private land, also Gothic soldiers under Theoderic owned land. But this is different, a different kind of thing from the form of payment of soldiers.

---

2 The text reads: "*Constantius patricius pacem firmat cum Wallia data ei ad inhabitandum secunda Aquitanica et quibusdam civitatibus confinium provinciarum*" (Prosper, *Epitom. Chronicon a.* 419).

WOOD: Yes, you do have more than one system operating right from the start. The other point that I would like to emphasize, is the point that you made on the shift from rent to property. This also goes with the point made by Levy (1951). Effectively *dominium* and *possessio* get confused totally and utterly. And it's in that context that it becomes more and more difficult to distinguish between what is usufruct and what is ownership.

GREEN: At the bottom of page 97, you are talking about the lexical reminiscences left by the Gothic language in southern France and you say they refer on the one hand to social and institutional status and on the other to war language. The terms you quote in brackets under social and institutional status ('companion' and 'troop') may belong to the 'Gefolgschaft', a military institution, so that my question is: how are you distinguishing between this military institution and war language?

JIMÉNEZ: What I wish to say is that the war language referred to military objects.

GREEN: You mean helmets, shields and so on. But then I think you are on tricky ground then to distinguish war language in that sense from a terminology of a military institution, the two are too close.

JIMÉNEZ: No, what I want to say is in connection with the place-names ending in the suffixes *-ingus/-ingos* or *-inga/-ingas* whose meaning 'the people of' supports the idea that rural settlements consisted of small military units which, therefore, were granted land to cultivate.

GREEN: But surely you run the danger of confusing two things here: a distinction, on the one hand, of endings in the place-names and a distinction between what the main body of the place-name indicates, whether a social status or war.language.

JIMÉNEZ: No, socially.

GREEN: Only socially. But then, how do you relate 'companion', 'band' and 'troop' to social status as distinct from military status?

JIMÉNEZ: Yes, probably I have extended this question. What I want to say is that the first Visigothic settlement consisted of troops around a chief and linked to some of them by such institutions as '*comitatus*', etc.

GREEN: May I make a suggestion? Why don't you say, at the bottom of page 97, that they refer to the social and institutional status, 'companion' and 'troop', and then omit 'and not to the war language'?
You keep your point and you avoid my difficulty.

JIMÉNEZ: I can do that. Thank you very much.

DÍAZ: You speak about the continuity of the langue d'Oc, but I am thinking about open countries in relation to the settlement in the fourth to the seventh century. I ask whether this was the same in all areas, because of the question of the influence of the Visigoths in the different areas where they arrived, originating different settlements in these different kingdoms.

JIMÉNEZ: You refer to the sentence: "In all the areas where the Visigoths were settled this continuity is attested"?

DÍAZ: Yes.

VELÁZQUEZ: On page 99, referring to place-names.

GREEN: I have three separate points which belong together here. The first one is not a question, it is just a comment: at the top of that page you are talking about Gothic place-names in southern Gaul and it's here merely that I would like to comment, that we suffer from the death of Gamillscheg, because although he investigated these in the thirties, and started revision of his multi-volume work in the sixties, he completed the revision only of the Frankish volume and never got on to the Gothic volume. So that some information on this problem, as far as his monumental work is concerned, is unfortunately out of date. My other point goes on to page 105, where just over half way through, you talk about a group of place-names more abundant in Aquitaine as a consequence of the Franks' colonization after 507. This, of course, is part of the big problem of Germanic place-names in France. In that we are dealing on the large scale with three linguistic groups with which we have to separate as far as possible, namely Gothic, Burgundian and Frankish. Quite apart from the paucity of linguistic material for Burgundian, it's extremely difficult distinguishing Gothic from Burgundian, because both are East Germanic languages and share basically the same characteristics, so that the means of distinguishing them are limited. They are not all that better when it comes to distinguishing either Gothic or Burgundian on the one hand and Frankish on the other, because there we are dependent on what is, after all, a limited number of phonological distinctions between these languages. As regards Gothic names in southern France, the difficulty is the fact that there is imposed on these Gothic names, and also on the Burgundian names, a Frankish top layer which makes it extremely difficult to distinguish one from the other. I am not asking you a question but merely, from my point of view, expressing my agreement. My last point on the place-name problem is on page 108 at the top, you refer to two Germanic ethnic names in place-names, *Taifali* and *Vandali*. The difficulty here is to distinguish in the case of such names between Germanic settlements as a result of conquest or occupation by these tribes, on the one hand, and on the other, while the Roman Empire was still in existence, the settlement of certain Germanic groups, not whole tribes, but smaller groups, in scattered areas within the Empire. We have in that context such French place-names as Allemanche, referring to the *Alamanni*, but miles removed from where the Alemannic tribe as a whole was at that time, or a name like Marmaigne, referring to *Marcomanni*, worlds removed from Bohemia, and Frisons, near the Frankish-Brittany border, worlds removed from Frisia. So that, when one comes across names like *Taifali* and *Vandali*, it doesn't necessarily mean that these are settlement areas occupied by tribes. It could refer back to earlier settlements at the time of the Roman Empire. And how to distinguish is another matter, but I merely want to draw your attention to that danger.

JIMÉNEZ: I agree, I agree.

SCHWARCZ: Concerning the *Taifali*, they were not a Germanic group and they were integrated into the Visigothic army after 376. In their original seats they were a Sarmatian group.

DÍAZ: I have perhaps a question there in relation with the question of place-names and personal names. I am sceptical sometimes about the possibility to follow the settlement from place-names or personal names.

JIMÉNEZ: In fact, it is very difficult. I believe I stressed this point.

DÍAZ: Yes, but in northwestern Spain we have a reference to the last years of the seventh century by Valerius of Bierzo (Aherne 1945), we have only two or three references to Germanic place-names or personal names, but in the ninth and tenth centuries, we have hundreds of place-name references, or especially personal names which are Gothic, in areas where the Visigoths never settled. Sometime it can be problematic to use these references.

JIMÉNEZ: It is not the same case in the eighth and ninth centuries. In the ninth century in *Hispania*, the Visigoths were a very important point of reference to originate the model of the kingdom of Asturias and later to launch the Reconquista.

VELÁZQUEZ: There are many Visigothic personal names, not many place-names.

JIMÉNEZ: And the place-names especially always have the problem that, until the eighth or ninth century, they cannot be confirmed by the texts. Hence, it remains a hypothesis.

VELÁZQUEZ: Do you want to say anything else about personal names and place-names?

GREEN: Yes on page 99. I don't know what Spanish usage is, but you talk about or imply a distinction between onomastics and toponyms. It's best in English to distinguish between personal names and place-names.

JIMÉNEZ: Thank you.

GREEN: In English, onomastics has to do with the origin of names of any kind.

VELÁZQUEZ: Concerning page 93, I would like to ask about a text of Sidonius Apollinaris. Euric had forbidden the inheritance from the mother in law and Sidonius can retain the *usum tertiae* of his mother in law. What does it mean? Is it the usufruct?

JIMÉNEZ: I don't know. There is a reference in Sidonius (*Epist*. VIII. 9. 2) to *sortes* and I don't know what it means. My first question related to that.

VELÁZQUEZ: I think it could be the third part of the usufruct in the inheritance of *bona materna*. But it is strange that this belongs to the mother in law. To the mother yes, but to the mother-in-law?

VELÁZQUEZ: Later, in effect, within the *bona materna* as something included.

WOOD: A general observation rather than a question. It has to do with the problem of the chronology in the chronicles. People have come to accept Hydatius's (*Chronica*, 69) date for the settlement in Aquitaine as 418 but, of course, Prosper says 419. Now that was dismissed on the ground that Prosper (*Chronica*, 1271, *a*. 419) is very often inaccurate in his dates. But actually Hydatius is inaccurate in his dates just as Prosper is. But Prosper was in Aquitaine in 419, so the chances are that his evidence is actually better than Hydatius'. Now this may not seem significant except in the crucially important relationship of the settlement to the re-institution of the Council of the Gauls. If it's 418 the Council of the Gauls is re-instituted after the settlement, if it's 419, which is Prosper's date, the Council of the Gauls is re-instituted before the settlement. And I think that one has to face that chronological problem. To that can then be added another chronological problem, which is that of the *Chronicle* of 452. Every single date in the second half of that, when you can check it, is probably wrong. So that one cannot speak of the Burgundians being settled in *Sapaudia* in 452, because all of the dates in the *Chronicle* for which we have any other evidence are wrong. So, I think that historians have to find a way of avoiding giving specific dates when it comes to 452. And I think that historians must be clear when dealing with the settlement of the Visigoths, because there is a problem with the relationship of the settlement and the re-institution of the Council of the Gauls. It is a straighforward observation on a problem of chronology.

SCHWARCZ: OK, I entirely agree.

WOOD: Nobody has followed me. [Laughter]

SCHWARCZ: I think that I did in my contribution in Paris (Schwarcz 1995:52 n2).

WOOD: Right.

RETAMERO: Very briefly, what does Margastaud mean? Page 99.

JIMÉNEZ: You have to read the work of Soutou (1964), where he explains that this place-name is one which is always associated with a river or a water place.

RETAMERO: Yes, but do you know the specific meaning of the word?

JIMÉNEZ: No.

References

Textual sources:

Claudian
> *Bellum Geticum*: see Hall (ed.) 1985:257 (ll. 492 ff., 546-7, 624-8).
> *Panegyricus dictus Honorio Augusto VI Cons.*: see Hall (ed.) 1985:268 (ll. 105-108).

Codex Eurici: see References at end of paper.

Hydatius
> *Chronica*: see Burgess (ed.) 1993.

Paulinus of Pella
> *Eucharisticos*: see Brandes (ed.) 1888.

Prosper
> *Chronica*: see Mommsen (ed.) 1892.

Sidonius Apollinaris
> *Epistolae*: see References at end of paper.

Bibliography:

Aherne, C. M.
> 1945   *Valerius of Bierzo. An Ascetic of the Late Visigothic Period*. Washington, D.C.: The Catholic University of America.

Brandes, W. (ed.)
  1888   See References at end of paper.
Burgess, R. W.
  1993   *The Chronicle of Hydatius and the Consularia Constantinopolitana.*
                  Oxford: Clarendon Press.
Hall, J. B. (ed.)
  1985   *Claudii Claudiani Carmina.* Leipzig: Teubner.
Levy, E.
  1951   *West Roman Vulgar Law: The Law of Property.* Philadelphia: University
                  of Pennsylvania Press.
Liebeschuetz, J. H. W. G.
  1990   *Barbarians and Bishops. Army, Church and State in the Age of Arcadius
                  and Chrysostom.* Oxford: Clarendon Press.
Martínez Díaz, G., & F. Rodríguez (eds.)
  1984   *La Colección canónica hispana*, vol. IV. Concilios galos. Concilios
                  hispanos (1ª parte). (*Monumenta Hispanica Sacra, Series canónica*).
                  Madrid: C.S.I.C.
Mommsen, T. (ed.)
  1892   *Chronica minora saec. IV. V. VI. VII.* (I) *Monumenta Germaniae
                  Historica. Auctores antiquissimi*, 9. Berlin: Weidmann. [Repr. 1981].
Schwarcz, A.
  1995   Senatorische Heerführer in Westgotenreich im 5. Jh. In *La noblesse
                  romaine et les chefs barbares du IIIe au VIIe siècle*. F. Vallet &
                  M. Kazanski (eds.), pp. 49-54. Condé-sur-Noireau: Association Française
                  d'Archéologie Mérovingienne.

KINSHIP AND MARRIAGE AMONG THE VISIGOTHS

GIORGIO AUSENDA

Center for Interdisciplinary Research on Social Stress, 6 C.da S. Francesco, San Marino (RSM)

1. KINSHIP AND MARRIAGE IN ANTHROPOLOGY

History of kinship theories

Lewis Henry Morgan was the first to realize the importance of kinship in the life of simple societies. He lived in Rochester in upstate New York and was a lawyer for the Iroquois who lived in the area. In the course of his work with them, he became interested in their kinship relations which were fundamental to understanding their jural relations. In time he became interested in comparing these patterns of relations, which he called 'systems', among as many simple societies as he could. He instituted a questionnaire survey and set out to obtain answers from American diplomats all over the world. The results of his research were published in 1877.

The only scientific paradigm available at the time in the biological and social sciences was Darwinian evolutionism which he adopted to classify and 'explain' his findings. Following the contemporary division of archaeology in three ages he chose to divide the evolution of mankind in three related epochs which he called "savagery", "barbarism" and "civilization" (Morgan 1963 [1877]: Preface).

Basing his comparison on the kinship terminologies he had collected, he divided his evolutionary paradigm into five stages characterized by different 'systems' which he defined as follows:

1. *The Consaguine Family*
   Founded on the intermarriage of brothers and sisters, own and collateral, in a group.
2. *The Punaluan[1] Family*
   Founded on the intermarriage of sisters, own and collateral, with each other's husbands, in a group. The joint husbands were not necessarily kinsmen. The same system could be originated by the intermarriage of several brothers, own and collateral, with each other's wives in a group, the wives not being necessarily each other's kin, although often this was the case in both instances. In each case the men in the group were conjointly married to the group of women.
3. *The Syndyasmian[2] Family*
   Founded on the marriage between single pairs, but without an exclusive cohabitation. The marriage continued during the pleasure of the partners.

---

[1] From the name of the corresponding Hawaiian custom called *punalua*.

[2] From the Greek *syndiàzein* meaning 'to couple'.

THE VISIGOTHS FROM THE MIGRATION PERIOD TO THE SEVENTH CENTURY:
AN ETHNOGRAPHIC PERSPECTIVE

4. *The Patriarchal Family*
   Founded on the marriage of one man with several wives, followed, in general,
   by the seclusion of the wives.
5. *The Monogamian Family*
   Founded on the marriage between single pairs with an exclusive cohabitation.

In Morgan's scheme there was a correspondence between the great evolutionary
divisions and the kinship systems he had devised in that the Consaguine was
supposed to be common during the phase of Savagery, the Punaluan was present
during Savagery and continued into Lower Barbarism, the Syndyasmian and
Patriarchal systems characterized Middle and Upper Barbarism, while the
Monogamian Family was the achievement of civilization.

Morgan introduced a broad distinction in the categorization of systems of
kinship, the notion that the kinship systems could be either "classificatory" in that
"consanguines are never described, but are classified into categories, irrespective
of their nearness or remoteness in degree to Ego" (Morgan 1963:403), while in the
"descriptive" system "consanguines are described either by the primary terms of
relationship or a combination of these terms, thus making the relationship of each
person specific" (Morgan 1963 [1877]:404). According to Morgan "the
development of the [descriptive] nomenclature...would probably never have
occurred...except when...the need [arose] of a code of descent to regulate the
inheritance of property" (Morgan 1963:404). This scope was attained by the
Romans and eventually followed by European nations (Morgan 1963:406). Thus,
the trend from classificatory to descriptive kinship systems followed the trend
from savagery to civilization.

Despite the shortcomings in his theory and the many errors in his categorization
of contemporary cultures, which were later exposed and criticized, Morgan had the
uncontested merit of discovering that kinship systems existed throughout the world
"which were similar to each other, but at marked variance with those known to
Indo-European- and Semitic-speaking peoples" (Leacock 1963:I-iii).

As a result of an expedition to the Torres Straits in the year 1898, W. H. R.
Rivers, a British medical doctor, developed a method for determining the relations
between kin categories in a given society, giving thereby the pertinent attributes to
all kinship terms involved. He described his method in an article by the title, "A
genealogical method of collection of social and vital statistics", which was
published in 1900 in the Journal of the [Royal] Anthropological Institute
(Penniman 1965:99). Based on his fieldwork Rivers also theorized that "kin terms
reflected antecedent sociological conditions" (Fried 1968:306).

River's method consisted in collecting the 'pedigrees' of several individuals and
asking them to specify the term of relation and the attendant relationship with the
individuals in their pedigrees, so much so that these became "real
personages...although [he] had never seen them, when identified in [his] book of
pedigrees" (Rivers 1968 [1910]:105 in Bouquet 1996:45).

With the tide turning against evolutionism in anthropology under the influence
of Franz Boas's cultural relativism at the beginning ot the twentieth century and

later of the functionalists, the study of kinship abandoned the evolutionary framework.

In a paper published in 1909 Alfred L. Kroeber attacked the "idea that either evolutionary or historical reconstructions could safely be made from kinship terms" (Schneider 1968:9). He applied Boas's methodology to disprove the "naive" evolutionism preached by Morgan and other early anthropologists by showing that "allegedly sequential elements can actually be found existing together in the same society at the same time" (Harris 1968:322). Kroeber's attack was directed also against Morgan's dichotomy between 'classificatory' and 'descriptive' kinship terminology in that, "A moment's reflection is sufficient to show that every language groups together under single designations many distinct degrees and kinds of relationships. Our word 'brother' includes both the older and the younger brothers and the brother of a man and a woman. It therefore embraces or classifies four relationships" (Kroeber 1909:17 in Fried 1968:307). Kroeber went on to propose eight different categories according to which terms of kinship could be classified: (1) difference between people of same and separate generations, (2) difference between lineal and collateral relationship, (3) difference of age within one generation, (4) sex of relative, (5) sex of speaker, (6) sex of person through whom the relationship exists, (7) distinction of blood relatives (consanguines) from connections by marriage (affines), (8) the condition of life (whether alive or dead, married or single) of the person through whom the relationship exists (Kroeber 1909:18-9 in Fried 1968:308-9). His conclusion against W. H. R. Rivers' finding that kinship terms "reflected antecedent sociological conditions" was in tune with a new 'scientific' paradigm which was coming to the fore during those years and was going to condition anthropological theory well into the 1940s. He maintained that terms of relationship reflect the 'psychology' not the 'sociology' of the interactions; they are "determined primarily by language and can be utilized for sociological inferences only with extreme caution" (Kroeber 1909:84 in Fried 1908:314). In 1952, after the wane of the psychological paradigm in anthropology, Kroeber revised his use of the word 'psychological' modifying his stance to a slightly different position by suggesting that kin term systems reflect unconscious and conceptual patterning as well as social institutions. The 'unconscious' is still there but in the company of other forces.

In the wake of the British triumph after World War I and the reorganization of the colonial empire, the work of Alfred Reginald Radcliffe Brown and Bronislaw Malinowski heralded the 'functionalist' approach in anthropology. The preceding history of social phenomena was henceforth neglected, also because in most cases it was impossible to detect as it became at best 'conjectural history', in favour of a synchronic analysis of the interplay of social institutions and the relations they generated. Everything, including magic and religion, could be explained in terms of their 'function' in the life of a social group.

Interpretations of kinship relations also took on a 'functional' varnish. In Radcliffe-Brown's words:

A system of kinship and marriage can be looked at as an arrangement which enables persons to live together and cooperate with one another in an orderly social life. For any particular system as it exists at a certain time we can make a study of how it works. To do this we have to consider how it links persons together by convergence of interest and sentiment and how it controls and limits those conflicts that are always possible as the result of divergence of sentiment or interest (Radcliffe-Brown 1950:3).

Radcliffe-Brown enunciated a series of explanatory principles whose existence, in greater or lesser intensity, could be detected in most kinship systems. Among them were the *cognatic* principle, whereby "all descendants of [Ego's] recognized ancestors, through both females and males are his cognates" (Radcliffe-Brown 1950:13); the *unilineal* principle according to which descent either through males or females is recognized and "used in the formation of recognised lineage groups" (Radcliffe-Brown 1950:14); the principle of the *unity of the sibling group* as it may "constitute a unity for a person outside it and connected with it by a specific relation with one of its members" (Radcliffe-Brown 1950:24); the *generation* principle involving respect and subordination for proximate ascending generation and the related principle involving the *merging of alternate generations* (Radcliffe-Brown 1950:29) whereby there is great familiarity between alternate generations, e.g. grandfather and grandson. Some of these principles are reflected in kinship terminology, especially the principle of the unity of the sibling group which is attested by "classificatory terminology in general" (Radcliffe-Brown 1950:33) and the "principle of lineage unity which is recognized in [the mentioned] tribes in other features of the terminology" (Radcliffe-Brown 1950:35).

Conditioned by their abhorrence for 'conjectural history', structural-functionalists were mostly concerned with synchronic explanations, hence their neglect of diachronic developments. This caused them to posit homeostasic equilibrium, whereby change vanished from the picture and was forgotten. This short-sighted view and the insistence on the reality of economic systems as contributing mainly to the maintenance of the social structure, rather than the fact that social structures utilize 'techno-economic' systems to adapt to changing circumstances, limited the explanatory power of functionalist theories (cf. Harris 1968:518), while the proofs of structural functionalist principles were mostly based on circular arguments.

After World War II a new approach to the theory of kinship was set forth by Claude Lévi-Strauss. His theory became known as 'structuralism' and, having started its career in anthropology, was later applied to most fields within the humanities. The concept of structure was still fundamental, albeit in a different perspective from that of structural functionalism, while 'functionalism' was no longer considered of any relevance. For Radcliffe-Brown, the 'structure' was an empirical reality "of which the component units are human beings" (1952 {1940}:190) or, in Lévi-Strauss's words, "nothing else than the network of social relations" (Barnes 1971:108), whereas for Lévi-Strauss the term 'social structure' has nothing whatever to do with empirical reality but "with models that can be built after it" (Lévi-Strauss 1963:279 in Barnes 1971:109).

The life of social groups is seen as based on several forms of communication which can be analyzed by building various kinds of communication structures (Barnes 1971:125-6). The three main "levels of communication are: women, goods and services, and messages". The structure of kinship and marriage in a given society shows how women are 'communicated' or 'circulated' (Barnes 1971:126). The system of marriage rules is predicated on the presence of the incest taboo and on the sexual division of labour (Barnes 1971:138). Lévi-Strauss's interpretation of the incest taboo is vaguely Tylorian[3] in that he sees it as requiring men to give their close female relatives to other men, thus linking different families, while the sexual division of labor is "nothing else than a device to institute a reciprocal state of dependency between the sexes (Lévi-Strauss 1956a:270-1, in Barnes 1971:139).

In contrast with structural-functionalist praxis, Lévi-Strauss's structuralism did not produce any propositions that could be tested (Barnes 1971:165). The merit of his work lies in the innovative 'linguistic' approach to the subject of kinship and marriage, whereby entirely new perspectives were uncovered which undoubtedly will be very useful as a basis for future research. Indeed he himself asked to be judged as a typologist rather than as an enunciator of propositions (Barnes 1971:166). This is indeed the limitation of the mechanical model he took from linguistics, whereby the patterns of phenomena such as language, in this case kinship and marriage, can be typologized before and after a change, the same as languages before and after a sound change, but they cannot be followed during the change, so that the cause of change remains unexplained. For this a 'statistical', i.e. historical approach is necessary as acknowledged by Lévi-Strauss himself (cf. Barnes 1971:127).

Genealogies and pedigrees

Kinship relationships and terminologies are obtained from genealogies collected in the 'field.' One should, therefore, be aware of the nature and meaning of genealogies. Among populations where genealogies represent one of the main socializing mechanisms, true 'biological' genealogies, especially beyond the second ascending generation, are a chimera. During my fieldwork I noted how there were several genealogical 'horizons': the lowest, generally reaching the second ascending generation, might actually, but not necessarily, be 'biological', the next highest, generally reaching the tenth ascending generation or thereabouts, serves to 'fix' the individual in society with respect to other individuals in his own

---

[3]   In discussing the advantages of 'exogamy' E. B. Tylor wrote: "Again and again in the world's history, savage tribes must have had plainly before their minds the simple practical alternative between marrying-out and being killed out" (Tylor 1889:267). In Lévi-Strauss's view, 'marrying-out' is the main consequence of the incest taboo.

kinship group and other connected groups, the last horizon, which can go back some forty or fifty generations to a god or a prophet, is the horizon which gives prestige to the individual's kinship group.

This is not the place to go into the mechanisms which produce genealogies, suffice it to say that they are not fabricated by individuals, but they emerge through a process of social recognition of the actual 'worth' of social groups in a process akin to linguistic communication. In the words of Barnard and Good, "...genealogies are not historical records of biological relations, but contemporary models for social relations...." (Barnard & Good 1984:9).

One should also distinguish genealogies from pedigrees. W. H. R. Rivers, the inventor of the genealogical method to obtain kinship terminologies and relations, considered pedigrees as tied to the personal names of the individuals mentioned by informants whereas genealogies reflected the "abstract system of relationships underlying these names" (Bouquet 1996:45). Commenting on River's perspective, David M. Schneider wrote: "Pedigree is a statement of actual biological relations between humans or animals. A race horse has a pedigree, which lists its dam, its sire, and its progenitors, but racehorses do not have a genealogy. A genealogy is a statement of social relationships, not biological ones" (Schneider 1984:55 in Bouquet 1996:63 note 4). Conversely "a genealogical statement becomes a pedigree when it is used to legitimize claims to status, office and so forth" (Barnes 1967:103 in Bouquet 1996:63, note 4).

Kinship systems and terminology

For Radcliffe-Brown, kinship terminologies had a social valence, in the sense that different individuals addressed by the same terms by Ego, i.e. the individual at the center of the kinship network surveyed, must be "structurally equivalent" using 'structure' in the sense of empirically observable relationships (Barnard & Good 1984:11). In Lévi-Strauss's view alliance and terminological structures were interchangeable or in his words, "the spouse is the spouse solely because she belongs to an alliance category or stands in a certain kinship relationship to Ego" (Lévi-Strauss 1969:xxxiv in Barnard & Good 1984:12).

Louis Dumont recognized two operational levels of kinship systems: the 'ideological' and the 'behavioural' (1980:343, n.1a in Barnard & Good 1984:12), and Rodney Needham (1967:43) further divided the ideological level into a 'categorical' and 'jural' one, in abeyance with field observation that "terminological structures (categorical)...[are] not necessarily congruent with...alliance structures (jural)" (Barnard & Good 1984:13). In other words terminology may equate certain structural roles which in the practice of that society are treated differently.

David M. Schneider pointed out "that a system of kinship terminology is not a single system of names for a single homogeneous universe of meaning" (Schneider

1968:13). In other words, one may use a kinship term not only to designate a kinsman, but as a term of respect such as 'uncle', used in many societies to designate older people, or 'father' used in our society to designate religious performers. Schneider goes on to describe kinship as a "system of symbols" (Schneider 1968b:18 in Barnard & Good 1984:175) which is yet another perspective worth taking into consideration.

One of the jural aspects of kinship systems is to supply the framework for rules of descent, inheritance and succession. *Descent* establishes the lines of transmission of group membership and its attributes. There are six logical possibilities in that it may be (1) patrilineal or (2) matrilineal; (3) double (when different sets of attributes are transmitted in the patriline or the matriline); (4) cognatic (when attributes can be transmitted equally through either line); (5) parallel (when different sets of attributes are transmitted from father to son and from mother to daughter) and (6) cross (when men transmit to their daughters and women to their sons) (Barnard & Good 1984:70-1).

The concepts of inheritance and succession should not be confused: the first concerns the transmission of property and the second the transmission of office (Barnard & Good 1984:70).

Corporateness is a concept which in simple societies is closely linked to kin groups. Corporateness stands for an ideology which promotes cohesion amongst several individuals or families toward collective action in religious, political or economic fields (Barnard & Good 1984:76). When engaged in fieldwork, the first aspect one perceives of a social group in a simple society is indeed its corporateness which may be more or less extended in time and space. Groups involved in corporate actions are termed corporate groups and their corporateness may be based on kinship or on proximity or both. Often corporate groups comprise some individuals held together by kinship ties and co-resident individuals with no other apparent reason for being part of the group.

Marriage

True to the synchronic approach, Radcliffe-Brown considered firstly marriage a "rearrangement of social structures" whereby "certain existing relationships, in most societies, those of the bride to her family, are changed" (Radcliffe-Brown 1950:43). The second important aspect is the acquisition by the husband and his kin of "certain rights in relation to his wife and the children she bears" (Radcliffe-Brown 1950:50). Thirdly, marriage should be considered "not simply as a union between a man and a woman" but "an alliance between two families or bodies of kin" (Radcliffe-Brown 1950:51). Nowhere does Radcliffe-Brown stress the importance of economic exchanges at marriage to the necessity of launching and giving the means of support to a new socio-economic unit grafted onto the social body. This observation is raised only in passing and set aside in favour of its symbolic aspects; "it is necessary to recognize that whatever economic importance some of these transactions may have, it is their symbolic aspect that we chiefly have to consider" (Radcliffe-Brown 1950:48).

Marriage is considered by Lévi-Strauss an exchange of women between groups of men (Barnes 1971:151). The notion of the exchange (of women) or reciprocity lies at the basis of the "universal form" of marriage (Lévi-Strauss 1969:143 in Barnes 1971:144). Because of its simple reciprocity mechanism, cross-cousin marriage (marriage between children of siblings of different sex) is considered the "elementary formula of exchange" (Lévi-Strauss 1969:129, 144 in Barnes 1971:148). Parallel cousin marriage (marriage between children of siblings of the same sex), which oftentimes takes place within the extended family, is alien to this kind of approach and Lévi-Strauss tries to prove, unconvincingly, that it "cannot take place without upsetting the exchange process" (Lévi-Strauss 1969:112 in Barnes 1971:148).

Sir Edmund Leach tried to define marriage as embodying a "bundle of rights" ranging from the "legitimation of offspring, access to the spouse's sexuality, labour and property and the setting up of affinal alliances between persons and between groups" (Leach 1955 in Barnard & Good 1984:89).

Despite the pessimistic assessment of contemporary theory that it is questionable "whether there is in fact a definable, cross-cultural phenomenon in the first place" (Barnard & Good 1984:90), I shall attempt to propose a definition to serve as a point of departure for the ensuing discussion. *Marriage in historical and contemporary society* (in which the socialization of children is entrusted to the kin group and genetic sex selection is not practiced) *may be defined as the socially acknowledged union between two or more individuals, generally but not necessarily of different sexes, to form and manage the elementary cohesive unit of a group which must be coherent with other existing units within the social group, to most of which the procreation, education and socialization of children for the continuity of that society, is entrusted.* In other words, marriage is the process through which the social structure renews itself. Marriage does not necessarily entail procreation as it is seen as producing an addition to the social group, not to the species.

The initial steps in the formation of a marriage alliance are the negotiations for the choice of spouses, which take into account, but not necessarily conform to, the limits set by traditional rules, the wedding ceremony and attendant economic exchanges between spouses and/or their kin groups, and the post-marital residence of the new couple.

The most widespread rules applying to the choice of spouses are those of *exogamy* which define the group of close kin relations within which Ego should not marry, and those of *endogamy* defining the limits of the kinship or social group within which Ego should marry (Barnard & Good 1984:91). In the ensuing discussion we shall see how, in the case of barbarian society, the traditional rules of exogamy were 'manipulated' by religious or political institutions for socio-political reasons. There are 'rules' concerning *preferential* choices of the kin category to which the spouse should belong; however, they are almost never *prescriptive* in that exceptions are quite frequent.

Wedding ceremonies are characterized by traditional symbolism and they entail material or symbolic exchanges between spouses and their groups. The main economic exchanges are *bridewealth*, according to which the bridegroom or his kin group offer wealth to the bride's group to compensate for the "rights to her labour, sexual services, or offspring...also provides the bride's family with the wherewithal to obtain brides for their own sons" (Barnard & Good 1984:115). *Dowry* flows in the opposite direction in that it is an economic contribution from the bride's father or kin group to the new couple or the bride herself. In addition to these main forms of exchange there are other ones such as *bride service* which involves labour prestations on the part of the bridegroom or his kinsmen to the bride's kin group, presents to the bride after the wedding to acknowledge her virginity, such as the *morning gift* which was widespread among Germanic tribes. Furthermore, bridewealth and dowry may exist simultaneously in that bridewealth may be reciprocated by the bride's kin group with a consistent dowry; there is also the possibility that bridewealth may not be given to the bride's kin but destined to make up the initial economic basis of the new couple. Because they are subject to the influx of the market's economic vagaries, as will be noted also in the case of the populations under study, bridal gifts change faster than the jural and symbolic aspects of weddings.

In some simple societies, probably including Germanic ones, marriage by elopement or abduction was made recourse to by young people in canonical relationships for which, however, marriage negotiations had either failed or not taken place, or sometimes to bypass marriage payments. This is not to say that this kind of marriage was traditionally approved, but it was very easy to offer and accept reparatory action and obtain forgiveness from the girl's kin.

The bridal couple's choice of residence is also important both from a political and economic aspect. The possible choices are described in anthropological jargon as *virilocal*, when the new couple resides with the bridegroom's kin, *uxorilocal*, when residence is with the bride's kin, *neolocal*, when residence is independent of both groups, *avunculocal*, when choice of residence is with the bride's father's brother, *duolocal* when spouses live separately, *ambilocal* where choice can be indifferently with the bride's or bridegroom's kin (Barnard & Good 1984:78-81).

Finally, the cohesiveness of the married couple is protected by rules of adultery restricting non-marital sex by both spouses.

We have not, so far, considered *parallel cousin marriage*, i.e. marriage between children of siblings of the same sex, generally brothers or close patrilateral male cousins. Contrary to Lévi-Strauss's contention that parallel cousin marriage upsets the reciprocity pattern (see above), parallel cousin marriage is widespread among agro-pastoral populations in the Middle East, North and East Africa. In his noted ethnography of the Basseri of South Persia, Fredrik Barth pointed out the prevalence of "cousin marriage" which produced a "higher proportion of patrikin, and especially agnates, present within the camp than other kinsmen" (Barth

1961:65). This type of marriage is improperly termed 'endogamous', as it is no more so than cross-cousin marriage, a term which has become accepted in anthropology. For Barth the "high frequency of endogamy within the camp [implies] a high degree of general close-kin marriage and close-knit kinship unity" (Barth 1961:35). Pierre Bourdieu, who did fieldwork among the Berbers of the Atlas, pointed out the pivotal role of brothers for structural cohesion among those agro-pastoralists and at the same time the fact that frequent lineage segmentation occurs between brothers "especially since they are likely to have divergent property interests. Parallel cousin marriage unites the offspring of these brothers and thus constitutes 'the ideological resolution, sometimes realised in practice, of this contradiction'(Bourdieu 1977:64)" (Barnard & Good 1984:168).

During the course of fieldwork with Hadendowa, Beni Amer and Rashaida in eastern Sudan, I ascertained that these social groups followed the rule of endogamy in that they married mostly within their close kin group. The closeness of marriages is such that affinal kin is indistiguishable from agnatic kin in that mothers are patrilateral kin as well as fathers (Ausenda 1995:23). The percentage of close cousin marriages is quite high or about 75 percent among Hadendowa (Ausenda 1987:196) reaching up to 90 percent and more among Beni Amer (Ausenda n.d.).

Close agnatic marriage should be kept in mind as the probable preferred pattern of Germanic populations before and during the early period of their settling in the Roman Empire as will be discussed below.

Influence of kinship in other domains

We have seen that kinship underlies several social institutions such as marriage, inheritance, succession and other jural areas. Even religion in simple societies reflects kinship links in that often ritual functions are invested in the head of the extended family.

One important feature of kinship is that its model can be extended to relations between groups. In discussing genealogies it has been rightly observed that these apply solely "when [one intends] to portray real or imaginary individuals" (Barnard & Good 1984:8). In other words genealogies should not be applied to groups, because groups as a whole, even when related, are linked by more complex paths than can be reproduced in simple genalogies. Nevertheless, reputable anthropologists, e.g. Siegfried Nadel (1943), have used genealogical diagrams to show the purported relationship between clans or clan sections. In fact, when talking to native informants, one realizes that the genealogical model is used to express their relative seniority and closeness, in that they may be 'brothers', i.e. issued of ancestors who were legendary brothers, or more distant relatives. In the 'genealogical' diagram of the relationships between sections of the dominant clan among Beni Amer, the ruling section appears as senior, whilst other sections are related but at a junior level (Nadel 1945:93).

Kinship was a primary legitimizing factor in the succession to rulership, and marriage among ruling houses was used, well into this century, to seal and legitimize alliances between nations. This was one of the main 'functions' of kings and princes and it is the decline of this function that has brought about the world-wide crisis of monarchy.

The previous discussion alerts us to the traces of kin-related phenomena in the texts and laws related to the ancient populations we are about to discuss.

2. KINSHIP AND MARRIAGE AMONG THE VISIGOTHS

Sources

It is obviously impossible to attempt to retrace through written documents the genealogical method of obtaining kinship relationships and terminology for the population under study here. In fact Visigothic genealogies are scarce and they serve mainly the purpose of legitimizing a ruler by attesting his descent from an antecedent hero or demi-god rather than portraying the actual 'horizontal' relationships between spouses and their kin.

However, the surviving laws, if properly examined, can give either directly or by implication, an idea of the workings of kinship and marriage among Germanic populations. In addition to the laws, we are fortunate in possessing substantial fragments of Wulfila's (AD 318-383) (Heather & Matthews 1991:152, no.45) translation of the New Testament and minor fragments of the Old Testament (Migne 1848:461 ff.).

The laws give us an insight into the jural relations of Germanic populations including, in varying proportions in the law codes of the various Germanic nations, kinship relations. Wulfila's translation of the Bible gives us a linguistic insight into Gothic kinship terminology, an important one at that because of the close relationship of the Gothic language with other Germanic ones whose texts have come down to us. Furthermore Wulfila's Gothic is probably the most ancient and complete Germanic text to have reached us.

The Visigoths were among the earliest populations to settle in the Roman Empire since their first arrival to settle as a group within the eastern *limes* dates back to the second half of the fourth century (Heather & Matthews 1991:135). As a result they were among the most 'acculturated' among 'barbarian' groups. This is immediately apparent when we pick up the *Leges Visigothorum* and, leafing through them, we note that there are very few which refer to customary law, especially concerning kinship relations and marriage. This is probably because these institutions had been rendered less important by sedentarization and the increasing importance of landed wealth, which required written transactions. These had pushed customary law, mostly concerned with movable wealth, into the background. In fact, prior to sedentarization, land was generally considered the common property of the tribe, clan or kin group rather than individuals. To put it succinctly, the *Leges Visigothorum* which have come down to us intact, are the most 'romanized', both in language and contents, of the laws of Germanic nations.

The earliest Visigothic laws were collected and written down during the reign of Euric in the year 469 at the earliest, or some time before 481 at the latest (Zeumer 1902:xiii). Subsequent kings revised the laws but substantially kept the Eurician code intact until King Chindaswinth and his son Recceswinth had the whole code 'modernized', revised and re-written to be issued in the year 654 (Zeumer 1902:xiv). His successor Wamba only added a few laws, but Erwig, who came to the throne in 680, decided to renew the complete body of Visigothic law. The revised law was issued in 681 (Zeumer 1902:xv).

Erwigs' successor Egica (687-702) took up the matter of Visigothic legislation in 693 deciding to revise it further. The revision consisted of adding new laws, criticizing some of those issued by Erwig and in some cases reinstating previous ones which had been abolished by his predecessor Erwig (Zeumer 1902:xv-xvi).

One can well understand that the various revisions and changes subverted the whole text so that only few traces of the early customary laws survived in the final version. In conclusion, we can only use the revised *Leges Visigothorum* as they have come down to us, to ascertain the possible presence of traces of previous customary laws bearing on kinship and marriage, which were probably written down in the earliest version of the Eurician code.

Only a few pages, some two dozen out of perhaps two hundred, have been found of the original version of Euric's code. In addition to these few remaining pages, it is generally held that the *Lex Baiwariorum* used the Eurician code as a source (Zeumer 1902:xvii). However, the *Leges Baiwariorum* are relatively late (von Schwind 1926:180-1). Another possible source are the *Leges Alamannorum* which have been dated to a period in which the Merovingian kingdom was *not* at the peak of its power, hence the second half of the seventh or the beginning of the eighth century (Eckhardt 1966:10).

The Langobards were also one of the Germanic nations which, in all probability, took much from early Gothic legislation. They had followed the Goths into Pannonia and thence into Italy only fifteen years after the latter had been conquered by the Byzantines. Furthermore, it is very likely that Langobards were converted to Arian Christianity by Gothic missionaries and that, if not their customary laws, at least the priorities in their legislative corpus may have been influenced by Gothic codes.

The methodology I shall follow will be to examine Langobardic law which is rich in aspects of kinship and marriage and, having highlighted them on this basis, compare them with similar ones among the laws of the *Alamanni* and *Baiwarii* and then with the surviving laws of the Visigoths to ascertain whether one can infer the previous existence of similar customs among the early Visigoths from traces or survivals in their late legislation.

Gothic kinship terminology

Terms for kinship relations can be found in the dictionary to Wulfila's translation of the Old and New Testaments (Migne 1848:1243-1510). Taken out of context, because obviously Wulfila only gave them 'biological' meanings (cf. Heather & Matthews 1991:159), their interest is mainly linguistic. However, they may be helpful in explaining the meaning of kinship-connected operations in Germanic laws which may use some of these terms in compound nouns.

Gothic[4]	**English**
ik	Ego
fader	father
aithei	mother
brothar	brother
svistar	sister
sunus	son
barn	child
dauhtar	daughter
avo	grandfather or grandmother
atta	father (great grandfather)
samakuns	*cognatus* (kinsman)
nithjis	nephew
nithjo	*fem. germana*
gadiliggs	*consobrinus* (cousin)
qens	wife (*queen*)

Other words connected with marriage or descent:

gabaur thi-vaurd	genealogy
wadi	gage
fadreins	*genus*, progeny
bruths	bride, daughter-in-law
bruth-faths	bridegroom
frauja	master
heiva-frauja	*pater familias*
frasts	male child
bloth	blood
gumeìns	*masculus*
thiuda	clan, nation (hence *thiudans* = chief)
thiudisko	'in the gentile manner' (adv.)
kunni	kin
knoda	progeny
liugan	marry

[4]   For a linguistic treatment of the author's interpretation of the terminology in Wulfila's translation of the Bible see the discussion on page 181, this vol.

liuga	marriage
magaths	virgin, maid
mavi	female child
sibja	*cognatio*
sibis	sib
vair	*vir*, man
viduvo	widow
faiho	livestock

We are missing the all important terms for paternal and maternal uncles and aunts and those for affines, except for the term for wife, *qens*, and we have only the terms of description but not those of address.

We know from the laws that the paternal uncle was the most important next of kin after the father. In the *Leges Alamannorum* XL (see Eckhardt 1966:99) *De patricidiis et fratricidiis*, the *patruus* comes right after the father and before the brother. In Rothari's edict the paternal uncle is called *barbas* or *barbanus* in its latinized form. The term is mentioned in Ro. 163 (Bluhme 1868:81) as referring to one of the closest relatives against whom someone might plot death. The closest relatives mentioned in that law, with the paternal uncle, were brothers and parallel cousins, i.e., the closest male agnates beyond the father.

The term *barbas* is again referred to in Ro. 164 as applying to a relative who could falsely accuse a nephew or cousin of being illegitimate, for purposes of inheritance and perhaps succession. Customarily the *barbas* stood in his brother's line of inheritance and became the heir if his brother's sons were disqualified by illegitimacy. In the line of inheritance, according to the same law, immediately after the *barbas* came parallel cousins, i.e. the *barbas'* sons.

The term is mentioned once more in Liutprand's law 145 (Bluhme 1868:172) which provided that if a niece died "*in capillis*", literally 'in her hair', i.e. while still a spinster, and an "altercation" originated about who should inherit her estate, provision was made for her *barbas*, under whose guardianship, *mundio*, she was, to inherit entirely her portion.

The *barbas* was a very important relative, next only to the father and brothers both in rights of inheritance and rights of guardianship over females. The importance of the paternal uncle is confirmed also in the *Leges Visigothorum. Lex* III, 1. 7. (Zeumer 1902:130) entrusts responsibility to the paternal uncle to decide about the marriage of nephews or nieces in case their father and mother died: "*tunc patruus de coniunctione eorum habeat potestatem*". The *patruus* is mentioned again in the same law as the person who, with the brothers, should consult with close kin about the possibility of accepting the request of a suitor.

This is in tune with kinship relationships among social groups with patrilineal descent where, in general, the father's brother is the most important kin next to the father.

Concerning what we now know of Gothic kinship terminology, this is already a considerable level of information which should help us place kinship operations in context. I shall discuss below a very complete list of Latin kinship terms in Visigothic law, but we shall never know, except for those derived from Wulfila's translation of the Bible, whether there were corresponding terms in Gothic.

Distinction between agnates and affines

This distinction should be highlighted as it marks a basic split in kinship terminology for most systems. The Langobards, whose succession was based on patrilineages, distinguished between agnates, i.e. relatives within the patrilineage, and affines, i.e. relatives on the maternal side. Corresponding terms have come down to us through the laws in Rothari's edict. Ro. 247 (Bluhme 1848:60) mentions the *gafan*, or agnate, as a relative on whom an impounding action could be carried out insofar as he was a "close relative and co-heir"; Ro. 362 (Bluhme 1868:84) allowed a plaintiff to choose the defendant's oath-takers "both from his agnates or his *gamahalos*, i.e., his relatives by contract (*confabulatus*) [sic]". Thus *gamahalos* were the affines, i.e., those who became relatives as a result of a marriage contract.

The importance of relatives as *sacramentales*, 'oath-takers', emerges also in the laws of other Germanic nations. *Lex Baiwariorum* VIII, 15 (von Schwind 1926:360) provides that a free man who, having become engaged to a girl, dismissed her against the law, should pay a compensation of 24 *solidi* to her parents and swear with 12 oath-takers *de suo genere nominatos*, 'chosen among his agnatic kin' (affines in this case are not mentioned), that he did not dismiss her because of envy for her parents nor for any other crime, but because he chose another one *propter amorem*, only because he had fallen in love with her (not for her wealth).

Gradually the veracity of oath-takers was recognized to be questionable. *Lex Visigothorum* II, 1. 23 (Zeumer 1902:70) states that the judge should ask for written proofs "so that one should not come easily [to taking] an oath", considered necessary only when he should not find any written documents or proofs". *Lex Visigothorum* II, 4. 2 (Zeumer 1902:95) makes it mandatory for witnesses to swear, while *Lex Visigothorum* II, 4. 13 (Zeumer 1902:104) forbids brothers, sisters, paternal and maternal uncles and aunts, nephews, nieces and both agnatic and affinal cousins to bear witness in a trial against a third party, "unless per chance those relatives of the same kin group should have a litigation amongst themselves".

Preferential marriage

One of the main characteristics of agro-pastoral populations to this day is their high degree of endogamy, i.e. marriage with close relatives within the lineage or corporate group (Ausenda 1995:23). In fact the great majority of present-day agro-pastoralists are characterized by unilinear descent and in most cases the paternal line is the privileged one. At the time of the invasion, the Langobards had a patrilineal descent system. This is shown beyond any reasonable doubt by the genealogies written in the prologues to their laws and in their histories. That they had a segmentary lineage system cannot be established beyond doubt, but is highly probable. The Langobardic term *fara*, attested to by contemporaries as meaning 'genealogy' or 'lineage', referred to the corporate groups by which the Langobards were organized when they migrated into the Italian peninsula and for some time thereafter (Ausenda 1995:35).

The high degree of endogamy found among agro-pastoralists may be dictated by economic considerations connected to their subsistence base which depended largely on the husbandry and management of livestock. Ethnographic research among agro-pastoral populations has shown that the management of a herd is entrusted to the sons of agnates who perform the various phases of the work in common. Common interest in keeping the herd together, so as to reduce the amount of work and risk, is a powerful conditioning force towards close kin marriage.

Fredrik Barth showed that FBD marriage was preferential among many nomadic pastoralists in the Middle East, especially among the Indo-European populations leading a transhumant existence between the sea shore and the Iranian mountains. Among the Kurds, for instance, the frequency of FBD marriage ranged as high as fifty percent (Barth 1954:167). Not only do agnatic parallel cousins have first rights to marriageable girls, but they are further motivated by a considerable reduction in a normally fairly high bride price (Barth 1954:167). This is a further indication that such close marriages are favoured for socioeconomic reasons.

Ian Cunnison reported that, among the Baggara Arabs of southwestern Sudan, up to fifty percent of first marriages took place within the corporate group (Cunnison 1966:89). The incentives to marriages within the corporate group are: lower bridewealth, one-third less than that required of an outside suitor, a simpler wedding ceremony, and finally the fact that a man who marries in the same camp retains for the use of his household the produce of his wife's cattle as well as his own. If he marries a woman from another encampment, his wife's cattle are not with him because her brothers retain them in their own camp (Cunnison 1966:91-3).

Ian Cunnison classified preferential marriage among the Baggara as follows: "The closest is father's brother's son, after this mother's brother's son and father's sister's son are equal, so long as they belong to the girl's own *surra* [encampment]; no special preference is given to mother's sister's son" (Cunnison 1966:91). FBD marriage is also preferential among the Libyan Bedouin, to the extent that a male parallel cousin has pre-emptive rights on his cousin, but a different bridegroom can only propose his candidacy after her paternal parallel cousin's consent (Peters 1960:44).

As far as the Langobards are concerned, practically no direct clue is available in their laws as to whether they had preferential marriage and whether this was with a parallel cousin. The adoption of Christianity must have caused considerable changes to occur with respect to pre-existing marriage customs about which practically nothing is known directly.

Marriage prohibitions

The early existence of preferential marriage among close kin can be inferred from later laws forbidding those marriages considered 'illicit' and 'incestuous.'

In Rothari's edict the only prohibition, mentioned in Ro. 185, is against marriage with a (widowed) step-mother or (widowed) sister-in-law or—for the widower—with a step-daughter; however, there is no specific law against close kin marriage, i.e. close cousins. Perhaps this is an indication that, until three generations after Langobardic settlement in Italy, endogamous marriages were still practiced.

On the other hand an 'early' instance of marriage prohibitions among the *Leges Baiwariorum* (VII. I; von Schwind 1926:317-8), considered by some to have been copied from the Eurician code written during the second half of the fifth century, forbids—considering them 'incestuous'—marriage with step-mother, step-daughter, sister-in-law (levirate), mother-in-law, daughter-in-law, brother's daughter, sister's daughter, wife's sister (sororate). The penalty imposed on the illicit couple was to be 'separated' and lose their estate to the royal fisc.

A law among the *Leges Alamannorum* has almost the same wording and the same penalty, but stresses also prohibition against parallel cousin marriage, *"filii fratrum, filii sororum inter se nulla praesumptione iungantur"* (XXXIX; Eckhardt 1966:99).

In the later *Leges Visigothorum* Chindaswinth substituted the law of the previous Eurician code with a wider prohibition (III, 5. 1; Zeumer 1902:119) which excluded from marriage persons "from the father's or mother's descent, and from the grandfather or grandmother or the wife's parents, also the father's wife or widow or left by his relatives...thus no one shall be permitted to pollute in a libidinous way, or desire in marriage close blood [relations] until the sixth degree of descent". The law exempts those persons who, "with the order and consent of the princes, before the law [was enacted] should have adopted this [form of] marriage". Again more than a hint that close-kin marriages were practiced in the early days and gradually prohibited by increasingly strict laws.

The *Leges Visigothorum* (IV, 1. 1 to IV, 1. 6; Zeumer 1902:171-2) give a clear and detailed list of the kin relations contained in each of the six prohibited degrees, and an exhaustive (Latin) kinship terminology is applied to each one.[5]

IV, 1. 1
De primi gradus natura.
Primo gradu continentur superiori linea: pater, mater; inferiori: filius, filia, quibus nulli alie persone iunguntur.

---

[5] For a diagram of forbidden degrees and a discussion of their relevance see *Current Issues and Future Directions*, the chapter on 'Kinship and Marriage' (pp. 488-495, this vol.).

IV, 1. 2
De secundi gradus adfinitate.

Secundo gradu continentur superiori linea: avus, avia; inferiori: nepos, neptes; transversa: frater et soror. Que persone duplicantur; avus enim et avia tam ex patre quam ex matre, nepos, neptis tam ex filio quam ex filia, frater et soror tam ex patre quam ex matre accipiuntur. Que persone sequentibus quoque gradibus similiter pro substantia eorum, qui in quoquo gradu consistunt, ipso ordine duplicantur.

Et ste persone in secundo gradu ideo duplices appellantur, quia duo avi, et paternus et maternus. Item duo genera nepotum sunt, sive ex filio, sive ex filia procreati. Frater et soror ex transverso veniunt, id est frater patris aut frater matris, qui aut patruus aut avunculus nominantur; qui et ipsi hoc ordine duplicantur.

IV, 1. 3
De tertii gradus parentela.

Tertio gradu veniunt supra: proavus, proavia; infra: pronepos, proneptis; ex oblico: fratris sororisque filius, filia, patruus et amita; id est patris frater et soror, avunculus et matertera, id est patris frater et soror.

IV, 1. 4
De quarti gradus consanguinitate.

Quarto gradu veniunt supra: abavus, abavia; infra: abnepos, abneptis; ex oblico: fratris et sororis nepos, neptis, frater patruelis, soror patruelis, id est patrui filius filiave, consubrinus et consubrina, id est avunculi et matertere filius, filia, amitinus, amitina, id est amite filius, filia, itemque consubrini qui ex duobus sororibus nascuntur. Quibus adcrescit patruus magnus, amita magna, id est avi paterni frater et soror, avunculus magnus, matertera magna, id est avie, tam paterne quam materne frater et soror.

Hic plus exponi opus non est, quan lectio ista declarat.

IV, 1. 5
De quinti gradus origine.

Quinto gradu veniunt supra quidem: atavus, atavia; infra: adnepus, adneptis; ex oblico: fratris et sororis pronepos, proneptis, fratres patrueles, sorores patrueles, amitini, amitine, consubrini, consubrine filius, filia, proprius subrinus, subrina, id est patrui magni, amite magne, avunculi magni, matertere magne filius, filia. His adcrescunt propatruus, proamita, hi sunt proavi paterni frater et soror, proavunculus, promatertera, hi sunt proavie paterne materneque frater et soror proavique materni.

Hec species nec aliis gradibus, quam scripta est, nec aliis vocabulis declarari potest.

IV, 1. 6
De sexti gradus extremitate.

Sextu gradu veniunt supra: tritavus, tritavia; infra: trinepos, trineptis; ex oblico: fratris et sororis abnepus [sic], abneptis, fratres patrueles, sorores patrueles, amitini, amitine consubrini, consubrine, patrui magni, amite magne, avunculi magni, matertere magne nepos, neptis, proprioris subrini filius, filia, qui consubrini appellantur. Quibus ex latere adcrescunt: propatrui, proamite, proavunculi, promatertere filius, filia, adpatruus, adamita, hi sunt abavi paterni frater et soror, abavunculus, abmatertera, hi sunt abavie paterne materneque frater et soror abavique materni.

Hec quoque explanari amplius non possunt, quam auctor ipse disseruit.

IV, 1. 7

De personis septimi generis, que legibus non tenentur.

Septimo gradu qui sunt cognati recta linea supra infraque propriis nominibus non appellantur; se ex transversa linea continentur fratris sororisve adnepotes, adneptes, consubrini, consubrine filii filieque.

Successionis autem idcirco gradus septem constituti sunt, quia ulterius per rerum natura nec nomina inveniri nec vita succedentibus propagari potest.

One may note that the sixth degree is considered the 'end' of forbidden alliances, at the same time the seventh degree is the last for 'succession', i.e. inheritance, because "by the very nature of things neither names can be found nor life can be extended to successors".

Langobardic laws concerning forbidden marriages also became stricter over time. Liutprand 33 (Bluhme 1848:123-4) forbade marriage with the widow of a cousin, but no further prohibitions were reflected in the laws. We know, however, that more extended prohibitions were made compulsory by the Church.

Indeed, from a letter addressed by Pope Zacharias to a Theodore, archdeacon in Pavia during King Liutprand's reign, one may infer that among Langobards it was still customary to marry between relatives linked in the fourth degree, that is, if the path was 'oblique', having the same grandfather (see above). On the strength of a similar permission granted to the Angles a century and a half before by Pope Gregory the Great, Theodore had requested the pope's permission to allow such marriages also among Langobards. This, however, was refused on the basis that it had been permitted to "rude people and having come to Christ recently", whereas the Langobards were to be treated as those who were "raised from the cradle within the Holy Catholic Church" (*M.G.H.*, *Epistolae* III, page 709, n.18; Italia Pontificia vi/1:174, n.3 in Bertolini 1960:477 and in Bullough 1969:323).

This shows that both Church and State were interested in forbidding close kin marriages. Their common concern becomes clear when one bears in mind the recognized difficulty the Church had, from the fourth century onwards, in expanding into the countryside, "because the world of peasants felt Christianity to be narrower, more restricted, less rich and, finally, less responsive to their spiritual requirements" (Manselli 1982:83). We are also told that "...the masses, especially the rural ones, were not, if only at very low levels, Christian" (Manselli 1982:84). In the case of the Visigothic kingdom in particular, "the problem of the eradication of paganism was not considered by the ecclesiastical hierarchy a pastoral, but a political, a policy problem, affecting directly the *respublica christiana*, and as such represented a question of public order" (Sotomayor 1982:662). Until then, in fact, "ecclesiastical organization was completely urban, legislation referred directly to the faithful of urban communities" (Sotomayor 1982:641). Manselli also noted that "resistance to Christianity was born from an intertwining of ethnic, family, in the sense of the extended family, and political problems" (1982:104) and, in the case of the Saxon stubborn resistance to the influx of Christianity that "it is not less interesting that [in trying to bend the Saxons to Christianity] *marriage relations were regulated* [in the *Capitulatio de partibus Saxoniae*] and sacrifices at water springs were condemned (Manselli 1982:97) [italics mine].

In conclusion, the strenuous effort to penetrate the countryside entailed a long-drawn battle against traditional religion, whose vehicle was the kin group, and substituting the authority of the elders of the kin group with that of a religious elder, the *presbyteros*. At the same time the king's rule was undermined by revolts on the part of the most powerful kin groups, clans or sections, whose conspiracies and murders menaced the power of the state (Diaz, this volume, p. 335). Thus Church and State became allies in trying to do away with the political power of extended kin groups utilizing all manners of impositions. One of the most effective among them was to destroy their cohesiveness by prohibition of close kin marriage.

Widowhood

Among Visigothic laws (III, 5. 1; Zeumer 1902:159), we have just seen the prohibition against marrying a widow of the father or of any relative, and in the *Leges Baiwariorum* and *Alamannorum* of marrying an (obviously widowed) stepmother or sister-in-law.

A more synthetic provision concerning the forceful remarriage of a widow is envisaged in *Lex Baiwariorum* (VIII, 7; von Schwind 1926:356-7). It condemns whoever "abducted" a widow and "forced her out of her dwelling" to a penalty of 80 *solidi* to the widow plus 40 to the fisc. This was a considerable penalty when one bears in mind that blood money for the murder of a free man was also 80 *solidi* in addition to an equal penalty payable to the authorities.

The provision for the remarriage of widows sheds further light on the original mechanisms of marriage and the changes which took place with sedentarization and christianization. A basic fact here was the economic disadvantage to lineage members when a widow left the lineage, partly because of her bride-price being a fraction, at most one half, of that paid when she was acquired by the lineage in the first place, partly because she took her wealth with her.

In fact, according to Ro. 182 and 183 (Bluhme 1848:43-4), when a widow remarried outside her deceased husband's lineage, she could take with her her *faderfio*, the so-called 'father's wealth' or dowry, and *morgingab*, her husband's bridal gift, which could be as high as one fourth of his estate. Against such losses of wealth, her deceased husband's agnates stood to earn only half her brideprice in addition to her guardianship fee. This was the reason for which they would try not to let her remarry outside the lineage.

During the early period these problems were allayed by the customary permission given to members of a lineage to take the widow of a deceased lineage member as their wife. Indeed Ro. 185 (Bluhme 1868:44) which forbids levirate (marriage with a deceased brother's widow) allows one to infer that it was common practice until then.

The close connection between levirate and widowhood is further proved by the sequential order of laws regulating widowhood and prohibiting levirate in

Rothari's edict. In fact Ro. 185, which declares levirate to be illegal follows closely behind Ro. 182 which sets the rules for a widow's remarriage. Ro. 182 transcended customary law in that it allowed a widow to remarry even without the consent of her deceased husband's relatives. If her deceased husband agnates failed to agree to her remarriage, they were forced to lose her *mundio*, guardianship, which reverted to her own kin or, if none were left, to the king's court.

The matter is further defined by Ro. 183. This law provided that the woman must be "delivered...by hand the same way as she was delivered to her previous husband". This meant that she must be married by a formal act so as to prevent illegal unions or concubinage with males in the deceased husband's lineage or corporate group.

As long as the lineage functioned as a corporate unit, the widow's choice for another husband within the lineage may have been fairly wide. After seventyfive years of sedentarization, the lineage may have lost some of its earlier strength. Thus the choice of a new husband within the lineage or corporate group became gradually narrower. From this stemmed the need for corrective legislation which went against customary law. This happened also because the social structure to which customary norms applied had changed in the meantime.

In 723 King Liutprand issued laws Li. 33 and 34 (Bluhme 1868:123-4) extending the prohibition against remarrying to the widows of first cousins or godparents. It seems that these laws implemented the decisions of a council held in Rome in 721 under the auspices of Pope Gregory II (Bertolini 1960:459). The probable reason for these two laws was that, since levirate had been forbidden by Ro. 185, families were trying to keep a widow's wealth within the boundaries of the close kin group by having her remarry a first cousin, or a godparent. In fact, the latter were probably not only relatives in a religious context, but also close kin, hence relatives in forbidden degrees concerning marriage.

In conclusion, the law concerning marriage prohibitions treats a widow as though, having married into a kin group, she herself had become part of the kin group, hence she must be forbidden to marry within the kin group of her deceased husband.

Incest

We have discussed prohibitions of marriage which, although defined as incestuous in some laws, are not incestuous by our standards. According to these, incest entails sexual intercourse, excluding that between husband and wife, between members of the nuclear family. Among simple societies in general, incest is not punished by human authority, because kin groups are autonomous to a large extent and not accountable to an outside authority on 'moral' infringements within the family. With the advent of civilization the punishment of intra-family crimes, beginning with murders within the nuclear family, gradually became the responsibility of the state.

While incest, in our meaning, is not mentioned in other Germanic laws, it is touched upon, even though indirectly, in the sense that it forbids sexual intercourse by father and son with the same concubine, in the *Lex Visigothorum* (III, 5. 5; Zeumer 1902:163-4). The law referred to mentions the previously discussed laws on 'incest' due to marriage within the forbidden degrees, and then goes on to condemn 'incest':

> ...however, since it appears to be no lesser crime to be stained in the paternal or fraternal bed, we add to the provision that none of his relatives may presume to fornicate with the concubine of his father or brother or with her, whether free or slave, whom he should know his father or brother to have fornicated with even once nor the father should pollute with the obscenity of rape one 'adulterated' by his son.

The penalty was the transfer of all the offender's estate, while still alive, to his heirs, and his permanent exile.

Wedding negotiations and betrothal

The engagement of a free man with a free woman must have been an elaborate affair because, in the cases in which marriage was not with close kin, it represented an alliance between the bridegroom and the bride's lineage. Despite the few glimpses of these ceremonies allowed to us by the dry prose of the legal texts, we gather the impression that the ritual preceding the wedding involved fairly lengthy negotiations. These went on for a matter of months with the participation of many lineage members as witnesses or guarantors to the transactions.

Among contemporary agro-pastoralists wedding negotiations are preceded by a formal request by the bridegroom's father or senior agnatic relative to the bride's father (Ausenda n.d.). This is discussed at length with all agnatic relatives both by men and women so as to be sure that no one else has priority to the bride's hand and that all close agnatic kin may be happy with the choice and no one might be unfriendly to the prospective bridegroom's family, a situation which would engender an unwanted crisis in the lineage or corporate group. In case of refusal by a relative of the bride, the bridegroom's father uses diplomacy and gives him presents to obtain his permission. In most cases this is finally granted, but in a few, of the order of one percent among Hadendowa, the relative remains adamant and the wedding does not take place. It is quite probable that some similar approach went on among Germanic populations before and after their sedentarization within the Empire. A mention of such negotiations may be found in the *Leges Visigothorum*; *Lex Visigothorum* III, 1. 7. provides that, in case of the father's death, a girl's *patruus* or her brothers should discuss with their next of kin "*si velit suscipere petitorem, ut aut communi voluntate iungantur, aut omnino iudicio denegetur*" ("if he should want to accept the suitor, so that they should be joined by common consent or he should be refused altogether through [their] judgement"). The procedure sounds entirely similar to the one described above for Beja tribes. However, we have no record of how these preliminaries were handled.

Considering the frequent mention in the history of Germanic populations of cases of kings requesting foreign princesses in marriage, it would seem that the initiative did indeed belong to the groom's family or lineage. From the *Historia Langobardorum* we know that the bridegroom was not supposed to be present at the negotiations, as the story of Authari accompanying the negotiators to the Bavarian court attests (*Historia Langobardorum,* III. 30), but we do not know the relationship between the negotiators and the prospective bridegroom.

In Rothari's edict the laws concerning marriage are enlightening as to the aspects of this important socioeconomic transaction. The pertinent ones are Ro.177 to Ro.184 included (Bluhme 1868:41-4).

Negotiations were of an economic nature and were brought to a final agreement between the bride's and the groom's families. This was made formal by a betrothal, an engagement ceremony, during which a contract was confirmed in front of witnesses or signed. The contract established the amount to be given as brideprice (Lang. *meta* or *metfio*, lit. 'wealth livestock', or more generally 'wealth'),[6] and may also have established the amount of dowry (Lang. *faderfio*, lit. 'father's livestock', or more generally 'father's wealth'), although this is not certain.

It is possible that the *morgingab*, literally 'gift of the morning [after]', was not established during the engagement negotiations. In fact, a later law by Liutprand, Li. 7 issued in 717 (Bluhme 1868:110), set down the procedure whereby the husband must show his relatives and friends "on another day", i.e. not on the wedding day nor the morning after, a written statement as to the amount he intended to give his wife in *morgingab*. Before Li. 7 *morgingab* was not normally the object of a written agreement.

The bridegroom's agreement to pay *meta* was guaranteed by a fidejussor, probably a wealthy elder among the bridegroom's next of kin. In fact Ro. 178 (Bluhme 1868:41) expressly allowed the guardian (Lang. *mundoald*) of a jilted bride to coerce a fidejussor to pay the agreed *meta*.

The betrothed were not present at the engagement ceremony. From the day of betrothal to the wedding day, the bridegroom was allowed (Ro. 178) a period of up to two years to fulfill his engagement, on penalty of losing both the *metfio* and the bride; after this period the bride's father was entitled to give her to someone else. Similarly *Lex Visigothorum* III, 1. 4 (Zeumer 1902:125-6) allowed a period of two years from the day of engagement to the wedding day; this could be extended by a further period of two years by "common consent" or because one "person should be absent out of necessity".

Ro. 179 foresaw the case that, during the engagement period, the bridegroom accused his betrothed of having been "adulterated". The law allowed the bride's relatives to "purify" her by means of an oath taken by twelve oath-takers. If one of the oath-takers failed, the girl was to be punished as an adulteress; if they all took the oath and "purified" her, the groom was obligated to take her as his wife; if he failed to do so, he must give her double the *metfio* he had promised.

---

6   For a linguistic treatment of the meaning of *meta* see discussion on pages 186-7, this vol.

In all likelihood, during the engagement period the betrothed never saw each other. This is borne out by the fact that Ro. 180 (Bluhme 1868:42) allowed the bridegroom to refuse his betrothed if she should turn out to be blind in both eyes, a disability which is fairly noticeable.

The *Leges Visigothorum* do not treat marriage negotiations in such detail. Two are concerned primarily with betrothal; these are III, 1. 2. and III, 1. 3. (Zeumer 1902:122-4). The first one confirms the higher authority of the father in the marriage negotiations in that, if a bride promised by her father should have gone against his will to someone whom she "wanted", they both were to be handed over with all their estates to the one who "*cum volumtatem patris sponsatam habuerat*", while her brothers or mother who consented to this "machination" should pay a penalty worth a pound of gold. The law was to be kept even if the father died before she had been 'given' in marriage. The second law mentioned establishes that even in the absence of a written agreement, the engagement ring and the promise given should in no way be violated and one party should not be permitted to change its mind without the consent of the other and, having provided for the dowry, the wedding celebration should be conducted.

The first law discussed asserts the father's customary authority in wedding negotiations, probably, as we shall see below, because he was customarily the 'owner' of the bride's *mundio*. The second law shows a desire on the part of the Visigothic lawgiver that the customary force of engagements may not be weakened by 'modern' changes in marriage customs.

Favourite season

There is always a season more appropriate to bridal negotiations and the ensuing wedding ceremony. The latter generally takes place during the yearly period of plenty which coincides with a season in which relaxation in the work for subsistence is possible, usually after harvest, when a population is primarily engaged in agriculture, or when pastoralists come together before scattering to take livestock to distant pastures. The periods most favourable for social gatherings and ceremonies are during the transitions between the cold and the hot season or viceversa. Quoting Ioan Lewis on the Somali:

> The favourite season for seeking a bride is the spring (*gu*) when, after the rains, water and pasture are abundant, and social life expands as people find themselves less heavily burdened with herding tasks. At this time of the year the two herding units— the nomadic hamlets and camel camps—are closer together than at any other period and the young camel herders drive their beasts close to the hamlets (Lewis 1962:12).

Among the Langobards, the traditional *gairethinx*, the warrior's assembly, took place at the beginning of spring. During this festive period, most of the Langobardic laws were approved and issued. It would seem that spring was also a likely choice for engagements and weddings.

Engagement ceremony

Among some agro-pastoralists, engagement does not involve an elaborate ceremony. When the bridegroom's father is informed that his request is accepted he visits the bride's family bringing gifts and food which he leaves with them (Ausenda n.d.). These are cooked and partaken of by the women and children in the bride's encampment. In fact, at the engagement ceremony, bride and groom do not come together and the festivity is a private one in the bride's encampment.

No description of the engagement ceremony can be found in the laws, but the fact that the engagement was transacted at the bride's father's residence leads one to believe that if there was a ceremony it may have been a 'private' one involving only the bride's relatives celebrating on whatever gifts the bridegroom's father and next of kin may have brought to the bride's family.

Wedding ceremony

On the wedding day a party with the *paranympha* and the *troctingi* (Ahistulf 15; see Bluhme 1868:201) went to fetch the bride from her household. The *paranympha* (the Germanic equivalent term is unknown) was the bride's lady-in waiting, in all probability she belonged to the bridegroom's lineage; the *troctingi*, literally 'escorts',[7] and possibly also jesters[8] were part of the wedding cortege. The presence of jesters at weddings is also found in contemporary ethnographic contexts and in particular among related European populations. Among the Serbs, weddings were attended by a jester who distributed the gifts brought by the bride to the members of the bridegroom's lineage; they made fun of the gifts, the recipients, and the effects the gifts would produce on them (Halpern 1958:196-8; Mijatovic 1914:62). Later, during the banquet, the jester made fun of everybody's contributions to the viands (Mijatovic 1914:62).

The wedding party led a war horse (Lang. *crosna*), as also related six centuries before by Tacitus concerning the *Germani* in general (*Germania* XVIII). The *crosna*, traditionally worth 20 *solidi* (Boretius 1868:868 - gloss: *crosna*) was the symbolic payment for the transfer of guardianship (Lang. *mundio*) from the bride's guardian (Lang. *mundoald*), generally her father or brother, to her husband. Now the father, or whoever was the bride's *mundoald* gave her her dowry (Lang. *faderfio*), which probably comprised also household goods and utensils, possibly loaded on an oxcart, as described by Tacitus for the earlier *Germani* (*Germania* XVIII), and the cortege made back for the bridegroom's paternal house where more ceremonies and festivities took place.

---

[7] For the etymology and the meaning of the term *troctingi* see the discussion on p. 187, this vol.

[8] The possible presence of jesters can be inferred by the meaning attributed to the term *troctingi* by a gloss in the *Liber Papiensis*, an eleventh-century commentary to Langobardic laws. This may mean that in the wedding cortege some of the 'escorts' were also jesters, as also attested in contemporary ethnographic examples.

On arrival at the bridegroom's house, the incumbent *mundoald* of the bride handed the *crosna* back to the bridegroom who was then supposed to give him a reciprocal gift, *launegild*, worth approximately 20 *solidi*, the value of the *crosna*. The bride's former *mundoald* now "handed over" the bride to the bridegroom. Ro. 183 (Bluhme 1868:43) was clear on the subject: "In fact, without the handing over [of the bride] we say that there is no certainty of anything". In other words, the handing over was the formal act validating a wedding. We do not know how long the festivities at the bride's and later at the bridegroom's house lasted. In all likelyhood their duration was proportional to the status and wealth of the parties involved. It would be interesting to compare these general remarks referring to Germanic weddings to mentions of wedding parties among the Goths.

Elopement and abduction

As discussed above (page 137), a less expensive alternative to the payment of bridal gifts and to the wedding ceremony is elopement. This may have been the case among Germanic societies because elopement is foreseen both in Langobardic and Visigothic law.

According to Ro. 188 (Bluhme 1868:45), whoever married a girl who had willingly eloped with him was liable to pay a penalty of 20 *solidi* for the offence deriving from the "unchaste treatment" of a woman (Lang. *anagrip*), in addition to 20 *solidi* to extinguish the feud. If the husband omitted to pay for the woman's guardianship (Lang. *mundio*) after elopement, he stood to lose all rights to her properties at her death. The total penalty corresponded to twice the average *meta*, but it may still have been convenient. In fact, no mention is made of the payment of a *morgingab*. The penalty increased considerably if the eloped woman had been previously promised to someone else. In this case her husband had to indemnify her previous betrothed by giving him twice the *meta* the jilted man had engaged himself to pay (Ro. 190). Li. 114 (Bluhme 1868:154) set a penalty also for the eloped woman: she should forfeit *meta* in case her husband died before having paid for her *mundio*.

The case was also foreseen that a girl could be abducted against her will (Ro. 191). The difference in penalty between elopement and abduction consisted in the payment of an extra composition of 900 *solidi*, a huge sum, one half to be given to the girl's relatives and one half to the king's court. In case that either elopement or abduction were simulated by her parents, possibly to free the girl from a previous less advantageous engagement, Ro. 192 (Bluhme 1868:46) decreed that the girl's relatives should indemnify her previous betrothed by compensating him with twice the value of the *meta* he was engaged to give.

The *Lex Visigothorum III, Titulus de raptu virginum vel viduarum* (Zeumer 1902:139 ff.) is much less lenient with a suitor who abducted a girl. Law III, 3. 1 punished with a penalty of one half of his estate anyone who abducted a woman who later happened to be freed before losing her chastity. According to law III, 3. 2, if the girl's parents succeeded in freeing her, her abductor must be delivered to the girl's parents and she should not be allowed to wed him under penalty of death for both. III, 3. 3 echoes Ro. 192 except that the penalty for the parents was to pay back to the jilted betrothed four times the 'price' he had paid for the girl (instead of twice according to Ro. 192). The time limitation for accusing the abductor of a virgin or a widow was 30 years; after this time "every accusation should lie dormant".

In conclusion, the Visigothic law, more 'modern' than the laws in Rothari's edict, did not condone elopement by mutual consent and was much harsher on individuals who abducted a girl to marry her, as it treated them as ordinary kidnappers. Since law and order had become the responsibility of the state, penalties against those who broke it became much more drastic than in earlier times when it was a matter of compromise between offenders and offended.

Post-marital residence

With regards to residence after marriage, indications in Langobardic legislation are fairly explicit. One may refer to Ahi. 15 issued in 755 (Bluhme 1868:201) which handed down a sentence in a specific case of defilement of a bridal cortege. While it was going to pick up the bride and escort her to her bridegroom, the procession had been humiliated by a shower of "filthy water and manure", intended as an insult to the bridegroom's lineage. The conviction that the bride went to her bridegroom is further confirmed by several laws in Langobardic edicts, more specifically By Ro. 182, 183, 188, and Li. 114, in all of which the expression *ad maritum ambulare*, "to walk to [her] husband", is used to define the action the bride must take in order to be married. The conclusion is that, in all probability, the residence of a newly married couple was virilocal, which is also consistent with the Langobardic descent system.

Visigothic law is also clear that brides were 'brought' to their bridegrooms. Among them III, 1. 2. (Zeumer 1902:123), discussed above in connection with marriage negotiations, makes it clear that the girl was 'handed over' (the verb used is *tradere*) to her bridegroom and that the girl in contention 'arrived' at the man ['s dwelling].

Marriage payments

Germanic customs considered several marriage payments, some of which took place before or during the wedding and some afterwards. Once more we obtain more information from Langobardic law. We shall then compare it with whatever information is available in Visigothic and other related law codes.

Among Germanic tribes the prevailing custom was for a brideprice to be tendered by the groom's to the bride's relatives. This was true during the first century, as related by Tacitus: "It is not the bride who offers a dowry to the bridegroom, but the bridegroom to his bride: parents and relatives participate and appreciate the gifts..." (*Germania* XVIII). In turn the bride gave to her bridegroom's relatives a few gifts. She also brought with her the *faderfio*, literally the "father's livestock", a kind of dowry.

The custom of brideprice is widely distributed even nowadays all over the world. The custom of a reciprocal gift from the bride's lineage to the groom's is less widely diffused. In black Africa, for instance, the custom of brideprice is encountered almost everywhere whereas dowry is very rare if not totally absent (Radcliffe-Brown 1950:46). Among pastoralists in the Saharan belt of North Africa, across the Middle Eastern deserts, along the African coasts across the Red Sea and further south, and among the pastoral populations of the Iranian plateau, one encounters both customs, i.e. a brideprice, as the basic transaction leading to marriage, and a reciprocal gift by the bride's parents to the groom or his relatives.

Among the Somali, for instance, the first gift is made at the time of betrothal while at wedding time reciprocal gifts occur between the bride's and the groom's lineages. The amount given in bridewealth varies according to the status of the parties involved and to the desirability of the marriage. The amount returned as dowry is in direct proportion to the value of bridewealth, being approximately one half and never exceeding two-thirds of the bridewealth (Lewis 1962:14). Bridewealth consists of several head of livestock in addition to horses, rare objects and rifles. The head of the bride's household, usually her father, keeps the horses which are prestige wealth *par excellence* and the rifles; he distributes livestock among his close kin. Relatives also contribute to the groom's bridewealth while the bulk comes from his own family.

Among the Basseri of southern Iran, bridewealth involves both a payment in cash, part of which should be used by the bride's father to provide and equip the bride's tent, and a payment in livestock, generally sheep, part of which may be given back by the bride's father to the bridegroom at the wedding (Barth 1961:18-9). In addition to brideprice, called *shirbabah*, or 'milk price', the bride is also given a *mahr*, considered "a divorce or widow's inheritance or fine, a stipulated sum, which is *the woman's share of her husband's estate* and which is also payable in the event of divorce" (Barth 1961:33) [italics mine]. During the betrothal period, the future bridegroom customarily brings gifts to his bride-to-be on various festive occasions and performs minor services for his future parents-in-law.

Thus, the Basseri, pastoralists of Indo-European stock, have three kinds of bridal exchanges, i.e. bridewealth from the groom's to the bride's family, dowry or a return gift from the bride's to the groom's family or relatives, and a gift called *mahr*, corresponding to "a share of the husband's estate" which belongs exclusively to the wife and is, therefore, interpreted as an "insurance" in case of divorce or widowhood (see above). The same articulation into three gifts, a bridewealth from the bridegroom's to the bride's kin, a dowry from the bride's kin to her future husband and a gift to his wife of a part of the husband's estate was customary also among Langobards at the time of sedentarization in Italy and for more than a century thereafter and pertained only to the class of free people.

It is very likely that the wedding procedure varied for the lower classes of clients, Lang. *haldii*, and slaves as in fact it does in present-day agro-pastoral societies between classes, but we have no clue in the laws concerning these eventual variations. It stands to reason that the written laws concerning marriage are those pertaining to the class of free men and women.

The three Langobardic bridal payments were: *meta* or *metfio*, corresponding to brideprice, *faderfio*, corresponding to a dowry, and *morgingab*, corresponding to a share of the bridegroom's estate given by him to his wife. There were, of course, wedding gifts on the part of friends which were partly reciprocated as will be discussed below. One may add the payment for the transfer of the girl's guardianship (Lang. *mundio*); this was not, however, strictly connected with marriage because it could occur also on other occasions, such as the death of the incumbent guardian or his default on account of his illtreating the girl.

The presence of the stem *fio*, 'livestock' (cf. modern German 'vieh'), in the compound nouns for both brideprice and dowry is indicative of the fact that in early Germanic society these payments were probably made in livestock.

According to the *Liber Papiensis*, a collection of Langobardic laws with appended comments and glosses, written during the eleventh century, *meta* was worth on average 40 *solidi* (*Liber Papiensis*, comment to Ro. 182; Boretius 1868:333). Recalling that the blood price of a servant girl was 30 *solidi* (Ro. 130, 134), and that the price of a cow was one third of the price of a mare, the price of a mare one third of that of a slave girl (see Ro. 332, 333, 334), the average value of *meta* among the Langobards was equal to approximately 13 cattle, or four mares, or one slave girl plus a mare.

We do not know the value of dowry, *faderfio*, as it is not discussed in the *Liber Papiensis*. Customarily it probably consisted of the bride's personal property to which gifts from the father may have been added according to the status of the bride's family. We shall discuss below the value of *morgingab* in connection with the evolution of economic exchanges at marriage.

A further exchange at marriage consisted in the gifts given to the newlyweds by their relatives and friends, a custom which is fairly ubiquitous among agro-pastoral societies in East Africa. The same custom was followed by the Langobards at the marriage of friends or relatives. In fact, Ro. 184 (Bluhme 1868:43-4) awarded the possession of wedding gifts given by [the bride's or the groom's] friends in exchange for token gifts distributed by the bride, to her husband, because he was the one who must give *launegild*, a reciprocal gift to the donors, if they requested it.

Among the *Leges Alamannorum*, law LV (Eckhardt 1966:112) refers to marriage payments in the case of the widow of a free man with no children who wanted to marry someone of her class:

> ...*sequatur eam dotis legitima, et quidquid parentes eius legitime plagitaverint, et quidquid de sede paterna secum adtulit, omnia in potestate habeat auferendi, quod*

non manducavit aut non vendidit. Dotis enim legitima 40 solidis constat aut in auro
aut in argento aut in mancipiis aut in qualicumque re, quod habet ad dandum.

The text is quite interesting because it confirms that the *Baiuwarii* also had marriage exchanges consisting of a *dotis* legally worth 40 *solidi*, probably the *meta* received at marriage worth the same amount among Langobards (see above), anything she took from her father's home, akin to the Langobardic *faderfio*, and anything her relatives should have left her by a *placitum*. One should note the fact that her 'dowry' could consist of "gold, or silver, or *mancipia* [livestock or slaves], or whatever thing [presumably real estate]".

Marriage payments were customary also among the Visigoths. Law III, 1. 5. (Zeumer 1902:126-7), having noted that "often different 'intentions' come up between people to be wedded", decrees that "anyone among the primates of our palace or among the 'seniors' of the Gothic people who should want to request to wed to his son the daughter of someone else or left by anyone else, or he should want to choose a wife for himself", as dowry (here again 'dowry' refers to the gift the Langobards called *meta*) counting all movable and fixed property, should not give more than 1000 *solidi*, and in addition he should have the faculty of writing a donation and giving 10 male slaves, 10 female slaves and 20 horses (worth altogether approximately 800 *solidi*, see page 157, this vol.); this second donation has been interpreted as the *morgengabe*, as confirmed by a short poem taken from an "ancient law":

> *Ecce decem inprimis pueros totisdemque puellas*
> *Tradimus atque decem virorum corpora equorum,*
> *Pari mulos numero: damus inter caetera et arma,*
> *Ordinis ut Getici est et morgingeba vetusta* (Zeumer 1902:127).

The customary giving of brideprice to the woman's next of kin is confirmed by *Lex Visigothorum* III, 4. 7. (Zeumer 1902:150); the case is discussed of a woman who might go to someone else's house to commit adultery, i.e. without being 'brought by the hand', and the man should want to have her as lawful wife, "he should give her kin the price [sic] requested by the girl's kin, or to her whatever he should have agreed with the girl herself".

We have further traces of the existence of *morgingabe* among the *Alamanni* (Alam. *morginaghepha* or *morgangeba*). *Lex Alamannorum* LIV (cod. A) or LVI (cod. B) (Eckhardt 1966:113) examines the case of a widow who should declare having received *morgangeba* from her deceased husband, and provides that she should "calculate how much it is worth in gold, or silver, or *mancipia* or horses, worth 12 *solidi*"; having taken an oath alone asserting, 'That my husband gave it to me and I must possess it'. This is what the *Alamanni* say '*nasthait*'". The last is a mysterious term with no clear meaning.

Concerning dowry, i.e. *morgingabe*, in the *Leges Visigothorum* we come to IV, 5. 2. (Zeumer 1902:198-9) which takes up the case of women who were allowed before then to do what they wanted with their dowry, the wealth given directly to them by their husband, hence *morgingabe*. The law sees fit to protect those "for whose birth marriage was agreed to", i.e. the woman's children. Having this aim it decrees that "a woman, who has children or nephews, who should want to give to the Church or to freed slaves or whomever she should want, should not have the faculty of giving more than one fourth [of her estate]" (Zeumer 1902:198).

In the previous section we have seen how among some populations bridal payments may be substituted by bride service, work performed for periods which could be as long as a few years, for the parents of the future bride. No trace of such institution can be found in the laws examined so far. This leads one to conclude that it did not exist in Germanic society, or in any case that it did not exist among the higher classes which seem to be the object of most Germanic legislation on the subject.

Evolution of marriage payments

The economic importance of marriage payments in Langobardic society may be inferred from the laws concerning customary exchanges of wealth during the engagement and wedding ceremonies. Li. 7 (Bluhme 1868:110) fixed the maximum amount of *morgingab* at one fourth of the husband's total estate (the same limit fixed by the previously discussed *Lex Visigothorum* IV, 5. 2), although in this case it is the husband's gift to his wife which is limited, whereas in the *Lex Visigothorum* it is the amount that the widowed wife can give to anyone she wants, but the result is the same, i.e. three-quarters of the father's estate must go to his agnatic heirs.

Li. 89 (Bluhme 1868:144) sets a ceiling on the value of brideprice (Lang. *meta*) to be given by noblemen: this was 400 *solidi* for "judges" and 300 "for the remaining noblemen". {We have seen (page 158, this vol.) that a slightly earlier *Lex Visigothorum* fixed the ceiling for brideprice to be given by a nobleman at 1000 *solidi*} Li. 103 confirmed the preceding laws, adding that whatever was given in excess of the statutory amount should "...not be stable". Ahi. 14. V (Bluhme 1868:200-1) provided that a husband could not will to his wife a greater usufruct than that pertaining to one half of his estate remaining after what had been given to her as *morgincap* [sic] and *meta* according to the law, if there were children from that wife alone. If there were also children from another wife he could give to the present one the usufruct of a third of his estate; if there were three, from a fourth of his estate, etc. These laws were meant both as a protection for legitimate heirs from a previous wife, in case their father should remarry, and as a brake on excessive lavishness on the part of suitors.

A comparison between the above discussed late laws and those concerning bridal payments, issued by Rothari, with Tacitus' account of bridal gifts shows that bridal payments underwent considerable change. Customarily brideprice (Lang. *meta*) included contributions from the bridegroom's agnatic relatives. It was given to the bride's parents who kept the main portion in the household and may have given some to their daughter on her wedding day and distributed some to their kin.

In the sixth century the picture had changed. According to the laws in Rothari's edict, the gathering and distribution of *meta* apparently involved only the bridegroom's and the bride's parents. *Meta* accrued to the bride in its entirety in the case, regulated by Ro. 178, that the bridegroom did not keep his engagement within the statutory period of two years. By Liutprand's time, a century later, probably in parallel with the decreasing importance of the lineage due to urbanization, *meta* had been reduced simply to a gift to the bride and had become an obligation on the part of the bridegroom alone.

The importance of *morgingab* increased with respect to *meta*, probably because it did not bind the bridegroom at the time of engagement, was given directly to the bride hence kept in the family, and could be given later, whenever the husband came into his estate.

The subsequent evolution of the three articulations into which the exchanges at marriage were divided is highlighted in the *Liber Papiensis*. The explanation to Ro. 182 (Boretius 1868:332-5) gives the example of a widow remarrying without her deceased husband's relatives' consent. *Meta* was given directly to the bride, no longer to her parents. It was worth, on average 40 *solidi*. The price of guardianship (Lang. *mundio*) was still symbolized by a harnessed war horse worth 20 *solidi*, and it was still paid to the bride's guardian. While the importance of *meta* had decreased, the importance of *morgingab* had increased considerably. A ceiling of one fourth of the husband's estate had been set for *morgingab* by Li. 7 and by the eleventh century the ceiling had become the accepted value of the transaction.

Although the value of *morgingab* is not given in the example, one may infer it from the penalty for failure to pay it. This was set at one hundred pounds of sterling silver (Lat. *librae*). The value of a *libra* was fixed at 20 *solidi* by Charlemagne's monetary reform. Since penalties in Langobardic jurisprudence generally were eight times the value of the forfeited good, one may infer that the average *morgingab* was worth about 12 *librae*, or some six times as much as the average *meta*. Dowry (Lang. *faderfio*) is not mentioned in the commentaries of the *Liber Papiensis* even if it was surely present as a customary exchange. Its importance was to increase during the following centuries, because of changes in the socioeconomic structure that do not pertain to the present discussion. On the other hand, except for some residual aspects such as the engagement ring, the customary 'gage' (Lang. *wadia*), to the betrothed, both *meta* and *morgingab* eventually disappeared.

Repudiation

Langobardic marriages must have been fairly stable, at least during the first century of their settlement in Italy, and repudiations rare. In fact, no provision is foreseen in Rothari's edict concerning the repudiation of a wife—the opposite was impossible. Two laws in the edict deal with the case of a husband having killed his wife. This too must have been a rare event because of the protection extended to a woman by her agnatic kin. Killing a woman without cause was tantamount to a blood offense to her lineage. This relationship was acknowledged by Ro. 166 (Bluhme 1868:38) which provided that a man suspected of having murdered his wife should prove his innocence by a judicial duel against his wife's agnates.

Ro. 200 was even more drastic in recognizing the rights of the wife's relatives; it condemned the husband proven guilty of his wife's murder to a penalty of 1,200 *solidi*, the highest in Langobardic legislation. This was to be paid, one half to the king's court and one half to those relatives "...who gave her to her husband and received [payment for] her guardianship". The beginning of a crisis in the Langobardic family structure may be detected in one of Grimoald's laws; Gr. 6 (Bluhme 1868:94), issued in 667, one generation after Rothari's edict, prohibited a husband to repudiate his wife "without a legitimate guilt". It called for a penalty of 500 *solidi* to be paid, one half to the king's court and one half to the woman's relatives.

Repudiation is not foreseen in the *Leges Alamannorum*. *Lex* LIII (E cod. B; Eckhardt 1966:110) sets a compensation of 40 *solidi* to a *sponsa* jilted by her bridegroom and an oath by the woman with 12 oath-takers *cum quinque nominatis et septem advocatis* (probably five agnates and seven acquaintances 'called' in as oath-helpers) that the suitor had not rejected her for a "vice or attempt" so that her reputation may be redressed. *Lex Baiuwariorum* VIII, 18. 14. (von Schwind 1926:359) foresees the repudiation of a wife with "no vice and for envy", fixing a compensation of 48 *solidi* to her relatives in addition to all marriage payments, *dotem*, she had a right to, according to her genealogy, i.e. brideprice and *morgengabe*. and the right to take with her everything she received from her parents, i.e., *faderfio*.

Leges Visigothorum III, 6. 1 and III, 6. 2 (Zeumer 1902:166-8) deal at length with repudiation and divorce. The former deals with the status of a woman who was repudiated justly by her husband, presumably because of having committed adultery. The law orders that no man should remarry her under penalty of being handed over with the woman to her prior husband, unless he should "know in an evident way that a divorce had been made between them either by a written agreement or in front of witnesses". In a case where the husband had left the woman unjustly, he should lose the dowry that she had brought to him nor should he keep any of the woman's possessions under penalty of being forced by the judge to make restitution.

Law III, 6. 2 is something of an anticlimax because, while the previous one recognized the necessity of making recourse to divorce, this one instituted that "no man, except for a manifest reason of fornication, should leave (repudiate) his wife and dare to 'make' a divorce between himself and his wife either through witnesses or by a written agreement", under penalty, in case he should trick her into obtaining a written agreement, of losing, after having made restitution, all his estate to his children. The husband who, having spurned his wife, took another one, was to be whipped in public with 200 lashes, have his hair 'abjectly' shorn and go into exile for the rest of his life, or remain in the hands of whomever the prince should decide to give him to. An interpretation of this seeming change of mind between two subsequent laws requires a study of the conditions of Visigothic society when these laws were issued.

Polygyny

Tacitus related that "...almost alone among barbarians they [the *Germani*] content themselves with one wife, excepting few who are sought after for several marriages not because of lust but on account of their nobility" (*Germania* XVIII). Polygyny was limited to lineage or clan heads because in simple societies marriage is the usual way of establishing alliances. Plural marriage may have become obsolete when Germanic populations gave themselves a king whose power became sufficiently established so that multiple alliances with other lineages were no longer necessary.

However, monogamy was limited to formal marriage with free women, while women of lower classes could be taken as concubines. Langobards took as concubines their *haldiae*, even when previously married, or their servant girls. The existence of concubinage among the Langobards until Rothari's time may be inferred by the numerous laws in Rothari's edict concerning the inheritance rights of illegitimate sons. The law was not very generous with illegitimate sons, Ro. 154 fixing the inheritance portion respectively for legitimate and illegitimate heirs. Each legitimate son was awarded two parts of his father's estate, whilst all illegitimate sons together were awarded only one part. Thus, if there were three legitimate and three illegitimate sons, each legitimate son would obtain 2/7 of his father's estate while the three illegitimate ones would obtain 1/7 all together, or 1/21 apiece.

Ro. 155 cautioned Langobardic free men that they did not have the right to give the same privileges to illegitimate sons as those pertaining to legitimate ones, unless the latter gave their consent upon reaching legitimate age on their twelfth birthday.

When the father had no legitimate sons but only daughters he might have taken concubines to increase his chance of having male heirs. In that case, legitimate daughters, as a group, received one half of the father's estate, illegitimate sons divided one third among themselves, while legitimate relatives or, in their absence, the king's court took the remaining sixth (Ro. 159, 160).

Law Ro. 156 confirms that illegitimate sons of concubines belonging to the father were free, although with diminished rights of inheritance. The same must have been true of illegitimate daughters, although their inheritance rights are not even mentioned. On the other hand, an illegitimate son, born from the union of a free man and someone else's servant girl, could become free only if his father "bought him" and emancipated him by the traditional ceremony of a public donation or *gairethinx*.

Concubinage must have reached extremes if King Liutprand's lawgivers felt it necessary, beginning in the year 725, to issue laws to curb these excesses. Li. 66 deals with the case of a master who took as his concubine the wife of one of his clients (Lang. *haldio*), or slaves, while her husband was still alive, and had children born of that union. The law decrees that in no case could these children become the master's heirs or free, nor could he donate to them any property "because the case is doubtful, whose son or daughter he [or she] may be, when both are alive, the slave and the master, he who had [her] before and he who took her afterwards".

In 734 Liutprand's legislators issued law Li. 140 according to which a free man who committed adultery with a servant girl married to his slave, or with a *haldia* married to one of his *haldii*, was condemned to free both his concubine and her husband. The law was aimed at repressing a condition which had gradually got out of control.

Although not expressly foreseen in the *Leges Baiwariorum* and *Alamannorum* it seems implicit that concubinage existed among them. Among the Visigoths it was explicitly recognized by *Lex* III, 5. 5, already discussed under the heading of incest, condemning the father or brother who 'adulterated' his son's, brother's or father's concubine. That concubinage by free men was tolerated is also proved by the harsh punishments meted out by *Leges Visigothorum* III, 2. 2 to III. 2. 4 to free women who 'mixed' in concubinage with one of their slaves or freed slaves. The penalty could be as harsh as death in case of adultery or one hundred lashes for a woman who should "join in marriage" the king's or someone's servant, whilst this last penalty did not apply to free men, except to those who fornicated with the king's or anyone else's servants.

Fornication and adultery

Among the aspects of marriage to be considered are fornication and adultery. These are severely punished, especially when committed by women, among social groups where a woman's chastity stands for the integrity and honor of her household and lineage. Among the Kababish of western Sudan, a girl could be killed by her father if she was found to have had a sexual relationship before marriage (Asad 1970:58). The same attitude prevailed among the Langobards during the early period. Ro. 189 (Bluhme 1868:45) allowed the girl's parents to "take revenge" on her. The penalty became less drastic with the passing of time until Li. 60, issued in 724 abolished any form of punishment or retaliation on the part of the girl's family, even in the case of a free woman fornicating with a client, *haldio*.

Among the *Leges Alamannorum* there is no specific law against a woman's fornication, the impression from other laws concerning sexual crimes, however, is of greater permissiveness. The *Leges Baiwariorum* are also more lenient with fornicating women in that fornication between a slave and a free woman (*Lex*

Alamannorum 7. IX; von Schwind 1926:357-8) entailed the handing over of the slave to the girl's parents for expiation or death, but no penalty for the girl.

Lex Visigothorum III, 4. 5 (Zeumer 1902:149) is almost as harsh as the law in Rothari's edict in that it exempts the father from penalty or "calomny" if he should kill his daughter "in adultery", hence fornicating, in his house; in cases where he wanted to spare her, he had the right of doing with her and the adulterer whatever he wanted.

Lex Visigothorum III, 4. 17 (Zeumer 1902:157) sentences a convicted harlot belonging to the class of free persons to receive 300 lashes in public and to be dismissed afterwards on condition that she should never again indulge in shameful vices nor ever come back to the city.

Concerning adultery among Germanic populations, we have an early testimony by Tacitus:

> Few are the cases of adultery among such numerous people, since their punishment is swift and given to the husband; having shorn her hair and stripped her in front of their neighbors, the husband expels her from his home and chases her all over the village with a whip; in fact there is no forgiveness for lost chastity: she will not find a [second] husband despite her beauty, youth or wealth. No one there laughs about vices, nor does one call being in tune with one's times to corrupt and be corrupted (*Germania* XIX).

We do not know whether Tacitus' remarks referred to a situation where the adulterers were caught in the act. In fact, in this case Ro. 212 (Bluhme 1868:51) sanctioned the husband's right to kill'them both and be exempt from paying their blood price.

If the suspected adulterers were not caught in the act, Langobardic law was more cautious. Ro. 213 instituted that the husband's accusation was not sufficient and that the accused had the right to "purify himself", either by having a judicial duellist (Lang. *camphio*) fight on his behalf against the husband's *camphio*, or by taking an oath. If he did not succeed in purifying himself, he was liable to death and so probably was the suspected adulteress.

Li. 121, issued in 733 instituted a lower level of adultery, when someone was found to be conversing shamefully with someone's wife, i.e. "having put his hands on her breasts or some other place which could be shameful", he must pay compensation equal to his own wergild to the husband. The latter was entitled to "take revenge" on his wife by whipping or by selling her into slavery, but he was expressly forbidden to kill or brand her. In a particularly heinous case of a woman committing adultery at her husband's instigation, Liutprand's lawgivers applied, in Li. 130, all the harshness of the ancient law so that the adulteress was condemned to death "in accordance with the previous [Rothari's] edict". The instigator-husband was condemned to pay the woman's relatives the same composition as if she had been killed unintentionally, or a sum equal to her brother's blood price. He also lost his wife's property either to her children or relatives and the adulterer was to be delivered to the woman's, not the husband's, relatives.

Leges Visigothorum III, 4. 1 to III, 4. 4 (Zeumer 1902:147-9) allow the husband of a convicted adulteress to take revenge both on her and the adulterer, "that he may do to them what he wants", including putting them to death. In fact III, 4. 4 briefly states: "If the husband should kill the adulterer with the adulteress, he should not be held for homicide".

In most cases of adultery, the law was much harsher with women than with men.

Interclass marriage

A fundamental aspect of marriage concerns interclass marriages which are the object of specific laws in many Germanic law codes. In this matter, however class is more important than kinship and this aspect is better discussed under the heading 'Social relations'.

Conclusion

The aim of this paper was not to give a definitive picture of the problem of kinship and marriage in Germanic society in general, and in the Visigothic one in particular, but to set down some points of departure that scholars may take or criticize, being alerted to some of the facets of this all important aspect of simple societies, in this case the early Germanic ones.

I believe I have shown how kinship and marriage pervaded numerous domains in the social, economic and political life of those populations. Not only was marriage a way of reproducing society, but it involved basic economic transactions which are indicative of the changes in subsistence which affected those societies.

Kinship regulated inheritance and succession and was of paramount importance to the political relations of those populations.

While, at present, only historical sources are available to allow one to go into greater detail concerning aspects of kinship and marriage of those populations, we should foresee and prepare for the time, close at hand, when more refined research methodologies, such as DNA identification, will allow scholars accurately to check the relationship between the skeletal remains of people belonging to ancient corporate units and find out whether and how they were related.

Once we are able to connect kinship to archaeology we shall be on the threshold of a qualitative jump which will allow us to reach a much greater understanding of those ancient populations and clear away the misinterpretations which are the main obstacle to our studies.

References

Textual sources:

[Abbr.: *Ro.* = *Edictus Rothari*; *Gr.* = *Leges a Grimoaldo additae*; *Li.* = *Leges Liutprandi regis*; *Ahi.* = *Leges Ahistulphi regis*; for all these see *Edictus Langobardorum*].

Capitulatio de partibus Saxoniae: see Boretius (ed.) 1883:68-70.
Edictus Langobardorum: see Bluhme (ed.) 1868.
Leges Alamannorum: see Eckhardt (ed.) 1966.
Leges Baiwariorum: see von Schwind (ed.) 1926.
Leges Visigothorum: see Zeumer (ed.) 1902.
Liber Papiensis: see Boretius (ed.) 1868.
Paul the Deacon
    Historia Langobardorum: see Waitz *et al.* (eds.) 1878.
Tacitus, Gaius Cornelius
    Germania: see Page (trans.) 1958.
Wulfila
    Old and New Testament in Gothic: see Migne (ed.) 1848.

Bibliography:

Asad, T.
 1970 *The Kababish Arabs.* New York: Praeger.
Ausenda, G.
 1987 Leisurely nomads: The Hadendowa (Beja) of the Gash Delta and their transition to sedentary village life. Doctoral dissertation, Columbia University, Dept. of Anthropology.
 1995 The segmentary lineage in contemporary anthropology and among the Langobards. In *After Empire: Towards an Ethnology of Europe's Barbarians.* G. Ausenda (ed.), pp. 15-45. Woodbridge: The Boydell Press.
 n.d. Beni Amer and Habab: A Diachronic Ethnography 1880-1990.
Barnard, A, & A. Good
 1984 *Research Practices in the Study of Kinship.* (Research Methods in Social Anthropology, 2). ASA Monographs. London: Academic Press.
Barnes, J. A.
 1967 Genealogies. In *The Craft of Social Anthropology.* A. L. Epstein (ed.), London: Social Sciences Paperbacks in association with Tavistock Publications.
 1971 *Three Styles in the Study of Kinship.* London: Tavistock Publications.
Barth, F.
 1954 Father's Brother's Daughter Marriage in Kurdistan. *Southwestern Journal of Anthropology* 10: 164-171.
 1961 *Nomads of South Persia: The Basseri Tribe of the Khamseh Confederacy.* Boston: Little, Brown & Co.
Bertolini, O.
 1960 Le chiese longobarde dopo la conversione al cattolicesimo ed i loro rapporti con il papato. In *Le chiese nei regni dell'Europa occidentale e i loro rapporti con Roma sino all'800.* (Settimane di studio del Centro Italiano di Studi sull'Alto Medioevo, VII). Pp. 455-492. Spoleto: C.I.S.A.M.

Bluhme, F.
1868   *Edictus Langobardorum.* In *Leges Langobardorum. Monumenta Germaniae Historica. Leges* (in Folio), 4. F. Bluhme & A. Boretius (eds.), pp. 1-234. Hannover: Hahn.

Boretius, A.
1868   *Liber legis Langobardorum Papiensis dictus.* In *Leges Langobardorum. Monumenta Germaniae Historica. Leges* (in Folio), 4. F. Bluhme & A. Boretius (eds.), pp. 290-605. Hannover: Hahn.
1883   *Capitularia regum Francorum*, 1. *Monumenta Germaniae Historica.* Hannover: Hahn.

Bouquet, M.
1996   Family trees and their affinities: the visual imperative of the genealogical diagram. *J.R.A.I.* 2 (1): 43-66.

Bourdieu, P.
1977   *Outline of a Theory of Practice.* Cambridge: Cambridge University Press.

Bullough, D. A.
1969   I vescovi di Pavia nei secoli ottavo e nono: fonti e cronologia. In *Pavia capitale del regno.* (Atti del 4° Congresso Internazionale di studi sull'alto medioevo). Pp. 317-328. Spoleto: C.I.S.A.M.

Cunnison, I.
1966   *Baggara Arabs: Power and the Lineage in a Sudanese Nomad Tribe.* Oxford: Clarendon Press.

Dumont, L.
1980   *Homo hierarchicus.* Chicago: University of Chicago Press.

Eckhardt, K. A. (ed.)
1966   *Leges Alamannorum. Monumenta Germaniae Historica. Leges nationum Germanicarum*, 5. 1. Second edition. [1st ed. by K. Lehmann 1888]. Hannover: Hahn.

Fried, M. (ed.)
1968   *Readings in Anthropology.* Vol.II, Cultural Anthropology. New York: Thomas Y. Crowell Co.

Harris, M.
1968   *The Rise of Anthropological Theory: A History of Theories of Culture.* New York: Thomas Y. Crowell Co.

Heather, P., & J. Matthews
1991   *The Goths in the Fourth Century.* (Translated Texts for Historians, 11). Liverpool: Liverpool University Press.

Kroeber, A. L.
1909   Classificatory systems of relationship. *J.R.A.I.* 39: 77-84.

Leach, E. R.
1955   Polyandry, inheritance and the definition of marriage. *Man* 55: 182-186.

Leacock, E.
1963   Introduction, to *L. H. Morgan - Ancient Society* [1877], pp. i-xx. New York: Meridian Books.

Lévi-Strauss, C.
1956   The family. In *Man, culture and society.* H. L. Shapiro (ed.), pp. 261-285. Oxford: Oxford University Press.
1963   *Structural Anthropology.* New York: Basic Books.
1969   *The Elementary Structures of Kinship.* London: Eyre & Spottiswood.

Lewis, I.
1962   *Marriage and the Family in Northern Somaliland.* (East African Studies, No. 15). Kampala: East African Institute of Research.

Manselli, R.
1982   Resistenze dei culti antichi nella pratica religiosa dei laici nelle campagne.
               In *Cristianizzazione ed organizzazione ecclesiastica delle campagne
               nell'alto medioevo: espansione e resistenze.* (Settimane di studio del
               Centro Italiano di Studi sull'Alto Medioevo, XXVIII). Pp. 57-108.
               Spoleto: C.I.S.A.M.
Migne, J. -P. (ed.)
1848   Martinus Turonensis - Ticonius - Ulfilas - *Grammatica et glossarium
               goticum. Patrologiae cursus completus. Tomus XVIII.* Paris: Publisher in
               rue d'Amboise, près la barrière d'Enfer, ou Petit-Montrouge.
Morgan, L. H.
1963[1877]   *Ancient Society.* New York: Meridian Books.
Nadel, S.
1945   Notes on Beni Amer society. *Sudan Notes and Records* 26: 51-94.
Needham, R.
1967   Terminology and alliance, II: Mapuche, conclusions. *Sociologus* 18: 39-53.
Page, T. E. (trans.)
1958   *Tacitus: Dialogue, Agricola, Germania.* Cambridge, MA: Harvard U. Press.
Penniman, T. K.
1965   *A Hundred Years of Anthropology.* London: Gerald Duckworth & Co. Ltd.
Peters, E.
1960   The proliferation of segments in the lineages of the Bedouin of Cyrenaica.
               Journal of the Royal Anthropological Institute 90: 29-53.
Radcliffe-Brown, A. R.
1950   Introduction. In *African Systems of Kinship and Marriage.* A. R.
               Radcliffe-Brown & D. Forde (eds.), pp. 1- 85. International African
               Institute. London: Oxford University Press.
Rivers, W. H. R.
1900   A genealogical method of collection of social and vital statistics. *Journal
               of the [Royal] Anthropological Institute* 30 (1): 74-82.
1968[1910]   *Kinship and social organisation.* London: Athlone Press.
Schneider, D. M.
1968a   Rivers and Kroeber in the Study of Kinship. In *Kinship and Social
               Organization of W. H. R. Rivers. Together with 'The Genealogical Method
               of Anthropological Enquiry', With Commentaries by Raymond Firth and
               David M. Schneider.* Pp. 7-16. London: The Athlone Press.
1968b   *American Kinship: A Cultural Account.* Englewood Cliffs, NJ: Prentice Hall.
1984   *A Critique of the Study of Kinship.* Ann Arbor, MI: Univ. of Michigan
               Press.
von Schwind, E.
1926   *Lex Baiwariorum. Monumenta Germaniae Historica. Leges nationum
               Germanicarum,* 5. 2. Hannover: Hahn.
Sotomayor, M.
1982   Penetracion de la Iglesia en los medios rurales de la España tardoromana
               y visigoda. In *Cristianizzazione ed organizzazione ecclesiastica delle
               campagne nell'alto medioevo: espansione e resistenze.* (Settimane di
               studio del Centro Italiano di Studi sull'Alto Medioevo, XXVIII). Pp. 639-
               670. Spoleto: C.I.S.A.M.
Tylor, E. B.
1889   On a method investigating the development of institutions applied to laws
               of marriage and descent. *J.R.A.I.* 18: 245-269.

Waitz, O. *et. al.* (eds.)
   1878   *Scriptores rerum Langobardicarum et Italicarum saec. VI-IX. Monumenta Germaniae Historica.* Hannover: Hahn.
Zeumer, K. (ed.)
   1902   *Leges Visigothorum. Monumenta Germaniae Historica. Leges nationum Germanicarum, 1.* Hannover: Hahn.

Discussion

GREEN: On page 132 (this vol.): "merging of alternate generations" (grandfather and grandson); my point in support of that is that modern German 'Enkel', 'grandson', goes back to Old High German *eninchili* (same meaning), which is made up of OHG *ano*, 'grandfather' and a diminutive ending, so that the grandson is designated as a 'little grandfather'.

DÍAZ: On page 133, the distinction between genealogy and pedigree might explain why some Goths—other barbarian tribes can be analysed—can become kings and others cannot. This is associated with lines of transmission of group membership and its attributes. The condition of being a Goth is not enough to reach the royal dignity, it is necessary to be included in other categories (not only the economic one). The problem is to recognize these conditions and categories.

JIMENEZ: On page 134, my question is: if genealogies are not fabricated by individuals, who fabricates them?

AUSENDA: One must keep in mind that genealogies begin in simple societies and they are based on oral communication. As such they have the characteristics common to oral phenomena. One should also realize that genealogies represented at one time the earliest form of history and the earliest maps of inter-group relations. Genealogies were the earliest form of history because, in the absence of calendrical know-how, events were connected to the names of individuals and viceversa. They also represented the earliest maps of inter-group relations in so far as these could be assimilated to genealogical kin relations. In simple societies genealogies are even the main way to account for populations of humans or animals. Genealogies were born and, for the greater part of their evolution, used in the absence of writing. They were written down only when former simple societies acquired writing.

As long as they were not written, the same as languages, they were subject to structural changes. Languages do indeed change through the action of individuals, but individuals are only the carriers of changes which are influenced by socioeconomic conditions that transcend the willful action of each individual. As a consequence of these oral characteristics, genealogies are made to reflect the on-the-ground social relations that suit a given group at a particular moment. For instance, the Hadendowa of eastern Sudan consider themselves descended from a founding ancestor 'Ahmed el Barakwin' who, according to legend, had migrated from the Hejàz. The seven most important clans among them are considered the descendants of seven sons, whereas less important clans are considered descendants of unnamed daughters (the names of women cannot be mentioned among Hadendowa) who had married sundry immigrants. Among the seven sons three have names which correspond to the patronymics of three important clans whereas four do not; their names correspond to the patronymics of less important clans made now to descend from daughters or grandchildren. The place of the less important clans have been taken over by clans which have grown in numbers and wealth during the last century to become more important than the previous ones which were reclassified to lower positions in the tribal genealogy. This is only one example among many which could be cited not only for tribes, but for sections, lineages and even families. In other words, genealogies change so as to reflect the on-the-ground reality, and it couldn't be otherwise.

When genealogies are written down, the process of adaptation is hindered and genealogies gradually lose their earlier function. This is the time when they can be fabricated by individuals. In the early Middle Ages genealogies were an important basis for the legitimation of rulers and noble families, hence it is quite possible that, when writing became widespread, they may have been fabricated to bolster rights of succession or other privileges. In present-day eastern Sudan genealogies are fabricated mostly by fakis or sheikhs who are paid by groups or heads of groups aspiring to a prestigious ancestor, generally a relative of the Prophet, and in contemporary Europe by specialists in heraldry who, for the right amount, can prove that the interested party is a descendant of a noble family. However, now that they can be written, notably by individuals, genealogies have lost most of their importance, as they no longer 'explain' the socio-economic relations of interrelated groups but only extol the individuals who requested their fabrication.

DIAZ: Referring to page 135 on the distinction between inheritance and succession. The concepts of inheritance (property) and succession (transmission of office) perhaps should not be separated, especially among aristocratic groups, since their prominent position is also subject to their economic condition, especially as far as the revenues from agrarian properties are concerned.

AUSENDA: Yes, inheritance and succession almost always occur together and their presence should also include descent, which signifies the transmission of group membership. However, this doesn't mean that they shouldn't be defined, hence recognized and studied perhaps in mutual relation but separately.

DE JONG: It's a more general point that troubles me, it concerned the simple societies you mention, on page 137, among which probably Germanic ones. Now the image you create, I think, is one of simple Germanic societies based on kinship, where kinship ethics have important regulating mechanisms.

AUSENDA: Not only regulating, cohesive.

DE JONG: I wonder, where do you situate these simple societies in time? As far as I can see from either Frankish or Visigothic legislation, we are not dealing with a simple society, but with a fairly complex one, and not with anything that is quite so Germanic. So, the image you conjure up of anything that was pristine Germanic and simple and that was subsequently manipulated by the Church and the state, which changed its kinship pattern into something quite different, is something I simply cannot accept, and it crops up in many parts of your paper.

AUSENDA: You are mixing various things together. I'm not saying that it becomes unsimple because it's manipulated. Two different things. Simple society is not only defined in time, it is also defined in space. You might have a society which is quite complex in Paris and very simple in the periphery. So, it's very difficult to say when a society is simple and how simple it is at a certain point in time. Obviously, Germanic society was simple before coming into the Roman Empire. Let's say five hundred years before, so that everyone is happy. From that time on, they still had some traditional customs which were engendered by the fact that they had been a simple society and that lingered on because of tradition. A glaring example of this lingering on of the customs of a simple society are feud and blood money compesation which are prominent in all the laws of Germanic kingdoms. In fact feud and blood money compensation are the paramount ways of controlling crime in a stateless, i.e. a simple society. So, I agree with you, look at the Franks, that was not a simple society when they were dominant in *Francia*, but originally they were a simple society. When you start dealing with these people you've got to think of what they were in order to understand what they are becoming. This is what historians do and anthropologists are trying to do. So, to understand what they become you've got to understand what their rules were and what they did, so that you may see which way they are going. I'm not saying that the Goths were a simple society when they were in Spain, they were mostly acculturated by that time. When I say 'Germanic society', I mean when they were Germanic east of the Rhine and north of the Danube and they behaved like a simple society. They probably didn't have a state, they probably didn't have one chief. A simple society, as you rightly said, has kinship as its main social background, not regulating but social.

SCHWARCZ: I want to say that you have to take into account the different concepts of this simple society. You should take a look at Germanic society when they enterered the Empire. There are two different concepts in addition to kinship, the concept of 'Gefolgschaft' and the concept of the 'house'. And after studying some years ago a synthesis of the political theory concerning the *Germani* I got the impression that kinship was not the most prominent social force. There was also the 'house' and the relation between the chief and his retinue which sometimes had stronger features.

AUSENDA: Sometimes, it's possible. But still, a relationship between the chief and his retinue does not make it into a complex society.

HEATHER: If I was right in understanding Procopius on the Ostrogoths, you have essentially three classes: free, half free and slaves. And certainly in the law codes these groups are not meant to intermarry with one another. How do you consider that; is that simple or more complex?

AUSENDA: Well, it all depends on how it behaves. East African societies are definitely simple societies and they have two or three classes. They have a dominant one, both client clans and individuals, because both can occur. Clans may be clients of the ruling elder of the tribe or they can be clients of individual nobles and they would have different treatment. It's very varied, and then you have slaves of course. The slaves are a minority in that society. It is still a simple society, where, despite stratification, the central authority is still quite elementary. Complex society is one where you have writing, complex religion with a non kin-related hierarchy, and where the transmission of information can be permanently recorded.

DE JONG: I have taken a closer look at your statement on page 138 that close agnatic marriage should be kept in mind as the probable preferred pattern of Germanic populations, again in the earlier period and your arguments for this, as far as I can see, come to a large extent from Langobardic law.

AUSENDA: Not only, but there are also prohibitions in Visigothic law.

DE JONG: Yes, that's precisely where I can't follow you because if there are prohibitions against marrying within the sixth degree, that's quite far.

AUSENDA: No, it isn't, it's quite close, it's the second parallel cousin. The sixth degree means you go back to your great-grandfather. That's very close. The fourth degree is your immediate, your first cousin, your uncle's daughter, that's the fourth degree. The sixth degree is one removed, which is very close. You wouldn't think of marrying a second parallel cousin nowadays. When Theodore of Pavia asked Pope Zacharias to allow the Langobards to marry within the fourth degree, it means he was asking the pope to allow parallel first cousin marriage, which had been allowed to the Anglo Saxons, as he wrote. Obviously there was parallel cousin marriage.

DE JONG: It depends on how you interpret this.

AUSENDA: You can say no, but I have obvious proof that it existed, because if it was prohibited by law it means that it was being practiced. Now, the reasons for which they didn't want people to do it might be the reasons you brought up, or those I indicated, or those pointed out by Goody or by someone else, but there is no doubt that it was legislated against.

DE JONG: What terminology does Theodore use? Is it *gradus* or is it *genus* or *geniculum*?

AUSENDA: It says degrees, *gradus*. And furthermore the relationships are specified with no uncertainty for all prohibited degrees. For the *de quarti gradus consanguinitate* it lists "*...frater patruelis, soror patruelis, id est patrui filius filiave, cunsubrinus et consubrina, id est avunculi et matertere filius, filia*", etc., which are undoubtedly parallel first cousins.

WOOD: Why is it Visigothic?

AUSENDA: Because those are the forbidden degrees, those which were preached against.

WOOD: That is a Roman list: it is not a Gothic list. The point I am making is that you are talking about people in Visigothic society, not necessarily about Visigoths.

AUSENDA: It is a Roman list in a Visigothic code. So obviously it applies to Visigoths. The person who wrote it down—and I must admit that he was an extremely thorough person—didn't leave anything out; he wrote down and described all the kin with whom marriage was forbidden in all degrees, for the group to which the law was addressed. As a matter of fact, one of the things I want to do for the coming publication is to draw a diagram of this list of prohibited degrees which will be quite interesting.[9]

WOOD: The early manuscripts do it.

DE JONG: There are diagrams from the eighth century.

AUSENDA: Well, all right, I'll draw a diagram in the twentieth century [laughter].

WOOD: My point is that this is legislation of the Visigothic state, deeply influenced by Roman law, and the list itself is Roman. It's not Gothic. There is the danger in taking this as an image of a traditional simple society, whereas it actually belongs to a mixed society, which is only Visigothic in the sense that it belongs to a Visigothic king.

AUSENDA: I am not saying that in Spain this was a simple society, but that they had parallel cousin marriage. If it was forbidden, it means that they obviously had it.

WOOD: But so did the Romans.

AUSENDA: It's possible that the Romans had it too, but I am not talking about the Romans. It would be easy to find out about the Romans by looking at previous Roman codes and searching for similar earlier prohibitions.

DE JONG: Could I finish my question. Parallel cousin marriage is one thing, if it is prescribed. If it is preferred that is the type of marriage you would want to make. It's quite another if there are people related in the sixth degree who may marry or may not marry. You see the difference? Do you mean that close agnatic marriage was the preferred pattern?

AUSENDA: It was preferred, not prescribed.

DE JONG: Well, that leaves the question. If it says, "...you should not marry within the sixth degree", can you draw the conclusion that parallel cousin marriage was the preferred model? I don't think so.

AUSENDA: If the law prohibited it, it means that some people did it.

SCHWARCZ: But it is still different to say that some would like to do it than to say that all of them preferred it.

AUSENDA: I am saying that it was the preferential model. I'm not saying it was prescribed. It was preferential, and I can see why it is preferential among the people I studied, because it cost less, because you are taking care of your paternal uncle's properties, because you are not splitting property, because you are not going out of the lineage. There are all kinds of economic reasons which underlie that choice. So, for me it makes perfect sense. It is not even discussed within the family, the father tells you "You marry that girl or woman", and it's between brothers or cousins and they are very happy and no one discusses it. This is in a simple society. And the father's paramount importance is even recognized in the *Lex Visigothorum*. I'm not discussing—we will come to that—I am not discussing why Church and state decided to go against this, obviously Church and state were hurt by the fact that these people intermarried so closely so they put their foot down and legislated against it. I don't know whether they did it in Roman times, your are telling me that. To show it you would have to look at previous Roman law.

---

[9] For both diagram and relevant discussion, see pp. 491-495, this vol.

DE JONG: I think early medieval acculturation can be explained to a large extent precisely by the fact that there was no preferred marriage: that anybody could marry anyone. 'Church' and 'state' were part of that society, the powerful could not step outside of society and look at it and say, "Now, let's manipulate this".

AUSENDA: I guess you haven't understood what preferred marriage means.

HEATHER: Yes, I've got a feeling that there is a problem there [laughter].

AUSENDA: Preferred marriage means that if I have a choice. I can marry anyone if they are marriageable. I have the choice but it is more expedient for me to marry my uncle's daughter because it keeps wealth in the family, it is only my preference, however, I am free to do anything I want. There are percentages. I have listed the percentages. Even in simple society, fifty, sixty percent. These are very high percentages, even though it is only preferential. If someone among the Baggara said, "I want to marry someone in Chad", everyone would think he was crazy, but they would let him do it. If there is an institution in the early Middle Ages which limited marriage choice it was precisely the Church and the state. So it is not true that in early medieval society anybody could marry anyone as you stated earlier, in fact there was not only preferential but prescribed marriage: you could not marry within the sixth degree of kinship.

DE JONG: I find that very interesting, and my only problem is the context which enlightens our understanding of seventh century Visigothic law, and I don't think that's the case.

AUSENDA: I have to explain several ethnological facts and I say that they apply to Visigothic law, so? I am saying that Visigothic law envisages the situation. It envisages the situation, because it forbids it.

HEATHER: But is it forbidding something that's happening a lot or is it forbidding something which might happen once in a while? That's the problem. Isn't that your problem Mayke?

DE JONG: Yes.

AUSENDA: We don't have a Ian Cunnison (1966) who studied those people at that time. We don't know what percentages married within which degrees.

DE JONG: Well, I agree, obviously. Still, I don't think it is right to say "it is forbidden and therefore it must happen all the time". That's not consequential.

SCHWARCZ: You do not forbid anything in law which doesn't happen. You only have to regulate things which happen.

WOOD: Yes, but how often do they happen?

SCHWARCZ: More than once is enough to disturb the legislators. If it is that seldom that it is once every twenty years you don't have to legislate against it.

HEATHER: However, there are cases in the Theodosian code which are obviously produced by one particular case that stimulates the law.

AUSENDA: Yes, but then they describe to you the case where it happened.

SCHWARCZ: The difference is that the Theodosian code is a collection of laws which were issued for special cases. Those are not general laws, they are collected because they are examples for one point in law. As for the so-called Germanic peoples' laws, they are general laws, whereas the Theodosian code is not.

HEATHER: But the Visigothic code is a living tradition, it's a collation like the Theodosian code, in this matter it follows exactly late Roman codes.

WOOD: Like Frankish law.

HEATHER: Absolutely. It might be happening a lot, but there is nothing to say that it is happening a lot.

SCHWARCZ: The difference is that in the Theodosian code you have for each law the day of its issuing and the person to whom it was sent. And the conventional opinion doesn't hold water because any law in the Theodosian code is such a single law, and they got into the collection because the collectors thought that they were important enough to apply them more than once.

HEATHER: No, they get into the law code because there is a principle at stake within them. It doesn't necessarily mean that it's happening a lot, just that there is a legal principle. And the Visigothic code tells you that if you come across a case—I think it's written in the preface—which is not governed by the Code, then you write to the king for a ruling. And that's what it is, a collection of individual rulings, just like the Theodosian code, some of which were generally applicable and others not.

SCHWARCZ: The thing which strikes us is that the Theodosian code is ordered into chapters and that the laws collected there are not placed in a very systematic order, whereas you can take, for instance, the *Lex Salica* or the *Lex Baiwariorum* and they are rather systematic already in their points. There is a development.

HEATHER: The order in the Theodosian code is quite systematic, except it is chronological rather than by subject.

SCHWARCZ: And I don't think you can say that the laws in the Theodosian code are there because they are only used once.

HEATHER: I didn't say that, I'm saying you can never tell.

SCHWARCZ: They were collected because they thought they were important enough to be preserved.

HEATHER: What I am saying is that you can never tell. In some instance they are very specific and you can actually tie them to one event. Other cases you cannot, but you don't know how general they are. I am sure this is the case with this stuff in the Visigothic law code.

AUSENDA: But this is not a particular case, this is a general law and only concerns the forbidden degrees of kinship of which it lists painstakingly more that 90. It means that before the law was issued they were not forbidden, which means that people married also within those degrees.

HEATHER: It means that maybe somebody did.

AUSENDA: I'm not saying that a hundred percent did.

DE JONG: We don't know, that's the point.

AUSENDA: We don't know, none of us knows either positively or negatively.

HEATHER: Can I just feed in one question of my own. Do you think there is any reason why preferential parallel cousin marriage is more applicable to pastoralist societies than to agricultural societies?

AUSENDA: It is just as applicable to agricultural societies. Whenever you have property which is better handled within the close family, you have a tendency for so-called endogamy, close kin marriage. It's not necessarily parallel cousin, but close kin.

HEATHER: Yes.

AUSENDA: It depends on the economic structure. Brideprice is lower, you don't have to have a big feast, you don't split your property, you keep it all together. There is a whole list of reasons for that.

RETAMERO: On marriage as a way of reproducing society, I would like to make some points. It is a general question, related to marriage. Specifically on the size of the groups. Do you think that we could agree on the fact that the size of peasant, pastoralist groups is closely related to the subsitence level of these communities?

AUSENDA: Yes, as long as they are independent. Do you know A. V. Chayanov's theory (1966)? As long as peasants don't have anyone exacting produce from them, and they are not in the presence of a market economy, they usually produce only as much as they think they are going to consume. Also because of the fact that in simple society storage of produce is a problem, because there are pests, floods, all kinds of difficulties, so one needs an organization which requires energy; energy means additional food. You have to be careful, you have to optimize. As long as you don't have someone else who gives you a field to till if you produce something for him you have more or less a subsistence economy.

RETAMERO: I have two additional questions on this page. How did overpopulation fare when peasant forecasts failed?

AUSENDA: They died because of malnutrition.

RETAMERO: Do they fragment?

AUSENDA: They are weakened by malnutrition and die because of diseases that a well nourished person would weather without problems. There is the so-called Body Mass Index, for short BMI. This is an index of nutrition, it is calculated by the ratio of the weight of an adult person (it is more difficult to apply to children) in kilograms divided by the square of his height in metres. The critical level under which a person is malnourished is 17. The index for all the people I studied hovers about 17. Mine must be around 30. You will see that if you are at that level of nutrition, you are always barely taking in what you need, and when there is scarcity you starve. There is nothing you can do about it. It doesn't help to work harder because of the drought or pests or whatever.

RETAMERO: I was thinking of infanticide or segmentation of the groups.

AUSENDA: Among these groups, men, male infants are, of course more valuable, because they are good for herding or other kinds of work. Girls are an enticement for young men to marry them and remain within the family, so they represent a second priority. So, when you have a very good ecological situation the percentages of males and females are more or less the same. When the ecological situation worsens, then you find that the number of females decreases with respect to the number of males. I found percentages as low as 40% for females as against 60% for males. There is no willful infanticide, but in a place plagued with malaria and all sorts of diseases, better care on the part of mothers for male rather than female babies makes a big difference. That is all it takes.

SCHWARCZ: There is a second point one gets in recent and ancient observations of people who live at a subsistence level, this is the custom of killing old people.

AUSENDA: They don't kill them, they just let them die. I've seen old people or sick people left in small straw huts at some distance from the main encampment and probably fed very little. They are not willingly killed.

RETAMERO: Could we envisage in which way an external demand, for example a fiscal demand could affect the group's composition at this level of susbsistence?

AUSENDA: It is a give and take, obviously. If you want someone to do more work for you, you have to offer them something in exchange. You cannot take away produce from them because they would starve. You have to give them land to till, tools, seed, protection and this will motivate them to produce a little more than what they eat. It all depends on how good your protection is. It's a question also of the market.

In the Gash, in eastern Sudan there are different people who work in different ways and they are sharecroppers. There are Hausa who work very hard, because they know how to store the produce, they live in villages, they put the sorghum in bags, so that pests do not easily get at it. The Hadendowa store sorghum in holes in the ground. So, they have to eat it all before the floods come in June. After that they have six months of leanness until the next crop comes in.

RETAMERO: Do you think that this kind of external pressure could be considered as the most important factor affecting the stability of the groups?

AUSENDA: I don't think there are such unbearable pressures. This is one of the widespread misapprehensions of civilized people.

RETAMERO: I am thinking of envisaging 'simple' societies during the Visigothic period, fiscally linked with the state.

AUSENDA: Simple society fiscally linked with the state in what sense?

RETAMERO: Paying tax, in kind or in cash.

SCHWARCZ: Simple society cannot easily accord with the existence of a state. It implies the existence of go-betweens, a stage which does not exist in simple society.

AUSENDA: No, well, you are talking about simple agriculture, agriculture practiced above subsistence level. You can have a peripheral part of society living at a 'simple' level within a state structure, because of the existence of a mediating stage like a landlord and if he exacts more tax or produce than in another place where the landlord asks for less, then they might leave. It's the same as if you had a mule or a donkey. If you keep beating it it will die, so you would not get anything out of it. This is the same with sharecroppers. When people say that they are treated as serfs, even so they have a measure of leisure which they probably wounld't have if they were left to their own resources.

I noted, both in Italy and in the Sudan, that peasants who are thought of as being very poor and having the worst part of the deal when there is an owner and, sometimes, a middleman who puts up the money for the agricultural season, are those who get most out of it. They eat part of the produce they cultivate and no one can check their production on a day-to-day basis. The paradox of Dufy, whereby, according to the documents he found, he concluded that sharecroppers only produced the seed for the following year....

RETAMERO: That's crazy.

AUSENDA: No, that's not crazy. The documents show what the people gave, not what they grew and what they ate. So, it obviously reflected a fraudulent return. It may even have been admittedly so.

RETAMERO: I cannot envisage a peasant sowing, preparing the fields and working during a whole year just for the seed.

AUSENDA: But he doesn't obtain only the seed. He obtains much more and he eats it or does other things with it and he does not tell the owner. Near San Marino, wy wife inherited some land worked by a sharecropper until five years ago. He was supposed to give her one half of everything he produced and she was supposed to pay for two thirds of the expenses. This went on until the man left because he was too old and his son did not want to be a farmer. Until the year he left, he produced 200 bottles of white wine of which he gave one half to my wife. My wife liked it and asked whether he could give her some more: no, he only obtained 200 bottles from the vineyard. The year after he left, the same vineyard produced 2000 bottles. Obviously he was not telling the truth. How are you going to check it? You have to be on call all the time; and you don't have the time to do it if you are the fisc nor do you have the time to do it if you are the landlord. You are happy with the 100 bottles he gives you and let it go at that. And when there are overseers, the situation doesn't change, because the overseer only takes a cut and closes his eyes.

The most difficult person to control is someone working in agriculture. In the case of pastoralists it is easier because you can count the animals. But when someone is working land it's more difficult to check.

RETAMERO: I'm not so confident that this was the case.

AUSENDA: It's done all over the Middle East, herders are given some livestock at the beginning of the season, before lambing or calving, a contract is made whereby they are given a certain number of head for a year's service, plus food, clothes, salt, tobacco, etc. and then they go out. If one comes back and says that hyenas ate many of them, word will get around and the following year he will not get a contract.

RETAMERO: How come that it should be impossible to make an assessment just before the harvest or even in the place where the wheat is threshed?

AUSENDA: You would be surprised how much produce can be robbed under your nose without your realizing it. I tried to measure sorghum production. It is extremely difficult, because when they are cutting it it's not all gathered and you have no idea of how much there is. They think that you are from the fisc, which was the situation in Sudan last January when armed police drove around the fields in jeeps, seizing bags of sorghum. Even so I don't think the fisc got more than 10% of what the tax called for, and that was under extreme duress. You ask them how many bags they are going to produce. The answer will be about half as many. What do you think the owner could do, he would have to sit there all the time and in various places at once and measure the whole production. I met a local school teacher who had been allotted ten feddan (approximately 10 acres) of sorghum as a kind of part salary. At harvest time he had moved to the field and stayed there day and night in a brush lean-to, and I imagine his family brought him food daily for the duration of the harvest and threshing operation. How many people can do that?

It's easier when there are machines, because the machines discharge directly into bags.

RETAMERO: I can see that it is a very complicated operation. But peasants do not move, pastoralists move. For example there are some references about how the Roman state taxed pastoralists in North Africa and the only way to control pastoralists was in the market place. It was the only moment in which pastoralists were controllable.

AUSENDA: Of course, but the Roman state was not as well organized as a family of Hausa or Hadendowa who know where to go and find their herder and can ask "Did you see Mohammed", "Yes I have seen him yesterday at the so and so wells". So they can track him down, and these people cannot migrate to another place, they have to remain in the vicinity. That was not the same for the Roman fisc, nor for that matter for the Sudanese fisc.

SCHWARCZ: I think especially in Egypt there are accounts of this way of assessing the peasants by going to them with an armed force and beating them up to get them to tell how much there was really around.

AUSENDA: The next thing that will happen in that case is that the peasants, if they can, will go away to another administration, so it is only when the state is desperate that it makes recourse to these methods.

RETAMERO: It actually depends on the effectiveness of the state, not on the very condition of agricultural activities and pastoral activities.

AUSENDA: With agricultural activities it is more difficult to assess production, with pastoral activities it is more difficult to locate the herds or flocks. Also because, whether your peasant sows wheat or beets or turnips or whatever, you cannot go there every day and count them.

RETAMERO: For instance, on a Visigothic slate there is the number of head to be delivered, their age and additional considerations.

AUSENDA: This proves my point. In other words Visigoths made contracts the same way as Beni Amer or Hadendowa, with the added advantage that they wrote them down on slates. I'll tell you another interesting story of camel herds up to 120 head that are herded by some five cameliers who let them graze through the bush by day and camp at night. As a naive anthropologist, I asked them how they kept track of all those camels which were dispersed in an area having a diamater of about one kilometre. Did they count their camels and how many times a day did they do it?

They looked surprised at the weird idea of counting their camels. They do not count their livestock, they recognize them by their 'genealogies'. They know the males, the females and the foals belonging to each female and they can immediately tell whether a camel is missing. This is why the work of anthropologists is fascinating, because it give one flashes of understanding in aspects that one couldn't understand except by being freed of the fetters of one's civilization.

DE JONG: I don't disagree with that, but I do think that you have to be careful making models from society A and applying them to society B. That's something different from getting flashes of insight.

AUSENDA: Apart from the fact that this morning the Far West was used as a model for Visigothic settlement and no one seemed to mind, the only thing I have been advocating all the time is to take insights from societies living at *the same* level of socio-cultural integration and seeing whether they even partially fit the situation under observation, with no pre-conceived ideas on how the society under study works, bearing in mind that no society is monolithic.

When Peter [Heather] talked about the ratio of nobles to clients, both Andreas and myself mentioned cases where the same ratios were encountered, so that this allows one to begin to think that he is not too far off the mark, it is something which can stand up.

JIMÉNEZ [upon reading the transcript]: I didn't use the Far West society as a model for Visigothic settlement, but in order to bear in mind that Visigoths were not necessarily nomadic people. They travelled on carts only while searching a permanent settlement. Their main difficulty is that their search lasted longer than they may have expected.

SCHWARCZ: It's a functional comparison, and of course you have to have the evidence, if there is no evidence you cannot argue that in this special society you can use the functional comparison.

DE JONG: Yes, OK.

RETAMERO: On your asking or suggesting the marriage season for weddings. I feel that the answer is implicit in your wording. We cannot know the answer because we know almost nothing about the peasant calendars during the Visigothic period.

AUSENDA: My hope was that someone would come up and say that they had read in the sources that Alaric had married so and so in May. This would give some insight into the situation.

HEATHER: One thing that occurred to me in relation to this doesn't really apply to later seventh-century Spain. There are a lot of references in Jordanes and in some of the *Variae* which make you think that there was an annual occasion when donatives were handed out to Gothic warriors and that would be an occasion for gathering, and for quite a lot of social business being done there.

AUSENDA: That was in May, wasn't it?

HEATHER: That was when the campaigns usually started, probably around that time, but I don't think we know exactly.

SCHWARCZ: Then of course the Roman army system was strictly regulated. You had to collect taxes, then you had to make sure that people were paid and you made the cities responsible for tax collecting, and you made those who collected also responsible for giving their pay to the officials and soldiers who should be paid by the state.

I have a remark concerning your first draft on the fact that acculturation began long before 376.

AUSENDA: I take your point., I will change the sentence to "the pace of acculturation quickened after their settlement within the Roman Empire". Do you agree with that?

SCHWARCZ: Yes, their acculturation starts, I think....

AUSENDA: ...five hundred years earlier, and then the exponential takes off.

SCHWARCZ: You have an exponential curve after 200 AD, and of course it is very stimulated by direct contact with the Empire.

GREEN: On page 139 I have three small points, small because I have a big one later. You refer to your edition of Wulfila as being Migne 1848. Giorgio [Ausenda], that is from any linguistic point of view unreliable and totally outdated. It must be Wilhelm Streitberg, Heidelberg 1928.

AUSENDA: You didn't like the list of names? That's all I took out of it.

GREEN: I know, that was the cause of the trouble. Second point, end of the next paragraph, you say that Wulfila's Gothic was probably the most ancient and complete Germanic text. It is certainly the most ancient, but it is certainly not a complete text.

AUSENDA: I take your point.

GREEN: And thirdly, three lines from the end you talk about the importance of landed wealth requiring written transactions. What is interesting for your point there, is the fact that the Ostrogothic deed of Arezzo includes the word *frabaúhtaboka*, meaning not a book but a document of sale. So that confirms your argument. This is borne out also in Wulfila's translation of the New Testament. That's all on page 139.

AUSENDA: Thank you.

DE JONG: [Referring to the middle of page 140]. So it's all we have of Euric, and there is nothing pristine about it, it is reconstructed.

HEATHER: It is not even necessarily Euric's. It can easily be Theoderic II.

GREEN: In the list you give here (page 141), Gothic and English, because you use the Migne edition is a number of misspellings which need correction. Secondly though, there are some mistranslations. Can I just seize upon three: first is the word *sunus*, certainly it means 'son', but you can't equate *barn* with it because that means a 'child'. The Gothic word *atta* means father, and there is no known linguistic connection with the Latin word *atavus*. It is best not to include that and certainly not the meaning 'grand-father', simply 'father'.

AUSENDA: Sorry, what's the difference between the word *fadar* and *atta*?

GREEN: None, *atta* has more of an emotional connotation.

AUSENDA: Is it an endearing form?

GREEN: No, it shows you the linguistic finesse of Wulfila in translating. When he translates the Lord's prayer, he doesn't say *Fadar unsar* but *Atta unsar* to try to develop the emotional link and closeness between the Christian and God the Father. That I think is the difference. Another example to seize on which would help your argument is the second word in the second list on that page, not *vadi* but *wadi* with a *w*. You translate that by 'gage', it means more a pledge or a legal security, but what you should seize upon for the argument of your paper is that this is the same word as English to 'wed' or 'wedding' and that ties the legal term up with your argument for marriage.

AUSENDA: Isn't it the same term as 'gage'?

GREEN: It's the same word as 'gage' but that comes from Frankish into Old French. Those are just a few examples but there are plenty others which I won't go into.

WOOD: On page 142, I want to raise a question which Dennis [Green] may be able to answer just as well as Giorgio [Ausenda], and it is quite simply to what extent the limitations of Wulfila's terminology are reflections of the relations which occur or do not occur in the Bible.

GREEN: Yes, obviously. The restriction of this terminology is dictated entirely by the restrictions of the lexis of the Bible.

WOOD: And one cannot move from this list to say anything about Visigothic kinship?

GREEN: No, one cannot.

AUSENDA: I agree with you. This is what I said. We know what the terms are but we don't know what they mean.

GREEN: No, that's not Ian's point.

AUSENDA: It is obvious that Wulfila only gave them biological meanings and they are only interesting from a linguistic standpoint.

WOOD: The point I'm making is that you write in your sentence that "we miss the all important terms for maternal uncle, and aunt and those for wife and so on". That sentence is historically meaningless, because we only have terms which are in passages of the Bible for which we have Ulfila's translation.

AUSENDA: That is why I say we were missing them, we don't have them. How do you want me to write it, instead of "we miss them"?

WOOD: I think you need to couch the passage in a different way.

GREEN: Something like, "Wulfila's text does not include...."

WOOD: The issue is that we cannot derive conclusions from this. If there were terms in the Bible which he could not translate, then that would be significant, but if there are nouns omitted in the Bible for which, therefore, we don't have the Gothic word, we can't give....

AUSENDA: Very good.

WOOD: Again on page 145, the question of stepmother marriage. Since this is against the Church canons, I wanted to know to what extent legal enactments are not indications of Germanic traditions but of clerical taboos. Moreover, can we assume that the regular reiteration of technical taboos is an indication that such taboos were regularly broken, or are we looking at a repeated statement about the purity of the people?

HEATHER: Is it worth mentioning that stepmother marriage is considered in both the sixth-century letter of Augustine to Pope Gregory and the seventh-century letter of Boniface to Pope Zacharias [in connection with prevailing barbarian customs]?

WOOD: It is also in Bede on Eadbald marrying the widow of Æthelberht.

HEATHER: Yes, as a general point though it is in those two letters.

WOOD: The point I was making is that you can't assume from a legal statement about step-mother marriage that it is a significant feature of Gothic society. The law may come from a different tradition.

HEATHER: That occurrence is also mentioned in the letters written for something that Augustine and Boniface, rightly or wrongly, thought they were encountering.

WOOD: Sure, but then I think you have argued from that point of view and not from the laws.

DE JONG: And it is in last year's paper [laughter]; it's all over the place. I would like to comment on that too, to the law on marriage within the sixth degree. It struck me that indeed the list of the kinship terminology is Roman and the terminology in this particular law is Roman and I have read that text as very much applied to both Visigoths and Romans, if it makes any sense at all to make the distinction at that particular point, because it is certain that in Roman legislation there was no prohibition extending to the sixth degree until this particular law. So, we do agree that this is a law intended for the whole population, possibly in view of purification. It is not specifically Gothic or Visigothic. Do you agree?

AUSENDA: It could be so or it couldn't. One would have to read the minds of the people who wrote it. There must be an expert on legislation here.

SCHWARCZ: Is there any possibility of doing this?

DE JONG: Well, I'm trying to get this out of the context of Germanicity. And in the later anti-Jewish laws it struck me that the marriage prohibitions define Gothicness and Christianity as completely overlapping concepts. A Christian Goth, in the sense of us, all of us, versus the Jews, is somebody who does not marry within the sixth degree. And the first thing the converting Jew is being made to do is to avoid marrying his kin within the sixth degree.

WOOD: On page 146, is the kinship list of *LV* IV relevant to the reconstruction of a Germanic kinship system? Giorgio, at some point in the paper you need to make a statement that the evidence that we have ceases to relate simply to the Visigoths as a *gens* of the pre-Migration or Migration Period, but comes to relate to the population of the Visigothic kingdom. Unless you make that distinction there is a danger in people assuming that this is a Germanic list, rather than a list directed to the kingdom as a whole.

AUSENDA: I take your point.

DE JONG: On Manselli's view, page 147. Yes, I think perhaps that we should be careful in citing Manselli, because he seems to subscribe to all sorts of ideas about peasants which are a bit romantic, I think. But, more important and more interesting on the same page are your remarks about the links between traditional religion and kinship, and I think we should ask ourselves what exactly is the traditional religion at the moment when these laws were issued against marriage between kinsmen. Most of those laws come from the seventh century. So, perhaps we should discuss what this traditional religion in the seventh century is.

AUSENDA: I only wish to argue that the people who wrote this thing on religion agreed on the idea that the Church had great difficulty in making inroads among the rural population, because the rural population didn't find Christianity suitable for its needs, and Christianity was considered oppressive and not adapted to their yearly cycle. So, I thought that this was exactly what I visualized for the reasons that Christianity had difficulty penetrating the countryside. You don't like it, but I do. We are on the opposite side of the tracks. You cite people who are of your opinion, and I cite people who are of my opinion, if you allow me to do so, especially when it is related in a book published by a respected historical institution. On the other hand, I will tell you something about my opinion concerning theories. Theories have to be simple and economical. This idea is simple and economical. I understand your idea of purity. I don't think it is simple or economical. So we have to weigh the two theories one against the other and we can go on discussing for the next few years until we find someone who will prove the validity of one theory or the other. You cannot ask me, because you don't like Manselli to give up the citation.

I don't like your theory, but I'm going to quote everything you say faithfully.

DE JONG: I think Manselli talks about....

AUSENDA: Not only Manselli, but Sotomayor. As I understand, Sotomayor was a great scholar and wrote more or less the same thing. The problem of the eradication of paganism was not considered religious but political by the hierarchy and the state.

WOOD: I think I would disagree there.

AUSENDA: On the fact that Sotomayor was a great scholar? [Laughter]

WOOD: The sources of the sixth and seventh century say exactly....

AUSENDA: OK, you give me the sources and I will add them to this discussion.

SCHWARCZ: That's the question of popular culture and popular religion. And there is a stubborn persistence of popular beliefs, they influence Christian beliefs and there is a lot of syncretism between them.

HEATHER: Well, yes. Christianity progressively redefines what Christianity is. What is perfectly good peasant Christianity in 600 is not by 700.

DE JONG: I think that is part of my problem. If Manselli says they were Christian only at the most rudimentary level, which ideal of Christianity does he then have in mind?

HEATHER: Yes, and anachronistic.

DE JONG: Yes, that's the point.

AUSENDA: I shall transcribe every criticism [laughter].

DE JONG: On page 150, *LV* III. Yes, that's an interesting text, *LV* III, that you cite there. It is on concubinage but I was struck when I read it by the fact that it was not only referring to concubinage as we would define it, it is also on incidental sex. So it is again about polluting sex in toto. It doesn't contradict anything you say, but it is a very interesting text. I thank you for calling my attention to it.

AUSENDA: Not only is it on incidental sex, but it comes closest to our idea of incest.

DE JONG: Our modern idea.

AUSENDA: Yes, our modern idea of incest.

DE JONG: It's a superficial similarity.

SCHWARCZ: On page 151, can marriage policy of kings be taken as an example for custom? I think that the marriage policy of kings is an international phenomenon in the early Middle Ages, and it is not only conducted by popular customs but it is dictated by policy and it is not always, I think, the father of the bridegroom who seeks the bride for his son, but it's also the other way around at times. For instance, if we shall take the policy of Theoderic the Great there has always been the assumption that he seeks to make political allies of other kings by sending his daughters to them and when he has no longer any daughters his more distant female relatives are used this way. And there is the custom of adopting kings by weapons, *adoptio per arma*, the German way. So, I would be indeed cautious with such parallels.

AUSENDA: I take your point, except for the fact that you have to do these things, that you talk about, saving face. In other words, he would send his daughters to those peoples, but at least he would have someone from the other side come and ask for them formally, because if he didn't, it wouldn't look good. So, he would at least, under a thin varnish, respect tradition. And the position was that.

HEATHER: And you've got that startling example of a Burgundian king who murders his son by Theoderic's daughter when he declares himself politically independent of the Ostrogoths.

SCHWARCZ: The other one is the Visigothic princess who was the first wife of Huneric the son of Geiseric, she gets her nose cut off.

AUSENDA: This has nothing to do with the negotiations preceding the marriage. It may happen.

WOOD: The Burgundians had been on bad terms with the Ostrogoths for a long period of time when Sigismer claimed to be Theoderic's heir. Sigismund then murdered him.

SCHWARCZ: Yes, that's a question of political expediency. You see for instance that the first Christian ruler of Bulgaria, Boris Michail, went back out of the monastery and deposed and blinded his son because he went against his policies of Christianizing the Bulgarians.

VELÁZQUEZ: On page 151, you say is it possible that the *morgingab* was not established during the engagement negotiation also in the Visigothic kingdom? You referred to the engagement negotiation and mentioned a law by Liutprand. But my question is do you think that in the Visigothic law there was negotiation, was it during the morning after?

AUSENDA: You know that *morgingab* is practically unmentioned in the *Lex Visigothorum*.

VELÁZQUEZ: Yes, but I will not say if the *morgingab* is preserving a formula, but I want to mention the *Lex Visigothorum* III, I. V about dowry. I want to say first that *donatio ante nuptias* and *morgingab* are similar in the society. *Morgingab* is a traditional Gothic gift and *donatio ante nuptias* is a Roman gift, but in the seventh century there is an assimilation between the two. But we have agreed that the law indicates that the donation was fixed during the negotiations not after them because in this law, the lawgiver says that the maximum is 1/3 of the patrimony of the father. I think that this concrete situation shows that this law reflects that the negotiation was before the wedding, before the establishment of the donation.

AUSENDA: You are not talking to a juridical specialist. I have absolutely no idea. If you want to know my feeling, it is that in the seventh century it was no longer a simple society and donations and marriage exchanges had changed considerably, it would be interesting to make a study to see exactly how and when they transformed. I cited it to show that there was a trace, and that they existed before. It's exactly the same as with marriage prohibitions.

In simple societies negotiations do not concern mostly the wealth being exchanged at marriage because it is tradition which regulates these exchanges. When you are amongst Hadendowa or Maori or whatever, you know you should give two cows or three camels or whatever. Wealth exchanges are not the central concern of those negoatiations. The most important part of the negotiations concerns whether your son or nephew can marry that girl and whether or not there is a closer relative who has priority to her. Indeed, you would have a mess in the family or a feud might ensue if that priority were not respected. That is what the marriage negotiation involves. With time, with landed property and all these aspects of wealth, obviously the question of wealth exchanges became much more important than when it consisted of two cows. The traditional exchange was based on the fact that if you wanted to launch a new family they had to have enough wealth to support themselves and their first child. Later it became more complicated. My interest here was to show that there was something called *morgingab* before. Later this may have been absorbed within a newly adopted dowry system and may have disappeared. These aspects evolved very quickly in two or three centuries, which shows that the socioeconomic situation changed considerably. That would be a worthwhile study in itself. I would be quite interested in reading such a study.

GREEN: Page 151, Langobardic *meta* or *metfio*. First it's far better to say not 'maid's livestock', but simply 'maid's wealth'. And similarly, two lines below on 'father's wealth', we cannot simply equate the etymology of a word with it's meaning at any one point in time.

AUSENDA: I meant literally.

GREEN: Yes, but the literal meaning may not have existed at the time that this word was used in Langobardic. It may have generalized or restricted its meaning. We don't know. You avoid all difficulies if you say simply 'maid's wealth'.

AUSENDA: Can I say the etymology of which is 'maid's livestock'?

GREEN: But then, I argue against you on the other term of that phrase, namely with 'maid'. I don't know what your thought processes were here. I suspect though that you equated <met> or <meta> with the English word 'maid'.

AUSENDA: No *magd*.

GREEN: Oh yes, *magd* but that is linguistically the same. But it cannot be. First, at this early stage of Langobardic, one would have to have not *e* but *a*, and one would also have, as in German *g*. One would have to have <magd> not <met>. I've got an alternative for you. I must admit I haven't had time to go into it, but I would suggest that you consider this. In OHG we have a word for 'payment' or 'reward', that word is *miata*. The earlier form of this was precisely *meta*, and that has the additional advantage of explaining why Langobardic in this context can use not merely *metfio* but *meta* by itself. Because a word for a 'maid' could not stand for 'maid's price' or 'maid's wealth', but if we take *meta* in the sense I proposed, the simplex could stand alongside the compound.

AUSENDA: It sounds like a very likely etymology, thank you very much.

GREEN: I come now to page 153, what you say about *paranympha* and *troctingi*. Here, Giorgio, I must disagree with you totally and unreservedly for a number of reasons. First, in the footnote on that page you venture to connect the word with the modern German word 'Trottel'. The first attested record of that German word is, believe it or not, 1833 and you would have, from the linguistic point of view, severe difficulties in linking the word *troctingi*, spanning centuries, with a word attested as late as that. You quote the word *paranympha*. The Greek form for this word is a feminine, but takes the form *paranymphos* with an *-os* even though it is a feminine. Latin has the form *paranymphus*, but in Latin it is a masculine. So that the Latin meaning of the word is a 'bride's male attendant', not a 'lady in waiting'. It is a male attendant of a bride, and as such this Latin masculine word is often glossed in the Germanic languages and the stem of the word used to gloss it, is a word which came up this morning, namely the stem <druht-> with its variants <droht->, <truht->. It means in Germanic a warband, a group of armed men, and the suffix <-ing> means someone belonging to...forming part of..., being a member of.... So the Germanic formation of this word is reasonably clear 'a member of an armed band', 'a member of a *druht-*'. But one can go further, because in the various West-Germanic languages, Old Frisian, Old English, Old Saxon, Old High German, this stem <druht-> is used precisely of a marriage procession where an armed band under a leader, the bride's male attendant, if you like, conducts the bride in a procession, guarding her, towards her new kindred. Let me just simply quote here from the *Lex Salica*, this is one example of many: "*Puella sponsata dructe ducente ad maritum*". In Old English we have for the male who does this forms such as *dryhtman*, *dryhtguma*, *dryhtealdor*, all glossing the Latin masculine *paranymphus*. But to get back to your precise word, we have in Old Saxon the word *drohting* and in Old High German *truhting*, both of them glossing Latin *sponsalis*, meaning a 'member of a marriage procession', or Latin *appetitor*, *procus*, meaning the 'man who courts or woos, a suitor', again in the context of marriage. And to provide further support I've got a list of six books or articles which deal with this word, one of them precisely on Visigothic marriage practice.

AUSENDA: I'm convinced. The only thing is that there is a gloss there in the *Liber Papiensis* which says *mimi* or *joculatores*.

GREEN: I cannot account for that. It may turn out to be another function of this stem, because it is used in Germanic of a banquet or feast, and therefore you may get the idea of *mimi* or your jesters taking part in a marriage feast.

AUSENDA: Furthermore, the law in question has both *paranympha* and *troctingi*.

GREEN: But the Germanic word glosses only *paranymphus* not *paranympha*. It's not easy to see how a lady in waiting conducted an armed band.

AUSENDA: That's a law of Ahistulf. The law says some people threw dung at a wedding cortege which was described as being composed *cum paranympha et troctingi* who are escorting to the bridegroom's house the bride they have fetched from her house. I have to take into account both words. Because the law mentions a *paranympha* too, so there obviously was an armed band with a lady in waiting.

SCHWARCZ: Well the gloss tells us what happened in the tenth century when the Goths were long gone.

AUSENDA: Yes, but the wording above is exactly that of the law of Ahistulf. The glosses are something else: they explain laws issued at the beginning of the eighth century, in which many customs were exactly the same as five centuries before, such as the war horse as part of the wedding cortege. Obviously those customs were not completely forgotten.

SCHWARCZ: No, but it changes its meaning. The gloss tells us what the man who made the gloss thought, not what it meant at his time.

DE JONG: On page 154, Giorgio [Ausenda] asks for wedding parties, and I have not exactly found one but I thought you might be interested in Erwig's law which is in 12, 3. 8 which defines how Jews should marry after they convert, which says *non aliter cum premisso dotis titulo*. So that suggests a written document where the *dos* is drawn up and they should do so *sacerdotali benedictione intra sinum sancte ecclesiae,* and that is I think the first mention in the Visigothic law of any priest blessing a wedding. We could think of this as late or early, and it's very early if you look at the rest of Europe. It's quite late if you look at Visigothic law, I just thought.

AUSENDA: Are you talking about wedding parties?

DE JONG: Well, if you think that a priestly blessing in church is a party. No, not exactly a party, but it does say something about the ceremony itself and I thought I'd note that because it is so rarely discussed.

AUSENDA: This is at the beginning of the transformation of matrimony into a sacrament that Ian was talking about last year. That he described as taking place in the eleventh century.

WOOD: That's right, it doesn't become a sacrament until the twelfth century.

DE JONG: It's very early, but probably this is an anti-Jewish law.

SCHWARCZ: And of course, yes, the priest is there to make sure that they are not following Jewish ceremonies.

HEATHER: I can't remember how much Venantius Fortunatus says about the marriages of Frankish princesses. He certainly talks at some length about two Visigothic princesses going to Frankish Gaul and some of the preparations are talked about at great length (Venantius, 6. 1; 6. 5).

DE JONG: The trousseau.

WOOD: In talking about Brunhild, Fortunatus concentrates on the Frankish celebrations. In discussing Goiswinth he concentrates on the relationship between her and her mother.

DE JONG: On page 155, proof that kinship networks were superseded by the state. This was something that I found puzzling in the *Liber Iudiciorum*: that if the people commit incest and they are separated, the children get to inherit. In Roman law the children are disinherited, they cannot succeed. I wondered about the difference between Roman and Visigothic law in this case, what you make of that.

VELÁZQUEZ: Sorry, I can't remember now the complete text of this Visigothic law.

DE JONG: We can discuss it later.

HEATHER: This reminds me of what Wendy Davies told me happened in later medieval Wales. It's that the state mobilizes via kinship relations in order to enforce legislation. Only in the later stages, very late, do you get reference to wide degrees of kinship being mobilized for law enforcement, but they are being mobilized by the state, by kings and princes.

DE JONG: I remember now what I wanted to mention about kinship and the state. There is a very interesting law 6 and 5. 14 again from Recceswinth's code where it says that if the kinsmen do not accuse, the *iudex* has to do so.

References in the discussion

Textual sources:

Augustine of Canterbury
> Letter to Pope Gregory: see Colgrave & Mynors (eds. & trans.) 1969
Bede
> *Baedae Opera Historica*: see Plummer (ed.) 1896.
Boniface
> Letter to Pope Zacharias: see Tangl (ed.) 1916.
Cassiodorus
> *Variae*: see Mommsen (ed.) 1894.
Codex Theodosianus: see Mommsen, Krueger & Meyer (eds.) 1904-1905.
Leges Ahistulfi regis: see References at end of paper.
Lex Salica: see Eckhardt (ed.) 1969.
Liber Iudiciorum: see Zeumer (ed.) 1902.
Liber Papiensis: see References at end of paper.
Venantius Fortunatus
> *Opera poetica*: see Leo (ed.) 1881.

Lex Visigothorum: see Zeumer (ed.) 1902
Wulfila
        Bible in Gothic: see Streitberg (ed.) 1919.

Bibliography:

Chayanov, A. V.
  1966   *The Theory of Peasant Economy.* D. Thorner, B. Kerblay & R. E. F. Smith
              (eds.). Chicago, IL: The American Economic Association.
Colgrave, B., & R. A. B. Mynors (eds. & trans.)
  1969   *Bede's Ecclesiastical History of the English People.* Oxford: Clarendon
              Press.
Cunnison, I.
  1966   *Baggara Arabs: Power and the Lineage in a Sudanese Nomad Tribe.*
              Oxford: Clarendon Press.
Eckhardt, K. A. (ed.)
  1969   *Lex Salica. Monumenta Germaniae Historica. Leges nationum
              Germanicarum,* 4, 2. Hannover: Hahn.
Leo, F. (ed.)
  1881   *Venanti Honori Clementiani Fortunati presbyteri Italici Opera poetica.
              Monumenta Germaniae Historica. Auctores antiquissimi,* 4, 1. Berlin:
              Weidmann. [Repr. 1981].
Manselli, R.
  1982   See References at end of paper.
Mommsen, T., P. Krueger & P. Meyer (eds.)
  1904-05   *Codex Theodosianus,* I-II. Hildesheim: Weidmann. [Repr. 1990].
Plummer, C.
  1896   *Baedae Opera Historica.* Oxford: Clarendon Press.
Sotomayor, M.
  1882   See References at end of paper.
Streitberg, W.
  1919   *Die gotische Bibel.* Heidelberg: Winter Verlag.
Tangl, H.
  1916   *Die Briefe des heiliges Bonifatius und Cullus.* Berlin: Akademie Verlag.
Zeumer, K. (ed.)
  1902   See References at end of paper.

SOCIAL RELATIONS IN THE VISIGOTHIC KINGDOM FROM THE FIFTH TO THE SEVENTH CENTURY: THE EXAMPLE OF MÉRIDA

IAN WOOD

School of History, University of Leeds, Leeds, GB-LS2 9JT

In many respects the Visigoths are the most accessible of the barbarian peoples in the initial stages of the Migration Period. They can be studied, like other barbarian groups, in their archaeology, in their origin legends and from their importance to Roman writers (Wolfram 1989), but they can also be studied, at least in part, on their own terms, through the *Life of St Saba* (Matthews & Heather 1991), and perhaps most significantly of all in the language of Wulfila's Bible, even allowing for the likelihood that the text was revised in Ostrogothic Italy. Once inside the Roman Empire they become a more problematic group. For all their importance to the narrative of the Fall of the Western Empire they remain curiously opaque until the seventh century. The evidence for even the greatest of their fifth- and sixth-century kings is poor, and the vast mass of the population present considerable problems of interpretation. Where and how they were settled first in Aquitaine and later in Spain, are issues which are not easily studied (despite Goffart 1980: see Jiménez Garnica in this volume). As Arians until the conversion of Reccared, even their Christianity is poorly evidenced and has to be reconstructed from fragments (Schäferdiek 1967).

True there are legal sources, even though the major Code, the *Liber Iudiciorum*, comes from the mid to late seventh century, being compiled by Chindaswinth (642-53) and his son Recceswinth (649-72) and then revised by Erwig (680-7). Leaving aside the problematic *Edictum Theodorici*, which is generally thought to be an Ostrogothic code, the one earlier Visigothic code to have survived largely intact, the *Breviary* of Alaric (484-507), is avowedly a codification of Roman law. There are, however, considerable fragments of the code of Euric (466-484), and more of Euric's code may be reconstructed from other sources. Further, the *Liber Iudiciorum* names numerous clauses as *Antiquae*, which usually indicates that they have been taken from the now lost code of Liuvigild (568-86).

What survives of the codes of Euric and Liuvigild, however, does not allow the reconstruction of the social history of a separate Visigothic *gens* in the fifth and sixth centuries. The legislation is heavily influenced by Roman law, to the extent that it is simply impossible to separate what stems from Roman and what from Visigothic tradition. This even holds true for the agrarian sections of Book 8 of the *Liber Iudiciorum*, whose similarity to the Byzantine *Eclogae* was once held to indicate the existence of Gothic communities in Asia Minor: it is simpler, however, to see both the *Eclogae* and the relevant books of the Visigothic code as both reflecting Roman provincial law (Collins 1983:28; Wood 1996:9). Further, the notion of a Gothic legal tradition may well be misleading: the Goths had long been

191

influenced by the Romans, and vice versa, and what traditions existed before the migration are likely to have been subjected to enormous pressure during the migrations of the fourth and fifth centuries. There are unquestionably certain sections of the law code which must have originated in the legislation issued for or by the Visigoths in the course of the fifth century, notably legislation relating to the settlement of the Goths (*CE* 276: *LI* V, 7. 2, VIII, 5. 2 & 5; X, 1. 1-16; X, 3. 5), and to the summoning of the Visigothic army (*LI* IX, 2. 1-7). In general, however, the legal evidence does not reflect the traditions of a Germanic *gens*, but rather the law of a post-Roman society, which was an inseparable amalgam of Gothic and Roman.

Although there are differences between the legislation of the *Breviary* of Alaric and that of Euric and Liuvigild, the inspiration behind the codes drawn up for the Visigoths themselves was largely Roman. It is important, however, to recognize the variety within what one may term Roman: the laws of the Roman provinces may have been the chief inspiration for Euric and Liuvigild, while Alaric's Roman lawyers simply abridged the *Codex Theodosianus*, a compilation of imperial edicts. Despite this variety, however, the fact that the law codes of the successor states were Roman in inspiration helps obviate one other problem: that of the personality or the territoriality of the law. Essentially, given the extent to which Gothic law was Roman, certainly by Liuvigild's time, and possibly by Euric's, the exact moment at which Visigothic law became territorial, even if it was as late as the reign of Chindaswinth (642-53) (King 1980), may have been a matter of comparatively little significance. The laws to which Roman provincials were accustomed would have differed less from that of the barbarian law codes than any simple comparison of the *Codex Theodosianus* and the *leges barbarorum* might suggest.

What the laws reveal is a mixed society, subject to a legal tradition which was largely Roman (Nehlsen 1983). Even the remarkable discussion of the family in the *Liber Iudiciorum* (*LI* IV, 1. 1-7 = *LRV* IV, 10. 1-8), with its seven degrees of kinship, comes from the *Lex Romana Visigothorum* and the *Sentences* of the Roman jurist Paul. The list provided by the code, therefore, is not derived from earlier Gothic traditions: it is is, rather, an account of the Roman family transposed into the Gothic world. In so far as the laws show us the Visigothic family in action it is not as a kin group, but as a household (on the absence of the kin group, King 1972:222-3). Certainly the laws, with their concern over marriage, women and children, present an interesting picture of the nuclear family (King 1972:222-50), but the issue most consistently present in the early laws is the relationship not of a man to his wife or children, but of a lord to his slaves. Time and again a distinction is made between those crimes committed by a slave with the knowledge of his lord and those committed where the lord is completely innocent. One of the relatively few early laws which does deal with the relations between a man and his wife, outside those that cover questions of marriage and adultery, states that the wife has no claim on anything gained by her husband in concert with her slave on an expedition, since she and the slave are both subject to the husband: equally, if a slave causes any loss on the expedition the husband is liable (*LI* IV, 2. 15 = *CE* 323). In the Visigothic laws it is the lord's household rather than his kin that we see in action.

In other words, by the late sixth century, if not earlier, one can no longer investigate the ethnology of the Visigothic *gens*. One can only study a mixed, or even a new, society. The drive towards social unification probably underlay Liuvigild's policies. It is implicit, at the beginning of the seventh century, in Isidore of Seville's decision to write a *History of the Goths, Vandals and Sueves*, which is essentially a territorial history, and is confirmed as such by the inclusion of the *Laus Spaniae*. Although there had been an attempt to keep Romans and Goths apart, that ended in the repeal, in Liuvigild's time if not before, of the ban on the intermarriage of Goths and Romans (*LI* III, 1. 1).[1] Thus the Visigothic kingdom of the sixth century was indeed a sub-Roman society, as implied by the laws. Whether or not there was legal unity in the time of Reccared, there was a sense of the growing unity of the various *gentes*: the Tome produced by Reccared at Toledo III (589) talks of the *gentes* under the king's rule (Vives 1963:110-11), while in his sermon following the council, Leander of Seville argued that Christ wished to form one Church of many *gentes* (Vives 1963:143). Yet unity did not mean uniformity. To study a society as mixed as that of the Visigothic kingdom of the sixth century from texts as normative as the law codes is to run the risk of looking simply at the imagination of lawyers schooled in the traditions of Roman Law, some of it going as far back as the 12 Tables (c.f. *LI* V, 7. 2 & 15).

In order to see this mixed society in action it is necessary to turn to a relatively detailed narrative source. On the whole the narrative sources for the Visigothic kingdom in this period are slight. The most significant exception is the *Vitas Patrum Emeretensium*, a work written by a deacon of the Church of St Eulalia in Mérida, probably in the 630s (Maya Sánchez 1992, with the translation and commentary in Fear 1997), but covering the history of the city's bishops between *ca* 530 and 605. Like all works of hagiography this presents problems of genre. The author admits his dependence on the *Dialogues* of Gregory the Great (*VPE* praef. 1), and clearly he had other sources of literary inspiration, including the *Life of Martin* by Sulpicius Severus and, more interestingly, the *Vita Desiderii* written by the Visigothic king Sisebut (Maya Sánchez 1992:108-13). Equally important, the author had an ecclesiastical agenda: specifically he was a deacon of the church of St Eulalia and was concerned to promote his saintly patroness (*VPE* 1, 22-3; epilog. 2). He was also concerned to extol the chief patrons of the Church of Mérida, especially the two bishops from whom the Church derived most of its wealth, Paul (530-60) and his nephew Fidelis (560-71), as well as Masona (571-605), the bishop who had done most to save the Catholic Church of Mérida from the threats presented by King Liuvigild and the Arian bishop Sunna. Yet over and above this the author does have a number of spiritual concerns, which are clearest in the three opening chapters on the deaths of the boy Agustus, abbot Nanctus, and an unnamed monk of the monastery of Cauliana. The story of Agustus in particular

---

[1] It should be noted that the ban was in origin imperial rather than Gothic.

is concerned with the justification of the innocent, in this case a young and illiterate rustic serving the church of St Eulalia (*VPE* 1), while the monk of Cauliana illustrates the significance of repentance, even after a life of sin (*VPE* 2). Penitence and penance recur again in the *Vitas*.[2] For all his ecclesiastical concerns, however, the author of the *Lives of the Fathers of Merida* does appear to allow an insight into the social working of a sixth-century Visigothic city. Moreover at a number of crucial points the text also allows comparison with the legal evidence.

Before looking in detail at the *Vitas Patrum Emeretensium*, it is, however, worth considering the extent to which a south Spanish city might have been representative of life in the Visigothic state. No detailed comparison can be made between Mérida and any other Visigothic city, not even the royal cities of Toulouse or Toledo, because comparable evidence does not exist: and the few short comments on other cities to be found in the chronicles are likely to refer to exceptional circumstances (Collins 1980:190-1). Moreover, Toledo, as a royal city, would doubtless have been an abnormal centre because of its association with the court. Both Mérida and Toledo, however, belonged to a world of Mediterranean cities, with far flung contacts (Collins 1980:202-5). The *Vitas Patrum Emeretensium* shows us something of the city's international connections. Abbot Nanctus came from Africa (*VPE* 3, 2): Bishop Paul was a Greek (*VPE* 4, 1. 1), as was his nephew and successor, Fidelis, who came to the city in the company of Greek merchants (*VPE* 4, 3. 1-3): Bishop Sunna was sent into exile on a boat that ended up in Mauretania (*VPE* 5, 11. 15). The world of Mérida, doubtless like that of other southern cities such as Seville, was thus an international world with a polyethnic community, and this community included Goths as well as Hispano-Romans, Africans and Greeks. The more northerly cities of the Visigothic kingdom may have looked rather different. So too, the cemetery archaeology of the Meseta may indicate a society with little in common with the southern *civitates*.[3]

A question, which is perhaps more important, is whether Visigothic Spain was dominated by urban or rural life. Certainly large parts of the *Liber Iudiciorum* are dedicated to farming, and therefore, by implication to life in the countryside. On the other hand, it is equally clear, for instance in legislation on bee-keeping, that people were expected to have access equally to urban and rural residences (*LI* VIII, 6. 2). Further, there is some legislation which seems more appropriate to urban than country life: prostitution is a more obviously, though not exclusively, urban matter (*LI* III, 4. 17): foreign trade is likely to have been almost entirely urban (*LI* XI, 3). More important, the main Visigothic officials, the *judices* and *comites* are likely to have been found in cities more often than in the countryside. Certainly the *Vitas Patrum Emeretensium* shows us a group of noble Goths, including several *comites*, in the city (*VPE* 5, 10. 1: c.f. Collins 1980:200-1). The implication is that the

---

[2]   The significance of penance in the Visigothic Church at this period is clear from Toledo II c. 11-12 (Vives 1963:128-9).

[3]   On the possibility of using the archaeology to detect kinship structures, see Ripoll in this volume.

civitas structure of the Roman world, in which an urban centre (*urbs*) presided over, and was inseparable from, its rural hinterland (*territorium*), continued in Spain as in Gaul and Italy. The likelihood is, therefore, that Visigothic, like Lombard, society was focused primarily on the town, although any wealthy Visigoth is likely to have had large rural estates, and that is where much of the slave population would have been found. Alongside the *superiores*, the great landowners, there were free men of lesser status, the *inferiores*, many of whom must have lived outside the city, whether in smaller towns, villages or in the countryside itself.

Despite the significance of life outside the cities, it is reasonable to assume that many of the more important aspects of Visigothic society were to be found in the great urban centres, and that city life in Mérida was not unrepresentative, at least of those centres with strong Mediterranean contacts. Moreover, the evidence of the *Vitas Patrum Emeretensium* is not confined entirely to the city: in the course of its narrative we travel out to the city's hinterland, to Toledo, and to Narbonne: we also meet King Liuvigild and members of the Gothic aristocracy, a wealthy Hispano-Roman landowner of Lusitania, as well as churchmen and lay people of Mérida, servile and free, and merchants from abroad. Although, as we shall see, the diocese and bishops of Mérida were unusually rich, an analysis of life as depicted in the *Vitas Patrum Emeretensium* is unlikely to be entirely misleading.

On family life and family structures the *Vitas Patrum Emeretensium* has little to say. Being concerned primarily with bishops, and to a lesser extent with monks and hermits, this is hardly surprising. As a result there is no narrative source for the fifth- and sixth-century Visigoths which allows us to see in action the highly schematic legal depiction of the family and inheritance to be found in the *Liber Iudiciorum*. The seven degrees of kinship, therefore, remain nothing more than a blueprint in our sources, and a Roman blueprint at that (*LI* IV, 1. 1-7). Equally lacking illustration is the pattern of inheritance, which was apparently changed by Liuvigild to allow equal rights to daughters as to sons (*CE* 320; *LI* IV, 2. 1); an important indication of the relatively good treatment afforded women in the Visigothic laws (King 1972:222-50).

Two families are, however, important to the narrative of the *Vitas Patrum Emeretensium*. The first is that of a Lusitanian noble, supposedly among the richest in the province, who is unfortunately not named (*VPE* 4, 2). An indication of the wealth of such a family may be indicated by the extraordinarily fine mosaics of the late Roman period to be found in Mérida itself, and the fact that the *missorium* of Theodosius was found on the site of a villa to the south of the city. When his wife's pregnancy went wrong the noble appealed to Bishop Paul, who had been a doctor, presumably trained in the Byzantine East, before coming to Mérida. Paul, after refusing to perform a caesarian operation supposedly because it would leave him ritually impure, was finally persuaded to do so, and, although the child was stillborn, he saved the life of the mother. The wife's survival was, however, the husband's chief concern: as a result of the caesarian, and in the absence of children, the couple gifted their property on Paul, half to be given immediately (perhaps the *bona materna* of Visigothic law) and half on their death. It was this gift which made Paul and later bishops of Mérida so powerful (Collins 1980:196).[4] In his account of this windfall the author may have exaggerated.[5] Controlling the cult of St Eulalia the bishops of Mérida had long been the beneficiaries of pious oblations. Yet clearly there was thought to be something particularly special about the estates aquired by Paul.[6]

Ritual impurity was a matter of significance to any bishop, who had to offer the sacrifice of the Mass regularly to God. Indeed a bishop's status depended, to some extent, on a claim to a relationship with God which was tested by the public perception of his ritual cleanness. Yet one may doubt whether impurity was the only factor that kept Paul from performing the caesarian operation. Doctors could face fines if a patient died in the course of a phlebotomy (*LI* XI, 1. 6), and one might wonder whether accidental death in the course of other medical treatment regularly gave rise to the payment of damages: indeed whether death during medical treatment might have left the doctor open to charges of murder (for the wergeld of a woman, *LI* VIII, 4. 16). There is, however, no question that doctors were highly prized in Visigothic society: effectively, according to the laws of Liuvigild, they were not liable to be incarcerated (*LI* XI, 1. 8). Further, in Mérida they were highly valued throughout the period covered by the *Vitas Patrum Emeretensium*. Already in Paul's day there were doctors attached to the Church at Mérida, and to these the bishop attempted to send the noble Lusitanian, who nevertheless believed that Paul alone had the required skill to deal with his wife's case (*VPE* 4, 2. 3-6). Masona, the successor of Fidelis, is noted as having built a *xenodochium*, where doctors treated slaves and free, Jews and Christians (*VPE* 5, 3. 4-6).

The second family relationship dealt with by the *Vitas Patrum Emeretensium* is, like that of the senator of Lusitania, of considerable importance to the narrative, but is equally abnormal within the social structures of the Visigothic kingdom. It concerns the family of Paul, himself a Greek (*VPE* 4, 3). According to the author, when Paul had been established as bishop for some while some Greek merchants came to Mérida, and he entertained them. The next day they sent a boy, Fidelis, with a gift of thanks. On questioning the child Paul discovered that he was his nephew. He asked the merchants to give him the boy, but they refused, saying that he was free and had been handed over by his parents to help them. They claimed that they would not be able to look the parents in the face again if they left the child so far away. Paul then threatened them, saying they would not get home if they did not hand over the boy, and explained that he was the child's uncle. At that point they accepted his gifts and left. Thereafter Paul brought up his nephew,

---

[4] Some indication of the later significance of Mérida's estates may be found in the Council of Mérida (666), where 13 out of 21 canons deal with property.

[5] Javier Arce expresses considerable doubts about the reliability of the *Vitas* as a source, Arce (n.d.).

[6] For a point of comparison see the estates acquired by Theudis through his marriage to a Hispano-Roman widow: Procopius, *Wars*, 5, 12, 50 (Dewing 1914/28:131).

Fidelis, appointing him as his successor, and leaving him his considerable wealth, gained from his obstetric skills.

This story, which in many respects reads like a romance, and may be a less than honest version of events, tells us nothing about the Visigothic family, but it does touch on the law in various interesting ways. Although the merchants apparently refused to give up the child on the grounds of a personal arrangement with his parents, the fact that he was not a slave put his case within the field of law. Both Euric and Liuvigild banned the sale of free persons (*CE* 290: *LI* V, 4. 11). Nor were parents allowed to sell children (*CE* 299; *LI* V, 4. 12). These clauses, of course, do not quite fit the situation described by the author of the *Vitas Patrum Emeretensium*,[7] and the *Liber Iudiciorum* may not have been applicable in the case on other grounds as well: even supposing Paul to have been subject to Visigothic law, as opposed to the Roman Law of the *Breviary* of Alaric, foreign merchants, at least in disputes between themselves, were subject to their own laws, administered by their own *telonarii* (*LI* XI, 3. 2). Nevertheless the story comes close to showing the bishop making an illegal deal, and it may well be that the wording, which suggests that the bishop did not intend to buy the boy, but rather asked that he should be handed over in return for gifts of the merchants' choosing, intentionally avoided any legal difficulties.

The story of the discovery of Fidelis is equally important for its implications for inheritance. Paul was careful not to leave his wealth directly to the Church, but to pass it on to his nephew and chosen successor (*VPE* 4, 4-5). Even though he had ordained Fidelis as the next bishop of Mérida, Paul realized that this would be challenged after his death, so he stated in his will that his property would go to the Church of Mérida if Fidelis was accepted as bishop, and that if he was not accepted Fidelis was free to do as he wished with the inheritance. When it was realized that Fidelis had the right to remove his wealth from the Church, opposition to his succession evaporated.

Paul here, as in his initial request for Fidelis, was effectively acting illegally, but in such a way as to forestall any opposition. Even since the Council of Antioch in 341 it had been illegal to appoint a successor and to consecrate him in one's lifetime, and this legislation was to be repeated at the second Council of Braga in 572 (cc. 1, 8) (Vives 1963:10, 12; Fear 1997:64 n82). On the other hand, because Fidelis was a relative of the bishop within seven degrees of kinship, Paul was not required to leave his property to the church of Mérida (*CE* 335; *LI* IV, 2. 12), although he could have done because he had acquired the property himself and not inherited it. By using his will to convey the property to Fidelis, and only to the Church of Mérida if his nephew was accepted as his successor, Paul could effectively blackmail the clergy into accepting his subversion of canon law.

Paul was careful to have his will written down. In his concern for documentation he was certainly in tune with the requirements of Visigothic law,

---

[7]   The law basically served to protect Spanish families and labour, rather than visitors to Spain (see also *LI* 11, 3. 3), merchants could not take paid labourers from the Visigothic kingdom.

which insisted on the inviolability of written pacts and agreements (*LI* II, 5. 2; also Euric, *Leges Restitutae* 15). The power of the written document indeed runs throughout the *Vitas Patrum Emeretensium*. When Fidelis was dying he freed many captives, gave alms and remitted debts, by *chirographis*. A woman, who was unable to get close to him to have her *cautio* signed, was instructed in a vision to go to the shrine of Cyprian and Lawrence and then to approach the bishop: as a result she was able to get the bishop's signature (*VPE* 4, 10).

When Masona was dying he freed his servants with charters of liberty, and with the charters he also gave them small properties. The archdeacon Eleutherius, who hoped to succeed as the next bishop, warned the servants to keep the estates intact, saying that he would hold them accountable for any loss (*VPE* 5, 13).[8] In fact the archdeacon was arguably correct in challenging the grants made by Masona, even though they had been conveyed in writing: a bishop could not alienate Church property without the approval of all the clergy (*LI* IV, 1. 2-3; also Fear 1997:101 n228). Nevertheless the saintly Masona rose from his sick bed, went to the altar of St Eulalia, and prayed. As a result the archdeacon collapsed and died. While the author of the *Vitas Patrum Emeretensium* was concerned for the privileges of the basilicas of Mérida when they were under threat from the Arian bishop Sunna backed by king Liuvigild (*VPE* 5, 5. 4), he was more relaxed in his attitudes when it came to the pious donations of his own saintly heroes.

For the most part Liuvigild is a villainous figure in the *Lives of the Fathers of Mérida*, but on one occasion, relating to the transfer of property to abbot Nanctus, he receives a favourable press (*VPE* 3, 8-15). Nanctus is the subject of one of the three chapters which open the *Vitas Patrum Emeretensium*, which deal with the holy deaths of non-episcopal saints associated with Mérida. He was an African, who arrived in the city, where he tried to keep himself from being seen by women (*VPE* 3, 1-7), though the author is careful not to present him as a misogynist: only fear of being led into temptation caused the abbot to avoid seeing or being seen by women (*VPE* 3, 3). When he was seen, as a result of a trick engineered by the widow Eusebia and the deacon Redemptus, he left for a hermitage in the country, and from there his reputation spread to the extent that the Arian king Liuvigild heard about him, and, despite their doctrinal differences, decided to endow him and his followers with income from an estate of the royal fisc. At first Nanctus refused, but he was pressured into accepting. The result was disaster. The *servi* on the estate were horrified on seeing him in scruffy clothes and unkempt hair, and some days later, finding him alone, they killed him. They were taken in chains to Liuvigild, who let them go free, committing them to the justice of God. Naturally they were soon overwhelmed by demons.

The granting of royal estates as benefices in the Visigothic kingdom is well evidenced in the laws, especially in military contexts (*LI* IV, 5. 5; IX, 2. 1 & 3). The grant to a Catholic holy man by an Arian king might be thought of, at first

---

[8]   On the property of bishops at the time of their death see the Council of Valencia (549), canon 2 (Vives 1963:61-2).

sight, as more surprising, though it is perfectly explicable in terms of Liuvigild trying to set himself up as the leading patron throughout his kingdom (Collins, 1980:212), and the support of Arian kings for Catholic clergy can be parallelled elsewhere. What is most interesting in the story, however, is not the property or grant, but the supposed reaction of the *servi* and their punishment. The *servi* react over the question of status: they want their lord to be recognizable as a man of importance. A comparable story, revolving around status although not around style, is told by Gregory of Tours, who relates the rise of the *servus* Andarchius, who ended up dispossessing his lord, Felix, and marrying his daughter. The senator's *servi*, appalled at this disruption of the social order, killed their new master (*Libri Historiarum* 4, 46). *Servi* in both Frankish Gaul and Visigothic Spain were, therefore, thought to want a master of appropriate status, which might or might not be associated with style. As for their punishment, being committed to the judgement of God, the author of the *Vitas Patrum Emeretensium* thought that this was a remarkable act on Liuvigild's part, though it may, of course, reflect an inability to prove a case against them.[9]

Whilst Liuvigild, on this occasion, acted with remarkable leniency, his son, the Catholic Reccared, is portrayed acting overharshly in the narrative of the *Vitas*. The context of the king's sentencing of Vagrila deserves to be set out in full. After his accession to the throne, and his conversion, Reccared returned churches which had been taken over by the Arians to the Orthodox. This prompted something of an Arian backlash. The *Lives of the Fathers of Mérida* refers to an uprising in Narbonne (*VPE* 5, 12; see also John of Biclar, *s.a.* 587, 589)[10] and dwells in considerably more detail on events in Mérida itself. There the Arian bishop, Sunna, with the backing of a number of Gothic *comites* and other nobles, attempted to murder Bishop Masona (*VPE* 5, 10-11). The latter, having refused to visit Sunna on the pretext of being too busy, invited him to the *atrium* of his own episcopal palace. At the same time he sent for the local *dux*, Claudius, a man of Roman extraction who was later to destroy the Frankish army sent to help the uprising in Narbonne (John of Biclaro, *s.a.* 589). Sunna's party decided to kill Masona and Claudius together, but their chosen assassin, Witteric, later king of the Visigothic kingdom, was miraculously unable to draw his sword. As a result, when everybody else had left, he confessed the intended crime to Masona, throwing himself on the bishop's indulgence. The bishop informed Claudius, who carried out an investigation, and discovered that Sunna and his followers were plotting to make a further attempt on the bishop in the course of the Easter procession. The *dux* then

---

[9] In Roman law, of course, the slaves would have been tortured automatically (*Codex Theodosianus*, 9, 1. 14).

[10] This chapter of the *VPE* is unusual in having nothing to do with Mérida or its bishops. It is presumably included because the general who defeated the Frankish army sent to support the rebels, Claudius (John of Biclar *s.a.* 589), was a friend of bishop Masona: yet the author of the *VPE* only mentions the Arian aspect of the uprising and not Claudius' victory. On the exclusion of secular material from the *VPE*, see Fear 1997:xx-xxii.

made his move, arresting those who offered no resistance and killing those who attempted to fight. Reccared was asked to judge on the matter: all were to be driven, chained, into exile—a point supported by John of Biclar (*s.a.* 588), who reveals that the secular leader of the plot, Segga, had his hands cut off and was sent into exile in Galicia. There was one exception, Sunna, who was offered another see on condition that he converted and did penance. Such a procedure cannot be inferred from the canons of the Third Council of Toledo (589), where on the one hand (c. 9) Arian churches had to be handed over to Catholic bishops (Vives 1963:127), while, on the other, Arian bishops who accepted Catholicism seem to have been left in post (Vives 1963:122-3). In fact the offer made to Sunna is remarkably similar to that required by the Frankish Council of Orléans (511) (c.10). That the bishop was not initially treated like the other conspirators may indicate that there was no real criminal case against him, though this does not seem likely, given the account of the same conspiracy in the Chronicle of John of Biclar (*s.a.* 588), where the plot is directed as much against Reccared as against Masona. It seems, therefore, that Reccared went out of his way to reconcile himself with the leaders of the Arian Church. According to the hagiographer, however, Sunna said he knew nothing of penance,[11] refused to convert, and was therefore set adrift in a boat with his companions: they were washed up in Mauretania, where Sunna was eventually killed.

One of the conspirators, Vagrila, had, meanwhile, fled to sanctuary in the basilica of St Eulalia (*VPE* 5, 11. 17-21). As a martyr from the Great Persecution, Eulalia could be seen as a patroness by Arians and Orthodox alike; indeed Liuvigild's attempt to get control of her tunic is an indication of the status she had in Arian eyes (*VPE* 5, 6. 12-21). Further, the fact that sanctuary is allowed in the *Antiquae* of the *Liber Iudiciorum* suggests that the practice was recognized by the Arians as well as the Catholics, at least in Liuvigild's day (*LI* IX, 3. 1-4). Having sought sanctuary Vagrila might have expected pardon, once he had promised to reform (*LI* IX, 3. 4), but his case was forwarded to Reccared, who judged that he, his wife, children and patrimony should all be handed over to the church of St Eulalia in perpetuity, and that he should always walk before the horse of the prior of the community. Masona, however, thought otherwise. He instructed Vagrila to take the horse of the deacon Redemptus, who was in charge of the basilica of St Eulalia, to the *atrium* inside the city walls, and there, taking the deacon's staff, the bishop freed the whole family.

The story of the attempt to murder Masona and of its aftermath raises a number of interesting points of law. First, Witteric, as an informer, was probably right to expect pardon: such at least was the case when the crime was theft (*LI* VII, 1. 3-4). Second, Claudius was right to investigate the accusation fully before acting (*LI* VII, 1. 5). Once he moved against Sunna's followers, he was entitled to kill those who drew their swords (Euric, *Leges Restitutae* 4; *LI* VI, 4. 2; VII, 2. 15). Thereafter the king's personal justice came into force (*LI* II, 1. 13). In one respect, however,

---

[11] See above, note 2.

Reccared seems to have acted unjustly. Vagrila could reasonably have expected that, whatever happened to him, his crime would in no way affect his wife or children (*LI* VI, 1. 8).[12] In defying the king's judgement Masona was arguably righting a legal wrong.

Thus far we have seen that the narrative of the *Vitas Patrum Emeretensium*, while it often impinges on the working of law, rarely coincides precisely with what might be expected from consideration of the law codes. Effectively we are faced with two types of source (hagiographical and legal) and two types of authority (religious and secular). There are points of overlap. Thus it is clear that the society depicted by the author is a legalistic society, used to written documents, and as such fits in with much else that is known about the Visigothic kingdom. At the same time we see Paul and Fidelis twisting the law to their own advantage, Reccared overstepping the bounds of justice, and Liuvigild, astonishingly, trusting entirely in the judgement of God. Of course, in this comparison the *Vitas Patrum Emeretensium*, as a hagiographical text, is as likely to be misleading as the secular laws themselves, since the narrative is necessarily an imaginative construct. Yet Paul's appointment of Fidelis is so far outside the canons that one might reasonably think that, in this episode at least, the hagiographer's account is reasonably accurate. Moreover, in his treatment of Nanctus, Liuvigild acts so much against the type of an Arian persecutor, and the Catholic Reccared, in his sentencing of Vagrila, is so patently not behaving as a just monarch, that one may regard these stories as having more than a grain of truth.

More important, the dislocation between the legal and hagiographical evidence shows that the laws are no sure indication of the workings of power, and that the twisting of law and the use of influence outside the strict practice of the codes were crucial to the functioning of society. Naturally, since the *Vitas Patrum Emeretensium* is a hagiographical text, the power structures that it explores are ecclesiastical, and because the author of the work was an inmate of the church of St Eulalia, the chief sources of power were the shrine and relics of the saint herself. Time and again the author attributes a happy result to the action of the saint. When he wished to outface his archdeacon the dying Masona prayed at the saint's altar (*VPE* 5, 13. 8-10). The conflict between Liuvigild, Masona and Sunna, is primarily seen as a conflict over control of the church and relics of Eulalia (*VPE* 5, 4-8). When the king decided to challenge the Catholics, Sunna attempted to take over all the basilicas and their privileges: in particular he tried to take over the church of St Eulalia. Masona refused to comply, and the king sent a command that there should be a public debate between the two bishops. This, the hagiographer insists, Masona won, with the help of the saint. Thereafter Sunna accused Masona of crimes, with the result that he was summoned to Toledo. There the king demanded the tunic of Eulalia. The bishop refused, claiming that he had burnt it,

---

[12] Reccared was clearly making an example of Vagrila: in condemning him and his successors he may have had Roman law on treason in mind. On the harshness of Vagrila's treatment, see Fear 1997:99 n213.

dissolved the ashes in water and drunk it, whereas he was in fact wearing it. He was sent into monastic exile, which came to an end when Eulalia appeared in the form of a dove, telling him that he was about to return to Mérida (*VPE* 5, 8. 1). As he entered the city with a huge crowd of well-wishers, Nepopis, the Catholic bishop who had been appointed in his place, scurried out with a small group of supporters (*VPE* 5, 8. 10-11).

It is not simply in major confrontations that bishops of Mérida brought the spiritual resources of their office to bear. Religious processions are a regular feature of the *Vitas Patrum Emeretensium*. The *atrium* of the bishop's palace collapsed in the course of a procession, which included the archdeacon in his alb, deacons with thuribles and the bishop (*VPE* 4, 6). The fact that no one was hurt was ascribed to the prayers of Fidelis and the merit of Eulalia. It was at an Easter procession that Sunna's followers intended to make a second attempt to kill Masona (*VPE* 5, 11. 2-3). Moreover there were as many boys dressed in silk in Masona's processions as you might expect to see in the king's (*VPE* 5, 3. 12). Such a display was clearly a sign of power, both of the wealth of the bishop and of the unity of the population behind him. It is no wonder that Liuvigild wished to break Masona's influence.

The significance of processions is further confirmed by the fact that they are the central element of two visions retold in the *Vitas Patrum Emeretensium*, both relating to Fidelis. In these cases, however, the processions reveal not the power of the bishop, but his holiness, though the two issues were, of course, related. On one occasion a servant of Fidelis was caught outside the town overnight, and, reaching the city gate while it was still locked, he saw a procession of saints, including the bishop, moving round the shrines of the city and its suburbs (*VPE* 4, 7). He was told by Fidelis to mention the story to no one. Another servant who did talk openly about a similar vision before seeing the bishop, was told to do penance and promptly died (*VPE* 4, 8). Like processions, visions were doubtless part of the armoury of the clergy: they could be exploited. At the same time they were part of the imaginative world of the people of Mérida and more generally of the early medieval West. However much some visions may have been fabricated, they were accepted, and although bishops are said to have tried to suppress visionary stories about them circulating during their lifetimes, they could certainly be used to enhance a bishop's posthumous reputation.

There was also the power of the church canons. Penance is mentioned on a number of occasions in the *Vitas Patrum Emeretensium*. A monk at the monastery of Cauliana outside the city began to steal food and drink, apparently within the community (*VPE* 2). For this he was whipped and imprisoned by abbot Renovatus: when this failed to correct him, the abbot left him to indulge himself, thinking that God would intervene. Eventually the man was restored to his senses on hearing children issue a warning about the judgement of God. The monk asked to be given penance, but Renovatus was not convinced of his contrition. However the sinner lamented for three days: as a result the abbot gave him penance, and the monk died announcing that his sins had been forgiven. As we have seen, penance was administered by Fidelis to a man who had told others of a vision he had of the bishop processing round the basilicas with a crowd of saints: the man died soon after (*VPE* 4, 8. 4). The young Agustus received penance on his deathbed, after seeing a vision of paradise (*VPE* 1). Offsetting these penances is the statement by the Arian bishop Sunna that he had no knowledge of the procedure (*VPE* 5, 11. 13). Clearly the author was concerned to show that even the most hardened sinner, like the monk of Cauliana, could be saved: and it was a mark of the extreme wickedness of the Arian Sunna that he rejected the opportunity not only to repent, but also to receive a Catholic bishopric. Yet behind the question of the infinite mercy of God, lay the power of the clergy: Renovatus, who had shown himself to be the mildest of men in his earlier treatment of the monk, was prepared to give the viaticum but not to prescribe penance until absolutely convinced of the monk's contrition. The opportunity for purification was strictly controlled; more particularly, it was controlled by the clergy, who decided who was and who was not sufficiently clean—an issue which points back to Paul's concern about staining his own hands in a caesarian operation.

Punishment in the *Vitas Patrum Emeretensium* is not always ordered by men. One step beyond penance is the judgement of God himself. This the monk of Cauliana suffered before he could do penance. The killers of Nanctus were hunted to death by demons, when Liuvigild was unable to sentence them (*VPE* 3,15). The king himself was beaten in his sleep by Eulalia for his treatment of Masona (*VPE* 5, 8. 3-4). Here an image of secular justice seems to have been brought into the world of divine retribution, since beating was a standard secular punishment, used particularly for slaves. The symbolism of a supposed beating of the king at the hands of a saint would have been particularly shocking.

God and, below him, St Eulalia are the great powers of the *Vitas Patrum Emeretensium*. Below them are rival human powers. Bishops and abbots could tap into their religious authority, that is they could exercise a spiritual patronage, but they too needed a more earthly power base, and much of their power seems to have stemmed from their ability to exercise earthly patronage. In a sense the story of Paul and Fidelis is the story of the creation of the secular power base of the bishops of Mérida, while the story of Masona is the story of that power being put to the test. By way of conclusion it is worth reconsidering the ways in which Paul and Fidelis established themselves as great patrons, and then looking at the implications of this for the history of Visigothic secular society.

According to the *Vitas Patrum Emeretensium* the power of the bishops of Mérida, which may well have been unique in the Spanish peninsula, derived, so far as we can see, from the gift of land which Paul received from the noble Lusitanian, whose wife he saved by his caesarian operation (*VPE* 4, 2. 15; 4, 5. 3). Paul himself used this wealth to ensure the succession of his nephew to the see of Mérida (*VPE* 4, 4. 3-5). It was, therefore, first and foremost in the episcopate of Fidelis that the Church experienced the benefits of this windfall. As the author of the *Vitas Patrum Emeretensium* remarks, perhaps out of local pride, Mérida was, as a result, the richest see in Spain (*VPE* 4, 5. 3). In describing the episcopate of

Fidelis, the author of the *Vitas* concentrates on two issues apart from the bishop's appointment: one is the various visions indicating the bishop's sanctity, experienced by clerics or monks of the city: the other is the bishop's patronage as expressed in his building and his care for his congregation.

Fidelis' patronage is seen in terms of building and good works. We are told that he rebuilt the episcopal palace, after its collapse, and then turned his mind to the church of St Eulalia (*VPE* 4, 6. 7-8; cf. Collins 1980:194).[13] At the end of his life he freed many slaves, helped the poor and remitted the debts of many (*VPE* 4.10.2). Masona was even more active, founding many monasteries and basilicas, as well as a *xenodochium*, which he staffed with doctors (*VPE* 5, 3. 3-6; cf. Collins 1980:194-5). Further, he provided wine, oil and honey dispensed from the *atrium* to the urban and rural poor (*VPE* 5, 3. 7). In addition he handed over 2,000 *solidi* to Redemptus, deacon of St Eulalia, to help those in need (*VPE* 5, 3. 8-9). Again, on his deathbed he made a number of grants, notably those to his slaves, which were challenged by the archdeacon Eleutherius (*VPE* 5, 13. 4). The bishop as patron, which can be inferred from the canons of the councils of Toledo (for the evidence, King 1972:60-1, 156-7), and from monastic rules, is an unmistakeable image presented by the author of the *Vitas Patrum Emeretensium*.

There is no narrative to show us secular patronage at work, but patronage is a matter of considerable significance in the law codes (King 1972:187-9). The issue of patronage is first sketched out in a military context. In Euric's code the donation of arms to a *buccellarius* forced him and his sons to remain with his patron unless everything received as a result of the patronage was returned. The daughters of a *buccellarius* were also subject to their father's patron, who was responsible in particular for their marriage (*CE* 310). Arms given to *saiones*, however, did not have to be returned, although anything else acquired while in service did (*CE* 311). This legislation is subtly less military when repeated in the Code of Liuvigild. Here there is a substitution of anyone in *patrocinium* for the term *buccellarius*, but the law is otherwise the same (*LI* V, 3. 1), while that on the *saiones* is simply repeated (*LI* V, 3. 2). There may be some significance in the change from *buccellarius* to *patrocinium*: the former with its exclusively military meaning may imply the workings of the *comitatus*, while *patrocinium* may suggest something closer to Roman clientship. Certainly other references to patronage in Liuvigild's code point towards a system of clientship: thus, anyone unfaithful to or wanting to leave a patron was to pay half of what he had acquired under him (*LI* V, 3. 3, see also V.7.13, where the client is explicitly a freed slave). In addition, a man leaving a patron had to return any land he had been given, and the new patron had to provide land instead (*LI* V, 3. 4). Not surprisingly a freed man who hit his patron could be returned to slavery (*LI* V, 7. 10).

To this extent the laws see patronage as a valid relationship within society. At the same time they see patronage as a centrifugal force which might challenge the king (King 1972:42 n5) and which constituted a threat to the working of law. If a

---

[13] For references to recent archaeological work in Mérida, and commentary, Arce (n.d.).

man sought a patron, a *potens*, in a law suit, his case should instantly be dismissed. Moreover the *potens* himself should be asked to leave the courtroom, and if he did not he was liable to the enormous fine of two pounds of gold; his slaves, if they refused to leave, should receive 50 lashes (*LI* II, 2. 8). A man refusing to confess the truth because of his relationship with his patron should be reported to the king, and then handed over to the judge or bishop (*LI* VII, 1. 1). Clientship was clearly regarded as a considerable threat to the working of the law. At the same time, secular patronage was also seen as endangering the Church: according to the third Council of Toledo (c. 1) it had supported Arianism (Vives 1963:19), and was a threat to Church order, according to the Council of Narbonne (589) (c. 5) (Vives 1963:147).

On the other hand it can be seen in a more neutral way, as part of the social structure. Like slavery, patronage tended to strengthen the household of an aristocrat, at the expense of the kin group. It also gave the client a certain amount of freedom vis-à-vis his own parents (*LI* IV, 5. 5). Further, and here the murder of Nanctus by his slaves is important, a patron's visible status was important even to his servile dependents. To have a scruffy master could be seen as worse than death (*VPE* 3, 11-12). Looked at in this way patronage was an alternative—or perhaps one should say various types of patronage provided alternatives—to a system of kinship, and this held true for episcopal or clerical just as much as for secular patronage.

From the point of view of the development of patronage it is possible to return to the more general issue of social relations in the fifth, sixth and seventh centuries. In all likelihood the main social bond among the Visigoths until the crises leading up to 376 had been the kin group. Arguably the royal murders of the second decade of the fifth century, notably that of Athaulf, show the continuing importance of the kin, at least at the very top of the Visigothic social order (see Orosius VII, 43. 8). Moreover, if there is any validity in the legends which attribute the catastrophic defeat of Roderic in 711 to the infighting between rival families competing for the kingship, some notion of kin groups remained for the whole Visigothic period.[14] On the other hand the kin group, except in the limited sense of the nuclear family, appears not to play a major role in the legislation of Euric or Liuvigild, whilst there are a number of important laws relating to patronage. Moreover, despite the obvious importance of kinship for Paul in promoting Fidelis, the narrative of the *Vitas Patrum Emeretensium* suggests the growing significance of the patronage of the bishops of Mérida, not least because of their vast wealth, arguably gained through Paul's obstetric skills. Given the weakness of the evidence one could hardly state that patronage had completely superseded kinship as the main cement in social relations by the time of Liuvigild, but it is at least a working hypothesis that there had been a substantial shift in that direction before the late sixth century, and that this shift was one aspect of the growing similarity between Romans and Goths in Visigothic society. The evidence

---

[14] I would not, however, subscribe to the arguments of García Moreno in *Francia* 1994.

for such a shift is, of course, slight. One cannot argue from the absence of legislation on kin and the presence of legislation on patronage in the codes of Euric and Liuvigild, since those codes only survive in fragments, and substantial sections of law dealing with kinship may have been dropped as outdated by Liuvigild, or even by Recceswinth. Yet there is an *a priori* case for thinking that patronage was of central importance. It was nothing new to the Germanic peoples. The *comitatus* is a military patronage-system par excellence. However significant it may or may not have been before the migrations, the migrations themselves are likely to have enhanced its importance (King 1972:222). Its significance in times of danger can be seen clearly in Procopius' description of the Ostrogothic war. Once the Visigothic state was secure, other types of patronage may have become increasingly significant: the Visigoths had before them the Roman system of clientship, and the ecclesiastical systems of patronage which flowed from the control of cult and from pastoral care. The absence of the kin in the *Leges Visigothorum* need cause no surprise. Social relations among the Visigoths settled in Spain were dominated by patronage and clientship rather than the family.

References

Textual sources:

[Abbr.: *CE* = *Codex Euricianus*; *LI* = *Liber Iudiciorum*; *LRV* = *Lex Romana Visigothorum*; *VPE* = *Vitas Sanctorum Patrum Emeretensium*].

Breviary of Alaric (*Lex Romana Visigothorum*): see Haenel (ed.) 1849.
Braga II (572): see Vives (ed.) 1963.
Codex Euricianus: see Zeumer (ed.) 1902.
Eclogae: see Ashburner (ed.) 1910 & 1912.
Euric
        Leges Restitutae: see Zeumer (ed.) 1902.
Gregory of Tours
        Historiarum libri X: see Krusch & Levison (eds.) 1951.
John of Biclar
        Chronica: see Mommsen (ed.) 1894.
Lex Romana Visigothorum: see Haenel (ed.) 1849.
Liber Iudiciorum: see Zeumer (ed.) 1902.
Narbonne (589): see Vives (ed.) 1963.
Orléans (511): see De Clercq (ed.) 1963.
Orosius
        Historia Contra Paganos: see Arnaud-Lindet (ed.) 1990/1.
Procopius
        Wars: see Dewing (ed.) 1914/28.
Toledo III (589): see Vives (ed.) 1963.
Vitas Sanctorum Patrum Emeretensium: see Maya Sánchez (ed.) 1992.

Bibliography:

Arce, J.
  n.d.   The city of Mérida (Emerita) in the *Vitas Sanctorum Patrum Emeritensium* (VIth century A.D.). In *East and West: Modes of Communication*. I. N. Wood & E. Chrysos (eds.). Leiden: Brill.

Ashburner, W.
  1910   The farmer's law. *Journal of Hellenic Studies* 30: 85-108.
  1912   The farmer's law. *Journal of Hellenic Studies* 32: 69-95.

Collins, R.
  1980   Mérida and Toledo: 550-585. In *Visigothic Spain: New Approaches*. E. James (ed.), pp. 189-219. Oxford: Oxford University Press.
  1983   *Early Medieval Spain: Unity in Diversity 400-1000*. London: Macmillan.

De Clercq, C. (ed.)
  1963   *Concilia Galliae A. 511-A. 695. Corpus Christianorum, Series Latina* 148A. Turnhout: Brepols.

Dewing, H. B. (ed.)
  1914/28   Procopius, *The Wars*. London: Heinemann.

Fear, A. T.
  1997   *Lives of the Visigothic Fathers*. Liverpool: Liverpool University Press.

García Moreno, L. A.
  1994   Gothic survivals in the Visigothic kingdoms of Toulouse and Toledo. *Francia* 21 (1): 1-15.

Goffart, W.
  1980   *Barbarians and Romans: Techniques of Accommodation, AD 418-594*. Princeton: Princeton University Press.

Haenel, G. (ed.)
  1849   *Lex Romana Visigothorum*. Leipzig: Wilhelm Bosser.

Heather, P., & J. Matthews
  1991   *The Goths in the Fourth Century*. Liverpool: Liverpool University Press.

King, P. D.
  1972   *Law and Society in the Visigothic Kingdom*. Cambridge: Cambridge University Press.
  1980   King Chindasvind and the first territorial law-code of the Visigothic kingdom. In *Visigothic Spain: New Approaches*. E. James (ed.), pp. 131-157. Oxford: Oxford University Press.

Krusch, B., & W. Levison (eds.)
  1951   *Gregorii Turonensis Opera*. Teil 1. *Libri historiarum X. Monumenta Germaniae Historica. Scriptores Rerum Merovingicarum*, 1. Hannover: Hahn.

Maya Sánchez, A. (ed.)
  1992   *Vitas Sanctorum Patrum Emeretensium. Corpus Christianorum* CXVI. Turnhout: Brepols.

Mommsen, T. (ed.)
  1894   *Chronica minora saec. IV. V. VI. VII.* (II) *Monumenta Germaniae Historica. Auctores Antiquissimi*, 11. Berlin: Weidmann.

Nehlsen, H.
  1983   Entstehung des öffentlichen Strafrechts bei der germanischen Stämmen. In *Gerichtslauben-Vorträge: Freiburger Festkolloquium zum fünfundsiebzigsten Geburtstag von Hans Thieme*. K. Kroeschell (ed.), pp. 1-16. Sigmaringen: Jan Thorbecke Verlag.

Schäferdiek, K.
  1967   *Die Kirche in den Reichen der Westgoten und Suewen bis zur Errichtung
                der westgotischen katholischen Staatskirche.* Berlin: Walter de Gruyter.
Vives, J. (ed.)
  1963   *Concilios Visigóticos e Hispano-Romanos.* Barcelona: Consejo Superior
                de Investigationes Científicas, Instituto Enrique Flórez.
Wolfram, H.
  1989   *History of the Goths.* Los Angeles: University of California Press.
Wood, I. N.
  1996   Roman Law in the Barbarian Kingdoms. In *Rome and the North.*
                A. Ellegård & G. Åkerström-Hougen (eds.), pp. 5-14. Jonsered: Paul
                Åströms Förlag.
Zeumer, K. (ed.)
  1902   *Leges Visigothorum. Monumenta Germaniae Historica. Leges* 1, 1.
                Hannover: Hahn.

Discussion

SCHWARCZ: The translation of the Bible as a means of christianization was part of Byzantine Church policy, as is shown especially by the translation of Cyril and Methodius. It is shown, I think also, by the Georgian, Abyssinian and Armenian versions of the Gospel.

HEATHER: Well, the Gospel text looks untouched. The Gothic Epistle text looks as if it's been re-worked against Latin subsequently.

GREEN: And also, linguistically, there are phonological differences between what must be hypothesized as being initially Visigothic as opposed to Ostrogothic.

HEATHER: It does look as though there was a continuous fight going on about what the correct biblical text was and the Epistles rather than the Gospels were the battlegrounds of theological argument, so that translation was certainly revised substantially in the West. Friedrichsen (1939) is very unclear whether he thought this was happening in the Visigothic kingdom or in the Ostrogothic kingdom. I suppose the Visigothic kingdom makes more sense, just because they have been there longer.

SCHWARCZ: Well, that depends on the date of the manuscript. And I think that the linkage being the sixth century would make it more plausibly Ostrogothic.

HEATHER: The actual manuscript is almost certainly Ostrogothic. That's where possible contacts between Ostrogothic biblical scholarship and Visigothic biblical scholarship might become important.

GREEN: Well, they certainly had links with Latin biblical scholarship.

SCHWARCZ: Of course there was an indirect discussion with the Latin biblical scholars in Italy and outside Constantinople there could not be found anywhere in the world at that moment a more advanced biblical scholarship.

DE JONG: Could I get you back from biblical scholarship to the Visigoths?

VELÁZQUEZ: On page 191, with reference to mixed society. I would like to make one point. I think I agree with you on the principal points which seem very important to me, and also on mixed society, and the difficulty of studying a society in the Visigothic kingdom from texts as normative as the law codes, although the laws reflect society at least to some extent. I would like to comment on the ambit of private law where there are some examples which may be taken into account to study the application of laws, e.g. the so-called Visigothic slates, which I cannot refrain from mentioning. There are also several slates which contain contracts of sale, exchange, and trial declarations, in Latin *condiciones sacramentorum* and so on. As, you know, yesterday I presented another very different text. However, I think that the letter from Tarra (Velazquez 1996) in the monastery of Cauliana to King Reccared is a strange but important text. It is an artificially rhetorical letter with a rhythmic structure, and I think that it could represent an example of the application of law, although it may be only a literary example, because the letter, I think, is based on a law of Chindaswinth, while it was seemingly written in the time of Reccared. This is problematic.

WOOD: Yes, it seems to me that both from what you said and from reading your paper, which is obviously dealing with the law, that we have very similar views about the problem of a mixed society and the fact that there isn't much point in trying to decide what is Germanic and what is Roman. What we have is evidence for a particular century.

GREEN: On page 192, on Germanic *gens* and sub-Roman society, my point is that I think that the contrast you make is probably a little too sharp, when you say that the legal evidence does not reflect the traditions of the Germanic *gens* but rather the law of a sub-Roman society. I would like myself to see that not so sharply, the one posed against the other. Cannot sub-Roman society incorporate something of the traditions of a barbarian *gens*?

WOOD: Yes I don't think I exclude that. I would specifically include what survives of Germanic tradition within sub-Roman society.

JIMÉNEZ: I want to express the fact that the Visigothic kings were compelled to legislate over their subjects in order to consolidate their authority, provided that the *consuetudo* of a kin group didn't exist within the Roman population. So, thanks to the law they could establish themselves over their other subjects.

WOOD: Surely.

DE JONG: But do you now imply that an elaborate kinship system did exist amongst the non-Roman population, the Visigoths?

JIMÉNEZ: We have no evidence whether the Visigoths had an elaborate kinship system or not. This, however, would have evolved considerably throughout the fifth century. The only fact that we know is that written laws appear when King Euric found it necessary in order to enforce his royal authority over the Roman-provincial population and not before, although the Visigoths were living alongside these Roman-provincials since 418-419.

WOOD: It's difficult to know whether the absence of the kin in the law means that the kin had no great significance or whether the law is only concerned with other areas of power. I don't think that we can talk about the kin in Visigothic Spain. Of course there are kin groups in any societies.

JIMÉNEZ: You don't think that they had kin groups?

WOOD: I don't think we can talk about them because we don't actually have the narrative texts, and there is thus no source that allows us to reconstruct a Visigothic family of the late sixth century to set against the law. This is where I think the documentation of the Visigothic state is so difficult. And it's where Gregory of Tours makes things so different for the Frankish kingdom; you can show families at work. We can't show families at work in Visigothic Spain, except at the highest possible level, and even then it's usually only for about two generations. We cannot assume from the lack of evidence, either that kinship is significant or that it isn't. We just cannot get at that problem. It seems to me to be an area which we just don't know about.

JIMÉNEZ: Hm, hm. I understand.

DE JONG: And there is an implicit assumption, I think, in mentioning kinship.

JIMÉNEZ: Probably, if we found some references about family and kin among the Franks too, it is because the conversion of the Franks to Christianity was more recent at the time when Gregory of Tours was writing. The problem with the Visigoths is that their conversion was in 376, one century and a half before.

WOOD: Yes, the Frankish narrative texts are better.

JIMÉNEZ: But about Visigoths in Spain we don't have as many narrative texts as in *Francia*.

WOOD: And so you have a difficulty: is the silence a significant silence or not? And because you cannot tell that, I think it is an area that we cannot investigate.

SCHWARCZ: I think there is a false assumption because I don't see any connection between Christianity and kinship structures. We have early medieval societies where the laws and the texts are all about kinship even centuries after the conversion, so I don't think that Christianization would have made any difference to existing kinship structures with the *Tervingi* and with the Visigoths. If we don't have them in the sixth century, we must assume that they weren't there in the fifth, at least not in that prominence for instance that the Anglo-Saxon laws gave them.

DE JONG: Even if they are given prominence you still have to ask yourself precisely in what context, because in many ways the state, if you want, and royal power, interfered. My guess in this case would be that precisely for the fact that this society has been in turmoil for one and a half centuries, before its conversion, well it does not give you very good chances of having all sorts of kinship and persistent features of the structure intact by the time they reach the seventh century.

HEATHER: A lot had happened since the time of Tacitus.

WOOD: And also, I think, the lack of a kinship structure or a lack of a significant kin, fits rather better with your argument about the Visigoths as an army. An army is going to be one area where....

JIMÉNEZ: Of course they were an army, but probably not all of them. Only some of them were part of the army.

WOOD: Sure, but within that context patronage systems are going to be much more important than the kinship systems.

JIMÉNEZ: Hm, hm.

DÍAZ: On page 192, I think that I am going to speak about the same subject [laughter], not about the historiographic tradition in Spain, but in general. The question is an old polemic on the balance between Roman and Visigothic traditions. And normally we pay attention to different elements. If we pay attention to the laws, and we study its formal elements, the linguistic connection with the past and a lot of elements of procedure, the elements of the *Lex Visigothorum* are essentially Roman. If we pay attention to the fiscal elements, taxes, administration in general, we find exclusively later Roman tradition. In all the elements of the organization of the state we find the Roman tradition. But perhaps not in the army; war is a very particular issue among the Goths, as is clear when they arrive and conquer the new place which is going to be their new state. But there is the question of their conversion to Catholicism which assumes their adaptation to the new situation. In this aspect the Roman or the Christian tradition are really the essence of it. But when we talk about a mixed society, we must recall one essential question, which is that only the Goths become kings. The central power, the idea of the control of all the resources of power are elements which only belong to the Gothic nation. And I think that the idea of a mixed society, of a balance between the Gothic and Roman elements, must have arisen on two different levels. The formal aspects concerning the control of the society and of power are based on the formal elements of the Roman tradition, they conform to the idea of provincial power; but to what extent is the preservation of power within the group accessory to Roman tradition? Indeed, we have here a strong element of Gothic tradition. Perhaps in relation to your war, with the paper of Gisela [Ripoll], we are going to discuss the symbolic elements which are elements of power of our religious institutions, we are going to lose the Germanic tradition. However, when we read in the Councils of Toledo the necessity of refusing to allow the Romans to reach the kingship and the royal dignity, we have elements of a Roman tradition. And if we can mention—in my paper I have written about it—some elements of the constant possession or preservation of power, it is because the elements of the old Gothic group show their capacity to become kings, and this is an element which, I think, is present throughout the Visigothic period. What do you say?

WOOD: I agree with you entirely that there is an element of power confined to the people who are of Gothic descent. I don't have a problem with that. When I am talking about mixed society, I am not talking about the very highest level of political competition.

RIPOLL: What do you mean by a 'mixed society' and how do you think that it can be explained historically?

WOOD: Well, I think that studying society implies the study of a larger range of social groups than simply the top.

RIPOLL: Yes I think you are right and that is a very interesting thought. One always talks about a Roman and a Visigothic society and, at present, of a mixed society. Actually the problem lies in the fact that one should not see two different social groups, but one social group alone which has nothing to do with national unity, that is a social juncture that answers a concrete historical moment.

DE JONG: Which perceived itself, yes as an ...

RIPOLL: It is quite probable that one may actually distinguish in a great social mass, on one hand, a social group where there are individuals of different origins and, on the other, an aristocratic group which was deeply hierarchic, the highest representative of which was royalty, in the end the king. I do not believe we can talk about a Visigothic society which takes on Roman tradition within the 'mixed society' of the sixth century, except that the Visigothic population lived with and had known for a long time Roman civilization. This means that the Visigoths, at this time, were already an inseparable part of the Roman world.

DÍAZ: Yes, well but they take all the symbolic elements of power in the Roman tradition of the Empire.

RIPOLL: Indeed, but Dr. Díaz' remark refers to the analysis, not so much of the society, but of those symbolic elements of power which I personally believe are different.

JIMÉNEZ: Sorry, I go on page 193 to my next question. It is the question of intermarriage between a Roman and a Goth. It is precisely because I think that the ancient laws of kinship were still alive among the Goths that Liuvigild or another king, I don't know which, issued a law voiding the prohibition of intermarriage between Romans and Goths. For this king it was absolutely necessary to weaken kinship in order to achieve one society, and the only way to eradicate kinship was to allow intermarriage.

DE JONG: What do you mean by the notion of kinship? If you want to integrate two different groups of people, where there is a previous different religious persuasion, why would you assume that one, for example in the situation of an extended family or something, I am sure....

JIMÉNEZ: Perhaps the term 'kinship' is incorrect, but what I want to explain is that probably ancient customs were still strong among the Visigoths and the only way to a unified society was to void the prohibition of intermarriage between the ones and the others.

SCHWARCZ: I don't think you can say that, because the prohibition of intermarriage is Roman law. It was issued precisely in the fifth century as an anti-heretic measure, and its application by the Visigothic kings is just taking over the Roman law of the fifth century. That has got nothing to do with keeping the *gens* together and long tradition of kinship structures. With the Visigoths, especially after the time between 397 and 419, I would not dare to postulate a kinship structure because an army on the move doesn't work along such lines but on military ones and on a recruitment basis. It is open to all who can bear weapons.

HEATHER: It just struck me about the law on intermarriage, that saying it is just taken over from Romans is problematic. The Roman law talks about barbarians, and I find it difficult to believe that Visigothic kings would have been ready to call themselves barbarians.

SCHWARCZ: You must take the Vandal example where the laws were turned around against the Romans just when they were issued by the Byzantine emperor.

HEATHER: I don't see why I must take it.

SCHWARCZ: You need not take it, but you should take into account the parallel examples of the fifth century because it is explicitly written by Victor Vita in his *Persecutio Africanae provinciae* from the Catholic point of view, that these measures were taken as retribution by Geiseric against the laws that were made in Constantinople against the Arians.

HEATHER: That's one context, but this is something that can be used for different purposes in different contexts. And I don't believe that kinship groups, extended kin had any important role in any of these Gothic groups for the reasons that you have all been talking about. But there is another element, which can sometimes get lost, and that is that the Goths actually create a kingdom by conquest, the Visigoths as much as the Ostrogoths, they do actually dominate it. They take over by military actions, campaigns are launched, so that the original situation has dominant Goths and subordinate Hispano-Romans. And even without having to overcome kinship, which I don't believe in, you do have to allow a passage of time for that original inequality to disappear through intermarriage and further political action, etc. In that kind of context, then this kind of ban on intermarriage and its disappearance could play another role. We have only 30 chapters out of 300 of the so-called code of Euric. It is quite likely that the Visigoths over time changed their ways. To say that it is simply taken over from the Romans seems to me to be reducing too much the number of possibilities of why one might use such a law.

SCHWARCZ: I would add one further point, namely that Euric and Alaric II formulated their laws when the Visigothic realm had its centre of power and the greater part of its territories still in Aquitaine where the Goths had been since 419. So the law was not defined merely for Euric's conquered Spanish territories, but for the whole territory where the Visigoths had been living together with a very mixed population for nearly 100 years.

AUSENDA: There are people who have been living together for two hundred years and they still do not intermarry.

SCHWARCZ: Yes, but not just because of customs.

AUSENDA: There is no law for intermarriage or non intermarriage but they just do not intermarry. Where I worked, there are six different ethnic groups; they are still ethnically distinct and they do not intermarry.

HEATHER: I don't see why it is so odd to think that it would have taken some time for people in inferior and superior positions to intermarry, really I don't.

DÍAZ: On page 194-5, whether Visigothic Spain was dominated by urban or rural life. I wonder if Visigothic Spain was dominated by the rural or urban worlds. The problem is that the evidence, you have to speak with a reservation, of Visigothic Spain is complicated. And if we have in our mind the *Vitas Sanctorum Patrum Emeretensium*, we have often a false impression about the balance, about the power of the city. Big areas in Spain, for example, in the whole north-central plateau especially, only Toledo, the capital, is an important urban area.

RIPOLL: Dr. Wood, on page 194, asserts that Toledo more than a royal town, was an "abnormal" centre. What is normal? [Laughter]. Maybe it would be worthwhile to put the question of what we mean by 'normal', on the grounds that this is directly implied in the urban phenomenon, in the urban texture of town life, etc.

DÍAZ: I have in mind another question. It is not only if the towns survive. That is not the question. It is where is now the centre of power. For example, what is subsidiary, the countryside on the city or the city on the countryside? It is a question we can discuss, I think.

WOOD: I think that is a problem, because the evidence doesn't survive to point you in one direction or another. But major political events described in the sources tend to happen in cities. Some things happen at major villas, like Gerticos. As far as one can see, the pattern is relatively similar to what has also been true in the Roman world; your aristocracy have vast landed estates, and in all sorts of ways their power comes from the land but, when they are seen to be doing something public, they do it in the city. And that's why I see the city as the focus of power even though the resources of power may be almost entirely rural.

SCHWARCZ: I don't see that you can make this strong contrast between the city and land in that period, because the Roman Empire was organized in cities, and the cities were cities which lived mainly by agriculture. So, it was quite normal and early and if you talk about the aristocracy, we must make a difference between the senatorial aristocracy and their continuation in the Visigothic kingdom, and the urban aristocracy which is a completely different thing, a bit lower in the stratum of society and had its main interest in the city, but lived also on the income from agrarian lands within the territory of the *civitas*.

WOOD: I agree entirely, but I think there is also an issue that needs to be raised. I don't think it is an issue that can be solved, although obviously I have a view on what the most likely answer to it is. But in addition to your Roman aristocracy there may well have been backwoods landowners who were perfectly powerful, but who never turned up in the city and who never turn up in the sources; we don't know. We don't know enough about what is happening in backwoods areas of *Hispania*.

RETAMERO: On urban and rural life. I think that there are 'rural lives' possible without urban lives, but the reverse is not possible.

RIPOLL: It is something we can only investigate using archaeological and epigraphic research. The only way to know what is happening to rural settlements and rural life is the transformation of the *villae* and I am not sure about what you have said. I think perhaps in the Visigothic period there remains strong connection between the *urbs* and the *territorium*. Not only one aristocracy in the city and one aristocracy in the *territorium*.

SCHWARCZ: That's what I said.

RIPOLL: OK and there is something very interesting in the transformation of the *villae*. All these big properties with all the luxury in the countryside they change a part of the functions of the architecture. At one time in one part of the *villa* we can have cemeteries, another part of the *villa* has been transformed in the late sixth century and in another part the proprietors have built a church; these structures and this private *oratorium* become a *parochia*. It is very interesting to see the transformation of these properties at the end of the sixth century.

AUSENDA: Are you basically describing the transformation of the *villa* into a town?

RIPOLL: I do not refer at any time to the transformation of a *uilla*, one of the specifically Roman buildings, into a town, but into a centre of production and exploitation.

AUSENDA: I know, the *uillae* in many cases gave rise to medieval towns.

VOICES: No, no, *villae*.

AUSENDA: Indeed, in France they are called 'villes'.

RIPOLL: We are referring to the Roman *uillae*, practically all organized around a central court or with porches along the façade, with a clearly defined residential area and another area destined to agricultural and livestock exploitation.

AUSENDA: Yes, but did any Spanish *villae* give rise to towns?

SCHWARCZ: The different towns come from castles not from *villae*.

AUSENDA: I don't know about Spain, but in Italy all the place-names ending in *-anum* were *villae*, as you call them, or *praedia*, and they all became towns.

WOOD: I think you need to be very careful about the word city. It may make sense in terms of the Italian, 'città'. A city in the English language is something like Milano. And you don't have *villae* turning into Milano.

AUSENDA: All right, what do you call them then, urban centres?

WOOD: They can be smaller than that: villages.

HEATHER: Large villages or rural towns.

RIPOLL: Peter Heather in this case is defining the *uicus*.

SCHWARCZ: They can't have come out of a rural *villa*.

HEATHER: I just want to mention this difference between the *urbs* and the *territorium*. I wonder if that might not give us another dimension, for thinking about town and country, in the sense that the urban centre can go to hell, when its buildings are falling down and so on, but another way in which the Roman idea of a town can live on is if the *territorium* is still being used as an organizational-administrative unit. What made me think of that is Gregory of Tours on the *civitas* still operating for western and southern *Francia* as the basis of organization of military levies. I've got a feeling, although I haven't really read it carefully, that the Burgundian and the Visigothic legislation of the seventh century implies that each city also had its own military officer organizing recruiting and then fining people who didn't turn up. This kind of thing would mean that, whatever was happening to buildings, they were still using the *territorium* of the city unit as a kind of governmental organizational space.

WOOD: But really that was what I had in mind when I said that the Visigoths focus primarily on towns. You could also say like Frankish society.

HEATHER: By having both *urbs* and *territorium*, they are making that distinction; that might actually answer Pablo [Diaz]'s concern, might it not?

SCHWARCZ: I don't see any parts in Spain, Italy, or southern France going completely to ruin. So, I don't think it is necessary for the town to disappear.

HEATHER: No, it doesn't have to disappear. It doesn't matter what is happening to Roman buildings and things; and I'm just interested in it as a spatial-governmental unit and the continuity of that, bringing that point to what might be happening to them.

Concerning page 194, all I would say is that I think Ian [Wood] perhaps has to say, although he is carefully avoiding it, something about the 'meseta' cemeteries. Because if there is a distinctive Visigothic element in the creation of these 'Reihengräber' cemeteries, then actually Mérida is not typical at all, and the distribution of power in Spain in the earlier sixth century would be focused on those areas.

RIPOLL: I didn't understand what you said.

HEATHER: If those 'Reihengräber' cemeteries in the North, on the plateau, if they are generated in some way by Goths, who have just conquered Spain, then in the first instance, in the earlier sixth century, to be an effective king that is your first area of potential political support that you have to relate to; if they are really Goths. That would change over time and, of course, if they are not Goths then this is not an issue. But, if they are Goths, then earlier sixth-century Gothic kings will have to play to this audience first, and Mérida and places like that will have been marginal.

RIPOLL: You don't think then that there are Goths.

HEATHER: I do. Ian might not, but I'm just saying that if you do think they are Goths, then that area would actually be alive with political electricity in the earlier sixth century.

WOOD: Yes, I do very specifically say that I'm talking about the world of Mediterranean cities. I mean to avoid getting into those problems. Again, the difficulty is that you've got archaeological sources but how do you turn that archaeology into sound history?

RIPOLL: I do not believe that presently the concept of 'Reihengräberfelder', with all its ethnic connotations should be taken into account. It is an obsolete classical concept in the archaeological literature of the first half of the twentieth century.

WOOD: They are not ethnic considerations if you look at the current work that has been done on Reihengräber found in *Francia*.

RIPOLL: One cannot talk about Reihengräberfelder in Gaul. There is no researcher who presently uses this terminology.

WOOD: I think perhaps you should look at work on *Francia* by James (1979).

RIPOLL: I recall that Edward James does not use this terminology and, in case he should, it would not be with the meaning of a Germanic ethnicity. Edward James believed in the process of acculturation of the Visigoths, not in the concept of ethnic differentiation.

WOOD: And Guy Halsall (1992).

RIPOLL: In the last few years the concept of 'Reihengräberfelder' has become obsolete precisely because it held to a Germanistic (cultural and ethnic) historiographical approach which cannot be proved archaeologically. The lining up, which is precisely what 'Reihen' means, is attested in a great number of cemeteries which do not necessarily belong to the Migration Period, they could be Roman or Islamic.

HEATHER: I don't think that there is really an argument between you.

JIMÉNEZ: On page 196. A suggestion in relation to this tale about Paul's power. According to *Lex Visigothorum* VIII, 4. 16 *Antiquae*, a woman arrived at her highest 'price' between the ages of 20 and 40, because it was then when she was fertile. This 'price' (wergild) was of 250 *solidi* and it had to be paid in case of a murder. So I think that Paul refused to do this operation on that woman fearing the woman's probability of death. This is most interesting in that one can see the price a woman reached at different ages. The woman was worth nearly nothing during her early age, then she arrived at a high 'price', and in her later life her 'price' decreased once more.

WOOD: Sure. I think, though, that that point that you've made can usefully be taken together with the law that I cited about doctors being held guilty in the case of certain deaths. Indeed, you wouldn't necessarily assume that the doctor was guilty of murder in every case that somebody died in the course of treatment. The point you make is right; this is the moment when the woman is most valuable. But it is also important that within the Visigothic code we have legislation to say that the doctors are liable in the case of certain specific deaths.

JIMÉNEZ: Was this case one of them?

WOOD: No, it doesn't say anything about whether or not death during childbirth is covered by the law. It might or might not be.

DE JONG: The comment I would make is that the problem was probably of ritual impurity, that seems very feasible. On the same page I was struck by your mentioning Masona who built a *xenodochium* where doctors treated these patients free, slaves, Jews and Christians. Now, if you think of the way in which the later seventh-century legislation considers Jews the utterly polluting enemy, this represents an earlier stage. I was struck by this image of an apparently still fairly open minded society.

WOOD: It's an astonishing account.

RETAMERO: Page 196, a short comment on Paul's wealth. Of course, part of this wealth, namely personal wealth, probably came from his obstetric skills, but I think that this part of his wealth by no means accounted for the wealth of the Church of Mérida as an institution: there is the wealth of Paul as a doctor and, when compared to his private wealth, the enormous wealth of the Church of Mérida. This is worth distinguishing because the origins are quite different. It's not the same to get money by obstetric skills, as to create the conditions—a fiscal mechanism or some other means whereby wealth is produced. Obstetric skills cannot create these conditions, the institution of the Church of Mérida can.

DE JONG: Can I latch on to that? That was something I can't make out, how much all the wealth is indeed the Church's, how much is Paul's personally.

WOOD: We are talking about property given to him by the senator; it is given to him and not to the Church. And it only becomes the Church's as a result of the Church accepting Fidelis as bishop.

HEATHER: Or so the hagiographer says.

WOOD: But it is such a strange point within the hagiography, that I think one must be inclined to believe it.

HEATHER: It is staggeringly candid.

WOOD: It sounds so right that I don't think this is hagiographic invention.

HEATHER: He has quite obviously blackmailed the Church.

RETAMERO: I am very sceptical that the wealth of the institution of the Church came from the personal wealth of a doctor.

WOOD: But the point is that this wealth is the entire estate of senator. Obviously the Church in Mérida must have had landed property before that. But what the hagiographer says is this bequest of the land property which....

RETAMERO: I think that the worst point of this fervent writer, which I find very hard to believe, is that Paul's personal wealth accounted for the whole wealth of the institution, i.e. for the *xenodochium*, for the basilica of St Eulalia and so on.

WOOD: Wealth breeds wealth anyway. Because you go on getting the income from estates and so on. But the point is not that this is the whole wealth of Mérida. Mérida obviously has wealth before. What we are told by the hagiographer is that this wealth makes Mérida richer than anywhere else.

RIPOLL: The Church of Mérida was one of the Churches in *Hispania* holding most property, these are distributed over the entire peninsula, not only limited to the estates received in the town of Mérida. They were used also for construction even in areas as distant as the North of the Iberian Peninsula.

RETAMERO: Do you think that the origin of this wealth lies in the medical skills of a doctor?

RIPOLL: The presence of the martyr Eulalia is such that one can see in the *Vitas Sanctorum Patrum Emeretensium* that there were many donations by private people to the Church of Mérida.

DE JONG: If I may just interfere for one moment. The problem seems to be that Ian [Wood] follows the story of the hagiographer. Then you subsequently all jump on him and say the hagiographer is wrong, but that's not the point.

DÍAZ: I think that the patron of Mérida had its origins, the same as St Eulalia, in the town's condition as a provincial capital, which was the condition which allowed it to become a very wealthy Church. And I think that in the hagiographical context of the *Vitas*, the example of Paul and the rich senator is a paradigmatic example, one out of a lot that the hagiographer most probably had the possibility of mentioning. But, the question is that if we take the Council of 666, the Council of Mérida, we can read this document as an organizational document concerning a big property, 13 out of 21 canons more or less are concerned with the organization and the preservation of the properties, and actually with the administrative organization of a big property. I think it is not the question of the senator. I think it is a paradigmatic example of the hagiographer, but the question is that the Churches, and some of them especially, we have here the case of Mérida, but we have in comparison the information of the monasteries, which are really enormous properties and they have two different faces, one is the spiritual one, the dogmatic question, but if we read the documentation of the Visigothic Councils in general, normally after Toledo V, we do not have dogmatic or Christological polemics, they are concerned with the properties of the bishop, the relation between the bishop and the Church, and these are really documents of economic importance.

WOOD: I think that a different point is being made about the wealth coming from this Lusitanian senator. Obviously you start with the point that Mérida, before Paul becomes bishop, must have wealth because it is a major cult centre. Then, what happens, as we are told by the hagiographer, is that a particular windfall comes. Now, of course, there will be other later grants from pilgrims and so on. But I don't think you can say that this grant by this senator is simply paradigmatic because Paul behaves so peculiarly over this wealth. He actually blackmails the Church. And for a hagiographer to admit that the bishop blackmails the Church into accepting his own nomination of his successor is such a strange thing that it is more than a paradigm.

HEATHER: Just a very small further point about the story. When I read it this summer, it struck me that this business about Fidelis happening to arrive sounded like a complete fairy story. The fact is surely that Paul actually sent for Fidelis in the first place, so he has to cover up this nepotism—subsequently followed up with such vigor by blackmailing the Church—which is actually planned and long meditated.

SCHWARCZ: You have to take into account Greek kinship structures [laughter].

HEATHER: "Well, look, I forgot it's my nephew! Amazing. Well, I'll make you bishop".

DE JONG: Yes, it sounds like the Great Desert Father stuff.

SCHWARCZ: On Catholic bishops on page 198. It is in the last line of the page that you regard a grant to a Catholic bishop by a king as rather surprising. I would say that the gift of an Arian king to a Catholic bishop doesn't suprise me, because we have other examples of this. It is political expediency to do so in a society where you have to reconcile Catholics and Arians. You do well to give, and even if you don't share his convictions, you have to respect a holy man. There are examples in Ostrogothic Italy, if you consider the *vita* of Caesarius of Arles and his contacts with Theoderic.

WOOD: I don't want to imply that grants by Arian kings to Catholic bishops are surprising—only that a grant from this king to this bishop is surprising. It sound as though Liuvigild tried to set himself up as the leading patron of Eulalia. You could draw plenty of parallels with the Burgundian kingdom.

DÍAZ: On page 201, on the application of the law and workings of power, I have doubts about the universality of the application of the law. When we read the Visigothic laws we read about some penalties, especially monetary penalties, when we read all the chapters in relation to property, they refer normally to big properties; when we read many chapters about power, we can't avoid thinking that probably the law was applied especially to one very specific segment of the social spectrum of the population. I had another question, Mayke asked me to be short and I will not speak about patronage, but very probably it is under this patronage that a part of the law was applied. We have old references, in the Councils of

Toledo, in general in Visigothic councils, when we read about the responsibilities of the bishops over their subjects. We have more information, for example, in the monastic rules about the old application of penalties in certain circumstances. I think of the *Lex Visigothorum* as evidence of the normative law of the kingdom, is very important in the situations close to the king and for the social group near the king, but probably it is not the day-to-day book of law in small villages and small towns.

WOOD: I would agree with you: it seems to me that a lot of what has been written about Visigothic law in the past has overemphasized the extent to which the Visigoths probably managed to enforce law. It is a point which Isabel [Velázquez]' paper supports very strongly. The only reason why I didn't go further is that I was very specifically trying to concentrate on the sixth century.

HEATHER: But in the ninth and tenth centuries, when you get the charters that Roger Collins works on (1985), there they really were using the Code. If they are doing it in the ninth and tenth century context, why are we so certain that they are not in the sixth and seventh? There you've got judges who know the law books and, as I understand it, according to the range of evidence that Collins is using, they're out in the sticks aren't they?

WOOD: Yes, but what is out in the sticks in the ninth and tenth centuries, given the reduction of the kingdom, is not necessarily out in the sticks in the sixth.

HEATHER: So, the argument would be that, because the kingdom is smaller or the area is smaller, in the ninth and tenth century that might be the reason why we would assume it doesn't work so well earlier.

DE JONG: On the other hand, if you look at certain laws and decrees themselves, in which the written word seems to aim at all the nooks and crannies of society, that is mind boggling. When you think about the professions of the Jews at their conversion, which should be handed over in writing to the bishop, at least those making the laws thought these texts might reach people.

WOOD: I think there are two points with regards to Collins' work. First his work on the laws has emphasized the extent to which they really are enforced. But if you look at his article on Mérida and Toledo, he emphasized the limitations of royal power. So you have a conflict between two approaches.

The other point I would want to make about Collins' work on the laws, is that twenty years ago, when the first of his papers came out, the question of literacy and written documentation in the early Middle Ages was a central matter of debate. Twenty years on we may want to modify conclusions in the light of new questions.

HEATHER: Yes, I am not going to insist on that; I'm just wondering why it is different.

SCHWARCZ: I think one must take into account who is doing the judging for whom. This is at the end of Antiquity, and I don't think you would then get the rural area people being judged by their landlord by the book of law, but according to custom and tradition. In the cities the court responsible for the Roman population is the *episcopalis audientia* and the bishop was in the role of the head of the city's administration. So I think that the range of the application of the law was restricted by practice.

DE JONG: You seem to be wonderfully sure of all these things that went on.

SCHWARCZ: I'm not so sure, but that's just a practical illustration of all we know about the development of justice from 400 onwards.

DÍAZ: Concerning spiritual power against temporal power of the bishops on page 202, I have a very simple question: what is the nature of the bishops' power and influence? Is it power or is it influence? If you can distinguish the two.

WOOD: He must have both. Anybody with the financial resources which the bishops of Mérida had by the second half of the sixth century, had power: but anybody who has access to something as significant as the shrine of Eulalia had a whole range of different powers which you might want to call influence.

DÍAZ: Of course, I think about the *Vitas*, the dispute between Masona and the opposing bishop, and the intervention of the *dux*. It seems that the ultimate power is just the power of the *dux*. And the bishop is influential and passionate; anyhow I am not going to speak....

WOOD: As soon as you get into a position where brute force is needed, you move beyond the normal power of the bishop. If you were to ask me, "Does the bishop have physical power?" then the answer would be "no". But if you ask if he has power, I think you have to say, "Yes, he does have power".

DÍAZ: Sometimes I think that it is a question between....

DE JONG: I wouldn't want to meet one of these guys.

GREEN: Yes, I just want very much to confirm what you say about processions being a part of the armory of the clergy and to confirm this not from the linguistic, but from the literary point of view, where processions, above all with litanies, processional hymns and refrains are very much the meeting point between Latin and vernacular, clergy and laity, and written and oral. That, I think, is important.

DE JONG: A remark about page 203 which contains lots of interesting material about deathbed penance and after having read this, I understand a bit more about it because it is the ideal way of death for the fallen élite. That one could carry this to the extent, that once you had taken a deathbed penance you should then die, was what went wrong with Wamba. He didn't. He fell short of the ideal. I think that's what's going on. Ian [Wood] and I talked a bit about why Sunna put off a penance, the opportunity of doing a penance. It is a problematic punishment for ecclesiastics, for clerics. But Ian says other rebellious ecclesiastics got that punishment.

WOOD: It's very difficult from the Council of Toledo to work out what punishment, if any, the Arian bishops receive. As far as one can see from the fact that a group of Arian bishops sign the Catholic statement of faith at the beginning of the Council, and that they still retain their titles as bishops, it seems that they were left in post. This is not the issue in the case of Sunna. The question then is, is his penance to do with his rebellion? It is not at all clear exactly what legal patterns are being followed at this moment.

AUSENDA: On patronage, very briefly. I was interested in trying to discover something about different kinds of patronage such as between *saiones* and *buccellarii* and the fact that it was a stratified society, because the law talks about *honesta persona* and *minor persona*, and *nobiles* and *minoris loci personae*, I was wondering whether I could open the discussion on that and let other people take the floor.

DÍAZ: No, because the patronage itself is a long, long question here. I think we can discuss about the conception of sociability only speaking about patronage. There is the question of the schematization of the society, the question of the central power and local powers. On these questions the discussion would be very long and we do not have the time now.

WOOD: I think there is a clearer point to be made. There are necessarily different types of patronage; there are patronages within the military context; there are clearly patterns of secular patronage, but for those we have scarcely any evidence whatsoever; and there is clearly religious patronage. Again, you are back with the problem in Visigothic Spain that, apart from the evidence for religious patronage, our evidence is normative. It would be nice to have a text which shows something about military patronage in operation, but when it comes down to it, for the sixth century at least you have a number of laws which simply say that there should be no patronage, but they don't tell you how it's been operating.

SCHWARCZ: So, that's what you would expect in a society that develops out of the old Roman system of secular patronage and the Gothic-Germanic system of 'Gefolgschaft'.

VOICES: Hm, yes.

HEATHER: The thing I have found interesting recently is whether *buccellarii* and *saiones* represent the start of a process which leads to the legal redefinition of the free class into higher and lesser freemen in the seventh century, which I think is probably the general assumption or whether that's the result of some other pressures.

SCHWARCZ: I think you are too late with this division of society, because we are talking of a Germanic society and the division into *honestiores* and *humiliores* is a thing of the third century.

HEATHER: No, I'm not, because the law codes actually place it in the seventh century. What I'm talking about is not that there aren't richer people and lesser people in the sixth century, but, as it were, the formal legal splitting of the free class which is certainly in the seventh century.

DÍAZ: I think that if we continue discussing about this question, we must analyse all the linguistic problems about the terminology, the evolution, the superposition of categories, etc. I think that it must necessarily be a long discussion. This is more complicated than it seems when we read some books about the Goths.

WOOD: That's right, I think that the problem is, in a sense, that one could write an article dealing only with the terminology of patronage. It would be a very specific and linguistic article, and obviously crucial would be the changes I point out in the shift from *buccellarius* in the *Codex Euricianus* to a more general *patrocinium* in the *Antiquae*. But that, in a sense, would be a technical article, simply dealing with terminology.

DÍAZ: Yes but not only an academic question, it's a long history of tradition. Because we need to speak about patronage, we must speak about all the explanations around privilege. It is a long question, yes it is a long question as we can see it in King's book.

References in the discussion

Textual sources:

Letter from Tarra to Reccared: see Velázquez 1996.
Lex Visigothorum: see References at end of paper.
Victor of Vita
> *Historia persecutionis Africanae provinciae*: see Petschenig (ed.) 1881:1-107.
Vita Caesarii episcopi Arelatensis: see Krusch (ed.) 1896:433-501; cf. Schwarcz 1997:1117.
Vitas Sanctorum Patrum Emeretensium: see Maya-Sánchez (ed.) 1992.

Bibliography:

Friedrichsen, G. W. S.
  1939   *The Gothic Version of the Epistles.* Oxford: Clarendon Press.
Collins, R.
  1985   Sicut Lex Gothorum continet: Law and charters in ninth- and tenth-century León and Catalonia. *English Historical Review* 100: 484-512.
Halsall, G.
  1992   The origins of the Reihengräberzivilisation: forty years on. In *Fifth-century Gaul: A Crisis of Identity?* J. Drinkwater & H. Elton (eds.), pp. 196-257. Cambridge: Cambridge University Press.
James, E.
  1979   Cemeteries and the problem of Frankish settlement. In *Names, Words and Graves*. P. H. Sawyer (ed.), pp. 55-89. Leeds: Leeds University Printing Service.
Krusch, B. (ed.)
  1896   *Passiones vitaeque sanctorum aevi Merovingici et antquiorum aliquot.* (I) *Monumenta Germaniae Historica. Scriptores rerum Merovingicarum, 3.* Hannover: Hahn.
Maya-Sánchez, A. (ed.)
  1992   See References at end of paper.
Petschenig, M. (ed.)
  1881   *Victor episcopus Vitensis. Historia persecutionis Africanae provinciae. C.S.E.L., 7.* Wien: Gerold.
Schwarcz, A.
  1997   Die Liguria zwischen Goten, Byzantinen, Langobarden und Franken in 6. Jahrhundert. In *Oriente e Occidente tra medioevo ed età moderna.* Pp. 1109-1131. Genova: Glauco Brigati.
Velázquez, I.
  1996   El *suggerendum* de Tarra a Recaredo. *L'Antiquité tardive* 4: 291-298.

JURAL RELATIONS AS AN INDICATOR OF SYNCRETISM: FROM THE LAW OF INHERITANCE TO THE DUM INLICITA OF CHINDASWINTH[1]

ISABEL VELÁZQUEZ

Dpto. Latín, Facultad de Filologia, Universidad Complutense, Campus Universitario, E-28040 Madrid

Transmission of texts

To best approach the Visigothic legislation we consider the publication of Zeumer in the *Monumenta Germaniae Historica* (1902) as well as his work on the history of Visigothic legislation (1898 [1944]), as texts of primary importance.

The works of Zeumer are venerable and of far-reaching magnitude and, as pointed out by Díaz y Díaz (1976:16) referring to the edition of 1902, "provide a foundation of work which is both serious and trustworthy". However, the problems posed by the transmission of a rich and varied manuscript tradition are enormous and remain unresolved to this day. Zeumer did not establish a *stemma codicum* to deal with the host of possible connections and the difficult relationships which can be glimpsed among the manuscripts of the different recensions: Recceswinth (R), Wamba (V) and Erwig (E).

The aforementioned study of Díaz y Díaz, whose very title "La *Lex Visigothorum* y sus manuscritos. Un ensayo de reinterpretación" (Visigothic law and its manuscripts, an attempt at reinterpretation), suggests the approach followed in this work, brought to light other manuscripts not used by Zeumer in his publication.

Díaz y Díaz's study also offered abundant and valuable clarifications of the manuscripts dealt with by Zeumer. But above all, his study highlighted the need to attempt a systematic study of the traditions of the manuscripts. This study would have to include codicological and formal aspects together with the geographical density and distribution of the manuscripts. Aspects of filiation and classification would also need to be dealt with.

Díaz y Díaz (1976) defined the *Lex* as a "living" text. In fact, the *Liber* was subject to changes, modifications, additions, new wordings or amendments and omissions, introduced by each of the kings who had a hand in the development of the legal system.

---

[1] This paper forms a part of the research project *Fontes iuris romani Hispaniae (FIRH)*, directed by Prof. J. M. Pérez Prendes and subsidized by DGICYT of Spain. I wish to thank Dr. Giorgio Ausenda for his kind invitation to participate in this symposium, organized by the *Center for Interdisciplinary Research on Social Stress*. I also would like to thank Richard Maher for translating my paper into English.

225

A priori we know which are the *Antiquae* laws, although the identity of the relevant king in each case is not so clear. We can identify the laws introduced by Chindaswinth or Recceswinth, and can recognize the modifications carried out by Erwig. However after analysing in depth the critical publication of Zeumer, the different levels in the text become somewhat blurred.[2]

In addition, from sources from the period itself, we know of the problems caused by copying the laws. It is imperative to distinguish between the copy of a law, that is, its inclusion in the *Liber Iudiciorum*, and how this law actually came to be included in the various copies of the *Liber* in circulation, and how long it took for the law to reach the judges and under what conditions this was carried out.

The letters from Recceswinth to Braulio of Saragossa, and vice versa are well known; for example, Recceswinth asked Braulio to amend and rectify the copies of the code in circulation in order to remove errors. In all likelihood the publication in question is the *Liber* or *Lex Visigothorum*. Furthermore law *LV* V, 4. 22, of Erwig, stipulates that all copies of the *lex* must follow the official text, with regard to its form as well as to its content.

This inevitably leads to a most careful comparative analysis of all the manuscripts. Many of the problems and aspects detected by Díaz y Díaz in his excellent study recommend an analysis of each manuscript as a statute *per se* and of the relationship between a particular manuscript and others paying special attention to geographical distribution and density. This analysis is an arduous task which has been carried out in part by the excellent doctoral thesis of Y. García (1997).

Possibly after studies of this type which apply philological perspectives, textual and codicological criticism and the internal study of the language itself and literary style of the Visigothic legislation—allowing us to view the problem through the eyes of a philologist—we may be in a position to undertake a new critical edition of the *Lex Visigothorum*—a colossal task, without a doubt, which requires an interdisciplinary approach—and to achieve a greater knowledge of the history of the legislation. This would be important not only for the *Lex Visigothorum*, but also for *Alaric's Breviary (Lex Romana Visigothorum)* and the code of Euric. In this sense, I believe that a comparative study of the various manuscripts will bring us closer not only to establishing the history of this evolution, but also to the ever thorny issue of the validity and application of the legislation, as we will see in due course.

In my opinion it is not sufficient to study isolated laws, making historians' assumptions, and much less to start out with preconceived ideas about the origin of the laws themselves. I sincerely believe that it is necessary to undertake the lexical study and the internal study of the texts. It would also be necessary to begin with the collection of laws pertaining, in principle, to each king and to study the traits and characteristics of language and style in depth.

---

[2] See the diagram (Appendix 1) on the laws of the *Liber* issued by various kings (adaptation of that proposed by Pérez Prendes 1991:34-36).

Territorial or personal application of the laws?

Another controversial issue concerns the validity and application of the legislation. As well known, the majority of studies on the legislation of the Visigothic period pose the issue of the Roman or Germanic influence upon Visigothic legislation as well as whether the Codes were of territorial or personal application.

It would be useless and indeed unnecessary to make a *status quaestionis* here on this issue. I would, however, like to make an observation. Generally many of the authors of studies on Visigothic legislation begin their analyses with a statement of principles or, at least, they allow their preconceptions to show throughout the study. They start out with Roman and territorial assumptions or with Germanic and personal assumptions giving rise to a controversy with their opponents. There seems to be a sort of determination, sometimes obstinate, to demonstrate the 'territoriality' of the laws or their 'personality', and comment on particular laws by establishing precedents either in Roman law (or in ancient Roman law) or, in Germanic customary law. Any element, sign or characteristic of the law is discussed in relation to one or the other viewpoint, on occasions strangely enough the same laws are used to achieve different purposes.

This situation leads more often than not to fruitless discussions with regard to the problem itself. Issues of far greater relevance are forgotten, i.e. the legislation itself, its content and the transformation of social reality throughout the centuries of Visigothic rule.

If the history of the ancient world, from the barbarians in the ambit of the Roman Empire to later societies in western Gaul and Spain, is the history of a process of struggle and resistance, of confrontations, but also of pacts and necessary coexistence, leading finally to a mix in seventh century Spain, why should the history of legal relationships be any different?

It is possible to talk of a legal system in the Visigothic period, which has many unique aspects and which constituted in the legal field the significant transfer in the West of the Roman imperial system to another socio-political structure which was formed as a result of the settlement of the Visigoths, first in *Gallia* and afterwards in *Hispania*.

The intention was to establish a common legal system for the inhabitants of the territories which were progressively controlled by the new power, conquered by the Visigoths. But, like in other situations, there was no rupture between one system and another, rather there was a process of development and evolution conditioned by transformations in society itself, as well as by the more or less forced coexistence of different peoples. The main group was the Roman population of *Gallia* and *Hispania*. These people, without a doubt, possessed the weight of a wholly vigorous cultural tradition assimilated at least by the élite, patterned after the classical Roman world and modelled on Christianity, adopted by the population after centuries of a romanized *modus vivendi*.

The second group, the Visigoths, had arrived in *Hispania* from the East through military movements and pacts (*foedera*) with the Empire looking for places to settle. These people were a minority with respect to the Romans but, through the extension of these pacts, grew in independence in contrast to the continuing decadence of the Empire. When the Empire collapsed, the Visigoths took control of the political system and replaced it with another, created and shaped by themselves, evolving appropriate means for the exercise of power (Ripoll & Velázquez 1995:42).

Legal system: means for the exercise of power

The legal system is perhaps the best and most effective means for the exercise of power in times of peace. As a result of this, at the time of greatest conflict, wars, struggles between Romans and Goths, among people of these same groups, depending on the pacts (*foedera*) with the Roman Empire, the laws of the various peoples were threatened, violated and subjected to the ups and downs of war. But when the Visigoths managed to settle in a relatively stable way in *Gallia* and began to extend the boundaries of their occupation, they entered into a far more stable and peaceful coexistence with the Roman world. They established political relations with the Empire and also experienced a process of increasing adaptation and romanization—which appears in every field of culture and in many ways of life and, of course, in the institutional forms of power—encouraged by the Roman cultural élite and the aristocratic classes who followed a policy of "if you cannot beat them, join them".

Both the poems and letters of Sidonius Apollinaris are exceptional evidence for this Roman attitude. The Visigoths began their adaptation process well aware that the Empire's political and administrative organization was superior to their own. In the end, the Roman cultural tradition was to their liking and the legislative system provided a well established political grounding for government. Due to the effort of the Romans and because of the wishes and convenience of the Goths, this inevitable conversion to the Roman world was useful to everybody. But, let us not forget that it was a process of adaptation in which elements of the Germanic world also played their part.

A prime example of this conversion is demonstrated by Orosius when talking of Athaulf:

> He was a fervent supporter of peace...who was wont to say: "*Initially I eagerly desired to erase the name of Rome and transform the Roman Empire into a Gothic Empire alone and that it would be called and would be—to express it in common terms—a Gothia that had been Romania, and that now, he who had been Caesar Augustus, would be Athaulf*". But on being convinced by experience that the Goths could in no way obey the law given their uncontrolled barbarism, and that it was not advisable to repeal the laws of the state, since without them a state is not a state, he chose to at least try to completely restore and boost the name of Rome with the Gothic forces and so be considered by posterity as the instigator of the restoration of Rome after not having been able to change it (*Hist. adv. paganos* 7. 43)

From this text we can pick out two points which are of interest for this discussion.

1) Goths could not obey laws because of their barbarism. Of course, they had their own laws which they did obey. These were customary laws which regulated the life and organization of their society. Orosius transmits these words of Athaulf from which, I think, it is necessary to understand that Goths would not have respected laws which affected their *modus vivendi*, especially in times of conflicts and disturbances, i.e. laws designed for a consolidated and moreover territorially settled state such as that of the Romans.

2) Without laws a state is not a state. Such a fundamental statement shapes the idea, already expounded, that the legal system is a basic instrument for governing and building a state.

For this very reason, as the Goths consolidated their settlements, they began to issue laws, conscious that establishing them in writing in the Roman style generated a firmer control than simple tradition. This is the most important and significant romanization of Visigothic law.

In this situation, the military domination of the Visigoths in the territories of Gaul required laws to be issued which affected both Goths and Romans, for instance concerning the distribution of land. Moreover, with the achievement of independence from Rome under Euric, the reality suffered a qualitative change as recalled by Sidonius Apollinaris in his letter to Leo 7. 3. 3, *"modo per promotae limitem sortis ut populos sub armis, sic frenat arma sub legibus"*.[3]

Now Euric could attempt to legislate with the help of his Roman advisers, using all the legislation which they thought useful from the Roman world. But we should understand that his position was strong. He acknowledged that it was convenient to make use of the Roman world, of Roman laws (I do not think that, judging from his character, he personally liked the Roman world), and that Avitus, Leo and the others attempted to include all that which was in accord with the Roman world. However, for the same reason, Euric would have given his approval only to those laws which did not contradict his customs, which did not force him unconditionally to abandon his Germanic customary law.

In my opinion there is no doubt that Euric attempted to legislate territorially for Goths and Romans. He did not limit himself to issuing laws relating to the *sortes* but rather to all facets of private life. But here also Euric would have had to take into account that if he really wanted to rule over everybody, he would not be able to legislate—despite being in power—for a population, for the most part Roman, which had seen its state destroyed and all its laws abolished.

From this arose the Roman nature of his code published certainly later than 475, most probably in 480 (accepting Pérez Prendes' hypothesis, 1991:69-71). Nevertheless the code has a Germanic flavour—which cannot be denied

---

[3] "Or having restrained people by arms now restrains arms by laws through the whole extent of his enlarged domains" (translated by W. B. Anderson 1965:411).

considering the arguments that have been put forth—and, above all, joint interests and intentions. However, neither can we ascribe exaggerated consequences to the code's application, of its scope as 'law', given the fragmentary nature of its preservation.

If we believe Isidore of Seville, "*Sub hoc rege Gothi legum instituta scriptis habere coeperunt, nam antea tantum moribus et consuetudine tenebantur*" *(Hist. Goth.* 35) ("Under this king the Goths began to write legislation as, before this, they were ruled by custom and usage"), it seems that it was only based on personal application—for the Goths—not on territorial application (King 1980:135-136).

But there is a fundamental question. When Isidore of Seville mentions the *Codex Revisus* of Liuvigild he notes, "*In legibus quoque ea quae ab Eurico incondite constituta videbantur correxit, plurimas leges praetermissas adiciens plerasque superfluas auferens*" *(Hist. Goth.* 51) ("Also on the subject of legislation, he corrected all those which seemed to have been established in a confused way by Euric, adding many laws which had been omitted and excluding a number of superfluous laws").

And what of the *LRV*? Isidore says nothing of this, as if it had not existed. It is clear that Alaric's *Breviarium* was issued, it was widely introduced in Gaul and is a continuation of the *Codex Theodosianus*, which incorporated *leges, iura* and various interpretations not exempt from inconsistency and disorder (Escudero 1995:207-8; Lambertini 1991; Morales 1995:121-33).

The famous statement of the *Breviarium (LRV)* in the *Commonitorium*: "*Providere ergo te convenit ut in foro tuo nulla alia lex neque iuris formula proferri vel recipi praesumatur*", must be understood as referring to the Roman laws which are used in the *LRV*, saying that these were the only laws to be used; but the lack of reference to the Eurician laws must not be understood as a repeal of the *CE* but rather as indicating a possible compatibility with it.

It is difficult to imagine that Alaric II—in view of the legislative experience of his father—would have legislated only for Romans, rather than territorially, above all taking into account his romanized frame of mind, his desire to be seen as the legitimate heir of the Empire. In this sense he may not have initially repealed the *CE* although he would have ended up doing so if it had not been for the defeat of Vouillé (Morales 1995:130).

With this I came to a crucial point: What was the application of *LRV* in *Hispania*? The fact that manuscripts are lacking in *Hispania*, with the exception of the, so called, *Legionensis palimpsestus* is definitely not in itself a clear indication, but it could reflect something which would be of no surprise: its limited or non-application in Spanish territory, not its absence. Theudis incorporated the law of 'legal costs' into the *Breviarium*, which is considered territorial, but to what extent was it valid as a legal code at least among the Visigoths? The period between the Visigothic settlement in *Hispania* and Liuvigild saw several modifications, and special situations, such as the Ostrogothic *interregnum*, which may have been of use for bringing *CE* up to date or as a replacement for both groups of laws.

The words quoted from Isidore in respect of the *CR* of Liuvigild make sense in this situation. If the real application of the *LRV* was very limited, it follows that Isidore would not mention it, but Isidore, who lived during a period sufficiently close to Liuvigild, during the reign of Sisebut, saw the *CE* in a larger-than-historical perspective. At that point, it would be perceived as old legislation replaced by that of Liuvigild; not in an entirely new legislation, but rather by a complete revision of the old one. In the light of the *CR* (which we only know indirectly through the *LV*) Isidore may have understood that those—now remote—laws were for the Visigoths of those—now distant—times, without trying to enter more deeply into the real situation of territories of Gaul controlled at that time by Euric.

On the other hand, the reference to confused and omitted laws may be a reflection of the unifying nature—aiming at synthesis—of this first legislative code. Confused in the light of the new accurate and complete editions; omitted in the light of innovations, although here we must realize that Isidore considers laws existing in the time of Euric, but not included in his code. This may refer to the incorporation of laws of Roman origin in the *CR* and at the same time may reflect a clear assimilation and acceptance, in the time of Isidore, of the laws included in the legislation of Liuvigild and successive kings.

But what does indeed seem clear is that the legislative intention of Liuvigild—the law *LV* III, 1. 1 being a primary example—was territorial. His policies, territorial, social and religious unification, bear this out. He was not successful on all fronts, but he managed to legislate for all inhabitants of his territory, although, like his predecessors, he had to seek balance among the Roman, Germanic and religious legal elements. His successors extended this code until eventually Chindaswint proposed a new global revision, the *Liber Iudiciorum*; perhaps he even managed to complete the task (King 1980), and undoubtedly his son Recceswinth issued it, newly extended. It was this *LV* which had a definitively territorial application and that provided the rules for the coexistence of the two peoples of different origin who were now united in the seventh century. As Pérez Prendes writes:

> The determining factors in the structure of Visigothic law is not the Roman legacy but rather the peculiar way of linking elements which were very varied in a whole which was no longer Roman but rather in which common Roman parts and canon law predominated (which many times meant writing things in Latin which were quite divergent from Roman law) accompanied by other legal traditions (1989:1105).

But, returning to the beginning, the *Liber Iudiciorum*, as it has survived, is a living organism full of re-elaborations, extensions, modifications which must be carefully analysed in order to understand this impressive legal system and the reality of the society where it was applicable. As a consequence of that, we can affirm that the legislative system in Visigothic *Hispania* is the result of a complex union and transformation of Roman *leges, iura*, traditions, etc., all from different origins (see App. 2).

Inheritance legislation

With reference to the vast legislative activity carried out by the Visigothic kings, I would like to concentrate on one specific aspect of private law: inheritance. The variety of factors reflected in inheritance legislation makes it one of the most interesting areas in private law. These factors include: family, property, family and social relations. Indeed, in my opinion, we can go even further in the area of inheritance and succession in Visigothic law: I think that the spirit of the law—if I may be allowed to refer to it in this way—provided an extra factor which also affected public life. This factor stems from issues raised by large inheritances, royal successions and donations. The possibility of making a will in favour of a third party became a matter of great importance when that third party was the Church, for example.

Furthermore, from my point of view, inheritance law allows us to see a reflection of this process of adaptation between two worlds, that I have already mentioned. This is only natural, because, precisely in the traditions of any people, it is normal to sense this topic as something deeply rooted. This is so because it directly affects important aspects in the way of life of the people and of their personal and family relations.

We start out from two quite different realities as far as origins are concerned: in the Roman world, the concept of the family, family relationships and the concept of property were based on the *patria potestas* of the *paterfamilias* and as a consequence of this, the *paterfamilias* had absolute freedom in making a will. In the Germanic world, family relations were based on links to the *Sippe*; blood ties determined how these relationships were understood and were decisive in deciding the rights of inheritance. As Tacitus (*Germania* 20) relates, the heirs were always the children and the *testamentum* was not used. If we combine this to their concept of property, based on the communal disposal of land, so far removed from the individual and personal nature of the Romans, we can see that the customs of both were quite different and necessarily clashed when they came into contact.

Nonetheless, the Roman world had undergone a clear historical evolution which progressively limited the power of the *paterfamilias* during the imperial epoch. This evolution, above all, regulated the inheritance rights of lawful heirs, to allow to the freedom of making a will. Although disinheritance was permitted, certain provisions were introduced in order to avoid the omission of lawful heirs.

This situation gave rise to the fact that, when the written laws of the Visigothic kings ruled on succession and inheritance, these two worlds were now not so irreconcilable. Saying this brings forward precisely the problem which I will tackle immediately and lays down the first premise of my exposition. The problem is this: inheritance law is a most clear example of how the points of view of modern legal historians—let us say Germanists versus Romanists—oppose each other, and how the same texts, and even the same arguments, are used to declare the nature of the same law as absolutely Roman, or absolutely Germanic and hence to conclude that the same is true of the entire legal system. In this sense, the famous *Dum inlicita* of

Chindaswinth (*LV* IV, 5. 1, named *la mejora* in Spanish[4]), was the object of an exhaustive study by Jorge de Lacoste in 1913. This study proclaimed the originality of the legal system established by this king, the *mejora* and its openly Germanic origin.

His opinions, many of which now are lacking in validity and have been superseded, were generally accepted except by a few authors. Many years later, Alfonso Otero published an extensive article (1963) in which he analysed systematically the Roman precedents of this law. Otero refuted the originality of Chindaswinth's law and examined all those Roman laws which could have led to the definitive establishment of the *mejora*. As for Otero he thought that the *mejora* did not have its origin in the *Dum inlicita* but rather in Roman law, especially in the famous *Constitutiones Feminae* of the *Codex Theodosianus* (*CTh* III, 8. 2). Other laws which Otero saw as complementing the *CTh* III, 8. 2, were *CTh* VIII, 18. 9 (*LRV* VIII, 9. 5) of Theodosius II and Valentinian III and the constitution of Theodosius I (*CI* V, 10. 1) from 392 AD, modified by Arcadius and Honorius (*CTh* III, 9. 1 = *LRV* III, 9. 1) in 398 AD. Also relevant, in his view, were *Novella* of Theodosius II, (*Nov.* 14 = *LRV* VII), from *ca* 458 AD, and (*Nov.* 35 = *LRV* XII) of Valentinian III.

Otero's analysis of these laws had two basic aims: firstly to demonstrate that the freedom to make a will in the Roman world was reduced, especially through restrictions on the possibility to disinherit: by the introduction of the *quota legitima* (it came to be the fourth part of the share *ab intestato*), by the possibility of bringing an action of *innofficiosi testamenti* (later in the third century), or of *innofficiosae donationis*, and, above all, by the restrictions on the father's possession of the *bona materna* established by *CTh* VIII, 18. 1 (= *LRV* VIII, 9. 1). The second aim of Otero's analysis, and the most important, was to demonstrate that these same laws were the source of the *mejora*. With reference to the first aim, the arguments are irrefutable. However what seems to me to be less clear is the assertion that the *mejora* has its exclusive origin in these laws, excluding the possible influence of other components. These other components could include a Germanic inspiration in the 'sistema de reservas' (system of life interests), as I will endeavour to examine, or this law may have been an attempt to adapt the legislation to the prevailing customs at the time of its establishment, or an attempt (not of less importance) by the legislators to control the inheritance system, as under this system—in relation to the wealthy upper classes—the law could have repercussions on social life.

The laws cited by Otero may be classified into two groups:

1) Laws relating to the *bona materna* and the *bona paterna*.

The most important law is Constantine's *CTh* VIII, 18. 1(= *LRV* VIII, 9. 1), which limits the *patria potestas*, establishing that the *potestas et ius fruendi res*

---

[4] This law goes by the name of *mejora*. At present, there is a law of *mejora* in the Spanish Civil Code. This legislation permits a person to apportion a third of his estate to favour any one or several or all of his right and lawful heirs. Section 823 of the Civil Code provides as follows: "Father or mother may apportion a third of their estate to favour any one or several of their natural or adopted children or offspring". In the following pages, I will translate 'mejorar' by 'to favour'.

liberorum suorum of the maternal possessions should remain in the father's hands, but repealed the *licentia* to deprive the children.

On the other hand, this law provides that, if the father frees his child, he must hand over to it the possessions of the mother, and the child must give a third part of this to his father (*muneris causa*). This part could be decided at the discretion of the judges, but the father would have the right to dispose of this part.

But, in reality, all the laws of title VIII 18 of the *Codex Theodosianus*—both those which were incorporated in the *LRV* as much as the others—follow this line of regulating the rights of the father over the *bona materna*. He could not dispose of them, sell them or donate them, but was entitled to life interest (*usufructus*).

Law *CTh* VIII, 18. 9 (= *LRV* VIII, 9. 5) touches on the same subject in the situation where the mother died intestate. Other laws—not used by Otero— prescribe similar rules when the possessions left by the parents of the deceased mother are in question, that is the grandparents to the grandchildren. In this case the father again does not have the right to dispose of these possessions, as a *CTh* VIII, 18. 6 (= *LRV* VIII, 9. 3).

2) Laws relating to *donationes ante (propter) nuptias*.

Otero (1963:23 ff.) provided a clear exposition of the gradual imposition of this type of *donatio* which originated in the East. Eventually, as Otero shows, this *donatio* reached a level comparable with the dowry and even came to be understood as a form of compensatory *dos - donatio ante nuptias*. This gave rise to terminological confusion in Visigothic legislation (Iglesias 1945:547; Watson 1968:229-32).

However, Otero does not comment on the possible impact of Germanic law or custom. There were several types of donation in the Germanic world: *Gerade*: *ornamenta nuptiale; Wittum: pretium nuptiale* (part of which were the marriage ring and token) and the *morgengabe* (morning gift). It appears that there was a strong relationship between the *Wittum* and the *donatio ante nuptias*, even in the existence of tokens, etc. (cf. *LV* III, 1. 3, and specially III, 1. 5). In this law, Chindaswinth established the amount of dowry for anyone that *ex senioribus gentis Gotorum filiam alterius vel cuiuslibet relictam filio suo poposcerit in coniugio copulandam*, and referred to several elements of the Roman laws collected in the text:

> Aut si forte, **iuxta quod et legibus Romanis recolimus** fuisse decretum, tantum puella vel mulier de suis rebus sponso dare elegerit quantum sibi ipsa dari poposcerit.

Chindaswinth brought together two hereditary customs (King 1980:155; Pérez Prendes 1989:1130), precisely in these aspects which were similar and comparable, where Roman legislation did not contradict Germanic tradition and could be used to draft the law technically and take advantage of the selfsame elements of the long Roman tradition.

Otero identified the fundamental Roman laws relating to the *donationes ante nuptias*, especially the aforementioned *Constitutiones Feminae* (*CTh* III, 8. 2 = *LRV* III, 8. 2 of Gratian, Valentinian I and Theodosius I in 382 AD), which Otero considered to be the "authentic origin of the *mejora*". In fact, in this law, we can read, that women who enter into a second marriage must hand over all the possessions deriving from the deceased first husband, to any or all of the children from that first marriage, but may not hand these possessions over to anyone else:

> *Id totum ita ut perceperint* **integrum ad filios**, *quos ex praecedente coniugio habuerint,* **transmitant vel ad quemlibet ex filiis**,*.... Nec quidquam eadem feminae ex isdem facultatibus abalienandi in quamlibet extraneam personam vel successionem ex alterius matrimonii coniuctione susceptam praesumant atque habeat potestatem possidendi tantum in diem vitae, non etiam abalienandi facultate concessa.*

Otero understood this law as the practical application of *CTh* VIII, 18. 1 for widows with children (childless widows could obtain *pleni proprietate iuris* over what they had received and would have power to collect and make a will in favour of whoever they wished). This was clearly a benefit or favour in the Roman world and furthermore, this law (*CTh* III, 8. 2) and its *interpretatio* had, in my opinion, a decisive influence in the elaboration of the aforementioned law of Chindaswinth (*LV* III, 1. 5). Law *CTh* III, 9. 1 (= *LRV* III, 9. 1) of Arcadius and Honorius, in 398 AD, confirmed this law *CTh* III, 8. 2, with the exception of the possessions proceeding from the *donatio*.

Otero (1963:31) also cited, as a clear precedent for the *mejora, Novella* 14 of Theodosius II from 439 AD (= *LRV* VII). The law compelled the man to dispose of the possessions proceeding from the woman in the same way as *CTh* III, 8. 2 (the *Feminae*) compels the women. In this *novella* the right of favour is equally confirmed:

> *Dividendi quoque res inter eos ipsos liberos parentibus pro suo arbitrio vel eligendi quem voluerint licentia non negamus....*

According to Otero (1963:34) "This right to choose or prefer is exactly the same as the *mejora*...Chindaswinth did nothing more than call it *mejora*". These (and other) laws relating to the *donationes* are indeed, as Otero maintained, a precedent for the *mejora*, but only in a general sense, in my judgement. In other words, they made it possible to favour one child from elements of the overall different estate: by the mother from the *bona materna* (gifts from the husband), by the father from the *bona paterna* (gifts from the wife). However these laws acquired several modifications in Roman common law.

Thus the *Novella* 6 of Majorianus considered *bona paterna* to be goods acquired by the mother *tempore nuptiarum*. But, more importantly, it now prohibited the mother from choosing—*meliorare*—in favour of one of the children, but the father was not prohibited from doing the same. *Novella* 1 of Severus repealed this law, but maintained the limitations on the rights of the widow over the *donatio*. The *donatio* remained as usufruct for the children—whether the widow remarried or not—and the ownership of the *donatio* was reserved, with no choice allowed. It was only possible to exercise choice in bequeathing the same usufruct of the goods.

Otero related these laws to Roman common law about the *donationes* and the *bona materna* with their corresponding laws in *CE*, especially 321, 322, 327 and 319, and *LV* IV, 2. 13; IV, 2. 14 and IV, 2. 18, as strictly related to the *Dum inlicita* (*LV* IV, 5. 1) of Chindaswinth, considering *CE* 321 in particular as "the immediate antecedent of the *mejora*" (Otero 1963:39). In agreement with this author, I think that these laws are precedents—in a general sense, as I have already said—and it can be maintained that the entire chapters (*Titulus*), about *De successionibus* and *De bonis maternis* of the *Codex Theodosianus* served as a foundation and had a more or less direct influence on many of the laws of the *CE* and the *LV*, and of course of the *LRV*. But this does not cancel out or deny Germanic precedents.

About the chronology of the laws

Before talking about the way that these laws of the *CE* adapt those of the *CTh* and preceded the *Dum inlicita*, a basic question of the chronology of the laws must be considered. If the Roman precedents of the *mejora* were adapted by the *CE,* where the *LRV* adopted the Roman laws directly, the following situation arises, which inevitabily relates to the problem of the validity and territorial applications of these codes of laws:

1) If the *CE* was replaced by the *LRV* and both had a territorial application, it would not be necessary to presume that there were explicit elements of the *CTh* in the *CE,* which were reproduced in the *LRV* afterwards. Since, if the *LRV* replaced the *CE*, then it is possible to attribute differences between them, precisely because it is indeed clear that Alaric's *Breviarium* had an openly romanizing motivation on the part of this king, who abandoned his father's code to adopt his own code composed of Roman laws. In such circumstances, the comparative study of the evolution of these laws should not be that which is traditionally done, ie:

$$CTh \longrightarrow LRV \; // \; CE \longrightarrow LV$$

but:

$$CTh \dashrightarrow CE \dashrightarrow LRV \dashrightarrow <CR> \dashrightarrow LV$$

2) If, on the other hand, the *CE* and the *LRV* had a personal application, then we must address parallel studies:

a) $CTh \longrightarrow LRV$ (which would end up in those laws which do not have an exact continuation).

b) $CTh \dashrightarrow CE \dashrightarrow <CR> \dashrightarrow LV$ (this type of comparison is normally presented even by upholders of the territorial theory).

3) However, following on from the second point, a strictly chronological sequence should be considered which perhaps might result in greater clarity:

$$CTh \xrightarrow[\text{Germanic influence}]{\hspace{3cm}} CE \dashrightarrow [LRV] \dashrightarrow <CR> \dashrightarrow LV$$

Using this approach I will attempt to demonstrate the following:

CE 321 (App. 3), which, following the influence of *CTh* 8, 18. 1; 8, 18. 8 and *Novella* 35, proclaimed (Otero 1963:40) the right of the father to the usufruct of the *bona materna* and the reservation of the *third part* of these goods in usufruct when the child reached 20 years, or the reservation of *half* of these goods in the case of marriage, should be considered as a legal emancipation, and a feature of Germanic law in accordance with the views of Zeumer (Zeumer 1944 [1898-1901]:302).

However, nothing was explicitly said here about the father's right to choose one of his children. It strikes me as somewhat strained to see in this law a *mejora* of the father based on an argument *e silentio* comparing it with *CE* 322 (App. 4). Precisely one of the most romanized facts of the CE is the supreme care (not supreme perfection) with which it was drawn up by Roman legislators. The establishment of written laws had the purpose and fullfilled the object of giving validity, permanence and effectiveness to the laws. If we examine, in general, the legal language of the Roman laws as much as the Visigothic laws, we can see the meticulousness and—at times excessive—precision with which they were drawn up to avoid misconstructions.

In my judgement Euric's laws on the matter of inheritance pursue a basic object: all remains within the scope of the *Sippe*. In a precise way *CE* 322 continued the ban of Majorianus and Severus, leaving the woman with only the possibility of leaving the usufruct of her goods to one of her children. It was not necessary, or perhaps not convenient, that the license to choose given by the *Novella* 14, which may be, logically, a reflection of the privileges of the *patria potestas*, was continued to be given in *CE* 321. Euric would not have seen the necessity or convenience of favouring (*meliorare*) one of his children. The situation in the *CE* would thus be equalized and he returned to the old Roman situation and continued with the Germanic: inheritance to the children—the *legitima*—of the Roman *intestati* and in general of the Visigoths. If *CE* 322 accepted the *Novella* of Severus, as Otero (1963:41) said: "as a guarantee of equal distribution among all the children"—and I believe that was a fundamental motive for a Visigothic king, such as Euric, with a mentality still very attached to his traditional concept of the family—it is easy to assume that *CE* 321 would not pick up the possibility of the election of the father—not abolished in Roman law, valid from the *Novella* 14—in order to guarantee this equality of goods and because the concept of *patria potestas* would not have been so relevant to him.

The result, in practice, was the prevalence of the concept of an equal lawful inheritance for all the children; *CE* 320 (App. 5) mentioned such an equality. However, here, notwithstanding that the reading of D'Ors (1960) of the first line is generally accepted (*Si parentes testati decesserint...*), I think that the first reading of Zeumer - *Si parentes intestati decesserint* - is more acceptable. It would be contradictory to give all the provisions that follow if a will had previously been made. The problem is again related to the romanized nature of the *CE*. Possibly the importance of the *testamentum* or codicil or the donations' *scripturae* is due to the fact that they were solemn documents which validated the provisions contained therein. And this feature is, perhaps, the most profoundly romanized trait of the *CE*. For this reason, in the case of the *intestati*, the norms must clearly be regulated to avoid the estate leaving the family sphere.

On the other hand, *CE* 320 continued some provisions which limited the rights of the woman. When the woman married without the consent of her siblings or their heirs (that is, she was going outside the main family), she lost her goods and, if she did not marry or was a religious person, she had the usufruct of the goods until her death, but the land should go back to her heirs (siblings, main family), being able to do what she wished with the remainder. On this point (*CE* 320. 5) the law insists on *intestati* because it was here making a new provision for an unmarried sister. I do not think that the law provided *intestati* at this point against an expression *testati*, written at the beginning. That is to say, the woman, in case she had no descendents, could not have the landed property. The *LRV* abandoned these provisions to reform the *CTh* (laws cited).

In *LV* IV, 2. 1 (App. 6) we see the beginning of *CE* 320 repeated with the reading *intestati* and reduced to the first provision alone, excluding the Eurician norms on inheritance in usufruct of childless sisters.

With reference to the above, we must mention *CE* 319 (App. 7). This law established that a widow could dispose of the goods bequeathed to her by her husband if she did not enter into an illegal union. It must be understood (Lacoste 1913:23, Otero 1963:43) that this was the case of a childless widow, since, although it is not explicity stated, it does say that these goods returned, on the death of the woman, *ad heredes donatoris legitimos revertatur*. If there had been children then it would have been specified by the term *filios*. However these donated goods could be left to anyone she wished provided that she did not enter into an illegal union.

This law is the origin of the *Antiqua LV* V, 2. 5 (*Maritus si uxori*. App. 8), attributed to Liuvigild. Otero (1963:43) assumed that this *Antiqua* was earlier than *LV* V, 2. 4 (*Si mulier a marito*. App. 9) and in its turn *LV* V, 2. 4 represented the general principle of life interest (*reserva*) for children with the power to dispose of a fifth part, and freedom of disposition when there were no children. *LV* V, 2. 5 would be the exception about the improper behaviour of the widow who was deprived of free disposition of the fifth part of the complete estate, if she had children and if she had not acted as provided in *CE* 319.

In my opinion the process is different. With *CE* 319 already in existence, law *LV* V, 2. 4 was issued. This law established that, apart from the dowry, *extra dotem* *(dos = donatio)*, any goods that the wife received from her husband, if there were children, remained in her possession until her death but that she could only dispose of a fifth part of the same. After her death the complete estate, less the fifth part, was transferred to the children. But if she was childless, she had the power to do anything she wanted with the donated goods. However, if she died intestate (which presupposes that in the preceding proposition she had been able to make a will and dispose of her estate as she wished) the goods returned to the husband if still living and, if the husband was deceased, then the goods passed on to his heirs:

> *Quod si ex ipso coniugio filii non fuerint procreati, quidquid mulier de rebus sibi donatis facere elegerit, liberam habeat potestatem. Ceterum si intestata discesserit, ad maritum eius, si suprestis extiterit, donatio revertatur. Sin autem maritus non fuerit, ad heredes mariti, qui donationem fecit, eadem donatio pertinebit.*

The law ends by saying that a similar approach was necessary in the case of men.

Once this law was issued, more than likely by Liuvigild, law *CE* 319 was reformed and clarified. In reality I do not see contradiction or impossibility in their coexistence (as Zeumer [1949]:335). What happened was that with the issuing of *LV* V, 2. 4, *CE* 319 needed to be revised. *CE* 319, which in its original composition, did not give rise to doubts—referring to the childless widows on mentioning the *heredes* of the husband and not the *filii*—now presented a certain ambiguity in the face of the terminological precision of *LV* V, 2. 4. For this reason Liuvigild (most probably) issued *LV* V, 2. 5 at the same time or after *LV* V, 2. 4 (not before), taking *CE* 319 and perfecting it. Thus he explicity added "*Si filios non habuerit*" and completed it with a fragment adapted from law *LV* V, 2. 4 itself about the fact that, if the wife died childless, then the donated goods must return to the husband if living or to his heirs.

Liuvigild, hence, produced a new law, *LV* V, 2. 4, and perfected and complemented an additional law, *CE* 319, which, when compared to the new law, proved ambiguous, and incorporated a further reform in the *Liber*, *LV* V, 2. 5. This case could well be an example of the legislative work carried out by Liuvigild and, as Isidore tells us, and we have noted earlier, "he corrected all those which seemed to have been established in a confused way by Euric, adding many laws which had been omitted and withdrawing a number of superfluous laws".

About the order of the laws in the Liber IV, Titulus II.

Studying the order of transcription of the laws in the *Liber Iudiciorum* is a productive exercise and fundamental to the history of the legislation, on the same lines as noted at the beginning about Díaz y Díaz' study (1976).

LV IV. II is the *Titulus: De successionibus*. One should recall that the first *Titulus* of book IV established the different classes and degrees of kinship. The second *Titulus* is made up of a series of *Antiquae* laws, based on *CE* and a series of laws from Chindaswinth and, later, laws which were incorporated into the *titulus* keeping a strict hierarchial order relating to degrees of kinship or the proximity in relation concerning inheritance.

The *Titulus* II of the *Liber* IV constitutes a meticulous and detailed collection of rules relating to inheritance. This collection comprises a complete panorama of the system operating in the Visigothic world of the second half of the seventh century which had been taking shape from the first moments of the *CE*. Thus this title begins with law (*LV* IV, 2. 1) on the inheritance of sons and daughters on an equal basis if the parents died intestate (excluding the rules regarding the landed property of the childless sisters in *CE* 320).

LV IV, 2. 2 (= *CE* 336) insists on the idea that children are first in the line of inheritance, then grandchildren and finally grandparents (parents of the deceased). *LV* IV, 2. 3 (= *CE* 336) established that if there were no heirs of the type listed above then collateral heirs would inherit.[5] The second part of CE 336 began with a very similar form: *Quando supradicte persone desunt*...but it is not preserved. It seems likely that it could be the same as the first part. The only difference is that *LV* has divided the content of *CE* 336 into two separate laws.

LV IV, 2. 4 is a law of a general character referring to the fact that all those who were family members should inherit (according to the established order) when the deceased did not make a donation, a will or did not express their intentions before witnesses:

> IIII. *Antiqua. Qui succedere possunt in eorum facultatibus, qui nec scriptis nec testibus suam alligant volumtatem.*

> *De successionibus eorum, qui sic moriuntur, ut nec donationem nec ullum faciant testamentum nec presentibus testibus suam ordinent volumtatem, qui gradu illis proximi fuerint, eorum obtinebunt hereditatem.*

I believe that this law is modelled on Roman tradition reflecting the equal status of the will and verbal donation among possible ways of expressing intention, and at the same time the definitive formulation of legitimate inheritance according to the Germanic 'spirit' and Roman tendency which were effectively contained in Roman common law in the West.

Next the law *LV* IV, 2. 5 of Chindaswinth appeared, which probably replaced another one of which there is no trace (or perhaps it is a new law). This law established that the brothers and sisters, who are children of the same father and mother are those who inherit on an equal basis. If they are children of different fathers then those who are of one father or one mother will be given priority.

Recceswinth was probably the king responsible for the new law *LV* IV, 2. 6, (App. 10) equivalent to *CE* 328 in its opening, concerning inheritance received from the grandfather and the grandmother, in which Erwig's addition confirmed the equality of the inheritance from both grandparents.[6] This and the following law conform to the 'principle of lineage'.

---

[5]   In Erwig's version it is emphasized that they received the inheritance "of the deceased who dies intestate" (*defuncti qui intestatus discesserit*). This preciseness is quite understable now since the original law in *CE* 336 was the combination of *LV* IV, 2. 2 and IV, 2. 3 On separating them in the later versions this declaration is a long way off.

[6]   One could think that the maternal grandfather was overlooked, since the law considers that in the first instance paternal and maternal grandfathers inherit on an equal basis. If the maternal grandfather is deceased, then the paternal grandfather and the maternal grandmother inherit. If both grandfathers are deceased, then the grandmothers inherit on an equal basis. At first glance it seems

The following laws are *Antiquae* and address lateral lines of kinship: *LV* IV, 2. 7 (= *CE* 329) to paternal and maternal aunts and *LV* IV, 2. 8 (similar to *CE* 331 of which only fragments are left) to nieces and nephews of brothers as well as sisters. After these laws (as well as *LV* IV, 2. 10 *Antiqua,* hence prior to this one) another follows from Chindaswinth *LV* IV, 2. 9 concerning inheritance by women. It is almost a recapitulation of the previous legislation referring to women: all possible female heirs (be they of father, mother, paternal or maternal grandparents, brothers, sisters, etc.) could receive inheritance on an equal basis with their brothers, "*nam iustum omnino est, ut, quos propinquitas nature consociat, hereditarie successionis ordo non dividat*".

Law *LV* IV, 2. 10 is, as mentioned earlier, an *Antiqua*: concerning the comparison of women with those of the same degree of kinship—with respect to inheritance—in the maternal line. So Chindaswinth, in drafting *LV* IV, 2. 9, summarized possible inheritance by women, expressly referring to the father or the mother, paternal and maternal grandparents, paternal uncles and aunts and their children, who should logically have appeared in *LV* IV, 2. 10. However, they had been included earlier in the *Liber,* perhaps because its wording was more general, comprehensive and had a wider application.

LV IV, 2. 11 (= *CE* 334) discusses inheritance between spouses when there are neither children nor relations within the seventh degree.[7] *LV* IV, 2. 12 (= *CE* 335) deals with the inheritance of religious persons whose goods—if they have no relatives—are transferred to the Church in which they are serving.

LV IV, 2. 13 looks at new viewpoints of inheritance after having dealt with all the possible types of heirs and inheritances. This *Antiqua* follows *CE* 321. In my judgement this is not immediately antecedent to the *mejora*. It merely establishes the usufruct of the father over the *bona materna* and the third part to which he is entitled, as I have suggested earlier.

LV IV, 2. 14 (= *CE* 322). On the disposal of the inheritance when the mother is widowed (cf. previous chapter).

LV IV, 2. 15 refers to something more removed in this order of processing: the goods acquired by the husband with the new goods of the wife and *LV* IV, 2. 16 is a law of Recceswinth (based on *CE* 325) on shared properties.

---

that nothing is said in the case where the maternal grandfather and paternal grandmother are the surviving grandparents. However manuscript V1 deals with this case: *Si avum maternum et paternam aviam*. This minority reading, I believe, offers the key. There may have been a type of 'haplography' perpetuated in the successive versions which had to be restored: *Ita quoque erit si <avum maternum et paternam aviam si> paternam et maternam aviam qui moritur relinquere videatur*. Whether possible or not, according to the hypothesis which I propose (perhaps it was only an oversight of the legislator), the following sentences of the law seem to me to be conclusive in order to lay down the equality of conditions for the four grandparents with regard to inheritance: *Et hec quidem equitas portionis de illis rebus erit, que mortuus conquisisse cognoscitur. De illis vero rebus, que ab avis vel parentibus habuit, ad avos directa lineas revocabunt.*

[7] Remember, for example, the gift made by the married couple of *Emerita* (*VSPE* 4, 2. 61 ff.) Bishop Paul cured the woman and saved her life. Then they—husband and wife—gave one half of their possessions to the Church and they also made a gift *mortis causa* of another half, when both died. In relation to this, see quota of free disposal (cf. *LV* IV, 5. 1, below).

LV IV, 2.17 is a further law of Recceswinth introduced in relation to the text of *LV* IV, 2. 18—of Chindaswinth and so on earlier—relating to children whose father died. This was a superflous law, drawn up in very rhetorical terms and quite unnecessary in view of *LV* IV, 2. 18, so that in Erwig's revision it disappeared completely.

We arrive thus at *LV* IV, 2. 18—known as the *Patre defuncto* law—which, according to Otero, is fundamental to the *mejora*, and is part of the *mejora* together with the *Dum inlicita* itself (*LV* IV, 5. 1) and *LV* IV, 5. 4. I will return to these afterwards. *LV* IV, 2. 18 was incorporated into the chapter on inheritance probably by Recceswinth given that its formulation moves away from inheritance law to concentrate more on donations, in this case *mortis causa* in general. In the *corpus* of Chindaswinth, it possibly came after *LV* IV, 5. 1 and 4, 5. 2, in the title *De naturalibus bonis*. Chindaswinth himself makes reference to a "*superiorem legem*" which he himself had published, undoubtedly the *Dum inlicita*. However, Recceswinth must have thought it best to include the law in the title *De successionibus,* as another case in this line of classified and ordered inheritance which had been prepared for this section of the book (*Liber*).

Law *LV* IV, 2. 19 follows, the last link in this chain of inheritances: posthumous children. These had to be considered equally as heirs.

The *Titulus* II of this *liber quartus* of *LV* concludes with a global law of Recceswinth: every free man or woman, noble or inferior, who left no heir of any kind, had the power to do what he or she liked with their possessions. All these laws progressively shaped legislation to implement the male-female equality in the domain of inheritance. In my opinion, this was the situation, when Chindaswinth issued the *Dum inlicita*, which is undoubtedly the highpoint of this comparison. It also opened a path to freedom (remembering the Roman tradition of freedom to make a will) so that it was possible to choose and dispose freely of a part of the inheritance which had to be left to the lawful heirs.

The *Dum inlicita* (*LV* IV, 5. 1) and the other laws referring to the *mejora*.

The *Dum inlicita* is the first law in the title *De naturalibus bonis* referring to donations and their regulation on the death of the donors and recipients, by which it is very closely related to the title *De successionibus*.

The text of the *Dum inlicita* may be arranged as follows:

1) *Rubrica:*

Flavius Chindasvindus Rex. De non exheredandis filiis; et quod iudicium ferant parentes de facultatibus suis.

2) Explanation of the reasons for issuing this law: unjustifiable disinheritance of the lawful heirs in favour of outsiders, to the detriment of the heirs and of the public interest:

Dum inlicita queque perpetrari cognoscimus, legem ponere secuturis oportune conpellimur. Plerique enim, indiscrete viventes suasque facultates interdum vel causa luxurie vel cuiusdam male volumtatis in personas extraneas transferentes, ita inoffensos filios vel nepotes aut non gravi culpa forsitan obnoxios inanes relinquunt, ut utilitatibus publicis nihil possint omnino prodesse, quos oportuerat cum virtute parentum iniunctum sibi laborem inexcusabiliter expedire.

3) Explicit repeal of the law which allowed the father or the mother, grandfather or grandmother the freedom to leave their inheritance to outsiders; even the wife could leave her dowry to anyone she wanted:

Sed ne sub ac occasione aut utilitati publice quandoque depereat, quod perire non debet, aut naturalis pietas suspendatur a filiis vel nepotibus, quam circa eos exerceri conpetenter oportet: ideo, abrogata legis illius sententia, qua pater vel mater aut avus sive avia in extraneam personam facultatem suam conferre, si voluissent potestatem haberent, vel etiam de dote sua facere mulier quod elegisset in arbitrio suo consisteret,

4) Establishment of a new moderate measure which would not deprive those who made a will entirely of their freedom, but would not allow the unfair exclusion from inheritance of the rightful heirs, because of an unjust will. They could dispose of a tenth part of their possessions to favour (*meliorare*) their children or grandchildren:

*sta magis servetur a cunctis moderata censura, qua nec parentibus vel aviis adimatur iudicandi de rebus suis ex toto licentia, nec filios aut nepotes a successione avorum vel genitorum ex omnibus repellat indiscreta volumtas. **Igitur pater vel mater, avus vel avia, quibus quempiam filiorum vel nepotum meliorandi volumtas est,** hanc servent omnino censuram, **ut super decimam partem rerum suarum** melioratis filiis aut filiabus vel nepotibus atque neptis ex omnibus rebus suis amplius nihil inpendant neque facultatem suam ex omnibus in extraneam personam transducant, nisi fortasse provenerit, eos legitimos filios vel nepotes non habere suprestes.*

5) Besides, those with children or grandchildren could leave a fifth part to the Church, to free servants or anybody they wished:

*Sane si filios sive nepotes habentes **eclesiis vel libertiis aut quibus elegerint** de facultate sua largiendi volumtatem habuerint, **de quintam tantum partem** iudicandi potestas illis indubitata manebit.*

6) Disinheriting children or grandchildren for trivial reasons was forbidden, although they could be punished or corrected:

Exheredare autem filios aut nepotes licet pro levi culpa inlicitum iam dictis parentibus erit, flagellandi tamen et corripiendi eos, quamdiu sunt in familia constituti, tam avo quam avie, seu patri quam matri potestas manebit.

7) If the children or grandchildren committed a grave offence against their parents or grandparents, they could be punished by the judge by whipping and also be deprived of their rightful inheritance:

Nam si filius filiave, nepos, neptis tam presumtiosi extiterint, ut avum suum aut aviam, sive etiam patrem aut matrem tam gravibus iniuriis conentur afficere, hoc est, si aut alapa, pugno vel calce seu lapide, aut fuste vel flagello percutiant, sive per pedem vel per capillos ac per manum etiam vel quocumque inhonesto casu abstraere contumeliose presumant, aut publice quodcumque crimen avo aut avie seu genitoribus suis obiciant: tales, si quidem manifeste convicti, et verberandi sunt ante iudicem quinquagenis flagellis et ab hereditate supradictorum, si idem avus et avia, pater vel mater voluerint, repellendi.

8) However, if they reformed they could be forgiven and their inheritance rights restored to them:

Tamen si, resipiscentes a suo excessu, veniam a suprascriptis, quibus offenderant, imploraverint, eosque in gratiam receperint paterna pietate aut rerum suarum successores instituerint, neque proiberi ab eorum hereditate neque propter disciplinam, qua correpti sunt, infamiam poterint ullatenus sustinere.

I have pointed out already that I do not consider *CE* 321 a precedent for the *mejora*. However, it is clear that there had been a process drawing the different hereditary estates closer, which is perfectly clear in the evolution of Visigothic legislation in the area of inheritance. This does not imply that the distinction was entirely cancelled out since, as will be discussed later, there are laws of Chindaswinth himself regulating the properties of women.

A number of observations can be made on the *Dum inlicita.*

Chindaswinth refers to the fact that if children are disinherited, they will not be able to cooperate with the public interest. This reveals a significant concern: public and social consequences could arise if hereditary estates left the family circle.

The statement that there are many people (*plerique*), who arbitrarily disinherit their children and grandchildren, suggests the perpetuation of Roman freedom in making wills—at least among people of Hispano-Roman origin and, perhaps, also those of Gothic origin—but this must be taken alongside the clear predominance of lawful and perfectly regulated succession. The existence of *testamentum* or *donatio* was maintained but one must conclude that even with the establishment of such provisions, the normal situation for everybody was to have their children as heirs. And on the other hand this was wholly logical. In any case, it seems that the *Dum inlicita* regulated inheritance both where a *testamentum* existed and where it did not.

In relation to the quotas established by the *Dum inlicita*, contrary to Otero (1963:57), I believe this law empowered the mother and grandmother as much as the father and grandfather, to favour (*meliorare*) and in the same proportions, with just one exception, the dowry (*donatio ante nuptias*), which had a specific regulation in the next law *LV* IV, 5. 2, *Quia mulieres.*

If we examine the text of the law we can see that there is a set of alternative conjunctions that serve to mention the different, but not neccessarily exclusive, possibilities. Men and women can favour (*meliorare*) without distinction.

Another non-excluding equivalence is expressed when the law makes reference to the consequences caused by the earlier law, now abrogated:

*Sed ne sub occasione **aut** utilitati publice quandoque depereat, quod perire non debeat, **aut** naturalis pietas suspendatur a filiis <u>vel</u> nepotibus quam circa eos exerceri competenter oportet.*

The provision is strictly formulated with an identical conjunction which mentions two possibilities for each group of persons, indicating the choice:

*Igitur pater **vel** mater, avus **vel** avia quibus quempiam filiorum **vel** nepotum meliorandi voluntas est.*

In this case, the order of words and the alternative seem to choose between each one giving rise to a parallel formally reflected:

pater vel mater, avus vel avia...filiorum vel nepotum

This seems to indicate that the father or the mother could favour (*meliorare*) the children, and grandparents—when there were no surviving children—could favour grandchildren, using also the right of representation which is, moreover, also regulated in another law, *LV* IV, 2. 18 *Patre defuncto.*

Daughters and granddaughters appear to be excluded, but this is not really so. When this situation occurs of wishing to favour, the following provision must be taken into account (*hanc servent omnino censuram*), that is, the strict formulation of the law:

*ut super decimam partem rerum suarum melioratis **filiis aut filiabus vel nepotibus atque** neptis ex omnibus rebus suis amplius nihil impendant.*

Alternative conjunctions are mentioned here which, although not perfectly established in accordance with classical rules, do make the text precise. *Aut* is equivalent to *atque*. Both conjunctions are used to add further possibilities, not to exclude them. *Vel* seems to indicate the different position of the children (sons or daugthers indiscriminately) on the one hand (when parents favoured them) and of the grandchildren (grandsons or granddaughters indiscriminately) on the other (when there are no surviving children and the grandchildren inherit).

In a subsequent paragraph, the law discusses again only *filios sive nepotes*, and *filios **aut** nepotes* with the same type of non-excluding disjunctions and with comparable terms used in the same way. It must be understood here that, as in the beginning, when the law talks of *filios* or *nepotes*, it does so in a generic sense, i.e. including daughters and granddaughters.

When dealing with the impossibility of disinheriting for minor misconduct, but with the possibility of punishment, the law uses a combination of elements, with an inversion:

*Exheredare autem **filios aut nepotes** licet pro levi culpa inlicitum iam dictis parentibus erit, flagellandi tamen et corripiendi eos, quamdiu sunt in familia constituti, **tam avo quam avie, seu patri quam matri** potestas manebit.*

*filius **aut** nepotes...**tam** avo **quam** avie, **seu** patri **quam** matri.* In spite of this, I would not dare to state that this careful order of words and disjunctive distribution (clearly made with rhetorical intention) rules out the possibility of a direct *mejora* for grandchildren.

The same situation arises in law *LV* IV, 5. 2, *Quia mulieres*, about dowry. The disjunctives are ambiguous:

*spretis filiis **vel** nepotibus...habens filios **aut** nepotis, **seu** causa mercedis ecclesiis **vel***

vel libertis conferre, *sive* cuicumque voluerit.... Nam tres partes legitimis filiis *aut* nepotibus, *seu* sit unus, *sive* forsitam plures.[8]

Here it seems that a woman could favour (*meliorare*) her children or grandchildren, or one of them, without distinction, such as we have seen above. Actually, I neither see an exclusion in the expressions "*seu causa mercedis ecclesiis* **vel** libertis conferre, **sive** cuicumque voluerit*", nor in the expressions "*filiis* **vel** nepotibus... filios* **aut** nepotes, etc."

Aut, vel or *sive* were not always exclusive in Latin and even less so in late Latin and the language of this period. The value of reckoning different possibilities also appears in other points of the *Dum inlicita*: when this law mentions several offences by children against their parents (see above).

Against such a possibility law *LV* IV, 2. 18, *Patre defuncto,* clearly states that only the grandchildren can be favoured, if there are no other surviving children. But we must take into account that this law talks of a *luctuosa hereditas* (see below). It also happens in *LV* IV, 5. 4, another *luctuosa hereditas* (see below).

I wish to emphasize that the use of conjunctions is different in Erwig's wording. Now we can see copulatives in these points: *filiorum suorum atque nepotum aliquid* and later *nec licebit filiis ipsis atque nepotibus* (see below).

Because of the word order, it seems that there is no direct *mejora* for the grandchildren in the *Dum inlicita*. However, here it is ambiguous as in *LV* IV, 5. 2, *Quia mulieres*. Perhaps Erwig allowed the direct *mejora* {Lacoste 1913:83 ff.; Otero does not accept it (1961)}, and perhaps even Chindaswinth allowed it. If the legislator (either Chindaswinth or Erwig) had no intention of favouring (*meliorare*) grandchildren directly, the text at least lays down a basis on which it might be done. On the other hand, we must remember that *Quia mulieres* was a law issued by Chindaswinth, hence a coherence among his different laws might be expected. We must also remember that *Patre defuncto* and *LV* IV, 5. 4 are laws of Chindaswinth. These exclude the direct *mejora* of grandchildren, but, as already indicated, both refer to *luctuosae hereditates* and it is, in my opinion, a different question.

Other expressions fundamental to the understanding of the text are: *super decimam partem rerum suarum...*and *ex omnibus rebus suis*, mentioning the source of the sum for the *mejora*.

In my opinion, the family estate is made up of a common whole formed by the *bona materna* and the *bona paterna* and its separation is not precisely determined in the text. On the other hand, both the quotas for the *mejora* and the fifth part of free disposal must start from the possessions that each one has *(paterna paternis, materna maternis)* originating from one's own family estate. I think that these are the principles of lineage (Pérez Prendes 1989:1135-36) and must have been fundamental. As a consequence, parents or grandparents could distribute their properties in three parts:

1) Quota of free disposal: **F D** 1/5. This was probably taken out of the total, leaving 4/5. These were dealt with a follows:

---

[8]   See the complete text below.

2) The *mejora*: **M** 1/3 of the remaining 4/5.
3) The right and lawful inheritance: **L I**, the remainder of the inheritance.

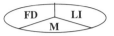

In the case of the mother this distribution might be made out of the *bona materna*, excluding the dowry (*extra dotem*) which had its own rules.

The *Dum inlicita* deals with the unfair situation arising when parents or grandparents (*pater vel mater aut avus sive avia*) under the law being replaced, had the power to leave their goods to outsiders, and adds:

> *vel etiam de dote sua facere mulier quod elegisset in arbitrio suo consisteret.*

The fact that the dowry is not mentioned, is not an incongruity or an oversight of the law. Strictly speaking, it describes the general case which occurred on repeal of the law; furthermore, the expression *vel etiam* gives an indication of how far it had gone. The law does not aim to legislate for the dowry, but rather seeks to state the situation which justified its issue. The particular problem of dowry is posed in the next law inspired by the same principle as the *Dum inlicita* and incorporated immediately afterwards as a complementary law.

This law on the dowry, *Quia mulieres, LV* IV, 5. 2 says that:

1) *Rubrica*:

> *Flavius Chindasvindus rex. De quota parte liceat mulieribus iudicare de dotibus suis.*

2) Until shortly before, women could dispose freely of their dowry, excluding children and grandchildren:

> *Quia mulieres, quibus dudum concessum fuerat de suis dotibus iudicare quod voluissent, quedam repperiuntur, spretis filiis vel nepotibus, easdem dotes illis conferre, cum quibus constiterit nequiter eas vixisse, adeo necesse est illos exinde percipere commodum, pro quibus creandis fuerat adsumtum coniugium.*

3) For this reason it now establishes that the woman can only freely dispose of 1/4 of the total dowry; the rest 3/4 is to be kept for children or grandchildren, or for one or many of these:

> *Denique constituentes decernimus, ut **de dote sua mulier, habens filios aut nepotes**, seu causa mercedis **ecclesiis vel libertis conferre, sive cuicumque voluerit, non amplius quam de quarta parte** potestatem habebit. Nam **tres partes legitimis filiis aut nepotibus, seu sit unus, sive forsitam plures**, absque dubio relictura est.*

I think that this is the right interpretation. Thus here we have a clear precedent for the possibility of dividing up the *mejora* established by Erwig in his modification of the *Dum inlicita*—if it had not been already thought by Chindaswinth—along the lines of *LV* IV, 5. 2. The interpretations, with which I am familiar, of this law are either silent about this phrase or uphold the contrary opinion without giving a reason (cf. Otero 1963:61 ff. with a diametrically opposed interpretation).

4) Only in the case where the woman had neither son, nor daughter, grandson nor granddaughter could she dispose freely of her entire dowry.

De tota interim dote tunc facere quod voluerit erit mulieri potestas, quando nullum legitimum filium filiamve, nepotem vel neptem suprestem reliquerit.

This was a considerable freedom compared to other rules in the laws. One would expect that it should be established that the 3/4 would go to the husband's family. But the dowry (*donatio ante nuptias*) had always obeyed a very special set of rules, see, for instance, the comments on *LV* III, 1. 5.

5) If the woman married for a second or third time, 3/4 of the dowry could not be given to the offspring of these new marriages. On the death of the woman, the 3/4 would necessarily have to go to the children of the first husband.

Verumtamen femine, quas contigerit duobus viris aut amplius nubere atque ex eis filios procreare, non eis licitum erit, dotem ab alio marito acceptam filiis aut nepotibus ex alio viro genitis dare; sed unusquisque filius filiave, nepos aut neptis ex ipsa linea procreati dotem, quam avus aut pater eorum concesserat, post mulieris obitum per omnia secuturi sunt.

Other facts must be taken into account. In no case is it possible to assume the amount of the estate, thus what the law does is to establish an identical *ratio* of these goods for each one of the possible members of the family who was going to inherit.

Otero (1963:44 ff.) assumes that only the father and grandfather could opt to favour (*meliorare*) a particular heir and infers that the third of the *bona materna, reservato usufructo*, when the child married, according to *CE* 321 and *LV* IV, 2.13, would be that which was used to favour (*meliorare*) in accordance with their theory that, as noted earlier, the *mejora* was already described exactly in *CE* 321.

I think this is not the case. Firstly it is not clear why a third of the *bona materna* was used to favour an heir in *CE* 321, and not half of that which is also mentioned when the children attained age twenty. However, I do agree with them concerning the computations of 1/3, 1/5, 1/10, etc. which appear in the Visigothic laws. They are taken from earlier Roman laws which are of great technical assistance and provide proportions which are always reasonable, adequate and suitable for each occasion. Actually, for reasons I will give later, I believe that the proportion of 1/3 used in *CE* 321 served technically as the 1/3 of Erwig but not as the *mejora* equivalent to the 1/10 of Chindaswinth.

Above all, regarding this third of the usufruct reserved to the father in *CE* 321, *LV* IV, 2. 13, I do not think that it can be assumed, as I argued earlier, that it was used to favour an heir, as Otero claims. In my opinion this would go against the general rules of succession which prevented one from disposing of something which was not in one's legal possession—that is, the *bona materna* in usufruct—which belonged to the children when their father died and the usufruct ended.

If we consider that the mother and grandmother could "*meliorare ex omnibus rebus suis*" (but *extra dotem*, which had its own set of rules) we can immediately show that 1/5 of free disposal in the *Dum inlicita* does indeed relate to the 1/5 of free disposal in *LV* V, 2. 4 which regulates, as previously seen, the goods *extra dotem*, since the law says: *De rebus extra dotem uxori a marito conlatis.*

As will be mentioned once more, it was said in this law that the woman would keep her possessions until death without being able to dispose of them except for one fifth:

> *Mulier usque ad diem obitum sui secura possideat et de quinta tantumdem parte earum rerum faciendi quod voluerit potestatem obtineat.*

As a result of that, the woman could dispose freely of 1/5 of those goods, the remaining 4/5 had to be shared among the lawful heirs and the *mejora* (1/10 of 4/5). In comparison with this, one must consider the coincidence between the 1/10 proportion of the *mejora* and the 1/5 of free disposal established by the law *Patre defuncto* (*LV* IV. 2. 18) also of Chindaswinth, which, as already stated, went into the legal *corpus* of this king immediately after *LV* IV, 5. 1 and IV, 5. 2. This law— the third of Chindaswinth relating to *mejora*—is undoubtedly based on *CE* 327 (see App. 10).

The law *Patre defuncto* (*LV* IV, 2. 18) establishes:

1) *Rubrica*:

> *Flavius Chindasvindus rex. Qualiter hereditatem parvuli parentes adsequi possunt.*

2) If the father dies (*patre defuncto*) and the child lives for ten days, is baptized and later dies, the mother has a right to the inheritance which would have gone to the child:[9]

> *Patre defuncto, si filius filiave decem diebus vivens et baptizatus ab hac vita discesserit, quidquid ei de facultate patris conpetere poterat, mater sibi debeat vindicare.*

3) The same situation with respect to the father, if the mother dies (*matre defuncta*):

> *Idemque matre defuncta non aliter defuncti filii portionem pater obtineat,<non>nisi natum filium filiamvel decem diebus vixisse et fuisse baptizatus edoceat.*

In my opinion, there is an incongruity in the text. It must be considered *<non>nisi* and not *nisi*. The reading of this phrase and the following endorses the change in the text.

4) If the father (when the mother died, *matre defuncta*) or the mother (when the father died, *patre defuncto*), who inherit from the child (predeceased and childless) do not have any other children, but have grandchildren of their children, these grandchildren will receive the *luctuosa hereditas*:

---

[9] I think that the mother has the life interest until this *luctuosa hereditas* is passed on to the other children, with the same set of rules as for the remaining goods: 1/10 for the *mejora* and 1/5 for free disposal, as written below. Again my interpretation of the text differs on some points from other authors (Otero 1963:68-9; Zeumer [1944]:186-7).

ita ut pater vel mater, quibus ista successio conpetit, si filios non relinquerint, integram et intemeratam eandem luctuosam hereditatem dividendam omnibus nepotibus derelinquat.

5) The father or the mother can reserve 1/10 for the *mejora* to a grandchild and 1/5 for free disposal as in the *Dum inlicita*:

Nec meliorandi quemcumque nepotum amplius quam decimam partem huius rei habeant potestatem. Nam si ecclesiis vel libertis seu cuilibet largiri de eadem facultatem voluerint, de quinta tantum partem secundum superiorem legem potestatem habebunt.

6) If there are no children, grandchildren or great grandchildren then the *luctuosa hereditas* (of the predeceased childless child) will go to other relations according to the nearest degrees of kinship:

Sin autem nec filii nec nepotes nec pronepotes suprestes extiterint, alii parentes, qui gradu proximiores fuerint, predictam facultatem procul dubio consequantur;

Here the wording of the law is confused and ambiguous (nor much better is Erwig's wording, although clearer) and it has sponsored too many interpretations. However, I think that a clarification of the aforementioned wording must be understood in the following lines:

...ea conditione servata, ut nepotes ex filio vel filia, qui patre vel matre supreste mortui fuerint, integram de rebus avi vel avie, quam fuerant pater eorum aut mater, si vixissent, habituri, percipiant portionem.

These seem to refer to the son or daughter of the predeceased child, but in reality it is again the grandchildren of the other children who have also died. This not very clever clarification—I would argue—is introduced into the law because of the innovative nature of the same: the hereditary prospects of the grandchildren, not only that of the inheritance that their parents would be slated to receive from their grandparents (of the children) if they lived and which they were directly entitled to as provided for in *LV* IV, 5. 1, but the hereditary prospect of a *luctuosa hereditas* of a predeceased uncle/aunt with no children, including moreover the *mejora* in the same form as in *LV* IV, 5. 1.

Inmediately after this point other provisions somewhat removed from the initial theme are outlined in the law. These provisions deserved their own chapter, forming another law, but the writers were not helpful. Moreover the clumsiness of the wording is surprising, including even errors of concordance (Zeumer [1949]:317) all the more so if the previous are analysed alongside the careful, detailed and precise, laws of Chindaswinth, although this does not mean that even the latter text is not difficult and challenging. Perhaps, as is traditionally held, Chindaswinth left his legal *corpus* prepared without finishing it off and his son Recceswinth preferred to leave it without modifications, or perhaps he modified it and got it wrong? We shall never know.

The other provisions are:

7) If the son, with wife and children, dies without having received completely (*implesset*)[10] from his father the portion of the inheritance due to him, and he himself, living with his father dies and his children die, the widow of such a son, will receive exclusively that which the father had previously withheld from his son, without being able to claim more from the father- and the siblings-in-law. However if the son had not received anything (*nihil ab eo portionis acceperit*), then the widow will only receive that which she was entitled to as a wedding gift:

> *Quod si filius, habens uxorem et filios, patre viventi recesserit, antequam ei pater suus omnem portionem, que ei contingebat, inplesset, et ipse cum patre vivens filios, quos reliquerat, vivente avo mortui fuerint, tunc illa relicta hoc tantummodo recipiat, quod in maritum pater antea sequestravit, nec plus illa vidua a socru vel cognatis requirat. Si vero filius cum patre in conmune vivens nihil ab eo portionis acceperit, tunc illa vidua tantummodo hoc accipiat, quod ei tempore nuptiarum maritus eius donationis titulo noscitur contulisse.*

8) Nevertheless (*vero*), if the deceased son, in spite of having allowed his father —showing him obedience—to own (*patrem possidere permiserit*) that part of the *bona materna* which was due to him, had left in writing that he would donate his part to his wife or any other person, this arrangement would be naturally upheld (if he was childless). The children would have inherited in accordance with the order established in the previous law, i.e. *LV* IV, 5. 1:

> *Si vero filius patris servans obedientiam res, que ei de materna successione conpetebant, patrem possidere permiserit, et postmodum eandem facultatem filio debitam, quam pater possidebat, idem filius uxori sue vel cuicumque concesserit, firma talis donatio in nomine uxoris vel cuiuscumque conscripta manebit; si tamen filii de eodem coniugio non fuerint. Nam si filii suprestes extiterint, ordo superioris legis incunctanter servandus est.*

With the interpretation I have just proposed, despite the difficulties in the wording of the text already mentioned, all doubts are clarified. The complete reading of the text turns out to be, in its entirety, clear and perfectly coherent with the fundamental law of the *mejora*, the *Dum inlicita*.[11]

Erwig's reforms of the *Dum inlicita*

Erwig carried out some modifications and clarifications to the *Dum inlicita* (Lacoste, 1913:76 ff.; Otero, 1963:51 ff.; Zeumer, [1949]:337 ff.):

---

[10] I understand here that the deceased son had already received a part of his inheritance, possibly the 2/3 of the *bona materna*, while the father had a life interest in the other 1/3 (according to *LV* IV, 2. 13, *Antiqua*, *CE* 321).

[11] A continuation of this law and closely related to it is *LV* IV, 5. 4 also of Chindaswinth. This law presents the case of a man married several times who has children from each of the unions. If one of the children dies *intestatum* and leaves neither children nor grandchildren, his brothers and sisters should claim the possessions of the predeceased child. In this law there are two *mejora*, now the third part of the inheritance. This law offers other problems that I will analyse elsewhere.

1) Increase of the *mejora* from 1/10 to 1/3.

2) He added that the *mejora* could be shared among children and grandchildren, and it could be divided, although he does not specify how:

> *Hoc tamen, rationis intuitu prelucente, observandum adicimus, ut pater vel mater, avus vel avia de supradicta tertia parte rerum suarum, si in nomine filiorum suorum atque nepotum aliquid specialiter scriptis conferre decreverint, iuxta testationis eorum ordinem cuncta erunt observanda perenniter; qualiter testatio talium de eadem tertia portione, iuxta quod eam in singulis voluerit prelargire, plenam et inconvulsibilem obtineat firmitatem.*

3) Those favoured by the *mejora* cannot act against the *mejora* established by their parents or grandparents, except when there is no condition concerning the future in the declaration of that *mejora*. This would suggest that this *mejora* could be given with certain conditions, but they are not outlined.

> *Nec licebit filiis ipsis atque nepotibus, qui de hac tertia portione aliquid meruerint a parentibus suis vel aviis percipere, quodcumque aliud iudicare, excepto si a parentibus vel aviis nulla ad futurum videatur pro conlatis rebus testationis condicio intercessisse.*

4) As with Chindaswinth 1/5 can be disposed of freely, but, in my opinion, here the *mejora* was first extracted. Then 1/3 for the *mejora*, and 2/3 to be divided between the lawful heirs and the quota of free disposal, which would now be 1/5 of 2/3 and not 1/10 of 4/5 (as with Chindaswinth):

> *Sane si filios sive nepotes habentes **ecclesiis vel libertis aut quibus elegerint** de facultate sua largiendi voluntatem habuerint, **extra illam tertiam portionem**, que superius dicta est, **quinta iterum pars separabitur**.*

If this hypothesis is correct, the increase in the *mejora*—quite considerable from Chindaswinth to Erwig—would now be truly extraordinary.

It explains that both the third part of the *mejora*, and the fifth of the free disposal must be considered separately from "*de propriis tantundem rebus*". This expression confirms the explanation proposed earlier for "*ex omnibus rebus suis*" in the version of Chindaswinth, expressed now in a more precise form:

> *Sed sive tertia rerum pars, que meliorandis filiis inpendi precipitur, sive quinta, que pro conlatione ecclesiarum vel libertorum seu quorumlibet inpensione separari iubetur, **de propriis tantumdem rebus separabitur**.*

7) It specifies that in the calculation of the 1/3 of the *mejora* or the 1/5 of the free disposal, goods coming from royal donations, over which the owner has complete freedom, must be excluded from the sum total of goods:

> *Nam quod quisquis ille per auctoritatem percipere meruit principum, nullo modo in adnumeratione huius tertie vel quinte partis quolibet titulo admiscetur, sed iuxta legem aliam, qui hoc a rege perceperint, habebunt licitum, quale voluerint de conlatis sibi rebus a principe ferre iudicium.*

As can be seen in the text, this refers to another law (*iuxta legem aliam*). This is undoubtedly *LV* V, 2. 2. This law is based on *CE* 305 and was issued by Chindaswinth in different terms but with practically the same content. Erwig extended the law by saying that, if the person who had received the royal donation died intestate, then the inheritance was transferred to the heirs according to the order established by the laws of succession.

Here, as argued by Otero (1963:54), Erwig's modification was a clarification of the law of Chindaswinth who did not specify it in his law, perhaps because he saw it as being implied since he himself issued this law on royal donations (*Donationes regie LV* V, 2. 2.).

The picture presented by these laws can be completed, for the period of Chindaswinth, with the laws relating to "*de bonis naturalibus*" also issued by him: *LV* IV, 5. 3 and IV, 5. 4, and the *Antiqua* IV, 5. 5.[12] I will discuss *LV* IV, 5. 4 subsequently.

Conclusion

Dum inlicita or law of the *mejora* (*LV* IV, 5. 1) is the main and most famous of a set of laws concerning inheritance included in the *Liber Iudiciorum* (*Lex Visigothorum*) which present a compact and perfectly established set of provisions regulating most aspects of family law. The chronology and order of these laws are consistent concerning the different degrees of blood relations. The legislation as a whole reflects the Visigothic monarchy's mentality regarding the construction of a legal system: its legislation was based mainly on the Roman legal tradition and any valid and useful aspects found in Roman laws were adopted by the new regime. All laws that suited the new situation were renewed and other new laws were issued to better fit the new circumstances of Visigothic society in the seventh century.

In this new society, not all differences were removed, but the political and ecclesiastical authorities of both groups, Goths and Hispano-Romans, considered law to be among the most important instruments necessary for coexistence.

The legislation regarding inheritance made it compulsory for a third of a person's estate to be passed on to his lawful heirs in stipulated proportions, allowing another third to be apportioned to any or several of the lawful heirs. However, as the remaining portion was disposable at will, i.e., could be left to any person or institution, even the Church, (or perhaps we should say, especially the Church), this legislation not only affected families but also the chosen beneficiary. Evidently, this legislation was of utmost importance not only on a personal and family level but also in public and social matters. That, however, is another story.

---

[12] This *Antiqua* is formulated concerning *leudes* and *LV* IV, 5. 3 concerning the donations that the parents gave to the children on the occasion of a wedding and which were considered excessive by the law.

References

Textual sources:

[Abbr.: *CE = Codex Euricianus; CI = Codex Iustiniani; Codex Revisus* (of Liuvigild);
CT = Concilium Toletanum; CTh = Codex Theodosianus; LRV = Lex Romana Visigothorum
(of Alaric II); *LV = Lex Visigothorum; V.S.P.E = Vitas Sanctorum Patrum Emeretensium*].

Braulio of Saragossa
          Epistulae: see Riesco Terrero (ed.) 1975.
Codex Euricianus: see D'Ors (ed.) 1960.
Codex Theodosianus: see Mommsen, Krueger & Meyer (eds.) 1904-1905 [1990].
Isidore of Seville
          Historia Gothorum: see Rodríguez Alonso (ed. & trans.) 1975.
Lex Romana Visigothorum: see Hänel (ed.) 1848 [1962].
Lex Visigothorum: see Zeumer (ed.) 1902.
Sidonius Apollinaris
          Poems and letters: see Anderson (ed. & trans.) 1965.
Vitas Sanctorum Patrum Emeretensium: see Maya Sánchez (ed.) 1992.

Bibliography:

Anderson, W. B. (ed. & trans.)
    1965   *Sidonius. Poems and Letters.* London: Loeb.
Caes, L.
    1950   La destinée de la Nov. Major. 6 d'après la formule de publication de la
                  Nov. Sev. 1. *RIDA* 4 (= Mélanges F. de Vischer III), pp. 223-227.
Calabrús Lara, J.
    1991   *Las relaciones paternofiliales en la legislación visigoda.* [First edition
                  1973]. Granada: Publicaciones de la Universidad de Granada.
Conrat, M.
    1903   *Breviarium Alaricianum. Römisches Recht im frankischen Reich in
                  systematischer Darstellung.* Leipzig: Aalen.
Díaz y Díaz, M. C.
    1976   La *Lex Visigothorum* y sus manuscritos. Un ensayo de reinterpretación.
                  Anuario de Historia del Derecho Español 46: 163-224.
D'Ors, A. (ed.)
    1960   *El Código de Eurico. Edición, palingenesia, índices* (=Estudios visigodos 2).
                  Roma-Madrid: Consejo Superior de Investigaciones Científicas (C.S.I.C.).
                  Delegación Roma. Cuadernos del Instituto Jurídico Español, n. 12.
García-Gallo, A.
    1936-41   Nacionalidad y territorialidad del derecho en la época visigoda, *Anuario
                  de Historia del Derecho Español* 13: 168-264.
    1974   Consideración crítica de los estudios sobre la legislación y la costumbre
                  visigodas. *Anuario de Historia del Derecho Español* 44: 343-464.
    1977   Del testamento romano al medieval. Las líneas de su evolución en
                  España. *Anuario de Historia del Derecho Español* 47: 425-497.
    1982   *Estudios de Historia del Derecho privado.* Sevilla: Publicaciones de la
                  Universidad de Sevilla.
García Garrido, M. J.
    1959   El régimen jurídico del patrimonio uxorio en el derecho vulgar romano-
                  visigodo. *Anuario de Historia del Derecho Español* 29: 389-446.

García López, Y.
1997   *Estudios críticos y literarios de la Lex Visigothorum.* (Memorias del Departamento Historia Antigua). Alcalá de Henares: Publicaciones de la Universidad de Alcalá de Henares.

García Moreno, L. A.
1989   *Historia de España visigoda.* Madrid: Editorial Cátedra.

Hänel, G. (ed.)
1848   *Leges Romanae Visigothorum.* Leipzig: Aalen.

Iglesia Ferreros, A.
1977-8   La creación del derecho en el reino visigodo. *Revista de Historia del Derecho* (Homenaje al prof. M. Torres López.) 2: 117-167.

Iglesias, J.
1965   *Derecho romano. Instituciones de derecho privado.* Barcelona: Ediciones Ariel.

Kaser, M.
1971-1975 *Das römisches Privatrecht,* I-II. München: C. H. Beck.

King, P. D.
1972   *Law and society in the Visigothic Kingdom.* Cambridge: Cambridge University Press. [Spanish translation 1981, Madrid: Alianza Editorial].
1980   King Chindasvind and the First Territorial Law-code of the Visigothic Kingdom. In *Visigothic Spain: New Approaches.* E. James (ed.), pp. 131-157. Oxford: Clarendon Press.

Lambertini, R.
1991   *La codificazione di Alarico II.* Torino: Giapichelli.

Levy, E.
1951   *West Roman Vulgar Law. The Law of Property.* Philadelphia: American Philosophical Society.

Maya Sánchez, A. (ed.)
1992   *Vitas Sanctorum Patrum Emeritensium.* Corpus Christianorum (CC) CXVI. Turnhout: Brepols.

Morales Arrizabalaga, J.
1995   *Ley, jurisprudencia y derecho en Hispania romana y visigoda.* Saragossa: Prensas Universitarias de Zaragoza, col. Textos docentes, Zaragoza.

Mommsen, T., P. Krueger & P. Meyer (eds.)
1904-05   *Codex Theodosianus,* I-II. Hildesheim: Weidmann. [Repr. 1990].

Otero, A.
1959   *Liber Iudiciorum* 3, 1, 5 (El tema de la dote y *donatio propter nuptias*). *Anuario de Historia del Derecho Español* 29: 545-555.
1961   La mejora del nieto. *Anuario de Historia del Derecho Español* 31: 389-400.
1963   La mejora. *Anuario de Historia del Derecho Español* 33: 5-131.
1971   Liber Iudiciorum 4, 5, 5. *Anuario de Historia del Derecho Español* 46: 129-140.

Pérez-Prendes, J. M.
1989   *Curso de Historia del Derecho español.* Madrid: Publicaciones Facultad de Derecho, Universidad Complutense.
1991   Las bases sociales del poder político (Estructura y funcionamiento de las instituciones político-administrativas). *Historia de España. Ramón Menéndez Pidal,* vol. III 1: *España visigoda. La monarquía. La cultura. Las artes.* Madrid: Espasa-Calpe.
1993   *Breviario de Derecho germánico.* Madrid. Publicaciones Facultad de Derecho, Universidad Complutense.

Reydellet, M.
1981   *La royauté dans la littérature latine de Sidoine Apollinaire à Isidore de Séville*. Rome: École française de Rome.
Riesco Terrero, L. (ed.)
1975   *Epistolario de San Braulio. Introducción, edición, crítica y traducción*. Sevilla: Publicaciones de la Universidad de Sevilla.
Ripoll, G., & G. Velázquez
1995   *La Hispania visigoda. Del rey Ataúlfo a Don Rodrigo*. (Historia de España, vol. 6). Madrid: Historia 16.
Rodríguez Alonso, C. (ed. & trans.)
1975   *Las Historias de los godos, vándalos y suevos de Isidoro de Sevilla*. (Estudio, edición crítica y traducción). León: Centro de Estudios e Investigación San Isidoro.
Watson, A.
1968   *The law of property in the later Roman Republic*. Oxford: Clarendon Press.
Zeumer, K.
1898-9   *Historia de la legislación visigoda*. [Spanish Transl. C. Clavería]. Barcelona: Universidad de Barcelona, Facultad de Derecho - 1944.
1902   *Leges Visigothorum. Monumenta Germaniae Historica. Leges nationum Germanicarum*, 1. Hannover: Hahn.

APPENDICES

1. Laws by Visigothic kings and Councils (Diagram based on Pérez-Prendes 1991:34-6).

Visigoth kings	Laws	Councils of Toledo
Theoderic I (418-451)	law-code?	
Theoderic II (453-466)	any laws?	
EURIC (466-484)	*Codex* (**480**?)	(*CE*)
ALARIC II (484-507)	Breviary or *Lex Romana Visigothorum*	(**506**) (*LRV*)
Teudis	(510-520//**531-548**)Law of costs (546), incorporated into *LRV*	
LIUVIGILD	(567/8-**572-586**)*Codex Revisus*	(**578**?, **580**?) (*CR*)
Reccared (586-601)	(*Antiquae*) laws: *LV* III. 5. 2; VI. 3. 7?; XII. 1. 2; XII. 2. 12	III *CT* (589)
Sisebut (612-621)	(*Antiquae*) laws: *LV* XII. 2. 13; XII. 2. 14	
Sisenand (631-636)		IV *CT* (633)
Chintila (636-638)		V *CT* (636)
		VI *CT* (638)
CHINDASWINTH (642-653)	a hundred laws (approx.):(new + amended) Issue of the law-code? (**643/4**?) *Leges Visigothorum* (*LV*) or *Liber Iudiciorum* (*LI*)	VII *CT* (646)
RECCESWINTH (649/653) (653-672)	ninety laws (approx.) Issue or revision of the law-code? (654) *LV*	VIII *CT*(653) X *CT* (656)
Wamba (672-680)	*LV* IV. 2. 13; IV. 5. 6; IV. 5. 7; VI. 5. 21; IX. 2. 8	
ERWIG (680-687)	more than one hundred laws (new + amended) Revision and new issue of *LV* (681)	XII *CT* (681) XIII *CT* (683) XIV *CT* (684)
Egica 44(687-702)	*LV* II. 1. 7; II. 1. 10; II. 4. 8; II. 5. 3; II. 5. 18; II. 5. 19; III. 5. 6; III. 5. 7; V, 7. 19; V. 7. 20?; VI. 1. 3?; VI. 5. 13; IX. 1. 21; X. 2. 5; XII. 2. 18	XV *CT* (688) XVI *CT* (693) XVII *CT* (694)
Witiza (698?/700) (702-709?)	*LV* V. 7. 20?; VI. 1. 13?	

2. Origin and evolution of the legislative system in Visigothic *Hispania.*

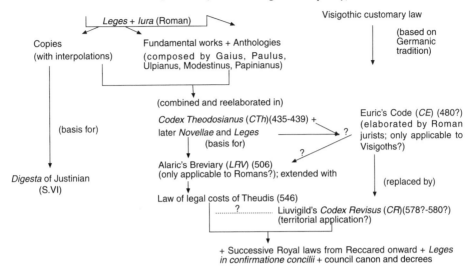

Leges + Iura (Roman)

Visigothic customary law

(based on Germanic tradition)

Copies
(with interpolations)

Fundamental works + Anthologies
(composed by Gaius, Paulus, Ulpianus, Modestinus, Papinianus)

(basis for)

(combined and reelaborated in)

Codex Theodosianus (*CTh*)(435-439) +
later *Novellae* and *Leges*
(basis for)

Euric's Code (*CE*) (480?)
(elaborated by Roman jurists; only applicable to Visigoths?)

Digesta of Justinian
(S.VI)

Alaric's Breviary (*LRV*) (506)
(only applicable to Romans?); extended with

Law of legal costs of Theudis (546)

(replaced by)

..........?.......... Liuvigild's *Codex Revisus* (*CR*)(578?-580?)
(territorial application?)

+ Successive Royal laws from Reccared onward + *Leges in confirmatione concilii* + council canon and decrees

Leges Visigothorum (*LV*) or *Liber Iudiciorum* (first issued during Chindaswinth's reign: 643/4)
(Issued or reelaborated? by Recceswinth in 654; again issued by Erwig in 681)
(territorial application)

Visigothic formulas (application of legislation) + common versions
Romance versions: Fuero Juzgo

3. *Codex Euricianus:* CE 321 (= *LV* IV, 2. 13):

[Beginning of *LV* IV. 2. 13 (*Antiqua*). *Ut post mortem matris filii in patris potestate consistant; et quid de rebus filiorum agere conveniat patrem: Matre mortua filii in patris potestate consistant. Quod*] *si marito superstite uxor forsitan moriatur, filii qui sunt eodem coniugio procreati in patris potestate consistant, et res eorum, si novercam non superduxerit, ea conditione possideat ut nihil exinde aut vendere aut evertere aut quocumque pacto alienare praesumat, sed omnia filiis suis integra et intemerata conservet. 2. Fructos tamen omnes pro suo iure percipiat <et> una cum filiis communibus consumat expensis. 3. Cum vero filius duxerit uxorem aut filia maritum acceperit, statim a patre de rebus maternis suam recipiat portionem, ita ut usufructuaria patri tertia derelinquatur. 4. Pater autem tam filio quam filiae, cum XX annos aetatis impleverit, mediam ex eadem quam unumquemque contigit de rebus maternis restituat portionem, etiam si nullis fuerint nuptiis copulati; medietatem vero dum advixerit pater sibi vindicet filiis post obitum relinquendam. 5. Qui autem novercam superduxerit, omnes facultates maternas filiis mox reformet, ne, dum filii cum rebus ad domum transeunt alienam, novercae suae vexentur iniuriis. 6. Eadem quoque de nepotibus forma servetur.*

4. *Codex Euricianus:* CE 322 (= *LV* IV, 2. 14):

Mater, si in viduitate permansit, aequalem inter filios, id est qualem unus ex filiis, usufrutuariam habeat portionem; qua(m) usque ad tempus vitae suae usufructuario iure possideat, ceterum nec donare nec vindere nec uni ex filiis .... e conferre praesumat. 2. Quod si eam filii hanc portionem matris <evertere> sive per neglegentiam sive per odiu(m) eorum forte prospexerint, ad millenarium vel ad comitem civitatis aut iudicem referre non differant, ut matrem suam contestatione commoneant ne res quas ad usu(m)fructum accepit evertat. 3. Nam usumfructu(m) quem ipsa fuerat perceptura *dare cui voluerit, filio vel filiae, non vetetur. 4. Verum si ex usufructuaria portione aliquid probatur eversum, filiis post mortem matris de eius facultatibus sarciatur. 5. Post obitum vero matris, portio quam acceperat ad filios equaliter revertatur, quia non possunt de paterna hereditate fraudari. 6. Quod si mater ad alias nuptias forte transierit, ex ea die usufructuariam portionem, quam de bonis mariti fuerat consecuta, filii inter reliquas res paternas, qui ex eo nati sunt coniugio, vindicabunt.*

5. *Codex Euricianus*: CE 320:

Si parentes <in>testati decesserint ..... de ea .... eas ad facu<l>tates ... sorores .... ccipient ... cum fratribus suis in terris vel in aliis rebus aequalem habeant portionem. 2. Quod si aliqua sine viro fuerit relicta, et ad coniugium expetens sponte transierit, totam portionem quam acceperat suis fratribus vel eorum heredibus relinquat. 3. Quod si ipsa virgo permanserit, quamdiu advixerit in rebus vel in culturis cum fratribus habeat portionem; post obitum vero eius terras ad heredes superius conprehensos sine mora revertantur, reliquas facultates cui voluerit donatura. 4. Circa sanctimonialem autem quae in castitate permanserit voluntate parentum, praecipimus permanere. 5. Quod si parentes sic transierit ut nullum fuerit testamentum, ea puella inter fratres aequalem in omnibus habeat portionem, quam usque ad tempus vitae suae usufructuario iure possideat, post obitum vero suum terras suis heredibus relinquat; de reliqua facultate faciendi quod voluerit in ei<u>s potestate consistat.

6. *Leges Visigothorum: LV* IV, 2. 1:

(Antiqua) Ut sorores cum fratribus equaliter in parentum hereditatem succedant. Si pater vel mater intestati discesserint, sorores cum fratribus in omni parentum facultate absque aliquo obiectu equali divisione succedant.

7. *Codex Euricianus*: CE 319:

Maritus si uxori suae aliquid donaverit, et ipsa post obitum mariti sui in nullo scelere adulterii fuerit conversata sed in pudicitia permanserit, aut si certe ad alium maritum honesta coniunctione pervenerit, de re(bus) sibi a marito donatis possidendi et post obitum suum relinquendi cui voluerit habeat potestatem. 2. Sin autem per adulteriu(m) seu inhonestam coinunctionem se miscuisse convincitur, quidquid de facultate mariti fuerat consecuta, totum incunctanter amittat, et ad heredes donatoris legitimos revertatur.

8. *Leges Visigothorum: LV* V, 2. 5:

(Antiqua): De rebus a marito mulieri concessis, vel si mulier fuerit adulterasse detecta. Maritus si uxori sue aliquid donaverit, et ipsa post obitum mariti sui in nullo scelere adulterii fuerit conversata, sed in pudicitia permanserit, aut certe si ad alium maritum honesta coniunctione pervenerit, de rebus sibi a marito donatis possidendi et post obitum suum, si filios non habuerit, relinquendi cui voluerit **[Erwig adds:** *secundum voluntatem testatoris] habeat potestatem. Ceterum si filios non relinquens intestata discesserit, aut ad maritum eius, si suprestis extiterit, aut ad heredes mariti, qui donationem conscripsit, eadem donatio pertinebit. Si autem per adulterium seu per inhonestam coniunctionem se miscuisse convincitur, quidquid de facultate mariti sui fuerat consecuta, totum incunctanter amittat, et ad heredes donatoris vel ad filios legitimos revertatur.*

9. *Leges Visigothorum: LV* V, 2. 4:

(Antiqua) De rebus extra dotem uxori a marito conlatis. Si mulier a marito extra dotem de quibuscumque rebus, quacumque donatione vel profligatione conquisitis aut illi debitis, quoquo tempore quodcumque donatum acceperit, si filii de eodem coniugio fuerint procreati, mulier usque ad diem obitus sui **[Erwig adds:** *secundum voluntatem vel ordinationem testatoris] secura possideat et de quinta tantumdem parte earum rerum faciendi quod voluerit potestatem obtineat* **[Erwig adds:** *Fructus tamen, sicut testator ipse, qui hoc testavit, expendendi vel utendi potestatem habere potuit, ita et illa, que usu hoc ad possidendum percepit, omnia, dum advixerit, sine cuiuslibet inquietudine, suis incunctanter utatur expensis; si tamen idem testator aliquam specialem testationem de ipsis*

*frugibus non instituerit]; post obitum vero suum reliqua integra et intemerata filiis ex ipso viro procreatis derelinquat, et nulla occasione [**Erwig adds**: cuiquam], exinde, excepto, ut dictum est, quintam partem, quicquam aliud mulier alienare praesumat. Quod si ex ipso coniugio filii non fuerint procreati, quidquid mulier de rebus sibi donatis [**Erwig adds**: iuxta prescriptum testatoris ordinem] facere elegerit, liberam habeam potestatem. Ceterum si intestata discesserit, ad maritum eius, si suprestis extiterit, donatio revertatur. Sin autem maritus non fuerit, ad heredes mariti, qui donationem fecit, eadem donatio pertinebit. Simili ratione et de viris precipimus custodiri de his, que ab uxoribus tempore quocumque donata perceperint.*

10. *Leges Visigothorum: LV* IV, 2. 6:
Flavius Gloriosus Reccesvindus rex. Si his, qui moritur, avos relinquat aut avias. Quotiens qui moritur, si avum paternum aut maternum relinquat, tam ad avum paternum, quam ad avum maternum hereditas mortui universa pertineat. Si autem qui moritur avum paternum et aviam maternam relinquerit, equales capiant portiones. Ita quoque erit, si paternam et maternam aviam qui moritur relinquere videatur. Et hec quidem equitas portionis de illis rebus erit, que mortuus conquisisse cognoscitur. De illis vero rebus, que ab avis vel parentibus habuit, ad avos directa linea revocabunt.

11. *Codex Euricianus: CE* 327:
In priore lege fuerat constitutum ut si patruus aus patrui filii cum matre.... vindicarentur. 2. Nos modo meliori ordinatione censuimus ut patre defuncto, si filius decesserit, omnem facultatem eius sibi mater dibeat vindicare, quae tamen sit post obitum vidua. 3. Si vero qui moritur filios, nepotes et pronepotes relinquerit, ipsi omnes habeant facultates, ea condicione servata ut nepotes ex eo filio qui patre superstite mortuus fuerit integram de avi bonis quam fuerat pater eorum, si vixisset, habiturus percipia<n>t portionem; 4. nam nepotes ex ea filia quae ante patre(m) mortua est de ea portione quam mater fuerat habitura tertia(m) portione perdant....

Discussion

AUSENDA: Two short points. One is where there is the word 'succession' I would call it 'inheritance'.

VELÁZQUEZ: I use inheritance and succession in a general sense; I'll revise it.

AUSENDA: The other thing that we discussed already is that you should try to find a Latin term for 'mejora'.

VELÁZQUEZ: Yes, but I said yesterday that 'mejora' is a juridical technical term in Spanish. I have to say that the 'mejora', I think, has its origin in the *Dum inlicita* of Chindaswinth. But, in one way or another, it is a law which has been preserved from the Middle Ages to the present day. For this reason, the *Dum inlicita* is most important, and nowadays when we talk in Spain about the 'mejora' we are talking about the technical term. I insist that it is an institution exclusive of Spain. And I'm sorry, but I don't know what it expresses now, with the reform of civil law in Spain, but until several years ago the 'mejora', improvement, existed in Spanish civil law. Because of this I use the term 'mejora' because it is exclusive to the Spanish juridical system. I might have to change it because it is a strange word.

AUSENDA: You don't have to change it, just add a footnote explaining what you said just now.

GREEN: Yes, on the first occasion give a short explanation.

WOOD: The simple translation 'improvement' doesn't actually help the reader who doesn't know what you mean by that concept. So you should provide a definition of it rather than a translation. Then you can leave it as 'mejora' all the way through.

AUSENDA: I would like to discuss the title, because there is some confusion of communication, due to my fault, because I thought it would be 'jural relations', instead it is 'juridical relations' and there is a difference. So, I was wondering, what you actually wrote about were juridical relations?

WOOD: I can see a difference between jural and juridical.

VELÁZQUEZ: In effect, there is a certain difference. However, it is also true that jural and juridical may be used as synonyms according to the dictionaries. I believe that the problem is due to the fact that in Spanish we have only one term, 'juridico', for the two words. I have used the word 'juridical' which is closest to the Spanish term. However, the content of my paper comes closest to that proposed 'jural relations'; although I have only dealt with one of the many aspects suggested by Dr. Ausenda; that is, I have concentrated on inheritance, not on property, war, blood money compensation, etc.

RIPOLL: I wish to speak briefly on a point that I believe important and that we Spanish scholars perceive quite well. The historiographic problematic, i.e. all the historical literature, practically of the entire twentieth century, tried to distinguish the meaning of the law for Visigoths and Romans always mixing the problems of ethnicity, territoriality and nationality. The exhaustive discussions do not reach a solution. The work done here concerning the *Dum inlicita* shows how the study of juridical and legislative problems can only be approached in this way, i.e. bringing to fruition a detailed philological analysis to try to understand what it means. This type of study of the question concerning the various laws is the approach that will allow in a near future to understand the meaning of juridical questions, etc.

DÍAZ: On page 226, a point on Visigothic law. The question is whether Visigothic law is a simple compendium or whether it is a text for scholarly consultation, for professional use in Spain. When we read about all the tradition of the historians of law, normally the Visigothic law is itself a mirror of the society. When we read, for example King's book (1972), we can find this question about whether the law is describing Visigothic society or not. When, in the work of the historians of law, in the Germanic and Spanish tradition especially, who have paid more attention to the *Lex Visigothorum*, we read about the *Lex Visigothorum*, there are two very different approaches; one of them is the technicalities of law, the Roman or non-Roman precedents of the same; and on the other hand there is the question of the social implications of the law. That is why I ask whether we are facing a simple compendium perhaps for the use of a narrow spectrum of people, or a real mirror of the society. In this case I think the whole introduction should be a discussion of this problem and later, in the second part of the work on the *Dum inlicita*, we will solve the technical question of the Visigothic law. I think it is a good thing to move beyond the old polemics about the legal question, because, if we speak about a technical question exclusively out of history, then we are not working in history.

VELÁZQUEZ: In the first part, I tried to explain my opinion, my point of view about territoriality or personality, about the transmission of the text, definitively about some of the problems the *Lex Visigothorum* poses. Indeed, I think that we can't talk about a concrete aspect of law if we don't begin by explaining our point of view about the general concept. For this reason, I explained my point of view about the legislative apparatus as a means for the exercise of power, and how the first legislative court of Euric is the first means, the first mechanism to exercise power. In fact laws are the basis for a state and for the power of the king. If we consider the chronology of the law, the different evolution, incorporation of law, by the successive kings, and if we consider the order of laws, for example, in the *Liber IV* of the *Lex Visigothorum*, I think the order of law is very significant, very important. We can approach the reality, the motive, the cultures, because the kings are obsessed with legislating.

RIPOLL: You say in your text and now you have taken the attitude that legislation is one of the best areas to study the meaning of the exercise of power. Do you believe that one can identify legislation within the structure of state power, as a sign of identity? Is legislation a sign of identity?

VELÁZQUEZ: Yes, but a sign of identity of the new kings, of the new generation. The first legislations of Euric and Alaric seek to imitate the Roman model—I am referring to the form not the contents—because to dispose of a legislative system such as theirs was a fundamental instrument for the exercise of power and moreover a sign of this power. Already at the end of the sixth century and in the seventh century, the *Lex Visigothorum* was a sign of the identity of this power and, in general, of the new society of *Hispania* in this era. It is neither a Gothic nor a Roman sign of identity, but rather a sign of identity of the new society.

HEATHER: In the seventh century, there is no ethnic terminology used in the laws.

VELÁZQUEZ: Yes, in the seventh century.

DE JONG: That's what I feel about the introduction, you just gave. Leave out *patria potestas*, leave out 'Sippe', and even more leave out Tacitus, when you talk about all this. I understand you just mention it as a background and you try to break through this opposition between Germanic and Roman, but somehow you seem to get the Trojan horse back in again. You say you cannot work with this opposition, I agree, but then, when you continue, you are still looking for things Germanic.

SCHWARCZ: I think you can't leave out of legislation the Roman law.

VELÁZQUEZ: I understand, but I think that the Visigothic kings, the new power used the Roman law technically, because I think that this is a mixed society and the legislation, the *Liber Iudiciorum*, is produced as a means of power and as a general legislation. Another thing is its real application. Roman law is used to construct this legislative-technical apparatus, but from Euric's code I think that this law tries to adapt to those things which are based on Germanic customary law, and which do not contradict Roman law. The difficult question is how the idea of Germanic cultural tradition is transmitted.

DE JONG: I can see that what you are trying to do is to show how they find common ground, but I think that for them it was of no importance whether this law was Roman or not. It was there, to be used and to be changed if no longer practical.

HEATHER: I think that I broadly agree with that, but in the early period, up to about 540, there is a further important dimension to Roman law, an ideological one, which means that Gothic kings will want to pay lip service to continuity within it, but we'll talk about that in a minute. But I am not disagreeing with you in the longer term, just in that specific early context.

DE JONG: Yes, that brings us back to Gisela [Ripoll]'s point about the law as a sign of identity.

HEATHER: That actually leads into the ideological point, so I might as well go on to the point which I was wanting to make on page 231, and take the two together. Your comments about textual transmission and accuracy reminded me of a text which I think is extremely interesting and significant: the minutes of the Roman senate. I'm sure you know it, where the Theodosian Code was introduced to the Roman senate in 439. And that is a staggering text, because you get a series of acclamations, where various points are made about this new law and the senators shout the points back, probably twenty times in certain cases, one of which is "Let there be no interpolations. Let the text be accurate". And the senators shout this ritually, twenty something times, I can't remember the exact figure. But this is tipping us off that law has more than a straightforward literal significance. Law means something else in Roman society. You have to think of the senate in Rome, all these people in their togas and they shout twenty times in a row, "Let there be no interpolations, let there be no interpolations, let there be no interpolations", they keep on doing it. It's an extraordinary scene when you bring it to life. And various other things, I think, help to explain this ritual significance of Roman law. It's part of an ideological construct about what being Roman is. Romans actually regard themselves—this is late Roman state ideology of the fourth and fifth centuries—they regard themselves as more civilized than anybody else in a particular way: they are more rational, defining rationality as the domination of the mind over the physical senses. So they are more rational, because their minds can control physical desires, usually sex, money and drunkenness, of course. But the Romans, in their own view, stand above this because of their higher rationality. In the bundle of ideas that go together, the great symbol of rationality is written law, this is the key thing. This is why we have that famous phrase from Athaulf about, "Goths cannot obey laws", meaning that he couldn't replace *Romania* with *Gothia*. This is why you get the other almost equally famous passage where the Byzantine historian Priscus (Blockley, frg. 11. 2; 1983:272) meets a Greek in the camp of Attila—people don't quote the punch line from that story—when the Greek turned Hun bursts into tears and agrees that Roman society is better because they don't have written Roman law among the Huns. So, written law and the steady continuance of procedures, is the total symbol of *Romanitas*: what's different about being Roman from everybody else. Thus you have to allow for that tremendous ideological loading on written law, at least in the early period, if not later on. And I think, in a very practical way, this very much explains why you get the *Lex Romana Visigothorum* in 506. You've got Frankish pressure on the kingdom, and we know that Clovis was making a play for the Catholic loyalty of Catholic landowners. He was trying it on, and Alaric II reacts by calling Church councils and also by issuing this law code, which is the great guarantor that Roman civilization is continuing, that the Goths belong among the civilized, that, as it were, civilization is safe with the Visigoths. Hence, in that early period, in say 500, law still has this tremendous ideological importance, and you have to deal with it as a symbol as well as a series of rulings about things.

DE JONG: Well, I would say it also was a joint symbol of identity.

HEATHER: Yes, that's right. By issuing that law code, Alaric is saying: "I'm part of the civilized world too".

SCHWARCZ: To embellish this argument which is absolutely right, may I draw your attention to Euric's legislation with other efforts to supplant imperial authority, and it's Euric who is the first Germanic king who doesn't take the title of *magister militum* but makes another person *magister militum* under his rule, and he is the first to make a *codex* because this is also a symbol of imperial authority.

VELÁZQUEZ: I will try to respond to these observations. I believe that basically I hold the same point of view. It is true that I state at the beginning that I am not going to work with the territorial-personal dualism and later I mention once more this Trojan horse, but I only wanted to underline some personal observations. I agree that the Visigoths tried to imitate the Romans and to romanize their people; and I know the example given by Heather about the approval of the Theodosian Code in the senate. I agree that Athaulf's phrase, "Goths cannot obey laws" and why he couldn't "replace Romans with Goths" must be understood in this context. However, this does not contradict my argument. In fact, I think that the Visigoths wanted to become romanized and, therefore, among other things, they tried to adopt Roman legislation. But I also believe that they tried to respect and keep some of their customs, and in the legislation they sought a compromise between their customs and Roman laws. I recall having said that the written laws are "the great symbol of Roman civilization".

GREEN: I have a point on page 225. It is the last paragraph where you quote to the effect that the *Lex* is a semi-live text. I have difficulties with the word 'semi-live'. I can understand that a text could be either for scholarly consultation, and therefore, if you like, dead, or a basis for the exercise of juridical activity and, therefore, live. What precisely do you mean by 'semi-live'?

VELÁZQUEZ: Yes. This paper of Díaz y Díaz (1976) talks about the different manuscripts of the law. There are many and some of them have been used by Zeumer, but others not. Díaz y Díaz explains the characteristics of these manuscripts from the codicological aspect. Zeumer's is a text which puts together the different laws issued by the kings. When a law is general and important, it is for everybody. The *Liber* assumes that this law is written in the *Liber*. In fact there existed a first edition, but the laws were added progressively. For this reason there are different manuscripts with different laws. In the *Liber* these are semi-live texts because, like a flower, it is growing. First an *Antiqua* law, we know the author, the legislator compiled various laws, we cannot identify the authors of all the

Antiquae, but we know some of them. For example, the *Antiquae* which were issued by Liuvigild. And after this, Reccared incorporated some other laws into the *Liber*, and later Sisebut did likewise. Then the *Liber* was growing until we arrive at Chindaswinth. I fear I am in agreement with King when he says that Chindaswinth probably made a revision, a new edition of the *Liber*. He abolished some laws, substituted some *Antiquae* laws with other laws of his own and probably made a new edition. If Chindaswinth didn't make a revision, it is certain that his son Recceswinth did. The *Liber* is a text which grows, which is extended. The situation reflects, in turn, the problems of the transmission of texts and, on the other hand, the application of the laws at different times and in different places.

GREEN: If I may make a suggestion, I think that needs amplification. When you use the term 'semi-live' here you need to explain it in such detail, I think the reader must be given help in your text. I don't know if others agree with me, but I certainly boggled at what precisely you meant by semi-live when I came across it. Ian, do you agree with me or not?

WOOD: Yes, I do. There might be a way of re-expressing it by saying that the law is about the living tradition of legislation within the Visigothic kingdom.

VELÁZQUEZ: Thank you, I will.

DÍAZ: On page 227, about validity and application of the laws. We are going to go on, more or less, speaking about the same thing. The crucial question is that Zeumer's edition is only a partial one, because not all the manuscripts were consulted at that moment and sometimes when we use some books or we read some questions, we see that some authors used in the past other manuscripts before this edition and we have more chapters of the law than we have in Zeumer's edition. For example, we find in some of these differences in the Spanish medieval translation of the *Liber Iudiciorum* with a lot of notes and different references. And if we keep in mind that in the legislation every *iudex* and every *dux* had one volume of the *Lex Visigothorum* and we doubt whether the *Lex Visigothorum* is a simple compendium or a text for scholarly consultation. It is very probable that every *iudex* had written down elements for interpretation. In this light we might ask ourselves whether that is a semi-live one or perhaps only a consultation book, or perhaps it was always used for the application of the law. Concerning this aspect, we have the question of the validity and application of the law. For example, when we read the *Vitas Patrum*, perhaps we find a coherence between one law and the other, but when we read, for example, the *regula communis* or the monastic documents of the North-West, we see elements that can raise a doubt about the real application, especially about the law of property for example. With all probability, in the areas of the North-West the *Lex Visigothorum*, the *Liber Iudiciorum*, faced an old tradition for which the application of Roman law was very difficult, the individual ability of granting gifts to other juridical personalities, for example, the ability of one man to give a property to a monastery is denied by all the members of the community who immediately go there and raise a conflict with the monastery. We have in the Spanish tradition a problem, because normally

711 is regarded as a total break, but this is not realistic, and in the ninth and tenth centuries we have a lot of '*fueros*' (local law codes). These are not local *leges* that are in force at the same time as the *Lex Visigothorum*; probably these 'fueros' are the expression not of a legal document but of a particular law. And it is the same with what is behind their application of the law: the proprietor, the abbas in the monastery, the bishop, probably used the *Lex Visigothorum* as a book for consultation at the same level at which they were using the old references. In the monastic tradition sometimes they were using penalties from the Old Testament, but they were used for the application and were in force together with the *Lex Visigothorum*. In this case, when we have one manuscript, and we have a lot of manuscripts with the *Lex Visigothorum* and the *Liber Iudiciorum*, we cannot think that it was the only one. But Zeumer put all that was common here and there in the manuscript he used. However, the most important things are perhaps the uncommon questions; the explanation is that they were using the law not as the Spanish constitution is used nowadays, for which perhaps we must think of the American one as a precedent. I think it is very important to renew investigations into the application of the law and on what level it is a mirror of the society and of reality.

VELÁZQUEZ: On page 226, I gave the example of the letters from Recceswinth to Braulio (*Ep.* 38-41). They are significant because Recceswinth asked Braulio to amend and rectify the several copies of the code in question in order to remove errors, because it was an important problem for the king that there were so many copies. Because of this he wrote these letters: perhaps this could be a clue for the bad application of the law. On the other hand you have mentioned the *fueros* after the seventh century. But we can also mention the Visigothic formulas. I think that these formulas are concrete examples and documents for the practical daily exercise of the juridical system. We realize the importance of written texts in the Visigothic world when we see a Visigothic slate which contains the *condiciones sacramentorum*, the formula for oaths is exactly the formula which we can see in the *Liber Iudiciorum* for the Jews. The text of this slate is fragmentary, but it can be read: *iuro per Deum et Patrem et Filium et per quatuor evangelia* and so on, but the oath does not include the Holy Spirit, *iuro per Deum Patrem et Filium* but not *Spiritum sanctum*.

DE JONG: Yes, I missed him already. Why?

VELÁZQUEZ: Because it is possible—I thought so some years ago—that this slate was written before the conversion of Reccared. However, I don't know the exact date. It may have been issued during the reign of Reccared. A mention of the year is not preserved. I don't remember exactly, but I believe that "*anno feliciter tertio regis*", would be 589. If the king was Reccared, but it could be even later since we don't know the name of the king, the official change in the formula *iuro per Deum et Patrem et Filium* and now *et Spiritum Sanctum* had not arrived to these *iudices* who were writing the slate, because from the change of the formula for oaths until its 'official' use in the judgements, quite some time could have gone by. The slate in question could be dated to 587 or later.

DE JONG: The poor *iudex* had no idea of what was happening.

VELÁZQUEZ: Yes, the poor *judex* without the necessary information.

GREEN: I have a point on page 235. At the top you use the wording 'common Germanic law'. I think I understand what you mean, but it is ambiguous. I take it you mean 'Germanic common law'. As it stands, that would read in English as meaning 'law common to all the Germanic tribes', shared by them all. You just need to reverse the words: 'Germanic common law'. [Changed to 'customary law'].

VELÁZQUEZ: Of course.

HEATHER: On page 227, on the supposed dichotomy between personal and territorial law, there is quite a nice article about it—overly complicated, I think— by Amory (1993) in *Early Medieval Europe* fairly recently on Burgundian law codes. There are various problems with the article, but one of the points that I think is right, is quite well made. It is that there isn't necessarily a head-on contradiction even between personal and territorial law. You don't necessarily have to choose between them. If you look at certain laws, they can be personal, they can be about Visigoths or about Burgundians, but also apply only within a defined territory. So, in a sense, the whole language of the debate is not right as well as much of the substance of it. You might find that article worth a look.

VELÁZQUEZ: Thank you, I shall read it.

SCHWARCZ: On page 233, on the use of the *Codex Theodosianus*. The information on the exact date of the laws should be mentioned.

RETAMERO: I think Constantine, page 233.

VELÁZQUEZ: Sorry, I forgot. I don't remember because I forgot to write it.

DE JONG: Could we please move back to page 234? I wonder about this text of Chindaswinth's law, in the middle of the page where you have the expression *ex legibus Romanis recolimus fuisse decretum*; you do not cite the earlier part of the text where Chindaswinth speaks of the *seniores gentis Gothorum* who have to do certain things 'because as we recall this to have been decreed in the laws for the Romans'. Wasn't the lawgiver talking about everybody? The *seniores* of the entire people, which he calls Goths, but which includes Romans and also some other goodies that are never mentioned. Roman law seems to be invoked just as a source to support the argument. So, there is no real opposition here between Goths on the one hand and Romans on the other which needs to be reconciled. What you have is probably the *Lex Romana Visigothorum* as an authoritative law book for all, do you see? Which is just incidentally drawn upon in a decree which is for everybody, referred to as Goths. Yes? You don't understand. Anybody who does understand?

HEATHER: I'll try [laughter]. I think Mayke means that by this date the usage *gentis Gothorum* actually means everybody in Spain, not Goths as opposed to Romans and that when the law goes on to talk about *legibus Romanis* it's kind of, I suppose, an academic intellectual reference, a technically pointed reference.

VELÁZQUEZ: Yes, but before he said "*nisi quantum nunc legis huius institutio continet aut si forte iuxta quod et legibus Romanis recolimus decretum. Si forte*", if perhaps, the king summarized his new *institutio* with Roman law.

DE JONG: You don't translate '*recolimus*', 'according to what we remember as having been decreed in Roman law'. It's very accidental. It is said in passing.

VELÁZQUEZ: The king assumes the Roman law. There is no contradiction with the new law.

DE JONG: No, but where is Germanic tradition? Germanic tradition crops up too much.

VELÁZQUEZ: No, I don't see Germanic tradition.

DE JONG: OK, good.

VELÁZQUEZ: I don't see Germanic tradition. I am in agreement with you. In this page I only try to demonstrate that *wittum* and *donatio ante nuptias* are similar concepts, but technically the instrument which the kings use is Roman law, it is a new revision of Roman law. But, because the *wittum* and *donatio ante nuptias* are similar in concept, because it is a gift, when a woman marries by the system of interchange of tokens, there is no contradiction between these two gifts.

DE JONG: No, I agree with that.

VELÁZQUEZ: And the *iuxta quod et legibus Romanis recolimus* is a recognition that the *Antiqua* Roman law is valid for the....

DE JONG: I think just your whole argument would be stronger if you wouldn't mention Germanic tradition.

VELÁZQUEZ: No, with Germanic tradition I only want to say that *uittum* and *donatio ante nuptias* are only similar. Probably it is a technical reference; because of this I haven't studied the concrete precedent of the law as Otero (1963:23) does. Indeed, I think that "*legibus romanis recolimus*" is a general reference. I think that in this law we can see Roman tradition but in it there is no contradiction with the existence of a Germanic custom of giving the gift, the *uittum*.

HEATHER: I would like to ask one question and then possibly offer a paradox, depending on the answer to this question. I didn't actually receive your paper, so I had to read it last night, quickly. Can you just summarize for us broadly what's happening in this sequence of legislation? Am I right in understanding that the individual is losing more and more control of various bits of land or various bits of the inheritance which are being designated for sons, grandsons, daughters, grand-daughters, but that, as well, by losing control of certain bits, one element is being defined, which you can then give away? Is that right? Are there two things happening side-by-side?

VELÁZQUEZ: The *Dum inlicita* tries to control the inheritance. This law establishes three parts. But, I think that the first part, the 'mejora', is connected to the freedom of inheritance in Roman law. Especially in relation to larger fortunes; it is necessary to establish a control in the mind of the king, of the legislator. I think there is a wish to control the most important part of the inheritance.

HEATHER: Two thirds.

VELÁZQUEZ: Two thirds, yes. The *quota legitima*, the legitimate inheritance is the most important. Only 1/5 is for free disposal. But in the *redactio* of Chindaswinth's law, the 'mejora' is 1/10, which is a small part. Later, in Erwig's edition, the 'mejora' is 1/3. Actually, I believe that the difference in Erwig's edition is even more pronounced.

We have two interpretations of a different form until now, because everybody thinks that first we take 1/5 of free disposal and then we take 1/3 of 'mejora'. However, I don't think this is the case in Erwig's edition. I think that first we take 1/3 of 'mejora' and then 1/5 of free disposal. This is very important and all of this means the intention of the legislator of controlling, establishing the inheritance, a very strong inheritance legislation. However, in this legislation it is still possible to have an element of freedom. This is a Roman concept, I think.

HEATHER: Yes, that is what I want to comment on. What came to my mind are two things. One is, it wouldn't just be kings who are worried about land being given away, it would also be the heirs, it would be the sons and the grandsons, the children and the grandchildren who would want to limit how much land is being alienated. And I think a lot of very good work on Frankish law sees royal courts as areas where accommodations and bargains and quarrels are worked out. So, I wouldn't be so sure that this is the king's royal agenda in the legislation. It might be partly, but it will also be partly the important children of nobles who are worried that daddy might give away all their money. Because of all these law codes in Spain, you think about kings doing things, but laws can be responses to requests, and, in something like this, the heirs are going to be terribly worried that a free gift would mean that they wouldn't get anything. So, don't forget the heirs.

VELÁZQUEZ: Yes, I understand but I am not forgetting: when I talk about the king, I refer to the king as a lawgiver, it's a general concept of king, in the abstract.

HEATHER: OK, I only said this because people have been talking about law codes as the foundation of state power, that phrase has turned up this morning. And that I think is a slightly misleading formulation in an early medieval context where the state does not stand outside the élites, the state is formed of élites and the legislation is a product of quarrels, bargains, whatever within the élite.

SCHWARCZ: I quite agree and I only want to give another parallel for the problem mentioned by Peter [Heather]. The *Lex Baiwariorum* starts with a chapter on donations to the Church, and one of the first paragraphs...orders anyone who wants to give anything to the Church, first to make an agreement with his heirs and then he must not give a donation to the Church without first consulting his children.

DÍAZ: A question about information. Is this the Visigothic concept of the king and the law: the law is an expression of the decision of the king? This is Isidore's implication about what the law is, that is the king. Later, in the concept of medieval Spanish tradition about the *Liber Iudiciorum*; the *Liber* is the law, not in relation to any authority. The starting point in the Visigothic period is the ongoing association between the king and the law and the revindication of one demand about the law, the last appellation possible is always the king. He is the supreme authority.

HEATHER: It's entirely late Roman. This is the late Roman concept of law. You are always allowed to suggest a law to the emperor, but he is the only one who can make laws.

WOOD: About Roman provincial laws. I think it is worth noting that the Farmer's Law, originally published as Gothic by Ashburner (1910-12), is now seen as being associated with Leo III's legislation. In fact, therefore, it is Roman law. So, I think you just need to add that there are other types of Roman law.

VELÁZQUEZ: Yes, I can mention this Roman provincial law, the most important really. But, as for this appendix, I had problems writing it, I had to fight with my personal computer [laughter]. But really the idea is clear, Visigothic customary law, Roman provincial law.

WOOD: The other point that I want to make was really very close to the one that Pablo [Díaz] made about the question of the manuscripts. What strikes me as extremely important in what Pablo was saying, and in what you are saying in this paper, is that the question of the difficulty of interpretation of individual laws and the question of the problem of manuscript transmission suggests that the traditional view of the success of the kings in ensuring the transmission of the correct text and its importance, is actually completely misplaced; that we need to think of the Visigothic code as looking much more, in its enforcement at least, like other barbarian law codes.

DÍAZ: Yes, but I think it's a question of time to have all the critical implications about the sources. The situation with these Spanish manuscripts is an exceptional situation in the European picture. I think, perhaps not to put it in question, but I think that only an elaboration of the Zeumer edition would consent a better picture and do away with the idea of a canonical text.

DE JONG: Yes.

VELÁZQUEZ: Most assuredly.

WOOD: This is something that Eckhardt's editions of *Lex Salica* have clarified for the Franks. We haven't caught on to the fact that the *Leges Visigothorum* pose similar sorts of problems.

DÍAZ: Yes. this theme is discussed in an article by Collins (1985) about the disputes concerning this theme. It is this very problem. In fact, when we take documents of the ninth century in Catalonia which are without the usc of the Visigothic law and later it is a question of civil law, one is not really faced with a rupture. However it is a very interesting, a really live question of the law. This is the problem of the historiographic tradition in Visigothic studies about using only a legal or also an institutionalist interpretation of Visigothic history. And we read King for example, and we read the pattern to suit, to pass off this situation only partially. However the problem is the long term interpretation of Visigothic history, and we as Zeumer, a splendid Zeumer because it is a problem of his time that emerges, on this point we alter all the evidence: when we find a contradiction between *Lex Visigothorum* and other sources, the other sources are incorrect. This is the traditional interpretation, when it may very well be the contrary. It is an ideological question, it is an idea for the future [laughter].

References in the discussion

Textual sources:

Codex Theodosianus: see References at end of paper.
Braulio
        Letters to Recceswinth: see Riesco Terrero (ed.) 1975:150-153.
Lex Baiwariorum: see von Schwind (ed.) 1926.
Lex Romana Visigothorum: see References at end of paper.
Lex Salica: see Eckhardt (ed.) 1962.
Lex Visigothorum: see References at end of paper.
Liber Iudiciorum: see Zeumer (ed.) 1902.
Priscus
        Fragments: see Blockley (ed.) 1983.
Vitas Sanctorum Patrum Emeretensium: see References at end of paper.

Bibliography:

Amory, P.
  1993   The meaning and purpose of ethnic terminology in the Burgundian laws. *Early Medieval Europe* 2 (1): 1-28.
Ashburner, W.
  1910-12   The Farmer's Law. *Journal of Hellenic Studies* 30: 85-108, 32: 69-95.
Blockley, R. C. (ed.)
  1983   *The Fragmentary Classicising Historians of the Late Roman Empire, Eunapius, Olympiodorus, Priscus, Malchus.* Liverpool: Praxis Cairns.
Collins, R.
  1985   'Sicut lex Gothorum continet': Law and charters in ninth- and tenth-century León and Catalonia. *The English Historical Review* 396: 489-512.
Díaz y Díaz, M. C.
  1976   See References at end of paper.
Eckhardt, K. A.
  1962   *Pactus legis Salicae. Monumenta Germaniae Historica. Leges nationum Germanicarum*, 4, 1. Hannover: Hahn.
King, P. D.
  1972   See References at end of paper.
Riesco Terrero, L. (ed.)
  1975   See References at end of paper.
Schwind, E. von (ed.)
  1926   *Lex Baiwariorum. Monumenta Germaniae Historica. Leges nationum Germanicarum*, 5, 2. Hannover: Hahn.
Zeumer, K. (ed.)
  1902   See References at end of paper.

AS COINS GO HOME:
TOWNS, MERCHANTS, BISHOPS AND KINGS IN VISIGOTHIC HISPANIA

FELIX RETAMERO

Departament de Ciències de l'Antiguitat i de l'Edat Mitjana, Universitat Autònoma de Barcelona, Edifici B, E-08193 Bellaterra (Barcelona)

According to the author of the *Vitas Sanctorum Patrum Emeretensium* (henceforth *VSPE*), sometime in the middle of the sixth century, an unespecified number of ships coming *de Orientibus* arrived at the shores of *Hispania*. As soon as the travellers, who were *negotiatores graecos,* reached Mérida, they proceeded, as it was customary to do (*ex more*), to visit the bishop, named Paul. The day after having been received in audience, the *negotiatores* sent a boy, Fidelis (*deferente puero nomine Fidele*), to present a gift (*munusculum*) to the bishop. Paul, *natione Graecum* himself (*VSPE*, IV. 1), observing the good nature of the adolescent sent by the *negotiatores (uidens adolescentem bone indolis*), eagerly interrogated him. It was then, unexpectedly, that Paul discovered that Fidelis was a nephew of his (*cognovit nomen sororis sue*). It seems that meeting Fidelis shook Paul profoundly. The *negotiatores* were then summoned by the bishop to his presence, and asked to leave Fidelis with him against a payment that they were allowed to set {*Puerum mici istum concedite et quicquid uultis a me postulate* (IV. 3)}. The bishop had even to threaten, in the first instance at least, the unwilling *graeci*, who nevertheless ended up by accepting the *pecuniam copiosam* offered by Paul. The bishop could thus hold Fidelis *ob consolatione captiuitatis* (IV. 3), and trained the boy with enthusiasm {*diebus ac noctibus strenue erudiuit* (IV. 4)}.

The author also says that, as the years went by, Fidelis was never reluctant to fulfill the wishes of the old bishop {*supranominato nutritori*—Paul— *suo dulci obsequio in omnibus obediret*—Fidelis (IV. 4)}. Paul decided thus to appoint his beloved nephew to be his successor in the bishopric, and the sole heir to his goods. These goods should be further inherited by the Church of Mérida, after Fidelis's death, *if* the *clerus Emeritensis* would be willing to accept the choice of Paul. This condition proved to be effective, as Fidelis occupied the episcopal seat in spite of the slanderous allegations made by some *pestiferi homines* (IV. 5). We are told that the wealth held by Paul, and eventually kept in the bosom of the Church for the bishopric of Fidelis, made the Church of Mérida the most opulent in *Hispania* {*ut illi in Spanie finibus nulla eclesia esset opulentior* (IV. 5)}.

Recent excavations have confirmed this opulence shedding light on the magnificence of some of the ecclesiastical edifices of Visigothic Mérida. Their location (Mateos 1992; 1995) in the city strongly suggests a layout similar to that of many late antique cities, as proposed by G. Cantino: some "punti forti", both inside and outside of the walls, of clustered dwellings.[1]

---

[1] "Si delinea allora un modello di città policentrica o polinucleare, articolata su una pluralità di 'punti forti' intramuranei e extramuranei, apparentemente indipendenti, in quanto non legati dalle maglie di una griglia geometrica di riferimento" (Cantino 1995:255).

It goes without saying that one of the most relevant *punti forti* in Mérida was the basilica devoted to St Eulalia. It is known from the *VSPE* (IV. 6) that the building, set up on a former *martyrium*, was restored and enlarged under Fidelis (560-571), the bishop who was once a sailor.

The author of the *VSPE* also mentions the reconstruction of the episcopal palace around the same period that the enlargement of the basilica of Saint Eulalia was made. Excavations have also allowed us to identify and to reconstruct the shape and the magnitude of the famous and luxurious *xenodochium* built to give shelter to pilgrims and sick people by Bishop Masona, who died in 605 (Mateos 1992):

> *Deinde xinodocium fabricauit magnisque patrimoniis ditauit constitutisque ministris vel medicis, peregrinorum et egrotantium husibus deseruire precepit* (*VSPE*, V. 3).

The pious author gives more details on the largesses of Masona. We are told, for example, that the bishop provided the basilica of Saint Eulalia with 2000 *solidi*. These funds were destined to give loans, after acknowledging receipt (*facta cautione*), to people who needed money urgently {*aliquis urguente necessitate adueniret* (*VSPE*, V. 3)}. The amount was possibly exaggerated, as observed by J. Arce (n.d.), but the practice in all likelihood existed.

The author also mentions the *thesauri* belonging to St Eulalia and St Iherusalem (*VSPE*, V. 6), and the carts transporting silver (*argentum copiosum*) and *ornamentum insignia* that the bishop Nepopis tried surreptitiously to remove when he ran away from Mérida (*VSPE*, V. 8).

Merchants coming from remote regions, a bishop paying lavishly for his nephew, magnificent buildings, amounts of money, luxury goods.... Both the *VSPE* and the archaeological reports provide us with plenty of signs of what is commonly known as 'wealth'.

This notion, as widely accepted but rarely argued, is often considered a measure of 'prosperity', for wealth, it can be assumed, embodies that part of the social production beyond the necessities of subsistence, so-called 'surplus'. Wealth is, therefore, thought to be a function of 'surplus', the latter being thus considered as the necessary and suitable condition from which wealth would *naturally* arise.[2]

The aim of this paper is firstly to try to highlight the scope and the significance of what we accordingly might call 'wealth'. To start with, I will discuss the building initiatives promoted by authorities, mainly bishops and kings, the diverse types of commerce, and the uses of money in the Visigothic period. Possibly, these three items represent some of the more conspicuous displays of 'wealth'. Lastly, the origins of 'wealth' will be discussed in the light of the Visigothic fiscal system.

---

[2] This supposed explanatory capacity of the notion of 'surplus' was strongly criticized by H. W. Pearson (1957), and G. Dalton (1960). The uncritical use of 'surplus' can obscure, first, the ways of controlling and capturing work—mainly peasant work—and secondly, the process by which the re^{...} of this capture were converted into wealth. In this sense, G. Dalton put into question that the 'e of "rulers, armies, priests, and other non-food producers" was attributable to the mere ty of a presumed pre-existing 'surplus', and stated that the use of this notion "as a cause of does not tell us how the surplus was caused" (1960:389-90).

Toledo was designated *sedes regia* by King Liuvigild in 580. In the last quarter of the sixth century there were two cathedrals, four abbeys, and one basilica, plus the important monastery of Agali {*pepinière d'évêques* (Ewig 1963:32)} outside the walls of the city (P. C. Díaz 1987:165-6). Also, written sources attest the existence of a *palatium* (Olmo 1992:348). The association of an ecclesiastical building, a basilica, and the *palatium* has also been found in Reccopolis (Olmo 1986; 1988; 1992), the short-lived city founded in 578 by King Liuvigild. According to John of Biclar, bishop of Gerunda, works to embellish the walls and the *suburbia* of the city were carried out at this time. The hoard of 90 gold coins found in the basilica (Barral 1976:86-92; Beltran 1972) seems to reflect the concentration of wealth in the city and its attachement to the Church.

Both the existence of *palatii* in different towns {those from Oviedo and Córdoba should be added to the list (Olmo 1992)}, and the proliferation of ecclesiastical buildings would clearly indicate that the case of Mérida was not unique, though it probably was the most conspicuous. These religious centres are normally considered as the focusses for concentrated population {the above mentioned "punti forti" (Cantino 1995:255; L. A. García 1977/78:319-21)}, as well as, more generally, the foundations causing the transformation of the urban layout and the creation or the revival of parts of the town. The same might allegedly apply to the countryside, where monasteries could be the *leitmotiv* for the organization of settlement (Gurt *et al.* 1994:169).

Both the proliferation (although the magnitude of this process has not been properly discussed) and the assumed leading position of religious foundations are usually referred to as 'Christianization'. This notion, however, only considers the resulting and self-evident dimension of a process that can scarcely be understood through this term. In other words, 'Christianization' might account for the importance of St Eulalia or for the virtuous influences of Bishop Paul, for example, but it is clearly of no use to properly understand the origin of the *pecuniam copiosam* paid by Paul for Fidelis, the 2000 *solidi* endowed to the basilica of St Eulalia, or the funds or the slaves needed to build up and sustain the magnificent *xenodochium*, and so on. 'Christianization' then only leaves room to stress how essential sainthood is to society:

> Mais on n'a sans doute pas marqué assez que la ville reste ou devient un lieu de sainteté aussi essentiel à la société que le monastère au milieu des champs ou dans une île (Février 1989:1392).

The *negotiatores* of the *VSPE* had indeed their audience with the bishop in the *atrium*. As it has been recently pointed out, the *atrium* was not the *palatium* itself, but a specific place of ceremony where the bishop showed himself and his entourage in solemn events. It was, then, an area in which the authority of the bishop, beyond his religious influence, was put on stage (Godoy 1995:135-7). One of these performances was the distribution of wine, oil, and honey *civibus urbis aut rusticis de ruralibus* (*VSPE*), following thus a tradition rooted in the Roman *curiae* (Godoy 1995:136).[3]

---

[3] In the same sense, P. C. Díaz has remarked that *magnanimitas* and *munificencia* were manifestations of lay powers, and not originally Christian virtues (1993:166).

Unless we accept the idea that the Church and its dwellings were sustained by offerings and legacies voluntarily made by its adherents, we have to admit that the basis of the wealth and the power of the bishops of Mérida or wherever could hardly have been different from that of the kings and the other Visigothic *magnates.*[4] The origin of this wealth is a matter which 'Christianization' obscures.

Apparently, the presence of *negotiatores* in *Hispania* was not an uncommon event during the Visigothic period. Besides the report given by the *VSPE,* there are some documentary references to the presence of *transmarini negotiatores* between the fifth and the seventh centuries. For example, Hydatius reports in his *Continuatio* on the arrival of *orientalium naves* in *Hispalis* in 456 (*Fontes Hispaniae antiquae,* IX.77; *cf.* De Palol 1950:141-2; L. A. García 1972:137). Likewise, four *Antiquae* contained in the *Lex Visigothorum* demonstrate the interest of the Visigothic state in legislating on the activities of these *negotiatores* (*LV* XI, 3; XII, 2. 18).[5]

L. A. García (1972) stressed the importance and spread of colonies of Oriental merchants. This author compiled scattered references to people arriving from the East, as well as the diverse epigraphical, archaeological, and numismatic Byzantine, or Byzantine-fashioned, remains found in some places in *Hispania.* According to him, this record proved the existence of a network of Syrian and Jewish colonies carrying on trading activities. In the same sense, P. de Palol pointed out the 'Mediterranean' features of Visigothic bronzes from the beginning of the eighth century, and attributed this influence to a 'constant' trade between the western shore of the Mediterranean and Byzantium (1950:113-4). More recently, finds of Byzantine and Vandalic coins have been also interpreted in the same way (Gurt & Marot 1994).

There seems to be, therefore, little reason to doubt the arrival of *graeci* in *Hispania* during the Visigothic period. The question remains, however, of the magnitude and the significance of this transfer of goods, men, and knowledge. First, *graecus* does not necessarily mean 'merchant'. Bishop Paul was *graecus,* but we are told that he came to Mérida as *peregrinus nihilque habens* (*VSPE,* IV. II. 18). Recently, J. Arce has argued that the *negotiatores* mentioned by the *VSPE* were also pilgrims themselves (Arce n.d.). This religious, but perhaps not unique, motive is also attested in some references gathered by L. A. García. For example, one of these alludes to the arrival to *Tarraco* of monks *qui ex clero graecorum veniunt* (1972:133). Now the question is whether monks or clergymen would have been involved in trade. Late Roman documentation certifies the frequent participation of monks in petty market activities, according to C. R. Whittaker: *emere aut vendere, ut plerisque monachis moris est* (*Sulp. Sev. v. Mart.* X. 6; *cf.* Whittaker 1983:169). In this sense, by the canon XIX of the Council of Elvira (*ca* 305-310), *episcopi, presbyteres et diacones* were prohibited from leaving their *loca*

---

[4]   Although documentation witnesses and stresses the importance of the offerings made by good-willing contributors (*Formulae,* VIII, IX, XXI; P. C. Díaz 1987; 1989:50-7; Gil 1972).

[5]   A. D'Ors attributed these laws to Euric (*ca* 476) (1958:468; 1960:4). Also, authorities tried to keep the rivers (*flumina maiora*) in good conditions for sailing (*LV* VIII, 4. 29).

for business (*negotiandi causa*) or to search out lucrative markets (*quaestosas nundinas sectentur*) by wandering about the *provinciae* (*circumentes provincias*). Instead, their business should be carried out by tied agents, *aut libertum aut mercenarium aut amicum aut quemlibet mittant* (Vives 1963:5; a better understanding in Arce 1993). These documentary mentions seem to indicate that, although the religious certainly undertook market activities, they tended to do it through middlemen, at least in the case of long-distance transactions. These references, although corresponding to an earlier period, run against the possibility that the monks mentioned by L. A. García (1972) would also have been merchants.

The epigraphical remains found in Tortosa, Ilici, Malaka, Astigi, etc., however, seem to offer much clearer signs of the existence of Oriental colonies in *Hispania*. The foundation of trade missions by distinguished communities is a well-known phenomenon.[6] In all likelihood, most of the Jewish communities settled in *Hispania* participated in trading or commercial activities. In this sense, Egica's law of 693 prohibiting the presence of Jews in the *cataplus* leaves no ground to doubt that they, as supposedly many others, effectively dealt with commodities in the market. But one must recognize that the legal sources mentioning Jews in a bad light can offer no proper idea of the scale of the trading activities they carried out. The more so if one considers that these laws can even give a distorting view, for, as in the case of the law of 693, these provisions were issued in an atmosphere of 'eschatological tenseness' in *Hispania*—and in Byzantium—at the end of the eighth century (Gil 1977). Moreover, as stated by A. & S. Sherratt, "...trading diasporas...are usually a temporary phenomenon...", and, "ethnically distinctive enclaves may continue to exist even when trade is no longer predominantly in their hands" (1991:356).

It is likely, therefore, that these onomastic and epigraphical remains from the fourth to the sixth centuries reflect the existence of oriental enclaves formerly engaged in trading activities, but not necessarily doing so currently. Significantly, there are no references to these 'colonies' during the seventh century (L. A. García 1972:154).[7]

Unfortunately, the *VSPE* does not inform us about the goods transported by the *negotiatores*, nor on the number and features of the ships, nor on the composition of the crew. We are only told that Fidelis was a *mercennarius*.[8] As for the goods, an *Antiqua* of the *Lex Visigothorum* records the products which *transmarini negotiatores* dealt with: *aurum, argentum, uestimenta uel quelibet ornamenta*

---

[6] For the Mediterranean Bronze Age, A. & S. Sherratt (1991); more generally, Curtin (1984). The closed character of these communities, on the other hand, favoured coalitions between traders, eased the circulation of trustworthy information, and thereby benefited transactions (Torras 1993:16-7).

[7] In the case of early medieval Gaul, J.-P. Devroey has recently pointed out, in the same sense, that, "Le concept de 'colonies' s'applique donc assez mal, dans l'état actuel de nos connaissances, aux implantations grecques ou syriennes de la Gaule médiévale" (1995:55).

[8] On the *mercennarius*, D'Ors (1958:480 n70), with bibliography.

(*LV* XI, 3).[9] The generic term of *ornamenta* probably referred to objects such as liturgical bronzes made in Italy from the sixth and the beginning of the seventh centuries (De Palol 1950; L. A. García 1972:142), or to jars such as that found at El Bovalar (Segrià, Lleida), made in a Coptic workshop (De Palol 1986; 1989:11).

Probably, the list of goods mentioned in this *Antiqua* is not exhaustive, but it does suggest a limited number of products exchanged.[10] According to A. D'Ors, other items should be added: slaves, wine, spices, and papyrus.[11] Anyhow, it seems that massive imports of foodstuffs were not common.[12] Instead, the goods mentioned in the *Lex Visigothorum* coincide with those imported to Amalfi from Egypt (spices and gold), and from Byzantium: "ceremonial clothes, eastern goods, jewels and 'objets d'art'" (Citarella 1968:533).

The seventh-century shipwreck at Yesi Ada (Turkey) and the ninth-century representations of Byzantine vessels allow a fairly accurate reconstruction of the ships on which the *transmarini negotiatores* sailed. They probably were

> ...less than 250 tons deadweight tonnage, were powered by a single lateen sail, were steered by two steering oars on the stern quarters, had curved stemposts and sternposts giving the hull configuration a rounded look, and had no deep keel (Pryor 1993:27-8).

We are far from the large corn ships of the Roman Empire carrying more than 300 tons of wheat (Garnsey 1983:124). It does not mean, however, that these small ships were not known and used during the Roman period. Wrecks from the first and second centuries found along the Catalan coast show vessels having a 9-10 m hull able to carry less than 10 tons, without deep keel to ease navigation in shallows, and with 'open' stems and sterns wich allowed embarking and landing at both ends of the ship (Casanovas & Rovira 1994). The ships of the *transmarini negotiatores* of the *VSPE* were thus probably built following a "classical tradition" "which began before 1400 BC..." and "lasted into the Byzantine period or even

---

[9] Isidore (*Etym.*, XIX-XXII, 21) also mentions the exotic clothes worn by pilgrims (*exotica vestis peregrina deforis veniens, ut in Hispania a Graecis*), but it seems to be an ethnographical comment, rather than a description of the traded *uestimenta*.

[10] Against the opinion of A. D'Ors (1958:474).

[11] The importance of the traffic in slaves has been recently stressed by B. F. Reilly in a book pointlessly entitled *The Medieval Spains* (1993). According to this author, "the only flourishing international trade was that in slaves from Slavic territories beyond the Elbe which found its way through Frankish Gaul in the Mediterranean (1993:24). The fact that "the most numerous finds of Visigothic coins outside of the realm itself have been in the Rhineland" would confirm this origin (Reilly 1993:24). If any, the validity of this assertion would be restricted to the case of the coins struck before the year 575 (see the maps of the distribution of coin finds in Barral 1976:147, 153).

[12] One should note, however, the large quantities of North African amphorae in the East of *Hispania* from the second half of the fifth to the mid sixth century, which suggest an "exceptional supply of Alicante and North-Eastern Spain" (Reynolds 1995:133-8, esp. 137; also Carandini 1983; Jarrega 1987; and Gutiérrez who considers the existence of a *gran relación comercial con el norte de África y con Oriente* 1995:178)

later" (McGrail 1991:84). This meant they did not have suitable attributes for open sea navigation, but for coastal voyages in sight of land.[13]

Apart from the constraints related to the small size of the ships and the problems derived from the normally high stowage-factor of luxuries (McGrail 1991:85), shipping patterns were conditioned, above all, by the meteorological and oceanographic characteristics of the Mediterranean. Thus, winds and maritime tides made voyages from south to north and from east to west much more difficult. That is why probably the *transmarini negotiatores* followed the safer and quicker route along the northern coast of the sea (Pryor 1993: xvii, 7, 87-90). On the other hand, navigation was almost non-existent in winter, as attested by a source of the fifth century reporting that the sea was closed from 11 November to 10 March (Pryor 1993:87). Moreover, the *Calendar of Córdoba* also records that navigation was avoided for 49 days from 7 March onwards, and that it was reputedly done *secundum intentionem Romanorum* (Pellat 1961:54-5).

All this leaves little room for thinking of a massive trade between the East and *Hispania* during the Visigothic period. Trade there certainly was, but it was concentrated in a few months of the year. Moreover, it involved a narrow range of high cost items which were carried in small ships. Finally, people voyaging on these ships might have been not only *negotiatores*, but they could have been mainly pilgrims and *legati*, as discussed below.

There are plenty of signs that in ancient societies trade was not the purpose behind the long-distance movement of luxury goods, normally referred to as *grand commerce*. For example, it is known that merchants from Ugarit in the Bronze Age also performed diplomatic functions (Knapp 1991:49). Similarly, *mercatores* voyaging between Persia and Rome were also considered as *legati* (Whittaker 1983:167). In 942, Amalfitan merchants (*malfatanin*) arrived to Qurtuba for the first time, according to Ibn Ḥayyân. Five months later, they came back accompanying an envoy of the lord of Sardinia and bringing "their precious merchandises: ingots of pure silver, brocades..." (*Muqtabis V*:365; transl. Barceló 1983:57).

Therefore, the movement of valuables from one place to another could have had a significance that was uncommercial, or more than commercial, depending on the purposes of the voyagers. For these non-commercial reasons, anthropologists have widely discussed the importance of gift-exchange as a way to redistribute wealth (Grierson 1961; Mauss 1966; Sawyer 1977, with bibliography). These movements of goods, normally called *munuscula* in early medieval sources (Grierson 1961:358), might have had, however, a political rather than redistributive dimension. In this sense, É. Benveniste pointed out that originally the gift:

---

[13] This type of seafaring was practised later on, in al-Andalus, by 'people from the sea', *baḥriyyūn*, whose activities were not inserted in any state organization until the sultan's intervention in the tenth century. The end of these *baḥriyyūn* coincided with the increasing dominion of the sea by the Italian cities, fairly evidenced in the attack and plunder of al-Mahdiyya and its suburb Zawīla in 1087 led by Pisans and Genoese (Ballestín, forthcoming; Barceló 1984a; Cowdrey 1977).

...c'est un don en tant que prestation contractuelle, imposée par les obligations d'un pacte, d'une alliance, d'une amitié, d'une hospitalité: obligation du *xeînos* (de l'hôte), des sujets envers le roi et le dieu, ou encore prestation impliquée par une alliance (Benveniste 1969:69).

The pacts involved in this conception of 'gift' were not only established between political powers clearly recognizable as states. This assumption is confirmed by many examples from different ancient societies, showing that agreements were also the principal and recurrent way, altogether with military pressure, to link alternative political forms to the state. B. D. Shaw has pointed out that the Roman state negotiated fiscal and military agreements with *gentes* located in the twilight zones where its control was seldom effective, whether in *Mauretania Tingitana*, in the mountains of *Isauria-Cilicia* in Anatolia, or in Gaul (Shaw 1986). One is struck by the recurrent difficulties that administrative staffs had in understanding these social organizations, and the way in which state officers frequently described the representatives or notable members of the communities they were dealing with as *seniores*, *principes* or *reges* (Shaw 1986:72). Thus, for example, the extension of royal authority by Liuvigild entailed the subjugation of a *senatus Cantabriae*, as well as the surrender of Aepidius, *senior loci* in the *Aregenses montes* (*Vita Aemiliani*; cf. Collins 1980:190).[14] Although the contents of such pacts obviously were different, the ritualistic sequence of the agreements was always the same:

> ...the negotiated agreement or *pax* struck between the two sides was formalized at a *colloquium* set up by *legati* from in either side...the *pax* or final agreement was then sealed by an exchange of *pisteis* or *pistia* (objects of good faith), by ritualistic gestures (such as the exchange of 'right hands'), and by the trading of hostages (Shaw 1986:80).

The achievement of the *pax*, understood as the variable involvement of *gentes* in fiscal networks and military organization, is also documented in the Visigothic period. Julian tells how *dux* Paul tried to obtain the help of Franks and Basques against King Wamba "by gifts and promises". The same author informs us about Wamba's campaign against the Basques. The king:

> *cum omni exercitu Vasconiae partes ingreditur...unde, acceptis obsidibus tributisque solutis, pace composita...*(Hist. Wamb., 10).

The fiscal significance of the *pax* imposed after the king "plundered the countryside and burned the houses...until the Basques of the locality gave hostages and gifts" is clear (Thompson 1969:221).

This political background to the movement of valuables is also attested in al-Andalus, during the Umayyad caliphate, when silk clothes from the *ṭiraz*, luxurious swords, *dīnâr*-s, horses, etc, were sent to the Berbers, who would, therefore, allow the circulation of the Umayyad coinage in the Maghreb (*Muqtabis*

---

[14] See also, M. Barceló (1984b:77-87) for the case of the treaty between King Jaume I and eighteen *senes* (*šaykh*-s, elders) and *sapientes* (*'alīm*-s, learned) in thirteenth-century Minorca.

VII, 166-7 (transl.); *Muqtabis V* 229, 334 (transl.). At this stage one should stress that valuables circulating in these political transfers are generally goods monopolized by the states in question. These goods normally related to the most common needs, e.g. clothing and food, become exclusive objects through this monopolized production, which does not necessarily imply direct control of all the phases of the production processes. It is precisely these distinctive features, the unequivocal fingerprints of power, that embody their social acknowledgement as 'wealth'. Behind the seemingly innocuous notion of 'luxuries' there lies, in many cases, the force to create exclusivity out the most common and daily objects. 'Wealth' thereby comes from authority. The workshop of liturgical bronze plates and vessels (De Palol 1950:105-7, 159-62) or the palace goldsmith's workshop founded by King Liuvigild in Toledo (Orlandis 1977:196) are examples of this exclusive production of a limited number of goods circulating in restricted circles.

That is not to deny, however, the possible commercial motives of the voyage of the *transmarini negotiatores* mentioned in the *VSPE*, but to suggest that their concerns might have been other than those generally attributed to mere merchants. Besides the possibility that they were pilgrims—or also pilgrims—as bishop Paul formerly was (Arce n.d.), they also might have been *legati*—or also *legati*—performing an ambassadorial function. In any case, Bishop Paul showed a great interest in these *negotiatores*. Both the fact that he ceremoniously received them in the *atrium* and the sending of *munuscula* by Fidelis—although eventually they did not suffice—fit well into both explanations of the voyage, political or commercial. The *negotiatores* acted as middlemen attached to the authorities: as envoys with diplomatic concerns and/or as agents involved in trading activities tied to, and controlled, by the bishop of *Emerita* and his entourage. The Church performed thus the same role in long-distance trade as the emperor and his court during the later Empire.[15]

In ancient societies, authorities generally favoured the activities of those agents, protecting them and even, if that be the case, forcing them to stop at the harbour.[16] Taxing purposes rather than the possibility of obtaining exotica or other merchandise are discernible behind this interest of authorities in trade. It is what M. Hendy accurately described as "the absolute control of trading time and space specifically geared to taxation" (Hendy 1993:336; Sawyer 1977:153). This control is fairly well illustrated by the *bandar*, 'quay of harbor, treasury, customs duty and storehouse', of the Malabar Coast described by Ibn Battûta {*Rihla*; Fanjul & Arbós (trans.) 1981:649}, and discussed by K. Polanyi (1968a:256-7).

---

[15] In spite of this replacement, however, "the institutions and even the practice of trade did not alter radically between the later Roman Empire and the Merovingian period" (Whittaker 1983:172, 179; on the attachement of the Jewish merchants to the Merovingian court, Devroey 1995:64-5; Laurent 1938:293; on "tied" and "controlled" trade, Hendy 1989a:14; 1993:335-7).

[16] As in the case of the city of Fakanawr in the fourteenth-century Malabar Coast, where ships were obliged to anchor at the harbour and to pay the *haqq al-bandar* {*Rihla*; Fanjul & Arbós (trans.) 1981:649; Polanyi 1968a:256}.

Trading activities thereby had to be confined to specific places to facilitate tax-collecting (Hodges & Whitehouse 1983:92; Sawyer 1977:151). These places were thus centers whose existence was attached to the presence of an administration controlling trading activities, in the same way that other public, open spaces in late antique and early medieval towns only survived if they were "protected by an active and vigilant civic authority" (Kennedy 1985:18).

In Visigothic *Hispania*, fiscal control of trade took place at the *teloneum*, the ubiquituous tax-office, and at the *cataplus*. As described above, Visigothic rulers legislated on the trading activities of the *transmarini negotiatores*. The first of the *Antiquae* mentioned above ordered that the sale of the specified goods (*aurum, argentum, vestimenta vel quelibet ornamenta*) done by a *transmarinus negotiator provincialibus nostris* had to be accepted as legal if the price of the sale was correct (*conpetenti pretio*), even in the case that the mentioned goods had been obtained by robbery (*si furtiva postmodum fuerint adprobata*). In his comment on this law, A. D'Ors pointed out the necessary conditions for a transaction to be legal: it should take place at the *cataplus* with the intervention of a *negotiator*, and the price payed for the good should be, according to him, "reasonable" and "moderate". A. D'Ors stressed that this expression did not carry the meaning of a "regulated price" set by the authorities, as happened, for example, in Byzantium and in ninth-century Italy where miners and washers were compelled to sell metal "at an appropiate price" to the administration (Hendy 1989b:17; López 1953:20). But, in spite of the hesitation of A. D'Ors, Isidore's description of the *teloneum* clearly attests the intervention of tax-officers on prices: *ibi (teloneum) enim vectigalis exactor sedet pretium rebus impositurus* (*Etym.*, XV. II. 45). This intervention, in fact, was a requirement which followed from the basic mechanics of fiscality, for prices were the necessary basis upon which taxes were assessed. In sum, it is reasonable to think of *ancient* prices as an effect of fiscal structures, and not as the result of an allegedly spontaneous concurrence of supply and demand. That is not to deny, however, that rarity, a quality embedded in the goods not necessarily consequent upon shortage, but on the narrow and restrictive conditions of their circulation, had some influence in the setting of prices, but it is to stress that prices in state-controlled trading centres were an administrative affair and resulted from fiscal provisions.[17]

Frequently, both 'long-distance' and 'local' trade are considered as embodying two different types of activity emerging from a unique human "propensity to barter, truck, and exchange".[18] Consequently, 'trade' is considered a single notion comprising a wide range of levels whose description—analysing distance,

---

[17] Moreover, the intervention of the Visigothic administration through the legal—and fiscal—device of the *competentia pretia* could entail the reselling of the goods previously bought at a 'moderate' price. Karl Polanyi (1957a) also attributed the setting of prices to administrative intervention on trade, but he did not consider the fiscal motives for such interventions.

[18] See the criticisms to this assumption made by H. W. Pearson (1957:329), K. Polanyi (1957b), and more recently, J. Torras (1993).

magnitude and value attributed to the goods involved, and the means of payment used—seems to be the main and, in some cases, even the sole concern of historical or archaeological study.

Such a conception of trade is mostly visible in the attempts to link every supposed level of trade with its corresponding—and, therefore, considered appropriate—monetary tool. This alleged adequacy implies the existence of as many diverse categories of monetary tools as there were levels of trading activitity in actual operation. That is, since exchange ranged from the every-day, most ordinary transactions to luxury commodities, precise monetary means were required, namely base-metal issues for petty commerce, gold coins for larger transactions, and silver for the 'middle-range' level of exchanges. There are plenty of examples of that. Thus, C. Howgego has recently suggested that later Roman gold issues were "suitable for larger transactions and unsuitable for small ones" (1992:11). It has been similarly argued that Merovingian gold coinage before *ca* 670, because of its high value, could hardly have performed functions apart from the "purchase of landed estates, of slaves and luxury imports". In the same way, silver *denarii* have been thought to have been mostly used for petty commerce during the last phase of the Merovingian period (Grierson & Blackburn 1986:95). The same has been said of the Vandalic silver coinage, considered the *monnaie courante* (Morrisson 1989:520). Similarly, Carolingian silver issues in Italy during the ninth century have been regarded as the optimum means to match the saving capacity of the "rural world" with "actual forms of exchange", and enabling a "certain degree of monetization of rent" (Toubert 1990:136)).

Sometimes, however, a monetary type is considered capable of satisfying a wide range of 'economic needs'. For example, it has been normally thought that Visigothic gold issues could hardly have been used as an adequate medium for whichever type of transaction, "because the value of the unit was much too high" (Metcalf 1988:15). That is why single-finds of Visigothic *tremisses* are considered as "mini-hoards", rather than accidental losses (Marques 1988:79; Metcalf 1986:317). However, at the same time the large number of coin-finds in the countryside (Barral 1976; Marques 1988) would also indicate, according to D. M. Metcalf, that "...coinage was being handled by people of a quite ordinary social level, and was not confined to the towns" and, therefore, "it is difficult to envisage any alternative explanations other than *the ordinary purposes of monetary exchange*" (Metcalf 1988:24, 32; my emphasis).

Thus we are led to think that Visigothic coins represented a "sound money" (I take the expression from Metcalf 1986:137), for they not only had to do with "the life of populous and wealthy cities", but they were used also in small places in the countryside (Metcalf 1988:21, 24). The pieces found in three houses at El Bovalar (Segrià. Lleida) have been interpreted in the same way (De Palol 1986:1989).

However, this interpretation that the Visigothic gold coinage performed a wide range of functions might be challenged, at least in some areas, by the recent identification of some bronze issues attributed to the Visigoths, which, according to M. Crusafont, would have been used as *pequeño numerario complementario*, mainly needed by *los estamentos comerciales de las ciudades de una cierta entidad* (Crusafont 1994:64-5). Obviously, all these considerations derive from the assumption that each monetary type, as defined by its metal content, would presumably have its corresponding purchasing capacity.

It seems then clear that these alleged monetary 'needs' attached to every level of exchange imply that both trade and money are conceived of as single notions embodying, respectively, different types of exchanges and monetary tools hierarchically arranged. It was precisely this conception and the recurrent mingling of trade and money that K. Polanyi criticized forty years ago.

Gift trade, administered trade and market trade were considered by Karl Polanyi to be not merely levels of the same basic activity, but distinct concepts involving different contents, functions and origins (Polanyi 1957b:262). These forms of trade might be ultimately reduced to two: marketless and market trading activities, the former being carried out by ancient states through systems of equivalences, and the latter corresponding to the dominant institution of the nineteenth century, the market, in which prices were determined by supply and demand (1957b:263). This discussion of trade was significantly followed by what Polanyi conceived of as the dichotomy between "all-purpose" *versus* "special-purpose" money (1968b). Among his contributions, one should stress two points: first, that trade should be regarded as a set of activities carried on in substantially different institutions; second, that trade, or 'trades', and money should be considered as separate institutions not necessarily conceptually intermingled. Polanyi referred to this as "the thesis of the *separate origins of external and internal trade, money, and markets* {Polanyi's emphasis (1968b:191)}.

Hopefully, this view should prevent what Karl Polanyi qualified as "modernizing approach to the problem", (1968b:181; see also Sawyer 1977:145). But, whether "modernizing" or not, the point is that many historians, archaeologists and numismatists stubbornly continue to match types of trade with types of coins.

Apart from protecting, promoting, and taxing long-distance trade, authorities could attempt to extend their control over all kind of exchanges, realizing the above mentioned "absolute control of trading time and space" (Hendy 1993:336). This purpose is fairly well illustrated by the *Novella* 15 of 444-45 issued by Valentinian III. This law contemplated that a *siliqua* per *solidus* should be levied *on every sale*, and, moreover, that transactions could only be held "at a defined place and time, through the decision of office-holders" (Hendy 1993:335).

Similarly, in ninth-century Mercia, royal authority extended its control from long-distance trading activities to "all buying and selling" in local market transactions (Sawyer 1977:153). The question, however, should not be regarded as the mere extension of the state taxes on new trading activities; above all, control over local exchange is closely related to the fundamental ability of the state to build up a broad fiscal network to capture and transform peasant work.

The extension of state control over local market transactions, as in the case of ninth-century Mercia discussed by Peter Sawyer (1977), poses the question of institutions involving exchanges whose existence could precede the intervention of any authority identified either by written sources or by the archaeological record. These institutions were recognizable in complex networks of markets held at fixed days. The schedule of different weekly, monthly, or annual assemblies implied a strict and thorough control both of time and of the places as to avoid interferences with nearby markets (Shaw 1981:45). Reasonably, the explanation of these different frequencies should be sought in the different and rigid rhythms determined by the peasant calendar. That is, their understanding is dependent upon the understanding of peasant logics.

As stated by Sawyer, these institutions were recognizable "in all parts of Europe—and beyond—both Roman and non-Roman": the Roman *nundinae* (Arce 1993; Frayn 1993; McMullen 1979), the Irish *oenach* (Sawyer 1977, with bibliography), or the Berber *sūq* (Benet 1957; Shaw 1981; Troin 1975) in the *siba* country (the land of perpetual dissidence) are examples of the spread and steadiness of these peasant assemblies. Sawyer also stressed that barter might be the prevailing method of exchange in these often 'coinless societies', and linked the absence of coins to the elaborate systems of gift-exchange, etc. which have been widely studied by anthropologists (Sawyer 1977:144).

Whatever the ways goods moved, however, the question now is the frequently neglected political dimension of these complex institutions. Studies of North African *nundinae* during the Roman period and of Berber modern *sūq*-s (Benet 1957; Shaw 1981; Troin 1975) oblige us, however, not to forget this dimension. 'Local' or, better, peasant markets indeed involved movements of goods, but they were also the central nodes connecting different peasant groups;[19] and moreover, the holding of these *fairs* constituted the most conspicuous display of complex forms of peasant management: setting rules, measures and devices to assess values and reckon time.

The example of extended royal control in ninth-century Mercia illustrates how authorities have always shown a fiscal interest in exchange, whether far-reaching or 'local'. Arguably, this recurrent concern to control exchange was due to the fact that the amount of fiscal revenue obtained from trading activities depended less on the nature of the goods traded than on the different ranges of operation entailed by the movement of products (whether barter, sales, loans, currency exchanges, etc.). Authorities should have been interested in increasing both the quantity of transactions and the number of ancillary operations. Ideally, this multiplication of trading activities to be systematically taxed needed to be concentrated into fewer places to make fiscal intervention easier. Hence, the fourteenth-century *bandar* on

---

[19] The discovery of single-finds of Arabic coins at Sant Rafel, in the island of Eivissa, along with additional evidence, suggests the existence of a rural market there between the end of the tenth and the twefth century (Retamero 1995). These coins would attest the inclusion of the peasant market in the fiscal mechanics; however, arguably its origin should be explained according to the peasant and political dimensions of the networks of settlements (*qarya*-s) linked to that market-place and market-time. On these Arabic and Berber peasant settlements in Eivissa, see Barceló (1997).

the coast of Malabar, Hamwic, Dorestad, the Visigothic *cataplus*, the *Novella* of Valentinian III, and the Babylonian *kar*.

Similarly, the extension of control over peasant trade entailed in many cases both the concentration and the numerical reduction of market places. A clear example of this practice was the simplification of the "complex geography of markets" in North Africa persistently carried on both by the Roman (Shaw 1981), and by the French colonial administration (Troin 1975:257). Possibly, both this repeated interest in taxing whatever movement of goods there was together with any attached operations, and the noticeably recurrent ways of achieving this goal, may have given the impression that such similarities would automatically correspond to institutions which were also substantially alike. That is to say, the overwhelming uniformity of intervention would have pervaded the regulated institutions so as to obscure their particular origins and characteristics. Therefore, it is reasonable to think that trade in its simplest form, meaning the mere movement of goods, would follow from the enhancement of the control of these institutions favoured by authorities. By the same token, the fact that 'local'-peasant trade institutions are so rarely mentioned in late antique and early medieval sources might reflect the extent to which state control of such local activities was incomplete or ineffective, whereas the relative abundance of references to centres related to long-distance trade would suggest that, in this area, actual state control was fully exercised. Nevertheless, such a notion would only account for one of the aspects involved in trade, precisely that privileged by the fiscal needs of the states.

This conception of trade does not simply represent another "modernizing approach to the problem". Isidore's testimony shows how the reduction of trading activities to mere buying and selling was related to state intervention. The illustrious bishop considered that, *"Mercatum autem a conmercio nominatum. Ibi enim res vendere vel emere solitum est"*, and immediately after he described the *teloneum* as the place where, among other things, *vectigalis exactor sedet pretium rebus inpositurus* (*Etym.*, XV. II. 45).

In all likelihood then, Isidore conceived *vendere* and *emere* as activities involving the use of money. In other words, he regarded trade with the eyes of a tax-officer. The *Codex Euricianus* attests the different meanings of *conmutatio* and *emptio* by equating the legality of both operations: *conmutatio talem qualem emptio habeat firmitatem* (*CE* CCLXLIII; D'Ors 1960:29). Doubtlessly, what made them different was the presence of monetary means in the latter. This tight relationship between 'selling' and money is sharply illustrated by the juridical distinction between 'barter' (*cambio*) and 'sale' (*vendida*) established in the medieval *Fuero Real* (III. 2. 1):

> ...ca si alguno da a otro cavallo por cavallo, o por mula, o da otra cosa cualquier por otra cosa que no diese dineros, esto es cambio, e no es vendida: mas doquier que se dé cosa cualquier por dineros, es vendida; y este es el departimiento entre la vendida y el cambio (Fernández 1955:373).

It is hard to know to what extent Visigothic authorities achieved a stable control of local trade as they probably did in the case of long-distance trade. Generally, sources are extremely elusive in this respect, although, as stated by Peter Sawyer, "After the collapse of Roman imperial authority in the West, local exchanges by barter or otherwise continued, although rarely mentioned in our sources" (Sawyer 1977:145).[20]

Possibly, hints of such institutions may be found in places where monasteries were established in the countryside. These may have been the cases of Melque (St. Martín de Montalbán, Toledo) and other monasteries and churches, and also the case of Reccopolis. According to L. Caballero, many of these centres were placed on crossroads and on pre-existing routes frequented by transhumant pastoralists. The same would apply to the site of Cancho del Confesionario {"probablemente en un paso ganadero" (Caballero 1989:75)}, where some fragments of Visigothic slates have also been found, and possibly to the sites of Navalvillar (Colmenar Viejo, Madrid), Perales del Río, and Aretxabaleta (Caballero 1988; 1989, with bibliography).

As suggested above, the control of local markets did not only make it possible to tax the movement of peasant products. Arguably, these institutions were not regarded by authorities as mere sources of revenues, but they could constitute the places, occupied and converted into monasteries and churches, where peasant production was captured and transformed into money.

As stated above, trade is thought to entail the need for an appropriate monetary means to match every level of trading activity. This systematic connection arises from the conception of the origins of money formulated by classical economics. Karl Polanyi described it as follows: at the beginning, "...the propensity to barter, truck, and exchange leads to individual acts of barter". As those acts increase, "...one of the commodities is adopted as 'money', on account of its suitability for indirect exchange" (Polanyi 1968b:195). Then, allegedly, precious metals having a commodity character were transformed to become metal money, and performed henceforward the functions as "means of payment", "standards of value", and "means of hoarding wealth or treasure" (Polanyi 1968b:196).

As far as this logical sequence, not necessarilly empirical, is considered a historical process (Polanyi 1968b:195), a different degree of social complexity is attributed to each 'logical-historical' step. This conception is embedded, for example, in the so-called dichotomy between 'natural economy' and 'money economy', the latter representing the uppermost level for it implies a higher degree of complexity than the former.[21]

A corollary of this would be that:

> ...those coin producers who are able to properly evaluate the different 'commercial needs' in any given society, and eagerly provide the adequate means to ensure the

---

[20] Probably the lack of references to these institutions impelled Karl Polanyi to think that "They cannot go unnoticed". It seems, however, that they really could; despite the fact that they "belong to the most penetrating everyday items of culture..." (Polanyi 1968a:256).

[21] Some historians and numismatists have obstinately ignored the criticism made more than sixty years ago by Maurice Bloch to this *pseudo-dilemme* (Bloch 1933).

exchanges, will succeed in enduring as the accepted or legitimate power (Barceló & Retamero 1996).

There is no need now to emphasize that ancient states were probably both incapable and unconcerned to put into circulation the suitable monetary means {e.g. see the criticisms by M. Hendy (1991)}.

In a recent article, M. Barceló and I have discussed what is defined as "the structure by which peasant work can be transformed into wealth through a disturbing social alchemy" (1996:56). The fundamental logic of this process is graphically presented as follows:

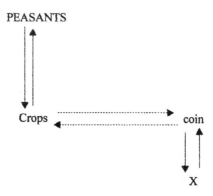

Fig. 8-1: Diagram of the relationship between crop and coin production.

This graph is intended to show the relationship between social subjects and their respective historical results. Then:

> ...a continuous line indicates a necessary relationship between different elements", whereas "a dotted line means that one element does not necessarily require the existence of the other. Peasant work is the center around which the whole revolves. At the oposite side of the graph, an unidentified subject [X] produces coins to enforce the relationship between peasant work and itself. In the middle of the schema there are the respective results of each social subject: crops and coins. This relationship, however, is far from being even. As the lines indicate, crops—the product of the peasant—do not necessarily require coins to ensure their existence. However, coins must be made exchangeable for crops to become money. Otherwise, they could never transcend their original condition as a product (Barceló & Retamero 1996:56).

The success of the intervention of X over peasant production, then, will be entirely dependent on "the ability of the coin producer to transform both coin and crops into money" (Barceló & Retamero 1996:56). Thus, volumes of coin production can be reasonably understood, in principle, as meaningful signs of such an extended control. Some case studies seem to confirm this basic connection between the size of coin issues and the scope of state intervention.[22]

As for the case of the Visigothic coin issues, no estimates of numbers of pieces struck are available.[23] The only known figure is that of the approximately 5000 surviving pieces corresponding to the period of the Visigothic regal coinage (*ca* 575-715). Despite the small size of the figure for a period of nearly 150 years— ridiculously low for Andalusian standards (e.g. Canto, Palou, Tortajada 1988), D. M. Metcalf has recently discussed the conditions which would explain the extremely low survival-rate of the specimens.

According to him, gold coins, the characteristic form of Visigothic issues, "generally have a very much lower loss-rate than silver" (Metcalf 1988). Moreover, future die studies are likely to confirm that "many thousands of dies were used" (Metcalf 1988:16-7). Even in the case that the social value of gold coins, the mechanism that allegedly would prevent high loss-rates, had resulted from the stuff they were made of,[24] and accepting that the number of dies used should tell its own tale,[25] the figure of 5000 surviving specimens for one century and a half in no way gives a sound ground to the optimistic consideration that "the Visigothic gold coins were produced in quantities totalling millions" (Metcalf 1988:17).

The fact that, in all likelihood, has caused D. M. Metcalf to envisage such an improbable quantity for Visigothic coin issues is the presence of currency in the countryside, as suggested by the distribution of coin finds in some areas. Thus, the use of coinage far beyond towns, as in the case of the Alentejo {"a peripheral region of the Visigothic kingdom" (Metcalf 1988:32)}, would supposedly reflect the wide scope of the monetary needs and therefore the enormous size of the issues.

The point at issue now does not concern the specific ways by which gold coins reached the countryside and were lost (or hoarded).[26] Clusterings of finds strongly suggest that coins were actually circulating in a monetary space understood as the sum of different factors: the monopoly over the assessment units, the determination of the monetary species being legal tender, and the establishment of

---

[22] See, for example, the case of tenth-century England (Sawyer 1977:154), and the unstable scope of state presence in the Balearic islands during the tenth-eleventh centuries, as suggested by coin finds (Retamero 1995).

[23] A recent approach to the relative numbers of circulating pieces can be found in Gomes, Peixoto & Rodrigues (1995).

[24] See the criticisms to this conception in Hennequin 1979.

[25] It is worth remembering that a die "is simply a tool", so that its activity may depend less on its technical capacity "that on the amount of bullion it is required to strike" (Grierson 1967:158).

[26] Whether their presence was due to military activities (questioned in Marques 1988) or whether they were carried by "merchants and other private individuals...buying and selling goods often over a distance" (Metcalf 1988:21).

ways and agents both to put them into circulation and to collect them (Aglietta & Orlean 1982:41, 44; Retamero 1995:25).[27]

As argued in a recent paper (Barceló & Retamero 1996), the text known as *De fisco Barcinonensi* (Vives 1963:54; see also Barbero & Vigil 1974:112-3; L. A. García 1971:244 ff.;Isla 1991:487-8; Thompson 1969:99) allows one to envisage the conditions for the making of a Visigothic monetary space.[28]

The text describes some of the basic operations carried out as part of the fiscal exercise. Firstly, Bishops Artemius, Sifronius, Galanus, and Ioannes, all of them *ad civitatem Barcinonense fiscum inferentes*, gave their consent to the instruction of the fiscal agents (*numerarii*) sent by Scipio, *comes patrimoniorum*. These orders consisted, in fact, of monetary assessments for taxed production, in this case, barley (*hordeum*). The basic measure used in the calculations was the legal, fiscal, bushel (*modio canonico*). This first evaluation served to establish further assessments for different fiscal concepts. (One should stress the coincidence, suggested above, of such an operation with the set of 'prices' in the *teloneum*). Then, the amount to be collected also had to take into consideration one extra *siliqua* for the work of each *numerarius* (*pro laboribus vestris siliquam unam*), and four *siliquae* for *inter pretia specierum*. One might wonder if this latter burden accounted for the losses derived from the existence of changeable and different levels of prices in non-controlled markets, or whether, in greater likelihood, these four *siliquae* were the added price for the further conversion of barley into money. Anyhow, all these fiscal assessments implied that the payment of the whole amount (fourteen *siliquae* for every nine-*siliquae modius*, taxes included), to be satisfied in the specific grain taxed (*inibi hordeo*), should include more than half a *modius* extra of barley for each basic fiscal-legal unit, the most important part of which was for the transformation of grain into coin.

The diagram of the Visigothic fiscal system suggested by this text may be represented by the graph of the following page.

As described in the *epistola*, the graph shows the involvement of the bishop (identified as *potentes*) in the fiscal process. Their participation was twofold and, apparently, somewhat contradictory, for they were held responsible for handing in taxes to the *fiscum* (*omnes episcopi ad civitatem Barcinonense fiscum inferentes*), and they had also to ensure the collection of crops. In other words, they were both subjects and high-status fiscal agents at the same time. It is easy to imagine the dramatic posibilities for fiscal evasion within this system.

Thus the connection between peasant production and coin supply did not entail any fiscal demand of actual coins from peasants, but from *potentes*. That is, coins

---

[27] However, it goes without saying that in some contexts coins by no means were considered monetary stuff; e.g. the Roman silver pieces in fifth-century *Britannia* (Blackburn 1988), or the *argentei* used to make necklaces found in burials in the area comprised by the rivers Rhine, Moselle, and Seine (Lafaurie 1987).

[28] The comments on this text closely follow the above mentioned study by M. Barceló and the author.

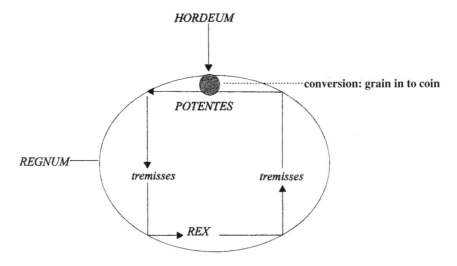

Fig. 8-2: Diagram of Visigothic fiscal system suggested by the preceding text.

did not meet peasant production at the lowest level of the fiscal process: the *numerarii* mentioned in the *epistola* collected (if they eventually succeeded in doing so) barley. This practice, contemplated in some *precariae*,[29] is also attested almost a century after the *epistola*, in Erwig's Edict of the XIII Council of Toledo (683): "...*fruges aridas et liquidas exinde in praeteritis annis unusquisque exactor collegit in ratione ipsius tributi...*" (Vives 1963:437). Coins then were *also* a tool in the hands of the king to dominate *potentes*.

Both the assessments of crops in terms of money and the legal-fiscal measure of capacity (*modio canonico*) embodying the instituted 'common language' were needed to generate a monetary space. This articulate administrative device accounted then, first, for the set of measures to individualize and to make workable units of account for peasant production, and second, for the necessary numerical values to evaluate these units (the 'price') and to carry on further taxing operations. Of course, coins were also assessed by means of the same monetary units, so as to make believe that both items, crops and coins, were exchangeable (Barceló & Retamero 1996).

It is precisely this phase of the whole process that eludes us, for the text of *De fisco Barcinonensi* does not inform us about who sold the grain, when, where, and to whom. But this operation must have happened, and in all likelihood the bishops who signed the *epistola* were involved in it. Otherwise, the transformation of crops into coins, and therefore, the conversion of both into money, would have been impossible. The fact that the assessments were calculated in monetary terms would, therefore, indicate that such an operation was already foreseen in the

---

[29] *Formulae*, XXXVI, XXXVII, Gil 1972:104-5: "*Et ideo spondeo me ut annis singulis secundum priscam consuetudinem de fruges aridas et liquidas atque uniuersa animalia uel pomaria seu in omni re....*"

arrangements made before the actual collection of taxes; otherwise, the subsequent burdens added to the initial *modio canonico* would have been reasonably expressed also in fractions of the legal measure of capacity, and not in monetary units.[30]

Buying and selling were therefore not only activities to be taxed, but operations by which crops and coins were converted one into the other, "only a way of making believe that both items were exchangeable" (Barceló & Retamero 1996). Apparently, then the movement could seem an exchange between different balanced goods. But, as the mentioned dispositions of the *Codex Euricianus* and the *Fuero Juzgo* highlighted, barter (*conmutatio*; cambio) and sale (*emptio*; vendida) were substantially different operations. And the difference did not arise from coins themselves, but from the conditions they embodied, that is, from those forming what was defined above as monetary space. The point is that these conditions did not result from social consensus; coins were not used in transactions as socially agreed 'sound' means of payment, in the same way that neither the *modio canonico*, nor *siliquae* were agreed measures.

Peasants then did not need to think of barley in terms of *siliquae* in so far as they did not need to handle coins to satisfy fiscal burdens (Barceló & Retamero 1996). But, of course, their production was "the center around which the whole articulation revolved" (Barceló & Retamero 1996). Some of the Visigothic slates found in the northern Meseta comprising lists of names and the duties of each person (M. C. Díaz 1966; Velázquez 1989; 1993) possibly attest the formative phase of the fiscal process, that is, that of the capture of peasant production. These documents include demands for crops expressed in *modii*, *sextarii*, etc., and, in the case of herds, both the number and the age of the specimens demanded are described in detail. There are also a few assessments in *solidi*, but *solidi* can hardly be considered a unit of account for cereals (otherwise, one must explain why two different sets of units were needed to reckon the same product) or, even more unlikely, for coins.

Therefore, as one may suggest from reading the *De fisco Barcinonensi*, the whole fiscal process was the outcome of linking two separate phases, namely the capture of peasant production, and its transformation into money. Obviously, the former was the principal one, but one may wonder at this stage whether any stable intervention in peasant production by recognizable and enduring organizations of non-producers would have been possible without the appropriate means to generate and to enforce the use of money.

Some hints suggest that the process failed more often than not during the Visigothic period. According to M. Hendy, the number of extant pieces minted by Reccared in *Barcinona* (no fewer than 26 *tremisses* recorded, contrasting with the

---

[30] This *by no means* signifies that monetary assessments always involved the use of coins. For example, the feudal sources of the tenth and eleventh-century Catalan counties include many references to *solidi*, *denarii*, etc. which however does not imply that coins were used (Retamero 1998).

13 specimens listed for the rest of the Visigothic period (Miles 1952:70-1, 202-4)) would indicate that an exceptional period of activity for this mint coincided with the issuing of the *epistola*. Therefore:

> There is in fact no clearer demostration of the direct connection between the extraction of state taxation, inevitably land tax, and the minting of coin, in the entire monetary history of the barbarian successor states, and fewer better examples of the general procedural continuity between those states and late Rome (Hendy 1989c:55).

It is precisely this exceptional production of coins, arguably attached to a momentary period of fiscal activity, which impels one to envisage an irregular effectiveness of the fiscal system in this area. In the same sense, the periodical cancellations of arrears in fiscal duties must be regarded as an acknowledgement of the failure of the state to ensure the steadiness of the fiscal practice.[31]

Whether the recurrent failures of the system were due to the reluctance of the *potentes* to contribute to the *fiscum*, or to difficulties in generating enduring and widespread links with peasant production or both, remains quite uncertain. The perpetual political conflicts between the king and the *gothi* clearly confirm the former. But it is equally clear that almost nothing is known either about the ways in which peasant production was captured or about the extent of this capture— even less on the organization of peasant production itself.

This limited scope of the Visigothic monetary circuit, as suggested here, would reliably account for the "structural thinness of Visigothic coin production", far below the quantities envisaged by Metcalf. Thus the low figures of surviving pieces would accurately reflect the reduced number of fiscal subjects responsible for handing over taxes in coin to the state (Barceló & Retamero 1996). It would follow, therefore, that the quantity of operations transforming crops into coins, and the number of points where these transactions were carried on, would be equally low, as compared, for example, with the magnitudes involved in the Andalusian fiscal system. Both the number of surviving pieces and the estimates of volumes actually struck,[32] clearly attest to a much more extended use of coins in al-Andalus. These different magnitudes would reasonably reflect two different ways of obtaining peasant production. In the case of the Visigothic state, as it was mentioned above,

> ...the only workable way...to ensure a widespread and recurrent tributary link with peasant work was through delegating to the *potentes* responsibility for the most delicate phase of the fiscal process, namely collecting taxes (Barceló & Retamero 1996).

Whereas, in al-Andalus, peasant communities (*qarya*-s) were held responsible for

---

[31] Isidore documented these cancellations in the reign of Reccared: "*...adeo clemens, ut populi tributa saepe indulgentiae largitione laxaret*" (*Hist. Goth.*; Rodriguez 1975:266). Similarly, Erwig's edict of 683 (L. A. García 1974:125-6; Vives 1963:435-7) and that of Egica in 691 (Vives 1963:480).

[32] See, for example, Canto, Palou & Tortajada 1988; or the 25 kilogrammes of coins and fragments of the tenth-century Haza del Carmen hoard (Córdoba), studied by A. Canto, as well as the quantity and distribution of coin finds (Balaguer, Barceló & Canto n.d.).

handing over taxes, at least during the Umayyad period (Barceló 1984-1985). Hence the volumes of coins involved and the necessity of a widespread network of local markets where peasant production could be transformed into coins on a very large scale.

Therefore, clusters of Visigothic coin finds in the countryside might reflect someone claiming calves or barley to be the same as *tremisses*. However, this regime did not necessarily entail peasants handling coins, although they might obviously be aware of what money could buy.

> Véritable problème de vases communicants: lorsque la circulation monétaire se fait plus intense s'effacent progressivement les formes rurales et la puissance sociale de la campagne; au contraire, ces formes rurales dominent quand il s'agit du phénomène inverse - comme si une économie monétaire recouvrait nécessairement une économie urbaine.

M. Lombard concluded in this way his discussion of the question posed by himself as the "liaison intime entre la circulation monétaire et le développement urbain" (Lombard 1957/72:51).

Many examples clearly confirm the link between the variable importance of the "essor urbain" as it was called by Lombard, and the magnitudes of coin production involved. One might compare, for example, the cases of Samarra[33] and the voluminous Abbasid coin issues (Noonan 1986), and of Madīnat al-Zahrâ' (more recently Vallejo 1995) and the magnitude of the tenth-century Umayyad issues (Canto, Palou & Tortajada 1988), with the size of Reccopolis and the proposed lack of Visigothic coin issues.

These rough comparisons, however, can offer meaningful orders of magnitude, and thus, a sound basis for properly discussing the scale of operations achieved by the Visigothic state, that is, its capacity both to control peasant production, and to transform it into socially recognizable forms of wealth.

As discussed above, wealth could result from exclusivity: precious metals monopolized by the state; workshops attached to the king or to the bishop producing clothes, jars, plates or jewels circulating in narrow circles of *potentes*, and goods arriving from abroad and administered at the *cataplus*. But neither gold, nor silk, nor liturgical jars could have been ever socially regarded as wealth outside of the intricate systems of value in which they were continuosly mirrored. It follows then that the exclusivity both of the making and handling of these so-called 'luxury' goods required an exclusive control of the assessing *corpora* used to reckon them, because measures not only show *how much* or *how many*, but also, and above all, *what* is valuable.

A monetary system could therefore be the most powerful tool for producing wealth in *ancient* societies. First, it entailed the possibility of valuing any good regardless of its physical features; in other words, *comites* or bishops could assess

---

[33] This city was created in the second half of the ninth century, and it "sprawled along the Tigris for *35 kilometres*" (Hodges & Whitehouse 1983:151. Authors' emphasis).

barley, calves, *uestimenta*, or gold using only *siliquae*. Moreover, as far as coins were introduced and required in fiscal payments, every good was made convertible into coin through its sale.[34]

One should note that the only kind of goods that had inescapably to be produced in fixed and repeated rhythms were foodstuffs (and human beings, as discussed below). Since coins returned to the *fiscum*, the whole process of capture and transformation eventually succeeded. Obviously, both the monetary magnitudes involved in the process and the bulk of monetary stuffs handed over to the state indicate the extent of this success. Consequently, as coins went back to the state, peasant produce was being definitively disengaged from its producers. In other words, the barley mentioned in the *epistola* signed by Artemius and his peers, since it was reckoned as money and made thus exchangeable, was taken out from the peasant domain. Needless to say, neither Bishop Artemius nor *comes* Scipio thought of barley in the same way as the peasants did. This intervention caused peasant estimates of production to take into account the part demanded by bishops, *comites* and kings, who were reckoning in *siliquae* and finally managing it as wealth.

Crops, removed from the peasant, could then be kept in store to be sold at favourable moments (for example, before sowing time), or to be distributed in ceremonial displays by the authorities, as described by the *VSPE* (see above, p. 273, this vol.), or, as suggested above, to be converted into coin to satisfy the fiscal demands of the king. That some of these operations were carried out in the town is clearly confirmed by the granaries found in Reccopolis (Olmo 1986; 1988), or by the existence of monastic stores in the towns, as revealed by the *Regula* of Isidore: "*Ad custodiendam autem in urbe cellam unus senior et graussimus monachorum cum duobus paruulis monachis constituendus est {Reg. Isid.*, 21; Campos & Roca (eds.) 1971; cf. P. C. Díaz 1987:87, 108}.

Because both crops and coins were considered money, of course the former could be used as a means of payment like the latter, but crops could not be used as easily as coins in many transactions (Polanyi 1968b:187). This apparently 'practical' motive, however, does not completely account for the interest of the king in handing out coins through payments instead of crops: coins, once put into circulation, remained recognizable objects bearing the sign of the authority, and therefore carried with them rules governing their use. Coins, thus, permitted one to take profits from their very use, for example, by forcing changes at favourable rates.[35] Obviously, such an operation could not be enforced if the monetary types involved could not be sharply distinguished from one another.

But, above all, coins were prefered in payments by the crown because, the more the social validity of coins spread, the more the king came to be the main owner— for he was the only legal producer—of these accepted means of payment and,

---

[34] Hence the value of coin hoards, which in monetary contexts become much more valuable as legal tender than as mere bullion.

[35] It is the case of the so-called 'monetary mutations'. See, for example, Bolin 1954.

therefore, the more he could acquire of whatever goods entered into the monetary mechanism. However, the repeated failure of Visigothic kings to ensure and to extend the conditions for coins to find their way back home tells another story, precisely the story of their weakness.

Neither Reccopolis nor any other royal foundation had an enduring and recognizable urban profile beyond the presence of the royal court and administrative and fiscal staffs. Their withdrawal could either provoke the total abandonment of a town or possibly its silent survival as a peasant site. One may wonder if it was the case of Córdoba before the conquest of Liuvigild.[36]

One may equally wonder whether the *transmarini negotiatores* would have come to Mérida without the presence of the bishop and his entourage. As discussed above, the presence of powers controlling—that is, taxing—trade only makes sure that written sources will reflect these activities, and particularly, that the mere movement of goods will be the aspect enhanced. However, state intervention through its monetary tools over trading activities might have caused the simplification of previous networks through which trade was carried out, embedded in a more complex system of social relationships. It follows then that, paradoxically, money could run against trade.

Nothing is known about the possible existence of these trading networks before the Visigothic conquest, precisely because very little is known about peasant production during the Visigothic period. And it is worth stressing that these institutions formed part of complex peasant systems linking production, exchange and political relationships. Trade then can be hardly regarded at this level as having a single dimension, i.e. as an activity entirely separate from peasant subsistence strategy.

Possibly, this unbreakable link made the absence of words meaning *commerce* a discernible activity in the study of Indo-European. Émile Benveniste stressed "le caractère nouveau de ce type d'activité", and stated that:

> ...les affaires commerciales n'ont pas de nom; on ne peut pas les définir positivement. Nulle part on ne trouve une expression propre à les qualifier d'une manière spécifique; parce que—au moins à l'origine—c'est une occupation qui ne répond à aucune des activités consacrées et traditionelles. Les affaires commerciales se placent en dehors de tous les métiers, de toutes les pratiques, de toutes les techniques; c'est pourquoi on n'a pu les désigner autrement que par le fait d'être 'occupé', d'avoir à faire (Benveniste 1969:145).

Conceivably, linguistics might also offer good grounds for suggesting when

---

[36] Only archaeology can solve this question. Some evidence clearly indicates that Visigothic towns were also peasant sites. For example, in Mérida, the *xenodochium* was set up in the *suburbia*, surrounded by fields (Mateos 1992). Isidore also mentioned grapes coming from the *suburbia* and sold in the *civitas* {(*Etym.*, IX; on the presence of vineyards, *horti*, etc. inside early medieval towns (Wickham 1988); for the case of *Complutum* in the Visigothic period (Méndez & Rascón 1992); on the sites of south-eastern *Hispania* (Gutiérrez 1995)}.

'buying' and 'selling', both attached to the notion of 'value', ended up restricting the comprehensive sense of 'trade' to these operations. According to Benveniste, the meanings of the Greek noun *alpháno*, the Indo-Iranian root *arh-,* and the Germanic verb *bugjan* ('to buy', in English) coincidentally bore the sense of 'acheter', étymologically, "libérer, racheter quelqu'un, pour le sauver d'une condition servile".[37] Thus the 'value', as entailed by the operations of buying and selling, resulted from the notion of 'merit' attributed to human beings: "La notion de 'valeur' prend donc son origine dans la valeur personelle, physique des hommes qui sont susceptibles d'être mis en vente" (Benveniste 1969:131-3).

Yet this sense is attested in one *Antiqua* of the *Lex Visigothorum*, where it was disposed that anyone who helped a fugitive must hand over another *servus equalis meriti*, if the fugitive had vanished.

The concept of 'buying' and 'selling' seems thus to have a twofold original meaning: the payment for freeing people, as indicated by linguistic evidence, and the use of coins reckoned as money, as suggested above. It is likely that the former preceded the latter, for the linguistic hints are older than the first known metallic coin issues, dating from the seventh century BC. Nevertheless, assessments made initially about people, and then giving rise to the setting of prices for releasing them from captivity, did entail monetary expressions; the more so if the operations of capture and release-sale were carried on regularly. In other words, the original notion of 'value', as established by linguistic evidence, would have entailed the use of monetary devices, consisting in the setting of prices, in order to establish enduring links with the subject communities, which regularly should pay for 'being released'.[38] These fiscal mechanisms involving monetary uses would have been originally conceived of as a substitute payment for giving people as hostages or as slaves. The case of the *pax* imposed by Wamba to the Basques (see above, p. 278) would then illustrate this step towards the establishment of enduring fiscal links, a phase in which further monetary assessments would have provided suitable devices to substitute a regular payment of products, whether in kind or in coin for the handing over of people. The case of the earlier fiscal treaties between the *Andalusi* state and some communities of the Balearic Islands in the eighth century may be understood in the same sense. One of the fiscal concepts imposed to the 'people' of Majorca and Minorca (*ahl Mayūrqa wa Minūrqa*) was the payment of the third of 'themselves' (*anfusi-him*). The precise meaning of this fiscal concept is unclear, but it probably implied payments satisfied in terms of actual people, as stated by Barceló, although such a practice would have been unsustainable if carried out regularly (Barceló 1994a; 1994b:15).

---

[37] The precise meaning of *bugjan* is 'to pay with arm-rings'. The Gothic word for 'value' and 'price' of a man is *waír* (giving 'worth', in English). I am grateful to Professor D. H. Green for this information.

[38] Significantly, the Gothic word *gawaír i* (from *waír*, 'value, price of a man') means 'peace', 'reconciliation'. See previous note.

Therefore, the impossibility of establishing enduring fiscal links on the basis of payments involving human beings would have impelled authorities to introduce a substitutory device, namely a new monetary set of equivalences, entailing the payment in kind or in coins in place of human beings. In the case of the Balearic Islands, coin finds suggest that they were not massively used until the eleventh century (Retamero 1995; 1996). This notorious presence would have precisely resulted from the steadiness and spread of the *Andalusi* fiscal network.

To sum up: 'value' and its attached monetary expression, 'price', constitute the core notions behind 'buying' and 'selling', conceived of as the predominating form of exchange. This conception is intimately related to the intervention of a recognized authority which controlled the measures, the means, the time, and the places where those operations took place. Its interest in the control and the enhancement of 'buying' and 'selling' did not exclusively result from the possibility of taxing these activities, but from their importance in the continuous process of converting human beings, goods and coins into exchangeable things through the intervention of money. Now the question posed is which historical form this process took in the beginning: whether it consisted in capturing previously instituted networks of exchanges and political contacts, or whether the original capture giving rise to the setting of prices was executed directly over people. Obviously these alternatives are not exclusive, and they may be ultimately reduced to whether the capture of production through fiscal links was preceded by the capture of human beings. If so, one should subsequently question when and how foodstuffs substituted for people as the main fiscal demand.

Monetization, therefore, appears to be a complex historical process by which sailors, barley, *uestimenta*, liturgical plates or coins could be equated with one another by using an instituted set of monetary measures. Wealth, then, was the resulting display of this control and capture of people and goods, mainly foodstuffs, through monetary means. Bishops, kings and the other Visigothic *potentes* did not only hold wealth, but they made the items normally identified with it go beyond their former social recognition. Therefore wealth was not conceivable nor recognizable as such when disengaged from a bishop Paul, a King Liuvigild or a *comes* Scipio. Without their intervention, barley and calves would have continued in their peasant way as barley and calves; coins would have been regarded as adequate stuff for necklaces, St Eulalia would have been venerated without her magnificent basilica, and Fidelis would have lived his life sailing on small wind-powered ships.

References

Textual sources:

[Abbr. *CE* = *Codex Euricianus*; *Etym* = *Etymologiae*; *Hist. Wamb.* = *Historia Wambae*; *LV* = *Lex Visigothorum*; *VSPE*= *Vitas Sanctorum Patrum Emeretensium*].

Fontes Hispaniae antiquae: see Grosse (ed.) 1947.
Historia Wambae: see Krusch (ed.) 1969.
Ibn Battūta, *Riḥla*: see Fanjul & Arbós (trans.) 1981.
Ibn Hayyān, *Al-Muqtabis V*: see Viguera & Corriente (trans.) 1981.
Ibn Hayyān, *Al-Muqtabis VII*: see E. García (trans.) 1967.
Isidore

> *Etymologiae*: see Lindsay (ed.) 1911.
> *Formulae Wisigothicae*: see Gil (ed.) 1972.
> *Regula sancti patris Isidori episcopi*: see Campos & Roca (eds.) 1971.

Lex Visigothorum: see Zeumer (ed.) 1902.
Vita Aemiliani: see Vázquez de Parga (ed.) 1943.
Vita Martini: see Codoñer (trans.) 1987.
Vitas Sanctorum Patrum Emeretensium: see Maya Sánchez (ed.) 1992.

Bibliography:

Aglietta, M., & A. Orléan
  1982   *La violence de la monnaie*. Paris: Presses Universitaires de France.
Arce, J.
  n.d.   Mérida en las *Vitas Patrum Emeretensium. The Transformation of the Roman World. European Science Foundation. I Plenary Conference*, Mérida, September, 1994. Leiden: E. J. Brill.
  1993   Mercados rurales (*nvndinae*) en la Hispania tardorromana. *Homenage a Miquel Tarradell*. Pp. 867-871. (Asociación Numismática - Museo Casa de la Moneda). Barcelona: Curial.
Balaguer, A. M., M. Barceló & A. Canto
  n.d.   *Corpus de hallazgos monetarios andalusíes*.
Ballestín, X.
  n.d.   La segmentación de grupos clánicos berberes y la actividad de los *bahriyyūn* (gentes del mar) en el Mediterráneo occidental durante la alta Edad Media (al-Andalus, al-Magreb, Siqiliyya), *20 años de al-Andalus. Homenaje a Pierre Guichard*. Granada, mayo, 1996. Granada: Universidad de Granada.
Barbero, A., & M. Vigil
  1974   *La formación del feudalismo en la Península Ibérica*. Barcelona: Critica.
Barceló, M.
  1983   The Earliest Sketch of an 'Oriental Despot'? (A note on the Exchange of Delegations between the Ottonides and the Caliphes of Qurtuba 338-339/950 - 367/974). In *L'Histoire à Nice*. Pp. 55-85. Nice: Université de Nice.
  1984a   Expedicions militars i projectes d'atac contra les Illes Orientals d'al-Andalus. In *Sobre Mayūrqa*. M. Barceló (ed.), pp. 59-76. Palma de Mallorca: Quaderns de Ca la Gran Cristiana.
  1984b   El tractat de Capdepera de 17 de juny de 1231 entre Jaume I i Abu Abd Allāh Muhammad de Manurqa. In *Sobre Mayūrqa*. M. Barceló (ed.), pp. 77-88. Palma de Mallorca: Quaderns de Ca la Gran Cristiana.
  1984-85   Un estudio sobre la estructura fiscal y procedimientos contables del Emirato omeya de Córdoba (138-300/755-912) y del Califato (300-366/912-976). *Acta Mediaevalia* 5-6: 45-72.
  1994a   Els *fulūs* de Tanǧa de finals del segle IH./VIId.C., els pactes més antics i el cas de Mallorca i de Menorca: una revisió. (Asociación Numismática Española). *Gaceta Numismática* 114: 5-18.

Barceló, M. *(cont.)*
1994b   Correccions a "Els *fulūs* de Tanǧa...". (Asociación Numismática Española). *Gaceta Numismática* 115: 63-64.
1997   *El curs de les aigües. Treballs en curs sobre els pagesos de Yabisa (290-633H./902-1235 d.C.).* M. Barceló (ed.). Eivissa: Consell Insular d'Eivissa i Formentera.

Barceló, M., & F. Retamero
1996   From Crops to Coin. Which Way Back? (Asociación Numismática Española). *Gaceta Numismática* 122: 55-63.

Barral, X.
1976   *La circulation des monnaies suèves et visigothiques.* München: Artemis.
1982   Transformacions de la topografia urbana a la Hispània cristiana durant l'Antiguitat Tardana. *II Reunió d'arqueologia paleocristiana hispànica.* Pp. 105-130. Barcelona: Institut d'Estudis Catalans.
1992   La cristianización de las ciudades romanas de Hispania. *Extremadura Arqueológica* 3: 51-55.

Beltrán, P.
1972   Un hallazgo de monedas de oro en la ciudad de Recópolis. *Obras Completas*, II. Pp. 170-176. Saragossa: Dep. de Prehistoria y Arqueología, Universidad de Zaragoza.

Benet, F.
1957   Explosive Markets: the Berber Highlands. In *Trade and Market in the Early Empires.* K. Polanyi *et al.* (eds.), pp. 188-217. New York: The Free Press.

Benveniste, É.
1969   *Le vocabulaire des institutions indo-européennes,* 1. *Économie, parenté, société.* Paris: Les Éditions de minuit.

Blackburn, M. A. S.
1988   Three silver coins in the names of Valentinian III (425-55) and Anthemius (467-72) from Chatham Lines, Kent. *Numismatic Chronicle* 148: 169-174.

Bloch, M.
1933   Économie-nature ou économie-argent: un pseudo-dilemme. *Annales d'Histoire Sociale* 5: 7-16.

Boldrini, E., & R. Francovich (eds.)
1995   *Acculturazione e mutamenti.* Siena: Università di Siena.

Bolin, S.
1954   Tax Money and Plough Money. *The Scandinavian Economic History Review* 2 (1): 3-21.

Caballero, L.
1988   Monasterios visigodos. Evidencias arqueológicas. *Codex Aquilarensis* 1: 31-50.
1989   Cerámicas de 'época visigoda y postvisigoda' de las provincias de Cáceres, Madrid y Segovia. *Boletín de Arqueología Medieval* 3: 75-107.

Caballero, L., & P. Mateos
1991   Excavaciones en Santa Eulalia de Mérida. *Extremadura Arqueológica* 2: 525-546.
1992   Trabajos arqueológicos en la iglesia de Santa Eulalia de Mérida. *Extremadura Arqueológica* 3: 15-50.

Campos, J., & I. Roca (eds.)
1971   *Santos Padres Españoles*, II. Madrid: Editorial Católica.

Cantino, G.
1995   Contributo allo studio della città tardoantica. *IV Reunió d'Arqueologia*
              Cristiana Hispànica. Pp. 235-261. Barcelona: Institut d'Estudis
              Catalans.
Canto, A., F. Palou & B. Tortajada
1988   Volumes of production of dirhams in al-Andalus during the years A.H.
              330 and A.H. 340 as calculated from die-link statistics. *Problems of*
              Medieval Coinage in the Iberian Area. M. Gomes & D. M. Metcalf
              (eds.), pp. 91-98. Santarém: Sociedade Numismática Scalabitana -
              Instituto de Sintra.
Carandini, A.
1983   Pottery and the African economy. In *Trade in the Ancient Economy.*
              P. Garnsey *et al.* (eds.), pp. 145.162. London: The Hogarth Press.
Casanovas, A., & J. Rovira
1994   Las naves grabadas de Ampurias. Un testimonio excepcional de
              embarcaciones romanas en aguas ampuritanas. *Archivo Español de*
              Arqueología 67: 103-113.
Citarella, A. O.
1968   Patterns in Medieval Trade: The Commerce of Amalfi Before the
              Crusades. *The Journal of Economic History* 28: 531-555.
Codoñer, C. (ed.)
1987   *Sulpicio Severo. Obras completas.* Madrid: Ed. Tecnos.
Collins, R.
1980   Mérida and Toledo: 550-585. In *Visigothic Spain: New Approaches.*
              E. James (ed.), pp. 189-219. Oxford: Oxford University Press.
Cowdrey, H. E. J.
1977   The Mahdia campaign of 1087. *The English Historical Review* 342: 1-29.
Crusafont, M.
1994   *El sistema monetario visigodo: cobre y oro.* (Asociación Numismática
              Española - Museo Casa de la Moneda). Barcelona-Madrid: Asociación
              Numismática Española - Museo Casa de la Moneda.
Curtin, P. D.
1984   *Cross-Cultural Trade in World History.* Cambridge: Cambridge
              University Press.
Dalton, G. (ed.)
1968   *Primitive, Archaic, and Modern Economies. Essays of Karl Polanyi.* New
              York: Anchor Books.
De Palol, P.
1950   *Bronces litúrgicos de origen mediterráneo.I. Jarritos y patenas litúrgicos.*
              Barcelona: Instituto de Prehistoria Mediterránea.
1986   Las excavaciones del conjunto de "El Bovalar", Serós (Segrià. Lleida) y el
              reino de Akhila. In *Los visigodos. Historia y civilización. Antigüedad y*
              Cristianismo, III. Pp. 513-525. Murcia: Univ. de Murcia.
1989   *El Bovalar (Seròs. Segrià). Conjunt d'època paleocristiana i visigòtica.*
              (Dip. de Lleida, Generalitat de Catalunya). Barcelona: Dip. de Lleida,
              Generalitat de Catalunya.
Devroey, J.-P.
1995   Juifs et syriens. À propos de la géographie économique de la Gaule au
              Haut Moyen Âge. *Peasants & Townsmen in Medieval Europe. Studia in*
              Honorem Adriaan Verhulst. J.-M. Duvosquel & E. Thoen (eds.) pp. 51-
              72. (Centre Belge d'Histoire Rurale, n° 114). Gent: Centre Belge
              d'Histoire Rurale.

Díaz, M. C.
1966   Los documentos hispano-visigóticos sobre pizarra. *Studi medievali*.
            7 (1): 75-107.
Díaz, P. C.
1987   *Formas económicas y sociales en el monacato visigodo*. Salamanca:
            Universidad de Salamanca.
1989   Monacato y sociedad en la Hispania visigoda. *Codex Aquilarensis* 2: 47-62.
1993   Marginalidad económica, caridad y conflictividad social en la Hispania
            visigoda. In *De Constantino a Carlomagno. Disidentes, heterodoxos,
            marginados*. F. J. Lomas & F. Devís (eds.), pp. 159-177. Cádiz:
            Universidad de Cádiz.
D'Ors, A.
1958   Los 'transmarini negotiatores' en la legislación visigótica. *Estudios de
            derecho internacional. Homenaje al profesor Camilo Barcia Trelles*.
            Pp. 467-483. Santiago: Universidad de Santiago de Compostela.
1960   *El Código de Eurico. Estudios Visigóticos, II*. Roma-Madrid: Centro
            Superior de Investigaciones Cientificas.
Ewig, E.
1963   Résidence et capitale pendant le haut moyen age. *Revue Historique* 230:
            25-72.
Fanjul, S., & F. Arbós
1981   *A través del Islam*. Madrid: Editora Nacional.
Fernández, R.
1955   La compraventa en el derecho medieval español. *Anuario de Historia del
            Derecho Español* 25:293-528.
Février, P.-A.
1989   Images de la ville dans la chrétienté naissante. *Actes du XIe Congrès
            International d'Archéologie Chrétienne. Lyon, Vienne, Grenoble, Genève,
            et Aoste, 1986*. Pp. 1371-1392. Roma: Istituto di Archeologia Cristiana.
Frayn, J. M.
1993   *Markets and Fairs in Roman Italy*. Oxford: Clarendon Press.
García, E.
1967   *Anales Palatinos del Califa de Córdoba al-Hakam II*. Madrid: Centro
            Superior de Investigaciones Científicas.
García, L. A.
1971   Algunos aspectos fiscales de la Península Ibérica durante el siglo VI.
            Hispania Antiqua 1: 233-256.
1972   Colonias de comerciantes orientales en la Península Ibérica, s. V-VII.
            Habis 3: 127-154.
1974   Estudios sobre la organización administrativa del reino visigodo de
            Toledo. *Anuario de Historia del Derecho Español* 44: 5-155.
1977-78   La cristianización de la topografía de las ciudades de la Península Ibérica
            durante la Antigüedad Tardía. *Archivo Español de Arqueología*
            50-51:311-322.
1982   Imposición y política fiscal en la España visigoda. In *Historia de la
            hacienda española (épocas antigua y medieval). Homenaje al profesor
            García de Valdeavellano*. Pp. 263-300. Madrid: Instituto de Estudios
            Fiscales.
Garnsey, P.
1983   Grain for Rome. In *Trade in the Ancient Economy*. P. Garnsey,
            K. Hopkins & C. R. Whittaker (eds.), pp. 118-130. London: The Hogarth
            Press.

Gil, I.
1972   *Miscellanea Wisigothica*. Seville: Universidad de Sevilla.
1977   Judíos y cristianos en la Hispania del siglo VII. *Hispania Sacra* 30: 9-102.
Godoy, C.
1995   *Arqueología y liturgia. Iglesias hispánicas (siglos IV al VIII)*, Barcelona: Diputación de Barcelona.
Gomes, M., J. M. Peixoto & J. Rodrigues
1995   *Ensaios sobre história monetária da monarquia visigoda*. Porto: Sociedade Portuguesa de Numismática.
Grierson, P.
1961   La fonction sociale de la monnaie en Angleterre aux VIIe-VIIIe siècles. *Moneta e scambi nell'Alto Medioevo*. Pp. 341-385. (Settimane di studio del Centro Italiano di Studi sull'Alto M.evo, VIII). Spoleto: C.I.S.A.M.
1967   The Volume of Anglo-Saxon Coinage. *Economic History Review* 20 (1): 152-160.
Grierson, P., & M. Blackburn
1986   *Medieval European Coinage. 1. The Early Middle Ages*. Cambridge: Cambridge University Press.
Grosse, R. (ed.)
1947   *Las fuentes de la época visigoda y bizantinas*. Barcelona: Librería Bosch.
Gurt, J. M., & T. Marot
1994   Estudi dels models de circulació monetària a les Balears: Pollentia (Alcúdia, Mallorca). *III Reunió d'Arqueologia Cristiana Hispànica*. pp. 223-233. Barcelona: Institut d'Estudis Catalans.
Gurt, J. M., G. Ripoll & C. Godoy
1994   Topografía de la Antigüedad Tardía hispánica. Reflexiones para una propuesta de trabajo. *Antiquité tardive* 2: 161-180.
Gurt, J. M., & F. Tuset
1986   Le commerce et la circulation monétaire. *Dossiers, Histoire et Archéologie* 108: 26-32.
Gutiérrez, S.
1995   La experiencia arqueológica en el debate sobre las transformaciones del poblamiento altomedieval en el SE de al-Andalus: el caso de Alicante, Murcia y Albacete. In *Acculturazione e mutamenti*. E. Boldrini & R. Francovich (eds.), pp. 165-189. Florence:Ed. all'insegna del giglio.
Hendy, M.
1989a   Economy and State in Late Rome and Early Byzantium: An Introduction. *The Economy, Fiscal Administration and Coinage of Byzantium*, I. Pp. 1-23. Northhampton: Variorum Reprints.
1989b   The Administration of Mints and Treasuries, Fourth to Seventh Centuries, with an Appendix on the Production of Silver Plate. *The Economy, Fiscal Administration and Coinage of Byzantium*, VI. Pp. 1-18. Northhampton: Variorum Reprints.
1989c   From Public to Private: the Western Barbarian Coinages as a Mirror of the Disintegration of Late Roman State Structures. *The Economy, Fiscal Administration and Coinage of Byzantium*, VII. Pp. 27-78. Northhampton: Variorum Reprints.
1991   East and West: divergent models of coinage and its use". In *Il secolo di ferro*. (Settimane di studio del Centro Italiano di Studi sull'Alto Medioevo, XXXVIII). Pp. 637-674. Spoleto: C.I.S.A.M.

Hendy, M. *(cont.)*
1993   From Antiquity to the Middle Ages: Economic and Monetary Aspects of the Transition. *De la Antigüedad al Medioevo. Siglos IV-VIII. III Congreso de Estudios Medievales.* Pp. 325-360. Madrid: Fundación Sánchez-Albornoz.

Hennequin, G.
1979   Monnaies et monnayages. *Annales Islamologiques* 15: 469-478.

Hodges, R., & D. Whitehouse
1983   *Mohammed, Charlemagne and the Origins of Europe.* Ithaca, NY: Cornell University Press.

Howgego, C.
1992   The supply and use of money in the Roman world 200 B.C. to A.D. 300. *The Journal of Roman Studies* 82: 1-31.

Isla, A.
1991   Moneda de cuenta y organización monetaria en la Galicia altomedieval. *Miscellània en homenatge al P. Agustí Altisent.* Pp. 487-510. Tarragona: Diputació de Tarragona.

Járrega, R.
1987   Notas sobre la importación de cerámicas finas norteafricanas (sigillata clara D) en la costa oriental de Hispania durante el siglo VI e inicios del VII d. de C. *II Congreso de Arqueología Medieval*, II. Pp. 338-344. Madrid: Comunidad de Madrid - Asociación Española de Arqueología Medieval.

Kennedy, H.
1985   From *polis* to *madina*: urban change in late antique and early Islamic Syria. *Past & Present* 106: 3-27.

King, P. D.
1972   *Law & Society in the Visigothic Kingdom.* Cambridge: Cambridge University Press.

Knapp, A. B.
1991   Spice, drugs, grain and grog: organic goods in Bronze Age East Mediterranean trade. In *Bronze Age Trade in the Mediterranean.* N. H. Gale (ed.), pp. 21-68. Oxford: Jonsered Paul Astroms Forlag.

Krusch, B. (ed.)
1888   *Fredegarii et aliorum Chronica. Vitae sanctorum. Monumenta Germaniae Historica. Scriptores rerum Merovingicarum*, 2. Hannover: Hahn. [Repr. 1984].

Lafaurie, J.
1987   Les dernières émissions impériales de Trèves au Ve siècle. *Mélanges de numismatique offerts à Pierre Bastien.* Pp. 297-323. Wetteren: Société Française de Numismatique.

Laurent, H.
1938   Marchands du palais et marchands d'abbayes. *Revue Historique* 178: 281-297.

Lindsay, W. M.
1911   *Isidori Hispalensis Episcopi Etymologiarum sive Originum.* Oxford: Oxford University Press. [Rep. 1966].

Lombard, M.
1957-72   L'évolution urbaine pendant le haut moyen âge. In *Espaces et réseaux du Haut Moyen Age.* Pp. 47-72. Paris/The Hague: Mouton.

López, R. S.
1953   An Aristocracy of Money in the Early Middle Ages. *Speculum* 28: 1-43.

MacGrail, S.
1991   Bronze Age Seafaring in the Mediterranean: a view from NW Europe. In *Bronze Age Trade in the Mediterranean*. N. H. Gale (ed.), pp. 15-20. Oxford: Jonsered Paul Astroms Forlag.
MacMullen, R.
1970   Market-days in the Roman Empire. *Phoenix* 24: 333-341.
Marques de Faria, A.
1988   On finds of Suevic and Visigothic coins in the Iberian Peninsula and their interpretation. *Problems of Medieval Coinage in the Iberian Area*. M. Gomes & D. M. Metcalf (eds.), pp. 71-90. Santarém: Sociedade Numismática Scalabitana-Instituto de Sintra.
Mateos, P.
1992   El culto a Santa Eulália y su influencia en el urbanismo emeritense (siglos IV-VI). *Extremadura Arqueológica* 3: 57-73.
Mauss, M.
1966   Essai sur le don: forme et raison de l'échange dans les sociétés archaiques. *Sociologie et anthropologie*. Paris: Presses Universitaires de France.
Maya Sánchez, A. (ed.)
1992   *Vitas Sanctorum Patrum Emeretensium*. (*CC*), CXVI Turnhout: Brepols.
Méndez, A., & S. Rascóm
1993   'Complutum' y el bajo Henares en época visigoda. *III Congreso de Arqueología Medieval Española*, II. Pp. 96-102. Oviedo: Universidad de Oviedo.
Metcalf, D. M.
1986   Some geographical aspects of early medieval monetary circulation in the Iberian Peninsula. *Problems of Medieval Coinage in the Iberian Area*. M. Gomes & M. Crusafont (eds.), pp. 307-324. Avilés: Sociedad Numismática Avilesina-Instituto de Sintra.
1988   For what purposes were Suevic and Visigothic tremisses used? The contribution of topographical analysis, illustrated by some comments on single finds from Alentejo, and on the mint of Elvora. *Problems of Medieval Coinage in the Iberian Area*. M. Gomes & D. M. Metcalf (eds.), pp. 15-34. Santarém: Sociedade Numismática Scalabitana-Instituto de Sintra.
Miles, G. C.
1952   *The Coinage of the Visigoths of Spain. Leovigild to Achila II*. New York: American Numismatic Society.
Morrisson, C.
1989   Le rôle du monnayage d'argent dans la circulation africaine à l'époque vandale et byzantine. *Bulletin de la Société Française de Numismatique*. [1989]: 518-522.
Noonan, T. S.
1986   Early Abbasid Mint Output. *Journal of Economic and Social History of the Orient* 29: 113-175.
Olmo, L.
1986   Recopolis. La ville du roi Leovigild. *Dossiers, Histoire et Archéologie* 108: 67-71.
1987   Los conjuntos palatinos en el contexto de la topografía urbana altomedieval de la Península Ibérica. *II Congreso de Arqueología Medieval Española*, II. Pp. 346-352. Madrid: Comunidad de Madrid - Asociación Española de Arqueologia Medieval.

Olmo, L. *(cont.)*
1988   La ciudad visigoda de Recopolis. *I Congreso de Historia de Castilla-La Mancha.* Pp. 305-312. Ciudad Real: Consejo de Publicaciones de la Junta de Castilla - La Mancha.
1992   El reino visigodo de Toledo y los territorios bizantinos. Datos sobre la heterogeneidad de la Península Ibérica. *Coloquio Hispano-Italiano de Arqueología Medieval.* Pp. 185-198. Granada: Publicaciones del Patronato de la Alhambra y Generalife.

Orlandis, J.
1977   *Historia de España. La España visigótica.* Madrid: Gredos.

Pearson, H. W.
1957   The Economy has no Surplus: Critique of a Theory of Development. In *Trade and Market in the Early Empires.* K. Polanyi, C. M. Arensberg & H. W. Pearson (eds.), p. 320-341. New York: The Free Press.

Pellat, C.
1961   *Le calendrier de Cordoue.* Leiden: E. J. Brill.

Polanyi, K.
1957a   Marketless Trading in Hammurabi's Time. In *Trade and Market in the Early Empires.* K. Polanyi, C. M. Arensberg & H. W. Pearson (eds.), pp. 12-26. New York: The Free Press.
1957b   The Economy as Instituted Process. In *Trade and Market in the Early Empires.* K. Polanyi, C. M. Arensberg & H. W. Pearson (eds.), pp. 243-270. New York: The Free Press.
1968a   Ports of Trade in Early Societies. In *Primitive, Archaic and Modern Economies. Essays of Karl Polanyi.* G. Dalton (ed.), pp. 238-260. New York: Anchor Books.
1968b   The Semantics of Money-Uses. In *Primitive, Archaic and Modern Economies. Essays of Karl Polanyi.* G. Dalton (ed.), pp. 175-203. New York: The Free Press.

Pryor, J. H.
1992   *Geography, Technology and War. Studies in the Maritime History of the Mediterranean (649-1571).* (Past & Present Publications). Cambridge: Cambridge University Press.

Reilly, B. F.
1993   *The Medieval Spains.* Cambridge: Cambridge University Press.

Retamero, F.
1995   *Moneda i monedes àrabs a l'illa d'Eivissa.* Eivissa: Museu Arqueològic d'Eivissa i Formentera.
1996   *Fulūs y moneda en Mallorca, Ibiza y Menorca antes del 290 H/902 d.C. Al-Qantara* 17: 153-169.
1998   Tādmekka, los taifas y los feudales. De nuevo sobre la moneda fiscal y la moneda feudal. In *L'incastellamento.* M. Barceló & P. Toubert (eds.), pp. 141-155. Roma: Escuela española de Historia y Arqueología en Roma - C.S.I.C.

Reynolds, P.
1995   *Trade in the Western Mediterranean, AD 400-700: The Ceramic Evidence.* (BAR, Int. Series, 604). Oxford: British Archaeological Reports.

Rodríguez, C.
1975   *Las historias de los godos, vándalos y suevos de Isidoro de Sevilla.* León: Centro de Estudios e Investigación "San Isidoro".

Sawyer, P. H.
1977   Kings and Merchants. In *Early Medieval Kingship*. P. Sawyer & I. Wood
            (eds.),pp. 139-158. Leeds: University of Leeds Press.

Shaw, B. D.
1981   Rural Markets in North Africa and the Political Economy of the Roman
            Empire. *Antiquités africaines* 17: 37-83.
1986   Autonomy and tribute: mountain and plain in Mauretania Tingitana.
            Revue de l'Occident Musulman et de la Méditerranée 41-42: 66-89.

Sherratt, A.& S.
1991   From luxuries to commodities: the nature of Mediterranean Bronze Age
            trading systems. In *Bronze Age Trade in the Mediterranean*. N. H. Gale
            (ed.), pp. 351-386. Oxford: Jonsered Paul Astroms Forlag.

Thompson, E. A.
1969   *The Goths in Spain*. Oxford: Clarendon Press.

Torras, J.
1993   La construcció del mercat. *Els espais del mercat. 2on. Colloqui
            Internacional d'història local.* Pp. 11-24. València: Diputació de València.

Toubert, P.
1990   *Castillos, señores y campesinos en la Italia medieval.* Barcelona: Crítica.

Troin, J.-F.
1975   *Les souks marocains.* Aix-en-Provence: Edisud.

Vallejo, A. (ed.)
1995   *Madīnat al-Zahrā'. El salón de 'Abd al-Rahmān III.* Córdoba: Junta de
            Andalucía.

Vázquez de Parga, L. (ed.)
1943   *Vita Aemiliani.* Madrid: Consejo Superior de Investigaciones Científicas.

Velázquez, I.
1989   *El latín de las pizarras visigóticas*, 2 vols. Madrid: Univ. de Murcia.
1993   Pizarras visigodas: nuevos datos y comentarios. *De la Antigüedad al
            Medioevo. Siglos IV-VIII. III Congreso de Estudios Medievales.* Pp. 419-
            436. Madrid: Fundación Sánchez-Albornoz.

Viguera, M. J., & F. Corriente
1981   *Crónica del califa 'Abdarrahman III an-Nāsir entre los años 912 y 942
            (al-Muqtabis V).* Saragossa: Anubar.

Vives, J.
1963   *Concilios visigóticos e hispano-romanos.* Barcelona/Madrid: Consejo
            Superior de Investigaciones Cientificas.

Whittaker, C. R.
1983   Late Roman trade and traders. In *Trade in the Ancient Economy*.
            P. Garnsey *et al.* (eds.), pp. 163-180. London: The Hogarth Press.

Wickham, C.
1988   La città altomedievale: una nota sul dibattito in corso. *Archeologia
            Medievale* 15: 649-651.

Zeumer, K. (ed.)
1902   *Leges Visigothorum. Monumenta Germaniae Historica. Leges nationum
            Germanicarum*, 1. Hannover: Hahn.

Discussion

WOOD: Can anything be said about the estates of Visigothic churches or of the
nobility? This relates in part to the methodological point I raised before about the

question of making comparisons between different barbarian kingdoms. The question: is can anything be said about the estates of the Visigothic nobility? And how you can use the information on the estates of the Church of Mérida more generally? Now the reason why I ask this, is that it makes a great difference whether all the estates of a church or individual are in one region or spread throughout the kingdom. The reason why it makes a great difference is, if you have, as in the Frankish kingdom, your aristocracy with estates scattered throughout the kingdom, individual aristocrats on their own estates have access to the whole range of goods; if you have salt pans, vineyards, olive groves and corn fields, you may actually need less of what we call trade, because you can bring things from several places. Can we talk about a non-trading pattern of distribution which runs through the estates of the Visigothic nobility or the Church, or do we simply not have enough evidence on the Visigothic nobility?

RETAMERO: I'm afraid we don't have enough evidence on the nobility's estates. I can only remember the case of the estates left by Vincent, bishop of Huesca, to the monastery of Asán, recently studied by P. C. Díaz (1998).

WOOD: So can we possibly argue a similar pattern for Mérida in terms of what is known of the Church holdings of Mérida.

RETAMERO: Yes. I'm afraid we have no evidence on the estates and provincial holdings either. But the existence of scattered estates, as in the case of Vincent, does not necessarily imply that *potentes* were able to select or manage the establishment of specialized and scattered agrarian areas so as to control a wide range of products, but this is only a guess.

WOOD: I know of nothing which suggests that we can talk about the estates of the great nobility.

DÍAZ: I think the central question concerns the relations. I think that the nobility had personal relations with the king, but 'central authorities' is an ambiguous term. The latter could not control the properties of this nobility and, actually, the process ran in the opposite direction since, normally, the members of the nobility held the central power even if we claim to understand who had control over large areas of territory, e.g. the northern plateau. In this enormous area we have no bishoprics, only in the peripheral areas, we have no mints in these areas, we have no other element which can be related to the central power, probably because in these areas the great proprietors are really self-sufficient and the problem is central. When we talk about taxes, the relationship between this nobility, and the central power is based on consensus. The problems of a small group need enormous consensus; when this consensus ends, power collapses. That was most probably the situation during the last few years of the kingdom. The proprietors held the power, and the *Lex Visigothorum* concerning the military laws of Erwig or Wamba is an expression of this situation. Actually in the last 40 years of the kingdom there was a central power, but only with very limited control over the many local powers. Concerning taxes, for example, we must recall Wickam's idea (1984) about the transformation of the old Roman scheme of taxation and the problem of revenues. The Visigothic army was not really an army, only perhaps the group around the king; it was made up of the armies of every great proprietor. The problem is to have a sense of 'kingdom'. I think they really had no control over this. Because it is curious, especially in the case of the Visigothic nobility, they made up the *aula regia*, they were the members that were around the king and the individuals that were going to hold the power in the administration and exercise probably, the greatest influence. We are not going to discuss the position of the Roman nobility now, especially bishops, because it is possible that they were answerable directly to the king or his closest representatives.

GREEN: A question on Greek merchants in Spain. Only for information, I would like to hear from you what you can tell me about these Greek merchants in Spain at large, what their frequency was, when they are first attested from, and how late they are attested, but also and more particularly, are they merchants from Greece or are they Greek-speaking merchants? You mention later Syrians, and I am particularly interested in that, and also what indications are there that these Greek merchants were Christian?

RETAMERO: On the evidence of the presence of Greek merchants in *Hispania* there is a very old article by García (L. A. García 1972) compiling all the references to Greek merchants. I don't know whether there is another article available. If I am not wrong, I think the first to mention Greek merchants is Hydatius, I shall check it. And whether they came from Greece or they were only Greek-speakers, I have no idea.

GREEN: But later you mention Syrians.

RETAMERO: Yes, I follow very closely on this point García, I'm afraid [laughter]. But I don't follow García, I follow the evidence compiled by García in his article. So that I can't give you more details on where they come from exactly, if they were only Greek-speakers, whether they came from Egypt, from Syria or from Greece.

GREEN: And what about their Christianity?

RETAMERO: The same applies to Christianity. My guess is probably they were Christians.

SCHWARCZ: In the fifth century I wouldn't expect anything else.

JIMÉNEZ: In the necropolis of Turuñuelo, Medellín (Badajoz), a gold circle brooch in repoussé with the representation of the Holy Kings, a theme which reflects a Syrian motif, was found. It comes from the late sixth century. Its Greek inscription says, "St Mary help the one who wears this". It allows us to believe that the owner was a Christian. Furthermore, among the archaeological remains of a sunken boat at Favarix in the north of the island of Minorca, we found a lamp with another inscription also written in Greek, which tells us who made it and where in Heliopolis (Palol & Ripoll 1988:277).

RETAMERO: There is also a reference to Oriental monks arriving at *Tarraco* (L. A. García 1972:133).

VELÁZQUEZ: There is a Greek inscription with an earlier mention of the name of the archangel Raphael (Gascó *et al.* 1993).

JIMÉNEZ: Is it on the slates?

VELÁZQUEZ: No, no, no. It is on a Greek inscription (Gascó *et al.* 1993).

DE JONG: With angels?

VELÁZQUEZ: Yes, Raphael, Michael. It is very fragmentary. It is interesting, it was published this year or last year. This inscription on a golden piece is earlier. The scholars who published it think it dates to the third century. There are also two slates with the mention of angels, one of them belongs to the seventh century and another was dated to approximately 750 AD.

WOOD: You have to come to San Marino to hear about new finds in Visigothic Spain [laughter].

GREEN: Thank you.

WOOD: On page 273, I have a comment where you make a point about *magnanimitas* and *munificentia* as an expression of lay powers and not Christian virtues. I think one could actually say that *magnanimitas* and *munificentia* can be Christian virtues precisely because they have been civic virtues. If you look at the work done by Martin Heinzelmann (1976) on the episcopal epitaphs of the Rhone Valley, one of his arguments is very precisely that episcopal virtues are late Roman civic virtues taken over. So, I don't think these two categories are exclusive.

RETAMERO: So, they could be considered as Christian virtues, but they previously were civic virtues.

DE JONG: Also on page 274, the question I would like to have clarified concerns the first paragraph of that page. As I read it now, what you are saying is that ecclesiastical documentation suggests that all these offerings were made voluntarily, but in fact there was power at play which made people give, but not voluntarily. I think you may be right and you could strengthen the argument by realizing that free gifts are so important in Christian ideology to disguise the element of tit-for-tat or *do ut des*. So, the usual phrase of charters would indeed be that we do this for nothing, etc. Well, it may very well be that what people are actually doing is not much different from giving to the secular power and then you have to see it in the guise of patronage; and secular and ecclesiastical patronage are not much different. Even if there are obvious differences it is a continuum, I think.

RETAMERO: I agree with you. Thank you.

VELÁZQUEZ: Page 274-5, on "Late Roman documentation certifies the frequent participation of ecclesiastics in the market".

RETAMERO: Yes, but not in *Hispania*.

VELÁZQUEZ: Not in *Hispania*. I don't want to bore you with Visigothic slates, but I am familiar with them. This Visigothic slate is a contract of sale which begins with *"Dominis honorabilibus fratribus"* followed by the formula of a contract of sale. *"Honorabilibus fratribus"* evidently refers to monks. Here is an ecclesiastic and a contract of sales for your references.

RETAMERO: Thank you.

DE JONG: Page 277, it is a question all the way. I want to know more about this calendar: I was wondering about the navigation being avoided for 49 days. Why is this? Did it have a liturgical background?

RETAMERO: I don't know why, I am directly recording the words of the calendar. However, they know the dangerous conditions of the sea, and they follow *secundum intentionem Romanorum*. This gives an idea of the antiquity of the knowledge of these dangerous conditions of the sea.

DE JONG: Which sea? The Mediterranean? In April or May?

AUSENDA: There is a whole book concerning navigation in the early Middle Ages published by CISAM with some three or four chapters concerning navigation in the Mediterranean. It is clear that they only navigated between May and September (Udovitch 1978:514, 530-33), only people who were very much in a hurry and were willing to risk their lives took to sea during unfavourable seasons, not only, but since merchant ships were very low and easy to sink, they were quite careful.

Sailors became more apt when they discovered the way of sailing against the wind, but this only started in the ninth or tenth century or even later.

DE JONG: So there is a factual basis there. Good.

AUSENDA: The 49 days are similar to the three days of Indian summer, or the 'khamsìn', the wind lasting 50 (*khamsìn* in Arabic) days which plagues southern Mediterranean countries with sandstorms in the spring. This is probably connected with the 49-day (seven weeks) adverse weather dreaded by the merchants who came to Spain.

On page 280 concerning the "appropriate price", you describe how the authorities interfered in the market to allow goods to be sold only "at an appropriate price", intimating that these authorities were in condition to set the prices of the goods sold in the market. I would wholeheartedly disagree with this interpretation in that the 'market' always emerges in the end and no one can throttle it. The first thing that would have happened to international trade, if word got around of authorities in a given market imposing political prices, would have been that merchants would have made their calculations and stopped coming to that market. I think that throttling prices on the part of authorities would have been the same as killing the hen laying the golden eggs. In fact, it stands to reason that authorities taxed purchases, because in an epoch where fiscal control was so difficult, taxation had to be carried out perforce at communication nodes, i.e. entrance to cities and markets; but in so doing the authorities must have been very careful not to compress the interests of the merchants. Taxing purchases of luxury goods was akin to an income tax levied on rich people. There is no other possibility because, if they should have started taxing their profits, the merchants would no longer come.

SCHWARCZ: That was not an income tax but a sort of Value Added Tax.

AUSENDA: That's right, however the tax on luxury goods affected only rich people, in this sense it was similar to a social income tax. OK, call it Value Added Tax.

RETAMERO: How, then, could we explain the repeated interest of authorities in controlling the places and the moments where goods were sold?

AUSENDA: They controlled them because they wanted to levy tax on them. I agree with you, but they did not impose the prices.

RETAMERO: Yes, I understand now. I don't remember now the exact source, perhaps it is Isidore (*Etym.*, XV. II. 45) who tells us that one officer at the *teloneum* did set the price and proclaimed it to the merchants. Of course, the final payment may eventually have been different. I'm considering the possibility that price could be identified with a fiscal assessment to evaluate the tax levied upon the trading activities. It is a fiscal device, it could be also a fiscal device. But you need to have a price.

AUSENDA: But it had to be a profitable price, or else the merchants would not come back.

HEATHER: Yes, you can only impose prices within limits. And there is quite a lot of information on price fixing in the tenth century and it's very clear that there is only a certain margin within which you can operate.

RETAMERO: I think that Isidore witnessed these assessments of the *pretium*.

HEATHER: Sure, you can set the price, but not any price. You cannot set the price at just any price that you want.

SCHWARCZ: We must take into consideration the fact that people in Antiquity had no understanding of economics in the modern sense, and, of course, authorities tried to do things which now we would think were completely senseless because they are not workable; one of the cases in point is for the state to try to impose prices, as in the famous edict of Diocletian. That couldn't work. And, of course, they imposed the *teloneum* on the goods, and they could do that because they fixed the places where they could control the trade and it was forbidden to sell the goods at any other point.

RETAMERO: It is also the case of the Byzantine *cataplus*.

AUSENDA: Yes, but what I am saying is that if the prices were not right, nobody was going to come and sell.

RETAMERO: What do you mean by a right price?

AUSENDA: A price that covers purchasing, cost, freight, risk, etc. and then one comes to that market to sell. If they didn't allow one to sell at that price, one would turn around and go and sell it somewhere else where there was a market. In other words, fixing the price that Isidore witnessed probably meant the overseer going around to various merchants of that product and finding out the price they were asking for and then fixing the prices he had just surveyed and thereby also fixing the tax he could levy on the purchases. Actually, he was also doing a favour to the merchants because he did away with competition in that market.

SCHWARCZ: But there was no competition, that's the point of it. You could take the example of Synesius of Cyrene! He tells us of one ship with shoes arriving in Cyrene, so the price plus the harbour fees had to be paid by everyone who wanted those shoes because there was no alternative.

AUSENDA: Andreas is right, he said that these people did not have theoretical notions about economics but they had very practical ones. So they knew that if they throttled prices the stuff would not come back. Wherever there was a flow of goods it was an extremely important 'carrier' to put taxes onto.

RETAMERO: Of course, prices should have been interesting for both merchants and authorities, so prices must have been within a reasonable limit. But on the notion of right price, the only one I can envisage is a price resulting from a bargain, not in a controlled market.

AUSENDA: In a controlled market, you bargain with the whole market at once. It is the authorities that make the bargain. They say, "...you sell at so much", and the merchants sell them at that price. So it's good for the market and it's good for the merchants. What would be the advantage to the authorities, if they left everyone free to bargain. The merchants would compete against each other as they would want to sell as quickly as they could and leave. This would cause a loss of money to themselves and to the tax authorities. So they are indeed fixing prices but in the sense that they are regulating the market. In essence, the authorities are fixing the minimum tax to be added to the price of the goods and paid by the purchasers.

RETAMERO: I would like to remark that 'control' evokes the idea that the authorities needed a monetary device to forcefully assess taxes.

AUSENDA: I agree with you. The only point where I don't agree with you is when you say, without qualification, that they fixed an appropriate price. You make it sound as if they went there and compelled the merchants to sell at any price the authorities wanted.

DE JONG: The question is not the price, you say it is another one.

RETAMERO: No, it is both of them: this previous monetary assessment to collect tax, to calculate tax, but it can be also the real price, the real payment for some goods. The case of precious metals monopolized by the state is an example. The main evidence in this sense is related to precious metals. I think we can hardly imagine a free market for precious metals, since the authorities are absolutely concerned with their control since they have their exclusive management. Of course, we can imagine free or less controlled prices for some goods, but, for example, in the case of precious metals, I think it is not possible.

AUSENDA: I don't think they could control even the prices of precious metals, because there are very stringent laws on the forgery of coinage. So, that means that precious metals were on the market. I visited Kassala, the main town in eastern Sudan several times, and gold was available there while there was famine and drought in the country at large, and it was sold at a price level close to the international price, which shows that the market of precious metals is impervious even to borders and customs.

SCHWARCZ: In Antiquity there was a fixed ratio of exchange between gold and silver from Constantine up to the higher Middle Ages. For centuries the relation between gold and silver did not change after Constantine's monetary reform. So you cannot compare it with modern times and, what's more, the mines in late Antiquity were state monopolies.

RETAMERO: You know perfectly well that exclusive access to precious metals or at least the aim to get an exclusive control of precious metals is widely attested in the sources.

DE JONG: I was struck by the point you made on page 278, which I think is very important. I would like to draw your attention to that again, which is the way gifts, mutual gifts, and agreements with what you call "alternative political forms to the state", and this is something which goes on certainly in waves up to the tenth century and after it, and it's very interesting to see if you can get a hold of the sources about how such gifts were defined on both sides. In relation to the Bretons, for example, the Carolingians said that they got tribute, on the other side the Bretons said that they gave gifts. But the important thing is to realize that states could exist on the basis of gift giving. Perhaps not states in the modern sense of the word, but quite persistent political conglomerations that were held together by the understanding on one side that they had subdued the other and the other pretending that they freely handed over gifts to them.

RETAMERO: I wonder to what extent any state could afford a steady organization only on the basis of circulating gifts.

DE JONG: I can see the point, but the rest of your paper is about how what looks like modern economics is not modern economics, it actually comes quite close to strategies of gift giving.

RETAMERO: It has a political dimension.

SCHWARCZ: Sorry I don't think you can do this for late Antiquity. You can do it for archaic Greece, but not for a later economy.

HEATHER: Maybe it was part of the post-Roman economy.

DE JONG: Post-Roman economy. Maybe, OK.

SCHWARCZ: This may go on on the eastern Frankish border but not in a particular town on the coast. Anyone who wants to talk about this Mediterranean trade in that period should take a look at the article of Dietrich Claude (1985b) and his book on trade in the Mediterranean (Claude 1985a).

DÍAZ: You speak of the existence of so many categories of monetary tolls at many different levels of trading activities. But on a theoretical level—we discussed it this morning—we must separate the old concepts of town and market and the agrarian economy of the late Roman Empire in the Visigothic period. Perhaps the agrarian economy can be self-sufficient, but only on a theoretical level. We can think about the necessities of these properties that consist in prestige, not only in relation to large properties, but also in relation to luxury goods imported from the East by the Greek merchants we have been talking about. The wealthy property owners are preoccupied by the accumulation of gold coins. It is strange that the ownership of large properties provides them with all agricultural necessities, but they do not have the possibility to control gold, they need a mechanism to transform peasant labour into wealth. You mention that on page 289: they need the market. But what does the market mean in the Visigothic period or in the late antique economy? Perhaps the financial capacity of these *possessores* implies that they can control prices. We have been talking about the lack of a theoretical concept of economics, but when we read the *Codex Iustinianus* or when we read another author of late Antiquity, we have a clear understanding that they have no theoretical ideas but very practical ones about economics. Perhaps the concept of

Visigothic economy is easier to understand not in terms of the Roman economy, but in terms of an agrarian economy. In the seventeenth century in Europe in agricultural areas the prices, for example in San Marino, were twice as much as those twenty kilometres away—there are many examples of this question in the seventeenth and eighteenth centuries—the situation is due to the fact that in this area the large owners needed to transform peasant work into wealth, especially in gold, and the monopoly of gold coins belongs to the state. The articulation of this was the theoretical self-sufficiency of the large owners, the need for a market especially for the towns, because towns normally do not have a large one. Where peasants are living who are working near towns is another question, but in Mérida, for example, they need a market and this relation needs a connection with the central power, which is the only source where it is possible to obtain gold coins to maintain this element. This is a problem to be solved, the model of the mechanism of actuation.

AUSENDA: On page 287, my question concerns the possible spread of enormous numbers of coins in the countryside; you cited someone who held that there was a great circulation of coinage in the countryside. Concerning the spread of currency in the countryside, it suggested that peasants were rich.

RETAMERO: No it is exactly the contrary. I said that the known figures of standing pieces do not permit us to envisage an enormous quantity of circulating pieces, as suggested, I think wrongly, by Metcalf (1986, 1988).

HEATHER: I don't think that's clear, because I was going to ask you what you thought about Metcalf too.

RETAMERO: I apologize for that.

AUSENDA: On this basis, I would like to recall that, as late as eighty years ago, before World War I, the rural economy in the Italian mountain ranges along the Alps was almost completely moneyless. In a village I studied, there were 52 families which produced everything they ate except for wine, salt and very few luxury goods. They even made their own medicaments from herbs and flowers. There were travelling craftsmen repairing chairs, cauldrons, and making baskets, and travelling salesmen selling seeds, and also travelling minstrels. There also were travelling buyers, buying rabbit and cat pelts, wallnuts and chestnuts, old clothes and shoes and also wax for candles.

Even those who were better off, in this case the family of the mayor of the village, had very little money, because they were "rich in land but poor in money". The little money they made by selling the few items described above was used to buy goods sold by travelling merchants or craftsmen who came their way. There was an annual fair in the central place of the valley, about ten kilometres from that village, on the occasion of the feast of Saint Roc in August and, as you pointed out, it coincided with a religious festivity and a pilgrimage of sorts. The main event at the annual fair was the domestic animals fair, where pigs were bought for winter fattening and cattle was bought and sold. Men made money while still young by travelling to neighbouring Switzerland to work as masons, they left in the early spring and came back as late as Christmas. The land was worked by the women and by the older men who no longer migrated to work. The women began to make some money in the nineteenth century, and went on until WW I, by breeding silkworms, whose 'seeds' were sold to them by travelling salesmen and whose cocoons they sold when 'ripe' to a local threading 'factory'. In conclusion, I doubt that in the early Middle Ages the countryside provided much impulse for monetary circulation and the few hoards found there may well be due to travelling merchants who, because they slept in barns and stables, may have not trusted themselves with carrying their small treasures around.

RETAMERO: Where was this?

AUSENDA: I thought you quoted someone who wrote that the countryside accounted for considerable monetary circulation.

RETAMERO: Yes it is Metcalf who wrote that, and that there was a lot of money.

SCHWARCZ: I am very sceptical.

HEATHER: I just may have misread it, but it seemed, when I read it, as if you were just reporting what Metcalf said without giving a firm indication about what you thought about the argument.

DE JONG: So try again.

HEATHER: You might add another sentence saying, "I think this is completely wrong" [laughter].

RETAMERO: I hope my opinion is clear now.

AUSENDA: Concerning the difficulty of collecting crops on the part of landowners, be they lay or religious, you describe on page 288-9, I already gave an example based on experience in Italy in the discussion of Dr. Jiménez's paper. I can add a further example from the Sudan here. In my experience both in the Sudan and in Italy I have come to realize that it is almost impossible to control the production and consumption of agricultural produce by sharecroppers as far as edible produce is concerned. In fact in Tokar, in the Red Sea province in Sudan, near the border with Eritrea, I was told by officials heading the agricultural scheme, akin to your bishops, that the most destitute among those who lived on the land were the sharecroppers, as compared to the owners of the land and the middlemen who provided the cash for the yearly operations. Having studied the situation I found out that the sharecroppers were those who drew most from the fields. I will not go into the details, but the main reason for that is that they 'eat' part of the produce without accounting for it to the owner, they graze their animals on the stubble or in the vicinity of their fields, they work at harvesting and threshing nearby fields obtaining in exchange about 1/9 of the harvest. Even if one wanted to, it would be almost impossible to control them.

People are wont to pity peasants as they do not realize that they are those who are on the land, closest to the produce and they can eat it or hide it with no practical possibility of control.

HEATHER: On page 288, on *potentes* and tax. This is the late Roman situation too. The model you have there is that taxation is a form of negotiation between the central state and local powerful people, and local powerful people and the peasants, and so on. I'm aware of the Spanish historiographic tradition on Visigothic Spain, which sees the state collapsing in the late seventh century as taxation goes into irreversible decline. Do you think this is correct? I ask because, as far as I can see, in the late Roman situation you get a kind of cyclical pattern of renegotiations. Different *potentes* come to power, and you cannot really talk about a local decline in taxation, I think it comes and goes.

RETAMERO: My guess is that the Visigothic state did not collapse in the sixth century. My opinion is that the Visigothic state was always collapsed [laughter].

HEATHER: Yes, but it didn't get worse.

RETAMERO: It was ineffective, the state had a fiscal system in which tax evasion had dramatic consequences. Peasants were not directly responsible for handing over taxes, but the *potentes*. If you cannot control one *potens*, you lose an enormous amount of tax. The system was always on the verge of collapse.

HEATHER: Well, what you see in the late Roman state, is that they play one *potens* off against another and that actually limits the degree of collapse. And I simply wonder, is there any reason to think that they are not doing the same in Visigothic Spain?

AUSENDA: Certainly the Roman Empire collapsed too.

HEATHER: But tax goes at the end, not paying taxes is not the cause.

SCHWARCZ: It's a part of the cause.

HEATHER: No, it's an effect.

DE JONG: Could I ask about the Visigothic state. Is it still widely believed that it was decadent towards the end? I thought that was....

HEATHER: Yes, this is surely the hidden agenda. Coming back in other ways.

RETAMERO: They are 'decadent' when they don't work.

DE JONG: They work very well.

HEATHER: It is still in García Moreno in a hidden way.

DE JONG: It is pretty awful in a way.

HEATHER: It may be pretty ramshackle, but is there any reason to think it is getting worse in the seventh century? That's my question. Obviously the whole thing was far from efficient, but is there any reason to think, as certainly García Moreno thinks or says, that it's getting worse in the course of the seventh century?

DE JONG: How well does the system work towards the end of the century?

HEATHER: Is it just the same?

RETAMERO: Just the same, yes. The only point could be the real effectiveness of the system, but the structure of the system was very weak. Of course it could work for some time, for a few years, but the system was a 'decadent' one.

DE JONG: Oh, no.

RETAMERO: In this way.

DE JONG: OK.

HEATHER: It is a serious question.

RETAMERO: I never used that word.

DE JONG: No, I don't want to use it either. I used it just to show how silly words can get.

AUSENDA: How come the Arabs flooded through Spain in 711 without any difficulty?

SCHWARCZ: After this I would like to put the question I have on this page which can follow after Peter [Heather]'s. It also concerns this model. I quite agree on the model of the working of the late Roman tax system. I only want to draw attention to the equation of *potentes* and bishops.

RETAMERO: It is the way sanctioned by the law of 371 saying *in serviant terras non tributario nexo, sed nomine et titulo colonorum.*

SCHWARCZ: That concerns the bishops. At the beginning of the fifth century the laws put the responsibility, which before that time was in the hands of the council of *decuriones*, in the court of the bishops.

On page 288, this also concerns the process of tax collecting and the question—we have discussed some examples already—concerning the way in which they were paid. I just wanted to draw attention to the fact that also at the beginning of the fifth century the payment of taxes was 'adaerated', transformed completely into money.

RETAMERO: Yes. But I was somewhat reluctant to use the term *adaeratio*.

SCHWARCZ: That's what I wanted to ask you.

RETAMERO: ...it implies that tax is converted into money, but it doesn't necessarily imply that kind is converted into coins. Kind is assessed in monetary terms. So, I prefer to talk about monetary assessment, and coins could or could not be used in transactions. That is why *adaeratio* can be a misleading term.

VELÁZQUEZ: What do you think of the assessment in *solidi* on slates?

RETAMERO: I have nothing to add to the evidence of the slates. I insist that I don't believe that these *solidi* referred to cereals, nor to coins. I don't know which goods are behind this monetary assessment.

VELÁZQUEZ: I think that probably it did not refer to money, it could be a unit of account.

RETAMERO: Of account of what?

VELÁZQUEZ: To allow for the establishment of units to do business, sales and so on.

WOOD: For the Franks and for the *Baiuwarii* there is a complete table of equivalences.

SCHWARCZ: Of course yes, there are also in our late medieval central European sources, *solidi* and *denarii*. That must be taken for German shillings and pfennig. People used the classical terms which had been in use since the time of Constantine.

DÍAZ: On page 288, it concerns once more the tax system. I think that the tax system, the fiscal system of the Visigoths may have been effective, but the problem was anachronism since, in the same way that the Visigoths took over elements of Roman law, they took over elements of Roman fiscality. The problem is that they did not have the constraining capacity to make the system work. We must take into consideration the use the Romans made of taxes: it was to pay the army. The Visigoths did not have a big army, they did not have to pay the army and they did not have the army to force the large landholders to pay. It was an anachronistic system and it was impossible to use it because the conditions were very different now. The Visigoths didn't elaborate a fiscal system according to the new conditions of the kingdom. I think that the problem was that the Visigothic state did not have the capability to capture peasant production because they did not have any possibility to constrain taxpayers.

DE JONG: Do you think the Romans did?

DÍAZ, JIMÉNEZ: Yes.

WOOD: The Franks didn't and they ended... [in a feudal economy?]

HEATHER: I can see it is very different. They did not have a professional army. You don't need tax to pay it and you don't have that threat of using the army on your taxpayers. But is it a problem or is it just different?

DÍAZ: Yes, but the problem is that the general scheme of the fiscal system of the Visigoths is a copy of the late Roman fiscal system, but the conditions were very different then.

HEATHER: Is it a copy or is it like the law, are they generating a new continuity?

SCHWARCZ: Not a copy, a kind of continuation of the copy.

DÍAZ: A continuation, but it is a new central power which is using the scheme.

HEATHER: Well, maybe they never needed it.

DÍAZ: The problem is the formation of the gold system.

HEATHER: You don't need so much gold, you just need a bit to pass out as gifts to your great men every so often. You don't need to put out huge amounts of salary, just your donatives to the army, and you just bring in ten percent of what the Romans used to bring in or five percent, but maybe that's enough in the new political circumstances. You're creating a kind of entity that has a less powerful centre. What I mean is that this is not necessarily a problem.

SCHWARCZ: Yes, the disappearance of the Empire was because the new structures were much cheaper than the imperial bureaucracy.

AUSENDA: Yes, I was thinking that the difference between Franks and Visigoths was that the Franks were more predatory than the Visigoths. Is it possible that the predatory attitude of the Franks allowed them to raid North and South, East and West, whereas the Visigoths were not as predatory?

RETAMERO: I think the difference between being predatory and having a fiscal system is a question of the regular basis of the fiscal activity. It might really be plunder, but when state control is regular it appears as legal fiscal links.

AUSENDA: When I talk about a state being predatory, I mean making war outside its borders.

HEATHER: As opposed to making war on the taxpayers.

AUSENDA: I think it was Ian [Wood] who noted that the Franks went out regularly and blackmailed their neighbours into giving them tribute so as not to be attacked. The Visigoths obviously didn't do that.

WOOD: Well, they had less opportunity; they didn't have the equivalent of the people east of the Rhine. They could beat up the *Vascones*, but the *Vascones* did not have that much money to pay.

DE JONG: There is this crossover: you substitute coins with land or you say coins instead of land. You know what I'm saying? If you apply this to a lot of early medieval economies without a fiscal system, that is if you don't have a fiscal system it's a gift system which works exactly the same way.

RETAMERO: There is a substantial difference: paying with land, you have very limited means of payment, whereas coins can be produced every year.

DE JONG: In other words land doesn't circulate. Yes, that's another problem.

RETAMERO: I would like to know the opinion of Professor Green about the statements of Émile Benveniste.

GREEN: On most issues I disagree strongly with Benveniste. There is one field where we meet on common ground and where I accept almost unreservedly what he says, but it is not in connection with your subject. It is in connection with something quite different.

JIMÉNEZ: May I ask a question. Don't you think that the real problem of the collapse of the Visigothic kingdom was that the Visigothic king did not create a new economic system applicable to a new social reality the same way as they had created a new legal system?

RETAMERO: I don't think a king could ever create an economic system.

JIMÉNEZ: Why not?

AUSENDA: I agree, kings do not do things. Kings are symbols.

JIMÉNEZ: Well, I want to say the Visigothic state, not the Visigothic king.

RETAMERO: Even the Visigothic state. Any state had very strong limits against creating what we call 'economic conditions'.

JIMÉNEZ: I don't think so but....

DE JONG: I think Margaret Thatcher didn't succeed either.

AUSENDA: When they raise or lower the interest rates, they are not imposing something on the market, they are following the market. Because, even if one tries to go against the market, it will push them in the direction it wants to go. When you believe that 'they' are doing things, it is not so, 'they' are floating on the surface of socio-economic trends. It is very difficult to reform an entire system, one has to change the mentality and the habits of the people involved, one usually has to have a crisis before changes can take place.

JIMÉNEZ: The crisis took place, it was the crisis of the Roman Empire.

AUSENDA: Yes, but then you had a period of 300 years, that's a long time. The Chinese Empire had recurring cycles of about 300 years between crises and changes of dynasties.

SCHWARCZ: Czechoslovakia and Yugoslavia are also examples of this.

AUSENDA: So did Russia. Russia was more powerful than the Visigothic state, yet its regime lasted only about 70 years.

SCHWARCZ: So, compared to that the Visigothic reign was quite successful.

HEATHER: Yes, you can say that even if you don't have all the information you might want. And instead of using these sub-Marxist models of economic collapse preceding political take-over, you can just think back to what happened at the battle of Hastings. Is that what happened to the Visigoths at Arab hands? It is at least as likely. Where the main political élite got killed all in one battle or in a couple of battles. It doesn't mean that the state had collapsed, it just means that the political élite died in battle and that's exactly what happened in Anglo-Saxon England.

AUSENDA: Well, that is very simplistic.

VOICES: No, no, it's true.

AUSENDA: If the Anglo-Saxon state had had an infrastructure holding them together, the Normans would have not been able to take over the country.

DE JONG: The Normans had success, precisely because the Anglo-Saxons had an infrastructure which they took over. You can look at it that way.

HEATHER: I think this kind of sub-Marxist model of disease of the late Roman Empire does not fit.

SCHWARCZ: Back to the Visigoths and the question of the Visigothic state. I think the most recent publications all agree that their fall was internal in a sense, but not due to decadence. You can easily show that there was internal strife immediately before 711, and for at least twenty years after 711, but that different quarreling groups followed a different policy also against each other. Some cooperated, some did not and that was why there was no recovery after 711.

DE JONG: Well, but quarreling groups are all over the place, also in states which proved quite successful.

HEATHER: There is also the problem of who you live next door to. Merovingian Gaul didn't have to live next door to a major Mediterranean Arab power.

DE JONG: This is precisely what Jinty Nelson said: the competition between aristocratic groups is an integral part of the vitality of the early medieval political constellations. You cannot say, well they quarreled and some sided with the wicked Arabs and the state collapsed.

SCHWARCZ: I did not say that, but just the contrary. There was more interest for the quarreling groups to side with the invaders, than to fight together against them.

AUSENDA: Anyhow, the 'causes' of the decadence and disappearance of 'systems' are still unknown, they are still a matter of speculation.

DE JONG: Yes, I am very sorry I mentioned the word decadence.

JIMÉNEZ: Yes, I am too.

HEATHER: Isn't that the problem that has been lurking in the background and it has to be confronted?

DE JONG: Definitely.

AUSENDA: I think one of the symptoms of collapse is demographic decline. I think there was demographic decline in the Roman Empire, demographic decline in Anglo-Saxon England and probably in Visigothic Spain.

HEATHER: There was no demographic decline in late Anglo-Saxon England, quite the reverse. Really, quite the reverse.

AUSENDA: You have the figures from Domesday Book and, if I am not mistaken, they amount to about 2 million people. That's not too many and this was some time after the Norman conquest.

SCHWARCZ: If we are talking about the Norman conquest, one should not forget that some years before the Norman conquest the English already were under Norse domination.

HEATHER: Well, I mean, the argument is showing that England was so attractive that lots of outsiders kept coming to it, that's the basic argument. So, in fact success can be a problem, can itself be a cause of failure.

Reference in the discussion

Textual sources:

Lex Visigothorum: see References at end of paper.

Bibliography:

Claude, D.
> 1985a   Der Handel in westlichen Mittelmeer während des Frühmittelalters. *Abhandlungen der Akademie der Wissenschaften in Göttingen. Philologisch-historische Klasse*. 3. Folge. Nr. 144.
> 1985b   Aspekte des Binnenhandels in Merowingerreich auf Grund der Schriftquellen. *Abhandlungen der Akademie der Wissenschaften in Göttingen. Philologisch-historische Klasse*. 3. Folge. Nr. 150, pp. 7-99.

Díaz, P. C.
> 1998   El testamento de Vicente: proprietarios y dependientes e la Hispania del s. VI. In *"Romanización" y "Reconquista" en la Península Ibérica: nuevas perspectivas*. M. J. Hidalgo *et al*. (eds.), pp. 257-270. Salamanca: Universidad de Salamanca.

García, L. A.
> 1972   See References at end of paper.

Gascó, F., J. Alvar, D. Plácido, B. Nieto & M. Carrilero
> 1993   Noticia de una inscripción griega inédita. *Gerión* 11: 327-335.

Heinzelmann, M.
> 1976   *Bischofsherrschaft in Gallien*. Munich: Artemis.

Metcalf, D. M.
> 1986   See References at end of paper.
> 1988   See References at end of paper.

Nelson, J. L.
> *Charles the Bald*. London: Longman.

Palol, P., & G. Ripoll
> 1988   *Los godos en el Occidente Europeo*. Madrid: Ediciones Encuentro.

Udovitch, A. L.
> 1978   Time, the sea and society: Duration of commercial voyages on the southern shores of the Mediterranean during the high Middle Ages. In *La navigazione mediterranea nell'alto medioevo*. (Settimane di studio del Centro Italiano di Studi sull'Alto Medioevo, XXV). Pp. 503-563. Spoleto: C.I.S.A.M.

Wickham, C.
> 1984   The other transition: from the ancient world to feudalism. *Past and Present* 103: 3-36.

VISIGOTHIC POLITICAL INSTITUTIONS

PABLO C. DÍAZ

*Facultad de Geografía e Historia, Universidad de Salamanca, c/Cervantes s/n,
E-37007 Salamanca*

Introduction: early political structures

The topic to be developed in this paper may at first seem evident from the title,
since it is clearly defined and limited, and at most only lacks a delimitation in time.
However, the development of the argument that I wish to make is full of obstacles.
In the first place, conceptual obstacles. What are the characteristics that permit us
to define an institution as 'political'? If we are looking at the past from the point of
view of current terminology, we should begin by defining *polity*, the form or
process of government, or *politics*, the science or art of government, or *political*, of
the state, of government, of public affairs in general. The equivalent words have
very similar meanings in most Western languages; it is the case of Spanish, my
own language of reference, which gives very similar dictionary definitions and
which includes a concrete definition under the Spanish word for *institution*: "an
organ instituted for governing or for carrying out a function of capital importance
for a State". It seems clear that a political institution is, in our current perception,
let us not forget, an organ of government. By means of an accumulation of these
institutions, a society with a complex structure administers its resources, imposes
and collects taxes, limits or abuses its power, legislates and administers justice, and
creates a bureaucracy for dealing with all these activities. It likewise defines its
boundaries and defends them, resorts to force if necessary to extend them or to
impede a foreign community from transgressing them, and for this it creates an
army, designs a foreign policy, etc. All of this is usually given the name 'state',
which in its ideal development in the modern world has been assimilated to the
'nation-state'.

However, it is not our intention here to situate the study of Visigothic political
institutions within a debate on the study of the state and its origins, where we
might consider that the concepts of politics and government are sufficient for
social analysis, casting doubt on the need for resorting to the concept of 'state'
(Radcliffe-Brown 1940:xi-xxiii). Nor shall we follow the historiographic debate
over the characterization of the Visigothic kingdom as a state or as a form of
state—a topic certainly of interest, but which teaches us more about the history of
the nineteenth and twentieth centuries, or about the different historiographic
currents, than about Visigothic history. In the Spanish historiographic tradition this
debate was charged with ideological connotations profoundly influenced by the
political evolution of the country (Torres López 1926; Sánchez Albornoz

© C.I.R.O.S.S.
San Marino (R.S.M.)

1972:157-499). We are going to maintain that a political institution is an organ of power sustained not by private positions of force, by the force of deeds, but rather by norms of public law applied to individual subjects of the law (Immink 1968:332-3), norms well-supported by a tradition commonly accepted by the majority, or better yet, by a written legal code; in both cases power is thus converted into a legal notion and the exercise of power develops into authority. The holder of this power, whether it be an individual or a group of them, acts by delegation of the power contained in the community, although in the long run it may become independent of the latter and build ideological mechanisms and formal resources to justify its position of power and for its perpetuation and build a tradition associated with the wielding of power, which it will endow with antiquity and surround with an aura of sacredness.

A community endows itself with political institutions when it has reached a certain level of economic and social stability, generally when it begins to move beyond those structures of blood relationship, the clan and lineage, the *sippe*, in our case, as the only elements capable of giving stability to the group. This process is difficult to document in the case of the Germanic kingdoms, owing especially to the existence of a broad historiographic tradition that has explained their social evolution by attending to the importance of some of the constituting clans and their descendants, which for some is more a comfortable means for reconstruction, accepted acritically as a necessary model, than a provable fact (Murray 1983:13-5, 31-4, 222-5), and where the clans are seen as military units, as territorial and settlement units, the fusion of which gave rise to the Germanic nations.

Within this scheme, the evolution of the Germanic peoples can be seen, on the one hand, as a continuum, that is, as an uninterrupted process that would have sustained a logical progression from the times of Caesar and Tacitus to the end of the fourth century, which is far from being certain, and on the other hand, as a process that was very similar for the different peoples or groups living on the periphery of the Empire, something which is equally debatable. This image evidently comes from the distortions made by the classical authors themselves, who used the interpretative categories and vocabulary from their own socio-political reality to describe phenomena or situations that were completely new to them. In their play of analogies they tended to group realities and groups that were probably very different in origin, or vice-versa, they identified split-off groups or factions as original and distinct, when they were practically indistinguishable from the group they came from. It is therefore probable that in many cases classical writers were identifying as great centralized units what were nothing more than circumstantial warrior alliances, and they made institutions that were absolutely limited in time seem permanent (Wallace-Hadrill 1979:1-4). Already on the Danube and just before entering the Empire, the Gothic subdivisions could, in moments of danger, act as *conspirantem in unum* (Ammianus Marcellinus XXVI. 6. 11; Rolfe 1935:II, 604), as warrior confederations, but once the danger was past they returned to their original components. Indeed, the key moment in the process of the political institutionalization of the monarchy was to be when it could survive the agglutinating circumstances with independence, or better yet, when it turned itself into a unifying element, which was not to occur among the Goths until Alaric I.

A knowledge of the exact level of political development reached by the groups of Goths at that moment might be of interest for understanding some of the characteristics of its subsequent evolution. It should not be forgotten, however, that in their contacts with the Romans and during their first wanderings in Imperial territory they underwent fundamental transformations and even adopted some elements as their own, elements which were to become an essential part of their mythical, cultural and political heritage. Even in the year 425 Philostorgius indicated that the differentiation of the Goths as a group separate from the Scythians was a recent fact (*Historia Eclesiastica* XI. 8; Bidez 1913:139). In this sense it should be noted that the tribal denominations Visigoths and Ostrogoths acquired political significance only in the fourth century, as tribal confederations created from smaller parental subgroups (Burns 1980:5-8), and were the product of fundamental readjustments caused by the Huns in Gothic society (Heather 1991:84-120). In reality, they replaced two large earlier units, formed after the end of the third century: on the one hand, the Greuthungian Ostrogoths, who occupied the land to the east of the Dniester, and whose destiny seems to be associated with a line of power capable of imposing itself at least temporarily as a royal family, the *Amali*; on the other hand we have the Tervingian *Vesi*, at whose head the sources place the oligarchic group of the *Balthi* (Wolfram 1990:13-5). The weight that these 'royal houses' had in the formation of Ostrogothic and Visigothic political units was doubtless magnified by their own dynastic propaganda and reached disproportionate success, due, above all, to the popularizing work of Jordanes (Wagner 1967; Cracco Ruggini 1978; Reydellet 1981:256-94; Heather 1991:34-67), but it seems certain that they were able to preserve Gothic political and cultural traditions, asserting their authority over a multiracial conglomeration that on more than one occasion managed to question their political leadership (Heather 1991:322-4). This multi-ethnic character should not be exaggerated, but, as was to occur in the case of the Franks (Wallace-Hadrill 1982:148-50), for example, this was not a homogeneous people but rather one with multi-racial confederations where the term *Gothi* was applied for convenience's sake, whereas the ethnic term would really only apply to the élite who were capable of monopolizing power and preserving it in spite of pressure from the Huns.

What were the traditions of power among these groups of Goths? The general impression is that the common Goths felt more identified with their local leaders, or with personal and limited warrior connections, than with the idea of a centralized monarchy (Heather 1991:320). This is a characteristic that probably marked a line of continuity from the *Tervingi* of the beginning of the fourth century to the most evolved and sophisticated phase of the Toledan monarchy. The *reiks* or chiefs that headed individual subdivisions (*kunja*) of the *Tervingi*, and who in case of necessity placed themselves under the orders of a *iudex*, a *iudex gentis* or a *iudex regnum* (Wolfram 1990:94), can be recognized, albeit that the cases are not exactly the same, in the *comites* with which the king of Toledo was supposed to reach a consensus on most of his actions (Heather 1991:322). However, as Wolfram (1990:95) has noted, the *iudex* was a dead end street from the institutional point of view, especially in the period of migrations when the armed group subordinated to its *reiks* (*rex?*), endowed with mobility, with solidarity from both relatives and clients, with discipline and unity in combat, as well as with immediacy in its relations with authority, displaced any other form of political organ at the heart of the community. We must not forget that in tribal societies the first element of unification is the state of war (Sahlins 1968:16-8) and that in the case of the Germanic tribes the essence of social hierarchy was ordered around an institution linked fundamentally to war, the retinues (*comitatus*) that united young warriors with their chiefs by means of strong ties of fidelity (Thompson 1965:48-60), which partially overcame the close bonds of kinship. During that migration process, the confederation of *reiks* demanded, probably as a mere functional necessity, subordination to a single command, a true *rex* at the head of the *exercitus Gothorum*, what Ammianus Marcellinus called *totius Gothiae* (XXX. 2. 8; Rolfe 1939: III, 310), an army which would now acquire a unitary nature, political subordination and a practical structure in *milena* and *centena* which would endure into documented periods (Wolfram 1990:97-9). It seems clear that the election of Athanaric as leader of the confederation derived from the needs of the war of 367-9 (Ammianus Marcellinus. XXVI.6.11; Rolfe 1935: II-602). The protagonism of the warrior leaders was to replace within this context the assembly-style political forms that included all the people known by Tacitus, and of which we find no trace in the Tervingian political structure (Wolfram 1990:104; Thompson 1966:47-9), nor in its subsequent evolution either in Toulouse or in Toledo.

This unitary *rex* constituted the political institution *par excellence* in the subsequent development of Gothic history, which was to force the creation of new structures of social control at all levels of society. And yet, in the strict sense it was a recent institution that was to take the form of such in the crucible of the years between the crossing of the Danube made by Alaviv and Fritigern and the settlement in Aquitaine—the period that went from detribalization to the formation of a permanent political structure within the Empire beginning in 418 (Heather 1991:223; Valverde 1994). A period lasting approximately fifty years and during which Roman influence on the Goths was to be so strong that sometimes any continuity with their tribal past is difficult to trace. The general idea is that contact with Rome not only altered political ideas or concepts of power, but also altered Gothic society in its totality, making it more hierarchical (Heather 1991:189). In this sense, it is possible that all this contact did was accelerate the foregoing process, since Gothic society already had an appreciable level of social differentiation (Thompson 1966:43-55), where *reiks* and *maistans* (Wolfram 1990:95) were situated in a position of clear superiority over the common people; these were military leaders with ties of kinship, on the one hand, and magnates, on the other, whose exact place is difficult to ascertain but which could be associated most clearly with an oligarchy whose power was measured in economic terms.

They would have headed the negotiations with the Roman authorities and been in charge of managing imperial subsidies and of administration, and, if it were the case, of distributing plots of land that came from the treaties with Rome (Thompson 1963a:107-9).

With these treaties, and taking as a starting point those of the year 376, and especially of 382, the Goths were to be accepted into the Empire under conditions of semi-autonomy. Their freedom was not recognized but, except for certain military salaries and the probable payment of taxes, they were allowed to develop their life as an organized group. None of their institutions of power were dismantled (Heather 1991:158-60). What is more, they were even capable of resisting imperial pressure, in some cases with overt indications of hostility towards the Empire; it is from this moment that "we are dealing with a nascent Gothic state, rather than a temporary and amorphous confederation" (Heather 1991:121). Their main objective at this time was probably to have land in which they could settle. A power structure associated with a territory and subjects over which to exercise that power are the ingredients necessary for an independent state. The process was not to be immediate.

When Isidore of Seville, with evident gaps in his information, looked to the past in an attempt to reconstruct the history of the Goths, he wrote that for many centuries they were governed by chiefs, *ducibus*, and then by kings, *regibus* (*Historia* 2; Rodríguez Alonso 1975:174), and a short time later (*Historia* 6; Rodríguez Alonso 1975:180; Rolfe 1939: II, 400) he seems to associate this change with the figure of Athanaric and says that he was the first to take charge of the government (*administrationem*) of the Gothic people, reigning (*regnans*) for thirteen years. Ammianus Marcellinus (XXXI. 4. 1; Rolfe 1939: II, 400) calls him *iudex gentis* or *iudex Thervingorum* and represents him as a negotiator before the Romans. It was with him that Valens achieved the peace of 369, he who in 380/1 offered soldiers in return for lands to cultivate (Iordanes, *Getica* XXV. 131; Mommsem 1961:92) and in exchange the Goths promised to obey the emperor as subjects (Zosimus IV.26; Paschoud 1981:II-288). In 381 Theodosius received him in Constantinople as intermediary and maximum representative of the Goths (Iordanes *Getica* XXVIII. 142-3; Mommsen 1961:95), and he died there a few days later. The emperor honoured him with a great funeral whose procession he presided over personally. However, not all the Visigoths agreed unanimously as to the posture to be adopted towards the Romans, nor was the figure of Athanaric accepted in a way that would correspond to the king of the entire confederation. Indeed, for some years, when he was obliged to take refuge in the mountains because of pressure from the Huns (Ammianus Marcellinus XXXI. 3-5; Rolfe 1939:III-394-418), he was abandoned by a great majority of his followers and was reduced to being leader of an isolated armed group, probably the one he had directed before his election as *iudex*. We can see then how with Athanaric the Visigoths had still not taken that qualitative step which would allow us to speak of a monarchy consolidated as a permanent political institution, and probably only in Theodosius' biased perception was Athanaric the great king to be received into Constantinople and over whose funeral Theodosius presided.

Indeed, the behaviour that the Goths were to display over the years following the death of Theodosius did not always correspond to that of a unitary people, subjected to a unanimously accepted leader and in search of lands to cultivate, as some contemporary testimonies would have us believe. Liebeschuetz (1991:83-5) has noted that envisaging the Goths as an agricultural people, even from the Roman point of view, as Priscus did (frag. 49; Blockley 1983:356) when he noted that before coming into the Empire many Goths had lived as farmers, may lead to error. In his opinion the behaviour of the Goths is best understood in reference to the behaviour patterns of a nomadic, or at least semi-nomadic people, which would explain why for forty years they adapted to an existence of constant movement. Sustenance would come from flocks, from some base area for grain collection and from periodical pillaging campaigns—wars from the Roman point of view—in order to obtain precious booty at the cost of the provincial inhabitants. This characterization as nomads or semi-nomads would equally explain some of their warlike behaviour, such as the permanent surplus of a young labour force ready for war, or the constant need for warrior chiefs to consolidate their situation of power through success and their corresponding generosity. However, the figure of Alaric can only be partially explained from this perspective (Heather 1991:325-8; Nixon 1992:65-7).

According to the testimony of Jordanes (*Getica* XXIX. 146-7; Mommsen 1961:96) between the years 395 and 400 Alaric had achieved an outstanding position among the Goths settled under the treaty of 382, and according to him this was because Alaric belonged to the *Balthi* family. However, as Heather (1991:196) notes, this is undoubtedly anachronistic. There is no reason to doubt that Alaric formed part of a family whose tradition would allow him to become a *iudex*, should this be the case, but the extent of his position at the head of an important group of Visigoths must be understood as a position attained in the midst of a struggle with other Goths who could wield those same rights, and not as a function of any preferential right. Who and what were those who could wield this right is an important question which we cannot answer. It is likely that the number of aristocratic families who in subsequent Visigothic history fought for the throne was already defined at this time, and their number was not necessarily high. As a comparative example it can be noted that the highest Burgundian nobility numbered no more than thirty families and perhaps only six among the Bavarians of the sixth century (Thompson 1963b:12). What is more, it is likely that Alaric gained his prestige while serving the interests of Rome, perhaps at the head of a group of barbarian *auxilia*, and because of that distinction asked for a promotion (Burns 1994:92-110). This does not mean that when he declared his interest in obtaining a Roman military command (Zosimus, V. 5. 4; Paschoud 1986:III-11) he aspired to an individual promotion, but the position of *magister militum*, no matter how much it served to strengthen or even provide political and military influence for the Gothic group that Alaric headed (Heather 1991:199-201), entailed the acceptance of Roman categories of power, absolutely subordinated to the emperor and in this case independent of a political command within the Visigoth conglomeration.

This approximation to Roman forms of power was now going to be decisive. Starting in 395 when he advanced towards Constantinople to demand from Theodosius' son the subsidies derived from the prevailing *foedus*, and during his wanderings through imperial territories up to the sacking of Rome, Alaric not only made himself essential to the group of Goths who followed him—probably not those settled in Moesia but only a part of those whom other *foederati* established in Epirus would join (Liebeschuetz 1991:77-9)—but, furthermore, the search for a new internal cohesion was also furnished with institutional mechanisms of power which looked more towards Roman models than towards their own tribal traditions. Hence, when the Goths *ordinant super se regem Halarico* (Iordanes, *Getica* XXIX. 146; Mommsen 1961:96), or in the opinion of Isidore: *Gothi patrocinium Romani foederis recusantes Alaricum regem sibi constituunt, indignum iudicantes Romanae esse subditos potestati* (*Historia* 12; Rodríguez Alonso 1975:190), we should not consider this a revival of an old monarchic institution but the creation of a newly fledged one. This process would have been associated with the 'invention' of a justifying tradition, a 'Stammestradition' which ensured power and its transmission within a particular ethnic or noble group (Wenskus 1961:54-82).

When, now probably as *rex*, Alaric signed the *foedus* of 397 with Arcadius, he received from him the appointment of *magister militum per Illyricum*, or perhaps *dux Illyrici* (Wolfram 1990:248-5). Without bringing into doubt the legitimacy which, in the eyes of the Goths, Alaric had as *rex* elected by his warriors, or by the *optimates*, and therefore possessor of an authority emanating from his own tribal traditions, the office granted by Arcadius, which legalized his position in the eyes of the Roman authorities, gave Alaric a pre-eminence which he would take advantage of in order to assert himself over the other *optimates*. This situation led to the future consolidation of the institution, but for the time being it made it a power subordinated to Roman authority. In a recent study Liebeschuetz (1992:75-83) wondered whether the Goths of Alaric were an army or a nation. The question is not new and can be traced as far back as D. Fustel de Coulanges (1891:291-302, 416-26), who already thought that Alaric was not the head of a nation but rather the head of an army, just as Athaulf would be later on, and that they were not a migrating people but rather an army of imperial soldiers in revolt against the Empire; for Fustel the ancient peoples had dissolved and only warrior bands, united by chance or by war, with no political organization, were coming into the Empire. The question may be rhetorical, but depending on the answer, Alaric may have been a mere military chief or an authentic *rex*. In reality, this is a problem that could extend to all the Visigothic kings up to Euric, for only then did the Visigothic monarchs stop acting, at least in theory, as authorities delegated by the imperial power.

The doubt as to the exact nature of the leadership that Alaric represented must, as a whole, be measured from his behaviour after the breaking in 401 of the treaty signed with Arcadius, the time at which he left the prefecture of *Illyricum* and started a series of raids which would culminate in the march on Rome, and finally in the attempt to reach Africa in which he would meet his own death. The decision as to whether Alaric I was a king or not follows a kind of fashion, where today the negative opinion is again asserted, although Herwig Wolfram believes that it must be accepted that it was with him that a new institution and doubtlessly a political identity were introduced, but neither was he able to create a *stirps regia* nor resolve the major problem of how a barbarian king and Roman power could be reconciled on Roman soil (Wolfram 1990:160). According to the narratives of Zosimus (V .36-50; Paschoud 1986:III 53-72) and Jordanes (XXIX-XXX; Mommsen 1961:96-9), it was probably during this period that Alaric managed to assert his authority over the majority of the armed groups who followed the Gothic *optimates*, but these authors are not precise enough to be able to affirm that the conscious imposition of a 'romanized' concept of centralized power was the work of Alaric. The defection of Sarus may reveal that not all Goth *optimates* accepted his leadership (Wolfram 1990:145). Indeed, at the time when Alaric called his brother-in-law Athaulf to his side (Zosimus V. 37. 1 and 45. 5; Paschoud 1986: III 54, 67) he did not seem to do so as an *auctoritas* recognized by the latter, but rather it seems to be a call to an equal. We also have the later reference to the moment when the prefect of the *praetorium*, Jovius, sent ambassadors to Alaric and asked him to appear accompanied by Athaulf (Zosimus V. 48. 1; Paschoud 1986: III 70), which perhaps reflects a Roman perception of equality between them. The very account that Jordanes gives of Alaric's burial (*Getica* XXX. 158; Mommsen 1961:99) is closer to the consecration of a Germanic warrior chief than to that of a *rex*, in the sense desired by the Romans and which would eventually take hold among the Goths. The sacred nature of the primitive German king, whether associated with his particular genealogy, derived from his ancestors and not his conquests, with his individual warrior *virtus*, or with his condition as representative of the moral life of his people, an individualized extension of the functions of the popular assembly which was sacred in itself, is a topic of specific interest but its projection into subsequent institutional evolution is very difficult to confirm (Grierson 1941:1-22; Höfler 1973:75-104; Schlesinger 1973:136-8; Wallace-Hadrill 1979:8-10).

The figure of Athaulf is perhaps more important when establishing the moment of the institutionalization of the Visigothic monarchy. According to the accounts of Orosius, Hydatius and Jordanes on the passing of power from Alaric to Athaulf, this was not so much a conscious act on the part of the former (Heather 1991:31), as an intentional use of kinship on the part of the latter (Wolfram 1990:161), who took advantage of this circumstance to construct a genealogy in his own interest, a myth about the family ancestry and his association with a family with preferential rights for occupying the office of *rex*. Furthermore it is in Athaulf that we find a conscious desire to emulate imperial power which culminated in his marriage to Galla Placidia, the last link in a chain of relations and negotiations with the emperor and his functionaries which involved, in principle, a new agreement with the handing over of land, now in the West. In the very context of this marriage to Galla Placidia, Orosius (VII. 43. 4-6; Zangemeister 1882:299-300) tells a story which, although suspect, is susceptible to a double reading: Athaulf, who had dreamed of destroying the Roman Empire and transforming *Romania* into *Gothia*, realized that the barbarism of the Goths could not be subjected to laws and that therefore they should preserve the laws of the Empire and exalt and restore Rome with the strength of the Goths. Beyond any observations that we might make concerning Orosius' ideology, the passage shows us that Athaulf was the first to assume that the political conceptions of the Goths, and in particular, their limited monarchical institution, would not serve for the governing of a kingdom (state, stable territory, or any other term we may use), and that for such an undertaking it would be necessary to have a complex scheme ideally modelled on the Roman Empire. It is even likely that he may have dreamed of uniting both nations in his son, whom he significantly named Theodosius. Olympiodorus (frag. 26; Blockley 1983:188) says that when this son was born Athaulf became even more friendly towards the Romans. The process was long and not always linear, in fact we can consider that it did not come to fruition until the time of Liuvigild.

Thus, while the figure of Alaric can still be explained according to the model of a military chief at the head of a semi-nomadic group, something like a soldier of fortune at the head of a professional army who made booty the essential source of his prestige, fed by his capacity to satisfy the demands of his followers (Liebeschuetz 1991:75; Schlesinger 1973:117-9; Wenskus 1961:313-6 and 409-12), Athaulf looked more decisively for new patterns of power. A land for permanent settlement and a territorialized power that was symbolically and formally capable of being assimilated to Roman patterns of power were his objectives. Athaulf, upon adapting, was only looking for an effective means of negotiating; he meant himself to be an authority acceptable to the eyes of Rome. It is interesting to note in this sense that Olympiodorus (frag. 24; Blockley 1983:187-8) not only underlines the *romanitas* of Athaulf, but even presents him dressed as a Roman general when describing his wedding in Narbonne.

This marriage, unwanted by the imperial family, meant his breaking off with Honorius and forced the Visigoths to move from Gaul to *Hispania* (Olympiodorus, frags. 22-3; Blockley 1983:184-6; Orosius VII. 43. 1-2; Zangemeister 1882:299), considered by Jordanes (*Getica* XXXI. 161-2; Mommsen 1961:100) as a voluntary move, where Athaulf was murdered in Barcelona by his own soldiers (Orosius VII. 43. 8; Zangemeister 1882:300). Although we do not know the exact reason for his murder, beyond its being an act of revenge directed by Sarus' relatives, it is likely that it entailed a struggle for power. This would mean that the pre-eminence of the *Balthi* clan was not unanimously accepted and that there was no unanimity as to who should be king. After the short-lived stay of Sigeric, Valia was elected king (Orosius VII. 43. 10; Zangemeister 1882:300; Hydatius, *Chronica* 37; Burgess 1993:82; Jordanes, *Getica* XXXII. 164-5; Mommsen 1961:100-1), and his behaviour again brings to mind an itinerant armed group in search of a stable situation, whether it be by occupying lands, by attempting to go to Africa, or by means of an agreement with the Empire. In this sense, the first *foedus* was signed with Rome in 416, according to which the Visigoths would act as a mercenary army in the service of Rome, and later there was a contractual treaty of settlement in 418 which meant the giving over of lands to the Goths in Aquitaine, *Novempopulana* and *Narbonensis prima*.

Alaric I, who is credited with having endowed the Goths with enough strength to intimidate the Empire, and who received almost unanimous confidence from his people and cleared the way for the permanent institutionalization of the monarchy, did not, however, resolve the matter of how imperial power and a barbarian king could be reconciled on Roman soil (Wolfram 1990:160). Athaulf's attempt to follow Roman models and even to seek a rapprochement by marriage did not solve the matter, which remained pending at the time of settlement in Gaul in 418.

Toulouse: the shadow of the Roman Empire

The definitive acceptance of the condition of *foederati* and the settlement of the groups gathered around Alaric and Athaulf within the borders of the Empire opened a new stage in which the overcoming of assumptions about delegated or subordinate power would mark the evolution of the monarchy and Visigothic political institutions. It was not by chance that at that time Olympiodorus (frag. 34; Blockley 1983:198) began to call the Gothic monarchy *archê*, undoubtedly in the sense of the Roman magistracy (Barnwell 1992:72-3).

It must be taken into account that, despite the growing feeling of unity that the Goths were acquiring, the settlement in Gaul must, in the first place, be measured in Roman terms, i.e., it responded to the Roman logic of using barbarians to defend their frontiers (Burns 1992:53-63; Pelliciari 1982:51-3), and in this case inner territories which were specially problematic (Bachrach 1969:354-8; Sivan 1983:12-4; Thompson 1982:251-5). As military colonists the Visigoths received grain and farmland in exchange for military service, but insofar as they were to be governed by their own rules of conduct and their own institutions, in practice they became a state within a state, a monarchy within the Empire (Burns 1994:283), where Valia or Theoderic I did not receive a Roman command, but were to all effects *reges Gothorum*, with civil and military authority over their people. However, the tribal system of behaviour now became a hindrance to institutional development and royalty did everything possible to repress old tribal customs in the interests of exercising their emerging power (Thompson 1963b:15-20). Thus the ascending populist tendencies of monarchic power gave way to other descending tendencies, where the monarchy intended to distance itself from the people or from the Gothic aristocracy, in order to mark its privileged position with divine ascendancy (Ullman 1961:19-21). Its success was probably not complete and in the same way that the Romans were to negotiate independently with the Visigothic nobility settled in Aquitaine (Burns 1992:62; Claude 1971:38), or that groups of Goths were to act independently (Heather 1992:87-8), the pressure from this nobility and its struggles with the king were to be essential elements in the subsequent institutional equilibrium, and in the strength or weakness that the monarchy would have in the future. Moreover, we must take into account the fact that the Gothic *optimates* also underwent the process of 'romanization' which affected the monarchy, and in the first place assimilated the concepts of wealth in landed property which defined Roman aristocrats. Moreover, if the king needed the support of the *optimates*, these in turn found in the monarchy the consolidation of their position with respect to the Gothic masses, and their justification with respect to Roman power (Vigil & Barbero 1974:379-93). This was probably one of the reasons why during the fifth century there were no rebellions on the part of the nobility, who obtained booty, especially lands, with the expansionist policy, in spite of having lost power to the king (Wolfram 1990:212).

The election of Theoderic I in 418 opened the way for the future Roman-Visigothic monarchy, from whence arose a new Gothic identity that was more newly created than remembered (Burns 1994:282; Claude 1972:1-7). Indeed, the same dynasty which was then being inaugurated, despite the fact that Theoderic was Alaric's son-in-law, was built upon new foundations (Heather 1992:87; Orlandis 1962:63; Wolfram 1990:174-6). From its primitive political regime, it preserved its tribal king, who was essentially a military chief (Latouche 1946:208-9), but the prestige of imperial dignities was added to this apparent simplicity. The Empire thus became the model which would culminate in Liuvigild's work (Claude 1971:61-4; Stroheker 1965:134-91), but right from the very moment of the settlement, the Visigothic kings adopted Roman titles and official functions, although in many cases altered and confused in content, and they sought to be near cities that had been ancient seats of Roman power (Bruguière 1974:231-3). The possession of a royal city and of treasure would, in the future, become synonyms for the possession of the whole kingdom (Wolfram 1990:205-6)

These factors were highly significant. The choice of a city as a royal seat, even if it was a secondary centre such as Toulouse, opened the way for the formation of a court and a central administration where the domestic services of Germanic origin and a chancellor-like bureaucracy of Roman origin were united (Stroheker 1937:90-1). Civil affairs continued in the hands of a Roman administration and the court was the essential nexus, since from there the king carried out supervisory duties through the *comites* (Barnwell 1992:78-80; Wolfram 1990:214). The title *comes* refers to a rank rather than to an office or function, for which the term *dux* or even *iudex* was used (Sánchez Albornoz 1959:374). These institutional duties were not yet exceedingly sophisticated in Toulouse, where we find references to the *comes ciuitatis* (*Codex Euricianus* 322; D'Ors 1960:39) or to the *comes armiger* (Sidonius, *Epistola* I. 2; Loyen 1970-II:6), on whose specific functions we have very little information, but which would undoubtedly entail an adaptation of diverse titles and traditions to the new circumstances of shared power (Barnwell 1992:81). The Goths were at the head of these positions of political control, but the Romans must have occupied an important place in the court, and sometimes in the army, at least as from 450 (Heather 1992:89-91), and although we do not know the exact title and form of address they received, they must have been essential when transmitting Roman customs, usage and laws. Roman administrative practice and ways of public life entailed the preserving of Latin cultural traditions at the expense of Germanic ones.

To what degree did the Visigothic king in Toulouse behave as a high imperial functionary, or did he see himself as a kind of emperor? The only significant text in this sense is the well-known letter of Sidonius (*Epistola* I. 2; Loyen 1970-I:4-8) which gives us a detailed account of the daily routine of Theoderic II. This well-known description may be partly reality and partly a reproduction of imperial models; in any case it brings to us a description both of the daily routine of the emperors, as well as of the routine of high-ranking Roman functionaries, such as provincial governors or the prefect of the *praetorium* (Barnwell 1992:72-3; Harries 1994:127-9). Probably, the image given by Sidonius responds to the divided personality that the Visigothic king would have for a few years, a Germanic king for his people, a patrician in the eyes of the Romans (Reydellet 1981:23, 69-80). Evidently, the description in the text fits the second image. We should not forget that Sidonius himself had taken note of Theoderic's Roman education (*Carmina* VII. 481-3: Loyen 1960:73) and how he helped Avitus to gain the imperial throne, and that this affected his appraisal of the Visigothic king, to whom he did not hesitate to assign the virtue of *civilitas*, formerly only attributed to a Roman monarch, and present him seated in his royal chair (the text uses *sella* or *solio*, but not *thronus*), accompanied by his main assistants. One might wonder how much of this is reality and how much is due to the image that Sidonius wished to create of Theoderic II, the most 'romanized' of all the Gothic kings (Rouche 1979:171); in any case, we must take into account the fact that his father already seemed to have been called *dominus*, just like Euric (Sivan 1983:110), who was addressed by Sidonius himself as *decus* and *columen* (*Carmina* XXIII. 2. 69-73 and 176; Loyen 1960:146-7, 151) and presented to us in his court, dictating treaties and issuing laws (*Epistola* VIII. 3. 3, 9. 4; Loyen 1970-III:87,104). He was also addressed as *dominus*, a title used until then by the Romans, to refer to the emperor or imperial magistrates, and dated documents by years of his reign (Wolfram 1990:204). The same title of *dominus* is given to Euric in an inscription commemorating the restoration of the Roman bridge at Mérida (Vives 1942: n° 363).

The legislative activity of the kings of Toulouse is another element of interest. It has been noted that the issuing of codes by Euric and Alaric II, and perhaps even by Theoderic I, should be seen as a continuation of the issuance of edicts that was proper to praetorian prefects; thus Euric's code should be called *edictum Eurici regis* (D'Ors 1960:3), and since King Euric proclaimed it, it was not intended to supplant the emperor but rather the prefect of Arles (Collins 1983:27-9; García Gallo 1974:343-467; Gibert 1956:26), and to build a kingdom limited to the southern territories of Gaul and *Hispania*, the old imperial diocese, a task in which he would probably have the help of some of the official representatives of Roman power, such as Vincentius Arvandus (Sidonius, *Epistola* I. 7: Loyen 1970-II:21-6). In any case, we should not forget that after Theodosius I, the image of the emperor was not so much that of a military leader as that of an administrator, someone who appointed people to office, and a lawgiver, and in this sense the symbolic value of Euric's legislative activity, and even more so that of Alaric II, is fundamental (Reydellet 1981:2-4, 60-2). The law to be developed now was in any case Roman law, constructed on the basis of vulgar Roman law by Roman jurists and in the language of that same law; not a single Germanic word can be found in Euric's code, not even in those norms with Germanic roots (Astuti 1970:327; Levy 1951:15-6). At present we will not go into whether these were territorial or personal codes but the early legislation of Euric and then the Breviary of Alaric II were clear attempts to provide the kingdom with laws legitimizing its own independence. The *Lex Romana Visigothorum* was a legal code issued before and legitimized by bishops and magnates, by the Gothic and Roman aristocracies, and in the letter of authentication accompanying each copy sent to each *comes civitatis* they were warned that in the future it was forbidden to use any other legal code on pain of death (Wolfram 1990:196). This seems to mark a qualitative difference between Euric and Alaric II; in the case of the latter we are clearly dealing with a *lex* rather than an *edictum* (Lambertini 1991:6 n. 2).

With Euric, the monarchy was now a fully established political institution, conceived independently from the Empire (Jordanes, *Getica* XL. 237; XLVIII. 244; Mommsen 1961:118-20; Sidonius, *Epistola* VII. 6. 4; Loyen 1970-III:44). A monarchy surrounded by the warrior-like attributes inherited from Germanic tradition and by the administrative legitimacy of imperial tradition from which it seems to have taken court practice, perhaps in imitation of Constantinople (Sivan 1983:108). A court which already had a *concilium regis*, into which members of the Gallo-Roman aristocracy would become integrated, as is the case of Leo, who, in the time of Euric, held the offices of *quaestor sacri palatii* and of *magister officiorum*, and who continued in the service of Alaric II (Sivan 1983:120-4). From this court, the control was also organized of the central administration and the government of cities and provinces by *duces* and *comites*, *rectores vel iudices prouinciarum, defensores ciuitatis* or *numerarii*, figures with military and civil functions, responsible for judicial or fiscal tasks, with Germanic titles in some cases, especially in the military institutions, and with Roman ones in the areas of the tax system or the administration of justice (Jiménez Garnica 1983:131-85; Wolfram 1990:202-22). We know the names of these and other offices thanks to Alaric II's *Breviarium*; in some cases they are no more than names and in their totality they form the *Officium Palatinum, Palatium Regis* or *Aula Regia*. On some occasions the terms seem to have been used for differentiated properly defined institutions; however, we must also accept the fact that sometimes they were used interchangeably and that the confusion may stem from the lack of definition of their composition and functions, as well as of the changes undergone throughout Visigothic history (Sánchez Albornoz 1946a:5-110).

The definition of this *Officium Palatinum* as a political institution undoubtedly depends on the characterization we give it. If we believe that it was made up of all those who were directly in the service of the monarch (King 1972:56), then what we have is a service bureaucracy and its political nature is ambiguous. If, on the other hand, as was to occur in the later development of the Toledan monarchy, we accept that the *Officium* was made up of the aristocratic élite of the kingdom, especially the Gothic élite, but in time also the Roman élite, that it included those holding important military and civil offices, and that the presence of the high clergy was also to be taken into consideration, then its nature was doubtlessly institutional. It is likely that this *Officium* was the result of the union of the Germanic tribal *comitatus*, the council of *optimates* whose opinion the Visigothic king had to take into account before his settlement in Aquitania, and the *Officium* of the praetorian prefect (Sánchez Albornoz 1946a:169). Taking into consideration the fact that the formation of this institution depended on the formation process of the monarchy as a whole, we must understand that although Euric is attributed with the formal organization of this *Aula Regia*, it was only really from the time of Liuvigild that it was fully developed (King 1972:13). Moreover, we should not forget that the most genuinely Germanic attribute of the Visigothic king was still his condition of warrior chief. The court was where the king was, and it was on these occasions that the *optimates*, who in political perception had become institutionalized after the Roman fashion, behaved in accordance with their traditions. The proclamation of Thorismund, after the death of Theoderic I on the Catalaunian Fields, corresponded to the trustees of the military power, to the Visigothic aristocracy; Jordanes' reference (*Getica*, XLI. 215; Mommsen 1961:113) to the Goths who raised him to the throne in the midst of a clamour of arms, should in no case be confused with an election made by the assembly of warriors. The same could be said with regard to the men who, armed with their spears, met with Euric before the taking of Arles (Hydatius, *Chronica* 238; Burgess 1993:120; Isidore, *Historia* 35; Rodríguez Alonso 1975:229), who were none other than the aristocrats with whom Euric discussed affairs during campaigns. In the same way, Sidonius' reference to the *veterum coetus* or to the *duces pariter Scythicusque senatus* was probably a preliminary step in the formation of this *Officium*, prior to its formalized creation with Euric (Jiménez Garnica 1983:154-6; Sánchez Albornoz 1946a:153-5).

The institutional consolidation of the Toulouse monarchy was interrupted in 507 when Alaric was defeated at Vouillé by Clovis, thus opening a period of political uncertainty and the beginning of the definitive move towards *Hispania*. The year before the Visigothic king had issued the *Lex Romana Visigothorum*, and that same year a great Catholic council had been held in Agde, which inaugurated a policy of great significance for the future of the successor kingdoms to the Empire, which we shall examine for the case of Toledo. Perhaps the Council of Agde and the promulgation of the *Lex Romana Visigothorum* can be seen as signs of a 'failed merger' (Wolfram 1990:200), a foretaste of the policies which Liuvigild and Reccared would carry out, and which were delayed by their defeat by the Franks. The death of Alaric II, in spite of the succession of his son Amalaric, called into question something that had not been debated since the time of Theoderic I, the right to transmit power within the *Balthi* family (Claude 1971:36-7, 46-8). The loss of control over a part of Gaul, the loss of at least a part of the royal treasure and the death of the king were to weaken the economic power and the prestige of the lineage of Theoderic I, and together with them its political and hereditary monopoly on the monarchy, which had never been based on an institutional principle; we might recall here the comments of Gregory of Tours (*Libri historiarum decem* III. 30; Krusch & Levison 1951:126), who, upon narrating the succession of usurpations that went on from Amalaric to Agila, pointed out that the Goths had adopted the reprehensible habit of killing their kings when they did not like them, replacing one king with another (Thompson 1963b:5). From this moment on, monarchical power was to become the subject of dispute among the family members of the traditional Visigothic aristocracy, the owners of great fortunes and dependants in *Hispania* (Vigil & Barbero 1974:380, 386). As from this moment, the political tradition of the nobles, and that of those who would fortuitously become kings, would have the same weight (Claude 1971:139-40, 201-3; Ewig 1976:21-3).

Toledo: the Visigothic monarchy

The disaster of Vouillé should be relativized (Wolfram 1990:243-5). It evidently meant an interruption in the institutional process. The end of the dynasty of Theoderic I opened new horizons for the monarchy, which, as already noted, was to become the central element of the Visigothic political disputes in the following period. Furthermore, for some years it allowed the kingdom to live under the protection of the Ostrogoths, who from Ravenna controlled as far as possible affairs in *Hispania*. In 511, even the Visigothic treasure was moved temporarily to the capital of the Ostrogoths, thus underlining the political significance of their submission (Procopius, *De bello Gothico* I(V). 12. 44-6; Dewing 1919:128-30). As R. d'Abadal (1960:55) has pointed out, the treasure was a talisman, the possession of which would define the legitimate continuity of the Visigothic monarchy until it was taken by Tarik in Toledo in the year 711. This "Ostrogothic Interval" (García Iglesias 1975:89-120) was not free of violent successions to the throne, even when in 549 Agila, the first king of an exclusively Visigothic line since the time of Alaric II, obtained the throne. The kingdom only really found a certain stability again after 572, when Liuvigild became sole king after the death of his brother Liuva with whom he had shared royal power. We shall not dwell on the political events which led him to subject to his authority the different regions of the Peninsula, which had acted with absolute independence of any central power, as well as the Suevian kingdom, and only the southern strip occupied by the Byzantines in the time of Athanagild (*ca* 551-552) remained out of his control. We are not interested here in Liuvigild's military campaigns, but in his initiatives to strengthen the Visigothic monarchy and the set of institutions of the kingdom—a formal renovation and at the same time a profound redefinition of the ideological mechanisms sustaining the new power of the State.

Liuvigild is presented by Isidore (*Historia* 51; Rodríguez Alonso 1975:258) as a formal renovator of the monarchy, the first one to present himself before his people on the *solium* and dressed in special royal robes, since previously, says the Bishop of Seville, both the seat and the apparel were common to the king and his people. This could be an anecdote if it were an isolated incident; however, this ritual exteriorization was part of a series of initiatives which aimed at placing the monarchy, finally, at the top of the pyramid of the social and political organization of Visigothic Spain. Dress and position symbolized a place given prominence over the people and the aristocracy, but they were not the only element to which Liuvigild resorted (Stroheker 1965:137-9).

In his plan of action, which seems consciously to emulate imperial Roman ways, the new royal seat, Toledo, occupied an important place. The choice of Toledo does not seem to have been the work of Liuvigild. In 546 Theudis had already issued a decree on procedural costs in that city, and Athanagild would have established his residence there (Ewig 1963:28). It was with Liuvigild, however, that it prevailed over the whole of the Peninsula. The choice of Toledo was not linked to its prior significance, it had neither been a centre of power nor a rich city, but under the geopolitical circumstances of the time its strategic location between Visigothic Gaul and the Byzantine territories in the South, and the particular ease of its defence, made it a fortunate choice. Liuvigild wanted to make of it a true *civitas regia*, a title it received at the third Council of Toledo, in an attempt to equate it with Constantinople. In time Toledo became a synonym of royal power; exalted and embellished by kings such as Wamba, it was the seat of the Councils of the Visigothic Church, whose political significance we shall come to. Its bishopric became metropolitan and its Church became the first in the kingdom (Rivera Recio 1955:3-34). Toledo was also the place where kings were anointed, when this became the custom.

Broadly speaking, we can say that "Liuvigild's reign saw the conclusion of a development that turned the Visigothic *regnum* into a Spanish *imperium*" (Wolfram 1990:245), and as another example of this, beginning in Liuvigild's time, the Visigoths minted their own gold coins which imitated imperial types. Apart from its economic significance, its symbolic value is equally manifest, just as it is in the fact that Liuvigild minted coins commemorating his victories. In the same way and as part of imperial emulation, Liuvigild founded a city which he called Reccopolis, something which at least two other Visigothic kings, Reccared and Sisebut, also did. In the case of Reccopolis at least, it seems clear that the city was never conceived of for utilitarian ends, or as a response to strategic or populational needs, but rather for merely "self-celebratory" reasons (La Rocca 1993:477-8).

At least two further aspects should be mentioned among those to which Liuvigild devoted attention and which, although not new, would in the future form part of the elements defining the Visigothic monarchic institution—on the one hand his role as a legislator, on the other, his religious policy. Liuvigild carried out a legislative revision which turned out to be less than perfect because it still did not overcome the separation between Goths and Romans. Thus in *LV* III, 1. 1 (Zeumer 1902:121-2), the king presented himself to a *populus*, but laws were still preserved which made distinctions between *Gothi* and *Romani*. Its form influenced by the *Corpus iuris civilis*, his *Codex Revisus* has not been preserved, although some of its laws were passed on as *Antiquae* to the *Lex Visigothorum*, a large code completed in the main by Recceswinth, with the advice of Braulio, bishop of Saragossa, issued in 654 after being revised by the VIII Council of Toledo. Moreover, Liuvigild devoted great effort to a unifying religious policy, perhaps with a Byzantine model in mind, but failed due to his insistence on taking the Arian creed as its theological reference, a minority creed which therefore distanced him from his Hispano-Roman subjects. Liuvigild aspired to a unity of kingdom, law and faith, which undoubtedly was an emulation of the Empire and specifically of Justinian (Stroheker 1965:139), but he failed.

Liuvigild, using his prestige and his power, managed to transmit power to his son Reccared. For this he resorted to the same mechanism that his brother Liuva had used with him, association to the throne, which had its precedent in the policy of the Roman emperors. In any case, Reccared was the optimal candidate because of his military prestige (Thompson 1969:92). Beyond the Catholic propaganda which associated his name with the definitive conversion of the Visigoths, and to the Third Council of Toledo, Reccared realized his father's policy of seeking a territorial rather than an ethnic monarchy. For this reason he advocated his own conversion and that of his people to Catholicism (Thompson 1960:4-35); evidently this entailed the elimination of religious barriers, but at the same time it entailed renouncing Arianism, which in practice had become a differentiating sign of identity (Heather 1986:289-318). Nevertheless, more important than the conversion itself, however much it helped towards a rapid fusion of Goths and Romans, was the Great Council held in Toledo in 589, which became the model for a form of government that was fundamental to the Western tradition. At the Council, when Reccared signed he put *Flavius*, the family name of the emperors of the Constantinian dynasty, before his name. John of Biclar, in the summary which he made of the event in his chronicle, compared him to the emperors Constantine and Marcian, who had presided at Nicaea and Chalcedon respectively (Barbero 1970:254-6). This Council also initiated a process of consecration of power and the imposition of the theories on the descending nature of power, sanctioned by the Catholic hierarchy, with which they intended to distance themselves even further from the nobility (Anton 1972:259-62; Claude 1971:77-80; Schaferdiek 1967:238-41).

The Visigothic Councils were a political institution in themselves, the supreme legislative assembly responsible for regulating the running of the state and the highest court in the realm (d'Abadal 1970a:90). By studying those of a general nature held in Toledo between 589 and 694, we can study the evolution of the monarchy, and what is more, that of a whole form of government which it would be erroneous to interpret in terms of Church-State relationship, because that reading would not have been understood by contemporaries (Wallace-Hadrill

1952:123). What we have is a mixture of ecclesiastic and secular administration, which, for example, allowed the use of excommunication as a political sanction, or permitted the king to pardon religious sanctions. These religious attributes of the kings were recognized and legitimized by the bishops. Thus, in Conc. Tolet. IV, *a.* 633: *...non solum in rebus humanis sed etiam in causis divinis sollicitus maneat* (Vives 1963:186), in this case in reference to Sisebut; or in the same way, with reference to Recceswinth in *Conc. Emerit., a.* 666: Praef: *...Et quoniam de saecularia sancta illi manet cura, et de ecclesiastica per divinam gratiam recte disponit mente intenta...*(Vives 1963:325); c.23: *ac deinde serenissimo atque piisimo et orthodoxo viro clementissimo domno nostro Reccesvintho regi gratia [e] impedimus opem cuius vigilancia et saeculaia regit cum pietate summa et ecclesiastica plenus disponit divinitus sibi sapiencia concessa* (Vives 1963:342). There are many other possible examples, but these will suffice.

The Councils brought together the bishops and magnates of the realm, a selection of them chosen from among the members of the palatine office or from the *Aula Regia*, and those that the king on occasion called companions in government, *quos in regimine socios* (*Conc. Tolet. VIII*; Vives 1963:265). In general the more important aspects of their agenda were always of a political kind and not, as would have been reasonable, of a theological or ecclesiast-ical-disciplinary nature. Despite the stipulation, for example in canon 18 of Toledo III, that the Council should meet annually, in practice it did so irregularly and on specific occasions, as a function of the political needs of the time, or of the king's need, for example, to legitimize his own ascent to the throne (d'Abadal 1970a:69-93), as was the case of Sisenand at the IV Council of Toledo, or Erwig at the XII, or Egica at the XV. In their evolution we find moments during which the king seems to be subject to the will of the Council, and others during which those gathered seem to act as puppets in the hands of the monarch. Hence, opinion as to what these Councils signified has not been unanimous. Formerly, they were considered to be instruments of the bishops to control the king's power. More recently, however, they have been interpreted as instruments that the king used against the nobility, at the same time involving the Church in the administration of the realm (Claude 1970:73-4, 98-100; Thompson 1969:277-9; Ziegler 1930:126-33). The king took the initiative of summoning all the general Councils in the seventh century; only in two (V and XV) is there no express evidence of this, but the king presided over them, which makes us think that even these met on his initiative. This prerogative was not vouched for by any law, and probably, rather than a show of strength of the monarchy, it was proof of its constitutional weakness. The king needed the Councils to be able to govern, and in them found protection and legitimization (Anton 1972:268; Valverde 1992:381-92). Besides summoning the meetings, the kings decided on the topics to be dealt with, which they usually made known to those attending at the beginning of the sessions by means of a *tomus*, the inclusion of any topic being considered legitimate (Schwöbel 1982:98-9), which was only approved if it received royal confirmation at the end of the Council, this being done by means of a law. If, furthermore, we take into account the fact that the king gradually asserted his right to name the bishops, which was sanctioned by the XII Council of Toledo in the year 681 (c.7; Vives 1963:394-5), we can understand the importance of the Councils as a political organ fundamental to the structuring and functioning of the Visigothic state (d'Abadal 1970b:65; Fernández Ortiz de Guinea 1994:159-67).

Essentially it is through the Councils that we can discover the real level that the development of the monarchic institution attained. Liuvigild received the power from his brother and managed to transmit it to his son Reccared; the latter, however, failed when he attempted to do the same with his son, Liuva II, who was defeated by Witteric in 602. The hereditary principle did not have the status of law even during the period 418-507, and after that, whenever an attempt was made to impose it, it failed. Probably because of this impossibility and in the face of the need to give stability and strength to the institution, the IV Council of Toledo, held in 633, under the presidency of Isidore of Seville, decided to issue a decree *pro robore nostrorum regum et stabilitate gentis Gothorum* (c.75; Vives 1963:217), establishing that "the king having died peacefully, the nobility of the whole nation, together with the bishops (*primates totius gentis cum sacerdotibus*), will in common agreement designate the successor to the throne, so that the concord of unity will be preserved by us, and no division will arise in the country and the people because of violence and ambition" (c. 75; Vives 1963:218). This elective principle was reproduced several times in subsequent Councils, such as that of Toledo VIII where it was noted that, regardless of the place where the king died, his successor should be elected by the vote of the bishops and the highest nobles of the palace, and not by the conspiracy of a few or by the seditious tumult of the rustics (c. 10; Vives 1963:283). In practice, the intention was to limit the inordinate ambition of the Gothic nobles, who not only considered themselves to be legitimate pretenders to the throne but who, in order to obtain it, repeatedly broke their oaths of allegiance (*fides* or *fidelitas*) to the legitimate king. The oath of allegiance is mentioned for the first time in the IV Council of Toledo, c. 75; by the end of the seventh century the entire free population was supposed to take it, those serving at Court were to take it directly before the king, and the rest were to take it before the functionaries who travelled around the kingdom (*LV* II, 1. 7; Thompson 1969:179; Zeumer 1902:52-3). In any case this oath and the *fidelitas* between the nobles and the king are analysed as essential elements in the formation of Visigothic feudalism (Barbero & Vigil 1978:126-54 against the point of Sánchez Albornoz 1942). In practice, the strength of the institution was systematically threatened by its instability, to the degree that at one point it seems that even a non-Goth aspired to the throne. This fact can de deduced from canon 3 of the V Council of Toledo, in 636, when the requisite to belong to the *Gothicae gentis nobilitas* was established for ascent to the throne, and was reiterated two years later: *nisi genere Gothus et moribus dignus provehatur ad apicem regni* (*Conc. Tolet.* VI, *a.* 638, c. 17; Vives 1963:244). Although in some cases it has been interpreted that "belonging to the lineage of the Goths as a condition to be chosen as king or to take part in the election of the monarch is an economic and social category which refers to the highest nobility" (Barbero & Vigil 1978:193; Barbero 1970:303), and would not have a strictly ethnic sense, there is no doubt that those who attained royal rank were always Goths, and certainly always from the highest nobility.

This reference is, however, interesting. Conversion to Catholicism coincided with the definitive abandonment of the Germanic language, clothing and probably the last remnants of the hereditary culture of the Migration Period. Unified in language, cultural assumptions, religious creed and in the application of law, the political monopoly had to be maintained by a show of strength on the part of the Gothic aristocratic group, by control of the army and of the administration. We should not forget that there were also many Goths who had no right to the throne, and that canon 75 of Toledo IV had eliminated any trace of popular tradition with respect to the election of the monarchy. Indeed the electors were, according to the Council canon quoted, Goths and Hispano-Romans (most of the bishops), but those eligible were the members of a restricted group of families who had inherited this right from the period of the migrations, a restricted group, but in practice, too large, thus multiplying the risk of attempts at usurpation.

Besides sometimes aspiring to the throne, the group also demanded that this exclusiveness be maintained, for example, in appointments to the highest offices in the administration or in the palace. We find an echo of this in *Conc. Tolet.* XIII, *a.* 683, canon 6 (Vives 1963:422), where access to these offices is limited for those of humble origin; or demands that legal guarantees be established to impede the king's arbitrariness from depriving them of the honour of their rank or from serving in the royal palace, and that if they were accused of any offence, they should be judged by their peers. We can see it in *Conc. Tolet.* VI, *a.* 638, canon 14 (Vives 1963:242) or in *Conc. Tolet.* XIII, a. 683, canon 2 (Vives 1963:416-8), where moreover the king was granted the legitimate right to remove anyone from office for reasons of inefficiency (*causa inutilitatis*) and replace him with someone more suitable (Barbero & Vigil 1978:122-4). In reality this struggle derived from the conviction of one same justifying tradition and of a practical fact: the new monarch needed to become rich in order to maintain his situation, which he defended, when necessary, with violence. We know, for example, that Chindaswinth inaugurated his reign with a violent repression of the nobility (Fredegar, IV. 82; Krusch 1888:162-3; *Cont. Isid. Hisp.* 26; Mommsen 1894:341), accompanied by confiscations which caused rejection on the part of the nobility, which the clergy also assumed. In this sense, the harsh epitaph of Eugenius of Toledo (*Carm.* XXV: *Epitaphion Chindasuinto regi conscriptum*; Vollmer 1961:250-1) reflects the sins of the king who is presented as adorned with all the vices. In general, the association of the clergy and the nobility against the kings who governed ignoring their interests seems evident, and Swinthila or Wamba could serve as examples (García Moreno 1975:152-84). In general, the aristocrats courted that power and systematically ignored their oaths of allegiance and the rhetoric of the sacred monarchy (Claude 1971:204-6; García Moreno 1975:144-6). All of this meant that the main characteristic of the Visigothic monarchy of Toledo was instability. Chindaswinth, in the prologue to *LV* II, 1. 8 (Zeumer 1902:53-4), recognized that the king had to take up arms more often against his own subjects than against foreign enemies. Although it should be made clear here that this law is within the context of the repression of the nobles, and is a law against treason, against any conspirator or rebel. This law was accompanied by another (*LV* II, 1. 7; Zeumer 1902:52-3) which abolished the right to beg pardon in cases of treason (Iglesia Ferreiros 1971:75).

In reality, the aspirations of this aristocratic group, i.e., their impatience to reach the throne, repeatedly put into question the elective ideal marked by canon 75 of Toledo IV. In practice, only Wamba was elected according to this system, and in general, the noble Goths seemed to have adopted from the monarchic conceptions of Isidore of Seville, reflected in the aforementioned Council, the principle that if a king "contrary to the reverence due to the laws, should exercise over the people a despotic power with haughty authority and regal arrogance, with offences, crimes and ambition, he should be condemned with a sentence of anathema, by Christ the Lord, and separated and judged by God for daring to act wrongly and lead the kingdom to ruin" (c. 75; Vives 1963:217-20). Isidore himself (*Etymologiae* I. 29; IX. 3. 19; Oroz & Marcos 1982:320-2, 768; and *Sententiae* III.48; Campos & Roca 1971:493-6) had elaborated on the right to resist a bad king whenever their evils were alleged (Barbero 1970:264-76; King 1988:140-2; Orlandis 1959:11-3; Reydellet 1961:457-466; Reydellet 1983:505-597). As a result, they repeatedly resorted to usurpation which the new king immediately took upon himself to justify, if possible confirming his accession through a council. In practice, procedures other than elections were never considered illegal, unless violence formed part of them, and even then, the Councils confirmed the kings under any circumstances, whether they had reached power through usurpation, hereditary succession or election according to the law, and this subsequent acclamation legitimized the new monarch (González 1977:54-68; Orlandis 1962:57-102; Sánchez Albornoz 1946b:76). Such legitimation really seemed unnecessary, since, beyond the indications already reflected in canon 75 of Toledo IV, there were no constitutional mechanisms for deposing a king. It could even be argued that, ultimately, the only valid mechanism for reaching power was force: he who gained the throne, by whatever means, "will subsequently obtain the allegiance of his subjects" (Iglesia Ferreiros 1970:679), which P. D. King (1972:24) has called an "occupative throne". Election could have been in practice no more than the acclamation of a *victor* (Wallace-Hadrill 1952:133).

Probably it was this impossibility to reach a single valid principle for succession to the throne which led the Church to use the extreme recourse for consecrating the figure of the king—unction. We do not know when this was established. Wamba was certainly anointed, but it does not seem to have been an innovation of that time. In fact, the IV Council of Toledo and Sisenand's desperate search for protection from the bishops may have been a propitious moment, without ruling out the fact that starting with Reccared the institution made sense (Barbero 1970:314-6). Unction was an original creation of the Visigoths, with precedents in the Old Testament, which ritually brought to a climax the process of consecration of the figure of the monarch, a consecration which, taken from the Christian literature of the late Empire, had been declared in Visigothic *Hispania* by Isidore. In his *Historia Gothorum*, Isidore had affirmed the divine origin of power, *"Aera DCLVIII, anno imperii Heracli X gloriosissimus Suinthila gratia diuina regni suscepit sceptra"* (*Historia* 62; Rodríguez Alonso 1975:274-6); and, with reference to the Old Testament, he considered that the unction administered to the king was a sacrament, *"sacramentum mysticae unctionis"* (*Quaestiones in Vetus Testamentum, in Genesin* 29. 8: Migne 1850:83, 269), where we seem to find a reflection of the similar opinion of Gregory the Great, *"ipsa unctio sacramentum est"* (*In librum I Regum Expositionum* IV. 5. 1; Ullman 1969:74); although W. Ullman (1969:74) considers that Isidore would have had no knowledge of the pope's points of view, and that when he wrote, unction did not exist as a practice. The king thus became one of God's chosen, but evidently the sacrament had to be administered by the bishops, which helps us to understand the role that they would play in the clericalization of the royal office (Ullman 1969:76). "Anointing was by its very nature a clerical monopoly" (Ewig 1976:23-4; Nelson 1977:2; Nelson 1987:143), and, ritually, the supremacy of the priests with respect to the princes was formalized, which was in agreement with the thought of Isidore, and which Gelasius had also elaborated in his time (Barbero 1970:303). This did not imply that subsequently they had the legitimate capacity for imposing their authority on the king. For example, the possibility of deposing a king was not raised, since the power conferred on the king came from God, and not from the electors (King 1972:46-8). In this sense we can interpret unction not as a show of strength of the monarchy, but rather as a show of its weakness. If unction replaced the charisma derived from the bloodline, from ancestral origin, with that derived from divine grace (Ullman 1969:54), to the point that unction took preference over election from among the reasons which made Wamba king, *"quem sacerdotalis unctio declarauit, quem totius gentis et patria communio elegit"* (Iul. Tolet. *Historia Wambae* 2; Levison 1910:501); or was the cause for Erwig receiving royal power, *"regnandique per sacrosanctam unctionem suceperit potestatem"* (*Conc. Tolet.* XII, c.1; Vives 1963:386), it is then reasonable that with time the Church should lose interest in defining what the legitimate system for the transmission of power was (Orlandis 1960:351). R. Collins (1977:45-8) considers that unction in itself was no guarantee of legitimacy, but rather only part of the process of the election of a new king, noting that, for example, Julian gives more importance to the place where it is performed—the *urbs regia*—than to the unction itself, and that Paul was also anointed without obtaining legitimacy thereby. Unction should keep the king away from violence and protect him from it (Wallace-Hadrill 1952:133), but in practice it meant the seizing of the institution whose unifying or centralizing aspirations were limited by the constant intervention of nobles and bishops (Barbero 1970:303).

However, it does not seem certain that the weakness of the king necessarily implied the weakness of the realm, at least not always. On the one hand something like the transpersonal nature of the State was achieved, the separation between the actual figure of the king and the idea of royalty, a separation between the *res propia* and the *publica utilitas* (Anton 1972:279-80). On the other hand, the usurpations of the seventh century, perhaps with the exception of that of Paul, did not seem to involve any attempt at separation. The tendencies towards centrifugal power usually associated with the economic processes of large land ownership and self-sufficiency of late Antiquity do not seem to have had a hand in the fall of the Visigothic reign. There seems to have been consensus regarding the monarchic institution as a defining element even of that Gothic past now formalized over a large territory, and that situation, barring exceptions, did not seem to displease the Hispano-Romans. The only purpose of the usurpers "was not to break the kingdom into a number of independent fragments but to replace the existing monarch by another of their own choice" (Thompson 1969:188), and nothing more.

The kingdom was composed of three entities, *gentem Gothorum, vel patriam aut regem* (Teillet 1984:524-5, 562-5), and this triple association was not fortuitous, but was repeated in almost all the Councils of Toledo between the IV and the XVII, and also in the *LV* (II, 1. 8; Zeumer 1902:53-4), although less profusely; we shall not now go into further considerations, but it is evident that the Visigothic state was upheld by principles of public law which distinguished perfectly between territory, people and king, where there was no place for patrimonialist conceptions. The king and his subjects exchanged mutual oaths of allegiance, but neither the territory nor its inhabitants were at the disposal of the king; he only governed them. The fact that the texts generally refer to *gentes Gothorum* or to *patria Gothorum* is probably because, as we have seen, in general terms the structure of active power was reserved for the Goths (d'Abadal 1970b:57-8; Claude 1972: 14-5).

Political control, administration at the specific level of the territory, of justice, or of taxes, just as in Toulouse, were not tasks exclusive to the king. With him were men in charge of bureaucrats of diverse categories and a series of institutions to advise the king in the tasks of government, in the issuing of laws or in the application of justice. Evidently, government had become more complicated since the Toulouse era, and this was reflected in a diversification of its organs and responsibilities. Their study, however, is highly problematic, since the information we have is scant and, furthermore, they were not regulated institutions, their functions mingle, their levels of action overlap and sometimes it seems that we are dealing with the same organ with different names, according to the level of action of the moment. R. d'Abadal (1970b:62-4) distinguished between the *officium*, the Council or *Aula Regia* and the assemblies of councils of the grandees, although references to the latter do not seem to be based on conclusive testimony; thus, the reference to, "*videtis cunctis sacerdotibus Dei, senioribusque Palatii atque gardingis*" of *LV* II, 1. 1 (Zeumer 1902:45), of Egica; or that assembly which Wamba summoned in Toledo to judge Paul, "*senioribus cunctis palatii gardingis omnibus omnique palatino oficio, seu etiam adstante exercitu universo*" (Iul. Tolet., *Iudicium* 5; Levison 1910:533), may have been nothing but a large meeting of the *Aula Regia*, in the second case of a public nature. The drawback of the *gardingi*, not generally testified to at these meetings, can be resolved if we take into account that the first references to *gardingi* do not appear in the sources until a little before 680, and that the king controlled who could be called to the meeting.

Those men in charge were, in general, members of the king's circle, of the *Officium palatinum* or of the *Aula Regia,* to whom we referred earlier, those whom Recceswinth considered *quos in regimine socios*. *Socii* was one of the names that the members of the entourage of the Germanic kings received during the period of the migrations (Jordanes, *Getica* XXVI. 135-6; Mommsen 1961:93) and it is used by Julian of Toledo to refer to the followers of the rebel Paul: *Ipsi Pauli omnes socii sui* (*Iudicium* 6; Levison 1910:534)). However, when studying them we find several problems. In the first place the sources of the era sometimes lead to confusion; thus, in Recceswinth's address to the VIII Council of Toledo, in 653, we read, "*Vos etiam inlustres viros, quos ex officio palatino huic sanctae synodo interese mos primaevus obtinuit ac non vilitas exspectabilis honoravit et experientia aequitatis plebium rectores exegit...*" and he addressed the same people shortly afterwards, "*In comune iam vobis cunctis et ex divino cultu ministris idoneis ex aula regia rectoribus decenter electis*" (Vives 1963:265). It seems reasonable to think that all the members of the *Officium* were also members of the *Aula Regia*, and that the latter institution included other nobles or functionaries who were not normally to be found in the monarch's circle, but who assumed their functions when they were in Toledo or wherever the Court was.

Seen in this way, the *Officium*, probably identifiable with the *cubiculum* that John of Biclar (*Chronica s.a.* 590. 3: Campos 1960:98) associated with Reccared, would be composed of the group of *primates* who had in their charge the administrative tasks of the realm centralized in the palace. We know little of them except their name, which we know from the signatures of the VIII, IX and XIII Councils of Toledo: *comes cubiculariorum, c. scanciarum, c. notariorum, c. patrimoniorum, c. spatariorum, c. thesaurorum, c. Toletanum* and *c. stabuli*. By their number we can appreciate that the administration of court affairs had become more complex since the times of Toulouse. As we have already indicated, its reorganization, but not its creation, must have occurred in the times of Liuvigild, although it would change and increase throughout the seventh century; C. Sánchez Albornoz (1946a:171-3) points out that in Toledo IV, *a.* 633, the choosing of the king still corresponded to the *seniores totius gentis* and to the *sacerdotes*, whereas in Toledo VIII, *a.* 653, reference is made to *maiores palatii* and *sacerdotes*. From their names we can infer their functions (García Moreno 1974:35-65), but in the same way it could be seen as a merely bureaucratic body. However, the level of professionalism reached by the Visigothic monarchy does not seem very high, and, in general, members of the higher nobility, supporters of the king, but also future usurpers, must have been placed in the most important offices. Hence, although the name may point to functions of administration, the *Officium* as a whole was a fundamental pressure and power group in the handling of the kingdom's affairs. We know, for example, that the *Officium palatinum* appeared with Sisebut

(612-621) sanctioning the law for the persecution of the Jews (*LV* XII. 2. 14; Zeumer 1902:420-3), and in such cases should be understood as a political body. Terms such as *optimates, primates, primi* or *maiores palatii* certainly referred to those who exercised the high offices of the *Officium*, but it is likely that on occasion they came to define those who could occupy them. It is also possible that in other cases they were honorary offices, as can be inferred from the duplication of functions, as seen in the signatures of the Councils, and that in general the *Officium* was an informal group with specific functions usually formed from among all the noble Goths, who as a whole formed part of the *Palatium regis* or *Aula Regia*, where we find references both to the Germanic entourage and to the *Sacratissimus comitatus* of Constantine (Sánchez Albornoz 1946a:181-92). From a reading of the second canon of the XIII Council of Toledo, one can infer that the condition of *palatinus* may have been either an honour or a service: *ab honore sui ordinis vel servitio* (Vives 1963:417), courtiers with or without an office. However, as a restricted *Officium*, we know that not all its members were of noble blood, but that on occasion these offices were occupied by individuals of very low social condition, even servants and freedmen, in some cases public and in some, private. Evidently, this construction of a court nobility or of a professionalized bureaucratic group, depending directly on the king, was an attack on the interests of the nobility and was rejected by them. Canon 6 of the XIII Council of Toledo in 683 (Vives 1963:422-3) attempted to put an end to this situation and the king accepted it and recorded it in the law ratifying the Council. But in practice these stipulations show that the king summoned to the highest offices those whom he considered appropriate, as can be seen in canon 2 of this same Council, when the king's right to replace those he considered incapable of occupying an office was recognized. Undoubtedly, within this *Officium* there must have been a *cursus honorum*, but we do not understand its characteristic progression.

The *Officium* was, then, the bureaucratic apparatus of the *Aula Regia* or *Palatium Regis*, but the fact that the handling of court affairs and the most important tasks of administration were in its hands caused the names to be confused sometimes even in legal texts (Sánchez Albornoz 1946a:177-8, 205-7). In a broad sense, this *Aula* or *Palatium* was in charge of advising the king, especially in legal matters, at the same time acting as the high court of the kingdom. Forming part of the *Officium*, besides the members, were other nobles of court circles, provincial dukes and counts of cities and of the army, as well as representative bishops of *Carthaginensis*. The *gardingi* did not form part of it, and, in spite of their great prestige, they were not included among the *seniores, primates* or *optimates*, but among the *mediocres* or *tertius ordo* (d'Abadal 1970b:63-4; opposed to Sánchez Albornoz 1946a:226). The *gardingus* was the king's companion and would correspond to the old companions of the Germanic chief, linked to him by special bonds of personal allegiance, or to the *domestici* of imperial Roman circles, his condition was essentially military (Wolfram 1990:240-2). As far as we know, there was no automatic mechanism for meeting, and they only met when summoned by the king; the frequency with which they did so would, to a good extent, define the king's disposition towards the nobility. In this sense it can be noted that Julian of Toledo shows us Wamba summoning the *primates palatii* as soon as he received news of Paul's revolt, so that they should decide whether to organize an expedition, and listening to their opinions, taking part in the debate, exhorting them in the face of their doubts and fears and finally convincing them of the need for the expedition, which they acclaimed (*Historia Wambae* 9-10; Levison 1910:507-10). Julian's description probably responds to the model for this type of meeting, but it does not enable us to know whether on any occasion the king did not manage to convince his nobles, or when the decision of the latter was contrary to his interests. Moreover, Wamba's meeting with his *primates* took place in Cantabria, in the midst of a campaign against the Basques, thus showing that the royal entourage, the members of the *Palatium*, travelled with the king. In any case, consultation of important decisions with the high dignitaries was, in ecclesiastical literature, one of the characteristics of a good prince (García Moreno 1975:183). But we must also take into account the fact that, as time went on, the number of the members of the *Aula Regia* became very high, even if only those who lived in the king's circle met, hence it is likely that meetings were summoned in a limited way, according to the issue, the circumstances or the monarch's will. In the same way that part of the members of this *Aula* had been elected, *mos primaevus*, by Recceswinth, to attend the VIII Council of Toledo (Vives 1963:265).

A suitable knowledge of the relationship between the king and the members of his *Aula Regia* would help us achieve a better understanding of the political structure of the Visigothic monarchy. Unfortunately, the information available is very scant. We know that the members of the *Aula*, who used to refer to themselves as *viri illustres*, enjoyed a privileged legal condition to which they responded with equally extraordinary duties of allegiance, loyalty and obedience (*LV* II, 1. 6 & 8; IX, 2. 8 & 9; Zeumer 1902:48-52, 53-7, 370-9; *Conc. Tolet.*, XVI. *Tomus*; Vives 1963:487-8). We also know that theoretically the king did not find his power limited by any of the institutions of the kingdom. As we have pointed out, the nobility tried to safeguard their interests from the arbitrariness of the king, but the latter did not feel obliged to consult them on his decisions if he did not want to, except on very limited occasions, and in case of disagreement, his will prevailed.

But in practice monarchs could not act at their own discretion; they needed the support of the grandees of the kingdom in order to maintain power. These grandees had concrete control of the government of the army, the provinces and the cities, where they carried out economic, administrative and judicial functions far from royal control, a delegation of power that in itself signified a limitation of the theoretical supremacy of the king (King 1972:72). In turn, in an unstoppable process of comings and goings, the king spent a part of the treasury buying, by means of favours and donations, the loyalty of these same nobles who would take advantage of any means to usurp the throne. The king, incapable of collecting taxes from the grandees with large properties who felt more and more autonomous, was finally obliged to turn to his own resources or to make confiscations in order to meet the expenditures of the state (Barbero & Vigil 1974:131-3; García Moreno 1975:148-50), something which inevitably led to the end of harmony with the aristocracy and once again made the king's position precarious. Likewise, the king, who was the head of the army, did not have an army of his own and had to resort to private followers, and although the nobles in their oath of allegiance to the king promised to come at his call when he required the presence of his *fideles*, the military laws of Wamba and Erwig make it evident that this was not complied with (Pérez Sánchez 1989:137, 155-70; Barbero & Vigil 1978:105-22). The king, to whom the legislation and the political-religious theory of the time conceded an almost unlimited power, and who occupied the central place regarding the political institutionalization of the realm, was in reality subjected to an enormously powerful propertied class, which no legal principle impeded from ascending to the throne, and to an ecclesiastical hierarchy whose economic and family interests were the same as those of the aristocracy. In this case it was not only important that the Church was in its totality the largest landowner of the kingdom, but also that it seems more than evident that there were family bonds between the high clergy and the great lay landowners (Claude 1970:112-14; Claude 1971:110, 204-6; Diesner 1969:32; García Moreno 1975:43-4). The kingdom maintained a balance that gradually swung in favour of the aristocracy. As the kingdom progressed, the petitions for protection of the king's family and his descendants increased, the non-fulfillment of the military obligations of the nobles became impossible to stave off, usurpations continued and right before the Moslem invasion the fulfillment of the principle by which political power ends up in the hands of those who hold military and economic power, which in this case was the great land-owning aristocracy, seemed imminent. The public nature of the struggle between the king and the nobility had degenerated into a conflict of economic interests (Barbero 1970:301), or, at best, of personal rivalry, but in which political differences are impossible to find (Thompson 1969:188-9). Governments that are concentrated in the hands of a few demand the complicity of many (MacMullen 1988:58-9); once this complicity ends, they fall.

Conclusion

As we reach the end of this chapter we can reflect on why we speak of 'political institutions' and not exclusively of the 'monarchy', since it is to the latter that we have devoted the greater part of our attention. In the strict sense we might put forward the idea that the only clearly defined and regulated political institution in the history of the Visigoths was the monarchy, and that the others that we referred to were either political instruments of the monarchy, or, regarding its relations of power with the clergy and the aristocracy, mechanisms for limiting or controlling its power. The king could count on the *Officium* or the *Aula Regia*, but these had no constitutionally defined political functionality apart from the person of the king himself. The aristocracy formed part of them by royal designation and their interests were essentially economic and not political, as shown in the history of the Kingdom of Toledo. The institutionalization of the monarchy and its instruments was, moreover, a long process that was interrupted by the Moslem invasion, and the evidence from the last stages of the kingdom seems to present a process of centrifugal disintegration with an ever greater imposition of private interests over public ones; one where the monarchy was becoming weaker and weaker.

What was left, then, of the old Germanic tradition? In this aspect we would have to differentiate between form and content. The Visigothic king had inherited the court tradition from the imperial court, i.e., his role as legislator and administrator of the realm. However, the exclusivist sentiment of a warrior caste, of an aristocratic minority with a right to the throne, was essentially Germanic. It is possible that their excessive eagerness for the throne was a way of claiming this exclusivity, although it is true that on a literary level the references to a particularized Gothic awareness disappeared with conversion. Probably the text of the *Vitas Sanctorum Patrum Emeretensium* (Maya Sánchez 1992), from the beginning of the seventh century, provides the last example (Claude 1972:19-21). As great landowners, the aristocratic Goths moved within Hispano-Roman circles of interest; they would have had the same cultural tastes, they could share administrative and even military responsibility with them. In the last instance, what made them different was their origin, a more or less invented tradition that allowed them to become kings. It is certain that after conversion, or even before, the feeling of bonding within a specific *sippe* was lost, but this did not impede noble Goths from being proud of their vaguely ethnic origin, reinforced by commemorative narratives of a glorious past, or by the intonation of self-identifying chants, a folklore tradition that would have fulfilled the educational functions that the material culture or the language could no longer perform, and to which Isidore of Seville seems to refer, with the name *carmina maiorum,* in his *Institutionum disciplinae* (Pascal 1957:426; Wolfram 1990:210, 324). It is likewise possible that certain concepts of honour or vengeance, the ancient *faida*, were still valid, although they were not transmitted, due to their 'patrimonial' nature, in the written sources (García Moreno 1994:1-15). It is in this patrimonial terrain where some Germanic elements can be traced, such as the Germanic dowry or *morgengabe* which can be identified in *LV* III. 1. 5 (Zeumer 1902:159) or in *Formula* XX (Gil 1972:90-4); however, they are very isolated and not very meaningful elements. We may also question whether all the aristocratic Gothic families had this right, or whether it was limited to a restricted and select group. It is likely that the purges and confiscations, the search for noble alliances and the natural process of economic concentration served to restrict the number of those aspiring to power, but in any case there were still too many of them at the time when the kingdom disappeared. All the cases of infidelities and usurpations seemed to occur within a restricted group of individuals who usually moved in the king's circle, a group more limited than the generic Hispano-Gothic aristocracy into which they were legally and economically integrated.

References

Textual sources:

Ammianus Marcellinus
    Rerum gestarum libri: see Rolfe (ed.) 1935.
Codex Euricianus: see D'Ors (ed.) 1960.
Concilia Toletana: see Vives (ed.) 1963.
Concilium Emeritense: see Vives (ed.) 1963.
Eugene of Toledo
    Carmina: see Vollmer (ed.) 1961.
Formulae Visigothicae: see Gil (ed.) 1972.
Fredegarius
    Fredegarii et aliorum Chronica: see Krush (ed.) 1888.
Gregory of Tours
    Libri historiarum X: see Krush & Levison (eds.) 1951.
Hydatius
    Chronica: see Burgess (ed.) 1993.
Isidore of Seville
    Etymologiae: see Oroz Reta & Marcos Casquero (eds.) 1982-3.
    Historia Gothorum: see Rodríguez Alonso (ed.) 1975.
    Sententiarum libri tres: see Campos Ruiz & Roca Melia (eds.) 1971.
    Institutionum disciplinae: see Pascal (ed.) 1957.
    Quaestiones in veteri et novo Testamento: see Migne (ed.) 1850.
John of Biclar
    Chronica: see Mommsen (ed.) 1894.
Jordanes
    Getica: see Mommsen (ed.) 1882.
Julian of Toledo
    Historiae Wambae regis auctore Iuliano episcopo Toletano: see Krusch &
    Levison (eds.) 1910:486-585.
Olympiodorus
    Fragmenta: see Blockley (ed.) 1983.
Orosius
    Historiarum adversus paganos libri VII: see Zangemeister (ed.) 1889.
Philostorgius
    Historia eclesiastica: see Bidez (ed.) 1913.
Priscus
    Fragmenta: see Blockley (ed.) 1983.
Procopius
    De Bello Gothico: see Dewing (ed.) 1919.
Sidonius Apollinaris
    Carmina: see Loyen (ed.) 1960.
    Epistolae: see Loyen (ed.) 1970.
Vitas Sanctorum Patrum Emeritensium: see Maya Sánchez (ed.) 1992.
Zosimus
    Historia Nova: see Paschoud (ed.) 1971-86.

Bibliography:

d'Abadal, R.
    1960   *Del reino de Tolosa al reino de Toledo*. Madrid: Real Academia de la Historia.

d'Abadal, R. *(cont.)*
1970a   Els concilis de Toledo. In *Dels Visigots als Catalans*. J. Sobrequés i
             Callicó (ed.), pp. 69-93. Barcelona: Edicions 62.
1970b   La monarquia en el Regne de Toledo. In *Dels Visigots als Catalans*.
             J. Sobrequés i Callicó (ed.), pp. 57-67. Barcelona: Edicions 62.
Anton, H. H.
1972   Der König und die Reichkonzilien in westgotischen Spanien.
             Historisches Jahrbuch 92: 257-281.
Astuti, G.
1970   Note critiche sul sistema delle fonti giuridiche nei regni romano-barbarici
             dell'Occidente. *Atti della Accademia Nazionale dei Lincei* 25: 319-348.
Bachrach, B.
1969   Another look at the barbarian settlement in Southern Gaul. *Traditio* 25:
             353-358.
Barbero, A.
1970   El pensamiento político visigodo y las primeras unciones regias en la
             Europa medieval. *Hispania* 30: 245-326.
Barbero, A., & M. Vigil.
1974   Algunos aspectos de la feudalización del reino visigodo de Toledo en
             relación con su organización financiera y militar. In *Sobre los orígenes
             sociales de la Reconquista*. A. Barbero & M. Vigil (eds.), pp. 107-137.
             Barcelona: Ariel.
1978   *La formación del feudalismo en la Península Ibérica*. Barcelona: Crítica.
Barnwell, P. S.
1992   *Emperor, prefects and kings in the Roman West, 395-565*. London: Gerald
             Duckworth & Co. Ltd.
Bidez, J. (ed.)
1913   *Philostorgius Kirchengeschichte*. Leipzig: J. C. Hinrichs Buchhandlung.
Blockley, R. C. (ed.)
1983   *The Fragmentary Classicising Historians of the Later Roman Empire.
             Eunapius, Olympiodorus, Priscus and Malchus. II. Text, Translation and
             Historiographical Notes*. Liverpool: Francis Cairn.
Bruguière, M. B.
1974   *Littérature et droit dans la Gaule du Ve siècle*. Paris: Presses
             Universitaires de France.
Burgess, R. W. (ed.)
1993   *The Chronicle of Hydatius and the Consularia Constantinopolitana. Two
             Contemporary Accounts of the Final Years of the Roman Empire*. Oxford:
             Oxford University Press.
Burns, T. S.
1980   *The Ostrogoths. Kingship and Society*. Wiesbaden: Franz Steiner Verlag
             GmbH.
1992   The settlement of 418. In *Fifth-century Gaul: A Crisis of Identity?*
             J. Drinkwater & H. Elton (eds.), pp. 53-63. Cambridge: Cambridge
             University Press.
1994   *Barbarians within the Gates of Rome*. Bloomington, IN: Indiana
             University Press.
Campos Ruiz, J. (ed.)
1960   *Juan de Biclaro. Obispo de Gerona. Su vida y su obra. Introducción, texto
             crítico y comentarios*. Madrid: Consejo Superior de Investigaciones
             Científicas.

Campos Ruiz, J., & I. Roca Melia (eds.)
1971   *Santos Padres españoles. II. San Leandro, San Isidoro, San Fructuoso.*
            Reglas monásticas de la España visigoda. Los tres libros de las
            "Sentencias". Madrid: La editorial católica S.A.
Claude, D.
1970   *Geschichte der Westgoten.* Stuttgart: W. Kohlhammer.
1971   *Adel, Kirche und Köningtum im Westgotenreich.* Sigmaringen: Jahn
            Thorbecke.
1972   Gentile und territoriale Staatsideen im Westgotenreich. *Frühmittel-*
            alterliche Studien 6: 1-38.
Collins, R.
1977   Julian of Toledo and the royal succession in late seventh-century Spain.
            In *Early medieval kingship.* P. H. Sawyer & I. N. Wood (eds.), pp. 30-49.
            Leeds: The School of History.
1983   *Early Medieval Spain. Unity and Diversity 400-1000.* London:
            Macmillan.
Cracco Ruggini, L.
1978   Come Bisanzio vide la fine dell'Impero d'Occidente. In *La fine*
            dell'Impero romano d'Occidente. P. Brezzi & S. Calderone *et al.* (eds.),
            pp. 69-82. Rome: Istituto di studi romani.
Dewing, H. B. (ed.)
1919   *Procopius, with an English translation. III. History of the wars, books V*
            and VI. Loeb Classical Library. London: William Heinemann Ltd.
Diesner, H. J.
1969   König Wamba und das westgotisches Frühfeudalismus. *Jahrbuch der*
            österreischischen Byzantinistik 18: 7-35.
D'Ors, A. (ed.)
1960   *El código de Eurico. Edición, Palingenesia, Indices.* Roma/Madrid:
            Consejo Superior de Investigaciones Científicas.
Ewig, E.
1963   Résidence et capitale pendant le Haut Moyen Age. *Revue Historique*
            230: 25-72.
1976   Zum christlichen Königsgedanken in Frühmittelalter. In *Spätantikes und*
            Fränkisches Gallien. Gesammelte Schriften (1952-1973). Munich:
            Artemis.
Fernández Ortiz de Guinea, L.
1994   Participación episcopal en la articulación de la vida política
            hispano-visigoda. *Studia Historica. Historia Antigua* 12: 159-167.
Fustel de Coulanges, D.
1891   *Histoire des institutions politiques de l'ancienne France, I. L'empire*
            romain. Les Germains. La royauté mérovingienne. Paris: C. Jullian.
García Gallo, A.
1974   Consideración crítica de los estudios sobre la legislación y la costumbre
            visigoda. *Anuario de Historia del Derecho Español* 44: 34-467.
García Iglesias, L.
1975   El intermedio ostrogodo en Hispania (507-549 d.C.). *Hispania Antiqua*
            5: 89-120.
García Moreno, L. A.
1974   *Estudios sobre la organización administrativa del reino visigodo de*
            Toledo. Madrid: Anuario de Historia del Derecho Español.
1975   *El fin del reino visigodo de Toledo.* Madrid: Universidad Autónoma.

García Moreno, L. A. *(cont.)*
1994   Gothic survivals in the Visigothic kingdoms of Toulouse and Toledo. *Francia* 21 (1): 1-15.
Gibert, R.
1956   El reino visigodo y el particularismo español. *Estudios Visigóticos I.* Roma/Madrid: Consejo Superior de Investigaciones Científicas.
Gil, I. (ed.)
1972   *Miscellanea wisigothica.* Sevilla: Universidad.
González, T.
1977   *La política en los concilios de Toledo.* Roma: Pontificia Gregoriana Universitatis.
Grierson, P.
1941   Election and inheritance in early Germanic kingship. *Cambridge Historical Journal* 7: 1-22.
Harries, J.
1994   *Sidonius Apollinaris and the Fall of Rome AD 407-485.* Oxford: Clarendon Press.
Heather, P.
1986   The crossing of the Danube and the Gothic Conversion. *Greek, Roman and Byzantine Studies* 27: 289-318.
1991   *Goths and Romans 332-489.* Oxford: Clarendon Press.
1992   The emergence of the Visigothic kingdom. In *Fifth-century Gaul: A Crisis of Identity?* J. Drinkwater & H. Elton (eds.), pp. 84-94. Cambridge: Cambridge University Press.
Höfler, O.
1973   Der Sakralcharacter der germanischen Königtums. *Vorträge und Forschungen* 3: 75-104. [4th reprint].
Iglesia Ferreiros, A.
1970   Notas en torno a la sucesión en el reino visigodo. *Anuario de Historia del Derecho Español* 40: 653-682.
1971   *Historia de la traición. La traición regia en León y Castilla.* Santiago de Compostela: Universidad.
Immink, P. W. A.
1968   Gouvernés at gouvernants dans la société germanique. In *Recueils de la Société Jean Bodin pour l'Histoire comparative des Institutions* 23: 331-393.
Jiménez Garnica, A. M.
1983   *Orígenes y desarrollo del reino visigodo de Tolosa.* Valladolid: Universidad.
King, P. D.
1972   *Law and Society in the Visigothic Kingdom.* Cambridge: Cambridge University Press.
1988   The Barbarian Kingdoms. In *The Cambridge History of Medieval Political Thought c. 350-c. 1450.* J. H. Burns (ed.), pp. 140-153. Cambridge: Cambridge University Press.
Krusch, B. (ed.)
1888   *Fredegarii et aliorum Chronica. Vitae sanctorum. Monumenta Germaniae Historica. Scriptores rerum Merovingicarum,* 2. Hannover: Hahn.
Krusch, B., & W. Levison (eds.)
1910   *Passiones vitaeque sanctorum aevi Merovingici.* (1) *Monumenta Germaniae Historica. Scriptores rerum Merovingicarum,* 5. Hannover: Hahn. [Repr. 1979].

1951   *Gregorii Turonensis Opera, Libri historiarum X.* Teil 1. *Monumenta Germaniae Historica, Scriptores rerum Merovingicarum,* 1. Hannover: Hahn.

Lambertini, R.
1991   *La codificazione di Alarico II.* Turin: G. Giappichelli editore.

La Rocca, C.
1993   Una prudente maschera antica. La politica edilizia di Teodorico. In *Teodorico il Grande e i Goti d'Italia.* (Atti del XIII Congresso internazionale di studi sull'Alto Medioevo). Spoleto: C.I.S.A.M.

Latouche, R.
1946   *Les grandes invasions et la crise de l'Occident au Ve siècle.* Grenoble: Éd. Montaigne.

Levy, E.
1951   *West Roman Vulgar Law. The Law of Property.* Philadelphia: American Philosophical Society.

Liebeschuetz, J. H. W. G.
1991   The Visigoths and Alaric's Goths. In *Barbarians and Bishops. Army, Church, and State in the Age of Arcadius and Chrysostom.* J. H. W. G. Liebeschuetz (ed.), pp. 48-85. Oxford: Clarendon Press.
1992   Alaric's Goths: nation or army? In *Fifth-century Gaul: A Crisis of Identity.* J. Drinkwater & H. Elton (eds.), pp. 75-83. Cambridge: Cambridge University Press.

Loyen, A. (ed.)
1960   *Sidoine Apollinaire. I Poèmes.* Paris: Les Belles Lettres.
1970   *Sidoine Apollinaire. II. Lettres (livres 1-V), and III (livres VI-IX).* Paris: Les Belles Lettres.

MacMullen, R.
1988   *Corruption and the Decline of Rome.* New Haven: Yale University Press.

Maya Sánchez, A. (ed.)
1992   *Vitas Sanctorum Patrum Emeretensium.* Corpus Christianorum. Series Latina CXVI. Turnhout: Brepols.

Migne, J.-P. (ed.)
1850   *Patrologiae Latinae. Cursus Completus. Tomus LXXXIII. Sancti Isidori Hispalensis episcopi, opera omnia.* Paris: Bibliothecae Cleri Universæ. [Repr. Turnhout: Brepols].

Mommsen, T. (ed.)
1882   *Iordanis Romana et Getica. Monumenta Germaniae Historica. Auctores antiquissimi,* 5. 1. Berlin: Weindmann. [Repr. 1982].
1894   *Chronica minora saec. IV. V. VI. VII.* (II) *Monumenta Germaniae Historica. Auctores antiquissimi,* 11. Hannover: Hahn.

Murray, A. C.
1983   *Germanic Kinship Structure. Studies in Law and Society in Antiquity and the Early Middle Ages.* Toronto: Pontifical Institute of Mediaeval Studies.

Nelson, J.
1977   Inauguration rituals. In *Early medieval kingship.* P. H. Sawyer & I. N. Wood (eds.), pp. 123-153. Leeds: The School of History.
1987   The Lord's anointed and the people's choice: Carolingian royal ritual. In *Rituals of Royalty. Power and Ceremonial in Traditional Societies.* D. Cannadine & S. Price (eds.), pp. 137-180. Cambridge: Cambridge University Press.

Nixon, C. E. V.
    1992   Relations between Visigoths and Romans in fifth-century Gaul. In *Fifth-century Gaul: A Crisis of Identity*. J. Drinkwater & H. Elton (eds.), pp. 64-74. Cambridge: Cambridge University Press.

Orlandis, J.
    1959   En torno a la noción visigoda de la tiranía. *Anuario de Historia del Derecho Español* 29: 5-43.

    1960   La iglesia visigoda y los problemas de la sucesión al trono en el siglo VII. In *Le Chiese nei regni dell'Europa occidentale e i loro rapporti con Roma fino all'800*. (Settimane di studio del Centro Italiano di Studi sull'Alto Medioevo, VII). Pp. 333-351. Spoleto: C.I.S.A.M.

    1962   La sucesión al trono en la monarquía visigoda. In *Estudios visigóticos III. El poder real y la sucesión al trono en la monarquía visigoda*. J. Orlandis (ed.), pp. 57-102. Roma/Madrid: Consejo Superior de Investigaciones Científicas.

Oroz Reta, J., & M. A. Marcos Casquero (eds.)
    1982-3   *Isidoro de Sevilla. Etimologías*. 2 vols. Madrid: La editorial católica S.A.

Pascal, P. (ed.)
    1957   The 'Institutionum disciplinae' of Isidore of Seville. *Traditio* 13: 425-431.

Paschoud, F. (ed.)
    1971-86   *Zosime. Histoire Nouvelle*. 3 vols. Paris: Les Belles Lettres.

Pelliciari, L.
    1982   *Sulla natura giuridica dei raporti tra Visigoti e Impero Romano al tempo dell'invasione del V° secolo*. Milan: Dott. A. Giuffrè.

Pérez Sánchez, D.
    1989   *El ejército en la sociedad visigoda*. Salamanca: Universidad.

Radcliffe-Brown, A. R.
    1940   Preface. In *African Political Systems*. M. Fortes & E. E. Evans Pritchard (eds.), pp. xi-xxiii. London: Oxford University Press.

Reydellet, M.
    1961   La conception du souverain chez Isidore de Seville. In *Isidoriana*. Pp. 457-466. León: Centro de Estudios San Isidoro.

    1981   *La royauté dans la littérature latine de Sidoine à Isidore de Séville*. Rome: Bibliothèque des Écoles Françaises d'Athènes et de Rome.

Rivera Recio, J.
    1955   Encumbramiento de la sede toledana durante la dominación visigótica. *Hispania Sacra* 8: 3-34.

Rodríguez Alonso, C. (ed.)
    1975   *Las historias de los godos, vándalos y suevos de Isidoro de Sevilla. Estudio, edición crítica y traducción*. (Fuentes y Estudios de Historia Leonesa, 13). León: Centro de Estudios e Investigación San Isidoro.

Rolfe, J. C. (ed.)
    1935-9   *Ammianus Marcellinus*. Three volumes. (Loeb Classical Library). London: William Heinemann Ltd.

Rouche, M.
    1979   *L'Aquitaine: des Wisigoths aux Arabes, 418-781. Naissance d'une région*. Paris: Éditions Jean Touzot.

Sahlins, M. D.
    1968   *Tribesmen*. Englewood Cliffs, NJ: Prentice-Hall, Inc.

Sánchez Albornoz, C.
1942   *En torno a los orígenes del feudalismo. I. I. Fideles y gardingos en la monarquía visigoda. Raíces del vasallaje y del beneficio hispanos.* Mendoza: Universidad Nacional de Cuyo.
1946a   El Aula Regia y las asambleas políticas de los godos. *Cuadernos de Historia de España* 5: 5-110.
1946b   El *senatus* visigodo. Don Rodrigo, rey legítimo de España. *Cuadernos de Historia de España* 6: 5-99.
1959   El gobierno de las ciudades en España del siglo V al X. In *La città nell'alto medioevo*. Pp. 351-391. (Settimane di studio del Centro italiano di Studi sull'Alto Medioevo, VI). Spoleto: C.I.S.A.M.
1972   *Los orígenes de la nación española I.* Oviedo: Instituto de Estudios Asturianos.
Schäferdiek, K.
1967   *Die Kirchen in den Reichen der Westgoten und Sueven bis zur Errichtung der westgotischen katholischen Staatskirche.* Berlin: Walter de Gruyter.
Schlesinger, W.
1973   Über germanisches Heerkönigtums. *Vorträge und Forschungen* 3: 105-141. [4th. reprint].
Schwöbel, H.
1982   *Synode und Könige im Westgotenreich. Grundlagen und Formen ihrer Beziehung.* (Dissertationen zur Mittelalterlichen Geschichte 1). Köln/Wien: Böhlau Verlag.
Sivan, H. S.
1983   Romans and Barbarians in Fifth Century Aquitaine: The Visigothic Kingdom of Toulouse, AD 418-507. New York: Columbia University Doctoral Dissertation.
Stroheker, K. F.
1937   *Eurich, König der Westgoten.* Stuttgart: Kohlhammer.
1965   Leovigild. In *Germanentum und Spätantike*. K. F. Stroheker (ed.), pp. 131-191. Zürich/Stuttgart: Artemis.
Teillet, S.
1984   *Des Goths à la nation gothique. Les origines de l'idée de nation en Occident du Vème au VIème siècle.* Paris: Les Belles Lettres.
Thompson, E. A.
1960   The conversion of the Visigoths to Catholicism. *Nottingham Medieval Studies* 4: 4-35.
1963a   The Visigoths from Fritigern to Euric. *Historia* 12: 105-126.
1963b   The Barbarian kingdoms in Gaul and Spain. *Nottingham Medieval Studies* 7: 3-33.
1965   *The Early Germans.* Oxford: Clarendon Press.
1966   *The Visigoths in the Time of Ulfila.* Oxford: Clarendon Press.
1969   *The Goths in Spain.* Oxford: Clarendon Press.
1982   The Visigoths in Aquitaine: why? In *Romans and Barbarians. The Decline of the Western Empire.* E. A. Thompson (ed.), pp. 251-255. Madison, WI: The University of Wisconsin Press.
Torres López, M.
1926   El Estado visigótico. *Anuario de Historia del Derecho Español* 3: 307-475.
Ullman, W.
1961   *Principles of Government and Politics in the Middle Ages.* London: Methuen & Co. Ltd.

Ullman, W. *(cont.)*
1969   *The Carolingian Renaissance and the Idea of Kingship.* London: Methuen & Co. Ltd.
Valverde, M. R.
1992   La iglesia hispano-visigoda: ¿fortalecedora o limitadora de la soberanía real? *Hispania Antiqua* 16: 381-392.
1994   De Atanarico a Valia: Aproximación a los orígenes de la monarquía visigoda. *Studia Historica. Historia Antigua* 12: 143-158.
Vigil, M., & A. Barbero
1974   Sucesión al trono y evolución social en el reino visigodo. *Hispania Antiqua* 4: 379-393.
Vives, J. (ed.)
1942   *Inscripciones cristianas de la España romana y visigoda.* Barcelona: Consejo Superior de Investigaciones Científicas.
1963   *Concilios visigóticos e hispano-romanos.* Barcelona/Madrid: Consejo Superior de Investigaciones Científicas.
Vollmer, F. (ed.)
1905   *Fl. Merobaudi reliquiae. Blossii Aemilii Dracontii Carmina. Eugenii Toletani episcopi Carmina et epistulae. Monumenta Germaniae Historica. Auctores antiquissimi,* 14. Berlin: Weidmann. [Rep. 1984].
Wagner, N.
1967   *Getica. Untersuchungen zum Leben des Jordanes und zur frühen Geschichte der Goten.* Berlin: De Gruyter.
Wallace-Hadrill, J. M.
1952   *The Barbarian West 400-1000.* Oxford: Basil Blackwell.
1979   *Early Germanic Kingship in England and on the Continent.* Oxford: Clarendon Press.
1982   *The Long Haired Kings.* Toronto: University of Toronto Press.
Wenskus, R.
1961   *Stammesbildung und Verfassung. Das Werden der frühmittelalterlichen Gentes.* Köln: Böhlau Verlag.
Wolfram, H.
1990   *History of the Goths.* Berkeley: University of California Press.
Zangemeister, C. (ed.)
1882   *Pauli Orosii historiarum adversus paganos libri VII. C.S.E.L.* 5. Wien: C. Geroldi.
Zeumer, K. (ed.)
1902   *Leges Visigothorum. Monumenta Germaniae Historica. Leges nationum Germanicarum,* 1. Hannover: Hahn.
Ziegler, A. K.
1930   *Church and State in Visigothic Spain.* Washington: The Catholic University of America.

Discussion

RETAMERO: On page 322 about the question *"conspirantes in unum"*.

DÍAZ: I use this reference from Ammianus Marcellinus several times. The idea is that in this moment of the Visigothic evolution we do not have a centralized institution. The political structure was similar to a confederation or to a momentary joining of interests to face a common enemy. I think it is not a unified state.

RETAMERO: Yes, but the thing that struck me is that the process you describe in your text is very similar to the description made by Ibn Khaldoun (1967), a fourteenth century historian, on how dynasties were born. Ibn Khaldoun describes and explains the same process in North Africa, how different groups came together to face a real or putative external threat; that was the pretext for different groups to join, as in the case of the Goths. The crucial point is how these alliances endure when the predominant group is no longer supported by the other ones but by mercenaries. Precisely this moment is when this already recognized dynastic power starts establishing a fiscal system.

DÍAZ: I think that the process of unification of the Visigoths—we have been speaking about it during the discussion of Peter [Heather]'s paper yesterday—can be compared with similar processes at different historical moments. I have not referred to Ibn Khaldoun in this case, but probably his insight about processes in areas of North Africa is a perception about not uncommon processes.

RETAMERO: According to Ibn Khaldoun, it was the only way by which dynasties were born. One could wonder whether the situation applied to the Goths.

GREEN: On page 322 about the lexicon of the Romans' own social-political reality. You talk of distortions made by classical authors from the fact they use a vocabulary not their own to describe foreign realities and groups. I accept that fully, but I would like to put it a little more broadly and to stress that they used their own conceptual conventions, applying to all barbarian peoples what may originally have been true of only one. The general term for that process is a term used by Tacitus himself, *interpretatio Romana*. In the case where Tacitus uses this expression, he has two points of comparison, a Roman institution and a Germanic one, he looks—and others do the same—for a point of comparison and links them up. We run the danger of assuming that all the other points, where there is no comparison possible, may in fact be identical. That I think is the broader context in which one has to place this *interpretatio Romana*.

DÍAZ: Well, this is a problem that normally we read in every book about Roman and Germanic relations. Sometimes when I read about how Romans, or Roman writers, or Roman Greek-language writers perceived Germanic barbarian reality, I read in comparison how the Spanish chroniclers saw the Indians in Mexico or Peru in the sixteenth century. It is very curious how the Spanish chroniclers of the American conquest used the terminology of the Castilian court, as they wrote about the 'king', about the 'viceroy', about all the figures known to them.

DÍAZ: In this perception, when we read the chronicles of the conquest of Peru we are led to believe that the crown of Castilia and Philip II were facing another king. In fact the chroniclers put it as if the king faced the king of France. This is caused by the use of an ethnocentric terminology.

GREEN: You think of a parallel in the New World, I can give you another parallel from another New World. The first European paintings of Australia depict Australian landscape as if it were a classical landscape.

DÍAZ: This is very interesting because in some cases, Indians who were educated as Spaniards, when they wrote about their own reality, used cultural models belonging to the Spanish tradition although they were Indians themselves; we have one or two cases. I think that this is a handicap—you are right about it— that we are faced with when we read Roman and Greek sources.

HEATHER: On the other hand, you know, you have to communicate by analogy, or else no one can understand.

DÍAZ: Yes, this is the solution here and everywhere.

HEATHER: This phrase "*conspirantes in unum*" is difficult. What does it mean? Which subdivisions are conspiring with which, and anyway Romans love to see barbarians conspiring. That's what they are doing all the time. Thompson (1966) gave this a very technical meaning, but I doubt it can really bear the weight that Thompson gives it, as a precise description of what's going on.

DÍAZ: Well, here, in this "*conspirantes in unum*", we must bear in mind the ideology of the Roman writers. Writing about *hostes*, sometimes they use *latrones*. Perhaps because in their perception, they use a concept which places the enemy at a lower level, they are *conspirantes* because they are seen through the Roman perspective. This may be a deprecatory use due perhaps to the barbarians' behaviour.

SCHWARCZ: Concerning *latrones*, I think it is only used when it is a small raid by war bands and not a full war. If they cannot make out exactly who is leading the group, then it is not a full scale operation then it is *latrones*. And when there is serious fighting it is not.

DÍAZ: Well, we have to analyse the context. They were not thinking about Germanic kings, but about 'enemies' at the northern borders of the Empire.

SCHWARCZ: But it was never used for *hostes* like the Persians.

DÍAZ: No, perhaps because it was a 'state', a 'partner' on a diplomatic level.

AUSENDA: This thing happens also in present day situations. The guerrillas fighting in southern Sudan are called bandits; whereas it is a full-fledged war.

DÍAZ: I think that in this aspect we can find parallels in every page of history. During the Spanish Civil War the chronicles of the nationalists, Franco's side, never described the enemies as a regular army, but as bandits, or traitors. Yes, we must think about this use in different contexts and apply it here.

HEATHER: You need to get out the concordance to Ammianus.

GREEN: Two points on page 324. The first is your use of *reiks* for 'chiefs'.

DÍAZ: It is not *reiks* in the plural.

GREEN: My real difficulty is where you follow Wolfram on page 324, where you put *rex* in brackets alongside what should be *reiks*. Now, Wolfram equates the Gothic *reiks* with the Latin *rex*. That adjective in Wulfila's Gothic can also be used as a noun, but we can be fairly precise about its range of meaning because we have got the biblical text which he is translating. It is quite certain that *reiks* is never used with the meaning of a 'king'. The word for 'king' in Wulfila's Gothic is always *thiudans*, a totally different word. And it's here that I have my doubts about the simplicity with which Wolfram makes this equation with no justification, linguistic or otherwise. I would accuse him here of an *interpretatio Romana* of a Gothic word which will not bear this particular weight. It will not bear it, not only because the Gothic word *reiks* nowhere has that function, but also because Wulfila uses it often with a pronouncedly negative and derogatory connotation, meaning more tyranny rather than kingship. So that I would be happier if *reiks* were not included in that context to avoid this difficulty. That is one point.

SCHWARCZ: A short remark on Wolfram's use of *reiks*, not meaning a king of the whole tribe, but a *regulus*. It may be better to use *regulus* rather than *reiks*.

GREEN: The highest up we can go with Wulfila's use of *reiks* is the idea of a chief.

SCHWARCZ: Yes, that's what Wolfram means in the context of the social reality of the Tervingian society, not the king in the sense of the Roman *rex Romanorum*.

DÍAZ: Well, the explanation is that concerning linguistic questions I am using second hand references, obviously because I have no knowledge of linguistics, and perhaps I should use the term *rex* in inverted commas.

GREEN: The second point is a similar one, namely on page 323, where again you follow Wolfram, if I am right in interpreting you here, when you say that *thiudans* is the equivalent of a *iudex*. Well, *thiudans* in Wulfila's Gothic means a ruler, literally someone who leads his people in the ethnic sense. Now it is true that *iudex* may share that meaning but, to the extent that it goes beyond that, it falsifies the Gothic terminology to imply that this wider range of meanings is present in Gothic.

SCHWARCZ: Yes, I think there is here a misunderstanding of Wolfram. About the position of Athanaric he says that he is not a *thiudans*, not a king, only a *iudex*.

GREEN: Yes, but here we have an equation between the two.

SCHWARCZ: Yes, but this is completely wrong because that's the point Wolfram is making about the *Tervingi*, that they don't have a *thiudans* that their *thiudans* is the *basileus*, the emperor.

DÍAZ: The use of Wolfram's text is a general reference, not an indication that he is called so by Wolfram. You can see Wolfram's text about this question.

HEATHER: I think Wolfram sees Athanaric as a *iudex* with ambition. [Laughter]

SCHWARCZ: Not as a king, because the *Tervingi* are a kingless society.

HEATHER: Yes. But if you talk with him and indeed in the printed version of his book, he thinks that Athanaric may have had it in mind to make himself a king so that his position, *ca* 370, is something beyond that of a *judge*. He is a kind of transition figure between a 'judge' and a 'king'.

SCHWARCZ: Yes, but of course he doesn't make it to kingship.

GREEN: Would you not avoid this if here you simply had *iudex* and then omit a *iudex* at the bottom of page 323?

SCHWARCZ: On page 323 you should use *iudex* instead of *thiudans*.

GREEN: Yes, either way.

SCHWARCZ: Because it is a sort of war leader, but it is clear that he is not a *thiudans* in the sense Wulfila meant, because he uses the word for the emperor.

DÍAZ: Well, I think it is a question of terminology. But we have different references about the *Tervingi*, and one should explain how this terminology was applied and, for example, the reference to a 'central authority' is part of it.

HEATHER: Yes, absolutely and the way round that this kind of study goes, is that you decide what you think the *Tervingi* were like, then you look for the appropriate terminology from books of the Bible.

DÍAZ: You see, the problem is the Bible.

SCHWARCZ: For the *Tervingi* 'rex' is used by Ammianus for Fritigern just before the battle of Hadrianople, because he never used it for Athanaric.

GREEN: And the point to make there finally, is that whereas *reiks* had this negative connotation, *thiudans* has an entirely positive one and can even be applied to the supreme imperial authority of Constantius II, in the Gothic calendar.

SCHWARCZ: Yes, and there it is.

HEATHER: My opinion is actually that the *Tervingi* had a permanent central authority and that, as Wolfram showed, the judgeship was clearly passing through one clan. So, therefore, that's one point where I differ a bit from Wolfram but not that much, because his idea of Athanaric's career and the kind of family history he constructs of him is moving in that direction. But you have to decide what you think the evidence suggests to you, and then look for the appropriate term.

SCHWARCZ: I would say that the term used for Athanaric should be *iudex*.

HEATHER: Yes, one might as well use *iudex*. But, what does *iudex* mean? It doesn't mean anything by itself, it is a mere term.

SCHWARCZ: Yes, but it shows that he perceived that it was not what one would have called a *rex* with the *Alamanni* or any other people he was acquainted with.

HEATHER: It shows that it is a different name. It doesn't show what the office is. You decide from the narrative what you think the office is, what the *iudex* does, how permanent he is, etc.

DÍAZ: Well, the idea of what he is implies a strange explanation really. One should bear in mind that it is a polemic, that it is an open question.

SCHWARCZ: Whatever it is, we don't want *thiudans*.

AUSENDA: On page 323, about the middle of the page, you wrote that "the élite...were capable of monopolizing power and preserving it in spite of pressure from the Huns". On the next page, referring to Sahlins, you rightly note that "in tribal societies the first element of unification is the state of war." How do you reconcile the expression "in spite" with the recognition of the fact that outside pressure contributed to cement tribal unity and the emergence of an élite? Would it not be better to say "because of the pressure exerted by the Huns"?

DÍAZ: Well, I think that it was not only in Germanic societies that war produced stronger links between groups. If we compare with the Greek polis, the leitmotif of the organization was war. I think that when Germanic tribes were coming into the Empire and facing its armies, war was a day-to-day situation. Perhaps war was one of the first unifying elements among human groups.

AUSENDA: Yes, but why did they scatter in front of the Huns? I wonder.

WOOD: There are two points here, Giorgio. One relates to monopolizing power, the other to preserving it.

AUSENDA: No: "monopolizing power because..." and "preserving it because...." Also "because".

WOOD: "In spite" means that the Huns could have destroyed them altogether.

HEATHER: There are all kinds of ways of reacting to the Huns. If you list all the kinds of Goths we know about in the Hunnic period, there are five or six different options that are clearly taken, maybe more.

On page 324, a question about political assemblies. It is essentially a Thompson (1966) point in origin that you don't have these Tacitean style assemblies, and I agree with him. In Ammianus you get no formal account of an assembly with something happening. However, you get a lot of references to consultation. Now, who is being consulted sometimes is not clear, but it happens often, particularly in the context of the Hadrianople narrative when, in the run-up to the battle, there are an awful lot of references to consultation. The point is that one must have some kind of assembly to consult, even if it is not a Tacitean style institution.

DÍAZ: Perhaps in this question about Thompson's point of view, where you can see ancient references in comparison to the fourth century.

HEATHER: Yes, and also an analytic ethnographic text with a narrative text.

DÍAZ: Sometimes in Visigothic sources of the Catholic period, we read some references that are difficult to understand from the day-to-day situation of the seventh century and I think that perhaps they are references to old traditions in political or military behaviour. It was the same in this case, a reference to an old reality that might have survived in the memory of the people but not in the sources.

HEATHER: This is where the fact of having to use Roman sources to understand something that is not Roman becomes really important. Since there are a lot of references to the giving of donatives, there has to be a moment of assembly, of communication between the leader and whoever it is that is assembled. That, in a sense, shows a continuous history of assemblies. I do think Thompson was pushing a bit hard to get a nice pattern, that all assembly and all consultation had gone out the window since the first century. It is clearly not true.

DÍAZ: I have considered the Thompson' reference in this case. My special area of investigation concerns the Visigoths after 418. For the period before that date I use Wolfram, Thompson and Heather, because I believe that they are the most qualified to discuss political institutions before 418.

SCHWARCZ: Just a remark about the consensus, it is not only necessary to have a kingdom of Toledo to reach a consensus. This is a thing which, in one way or another, in politics has to be reached nearly always. A king cannot do without at least the tacit consensus of the élite. In the case of the Goths there must be the consensus of the army before the battle and of its leaders in the council.

DÍAZ: Well, I think it is related to an indication about the war and its meaning. I think that the war is not only tactics, not only the battle, it is their self-confidence about that war and the need to reach a consensus before the battle. We have many indications, not only about the Roman army, which was the standing army during this period, but also from Greek history.

SCHWARCZ: Yes, but if you take the descriptions of the battles in Ammianus, it is clear that the emperor has his chief officers to a council before the battle to reach consensus about the tactics.

DÍAZ: When I was speaking about the Greeks' sense of history, it was not only about the tactics, it was about the consensus, "We are going to the battle together, are we sure that we are going together?" Later, the *strategòi* discuss the tactics. This is the second question. It is necessary before that that one must be sure of going to war in some sort of confederation. I prefer to compare this case to war in the Greek polis, better than in the Roman army, where the discussion was limited to tactics.

JIMENEZ: I think that at the battle of Guadalete in 711 the consensus between the nobles and King Roderic disappeared, and thus the battle was lost.

DÍAZ: And when Wamba went to the Basque country, before attacking, he met the members of the aristocracy to decide about the opportunity of making war, probably because he was looking for consensus. These were the members for whom the law on military obligations was issued in the same period, because of the difficulty of getting the aristocrats to fight together.

HEATHER: In many ways, I suppose, the interesting description does not concern the central authority but those whom the central authority must consult with.

DÍAZ: I am very interested in the formative process, and the occasional trends that explain further evolution.

SCHWARCZ: A parallel to this can be found also in the Roman Empire. If you read Procopius, at the beginning of the war against the Vandals Justinian has to find consensus in the *consistorium*.

GREEN: On page 324, about *maistans* as a Gothic term of social differentiation. I have my doubts as to whether one can think of this word as evidence for social differentiation in Gothic society. It may be so, but there is an element of doubt. The word *maistans*, an adjective used as a noun in Gothic, means literally biggest, and it translates the Greek word *meízon* meaning bigger. The fact that the Greek word may be used technically as a term of social differentiation doesn't mean that Wulfila, when forced to find a Gothic equivalent in translating the Bible, used a word which was in use technically of social differentiation in Gothic. It may, but need not have been, it could be a mere compulsion of translation and of finding the nearest linguistic equivalent which guided him in this direction without necessarily meaning that *maistans* was a term of social differentiation in Gothic society. I think one has to be much more cautious in adducing that word in that context.

DÍAZ: Yes, I think that my usage is somewhat doubtful, *maistans* means 'magnates', the 'biggest' ones in Spanish. Perhaps in English it is not the same word. Biggest in a social sense, not in a military sense nor in authority. I perceive here two levels of authority, of the *reiks* at a personal level, and of the *maistans* at the political, social and economical levels.

GREEN: No, we can be fairly clear, whatever meaning we attribute to it that *reiks* was a term of social differentiation in Gothic, but we cannot be sure about *maistans*. To lump the two together, as you do here, creates a false impression.

DÍAZ: Perhaps I can re-elaborate the sentence, because the idea, I think, is the same.

HEATHER: On page 324-5, the theory about hierarchy is not clear, I think. How hierachical Gothic society is at this point. It is a general comment on the discussion in the first paragraph. Again I am thinking about that Ostrogothic material. It is later, but on the other hand there are an awful lot of people still involved to some degree in the political process there. So I'm just worried about making fourth-century Gothic society too hierarchical. Clearly it is a lot more hierarchical than it is likely to have been before the third century. If one thinks, as it were, of a chronological process between Tacitus and seventh-century Spain, I think there is a tendency to make a lot of this process happen in the fourth century, whereas it seems to me that, not that it definitely hasn't happened in the fourth century, but that the evidence at least throws some doubts on it, and leaves open the other possibility of a longer and a shorter chronology for the emergence of a kind of dominant oligarchic nobility in Gothic society.

DÍAZ: The problem is perhaps an historiographical one. When I try to explain the growth of this political institution, I attempt to put it in relation to the social evolution of the group. When I read Thompson's studies about the fourth century, the *Passio sancti Sabae*, or other texts he uses, I find enough elements to build a model. It is not a certitude here, it is a model that might explain the social relations within the group. If the political institutions are a mirror of this, we may accept this interpretation or not, but I accept the model that Thompson proposed (1966). However, if I discard Thompson's model, the relations within the social group or the questions about the position that everyone has in the group and why anyone can or cannot become king, are very difficult to explain. In my perception, I need to have more than only concrete dates. I need, especially in this long evolution, to look for the relation between the political institution that we are looking at and the social relations in the group that is generating those political institutions.

HEATHER: Yes, I am not quarreling in the slightest with that. I'm simply saying that the evidence leaves open more than one possible construction. Thompson was very keen to look for nobility and hierarchy. You can easily see it in the *Passion of St Saba*. In one example you see in the village the work of solidarity and the exclusion of central power: they pretend to sacrifice and they protect the Christians in their village. The central power needed force to have this local community respond to its commands, and yet the local community can mediate the effect of those commands. You can describe this exchange either as showing the importance of hierarchy or local solidarity. Thompson had a particularly Marxist agenda about the importance of hierarchy; from his first book on the Huns in 1948, the model is the same.

DÍAZ: But perhaps this is a question of the emphasis that you put on a particular level of interpretation.... I can think about Thompson once again but I have been thinking about Thompson's interpretation many times before coming here.

AUSENDA: On page 325, when you talk about Athanaric, you note that "Ammianus...represents him as a negotiator before the Romans." I would like to note that clan heads become tribal chiefs especially through the fact that they are in a favoured position, both geographically and socially, to negotiate with the foreign overlords, and thus become tribal chiefs, more on the strength of the prestige they acquire by dealing with the foreigners than by internal recognition.

DÍAZ: Yes, here once more we have the problem of what was the perception of the Romans about Germanic kings. There is an indication about when Theodosius received Athanaric in Constantinople and it seems it was Theodosius who decided, "You are the chief". It might be a humorous interpretation, but he was more a king for Theodosius than probably for the people that he was leading at that moment. Theodosius needed a king and someone to negotiate with.

AUSENDA: But it is a closed circuit, the other 'appointee' benefits as much as the foreign overlord from the appointment.

DÍAZ: Yes, we have many references where the authority seems not to have it origin in the Germanic group, but in the Roman perception of the power of this group. The problem is that we have only the Roman sources to interpret it from.

HEATHER: Well, you can do better than that with the *Tervingi* because Athanaric's father has been a hostage in Constantinople.

SCHWARCZ: You must be very careful with the passages you take from Jordanes about Athanaric, about making treaties with soldiers for him, because in contemporary sources that's exactly what he did not do, just the other way round, he made treaties in 369 which stipulated that they didn't give soldiers and didn't get *annonae* in return.

AUSENDA: On page 326 you mention the "behaviour of the Goths is best understood in reference to their behaviour patterns of a nomadic or at least semi-nomadic people, which would explain why for forty years they adapted to an existence of constant movement." I appreciate your evaluation which strengthens my erstwhile opinion, discussed in a previous meeting, that Germanic tribal customs could be better understood by referring to an erstwhile nomadic or semi-nomadic socio-cultural condition.

DÍAZ: I use here the word nomadic only as a possible explanation to understand some elements of behaviour of Alaric's Visigoths. This is my only intention when I introduce this term. I offer this interpretation in case it can be useful to understand some questions. We can use 'migratory population' instead.

SCHWARCZ: It is misleading, because when they move into the Empire after 382, they certainly are not nomadic economically. This is a military organization.

HEATHER: That's right, it is a military and political phenomenon. This is what is driving their behaviour, not their economic forms. It has economic connotations, but that is not the same.

SCHWARCZ: It certainly was with the Goths.

DÍAZ: I think this opinion is not mine.

SCHWARCZ: They are not nomadic. When they move, they are paid as Roman soldiers. And, if you look at the sources of the fifth century, where Theoderic the Great and Theoderic Strabo march around in the Balkans, you even get a notice that the emperor was asked to send officials to check the receipts they gave to the citizens from whom they took the money and the wheat to feed the soldiers.

JIMÉNEZ: On page 329, about Athaulf and his wish to emulate imperial power, I do not agree with that idea. I do not think that it was Galla Placidia who wanted power by a future son. We should not forget what Orosius says about Galla Placidia's advice being behind all his resolutions. And when their son was born, he was named with a Roman name, rather than a Visigothic one.

DÍAZ: Yes, probably, but Athaulf was the leader at this moment and he must agree.

SCHWARCZ: Of course the people and the king had to decide the policy, but Galla Placidia had a strong position as sister of the emperor and she actually came to be regent for her son Valentinian III.

HEATHER: And, of course, Honorius didn't have any children when Athaulf and Placidia's son was born. Naming the child Theodosius carried a lot of electric charge.

AUSENDA: On page 329, about the murder of Athaulf, I think that even if it was a political thing, it was couched in a feud, because had it not been in a pattern of family feud, the murderer would have been left to defend himself on his own resources.

SCHWARCZ: Rather than a simple family feud, it is more a question of duties of a retainer in the case of Athaulf's murder and a family feud in the case of Athaulf and his successor. A retainer of Sarus killed the king, and this was more a question of the duties of 'Gefolgschaft'.

DE JONG: On page 330 on the royal privileged position versus Gothic aristocracy, just a point concerning which I was going to oppose you until I discovered what you meant in the Spanish text, on page 330, you cite Ullman and the expression you should use is not 'declining' but 'descending' and then not 'rising' but 'ascending'. Then we all know what you mean. Declining tendency suggests that something is going fairly wrong.

DÍAZ: I am sorry, it was my own translation into English of the Spanish edition of Ullman's book.

HEATHER: On page 332 about Sidonius and Theoderic, just the context of the famous letter of Sidonius about Theoderic (*Ep.* 1.2). The point of its context is that this letter is written by Sidonius to at least one other Gallo-Roman and probably to several. I don't think there is any doubt that the whole point of this description is to sell Theoderic as a member of the new Roman political establishment; and the new Gothic-sponsored régime of Avitus. The audience is not at all Gothic. The careful presentation is of Theoderic as a Roman-style ruler, as a member of civilization. When you look at all categories that are picked up in that description, they respond and answer to the general Roman prejudices against barbarians. It's all about not drinking alcohol and so on. Iit reminds me very much of Mrs. Thatcher comment after meeting Gorbachov the first time that, "We can do business with this man". This description is just saying "He is one of us, a Gallo-Roman".

DÍAZ: Yes, I think that it is the same use that Theodosius made of Athanaric's legacy. Here, Sidonius Apollinaris wants a "Roman" king, and this is the description he makes of Theoderic.

HEATHER: They are reasonable allies. Athanaric and Theodosius are slightly different. Theodosius had just lost against Goths and Gratian had re-taken control of the Gothic war from Theodosius, and Theodosius had retreated to Constantinople. Theodosius wanted to present himself as actually being successful against the Goths and Athanaric came to Constantinople with a hundred to hundred and twenty people, not too many.

SCHWARCZ: That was his personal retinue.

HEATHER: Absolutely, and Theodosius was pretending that Athanaric was still important in terms of Roman or Constantinopolitan visions of the war. It is a bit different.

SCHWARCZ: There is another difference, the personal history of Sidonius Apollinaris. He was one of the leaders of the resistance against the Visigoths, now he had to make up with the new régime and explain to the others why he was doing it.

HEATHER: Not at this moment. Sidonius's behaviour is actually very consistent. He is very happy to work with Goths as long as they are allies of the Empire. It is when Euric becomes independent that he starts resisting Gothic ambitions.

DÍAZ: Yes but really, I think that we must read not only this letter but all Sidonius' production. Samuel Dill (1895) wrote about Sidonius' perception of fifth-century chaos. Indeed I think that it is not only Sidonius' personal position, it is the position of one part of the Gallic aristocracy about the new political situation and they need to identify the king of the Goths with the emperor; so perhaps they transformed reality according to the model of Roman power and, in theory, he was the emperor's representative. I think that this might have been the situation.

HEATHER: Yes, but the thing I would note, is that whichever bit of Sidonius you are reading, you have to put it in chronological context. Because different members of the Gallo-Roman élite reacted differently. They all had to go in the Gothic direction in the end, Euric actually created a kingdom and it was a Gothic kingdom and there was no choice. But they have different rates of moving; some faster, and some, like Sidonius, who would prefer not to move at all. You cannot take a decontextualized Sidonius, you lose half the point to it.

SCHWARCZ: May I draw attention to the bibliography, to the commentaries to Sidonius Apollinaris in André Loyen's studies and edition of Sidonius? The other remark I would like to make is about the figure of Euric who is central to the whole concept, because he is the first who really shaped himself on the model of the emperor and did things only an emperor did. And I wanted to point out that it was the strategy which you noticed very well by drawing attention to the fact that Euric wanted to be *dominus*.

HEATHER: Indeed, there is a big jump between Theoderic II and Euric. And I am sure that's why Theoderic II is murdered: a different vision. He wanted to operate within the Roman context; others like Euric wanted to be completely independent. On page 335, about the move to *Hispania*. This may just be a problem in translation. At the changeover from page 334 to page 335, you have the beginning of the definitive move towards *Hispania* coming after the battle of Vouillé or the battle of 507. At least according to the *Chronicle of Saragossa* (*s.a.* 494, 497), it's happening before, which makes this the final stage in a process. The point is very minor.

DÍAZ: Yes, but my intention in the Spanish version....

HEATHER: I made the point because it would give the wrong impression. On page 337, about Liuvigild. Well, we talked about it yesterday; and the question is just, "how stupid was Liuvigild?" How much of a minority were the Arians, or not quite Arians, but his compromise theological position.

DÍAZ: Yes, I think that he really was stupid.

HEATHER: But in the normal narrative accounts you get this included.

DÍAZ: But Liuvigild is very contradictory and he is looking for a solution in bringing together the Christian factions. He is groping in the darkness, and perhaps in the perception of Stroheker (1965) about Liuvigild's primitivism, he attempts to retain the old elements of identity—Arianism is one of them—and the discussion with Masona about the temptation to combine Arianism is better. I think it is really a stupid attempt at unification.

HEATHER: It just interests me a bit also like the Vandal king Huneric's persecution, as to how ridiculous these people were being in promoting hopeless persecutions, or whether our Catholic sources are misrepresenting the degree of common ground and the possibility of success.

DÍAZ: But in any case, if we read with attention the *Vitas Sanctorum Patrum*, the discussion between Masona and his counterpart, the Arian bishop, is a central question of the self-definition of the ideology of the monarchy. In fact I think that Liuvigild's intention to Arianize all the Catholics was a stupid, but an important idea.

HEATHER: But he didn't; that wasn't his intention. He took account of the Council and the theological compromise he made. It's not right to say that he was trying to Arianize.

SCHWARCZ: I compared Liuvigild's formula with that of Wulfila given in the *Maximini dissertatio*, and there is no difference at all in the Christological question.

VELÁZQUEZ: On page 338, about the difference in government relations between Church and state, or a mixture. I realize that there is a difference, but now I cannot understand it in Spanish. I don't understand the difference between Church-state relations and a mixed ecclesiastical and political administration and what the difference would be, the precise difference. Must I understand this sentence in modern terms, in political language?

DÍAZ: I think that the expression is only an anachronism and that it is not possible to understand the relations between Church and monarchy in modern terms.

AUSENDA: On page 338, the king needed Councils for protection and legitimation, you mentioned the king summoning general Councils and that "probably, rather than a show of strength of the monarchy, it was proof of its constitutional weakness; the king needed the councils to be able to govern and in them found protection and legitimation." This is confirmed by what you wrote on page 346 about the habit of consulting with the high dignitaries.

DÍAZ: The position of the king in the Councils is a part of this peculiar relation between the Church and the king. When we read John of Biclar's chronicle (Campos 1960) about the third Council of Toledo, he compares this Council and Reccared's role in it with Constantine and the Council of Nicea, and with a Byzantine emperor, Marcianus, in the Council of Chalcedonia. In the Catholic period all the kings continue this practice: they are at the head of the Church, and at the head of the Councils, they open the Councils. In the last years of the seventh century they often use this privilege to appoint the bishops, etc. I think that this comparison was made because the king considered himself the same as Constantine in a way, that he was at the head of the state in every respect.

DE JONG: Do you mean that good kings could do without the trappings of bishop and Councils?

HEATHER: Strong kings.

DE JONG: Well, yes. There is a problem there.

DÍAZ: Yes, the situation was not always the same. Not every king had the same relationship with the Church. Sometimes a new king needed the Church and the Councils, at other times he didn't.

SCHWARCZ: I think we must take into account the point you made just now about the practice with general Councils: it was the emperor who was responsible for the Church, but the emperor was not present at the general Councils, they were presided over by a representative of his, and a military one at that.

DÍAZ: Actually this is a simplification. Normally the king opened the Council and read a speech with the elements and the topics to be discussed, and afterwards he left the Council. Then the Council, normally in Toledo, continued in the presence of the metropolitan of the province.

SCHWARCZ: It is called by the king and he opened it formally and he presided over the Church. And one must also take into account the practice of governing southern Gaul with the Council of the seven provinces. One must also take into account that these institutions change in time. It is not a sign of the kingship weakening, but of continuity in that these regional powers, formed around ecclesiastical institutions.

DÍAZ: But in this long evolution, especially after the Liuvigild-Reccared reform, the old models, whether Germanic or Roman, should be considered only a distant echo, because the evolution of the Visigothic state is autonomous. I believe it was a new reality and a very peculiar evolution, and when the kings of the seventh century used some elements, they were not thinking of the Roman imperial model, but of their predecessors, Liuvigild or Reccared.

HEATHER: But I think Mayke [de Jong] is making a more general point that kings cannot rule without consensus. Autocracy exists as an ideology, but not as a reality and Councils do not, therefore, start by themselves.

SCHWARCZ: Probably they would.

DE JONG: On royal succession and consecration. I would like to follow up on the discussion on pages 338 and 339 of your paper. You seem to suggest that kings who had themselves anointed were by definition weak kings: they lacked the charisma derived from the 'bloodline' and 'ancestral origin'. That's what was long said about the Carolingians. I do have some problems with this image, for you also seem to imply that anointing really distanced the king from the aristocracy and the people. This is true to a certain extent, but if you compare the Visigoths with the Carolingians, a case could be made for the anointing not only sacralizing the king, but also the *gens* in the sense of the élite of the kingdom. As Janet L. Nelson has pointed out, royal consecration under the Carolingians went very well with the politics of consensus: kings who ruled with their aristocracy (*fideles*), who shared in the exaltation of kingship. Significantly, in the Old Testament David was anointed twice, once by Samuel, who could stand for the bishops, and once by the elders of Juda, who could be taken to signify the aristocracy. Now, if we take this further and look again at the situation concerning Paul and Wamba, I don't think anointing says much about the strength and weakness of the monarchy. It was a very powerful symbol, and it looks as if Paul wanted it too, for precisely the same reasons that Wamba did. The image projected by *Historia Wambae* is one of *electio* and *unctio* being in perfect harmony. On the one hand, there is not only the king but also the *gens* which is consecrated, on the other hand, the element of the *acclamatio* is emphasized. What I'm trying to say is that things get more interesting once you move away from your perspective, according to which the Church increasingly dominated weak kings and the 'authentic' Gothic aristocracy which might have lent the monarchy real strength. To my mind, anointing was about reinforcing the bond between king and élite within a biblical frame of reference which did not necessarily clash with 'lay' aristocractic values.

DÍAZ: I think that this question is more interesting in relation to your paper. We have spoken yesterday about it: they are connected. The same thing must be explained in the context of the impossibility to define an accepted system for the succession of kings. And the problem is that many aristocrats had the possibility to become kings.

DE JONG: The chances for aristocrats in Spain were surely better than for their Carolingian counterparts.

DÍAZ: But when one of them became king, he tried immediately to transform royalty into an exclusive monopoly.

DE JONG: I don't deny that competition for kingship was fierce, but at a certain point a consensus had to be reached as to who was the legitimate king—and by that stage it was no longer a matter of usurpation or pretending, but of enhancing the position of the new king in order to profit from his favours.

DÍAZ: There are references the Chindaswinth-Recceswinth period, that at the moment the king ascended to the throne, that is when Recceswinth became king, he killed 500 members of the aristocracy, in order to avoid the possibility that one of them should become king. He attempted to start a new dynasty by his sons' succession. This is a constant event in all seventh-century history. Probably it is in this context of feud when the purpose of anointing was that when an aristocrat became king, he was consecrated and was king as long as he lived.

DE JONG: I'm sure you are right, but I am trying to interpret it a bit differently, with an eye on contemporary sources and their role in creating and legitimizing new kings. The language used in these texts is important, and it does not support the image of an aristocracy always out to usurp kingship.

SCHWARCZ: Just one word after this example, well that's what Clovis did with all his relatives, after he was made king, it was a question of political expediency.

GREEN: On page 344 about *gardingi*. *Gardingi*: the suffix *-ing* denotes 'membership of' or 'belonging to' and the stem *gard* means literally a household, but here more specifically a contraction of Wulfila's word *thiudangardi* meaning kingdom, or the power center of the kingdom, the royal palace. So *gardingi* means literally members of the royal palace or the *aula regia*. But again notice it is *thiudans* in the sense of king and not *reiks*.

DÍAZ: Yes, the problem of this word is that we have the reference only in late sources, and it is normally considered an anachronistic term. It is a problem because of the interpretation of *gardingus* as a group, a personal guard of the king. They are not members of the great aristocracy, but a group of personal guards of the king. It is difficult to give a precise evaluation.

WOOD: On page 345, why did the Visigoths look so different from the Franks? I would pursue the issue of the relationship between the nobility and the king, following the lines of what Mayke [de Jong] and I said. Take the phrase *morbus Gothorum*. Yet the Franks murdered kings; they murdered just about as many kings as the Visigoths, but nobody ever stops to talk about the *morbus Francorum*. It seems to me that the murder of kings actually shows that nobles were interested in court. You don't murder people if you don't think they are interesting or worth dealing with. And the force of royal murder, it seems to me, is like the force of civil war; it doesn't necessarily destroy; it can unify. In fact I would argue that Frankish royal succession is rather more complex. But the crucial question is, when does the nobility lose interest in court? You might argue that the majority were always alienated from the court, but episcopal witnesses don't support that line. Does the alienation only come in Visigothic Spain between 700 and 711? In which case you have to say that this is precisely the time it happened in *Francia*. So, it seems to me that you have a possibility of reading Visigothic history as almost exactly parallel to Frankish history. And the issue then is whether the problems we are faced with have more to do with the development of modern historiographical traditions than with what actually happened in the seventh and eighth centuries.

DÍAZ: Yes, but the evidence is not clear. I have to search more carefully for this comparison; I think that everyone, Franks, Visigoths and Langobards have a particular evolution and it is evident that the comparison between one and the other can help to understand the term.

HEATHER: Picking up this theme which is developing through the contributions of Mayke [de Jong] and Ian [Wood], on page 347 at the start of the Conclusion, it seems to me that you tend to write about the monarchy as an institution that works from the top down. And it seems to me that some of the things that Mayke and Ian and Andreas and myself might say, on the basis of what one knows about the Frankish realm, is that monarchy is a kind of aristocratic institution as well, and that the two elements have to be taken together. In a sense, I would echo Ian, I do think it's the kind of sources that survive from Spain, like law codes, which have the king's name on, which make you think in terms of kings downwards. And there is certainly some of that, but monarchy is also created by negotiation and consensus, the Visigothic one and all of this has to come in to a greater extent in any comprehensive account.

AUSENDA: I just wanted to ask what you mean by 'patrimonial'.

DÍAZ: Patrimonial? In what context here?

AUSENDA: Page 348 "due to its patrimonial nature".

DÍAZ: Oh well, it's in inverted commas. Well this is a description of the monarchy as an element of public law or an element of patrimonial law, i.e. family ownership. And the conclusion is that the Visigothic monarchy was an element of public and general interest, an element of state or an element of government, not only a question of the power of a group or the power of a family.

DE JONG: Yes, in the García Moreno article (1994) the concept of patrimony is used to explain why sources do not talk about certain things. Yes? And I must say that I thought this very strange argument *ex silentio*, to say it was not discussed it was so important, it is all patrimonial that it was not discussed, etc.

SCHWARCZ: And it's misleading because in late Antiquity and in the early Middle Ages, the *patrimonium* in relation to the king mean the things and the estates he owned in his private possession; and there is the function of the *comes patrimonii* who is one of the highest functionaries in Odoacer's realm and in Ostrogothic Italy. So it is better to find a different *terminus technicus* from this one.

References in the discussion

Textual sources:

Ammianus Marcellinus: see References at end of paper.
Chronica Caesaraugustana: see Mommsen (ed.) 1894.
Julian of Toledo
      Historia Wambae: see References at end of paper.
Maximinus episcopus Gothorum.
      Dissertatio contra Ambrosium: see Hannan (ed.) 1958.
Passio sancti Sabae Gothi: see Delehaye (ed.) 1912.
Sidonius Apollinaris
      Epistolae: see References at end of paper.
      Opera: see References at end of paper.
Vitas Sanctorum Patrum Emeretensium: see References at end of paper.

Bibliography:

Campos, J.
    1960   See References at end of paper.
Delehaye, H. (ed.)
    1912   Saints de Thrace et de Mésie. *Analecta Bollandiana* 31:161-300.
Dill, S.
    1899   *Roman Society in the Last Century of the Western Empire*. London: Macmillan & Co., Ltd.
García Moreno, L.
    1994   See References at end of paper.
Hannan, A. (ed.)
    1958   *Maximinus episcopus Gothorum. Dissertatio contra Ambrosium. Patrologiae Latinae Supplementum I.* Paris: Bibliothecae Cleri Universae.
Ibn Khaldun
    1967   *The Muqaddimah, translated by Franz Rosenthal.* London: Routledge & Kegan Paul.

King, P. D.
 1972   See References at end of paper.
Loyen, A. (ed.)
 1960/70   See References at end of paper.
Mommsen, T. (ed.)
 1894   See References at end of paper.
Nelson, J.
 1987   See References at end of paper.
Stroheker. K. F.
 1965   See References at end of paper.
Thompson, E. A.
 1948   *A History of Attila and the Huns.* Oxford: Clarendon Press.
 1966   See References at end of paper.
Wolfram, H.
 1990   See References at end of paper.

ADDING INSULT TO INJURY: JULIAN OF TOLEDO
AND HIS HISTORIA WAMBAE

MAYKE DE JONG

*Department of History, Utrecht University, Kromme Nieuwe Gracht 66,
3512 HL, NL-Utrecht*

"Did everything happen in Spain two centuries earlier?" The Dutch student who once asked this question in a seminar on Louis the Pious had a number of striking similarities between seventh-century Visigothic Spain and the Carolingian kingdoms in mind: a close co-operation between rulers and bishops, a clear conception of kingship as divinely ordained (including a royal *ministerium*), an overwhelming preoccupation with moral purification of the realm ('*correctio*') and a formidable impact of Old Testament notions on both law and liturgy. The Visigothic king Wamba (672-680) seems a particularly intriguing case in point. Not only did his anointing in 672 look like a precedent for Pippin's inauguration in 751, but Wamba's reign ended in 680 with the king undertaking a penance. Falling seriously ill, he received the tonsure and the religious habit of the penitent and handed over his realm to his chosen successor, Erwig. Did this serve as a useful model for the bishops who in 833 imposed a public penance on Louis the Pious? Supposedly, the rebellious Carolingian episcopate also relied on the efficacy of the penitential ritual, which was to prevent the monarch's return to the throne.

It is on Wamba's history that I shall concentrate in this paper, but not in order to detect Visigothic influence on Carolingian ritual, royal and otherwise. Carolingian ecclesiastical leaders had ample access to a substantial corpus of Visigothic canon law and liturgy (Fontaine & Pellistrandi 1992), but this does not warrant an automatic explanation of certain similarities in terms of 'influence'. The reception of older tradition is never self-evident, for it takes a specific historical context for such models from the past to become useful to the present. Another question I will avoid is the following: 'what really happened to Wamba in 680?' From the 880s onwards, Bishop Julian of Toledo (680-690) was accused of helping his ally Erwig to the throne by forcing a deathbed penance onto the poisoned and therefore unconscious king. This tale has gained tremendous influence in modern historiography, although Julian has also found his defenders.[1] The most recent

---

[1] For a review of the evidence, see Murphy 1952:15-9 and Hillgarth 1976:xi-xii. The Chronicle attributed to Alfonso III and others (883) is the primary source for accusations of foul play, and also for the persistent idea that King Wamba was unconscious when penance was administered to him. The only contemporary source, the *acta* of the Twelfth Council of Toledo (681), merely state that Wamba received his penance 'in the event of inevitable need': "*Idem enim Wamba princeps dum inevitabilis necessitudinis teneretur eventu, suscepto religionis debitu cultu et venerabili tonsurae sacro signaculo, mox per scribtuarum definitionis suae hunc inclytum dominum nostrum Ervigium post se praeelegit regnaturum, et sacerdotali benedictione unguendum*" (XII *Tolet.* c. 1; Vives 1963: 386). Without

373

assessment by Roger Collins (1995: 78) that 'the worst he [Julian] can be accused of [is] taking advantage of an unexpected occurrence' seems fair enough, but given the nature of contemporary sources (and Julian's near dominance of them) the 'reality' of 680 must remain elusive. As with Louis the Pious, the crucial questions are not whether Wamba was forced to become a penitent, but why a public penance, be it in the face of death or political deadlock, was something that might be expected from a king, and why this ritual was considered to be efficacious and therefore binding. Even if one suspects Julian and Erwig of a vile conspiracy, its success must have been predicated on the more widely shared conviction that penance was an honourable way out for a ruler who had run out of options. After all, Louis the Pious's humiliating public penance of 833 was preceded by a very different one in 822, which the monarch undertook of his own accord, setting a glorious example and enhancing his reputation; Louis helped to shape the penitential rituals which eventually would be used against him (De Jong 1992; 1997). Moreover, Wamba was not the only Visigothic king to leave the political scene as a penitent, after having duly designated his successor. Chindaswinth had done so in 653 (Fredegar, *Continuationes* IV, c. 82; Kusternig 1994:256), and Erwig did the same in 687 (*Laterculus Visigothorum* c. 49; Mommsen 1898:408). Whatever the political pressures involved, something of a pattern suggests itself: the old ruler stepping down as a penitent, with his honour unimpaired, while a potentially disruptive struggle for succession was contained by a *designatio*.

The problem of kings 'opting out' by means of public penance will be given due consideration elsewhere. This paper concentrates on the representation of ritual in the dossier of texts concerning Wamba. The background to the penances of both Wamba and Louis was indeed similar, namely an interdependence of secular and religious power. Even if this alliance temporarily broke down, as it did in Soissons in 833 and may have done in Toledo in 680, it was still a tremendous political force to be reckoned with. In both societies clerics consciously presented themselves in the guise of the Old Testament priesthood. They were the ritual innovators who furnished monarchs with new symbols of power and with new models of rulership. Again, there is nothing self-explanatory in the adoption of Old Testament models. The clergy of the Byzantine Empire never anointed their rulers, and neither did Western kings until the seventh century; in Byzantium, monks were not a separate caste, as they became early on in the West. To say that from the seventh century onwards "kings moved into an ecclesiastical atmosphere"

---

mentioning Wamba, the following decree discusses the problem of deathbed penances being administered to unconscious sinners, who upon recovering refused to remain in the penitential state. The council decided that such penitents were bound to the consequences of the rite, but threatened with a year of excommunication future bishops giving penance to those not expressly asking for it (Vives 1963:387-9). The enigmatic reference to 'inevitable need' may well have served to cover up political pressure on Wamba to give up his throne; likewise, it is easy to see why the decree about unconscious penitents has been interpreted as an indirect comment on Wamba's fate. However, there are equally good reasons to assume that the two decrees were not connected. Yet historians remain 'deeply suspicious' of Julian and Erwig (King 1972:19 n4).

(Wallace-Hadrill 1971:47) confounds the issue, for the ecclesiastical atmosphere was not determined by 'The Church', but by the societies of which clerics were a part. The ideal of one's own *gens* as a chosen people, a New Israel, became relevant to a number of early medieval political communities, notably the Irish, the Anglo-Saxons, the Visigoths and the Franks. This identification of one's own *gens* with God's elect bound together the ruler and his people, however diverse its (ethnic) background. Yet it also imposed far-reaching demands. To be marked out as the New Israel implied extensive—but never uncreative—borrowing from the Old Testament in matters of law and liturgy: the levying of tithes, the observance of the Sunday, the use of unleavened bread in Mass, the anointing of kings, the oblation of children, the offering of sacrifices to a vengeful God. Above all, it implied the adoption of exclusive *mores*, particularly in the sexual domain. Hence, both Frankish and Visigothic rulers assumed responsibility for the *correctio* of their subjects and the purification of the realm.[2]

Janet L. Nelson asked the crucial question: "Why were these categories of persons [i.e. priests and kings] specially and now so emphatically marked off from other members of the *populus christianus*?" For this was the significance of anointing: "The reinforcement of stratification, the sharp delineation of restricted channels of access to supernatural power, the specification of those offices which guaranteed the identity and continuity of new political communities. Ritual, in the hands of barbarian priests, defined the holders of theocratic power" (Nelson 1986a: 279-8). Julian of Toledo would not have enjoyed being called a 'barbarian priest', but he certainly was engaged in defining theocratic power. His compilation of texts about the events of 672-673, known as the *Historia Wambae*, forcefully projects the image of a unified Christian *gens* and its king. In this process of definition, the issue of correct ritual loomed large. What constituted 'good' and therefore efficacious ritual, how could it be identified, and how could one recognize its dangerous counterpart? If anything, Julian was a ritual specialist, inventing tradition as he went along. Even if Visigothic kings before Wamba had been anointed[3] it was Julian who grasped the significance of this rite, and recorded it for posterity. By his own account Julian wrote a 'a *narratio* intended to raise the souls of the *iuvenes* to the sign of virtue' (*HW* c. 1). Hence, Collins (1977; 1992) has argued that the *Historia Wambae* was written for the education of young princes and nobles in Toledo's *aula regis*. This is entirely possible, but if so, these young courtiers were to be educated in the art of interpreting *signa*, in the sense of symbols, for this was what Julian's '*History*' was all about. The text is an exercise in the 'good ritual' of legitimate kingship contrasted with its disorderly and rebellious counterpart. It therefore offers not so much a 'description' of a royal

---

[2] Cf. Kottje 1970; Staubach 1984; De Jong 1996. See also the issue of *Early Medieval Europe* (1998/3) on 'The Bible and Politics in the Early Middle Ages', with contributions by Mary Garrison, Yitzhak Hen, Bart Jaski, Mayke de Jong, Rob Meens and Ian Wood.

[3] Cf. King 1970:48-7; Claude 1971: 155. However, Reydellet (1981:567) contends that there is no proof for any earlier anointing, and I find his arguments convincing.

anointing, as a strategic window on rituals of royalty in the making.[4] Moreover, Julian's elaborate metaphors provide revealing clues to the obsessions and fears of a highly influential member of this singularly paranoid society.

Julian and Wamba

Bishop Julian of Toledo was born in the early 640s, most likely before 644. According to the so-called Chronicle of 754 he was of Jewish descent. His later successor as metropolitan bishop of Toledo, Felix (693-*ca* 700) produced a brief biography (the *Elogium Sancti Iuliani*), which describes Julian as the pupil of Bishop Eugenius II of Toledo (646-657). This early training under Eugenius' wing no doubt gave him a thorough grounding in theology, poetry, liturgy and grammar. When Eugenius—the intellectual grandchild of Isidore of Seville—came from Saragossa to Toledo, something of a 'school' of Toledo emerged, with bishops actively engaging in theological and literary production (Collins 1992:9-12). Many of Julian's works are now lost, though, as Collins remarked (1995:77), "some of his compositions doubtless rest undetected in the great corpus of the Visigothic or 'Mozarabic' liturgy". He was a skilled theologian, who became deeply involved in the controversy over the Three Chapters. Two of his works were dedicated to his friend King Erwig (680-687): the still extant anti-Jewish *Liber de Sextae Aetatis Comprobatione*, and the now lost *Libellus de Divinis Iudiciis*.

Julian's friendship with Erwig contributed much to his later notoriety, but as far as we know, he initially entertained equally good relations with Erwig's predecessor Wamba.[5] Of the latter's origins nothing is known, except that he was an aristocrat who became king not by virtue of royal blood or designation, but by election. Wamba was elected to the throne after the death of Recceswinth (649-672) who apparently had no male heirs, to be anointed 19 days later (19 September 672) in the *sedes urbis regiae*, Toledo. All this information we owe to Julian. His *Historia Wambae* forms the centre piece of a dossier consisting of four documents. In most manuscripts[6] the *Historia* is preceded by a brief but provocative letter from the rebel Paul, 'the anointed king of the East', to his adversary 'Wamba, king of the West', and followed by two more extensive texts, the *Insultatio* and the *Iudicium*.[7] The latter, presented as the record of the rebels' trial in 673, is phrased

---

[4]   About the literary portrayal of 'good' and 'bad' ritual, see Buc 1997, and the author's forthcoming book on *Dangerous Ritual*. I am much indebted to Philippe Buc for his willingness to share his ideas and unpublished work with me.

[5]   On Wamba's good relations with the Church, see Hillgarth 1976:xiii. However, XII Tolet. c. 4 (Vives 1963:389-92) does reveal tension between Wamba and the episcopate, for example over the king's institution of a new bishopric in Toledo's suburb. Collins (1995:76) calls Wamba's reign 'a trying time for the Church'.

[6]   The manuscript tradition is still best outlined by Levison 1910:487-99. See also Hillgarth 1976:214-16. Only sixteenth-century manuscripts are now extant.

in juridical language, with much predictable attention to details of criminal activity (who did what and where). The *Insultatio* is perhaps the most intriguing part of Julian's compilation. To some extent its vitriolic and highly rhetorical invective is indebted to a fifth-century model, the 'Altercation between Church and Synagogue' (Hillgarth 1970:301-2), but judging by the *Historia Wambae*, verbal insult of one's enemies was part and parcel of contemporary battle tactics, literary and otherwise. Generally it is agreed that Julian put this compilation together shortly after 673, when Wamba was firmly in the saddle after having suppressed a rebellion in 'Gaul' (*Septimania*) (Collins 1992; Teillet 1986). According to Hillgarth (1976: ix) the *Historia Wambae* in the strict sense of the word may even have been commissioned by Wamba himself, "for it bears the stamp of official history". Collins (1995:113) argued that a "potential flaw" at the heart of the Visigothic political system was the need for the new king to prove himself in battle, even after an apparently legitimate succession; until the new ruler had been victorious in war, his authority remained frail. From this point of view, Julian's *Historia Wambae* served to provide watertight proof of Wamba's new authority, for not only does the History emphasise the king's legitimate election and his subsequent unction in the *urbs regia* Toledo, but it also highlights his victorious suppression of a rebellion led by the 'usurper and tyrant Paul'. Some have stressed the panegyrical nature of Julian's work, primarily because of his efforts to set up Wamba as the ideal Christian king (Berschin 1988:201; Claude 1971:154; Teillet 1986), though Collins (1977:40) has noted that if Julian had panegyric in mind, he had a "most peculiar way of going about it". The *Historia Wambae* in the strict sense of word does not easily fit panegyrical traditions, let alone the compilation in its entirety. The relation between three of the four documents has been recently re-examined by García López (1993). In her view the *Iudicium* is an authentic document dating from 673, but *Historia* and the *Insultatio* bear the stamp of the Twelfth Council of Toledo (681) and must at least have been revised afterwards, if not written from scratch, according to its pronouncements.[8] Whatever the case, the *Insultatio* is an integral part of Julian's dossier, and a key to one of its central purposes: the literary *damnatio memoriae* of those who dared to upset the delicate balance of power and the fragility of legitimate kingship, be it at the beginning of Wamba's reign, or of that of Erwig's. Through the damnation of perfidious Gaul

---

[7] The *incipit* of the *Insultatio*: "*Incipit insultatio vilis storici in tyrannidem Galliae*" ("here begins a humble historian's diatribe against the tyranny of Gaul"). The ending ("*explicit insultatio vilis provinciae Galliae*", i.e. "here ends the insult of the vile province of Gaul" fits the contents better. The full title of the *Iudicium*: "*Iudicium in tyrannorum perfidia promulgatum*" (cf. Levison 1910:526-9). References to the *Insultatio* are not consistent: "*Insultatio in tyrannidem vilis Galliae*" (Hillgarth 1970:301), "*Insultatio vilis provinciae Galliae*" (James 1980:224). I would opt for the latter.

[8] Levison (1910:491) already thought that the *Iudicium* was not Julian's work, but that of an anonymous palace cleric. García López's carefully argued interpretation deserves serious consideration, although the argument may prove to be circular because of Julian's dominance of the evidence, including the conciliar legislation of 681.

and its allies, the 'outsiders' (*externae gentes*), Julian provided his audience, the élite with access to the *aula regis*, with a blueprint of their true identity: the Goths as God's elect.

Though only treating the events of one year (September 672-September 673), the *pièce de résistance* of the compilation, the *Historia,* is a finished product with a coherent structure. Dates play a significant role: Wamba's armies entered rebellious Nîmes on September 1st 673, precisely one year after his election (*HW* c. 16). The text is constructed as a *historia*, a chronologically ordered record of contemporary history: Wamba's victorious dealings with his opponents, for the edification of youth and posterity. Its didactic purposes are made clear by its author (*HW* cc. 1, 30), but one may well wonder if Julian had only the future powerful of the *aula regis* in mind. If so, he must have hoped they adopt the sense of exclusive identity and group cohesion he sought to instill in the élite of the kingdom. The *Historia Wambae* is about the virtuous *gens* and *patria* of the Goths, beset by perfidious external enemies, but inexorably led to victory by God and its divinely elected king.

The *Historia Wambae*: good and bad ritual

In Julian's *History* some central themes emerge which are vital for the understanding of the other parts of his compilation. These themes are interconnected, but have to be separated for purposes of analysis. In order to evoke Julian's perceptions and preoccupations, I follow his structuring and interpretation of events as much as possible. However, the reader should keep in mind that I am not a Visigothic bishop, and neither do I subscribe to Julian's world-view.

The bare outline of Julian's story is as follows. After having been duly elected and anointed in September 672, Wamba was faced with a revolt in Gaul, led by Hildericus, count of Nîmes, Gumildus, bishop of Maguelonne, and an abbot called Ranmirus, who usurped the see of Nîmes. Wamba sent his *dux* Paul to deal with the uprising, but the latter, fired by ambition to become king himself (*regni ambitione illectus*) became unfaithful to Wamba (*spoliatur subito fide*). With his Visigothic allies, Count Ranosindus and the *gardingus* Hildegisus, he set up a rival kingdom. The king learned of this while on campaign against the Basques; having subdued them, he devoted his attention to Paul's insurrection. One after the other, the rebellious cities fell into his hands. The centres of rebellion, Narbonne and Nîmes, only fell after persistent fighting; when Nîmes was taken on September 1st 673, Paul and his followers fled to the safety of the arena, where they held out for two days, until the victorious Goths entered the city and dragged them from their hiding place. Paul was sentenced to death, but Wamba spared his life, converting the death sentence into *decalvatio*.[9] He was publicly humiliated, first in Nîmes, where he spontaneously deposed his *cingulum*, and then in Toledo itself, which he

---

[9] (*HW* c. 27). Whether *decalvatio* really meant 'scalping' or merely a shameful shaving of the head akin to tonsure remains a vexed question. King (1970:90) thinks the former was the case, but I now tend to agree with Lear (1965:159-60), who to my mind convincingly argues for the latter. That *decalvatio* and tonsure were connected is apparent from VI *Tolet.* (638) c. 17 (Vives 1963:245) which

entered barefoot and shaven on a cart drawn by a camel. Wamba headed this victorious procession, crowned with laurels.

Julian's *History* opens with the best of good ritual: Wamba's election and subsequent anointing in Toledo. The future king was sought out and the entire *gens* and *patria* beseeched him to become their ruler, declaring they wanted no other. In the tradition of saintly humility, he initially refused their supplications, declaring that he was not up to the task, and much too old. Wamba eventually relented, and was duly elected king in the rural villa Gerticos on September 1st 672 (*HW* c. 2). He then postponed his unction for 19 days, in order to return to the *urbs regia* Toledo. This was one of Julian's central messages: it was only here that a king could receive the real sign of consecration (*vexilla sacris unctionis*). Moreover, Wamba's self-control indicated that he was not a usurper, driven by haste and ambition, but a true monarch (*HW* c. 3). This was revealed on the day of his unction in Toledo, when Wamba already distinguished himself by royal behaviour (*regio iam cultu conspicuus*), having pledged his faith to his people (*HW* c. 4). Kneeling, he received both blessing and anointing. Then a column of smoke arose from his anointed head, out of which emerged a bee—a sure sign of future divine favour (*signum salutis*).

Julian contrasted this good ritual with its bad counterpart. The usurper Paul had himself designated by one of his followers, a certain Ranosindus. It was only this follower who said *he* wanted Paul for a king, rather than the entire people of the Goths—at which point Paul forced all present to an oath of fidelity (*HW* c. 8). Julian's point is clear: whereas Wamba became king through divine election and with divine favour, showing admirable self-restraint, Paul rushed his fences, having himself proclaimed king without proper *consensus* on the part of both his aristocratic followers and his army.

Presenting Wamba's adversaries as masters of 'bad ritual' was part and parcel of Julian's rhetorical strategy; he depicted them as the quintessential bunglers of the most vital ritual occasions. When Wamba victoriously entered Narbonne through city gates burned down by God's hand, Paul's *dux* and deputy Wittimir fled to St Mary's church, seeking asylum. But Wittimir defeated his own purpose by doing so without due reverence (*sine reverentia loci*) and hanging on to his sword, all the way to the altar; 'our people', of course duly disarmed, got at him while he hid behind the altar by throwing a board *(tabula)* at his head, at which point Wittimir prostrated himself and was captured (*HW* c. 12). In a similar vein, Paul was said to have committed the ultimate sacrilege: the robbery of a precious liturgical vase and crown (*HW* c. 26). Given Julian's technique of creating two mirror images of kings conducting ritual, one good and one bad, it was Wamba's task to correct Paul's abomination. Once having captured Paul's treasure, he anxiously guarded it, not because of avarice, but with the intention of returning any consecrated objects to

---

excluded those who had been 'decalvated' or tonsured from royal succession. However, according to the *Iudicium* (c. 7), Paul's death sentence was converted into blinding, a discrepancy which (among others) led García López (1991:123-4) to think that the document may be older than the *Historia*.

God. All this was part of Wamba's earnest efforts to rebuild Nîmes after its destruction, which should perhaps also be interpreted in the context of good ritual: a true king may initially cause devastation and death, but when all is said and done, one knows his true royalty because a king rebuilds, reconstructs, and restores both material wealth and social order. As he did several days later in Narbonne: '*mira pace componit*' (c. 28).

Significantly, Paul's imminent defeat was marked by his spontaneous (and divinely inspired) abandonment of his quasi-royal trappings: thus we see the divine undoing of a ritual which had got out of hand. On the 1st of September, one year after Wamba's succession, Paul relinquished the *regalia indumenta* he owed to tyrannical ambition rather than to just order (*HW* c. 20). This did not put an end to false ritual, however. Paul, still ensconced in the Nîmes arena, sent out an envoy to negotiate about his fate, asking Wamba's forgiveness. Bishop Argebadus of Narbonne duly proceeded to Wamba, but unfortunately he did so in the very clothes in which he had said Mass and buried the dead rebels. Meanwhile, he had refused a Christian burial to fallen enemies. Meeting Wamba and his tremendous army four miles out of Nîmes, the bishop made a fruitless attempt to perform proper ritual, so he got off his horse and prostrated himself, asking forgiveness on Paul's behalf. Wamba, who knew how to respond to an *occursus* when he saw one, took the bishop's horse by the bridle and ordered his men to get Argebadus back on his feet. Argebadus then lamented 'we have sinned, *sacratissime princeps*', and confessed to have 'polluted' (*maculavimus*) the faith due to the king (*HW* c. 20). But then the bishop asked too much, again revealing that whereas his ritual wherewithal was sadly deficient, the opposite party had plenty of it. In his liturgical garb polluted by death he dared to ask Wamba to refrain from any sort of revenge, something the king firmly refused to promise. Any clemency would be for the people of Nîmes, not for the insurgents still holed up in its arena (*HW* c. 22).

Subsequently, King Wamba proceeded to Nîmes with great pomp and splendour (*cum terribilis pompae et exercitum admiratione*); all were overwhelmed by the valour of his warriors (*quae species iuvenum*).[10] There was even a clear sign of divine protection and correct ritual, observed by a foreigner and therefore all the more credible. This *homo externae gentis* (c. 23) saw angels flying above the victorious procession and Wamba's *castrum* outside Nîmes. This may be a direct reference to the *Ordo quandum rex cum exercitu ad prelium egreditur* composed in 672 for Wamba's accession to the throne (Férotin 1904:150-1; Díaz y Díaz 1965:79-80; Díaz y Díaz 1980), which contains the following benediction: "*Sit deus in itinere vestrum, et angelus eius comitetur vestrum*". It is tempting to think that this *ordo* was one of Julian's own compositions "resting undetected in the great corpus of Visigothic liturgy" (Collins 1995:77), but it could also be argued that angels flying over victorious armies belonged to the imagery on which any liturgist might draw. Be this as it may, the entry into the city was an uplifting

---

[10] For a penetrating analysis of this depiction of triumphal celebrations, juxtaposed with Paul's 'parade of infamy', see McCormick 1986:308-12.

spectacle, except for those who still hid in the arena. Paul, having been duly dragged from his hiding place was forced to face Wamba by two strenuous *duces* on horseback, who held him by the hair as if he were a female servant. Bad ritual should be answered in kind. This was the first of the three stages of 'the tyrant's' humiliation. Falling from the heights of *superbia* to the depths of humility (*HW* c. 25), Paul prostrated himself and took off his military belt (*cingulum*) as soon as he had to look Wamba in the face.[11] The latter proved himself a benign victor, granting life to Paul and his associates, and sending most of their Frankish and Saxon allies home, "so they could not say that they had been vanquished by an inclement conqueror". (*HW* c. 25) Obviously, reputations could be made or broken by disgruntled aliens bad-mouthing the Goths at home.

Julian's *Historia* culminates in the four last chapters, which are about Paul's successive humiliations. On the third day after Wamba's victory, Paul and his associates were brought in front of the enthroned king. According to the *antiquus mos*, Paul bent his neck for the royal feet, at which point he was sentenced to death by all present, but the king converted this sentence into *decalvatio* (c. 27). After returning to Spain entirely unafraid of Gauls, Franks or other outsiders, and completely contemptuous of barbarian *gentes*, the king felt able to send his troops home. Then he victoriously entered Toledo, the *urbs regia*. Julian's History leads up to this ritual climax, described in the last chapter (*HW* c. 30). A long procession headed by a laurelled king comprised both the royal servants, all proceeding according to order, followed by the picture of disorder: Paul and his associates, heads and beards ignominiously shaven, barefoot and in squalid clothes, on waggons drawn by camels. This procession represented a 'parade of infamy' (McCormick 1986:314), but also a theatrical enactment of a *iudicium dei*, which Julian considered the most vital of all rituals. Whereas all battles fought by Wamba against Paul were in fact divine judgements for which Wamba and his army thoroughly prepared themselves (*HW* c.10), Paul only managed to provoke God with his mindless bragging. By declaring loudly that Wamba's marching up to Gaul did not worry him in the least, he invoked a divine judgement (*HW* c. 11): God's hand set fire to the gates of Nîmes, paving the way for the victorious army (*HW* c. 12). It was this *iudicium dei* which needed to be re-enacted, time and again, in the successive rituals of humiliation imposed on the vanquished.

Many cultural traditions impinged upon Julian's outlook, but it should be noted that his perception of 'old custom' (*antiquus mos*) owes as much to the Old Testament as to any other cultural heritage, be it late antique, Byzantine or Visigothic. Paul's humiliation by Wamba, the foot set on his neck (*antiquorum more curba spina dorsi vestigibus*, *HW* c. 27) echoes Old Testament models.[12] The same goes for his portrayal of orderly and disorderly conduct in both armies. Here,

---

[11] About the *cingulum militiae* as the symbol of military might, high political office and the duties of 'ministry' (*ministerium*), see Leyser 1984 and De Jong 1992.

[12] 3 Reg. 5. 3, Jos. 10. 24 and Ps. 110. 1. Cf. McCormick 1986:330; Teillet 1986 gives other examples.

as so often with regard to early medieval texts, the work of Mary Douglas (1966) provides an enlightening perspective.

Purity and danger

In the *Historia Wambae* the motif of good and bad ritual is intricately connected with that of order and purity. Good ritual evokes a sense of social belonging and continuity in those present, through the shared recognition of familiar symbols. Well-performed ritual is the hallmark of proper order, as Julian did not tire of pointing out. Whereas Paul rushed into kingship, receiving his *regalia* not by virtue of *ordinatio* but through blind ambition (*HW* c. 20), Wamba duly observed the *cursus honorum* before he succeeded to the throne (*HW* c. 4). Abbot Ranimerus became bishop of Nîmes in a most disorderly fashion, for he was consecrated by two bishops from a foreign people (i.e. the Franks, *HW* c. 6). Disorder reigned in the ranks of the insurgents of Nîmes, for once they knew their end had come, they turned on each other, slaughtering each other like animals (*parebant animalium greges*) and turning upon their leader (*HW* c. 19). Paul's Frankish allies fled in such a disorderly fashion that they left everything behind, not only men who could not keep up with them, but also cattle and treasure. Their flight was so 'sordid' (*sordidus*) that they left no trace whatsoever (*HW* c. 27).

Like order, purity was a condition for successful ritual as well as for victory. The Goths could only enter the ordeal of battle with confidence as long as they punished the rapists in their midst (*HW* c. 10). Keeping the biblical example of the priest Eli in mind, who neglected to correct his lascivious sons and therefore perished (1 Reg. 4, 17, 18), Wamba kept his army 'to God's rules' (*sub divinis regulis*), and could therefore confidently face the impending battle.[13] Offenders were punished by circumcision, 'a most bizarre punishment' (McCormick 1986: 312) indeed, except that it fits the logic of Julian's discourse: those creating moral disorder en route to the battlefield were turned into the epitome thereof. Wamba cleaned up Narbonne by driving out the Jews and purged the polluted land by 'the new baptism of justice'(*novo iudiciorum baptismate purgata*) (*HW* c. 27). Through these metaphors of purity and danger runs the undercurrent of gender. Whereas Spain is ruled *viriliter* by a valiant king (*HW* c. 4), Gaul is an unfaithful whore, or even the male prostitute of the Jews (*HW* c. 5). "They", the rebels, had the gall to say that "we" were only women, and therefore presented no military challenge (*HW* c. 9), an insult which rankled so much that it is countered not only in the *Historia*, but also in the *Insultatio* and the *Iudicium*. Yet in the *Historia* the representation of disorder in sexual terms remains a secondary theme; it was only fully developed in the *Insultatio*.

---

[13] *HW* c. 10: "*...si purgati maneamus a crimine, non dubium erit, quod triumphum capiamus in hoste*".

Public and secret, Goths and aliens

Virtuous Goths do things openly, perfidious Gauls do them in secret; this was one of Julian's other messages to his audience. Refusing Wamba's fair offer of peace, Paul's *dux* Wittimir also avoided an open confrontation; instead, he hid within the walls of Narbonne (*HW* c. 12). Likewise, the rebels in Nîmes did not come out to do open battle, but crept behind their walls (*HW* c. 13). This stood to reason, for Gauls were infamous for putting their trust in walls instead of in men (*HW* c. 17). When the rebels did go into battle, finally, they hid their banners (*bandorum signis absconditis*), in the futile hope that their army would not be recognized (*HW* c. 16). Paul and his inner circle persistently hid in the arena of Nîmes (*HW* cc. 18, 22, 24), leaving the fighting to others. Once forced to leave his lair, Paul was exposed on the walls of Nîmes in a way which Julian deems *viriliter*, for it was done openly (*HW* c. 24). Such was the way of the Goths, who never went into hiding. On the contrary, Wamba's victorious campaign in Gaul was a highly visible spectacle, accompanied by pomp and splendour. Once Nîmes had been taken, Wamba established himself four miles away from the city *in plana cum exercitum*, where he erected a splendid fortification. Here he waited for Paul's Frankish allies to attack him, but these were so frightened that they fled in haste, vanishing instantly (*HW* c. 27).

To hide oneself was one aspect of Gaul's deviousness; the other was its reliance on outsiders. The rebel Ranimerus was consecrated bishop of Nîmes by two bishops from an alien *gens* (*HW* c. 6), Paul invoked the help of Franks and Basques (*HW* c. 13), and Nîmes could not withstand Wamba's might without seeking the aid of *externae gentes* (*HW* c. 13). These were invariably frightened out of their wits by Wamba and his Goths (*HW* cc. 17, 24, 27), but he treated Franks and Saxons leniently, so they would not return home with tales of a vengeful victor (*HW* c. 25). Alien *gentes* were to be distrusted as a matter of course, but they were not as bad as the insiders/outsiders who poisoned the roots of the Gothic *patria et gens*: Gauls, rebels and Jews.

Julian's frame of reference precludes the notion of any 'Gothic survivals' (García Moreno 1994). In Julian's view, 'we' (including himself, a cleric of supposedly Jewish origin) are the Goths, as opposed to the *externae gentes*; Gothic identity is embodied by both *gens* and *patria*. The latter is clearly a territorial notion, but the former has nothing to do with ethnic identity.[14] At best it is an ethnic label encompassing all those who are neither dishonoured nor 'other'. The same notion was expressed in 638 by the Sixth Council of Toledo, which restricted royal succession to someone who is *genere Gothus et moribus dignus*; 'un-Gothic', and therefore excluded from the throne, those who had been tonsured, 'decalvated', or were of either servile or 'foreign' (*extraneae gentis*) origin (VI Tolet. c. 17, Vives 1963:245). Julian's *History* attempted to define quintessential Gothicness, embodied by a divinely ordained king, but shared by his virtuous *gens*; he did so in terms of the moral purity of the New Israel.

---

[14] For a survey of the by now copious literature on ethnogenesis, see Pohl 1994; 1998.

Adding insult to injury

One of the threads running through the *Historia Wambae* is public insult. Julian
larded his history with rhetorical vituperation, which he often presented as public
speech. The rebel Hildericus delivered the legitimate bishop of Nîmes into the
hands of the Franks, so they might ridicule him (*in Franciae finibus Francorum
manibus tradidit inluendum*) (*HW* c. 6). At various occasions, Paul publicly
mocked Wamba, saying he could no longer support him as king (*HW* c. 8), and
declaring that Wamba's armies did not worry him at all (*HW* c. 11). Battles started
with ferocious insults. Paul's *dux* Wittimir opened hostilities in Narbonne with a
barrage of insults from the walls, pouring *maledicta* over the king and his army
(*HW* c. 12). Such adverse intimidation tactics invariably got the army in the proper
fighting spirit. Julian's depiction of the crucial *iudicium dei* of Nîmes began with
one of the rebels climbing the walls to tell the opponents that their king was
despicable, and that their would be no mercy for them if they were vanquished
(*HW* c. 14). 'I insult your king' (*insultatione inludere*, c. 14) was a game also
played by the Goths, with the difference that in their case there was no *lèse-
majesté* involved. The nature of the invective becomes clear from Wamba's speech
to his own army, which revolved around the pressing need to teach a lesson to
those who had dared to say that 'we' are only women (*HW* c. 9). Female weakness
is also the crux of the insult delivered by Paul in his speech to his own army: once
upon a time the Goths were to be feared, but those days are bygone, for they have
become degenerate (*HW* c. 16). Appropriately, Paul's downfall was heralded by the
ultimate insult: a member of his own *familia* publicly declared that he had
promised more than he could deliver, and was no longer capable of protecting his
own (*HW* c. 20).

   Insult was one of the themes of the *Historia Wambae*, but it was the substance of
the *Insultatio*. Like the vilifying speeches in the *Historia*, the invective in the
Insultatio is a literary work of art, though this is not the same as saying that it had
nothing to do with the realities of warfare. Julian's vicious metaphors were not
only for private literary consumption; they aimed to vindicate the insulted home
front and to humiliate the insulters. After having consequently referred to 'Goths'
in his *History*, the *Insultatio* only speaks of *Spani* and *Spania*, which may mean
that Julian now adopted the terminology of his primary audience, perfidious Gaul.
The only way to do justice to Julian's prose would be to present an integral
translation. *Faute de mieux*, here follows the gist of his first chapter: Where are
you now, Gaul, with your so-called liberty? Where is the exuberant voice, with
which you declared Spanish men to be weaker than women? What future will you
have if you destroy honest work and avoid good council? You pile crime upon
crime, are devoted to perjury, and love Jews more than the believers of Christ.
Following the law of adultery (*lex adulterii*) you think that all you do is virtuous:
whoring like animals, putting a knife in the back of your friends, killing innocent
souls. You pretend to be hospitable, receiving man, wife and children, but offer

them wine mixed with blood; you kill the man and the children, and take the wife into your adulterous bed.

So much for an impression of Julian's style of insult. His metaphors centre upon sexuality and illness. Gaul is the patently female source of scandal, evil, blasphemy, prostitution and perjury (*Ins.* c. 2). As if all this coming from her breasts was not enough, she preferred a usurper above its legitimate monarch, not through *ordo* but through perfidiousness, not through *virtus* but through treason. Who has ever heard of a woman who, already married, took another man with impunity? The uterus of Gaul's soul produced a wealth of trickery (*ubertas dolorum, Ins.* c. 3). Gaul may have taken foreign counsel, but she conceived of this monstrous birth. If it was of alien origin, why did she cherish rather than abort it? If it was a monster, why did she not kill it before it began to grow? After all, the killing of *informes* and monsters is what *ordo* demands (*Ins.* c. 4). Gaul has become frenetic, and has therefore lost her memory. But her frenzy is worse than that of those who are legitimately ill and cannot be held responsible for their acts (*Ins.* cc. 2, 6). If Gaul ever regains its memory, she should know against whom she raged (*Ins.* c. 2). She has now been slain by the Spanish army and its legitimate king (*Spanorum exercitus cum ordinato principe*), because the head cared about the sick part of the body (*Ins.* c. 7). Whereas Gaul stands for *crudelitas*, *dolor* and *peremptio*, 'Spain' harbours *pietas*, *pax* and *defensio* (*Ins.* c. 8). Metaphors of illness blend into those of sin and penitence. Gaul has to clean herself from pollution by doing penance (*Ins.* c. 7) and should benefit from the *asperitas correptionis* of Julian's insults: '...*tibi insultasse sit utile*'.

The 'utility of insult' may be the key to Julian's entire dossier. It opens with Paul's taunting letter to Wamba, who is not only presented as 'the Western king', but also as the king of the Wilderness. He roams the uninhabitable mountainous regions, skirts the edges of forests, tames wild animals and vomits the venom of adders - but if 'the lover of stones and woods' has enough of this, he should say so, for then a great army awaits him to do legitimate battle (Levison 1910:500). Whether this letter really came from Paul or was concocted by Julian remains a moot point.[15] Its significance can only be guessed at in the context of Julian's compilation, which opened with Paul's insult and ended with the text of the *Iudicium* pronounced over him by the victorious Goths. The latter comprises the record of the insurgents' trial and punishment (death, converted into blinding, and confiscation of their goods), but it also phrases in juridical language what Julian had already expressed in different terms in the earlier parts of his dossier: the rebels were struck by *infamia*. The *Iudicium* opens with the proclamation of the reasons why the rebels, who have turned upon their *patria*, have become infamous (*titulos infamiae suae, qui evasores sunt patriae*); these should be made known posterity (*Iud.* c. 1). Judging by the *Iudicium*, one of the insurgents' worst

---

[15] The riddle of the enigmatic 'Letter from Paul' remains to be solved: cf. Berschin 1988:202. Debates about this letter's 'authenticity' (e.g. Claude 1971:156) do not seem to take the argument much further. Even if Paul's *intitulatio* is in line with current terminology, as Wolfram (1976:72) has pointed out, this says little about Paul's supposed authorship. One might trust Julian to come up with the expression '*Flavius Paulus rex orientalis*'.

transgressions had been their attempt to defamate Wamba by calling him a *rex infaustus* (*Iud.* cc. 2, 6), which might roughly be translated as an 'unlucky' king, unable to bring his people peace and prosperity; this very defamation was now used against Paul and his fellow conspirators, who openly performed '*infausta perfidia*' and therefore created 'scandal', *scandalum*. The concept of *infamia* was a central one in Visigothic legislation; it barred men from giving testimony, which spelled nothing short of a disaster in any litigious society (King 1972:89, 102-4). Wamba himself had struck all those who deserted from the army with *infamia*, a law which supposedly wrought such havoc in society that it was instantly repealed by his successor Erwig (XII Tolet. c. 7, Vives 1963: 394-5). Although the juridical expression itself was only used in the *Iudicium*, Julian's dossier on 672-673 was geared towards publicizing the *infamia* of Paul and his associates. This was the framework of his *History* and *Insultatio*, and the ultimate aim of his vitriolic prose. The closing sentences of the *Iudicium* express the fervent wish 'that the name of the rebels may entirely disappear from the earth, and that future generations may flee from imitating their dismal memory contained in this document'.[16]

Conclusion

Instead of wiping Paul and his allies from the face of the earth, Julian of Toledo gave them a place in history. He also provided future historians with a privileged source: the earliest text which clearly records an instance of royal anointing. But is 'recording' the right word? As an inventor of liturgical tradition Julian played in the same league as his Carolingian colleague Hincmar of Rheims (García López 1993:132-3, with reference to Nelson 1986a and b). This sophisticated compilation was a didactical work, in that it educated its courtly audience, young and old, about the boundaries of Gothicness. In Julian's view, these were primarily defined by correct ritual and the ability to distinguish the latter from its disorderly and subversive counterpart. In a similar vein, Julian's vituperation and vicious metaphors were all about distinguishing 'them' from 'us', thereby creating a world of Gothic order threatened by alien forces. There is nothing new or surprising about the evocation of *Feindbilder* to reinforce internal cohesion, precarious or not. Yet historians using the *Historia Wambae* as a source for the first instance of royal anointing should remember that this was a text which aimed to strengthen a common identity, with the portrayal of correct ritual as its central strategy. This makes Julian's work less of a 'reliable' historical source than it has often been taken to be. On the other hand, the *Historia Wambae* and its appendices go a long way towards explaining the mental framework within which Christian humility (in the received, New Testament sense of the word) could become effortlessly integrated into early medieval conceptions of humiliation and *infamia*. 'Barbarian

---

[16] Levison (1910:535): "*...ut seditiosorum nomen funditus a terrae dispereat et lugubrem eorum memoriam his titulis denotatam sequutura saecula imitari refugiant*".

priests' were innovators indeed. Whether Julian's ideas about moral purity, infamy and revenge were 'ecclesiastical', 'Roman' or 'Visigothic' is of little significance. His notion of 'old custom' (*antiquus mos*) owed as much to the Old Testament as to late antique and Byzantine models. What one encounters in Julian's work is something new, the result of a blending of cultural traditions in which the Bible in general, and the Old Testament in particular, served as a catalyst. Is this not the crux of the process that is nowadays called 'ethnogenesis'?

Acknowledgements—I am grateful to Roger Collins, Rosamond McKitterick and Chris Wickham for their comments on an earlier version of this paper, and to the participants of the 1996 San Marino Colloquium for their stimulating discussion.

References

Textual sources:

Councils of Toledo: see Vives (ed.) 1963.
Fredegar
         Continuationes: see Kusternig (ed.) 1994: 42-271.
Julian of Toledo
         Historia Wambae: see Krusch & Levison (eds.) 1910: 500-535.
Lex Visigothorum: see Zeumer (ed.) 1902.
Laterculus Visigothorum: see Mommsen (ed.) 1898.
Liber ordinum: see Férotin (ed.) 1904.

Bibliography:

Berschin, W.
    1998   *Biographie und Epochenstil im lateinischen Mittelalter* 2. Merowingische Biographie, Italien, Spanien und die Inseln im frühen Mittelalter. Stuttgart: Anton Hiersemann Verlag.
Buc, P.
    1997   Martyre et ritualité dans l'Antiquité tardive. Horizons de l'écriture médiévale des rituels. *Annales. Histoire, Sciences Sociales* 52: 63-92.
Claude, D.
    1971   *Adel, Kirche und Königtum im Westgotenreich*. (Vorträge und Forschungen, Sonderband 8). Sigmaringen: Jan Thorbecke Verlag.
Collins, R.
    1977   Julian of Toledo and the royal succession of kings in late seventh-century Spain. In *Early medieval Kingship*. P. H. Sawyer & I. N. Wood (eds.), pp. 30-49. Leeds: University of Leeds.
    1992   Julian of Toledo and the education of kings in late seventh-century Spain. In *Law, Culture and Regionalism in Early Medieval Spain*, item III. R. Collins (author). Aldershot: Variorum Reprints.
    1995   *Early Medieval Spain. Unity in Diversity, 400-1000*. [2nd ed.]. Houndsmill & London: Macmillan Publishers.
Díaz y Díaz, M. C.
    1992   El latin de la liturgia Hispanica. (1965). [Repr.] In *Vie chrétienne et culture dans l'Espagne du VIIe au Xe siècles*, item V. M. C. Díaz y Díaz (author). Aldershot: Variorum Reprints.

Douglas, M.
1966   *Purity and Danger. An analysis of the Concepts of Pollution and Taboo.*
            London: Routledge.

Férotin, M. (ed.)
1904   *Le Liber ordinum en usage dans l'Eglise Wisigothique et Mozarabe
            d'Espagne.* (Monumenta Ecclesiae liturgica, 5). Paris: Firmin-Didiot.

Fontaine, J., & C. Pellistrandi (eds.)
1992   *L'Europe héritière de l'Espagne Wisigothique: colloque international du
            C.N.R.S. tenu à la Fondation Singer-Polignac.* Madrid: Casa de
            Velasquez.

García Lopez, Y.
1993   La cronología de la 'Historia Wambae'. *Anuario de estudios medievales*
            23: 121-39.

García Moreno, L.
1994   Gothic survivals in the Visigothic kingdoms of Toulouse and Toledo.
            Francia 19: 1-15.

Geary, P. J.
1983   Ethnic identity as a situational construct in the early middle ages.
            Mitteilungen der anthropologischen Gesellschaft in Wien 113: 12-26.

Hillgarth, J. N.
1970   Historiography in Visigothic Spain. In *La storiografia altomedievale.*
            (Settimane di studio del Centro italiano di Studi sull'Alto Medioevo,
            XVII). Pp. 261-311. Spoleto: C.I.S.A.M.

1976   *Sancti Iuliani Toletanae sedis episcopi opera*, 1. (Corpus Christianorum,
            Series Latina 115). Turnhout: Brepols.

James, E.
1980   Septimania and its frontier: an archaeological approach. In *Visigothic
            Spain. New Approaches.* E. James (ed.), pp. 223-241. Oxford: Oxford
            University Press.

de Jong, M.
1992   Power and humility in Carolingian society: the public penance of Louis
            the Pious. *Early Medieval Europe* 1: 29-52.

1996   *In Samuel's Image. Child oblation in the early medieval West.*
            Leiden/New York/Köln: E. J. Brill.

1997   What was *public* about public penance? *Paenitentia publica* in the
            Carolingian World. *La Giustizia nell'alto Medioevo (secoli IX-XI).*
            (Settimane di studio del Centro Italiano di Studi sull'Alto Medioevo,
            XLIV). Pp. 883-902. Spoleto: C.I.S.A.M.

King, P. D.
1972   *Law and Society in the Visigothic Kingdom.* Cambridge: Cambridge
            University Press.

Krusch, B., & W. Levison (eds.)
1910   *Passiones vitaeque sanctorum aevi Merovingici. Monumenta Germaniae
            Historica. Scriptores rerum Merovingicarum*, 5. Hannover: Hahn.

Kusternig, A. (ed.)
1994   *Chronicarum quae dicuntur Fredegarii continuationes, Quellen zur
            Geschichte des 7. und 8. Jahrhunderts.* (Ausgewählte Quellen zur
            deutschen Geschichte des Mittelalters, 4a). Darmstadt: Wissenschaftliche
            Buchgesellschaft.

Lear, F. S.
1965   *Treason in Roman and Germanic Law.* Austin: University of Texas Press.

Leyser, K.
1984   Early medieval canon law and the beginnings of knighthood. In *Institutionen, Kultur und Gesellschaft im Mittelalter, Festschrift für Josef Fleckenstein zu seinem 65. Geburtstag.* L. Fenske, W. Rösener & T. Zotz (eds.), pp. 548-566. Sigmaringen: Jan Thorbecke Verlag.

Linehan, P.
1993   *History and Historians of Medieval Spain.* Oxford: Clarendon Press.

McCormick, M.
1986   *Eternal Victory. Triumphal Rulership in Late Antiquity, Byzantium and the Early Medieval West.* Cambridge/Paris: Cambridge University Press.

Murphy, F. X.
1952   Julian of Toledo and the fall of the Visigothic kingdom in Spain. *Speculum* 27: 1-27.

Nelson, J. L.
1986a   Symbols in context: rulers' inauguration rituals in Byzantium and the West in the Early Middle Ages. In *Politics and Ritual in Early Medieval Europe.* J. L. Nelson (author), pp. 259-281. London/Ronceverte: Hambledon Press. [Orig. 1976].
1986b   Kingship, Law and Liturgy in the Political Thought of Hincmar of Rheims. In *Politics and Ritual in Early Medieval Europe.* J. L. Nelson (author.), pp. 133-171. London/Ronceverte: Hambledon Press. [Orig. 1977].

Pohl, W.
1994   Tradition, Ethnogenese und literarische Gestaltung: eine Zwischenbilanz. In *Ethnogenese und Überlieferung. Angewandte Methoden der Frühmittelalterforschung.* K. Brunner & B. Merta (eds.), pp. 9-27. Munich: Oldenbourg.
1998   Telling the difference: signs of ethnic identity. In *Strategies of distinction. The construction of ethnic communities, 300-800.* W. Pohl & H. Reimitz (eds.), pp. 17-69. Leiden/Boston/Köln: E. J. Brill.

Reydellet, M.
1981   *La royauté dans la littérature latine de Sidoine Appollinaire à Isidore de Séville.* Rome: Bibliothèque des Écoles Françaises d'Athènes et de Rome, 243.

Teillet, S.
1986   L'Historia Wambae est-elle une oeuvre de circonstance? In *Los visigodos. Historia y civilización. Antigüedad y Cristianismo, Monografias sobre la antigüedad tardia*, vol.3. Pp. 415-424. Murcia: Universidad de Murcia.

Vives (ed.), J.
1963   *Concilios visigóticos e hispano-romanos.* Barcelona/Madrid: Consejo Superior de Investigaciones Científicas.

Wallace-Hadrill, J. M.
1971   *Early Germanic Kingship in England and on the Continent.* Oxford: Clarendon Press.

Wolfram, H.
1967   *Intitulatio. Lateinische Königs- und Fürstentitel bis zum Ende des 8. Jahrhunderts.* (Mitteilungen des Österreichischen Instituts für Geschichte, Ergänzungs-Band 21). Graz: Hermann Bohlaus.

Zeumer, K. (ed.)
1902   *Lex Visigothorum. Monumenta Germaniae Historica. Leges nationum Germanicarum*, 1. Hannover/Leipzig: Hahn.

Discussion

HEATHER: I wondered if to some extent Chrstianity comes to play this powerful role because it transcends biological background. In other words it is particularly useful to medieval kingdoms in a kind of post-Migration Period phase, because it's not about where you were born or where your ancestors might have been, it's about current purity now, which is accessible to everyone if they behave that way.

DE JONG: I am glad you bring that up because it is important. That's one side of the problem; but apart from this universal appeal of Christianity, there is also a particularist version thereof which emphasized the exclusiveness of the chosen people. This is why the Old Testament was such an important source of inspiration. So there is this notion of the *gens* being the only true New Israel. I think Christianity was so powerful precisely because these two notions, universality and exclusiveness, could exist side by side.

WOOD: On page 373, should deposition/penance be compared with *decalvatio*? My question is concerned with the possibility of a comparison with the Merovingian state, and it is whether deposition and penalty in the Visigothic world should be compared not just with Merovingian *decalvatio* but also the Merovingian practice of deposition and tonsuring.

DE JONG: I think these are related phenomena. Of course there are differences of degree: giving someone a haircut is not the same as pulling his hair out. Yet all these punishments were public and dishonourable; in one way or another they expelled a person from society. Although I must say it was in a Visigothic text that I encountered *decalvatio* for the first time as a very clear and regular practice. As far as I know, in Merovingian texts you only find it in very specific contexts, whereas in Visigothic anti-Jewish law it is a normal punishment. So, the answer is yes.

JIMÉNEZ: Yes, I wish to recall the fact that the striking similarities between seventh century Visigothic Spain and the Carolingian kingdom can be explained not only because Carolingian ecclesiastical leaders had ample access to a corpus of Visigothic canon law and liturgy, as you say, but because they received the Visigothic pattern directly from Visigoths above all intellectual and ecclesiastical Visigoths who moved to Gaul after 711. This topic is very well studied in a book edited by Fontaine and Pellistrandi (1992).

DE JONG: Thanks for reminding me.

SCHWARCZ: One page 373, on deposition by penance. We have to discuss the point we already discussed in private, namely the difference between deposition by canons and consecration after deposition. When I read your paper it came to my mind that I think the first example of a Christian connotation in the deposition is that of the emperor Eparchius Avitus. He was consecrated as bishop of *Placentia* after his deposition. And I thought that this might have been something of an example for the later periods.

WOOD: Within the Visigothic context this may be of particular significance; he is an emperor raised by the Visigoths and he came from Aquitaine, which remained Visigothic until 507.

DE JONG: Yes, this is also perhaps something I should stress: the social and political role of public penance was much much more important, much earlier in *Hispania* than elsewhere.

SCHWARCZ: And I should like to point out that the first example for public penance is the one done by Theodosius I in 390 after the massacre of Thessalonike.

DE JONG: Yes, you are absolutely right, but this is a complicated case, for, according to the Theodosian model, the ruler humiliates himself voluntarily and, therefore, he is exalted even more. On the other end of the scale there is public penance as a really dishonourable punishment. Anything in between is also possible.

HEATHER: And, in relation to voluntary humiliation which you get onto on page 374, you may want to control your discussion using Neil McLynn's new account of the Theodosius-Ambrose incident in his book on Ambrose (1994), which is, I think, very interesting and very convincing about the voluntary element in Theodosius I's action.

GREEN: On page 374, on the models in the Old Testament, you say that there is nothing self-explanatory in the adoption of Old Testament models. Many years ago I wrote a book on Crusading literature (1966) and its connection with Old Testament models and I'm interested in what you might have to say in this earlier period. You say it is not self-explanatory, but would you volunteer at this stage a general explanation along what lines the model was conceived? I'm interested in seeing if there are any parallels between your period and my later one or any differences.

DE JONG: I would agree with Janet Nelson (1987) that the essence of the matter is the very special relation between a ruler and his people with God, in the sense of a chosen people. But perhaps I should ask you what you mean by 'model'. Certain passages from the Old Testament, certain practices?

GREEN: It is you yourself who use the word 'model'; I took it from you.

DE JONG: Twenty years ago Nelson wrote an excellent article (1986) in which she suggests that the whole issue of priestly ritual purity does not come up as much in Byzantium as it does in the West. For example, the distance between those anointed—it is not only the king but especially the priestly caste—and ordinary people was much greater in the West than in the East. Peter [Heather] and I talked about this. He has doubts whether this is true, and says that similar tendencies were operative in Byzantium, so I suppose I should do some more homework.

GREEN: What about the specific justification or non-justification of warfare by Israel's model.

DE JONG: Yes, that reminds me of Emperor Lothar I who says in one of his letters that he liked Joshua best of all the biblical books because Joshua, like him, had to fight lots of battles. Liturgy concerning warfare is full of Old Testament texts and reminiscences. There is Visigothic liturgy for a king going into battle—perhaps connected to Wamba—which derives its language almost entirely from the Old Testament. But I think I haven't answered your question.

GREEN: If we can trust Philostorgius on this, Wulfila omitted from his translation of the Bible the books of Kings precisely because he didn't want to inflame the warlike spirit of his fellow Goths any further by giving them this model.

DE JONG: Ha. ha, great. Like Benedict.

HEATHER: Is it worth making some sort of general and very simple point that you've got Christianity with a hallowed literature which is the Old Testament and the New Testament, and actually the New Testament, apart from the passage about "Render onto Caesar", is quite useless when it comes to ordinary relations within the state and models of ruler-subject behaviour? So, in your hallowed Christian texts you are almost bound to hunt in the Old Testament for stuff, because the New Testament does not give you anything.

DE JONG: That's what you see time and again in political treatises of the Carolingian Age: lots of Old Testament, quite a bit of Church Fathers, and very little New Testament. Aren't parts of the New Testament, if taken literally, a recipe for subversion?

WOOD: On page 374 about Celts anointing. I merely wanted to make certain that the Celts were not left out of this, although there is a tendency to assume that Gildas is speaking figuratively when he says that kings were anointed. I see no reason to believe that this is figurative: it is just as likely to be an actual statement about Christian Celtic kings being anointed in the early sixth century. And, even if it is only figurative, Gildas earlier than anybody else is casting society entirely in Old Testament terms. And I do think that it is worth not forgetting that there is this earlier tradition.

DE JONG: You are totally right. The main reason why I don't go into Gildas is that I didn't have time to go into it yet.

WOOD: He also has kings going into monasteries voluntarily and otherwise.

DE JONG: Yes. That will be something for my sabbatical.

SCHWARCZ: On page 374, kings in an ecclesiastical atmosphere. I just wanted to remark on your criticism of this passage written by Wallace-Hadrill (1971) because to my mind emperors and kings were in an ecclesiastical atmosphere from the fourth century onwards, from the time of Constantine and especially of Theodosius I and for the Visigothic kings we have the description of Sidonius Apollinaris at the court of Theoderic II.

DE JONG: Yes, quite.

RETAMERO: On page 374, on kings in an ecclesiastical atmosphere. Probably I didn't understand your sentence. You mean that the Church institution had nothing to do with the creation of this ecclesiastical atmosphere?

DE JONG: No, what I mean is that I try not to think of 'the Church' as a closed independent institution. I think 'the Church' consists of certain people who share to a large extent the prejudices and concerns of their own society. This is one of my hobby horses, which I try to stick into many papers. Yes, because the clergy also lived in that society.

GREEN: On the top of page 375 when you talk about various barbarian people as a new Israel, I'd like to take up your reference to the Franks and ask you if you know a fascinating example from Old High German literature, Otfrid von Weissenburg, a Frank, who wrote in Frankish rhymed verse a Gospel harmony with interpretation, mainly a life of Christ but with a theological exegesis. In one of the prefaces he sets himself a double task, the first is praise for the Franks as a new Christian people and the second is a justification of his own task in using a barbarian vernacular for this theological purpose. When praising the Franks, he makes a short description of the land of the Franks which has been shown, I think quite conclusively, to be based on biblical descriptions of the promised land as a land flowing with milk and honey. So that, tacitly and implicitly, there is a link between the land of the eastern Franks and the promised land. Secondly, when justifying his task in doing this in the vernacular, he makes reference to the three sacred languages used on the inscription on the cross, Hebrew, Latin and Greek, but in his actual argument in this preface he makes reference to three languages, they are Greek, Latin and Frankish. So that again tacitly, Frankish has replaced Hebrew.

DE JONG: Well, thank you, I would be grateful for this reference.

HEATHER: On page 375, just the point that Mayke mentioned in her introduction that we talked about. I think Byzantium is slightly different but actually deeply similar. Then, for example, there was in Byzantium a different ideological explanation of the emperor's relationship with God, which put the emperor much closer to God, and I think the intervention of ointment-wielding bishops would be less appropriate. But at the same time, as Andreas [Schwarcz] said, that emperors had been thoroughly Christian and sacred for a long time; and particularly after the Arab invasions, Byzantium goes through a crisis of identity when it loses three quarters of its land, revenues and so on. And you get strong reflections in Byzantine apocalyptic literature of the inhabitants of Byzantium as the chosen people as well. And I think this is very much the air of the times. Byzantium, I think, is thus a variation on the theme, not different.

DE JONG: OK, I will look it up.

DIAZ: I have some general questions on page 375 about the meaning of anointing and the start of the anointing ritual. Perhaps the anointing was the most significant among the rituals of the Visigothic context of power of the monarchy. But I am not sure about the starting point of the anointing ritual and I think that the meaning of the anointing can be discussed. We can think of several possibilities for its meaning. Normally we study the anointing ritual among the relations between the monarchy and the Church, and in this approach to the problem, in the Visigothic history of the seventh century there were more propitious moments for the anointing ritual than at Wamba's accession to the throne. Probably a moment of weakness of the monarchy and a moment of strength of the Church. On the other hand we must understand the anointing within the elaboration of a sophisticated theory about kingdom and legitimacy. I think that the *Historia Wambae* was a very ideological work and the intention of the bishop of Toledo is to remark that it is the anointing that gives legitimacy to the king and, moreover, there is an ecclesiastical ritual, the penance, that deposes the king. The principal significance of the anointing ritual is especially an indication of the strength of the Church. But in any case we must think of another interpretation concerning the ritual. Sometimes we read that anointing is an indication of the strength of the king in the sense that the Church confirms a good choice. You spoke about it but I think it can be discussed.

DE JONG: Well, what to say? Perhaps about this text being ideological, well yes, I concentrate precisely on that aspect; it is because it is so ideological that it is interesting. So, it's not a matter of saying "Look, here we have what Julian says about his anointment and, therefore, this must be a covenant". On the other hand, what I would also be careful about saying, "Oh well, this Julian is a bishop, he is ideological, so reality must be exactly the opposite of what he says". Historians do that all the time. As far as the strength and weakness of the monarchy is concerned in relation to anointing, that's an interesting point. I don't know, I don't think that there are rules for that. It is often said that anointing happens because the future king is weak. You say that in your own paper and I will question you about that, because I don't think it necessarily happens that way. But apparently you have your doubts yourself. Right? We'll discuss it further.

SCHWARCZ: On page 375, on the role of the priests. Your citation of Janet Nelson. I'm not so happy about this restriction of the access to supernatural power to barbarian priests, because heathen religion works otherwise. Which ritual is used by priests, which religious ritual is used by military leaders, which is used by the head of the community, of the rural community, which is used by the head of the realm depend on circumstances.

DE JONG: Yes, so what are you worried about? Oh, you have 'barbarian' of course there. I left that in. You probably wouldn't want to phrase it that way nowadays. When Jinty Nelson wrote this she still used the word 'barbarian'.

SCHWARCZ: No, it is not the word 'barbarian' but it is the restriction to a special group of people.

DE JONG: Well, this may not be the norm in the type of religion you discuss in your paper, but certainly in various medieval societies the priests are trying to monopolize ritual. Or not?

SCHWARCZ: I would say so. Of course, yes, but I am not so sure about this connection between what you call 'pagan' religion and Christianity.

WOOD: Jinty was not referring to that when she talked of barbarian priests. They were actually Christian priests in the eighth or ninth centuries. It is a deliberately shocking use of the word 'barbarian'.

SCHWARCZ: That's what was quite clear from the passage.

DE JONG: "Barbarian priests innovated" is wonderfully short. That's what I like about it.

GREEN: But the shock is a useful one.

VOICES: Yes.

WOOD: You should perhaps put a gloss in the published version when Jinty's quotation is taken out of context; it is not entirely clear that she is talking about Christian priests.

SCHWARCZ: That's it.

RETAMERO: On page 376, on "paranoid society". Just a comment on the expression "paranoid society", such a strong word. I don't know whether this term properly describes traits or explains something relevant of any society, such as 'decadent', for example.

DE JONG: Felix [Retamero], I agree it is not proper scholarly usage to speak of a 'paranoid society', but I hoped you would sit up and think about it. Because I really wonder what on earth is going on in the last decades of the seventh century, especially with Erwig's legislation. And it is, let's say, the kind of intense persecution that you only encounter much later in the Middle Ages in very different situations.

HEATHER: I mean, maybe the problem is the word 'society'. One of the questions is how big a group are we talking about, as big as the power brokers within the Visigothic kingdom? Are we talking about Julian and ten to twenty people, as it were, and their obsessions, or are we talking about a much bigger ruling group? In a sense, coming back to the point that was made yesterday concerning Roger Collins's book (1989), for instance, if it is indeed right that when the Arab invasion took place, an awful lot of groups were ready not to be a part of the Visigothic state and to ally with the Arabs against rivals and so on? What you might actually be seeing, is an over-narrowing of the political élite, leaving too many people out. And that might make it easier, then, to envisage how, in a sense, really odd things start to happen. Because if you are talking about very few people, then the inherent logic of doing something odd like this massive persecution of Jews or whatever, becomes easier to explain than if you've got to explain why five hundred or a thousand people suddenly decide that they are going to persecute Jews.

DE JONG: Yes, I agree, that is an absolutely valid point. What bothers me there, is the numbers.

HEATHER: I was guessing.

DE JONG: Yes, but you are also suggesting that they are very small indeed.

HEATHER: No, I was simply setting up two hypothetical ends of the spectrum of possibility. I am not trying to suggest that the numbers I pulled out of the air there have any relationship to what was actually going on.

AUSENDA: I believe that one should take into account that the lashing out against Jews might be important because Jews are the people who handle most of the trade of prestige goods. They were obviously very useful to the kingdom at given moments, and they probably were not as useful at other moments, depending on the economy. It might be a move to bring in austerity. Because if the Jews were singled out this may have reflected on trade.

DE JONG: The problem is that they are not being singled out, they are in a whole range of people being persecuted.

HEATHER: The problem is very similar, I think, to Peter Brown's (1982) approach to iconoclasm in Byzantium where he is looking for societal crisis, when actually, I think, what you are looking at is an ideological line which is exploited within the élite of the Byzantine Empire. Within that, a very small group, there are elements of crisis, but actually most of what is going on is happening in the centre at court. So that, as it were, is an example of paranoid or deliberately manipulated elements at court, not a whole society going through a sudden change of vision.

SCHWARCZ: I would agree and I would like to point out that you must take into account the further religious debate which is going on in late Antiquity and in the early Middle Ages especially in Byzantium and also the theological debate which is going on in Visigothic *Hispania*. There is a sharpening of the anti-Jewish legislation in Justinian's reign because he personally tried to convert them as a whole to Christianity and he was a studied theologian himself who published theological works. For the later Visigothic kings, that applies too, and it is a tradition of a rigid Orthodox Christian Church going back to Justinian and his direct intervention into Church affairs which is the example, I think, for the Visigothic policy in the seventh century.

DE JONG: Well, both of your remarks are very useful.

AUSENDA: Concerning Wamba's election (page 377, this vol.), in your original draft you quoted Collins's remark on the voluntary choice of a child as king on the part of the nobility rather than having recourse to so-called elections. The term 'election' is misplaced if understood in the modern sense. In a stratified society, as that of the Goths, legitimacy is all important to uphold the right to rulership. In general, excepting the case of a ruling family without descendants, the choice of rulership was restricted to the agnatic kin of the incumbent, hence the election procedure consisted in a council of elders belonging to the ruling and allied noble families choosing, among the agnates, the individual considered best for their collective interests. The choice was then presented to the assembly of freemen who acclaimed the chosen one. The choice of a child might be a political answer to a difficult situation where the most qualified agnate was considered dangerous by the elders, hence a child under the guardianship of a trusted elder was preferred. Of course, as in all manifestations in simple societies there is no set rule, but a governing tradition which may be transgressed or contravened.

SCHWARCZ: Well, but I don't think that that is quite true. It is also cognatic group relatives and sometimes the necessity to take your wife out of the royal family. In the case of the Langobards, for instance, you even have a widow.

AUSENDA: But you don't know whether the widow was acting under the influence of all the others around her. Of course, yes but it's the marriage which is necessary to confirm the relation.

DE JONG: So, it's just a word, but it can be misleading, I agree.

VELAZQUEZ: On page 375, I would like to know Mayke's opinion about the letter from Paul to Wamba. I think that's perhaps a later scholarly product in the circle of Julian of Toledo. We talked yesterday about this point, because, in spite of it being a rethorical and literary product, I believe it is an important document. In fact Paul had proclaimed himself *rex unctus* and anointed as an important symbol of power.

DE JONG: Well, this is the most difficult bit of the whole question. It is a literary text, whatever way you look at it, because it is in this compilation. But the important thing is that Julian ascribes it to Paul, that's all we have. Then you can only ask yourself, why did Julian want to present Paul as a *rex unctus*. This is strange, given that he is also trying to show the world that Paul is perfidious and dishonourable. The rest of it is also a very strange document. Why does the so-called Paul present Wamba as a wild man roaming the woods? I don't know, I have not a clue. Any ideas?

AUSENDA: Is there any reason why this man is called Paul and not a Germanic name?

DE JONG: Yes, we talked about that over beer yesterday. Was he Roman perhaps, or not? But we also talked yesterday about the dangers of linking someone's Roman name with Roman descent.

HEATHER: I have one thought for you, I was going to make in relation to page 379-80. It can go now, I don't know if this is right at all. When the fourth-century Roman historian Ammianus Marcellinus talks about the creation of emperors (*AM* 25. 5-6; cf. Matthews 1989: ch. 9), there is no single way of creating an emperor, but for the creation of an emperor to be done right, there are various things that ought to happen and what they are is very clear from his accounts of different imperial elections. And in the elections of emperors that he considers usurpers, he always makes the usurpers try and do these things but they always get at least one of them wrong. So, for instance, the usurper Procopius cannot find a proper purple robe and he presents himself waving a bit of purple rag at a crowd in Constantinople. I am sure most of this is actually fantasy on Ammianus's part, but it is fantasy to portray a deeper truth, which is what classical historiography is all about. The deeper truth is that these men are usurpers. And I wondered if, in a sense, a lot of what is going on in the corpus about Paul is exactly this kind of thing. You see Paul trying to do it, but unable to do it quite right. And this actually by itself makes the point that he is a usurper because he cannot do it right.

DE JONG: That's something I did try to convey in my analyses.

HEATHER: Yes it is because you conveyed it that made me think about the answer. But I wonder if one could take that same line about the letter, if that might be fruitful.

DE JONG: I think so, for many reasons. Paul was the subject of *historia* of this type; he is portrayed as someone who actually bungles royal ritual and, therefore, is unworthy of kingship. I am very interested in the 'insulting speech' as a literary genre, and I should have a closer look at Ammianus.

HEATHER: I think it might well work. It's this idea of truth but not necessarily literal truth. I think it is a very powerful one.

DE JONG: Exactly, thanks.

AUSENDA: On page 378, on scalping, in your original draft you mentioned "the vexed question whether *decalvatio* really meant scalping or merely shaving the head". Scalping, unless performed on a very small area of the skull, entails death as one can readily ascertain by consulting a specialist in anatomy. On the other hand shaving hair, from Samson on down, is considered a sign of weakness and defilement, and an appropriate symbolic punishment for someone who attempted to raise himself above his status or lowered his status by some infamous act. At the end of WWII this was the penance imposed on women who had consorted with Germans. That *decalvatio* meant having one's hair shorn is also borne out in the *Leges Visigothorum* (III, 4. 17; see Zeumer 157, line 18) where an *ancilla* caught exercising prostitution is *decalvata*, and given back to her *dominus* who must send her far from the city. Had she been scalped they could not have given her back to her *dominus*, hence they would have had to pay her wergild. Here again one cannot be absolute, all one can say is that, in general, *decalvatio* meant having one's hair shorn, but it is possible that in some cases, especially when bloodthirsty individuals were in charge and willing to risk paying the victim's wergild, the procedure was extended a few millimetres below the surface.

DE JONG: Yes, I would like to think you are right, but unfortunately I don't. There is a whole scholarly debate about this in the nineteenth and the early twentieth century. If you look at the texts carefully, it is quite clear that there must be some kind of maiming involved, of disfigurement and something more than cutting of hair which could grow again. I do not know exactly how they did it and I also worry about the question whether somebody who has been *decalvatus* could live, but you can also wonder what happens to someone who got one hundred or two hundred lashes, which occurs regularly in this legislation [between this discussion and the final draft, De Jong changed her opinion, see note 9, page 378, this vol.].

AUSENDA: It all depends on how they give the lashes.

DE JONG: But now look at this text. Paul, according to the *Iudicium* was blinded, according to the *Historia* he is *decalvatus*. That means that blinding and *decalvatio*, if they are so interchangeable, must somehow be equally severe.

SCHWARCZ: There is no question of that in this case, but I want to point out that it must have meant something different in different texts. In the case where people are *decalvati*, and later let their hair grow again, it can't have meant scalping, as for instance for one of the Merovingian kings. In other texts it is quite certain that it is something more gruesome and to the point that the person actually could have died from it. I would take the description that Victor of Vita gives in his *Historia persecutionum Africanae provinciae* of the way Vandals were punished if they were caught attending the Catholic service. And, according to this description, and Victor of Vita is in any circumstance very attentive to detail, the king had special guards watching the Catholic churches in Carthage, and if they saw someone with the hairdress of a Vandal, they took him by force and with iron combs they tore off his whole hair with the hide under it. Sometimes people died immediately after this. To attend the right cult and ceremony is the sign of belonging to a group. And it was necessary for a Vandal to wear this special hairdress and to attend Arian service.

AUSENDA: This is what I said, that if you scalp people they die. So if they are returned to someone, they are obviously not scalped, or they couldn't be returned. So you've got to make up your mind. I'm not saying that they did not do it. I'm saying that bloodthirsty people may have done it if they wanted to kill the man. But I believe that in the great majority of the cases the hair was shorn (not just cut). Because one always has to account for the effects both physical and symbolic.

SCHWARCZ: But just for this reason you have to make use of the sources.

AUSENDA: I agree with this, absolutely, and also if you take the hair out, it all depends on how you do it. If the man went down deep he may have taken out the scalp, if he didn't maybe he wouldn't have produced any wounds. Concerning lashes, a Combonian brother was lashed in Sudan as recently as twelve years ago because a bottle of whisky was found amongst his belongings. The lashing was mainly symbolic because they didn't want the brother to die, they just wanted to show everyone that they had jailed a priest and lashed him in public. There again, you have a great amount of variability in the spectrum of the same penance. Fifty lashes are enough to kill somebody, and it also depends on the type of rope or stick, and the strength by which they are administered.

DE JONG: But we don't know what exactly happened. If you want to fantasize about the whole thing you could perhaps imagine something intermediate, something which disfigured someone permanently, because that's the essence of the whole thing, without necessarily killing him.

HEATHER: But you can go deep in the front and then just do the hair further back. So that leaves a mark on the forehead.

AUSENDA: You could patent that.

HEATHER: I told Mayke that one of my wife's ancestors was scalped out in the West of the US and survived. They put a metal plate on her head. Then she died later because the lid of a box fell on the metal plate and smashed into her brain.

DÍAZ: On page 381 about *decalvatio* and *antiquus mos*. Especially about the meaning of anointing and the meaning of the information in the *Historia Wambae*. *Decalvatio* is a public punishment against Gothic aristocracy and when we read the *Historia Wambae*, the *Iudicium* against Paul is *antiquus mos* and the last punishment is there but we find *decalvatio* in the text. The influence here is the intention of Julian in the *Historia Wambae*, the influence of the Church because this *antiquus mos* is probably a *iudicium dei* or *iudicium publicum* in the *urbs regia* in Toledo, where we can interpret the opposition between the *barbaritas* of the *antiquus mos* and the *decalvatio* against the *civilitas* of the *urbs regia* and against *Christianitas*. In the new perception the place is not anywhere, the place is the *urbs regia* where the anointing of Wamba was confirmed and it is in the *urbs regia* where the last exibition of the *traditor* was realized. And the Church acts the same with the anointing ritual. If we use this interpretation, the anointing was a manifestation of the strength of the Church, it is a manifestation of the transformation of the old Germanic monarchy into a Christian monarchy. In this case we can use the same interpretation as in the ideological intention of Julian. The punishment against Paul is not only an *antiquus mos*, it is confirmed in the *urbs regia*, it is confirmed by other institutions, especially the Church. I think it is an idea, because I still think that the *Historia Wambae* is the most ideological text of the Visigothic sources, the Visigothic production.

DE JONG: I think it is an interesting idea that the *decalvatio* takes place outside Toledo according to *antiquus mos*, and the *iudicium dei* in Toledo. I am rather unhappy with someone speaking of the Germanic monarchy in 680 being Christianized. I mean if you look at the type of Visigothic kings about 100 years before, you don't need to Christianize all that much any more.

DÍAZ: Indeed, we should read not only this text but all the sources concerning the relation between the Church and the monarchy. And, if we read not only the *Lex Visigothorum* but also the Councils of Toledo, we have both points of view. In fact, I keep on thinking that the Gothic aristocracy had a clear idea about its own identity, the exclusive possibility of this Gothic aristocracy to become kings. One needs some elements that justify this position.

DE JONG: Perhaps we should talk about how you should interpret the expression *gens Gothorum* in 680.

AUSENDA: On page 381, you mention Paul taking off his *cingulum* which you translate as 'armour'. I understand the *cingulum* to be the belt or strap holding the sword to the shoulder or to the waist. In other words the man was surrendering his sword, a sign of surrender until WWII.

DE JONG: Yes, I'll change that. But the important thing is that *cingulum* is an expression which has a practical connotation but also a symbolic one. The symbol stands for the man's public office.

SCHWARCZ: No, in this case, it is not, because the belt is a sign of office. In late Roman military times it is also a sign of status.

GREEN: On page 385, I would like to make two linguistic points, neither of them really serious. You refer to the "uterus of Gaul's soul" producing a wealth of trickery. Your use of the word 'uterus' there has an irony of which you may not or may be conscious, when you are talking about the *Historia Wambae*. The name of this ruler 'Wamba' is attested in Gothic, where it means 'stomach' and in other Germanic languages (English 'womb') it means precisely 'uterus' and this suggests that the name of this king may in effect be a nickname, he may have had a pot belly, a beer belly, and he was called as such, a nice irony, unconscious though it may be in your use of the word 'uterus' there.

DE JONG: I will add this one to my metaphors.

GREEN: My other linguistic point—I didn't bring it up when we were talking about *decalvatio* because it only remotely belongs to it. Latin loanwords in Gothic can be divided in two groups, trade and warfare. Amongst these, one particular word, namely Latin *capillare*, 'to have your hair cut', comes into Gothic as *kapillon*, not in the sense of scalping but in the military sense. A Germanic mercenary, used to having his hair done in a Germanic hair knot, had to have his hair cut if he was a member of the Roman army. It is this military context which explains why a word for having a haircut should have been taken over from Latin into Gothic as one of many military terms which come across at this time. Neither of these points is meant to be serious.

DE JONG: Ah, well, thank you anyway.

DÍAZ: This is a reflection about this meeting. Most of us are participating in the meeting of the 'transformation' project and we spoke yesterday about the 'mixed society' and we are here mixing in different historiographical traditions. Anointing was a very important element in the Spanish research on Gothic history, perhaps not always with outstanding results because in one line of investigation the anointing was used to justify the Church and state relations in many cases. But in this long-term reflection there are outstanding works and perhaps it is interesting to take into consideration some of them. Well it is only a Spanish production. For example, there are two very contrasting approaches, one by Orlandis (1962), perhaps he belongs to the most Catholic interpretation about what anointing means, but in any case he knows very well the sources; on the opposite side in the very old, perhaps ideological perception of historical materialism, we find Abilio Barbero (1970), but in one work of the nineteenth century I believe we can find all the possibilities concerning the anointing and this is very important. Well, I read with a lot of interest Ullman's book (1969) about the Carolingian renaissance with many indications about anointing and with reference to the Visigoths. I believe that if we mix our impressions here, it is necessary to mix historiographical traditions to understand some problems, because perhaps this is one of the most interesting questions in the *Historia*.

RIPOLL: I think that Abilio Barbero's is a very good book.

DIAZ: Yes, an outstanding one. I think it is the best work in the scholarly production concerning Visigothic anointing.

RIPOLL: It is very easy to have it and his work was published.... They have published it in a general book.

References in the discussion

Textual sources:

[Abbr. *AM*=Ammianus Marcellinus]

Ammianus Marcellinus
> *Res gestae*: see Rolfe (ed.) 1950-2.

Julian of Toledo
> *Historia Wambae*: see References at end of paper.
> *Iudicium*: see Krusch & Levison (eds.) 1910.
> *Letter from Paul*: see Krusch & Levison (eds.) 1910.

Otfrid von Weissenburg
> *Das Evangelienbuch*: see Erdmann (ed.) 1882.

Victor of Vita
> *Historia persecutionum Africanae provinciae*: see Moorhead (trans.) 1992.

Bibliography:

Barbero, A.
1970   El pensamiento politico visigodo y la primeras unciones regias en la Europa medieval. *Hispania* 30: 245-326.

Brown, P.
1982   A Dark Age Crisis: Aspects of the Iconoclastic Controversy. In *Society and the Holy in Late Antiquity*. P. Brown (ed.), pp. 251-301. London; Faber & Faber.

Collins, R.
1989   *The Arab Conquest of Spain 710-797*. Oxford: Blackwell.

Enright, M. J.
1985   *Iona, Tara and Soissons. The Origins of the Royal Anointing Ritual.*
             Berlin: De Gruyter.
Erdmann, O.
1882   *Das Evangelienbuch.* Halle: Waisenhaus.
Fontaine, J., & C. Pellistrandi (eds.)
1992   See References at end of paper.
Green, D. H.
1966   *The Millstätter Exodus. A Crusading Epic.* Cambridge: Cambridge
             University Press.
Krusch, B., & W. Levison (eds.)
1910   See References at end of paper.
Leyser, K.
1984   See References at end of paper.
McLynn, N.
1994   *Ambrose of Milan: Church and Court in a Christian Capital.* Berkeley, CA:
             University of California Press.
Matthews, J. F.
1989   *The Roman Empire of Ammianus.* London: Duckworth.
Moorhead, J. (trans.)
1992   *Victor of Vita: History of the Vandal Persecution.* Liverpool: Liverpool
             University Press.
Nelson, J. L.
1986   See References at end of paper.
1987   The Lord's anointed and the people's choice: Carolingian royal ritual. In
             Ritual of Royalty: Power and Ceremonial in Traditional Societies.
             D. Cannadine & S. Price (eds.), pp, 137-180. Cambridge: Cambridge
             University Press.
Orlandis, J.
1962   La sucesión al trono en la monarquía visigoda. In *Estudios visigóticos
             III. El poder real y la sucesión al trono en la monarquía visigoda.*
             J. Orlandis (ed.), pp. 57-102. Roma/Madrid: Consejo Superior de
             Investigaciones Científicas.
Ullman, W.
1969   *Principles of Government and Politics in the Middle Ages.* London:
             Methuen & Co. Ltd.
Wallace-Hadrill, J. M. (ed.)
1962   *The Long-haired Kings and Other Studies in Frankish History.* London:
             Methuen.

GISELA RIPOLL LÓPEZ

Dep. de Prehistoria, Historia Antigua y Arqueología, Universidad de Barcelona, C. Baldiri Reixac s/n, E-08028 Barcelona

Symbolic life or everyday symbolism: the limits of the question and definition of the subject

In the first instance, the subject that is considered in the following pages[1] requires a definition of what is understood by the word 'symbol'. The most frequent definition in any dictionary is that which considers a symbol to be any object, design, sign, act, etc., conventionally accepted as representing some person, abstract idea or quality. This kind of definition has been adapted by historians of symbols such as E. R. Goodenough (1953-1968:40), who, taking as a starting point a quotation from Ovid (*Heroides* XIII, 153): *Crede mihi; plus est quam quod uideatur, imago*, states "That is, a symbol is an image or design with a significance, to the one who uses it, quite beyond its manifest content. Or for our purpose we may say that a symbol is an object or a pattern which, whatever the reason may be, operates upon men, and causes effect in them, beyond mere recognition of what is literally presented in the given form". From this it can be deduced that a symbol, as expressed by J. Chevalier and A. Gheerbrant (1973: xiii), has the exceptional property of synthesizing in a tangible form all the influences of the unconscious and the conscience, as well as instinctive and spiritual forces, whether in conflict or in harmony within each human being.[2]

These comments provide an introduction to the subject of what symbolic life must have meant in the Visigothic world, above all in the Iberian Peninsula, for this is where most material and literary forms of expression of this people are to be found, although what is involved by the application of terminology of this type, not so much to the plastic arts, but within a historical perspective, needs further consideration. I would like to emphasize this aspect since, although we can determine that any system of symbols is indicative of a system of moral or spiritual values, we should also point out, as a methodological principle, that the

---

[1]   The title and the subject matter of this paper were suggested by Dr. Giorgio Ausenda, whom I would like to thank for inviting me to take part in the seminar organized by the *Center for Interdisciplinary Research on Social Stress* in September 1996 (San Marino). The problem of symbology in the Visigothic world is extensive, above all as far as literary sources are concerned, and for that reason the scope of the contents has been restricted. I would also like to express my thanks to Dr. P. Banks for translating this text from Spanish into English.

[2]   A full bibliography concerning symbols would be of considerable length; the following however, are fundamental works: J. Baltrusaitis (1972); M. Eliade (1952), C. G. Jung (1967).

relationship between symbols never reflects a logical relationship, because symbolism is never only logical and neither does it contain a rational pattern of logic.

What has been said above enables us to define the subject to be considered. On the one hand, I will endeavour to offer an approach to the symbols used by Visigothic society that finally came to constitute a system of symbols, in response to this idea of a system of moral or spiritual values. On the other hand, knowledge of these symbols will provide an opportunity to know how they formed part of certain aspects of everyday life, thereby transforming the latter into what might be defined as a symbolic life.

This kind of subject can very easily lapse into an analysis of iconography and decoration. However, insofar as it is possible, I will avoid reverting to pure art history in order to extract from the system of symbols not only the meaning of the iconographic language, but also the essential social aspects needed to understand them in historical terms. As Paul Zanker (1987) has demonstrated for the Augustean period, the complete set of images and symbols are the internal reflection of a society and its values. Nevertheless, from the very beginning, those who have studied the problem of interpreting symbolism have run the risk of subjectivity and have resorted to the inter-relation of several disciplines for a correct interpretation. It is no coincidence that E. R. Goodenough (1953-1968:38), when considering the question *What is a symbol?*, replies:

> An objective approach to ancient symbolism is possible only for those who are ready to combine historical with psychological techniques. Use of the techniques of either one of these sciences without aid of the other has heretofore resulted in pure subjectivism. The study of religious art by the 'scientific' historians of the last half century has been done with great skill and erudition in identifying the figures represented.... What has been done in this way is of permanent importance, and has earned such scholars the right to call themselves scientific. Most of them have suddenly ceased to be scientific, however, as they have exhausted the possibilities of such study, and gone on to assert what religious values the figures did or did not have.

Signs of identity or differentiating factors

I would like to stress, however, that the search for the symbols of the Visigothic people involves the identification of a series of signs of identity which may be very difficult to interpret in historical terms as a result of the changes imposed by the passage of time and the subjectivity inherent to historical perspectives and interpretation. A valid identification of these signs is feasible when differentiating factors are distinguished, and this is only possible if there exist two or more groups, characterized by their origins and religion, at conflict, within the population (Wolfram 1993), each with their own law codes and language.

What is clear is that at the moment when the Visigoths arrived in the Iberian Peninsula, this people was in the throes of the process of adaptation or acculturation to Roman culture, an aspect which cannot easily be ignored. It is important to remember that the reason behind this process lay precisely in their conversion to Arianism, which, as yet another form of Christianity, was inseparable from Latin culture, as was demonstrated by Henri-Irenée Marrou (1977:159). The arguments of this scholar are based on the idea that the conversion implied the loss of a national culture and the rapid adoption of a Latin-based Christian culture under Ulfila.

As regards the analysis of signs of identity, it should be pointed out that from the first moment when the two groups began to live alongside one another there existed various factors that were to mark the differences between them, and even lead to opposition and rejection. These, however, gradually faded away, which made it possible for the acculturation process that took place in *Hispania* in late Antiquity to be consolidated.

These differences should be understood by means of the concept of "the Other", what historiographical works call *l'image de l'autre* or "otherness" in contrast with the "identity", which, in the words of E. Benito-Ruano (1988:15), is defined as: "the multiple subject that, in the eyes of a culture, of a society, of a state, of a generation, of any human group, or simply of an individual, appears as someone or something that belongs to the same kind, yet at the same time as something radically different".

One of the most significant differentiating factors, which can thus be considered as a sign of identity, was that of religious denomination, arising from the opposition between Catholicism and Arianism. On the arrival of the barbarian peoples, the official religion in *Hispania* was Catholicism, although pagan survivals continued, especially in rural areas, together with small groups of heretics, to more precise Priscillianists, especially in the North-West, and the Jewish religion, as a consequence of the presence of people professing this faith. In the initial stages, the Arian faith of the Visigoths led to open opposition with the Hispano-Roman Catholics. Some scholars see an apparent conflict between what can be called the *fides Gothica*, defended by the Visigoths, and the *fides Romana*, the banner under which the Romans aimed to maintain or restore earlier concepts of the Empire (Godoy & Vilella 1986).

From the time of Reccared onwards, with the official conversion of the Visigoths to Catholicism, this differentiating factor lost strength, although there had been previous attempts at bringing the two doctrines closer together and important theological debates, and in spite of certain later revivals under kings such as Witteric or among rebellious nobles who used it as a basis for their uprisings.

The identification of each of the groups among the population, on the one hand *Gothia* and on the other *Romania*,[3] with a specific type of religion, as is the case

---

3   This identification was clear from the time of Athaulf, as can be seen from the following lines of Orosius: (*Adv. pagan.*, VII, 43,5): *... se in primis ardenter inhiasse, ut oblitterato Romano nomine Romanum omnem solum Gothorum imperium et faceret et vocaret essetque, ut vulgariter loquar, Gothia quod Romania fuisset et fieret nunc Athaulfus quod quondam Caesar Augustus.*

with the *fides Gothica* and the *fides Romana*, enables them to be considered as signs of identity forming an integral part of a system of spiritual and moral values, even though they were also used in political matters. It is sufficient to recall, for example, the struggle between Liuvigild and his son Hermenegild (Saitta 1979).

After the totally effective mixture of the population at all levels following the repeal of the law prohibiting mixed marriages (although there had been precedents for these) (Jiménez Garnica 1985), this situation was to change dramatically, and land was divided and distributed by means of inheritance, sales and other agreements. From this state of affairs, it can be deduced that the land-distribution question was one element which identified different groups among the population, and, although this should only be accepted with the necessary degree of prudence, a sign of identity or a symbol of moral or spiritual values may have been derived from it.

An important element determining a people's identity is language. This aspect will not be dealt with at length here, but I would like to highlight certain aspects that suggest a degree of approach and assimilation between the two main groups among the population in the Iberian Peninsula, rather than suggest that language was a differentiating factor. There is nothing to suggest that the Visigoths still used their language on their arrival in *Hispania*. After a long period of contact with the Roman Empire, starting with the first advances on the Danube frontier, and continuing with their subsequent settlement in *Gallia*, their level of acculturation was considerable. Even if there was a certain use of the Gothic language, as was the case in the Arian liturgy, this does not mean that it was understood. All that has really survived of this language and all it has contributed are a number of lexical items and some personal names (Díaz y Díaz 1981).

Careful reinterpretation and a new analysis of the archaeological material, particularly of funerary items, enable us to qualify the traditional view expounded above as regards differentiation and confrontation. The cultural situation in *Hispania* from the late fifth century to the early eighth century was highly varied and the importance of differentiation and confrontation was at times only relative, since, as was stated above, the arrival of the Visigoths involved the adaptation of the great mass of the population and a mutual process of acculturation, which had started prior to their settlement in the Iberian Peninsula. In all likelihood, if the process, which started in a clear form in the time of Alaric, is understood as a whole, as J. H. W. G. Liebeschuetz (1992:83) stated:

> The time had been when Roman citizenship was so attractive that the inhabitants of the Empire, whether Gauls, Britons, Illyrians or North Africans, were eager to accept all the privileges and duties and patriotic emotions that went with it. In our period, Roman civilization, especially its language and Christian religion, still exerted great attraction, but Roman citizenship had ceased to do so entirely. If Roman citizenship had retained its attraction, the Goths and other Germans would after a few decades have become patriotic Romans, and the Empire would have re-emerged after a time, even in the provinces flooded by barbarians. Instead, patriotic community-building forces radiated from Germanic war-bands and emerging Germanic kingdoms, and the political unity of the Roman world was irreversibly broken".

Personal adornments as signs of identity (sixth century)

One of the main elements giving insight into Visigothic symbolic life, or the series of symbols that structured the main lines of everyday symbolism, is to be found among what are known as personal adornments, since they provide indirect information not only about an individual and a social tradition, but also about a series of manufacturing techniques and ornamental styles, as well as about a series of motifs that hint at a common inner world shared by contemporary society.

J. D. Richards (1995:56), in his analysis of the Anglo-Saxon world, referred to this in the same way:

> My own research has focused upon the role of symbolism in Anglo-Saxon burial. An Anglo-Saxon burial can be interpreted as a complex piece of communication. On one level it signifies ideas of the afterlife and the needs of the dead. On another level, the grave represents the identity of the deceased. It might be said that the symbols indicate the status of the deceased, although this begs the question of how status is defined. It is the task of the analyst to attempt to identify those aspects of identity which are represented in the burial rite. These may include gender, age set, wealth, and kin group, as well as race and tribal and sub-tribal groupings. But it is important to remember that these are all cultural constructs, rather than natural categories. Mortuary behaviour reinforces cultural differences and helps classify Anglo-Saxon society. It is a means of describing and defining social identity.

J. D. Richards' work represents a great advance as regards the meaning of symbolism in the Anglo-Saxon world although certain scholars have called for more analysis of dynamic aspects. Such is the case of Heinrich Härke (1992:149):

> In recent years 'symbolism' has been used as an explanation of variability in the Anglo-Saxon burial rite, but so far symbolism has been treated as a largely static phenomenon. Thus, a number of important questions have not yet been tackled: how a symbol can change its meaning, how it may be replaced over the time by another of identical, or similar, meaning, and how symbols may become redundant because of changed circumstances.

The starting point for the study of personal adornments is the archaeological material found in graves on cemetery sites. The tomb should be interpreted, according to the definition of P. A. Février (1984:164-83)), as an "interval" between the person's death and resurrection. The physical body must have a place where it can rest or wait, that is to say a material infrastructure in order to pass on to the afterlife, to the eternal condition of man. For that reason, the paralysis of the body, or in other words the prolongation of earthly life, takes place within the grave and it must be accompanied by its personal goods, the adornments, in order to pass onto heavenly life or life beyond the tomb. Only objects of personal adornment appear, for the new systems of values expressed in the later Roman Empire showed that the status of the soul was immaterial; it did not need to be accompanied during this "interval" by specific funerary deposits. In short, the tomb is a material expression of the hope for resurrection (Ripoll 1989:412-3).

The majority of cemeteries, in which burials reflecting the initial stages of Visigothic settlement in the Iberian Peninsula are recorded, are to be found scattered over the central area of the Castilian Meseta in particular. This distribution was largely a result of the process of accommodation and integration of the Visigoths within the Roman population, of the repeal of the law concerning mixed marriages and of the conversion of the majority of the Visigothic population to Catholicism. Archaeologically speaking, evidence for these alterations is presented by inhumations, by the gradual abandonment of the typically Visigothic form of dress and, at the same time, by the adoption of a new form of dress and, with it, objects of personal adornment in a new style (Ripoll 1997).

From the outset it should be pointed out that these cemeteries and their grave-goods enable us to trace a certain mixture of Romans and Visigoths in the population.[4] Analysis of the cemetery of El Carpio de Tajo in the present-day province of Toledo is of particular interest for studying and illustrating this phenomenon.[5] The importance of the cemetery lies in the fact that it is one of the largest funerary groups known from *Hispania* for this period and that closed burials were found which enable relative dates within the cemetery to be established. Furthermore, a plan showing the distribution of the burials is available, which makes it possible to produce a topo-chronological study. Thus, El Carpio de Tajo is a site of fundamental importance for our knowledge of the funerary archaeology of the closing decades of the fifth century and the opening ones of the seventh century, as well as for the process of acculturation.

Although the analysis of this cemetery is strictly archaeological, it cannot be doubted that certain points of historical importance can be inferred from it, and it is quite probable that these may also be detected in other cemetery sites with comparable characteristics, as might be the case of Castiltierra and Duratón in the province of Segovia, or that of Cacera de las Ranas in the vicinity of Aranjuez (Madrid). As far as currently known, all these cemeteries reflect rural settlement sites.

As regards El Carpio de Tajo, this is one of a series of characteristic burial sites; it must have been related to a still-unknown rural settlement, perhaps a *uicus*,

---

[4] The information concerning this point offered by the slate tablets with Visigothic cursive writing is highly informative, since the mixture of names of Germanic and Roman origin is a constant feature. This phenomenon is particularly clear in the case of those pieces that are of value as legal documents and which basically deal with matters referring to dependent peasants or serfs etc. In the initial stages of Visigothic settlement some Visigothic individuals may well have adopted names of Greek or Latin origin, in view of the cultural superiority and prestige of Roman culture. However, it is also highly likely that at a subsequent date, when integration of the population was well-established and the *tria nomina* had effectively disappeared, that names of Germanic origin re-emerged, certain signs of identity thus being recovered. Cf. especially Velázquez Soriano (1989); Ripoll and Velázquez (1995).

[5] All the documentation concerning the cemetery, the study of the personal adornments and of the plan, its historical interpretation and a bibliography on the subject are to be found in Ripoll 1993-1994. An initial publication without the plan, but with an analysis of all the personal adornments, can be found in Ripoll 1985.

which it undeniably reflects. Taking into account the number of graves (although the number of re-used graves remains unknown) and the fact it covers a maximum time span of a hundred and fifty years, it can be seen that the community was of limited size. Such cemeteries and communities are characteristic of the centre of the Iberian Peninsula and they were particularly associated with agricultural and herding estates.[6] The cemetery was located overlooking the River Tagus valley, on the top of a rise on the right bank. It was therefore situated to the west of *Toletum*, a city whose historical importance was considerable as from the mid-sixth century. It thus fell within the zone of influence of the royal town, although there is no element in the cemetery that might suggest a connection between this funerary site and the city. The whole area to the south of the Sierra de Gredos and the north of the Montes de Toledo was densely populated in late Antiquity, a dispersed pattern of settlement, knowledge of which continues to grow, being particularly noticeable (Yañez *et al.* 1994; Ardanaz 1990). Nevertheless, within this area, the cemeteries of El Carpio de Tajo and the above mentioned one at Cacera de las Ranas in Aranjuez (Ardanaz 1991), both reflecting, as far as is known, rural settlements, continue to be the largest and best known funerary sites at the present time.

At El Carpio de Tajo a total of 285 inhumations were found, many of which contained articles of personal adornment, the majority being classifiable as items of female jewellery; the time span ranged from the late fifth to the late sixth centuries. The types of material found enable some burials to be considered as typically Visigothic, while others may have belonged to the Roman population, or at least they were not characteristic of Visigothic dress. We are thus faced with a cemetery site that should be identified with a centre of mixed population, Visigothic and Roman, rather than one representing exclusively Visigothic social structures. The chronological evolution of the use of this funerary site is also of interest, for it demonstrates the gradual integration of different groups within the population. The earliest burials, known as foundational graves, seem to represent late fifth-century Visigothic individuals. By the early sixth century, the funerary space had been defined, and typically Visigothic burials and those possibly attributable to Romans occupied the different sectors, without specific zones being defined. With the advent of new generations, the funerary site was gradually more densely occupied until an uncertain moment in the late sixth or early seventh century when it was abandoned. Spatial organization was implemented on the basis of social and/or family groups.

From this layout one can infer that, as a result of the passing of time and contact with Romano-Christian civilization, the kinship system gradually weakened at the same time as the conjugal family gained in importance. It is highly likely that the first nucleus of occupation of the cemetery—the foundational one—reflects a kinship system, and this gradually gave way to burials governed by a nuclear

---

[6]   This question has been considered in Ripoll (1989:399-403). For a recent reconsideration of the subject, Bierbrauer (1992:34; 1994:168). On the social and economic conditions of dependence cf. Wolfram (1983:178-187).

family structure. This analysis and working hypothesis illustrates not only the process of acculturation, but also the incorporation or assimilation of Roman individuals into Visigothic family groups. From all this one can conclude that the settlement site that was related to El Carpio de Tajo comprised a mixed population, in which Romans and Visigoths lived together, and not only people of Visigothic origin, as has hitherto been supposed.[7]

The model proposed for El Carpio de Tajo enables us to perceive that, during the sixth century, the Visigothic group, like the Roman one, had certain signs of identity based on objects of personal adornment, the result of their clothing traditions. Some researchers define these personal objects as a Gothic national costume (Bierbrauer 1994:166).[8] It is also of interest to emphasize that these signs were only associated with female dress, since we have no knowledge of male personal adornments. It is also obvious that not all women in a rural context were buried with their personal adornments as there are burials without any grave goods. One can thus infer that different social classes were in existence and that some women in the countryside enjoyed a higher social status, if it is accepted that metal objects are a sign of power or of class, as well as a sign of identity.[9] These moveable objects of personal use that women took with them to the grave formed part of the share of the patrimony reserved for the dead (*Totenteil*); in other words there existed individual property that did not form part of the common family heritage. It is quite probable that these personal adornments were the *ornamenta muliebria* that the wife received from her *Sippe* at marriage and that they belonged to her throughout her life.[10]

In addition, what has been said above supports the working hypothesis that one of the most widely developed activities throughout the sixth century was metalworking, which should perhaps be taken as a differentiating element between the groups within the population, since, as H. I. Marrou supposed (1977:142), there was clear "technical superiority on the part of the invaders in metal-working". In contrast, gold- and silver-working were of greater importance in the

---

[7] This same phenomenon has been detected in other cemeteries, such as that of Duratón in the province of Segovia, the distribution plans of which were drawn up by Bierbrauer (1980a: figs. 2-4), who reconsidered the subject in 1992 (28-34). Mixed populations have also been traced through the study of cemeteries in Pannonia (Bierbrauer 1980b:141).

[8] I find it difficult to accept the terminology of 'Gothic national', since, despite a certain historiographical tradition, the exact limits of the 'nation' for the Visigothic kingdom of Toledo have not yet been correctly established. The bibliography is extensive, although the question was dealt with indirectly by Wolfram (1992) and previously by Teillet (1984).

[9] Jiménez Garnica (1995) should be consulted on the importance of women in the Visigothic world.

[10] The complexities of moveable property and its transmission are reflected in the jurisdiction laid down about personal rights (Pérez-Prendes & Azcarraga 1990:146; Pérez-Prendes 1993:39), which it is difficult to detect in archaeological terms (Ripoll 1993/94:243).

seventh century and they are largely known thanks to the strength of the palace workshops operating around the court of Toledo.

Before continuing the discussion further, I would like to make a series of historiographical observations that have marked research on these small items of personal ornamentation, by and large found, as has already been noted, in cemetery graves, and which, as a result, define some of the main characteristics of the world of symbols among the Visigoths. Early twentieth-century German scholars had a profound influence on the fundamental lines of research pursued through their efforts to distinguish, on the basis of these objects, the Visigothic people as a Germanic ethnic group or race completely different from the rest of the population of the Iberian Peninsula.[11] It was not until the 1950s that a new generation of archaeologists demonstrated the continuity of the Roman world within the Visigothic horizon.[12] It has thus proved possible to evaluate the real impact of Germanism—only present in certain burials in the cemeteries of the central Meseta—alongside the strong Roman current that can be detected in all underlying levels in the Iberian Peninsula, as well as the various other influences that might have affected the population of *Hispania*, not only the Roman and Visigothic sectors of society, but also all those social groups of oriental origin to be found the full length of the Mediterranean and Atlantic coastline (Ripoll 1997).

The study of the material resulting from Visigothic-period funerary sites has enabled me to establish, in general terms, a number of typological groups with very relative chronologies (Ripoll 1991a; 1991b). The selection of the material on the basis of what are known as 'closed finds' was carried out starting with the objects of personal adornment found in association with each other in Visigothic-period cemeteries, basically Duratón, Madrona and Espirdo (Segovia), El Carpio de Tajo (Toledo), Deza (Soria), Herrera de Pisuerga (Palencia) and Estagel (Pyrénées Orientales).

The majority of the surviving objects are *fibulae* which were used to hold the cloak at shoulder or chest level, in addition to belt buckles of various types. Among the standard personal adornments of Visigothic type datable to the late fifth and early sixth centuries, a wide variety of *fibula* types should be noted; earliest in the chronological series are the brooches known as 'Silberblechfibeln', which were usually made by joining together a series of plates or, alternatively,

---

[11] It is obvious that this was a historiographical tradition that developed in the nineteenth century, but these scholars' works made the wealth and significance of the characteristically Visigothic funerary material of the Iberian Peninsula more generally known. More specifically, I refer to the works of Götze (1907), Aberg (1922) and Zeiss (1934), and subsequently those of Reinhart (1945) and Werner (1946).

[12] In particular, I refer to the work of Professor Palol. His contribution at Spoleto marked an important step forward in Spanish Visigothic studies. Although he declared himself to be a Romanist, he attributed Germanic characteristics to the personal objects (1956:63). It is of interest to mention his recently published general summary of archaeology, as it includes all his views (Palol 1991), as well as his historiographical reflections (Palol 1995).

were cast in bronze (fig. 11-1). There is also a wide variety, in typological and decorative terms, among belt buckles. The latter are nearly always distinguished by their polychrome decoration, since the majority exhibit incrustations of semi-precious stones or garnets, or surfaces covered with *cloisonné* (designs of patterns of small cells) containing coloured glass. There are also certain types of belt buckles, above all in the earliest phases, which consist of rectangular plates of iron or silver with hardly any decoration or with only a few isolated stones set *en cabochon*.[13]

Among all these products belonging to the initial stages of Visigothic settlement, the so-called eagle-brooches stand out.[14] Even though they cannot be considered to be specifically characteristic of the Iberian Peninsula, as they appear elsewhere such as Domagnano (Republic of San Marino), they are marked by the particular personality of the brooch-makers and metalworkers of the Peninsula. Two different types exist: those produced by means of the *cloisonné* technique, with remarkable examples from the cemeteries of Alovera and Espinosa de Henares (Guadalajara), Duratón (Segovia), La Jarilla (Galisteo, Cáceres), Tierra de Barros (Badajoz), etc. In the second type, the eagle was cut out of, or cast in, heat-gilded bronze sheet, with incised geometric decoration. Examples of this latter type were found in the cemeteries of Madrona and Castiltierra (Segovia) and Deza (Soria). It is very probable that this second type is a product of Hispanic workshops alone and is a forerunner of the seventh-century eagle brooches cut out of gold sheet, which probably formed part of the personal attributes of the highest social classes. As far as their possible symbolism is concerned, since there is neither textual nor archaeological evidence to support the view, it is difficult to accept that we are faced with a sun symbol, and therefore by extension a representation of royalty. The Western tradition interprets the open-winged eagle as expressing the freedom of flight in order to achieve knowledge of the *pneuma*, and for this reason the Christian tradition assimilates this bird with the one responsible for carrying on its wings the soul of the deceased to the presence of God. Neither do we know if the latter was the symbolism that it was thought to transmit through the use of eagle-brooches as an element of personal adornment.

The objects of personal adornment that have so far been described, which appeared at the end of the fifth century and continued in use until the second half of the sixth century (fig. 11-2), represent the only elements that could be considered as signs of identity. An interpretation at two levels can be derived from

---

[13] The development and appearance of all these materials, together with their detailed study, can be followed in Ripoll (1991a:134-40; 1998b:41-66). As regards the cloisonné-decorated belt plates, it should be noted that my types A and B appear in association with plate brooches and are thus of a relatively early date. As James (1977:249; 1980:236) has suggested, they may have been manufactured in the *Narbonensis*.

[14] The bibliography concerning eagle-brooches is long and complex, since, in addition to the dispersed nature of the finds, one has to take into account some forgeries produced in the 1930s. For an overall view, Ripoll (1991a:168-72, 178-81).

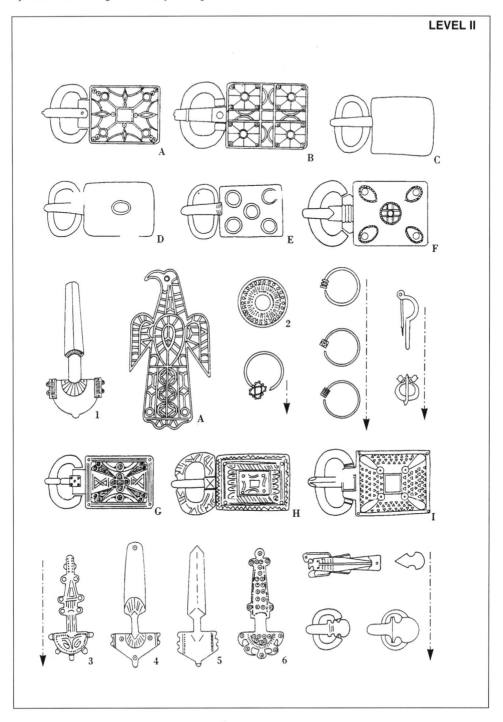

Fig. 11-1: Personal adornments, II level (480/90 - *ca* 525) (Ripoll 1998b).

their presence: first, the significance that these pieces acquired within the tomb, as elements accompanying the deceased in their life beyond the grave; and secondly, the very identification of the person buried with these objects. I do not consider that these signs of identity reflect a concept or the assimilation of race, ethnic group or nation, but rather an identity of a personal nature, which was developed within that person's own social group.

Personal adornments and the loss of, or change in, signs of identity (seventh century)

With the passing of time and in view of the advanced state of the process of acculturation, Visigothic fashions gradually gave way to more Latin-Mediterranean ones, no longer centred upon the Castilian tableland, but which rather responded to a demand from the whole Iberian Peninsula. Conversion to the Catholic faith both on the part of rural and urban inhabitants is likely to have implied an abandonment of the old Visigothic traditions of dress, and, as a consequence, the adoption of more general habits of dress in fashion at that moment. This phenomenon is also attested by the progressive abandonment of the cemeteries of the central Meseta. It is, for example, the case of El Carpio de Tajo in Toledo, of Castiltierra and Duratón in Segovia, of Herrera de Pisuerga in Palencia, etc. If this argument is correct, and the archaeological evidence seems to corroborate it, we are faced with a change in mentality and in focus as regards the system of symbols or the signs of identity.

On the other hand, the intrusion of these new Latin-Mediterranean fashions indicates a decline in production on the part of the Visigothic workshops and the increased development of other Hispanic production centres with certain undistutably local connotations. The personal adornments of the late sixth and the entire seventh centuries were marked by the Mediterranean influences to which allusion has been made, but also and more specifically by Byzantine products of great craftmanship, which circulated around and reached all the ports of the Mediterranean. The output of brooch-makers and fine metalworkers thus responded to such contemporary tastes and fashions, it being possible to detect the various influences derived basically from non-peninsular products that were imitated and manufactured in local craft workshops. In view of the large number of archaeological finds and their widespread distribution in regions previously with only a limited Visigothic population, basically in the *Baetica*, the demand must have been fairly high and their manufacture must have been centred upon major urban centres, from which they were distributed and placed on sale. Almost 70% of the known lyre-shaped belt buckles come from a production centre not far from the city of *Hispalis* (present-day Seville), which enables us to state, although not without a degree of doubt, that a production centre existed in this region. Other workshops existed in the Peninsula, but for the moment only the existence of one of the most important in the Seville region, the products of which were even

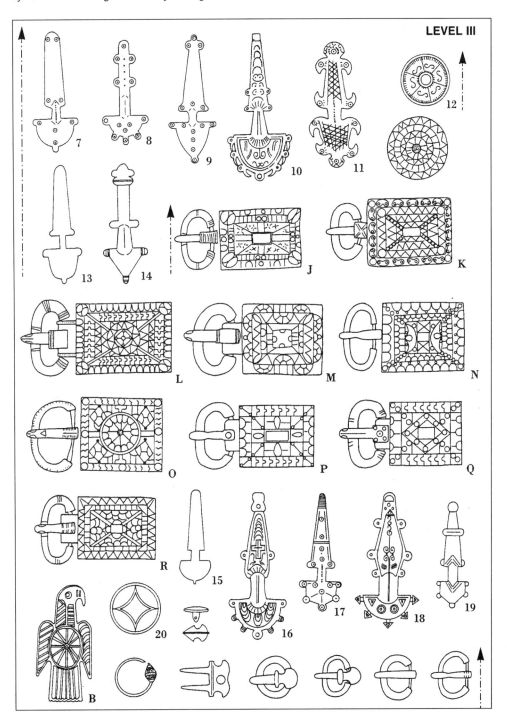

Fig. 11-2: Personal adornments, III level (*ca* 525 - 560/80) (Ripoll 1998b).

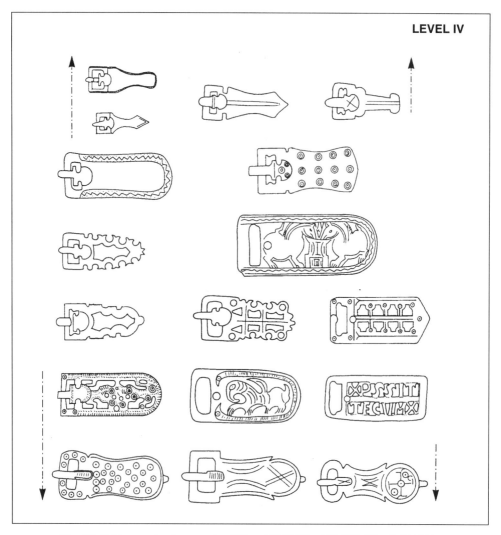

Fig. 11-3: Personal adornments, IV level (560/80 - 600/40) (Ripoll 1998b).

distributed as far as the other side of the Pyrenees, as is shown by the finds made in the *Narbonensis*, can be confirmed (Ripoll 1998b).

What are known as stiff-plate or openwork belt buckles are characteristic of the period lasting from the late sixth century until well into the seventh century (fig. 11-3). Production of these pieces seems to have started in an Italian workshop which distributed its products all over Europe and the Mediterranean world around the year 600 (Fingerlin 1967). They are found widely distributed in the Iberian Peninsula, but the most noteworthy finds have been made in the *Baetica*, although the discoveries from the central Meseta should not be ignored.

Some of the scenes that appear on these plates depict griffin-type animals, or human masks (fig. 11-4), or even the scene of Daniel in the lions' den. The

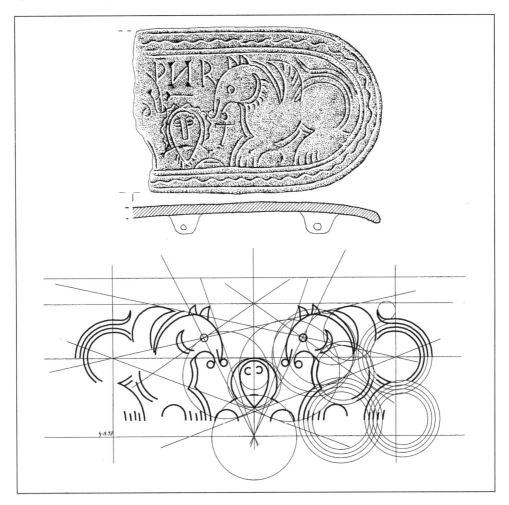

Fig. 11-4: Plaque from the area of Seville and restitution of the scene (Ripoll 1998b).

appearance of griffins, in general in isolation, or facing a human mask, symbolizes the two natures of Christ, the human and the divine. Some scholars have wondered whether this is a representation of Christ—or of Wodan, as the god of death (Lorren 1976:380). The Greek tradition identified griffins as monsters that guarded the treasure of the land of the Hyperboreans and Dionysius' krater full of wine. The Christian tradition considered griffins as guardians of the souls of the dead, and for that reason they appear facing a crater or a human head. This type of image, together with the scene of Daniel in the lions' den, alludes to the world of the dead, in other words it is symbolic of the immortality of the soul and divine protection. They form part of an iconographic or symbolic programme assimilated by and within a purely Christian tradition that no longer has any connection with Germanic mythology or Visigothic traditions (Ripoll 1998b:76-90).

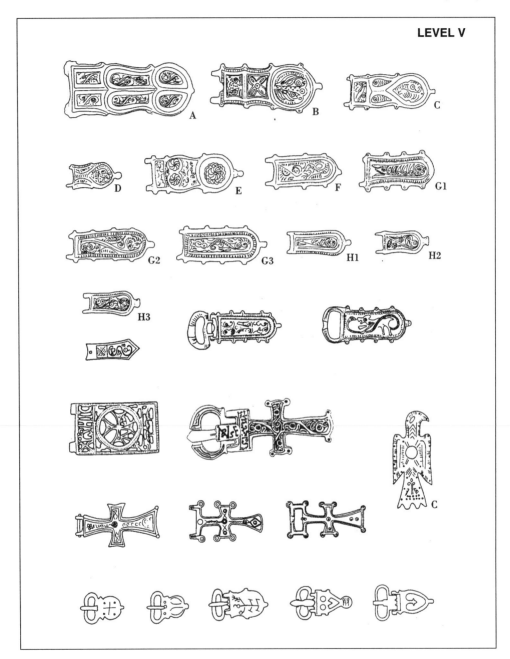

Fig. 11-5: Personal adornments, V level (600/40 - 710/20) (Ripoll 1998b).

    The most frequent personal adornments in the seventh century are what are known as lyre-shaped belt buckles, so called because of their lyre-shaped plates. Be that as it may, their typological variety is great, as is the decoration of these pieces, which ranges from simple geometric decoration, through schematic plant or animal designs, even to figurative patterns (fig. 11-5). Generally speaking, they were models of eastern origin of 'Trebizond' type, made in the workshops of the *Pontus* area, and copied by craftsmen in the Iberian Peninsula. The key motif in the decoration of these original models was a scene from the Physiologus fable (Werner 1988; Ripoll 1996), which was copied by Hispanic workshops, although they had some difficulty in understanding the design, so that the representation became increasingly distant from the original motif. It is also common to find totally distorted depictions of griffins forming part of plant shoots. The iconographic continuity between the late sixth-century material and these fully seventh-century pieces is demonstrated by the decoration of the lyre-shaped belt-buckles with schematic designs or griffins depicted in various ways (fig. 11-6; Ripoll 1998b:127-78).

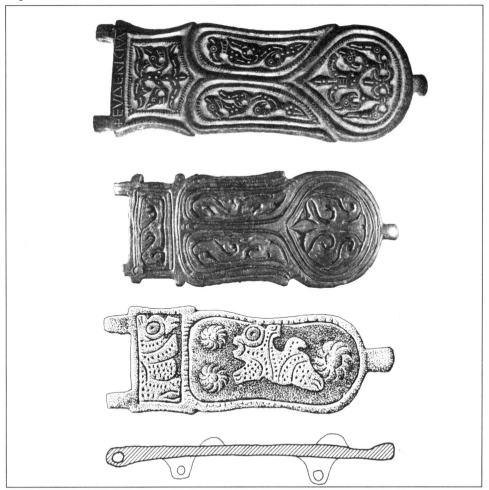

Fig. 11-6: Plaques of lyre-shaped buckles. Hinojar del Rey (Burgos; MAN 61787); unknown origin (MAN 59988); area of Seville (RGZM) (Ripoll 1998b).

It is of interest to emphasize that the distribution of these lyre-shaped belt plates covers the entire Iberian Peninsula, although they are largely recorded on the eastern and southern coasts, with very few examples being recorded from the Castilian plateau and the north of the Peninsula.

Among the characteristic materials of the seventh century there also appear small belt-buckles of Byzantine type, and cruciform ones, which became increasingly abundant, the areas of expansion and distribution of which coincide with those of the above mentioned lyre-shaped belt-plates (Ripoll 1998b:178-201). This leads one to accept that the large cemeteries of Visigothic tradition scattered across the central Meseta were in the course of being abandoned in the early seventh century, when such personal adornments started to be produced on a massive scale.

It is quite probable that the craft workshops that made the material that has just been described also manufactured various objects destined, as far as is currently known, for liturgical use; these include Eucharistic patens and jugs (Palol 1950). As far as censers or thuribles are concerned, examples imported from elsewhere in the Mediterranean basin are known, but locally produced examples have not been identified.

Reference has previously been made to the importance of 'Romanism' and 'Germanism', to which should be added, after what has just been said and in the light of the personal adornments, the intense impact of 'Byzantinism'. I consider that we should evaluate the Byzantine element itself, common in all the regions of the Mediterranean basin, for it clearly marked late sixth and seventh-century cultural and artistic expression.

From the moment when personal objects ceased to be considered as such, one can start to obtain a clearer idea of the individuals who made up sixth and seventh-century society, and of how the settlement of the Visigothic people in the Iberian Peninsula subsequently developed. Apparently, even from this moment onwards, we can talk of a single community without any specifically Visigothic signs of identity. The symbols were now common to the entire Mediterranean world of Western Christendom. The distribution within the Iberian Peninsula of personal objects alone, especially the lyre-shaped belt-buckles, may suggest that mixed marriages were already commonplace and that no differentiation could be made between the two main constituent groups in the population on the grounds of ethnic-derived ways of dress.

This loss of or change in signs of personal or social identity attributable to the Visigoths is likely to have been subsequent to the III Council of Toledo, since this council marks the apparently definitive political unification of the Iberian Peninsula, even if the numerous rebellions against it are taken into account. Even though the period under consideration dates to after the Third Council, all the available evidence would seem to indicate that there was a fairly significant development in such items of personal adornment around the middle of the seventh century, basically coinciding with the renaissance that took place in Recceswinth's reign. This is witnessed by imitations of coinage and the hoards from Guarrazar and Torredonjimeno, the Byzantinizing spirit of which indicates that this trend trickled down from royal court circles to the personal adornments worn by the inhabitants.

As an immediate conclusion, one may propose that the situation as regards symbols and signs of identity at the turn of the sixth and seventh centuries was clearly in a state of flux. Symbols, as was stated at the beginning of this paper, are systems of moral and spiritual value, and if they are in a process of change or mutability, this means that society itself is changing. The clear signs of identity of the Visigoths in the sixth century, represented by objects of personal adornment, were to change their symbolic contents in the seventh century and no longer act as a distinguishing element—insofar as origins and the social group were concerned—between two groups within the population.[15]

I have put forward a series of factors that I consider to be plausible vehicles of change as regards symbols or of changes in mentality, although any analysis of this type must harbour some doubts as to the veracity of the statements. I consider that H. Härke's words (1992:165) on the possible influences of changes in the Anglo-Saxon horizon reflect the same problems as in *Hispania:*

> This cannot have been due to the spreading influence of Christianity alone, not least because the decline of the grave-goods custom was paralleled in Continental Western Europe where Christianity had taken hold much earlier without affecting the deposition of grave-goods in any noticeable way. Looking at the Anglo-Saxon weapon burial rite in isolation, it is probable that it was phased out after its one remaining, symbolic function had become redundant because of the stabilisation of the social and political system, or even more likely, it was replaced by other, archaeologically invisible symbols which accompanied the living, but not the dead.

Before ending this section on the personal adornments of the seventh century and the loss of certain signs of identity, I would like to reflect briefly on the possibility of establishing certain iconographic parallels between sculpture and personal objects which may refer to a world of symbols.

Among the iconographic motifs used by brooch-makers on objects of personal adornment from the late sixth to the early eighth centuries, schematic plant elements, such as vine leaves and the tree of life, stand out, as do animal themes, such as birds, felines and fantastic quadrupeds, and themes from both the Old and the New Testaments, such as the case of Daniel in the lions' den etc.

These themes found on objects of personal adornment have obvious parallels in works of sculpture[16]. Particular mention should be made of the output of the important sculpture workshops of *Lusitania* such as *Olisipo* (present-day Lisbon)

---

[15] It is quite probable that we are dealing with a distinguishing element of an 'ethnic' nature although it is difficult to confirm this. What is, however, certain is that it was a distinguishing factor at a social or social group level.

[16] Many works have been published on Hispanic architecture and sculpture in this period, and the bibliography cannot be presented here. A good summary can be found in Palol and Ripoll (1988) and in Palol (1991) although Godoy's work (1995) should also be noted.

and *Emerita Augusta* (modern Mérida), to which should be added the workshop of *Toletum* (modern Toledo), the external friezes on the apse at Quintanilla de las Viñas (Burgos) and the frieze from the chancel arch of the same church. The decoration of the imposts over the transept capitals of the church of San Pedro de la Nave (Zamora) also stands out. All these sculptures have motifs with roots in late Roman mosaic designs, as well as in eastern silks, manuscripts and ivories that reached western ports without difficulty thanks to the *negotiatores transmarini* and Syrian traders (Palol & Ripoll 1988:233).[17] From the *Vitas Sanctorum Patrum Emeretensium* it is known that oriental silks were greatly valued by the sixth- and seventh-century population. It is quite possible that the artisans of contemporary *Hispania* found inspiration in material from the Orient and even in the sculptural material to which reference has been made.

As already mentioned, certain problems arise from the sculpture, in particular the chronological limits of the latter have still not been accurately defined, since in very few cases do we have reliable information that enables us to date and study the great production centres of decorative sculpture. One should not forget that nearly all the sculpture that seems to belong to the sixth and seventh centuries has been found out of context; that is to say, there is no archaeological or architectural evidence as regards its findspot or location, a fact that restricts our ability to study it.

Be that as it may, what can be stated is that it combined both continuity from the underlying late Roman background and clear innovations, derived from Mediterranean decorative tendencies, particularly from the eastern Mediterranean. Certain decorative models mainly based on geometric and ornamental designs must have existed in the different workshops, the presence of figurative models being limited, with the exception of certain pieces, such as the transept capitals of San Pedro de la Nave or what is known as the pilaster of San Salvador, located in the Toledo church of that name, although it has no known provenance.

The problems involved are clear: stylistic criteria cannot be used alone to date the different sculpture workshops. The same is true of ecclesiastical structures in rural areas. Reference was made previously to the most noteworthy buildings erected in the seventh century, among which several churches stand out: these include San Juan de los Baños (Palencia), Quintanilla de las Viñas (Burgos) and San Pedro de la Nave, all of which were located in what has been called the area of influence of the Toledo workshops.

To conclude this section, I would like to mention two examples that support the existence of a common repertoire of themes among architects, sculptors and

---

[17] One should remember that there was very precise legislation about them: *LV Antiqua* XI, 3. 2: *Cum transmarini negotiatores inter se causam habent, nullus de sedibus nostris eos audire presumat; nisi tantummodo suis legibus audiantur aput telonarios suos*; and that the products that they imported are also known from the law codes: *LV XI, 3. 1: Si quis transmarinus negotiator aurum, argentum, vestimenta vel quelibet ornamenta provincialibus nostris vendiderit, et conpetenti pretio fuerint venundata, si furtiva postmodum fuerint adprobata, nullam emptor calumniam pertimescat.* D'Ors (1958) and Saitta (1987:80-3) may be consulted on this question.

brooch-makers. In other words, elements that we might run the risk of defining as signs of identity or symbols with a moral or spiritual message, datable to the late sixth or seventh century.

The first example is provided by images of birds enclosed within circles of plants, which appear both in the external friezes of the church of Quintanilla de la Viñas and on the belt-plate from La Guardia (Jaén). In the case of this belt-plate, the decorative motif is of openwork design and there are three circular plant roundels, each of which encloses a long-necked bird with a down-turned beak.

The second example that should be noted is that of the scene of Daniel in the lions' den. The scene appears on one of the capitals of the church of San Pedro de la Nave. An inscription in the uppermost frieze of the capital identifies the scene: UBI DANIEL MISSUS EST IN LACUM LEONUM (Palol & Ripoll 1988:236). The same design, although handled in a different way, can be found on a belt-plate from the region of *Hispalis* (present-day Seville) (Ripoll 1993a:248-9, 559; 1998b:91-105). This belt-plate falls typologically within the category of stiff plates, and two lions appear in two horizontal registers in the decorated part; alongside the lions' heads there appear two small birds, perhaps doves (fig. 11-7). The far end is occupied by a human head with abundant hair surrounded by a two-headed serpent. This scene has a long history and symbolizes the figure of Christ,

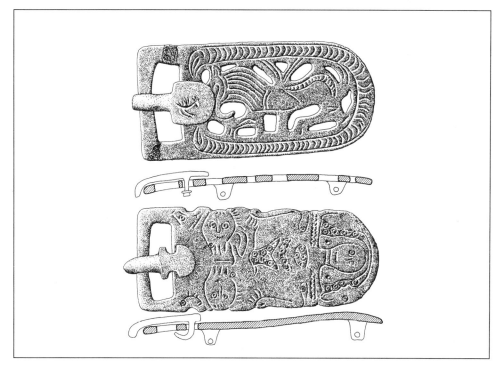

Fig. 11-7: Belt buckle with griffin from the area of Sevilla; belt buckle with the scene of Daniel in the lions' den from the area of Sevilla (RGZM) (Ripoll 1998b).

who has made death harmless. For this reason, the depiction performs an apotropaic or evil-eye function by evoking divine protection, at the same time as it represents immortality. The appearance of a two-headed serpent, which in Germanic mythology symbolizes men's souls,[18] is illustrative of the conjunction of two different traditions, since, as a consequence of its role in Genesis, the serpent came to be considered a symbol of evil, associated with the punishment for sinners.

In the previous pages one has seen that the chronological problems of sculpture and architecture are almost identical to those of the funerary material. In other words, the various working hypotheses proposed by different scholars, including those put forward here, are fragile, even extremely fragile, since the chronology of the assemblage of materials to which reference has been made is only supposed or relative, and for the moment nothing enables us to confirm these dates. At the same time, as a result one may infer that all the suggestions made as regards the existence or loss of possible signs of identity on the basis of the range of symbols are no more than that: suggestions or working hypotheses.

The work of goldsmiths as the insignia of power

Indirect reference has already been made to the existence of palace workshops that worked within the ambit of the court and were controlled by a palace goldsmith known as the *praepositus argentariorum*. After the establishment of the court in Toledo, the activity of the palace workshops may well have increased, as the number of royal gifts, whether for reasons of thanks, or for commemorative purposes or because of marriage alliances, also grew. The importance for these workshops of Liuvigild's adoption of Byzantine court pomp and ceremony as the true and only sign or symbol of power has long been known. The high quality of the palace products was reflected in the literary sources, above all the Islamic ones, and is also known from several treasure hoards largely dated to the mid-seventh century, such as those of Guarrazar (Amador de los Ríos 1861) and Torredonjimeno (Hübener 1975). The objects making up these hoards have always been considered insignia of authority, at least from the time of Reccared onwards and throughout the seventh century (Wolfram 1992:377). Although it is not my aim here to study what the royal insignia were, as this falls within the field of the concept and exercise of authority,[19] it is of interest for our knowledge of symbolic

---

[18] The study and symbolism of two-headed serpents takes as its starting point the gravestone from Niederdollendorf (Bad Godesberg, Rhineland). The first study was carried out by Böhner (1944-1950) and more recently by Krause (1991) although without adding to the symbolism of the serpent motif.

[19] The subject is a broad one, above all from the literary point of view. See in particular the works of Barbero (1970), Reydellet (1981:479-597), Ripoll and Velázquez (1995:42-75) and a study on the crown as an insignia of authority in Delgado Valero (1994).

life to outline what these collections of crowns and processional crosses meant within Visigothic society.

I am of the opinion that the importance of the Guarrazar hoard warrants our considering it, even if only briefly (Ripoll 1993b:53-9). The first discoveries took place at the point known as Huertas de Guarrazar in the province of Toledo in the middle of the nineteenth century. The treasure was probably hidden because of the danger represented by the Arab advance. From the very moment of its discovery, various searches, interventions, sales and thefts led to this hoard, like that found at Torredonjimeno in the province of Jaén, suffering a sad fate, until 1943 when all the material was brought together again in the Museo Arqueológico Nacional in Madrid, with the exception of one crown and some cut-out letters which continue to be preserved in the Musée de Cluny in Paris (Caillet 1985:218-27). It is made up of several pieces of jewellery, with a clear votive intention, dated to the seventh century. In other words, it was an offering. The crowns and pendant crosses, as well as the processional crosses, all belonged to the same church and were hidden as a precautionary measure in light of the imminent threat posed by the arrival of the Muslims in 711.

One of the votive crowns stolen from the Real Armería was of supreme importance for establishing the chronology of the treasure hoard. A series of letters were suspended from the band of that crown, spelling out +SV[IN]T[H]IL[A]NVS REX OFFE[RE]T (King Swinthila gave this). Thus we know that the crown was presented by the Visigothic king Swinthila, who reigned from 621 to 631. The other crown from the hoard, that of Recceswinth, also bore a series of cut-out pendant letters. The letters spell out RECCESVINTHVS REX OFFERET (King Recceswinth gave this), again naming the individual who commissioned the crown. The votive crown may be dated with precision between 653 and 672, the period of King Recceswinth's reign, and is a supreme example of the high standard achieved by Toledo court goldsmiths. The crown's decoration gives coherence to the other objects in the treasure, especially to the processional cross whose ornamentation is virtually the same. The dates of the reigns of Swinthila and Recceswinth (621-631 and 653-672) provided a chronology for the entire treasure, which while not absolute, affords an approximate date for the objects.

Two more crowns are of interest since they refer to offerings made by members of high social status or of high ecclesiatical rank, as is the case of one offered by an unknown person, Sonnica, on which there is an inscription engraved on the pendant cross distributed over several lines reading: IN D[OMIN]I / NOM/INE OFFERET / SONNICA / S[AN]C[T]E / MA/RIE/ IN S/ORBA/CES (In the name of God Sonnica offers [this] to Saint Mary in Sorbaces). An incorrect use of the accusative instead of a plural locative ablative can be seen in the word *Sorbaces*, from which it can be deduced that *Sorbaces* is not a place-name but a descriptive designation, that is, an area of *serbales*, or service trees. This allows us to establish the origin of the crown as Toledo, where there are many such trees. The personal name Sonnica does not refer to a Visigothic monarch; it may refer to an individual of high rank in the Toledo court during the reigns of Swinthila and Recceswinth, the period during which the Guarrazar hoard was formed. The other inscription, also formed by letters hanging from a crown, was dedicated by an abbot by the name of Theodosius: +OFFERET MVNVSCVLVM S[AN]C[T]O STEPHANO THEODOSIVS ABBA (this small gift was given to Saint Stephen by Abbot Theodosius).

The use of votive crowns to decorate church altars was customary in the seventh century Byzantine world. Documents reveal that the practice was widespread throughout the Visigothic kingdom by the time of Reccared's reign, and that, after 589 and his conversion to Catholicism, he offered a crown in the name of Felix, the martyr of Girona, which later, sources tell us, the usurper Paul placed upon his own head when he rebelled against royal authority. These votive crowns and processional crosses, in general, were offerings made to a church on the part of specific rulers, although courtiers and sometimes abbots made such offerings as well. This is borne out by the two royal votive crowns of Suinthila and Recceswinth; another given by a person of high rank—possibly Sonnica; and lastly the crown of the abbot Theodosius.

The Guarrazar treasure hoard, like that of Torredonjimeno, confirms the artistry of Visigothic court goldsmiths. A perfect blending of Roman traditions with those of the Byzantine East produced a royal art of superior quality. Byzantine influence is evident when we compare the Guarrazar treasure hoard—the crowns, crosses, and the processional cross— with the Theodelinda Treasure, dated to about 600, in the cathedral treasury in the Italian city of Monza, or with the famous cross from the treasury of the *Sancta Sanctorum*, formerly in the Vatican.

The Guarrazar treasure hoard can be considered as a synthesis of the symbols or the insignia of authority that appeared from the time of Liuvigild, among which the royal mantle, the canopied throne, the diadem, the minting of coinage, the construction of a *praetorium* in the *sedes regia* of Toledo, the foundation of cities such as *Reccopolis* or *Victoriacum*, etc. stand out. All such insignia, referring to the wielding of authority had their origins in the Byzantine world and were passed on to the West. They were perpetuated into the Middle Ages. In contrast, the few signs of identity referring to a world of symbols that can be detected in the sixth century gradually disappeared as from the following one although a few iconographic recollections did survive in what is known as Asturian art.

References

Åberg, N.
  1922   *Die Franken und Westgoten in der Völkerwanderungszeit.* Uppsala: Vilhelm Ekmans Universitetsfond.
Amador de los Ríos, J.
  1861   *El arte latino-bizantino en España y las coronas visigodas de Guarrazar. Ensayo histórico-crítico.* Madrid: Real Academia de San Fernando.

Ardanaz, F.
1990   Hallazgos de época visigoda en la región de Madrid. In *Madrid del s. IX al XI*, Catálogo de la Exposición, pp. 31-39. Madrid: Comunidad de Madrid, Consejería de cultura.
1991   Excavaciones en la necrópolis de Cacera de las Ranas (Aranjuez, Madrid). In *Arqueología, Paleontología y Etnografía*, 2. Pp. 257-266. Madrid: Comunidad de Madrid, Consejería de Cultura.

Baltrušaitis, J.
1972   *Le Moyen Âge fantastique. Antiquités et exotismes dans l'art gothique.* Paris: A. Colin. [First publ. 1955].

Barbero, A.
1970   El pensamiento político visigodo y las primeras unciones regias en la Europa medieval. *Hispania* 30: 245-326.

Benito Ruano, E.
1988   *De la Alteridad en la Historia*, Inaugural lecture, Real Academia de la Historia. Madrid: Real Academia de la Historia.

Bierbrauer, V.
1980a   Frühgeschichtliche Akkulturationsprozesse in den Germanischen Staaten am Mittelmeer (Westgoten, Ostgoten, Langobarden) aus der Sicht des Archäologen. In *Longobardi e Lombardia: aspetti di civiltà longobarda.* Pp. 89-105. (Atti del 6° Congresso internazionale di studi sull'Alto Medioevo, Milano, 21-25 ottobre 1978). Spoleto: C.I.S.A.M.
1980b   Zur chronologischen, soziologischen und regionalen Gliederung ostgermanisches Fundstoffes des 5. Jahrhunderts in Südosteuropa. In *Die Völker an der mittleren und unteren Donau im fünften und sechsten Jahrhundert.* H. Wolfram & F. Daim (eds.), pp. 131-142. (Österreichische Akademie der Wissenschaften, Denkschriften, 145). Vienna: Österreichische Akademie der Wissenschaften.
1992   Die Goten vom 1.-7. Jahrhundert n. Chr.: Siedelgebiete und Wanderbewegungen aufgrund archäologische Quellen. *Peregrinatio Gothica* 3: 9-43.
1994   Archäologie und Geschichte der Goten vom 1.-7. Jahrhundert. Versuch einer Bilanz. *Frühmittelalterliche Studien. Jahrbuch des Instituts für Frühmittelalterforschung der Universität Münster* 28: 51-171. [For the Visigoths cf. particularly p. 152-171].

Böhner, K.
1944-1950   Der fränkische Grabstein von Niederdollendorf am Rhein. *Germania* 28: 63-75.

Caillet, J.-P.
1985   *L'antiquité classique, le haut moyen âge et Byzance au musée de Cluny.* Paris: Réunion des Musées Nationaux.

Chevalier, J., & A. Gheerbrant
1973   *Dictionnaire des symboles. Mythes, rêves, coutumes, gestes, formes, figures, couleurs, nombres.* [1st ed. 1969] Paris: Éditions du Seuil.

Delgado Valero, C.
1994   La corona como insignia de poder durante la Edad Media. *Anales de la Historia del Arte, Homenaje al Doctor Azcárate* 4: 1-17.

Díaz y Díaz, M. C.
1981   Le latin du Haut Moyen âge espagnol. In *La lexicographie du latin médiéval et ses rapports avec les recherches actuelles sur la civilisation du Moyen Age.* Pp. 106-114. Paris: Éditions du C.N.R.S.

D'Ors, A.
1958   Los *transmarini negotiatores* en la legislación visigótica. In *Estudios de Derecho Internacional. Homenaje al Profesor Camilo Barcía Trelles.* Pp. 467-483. Santiago de Compostela: Univ. de Santiago de Compostela.

Eliade, M.
1952   *Images et symboles. Essai sur le symbolisme magico-religieux*, Paris: Éditions Gallimard.

Février, P.-A.
1984   *La tombe et l'au delá.* In *Le temps chrétien.* Pp. 164-183. Paris: Éditions du C.N.R.S.

Fingerlin, G.
1967   Eine Schnalle mediterraner Form aus dem Reihengräberfeld Güttingen, Ldkrs. Konstanz. *Badische Fundberichte* 23: 159-184.

Godoy, C.
1995   *Arqueología y Liturgia. Iglesias hispánicas (siglos IV al VIII).* Barcelona: Port de Tarragona - Universidad de Barcelona.

Godoy, C., & J. Vilella
1986   De la *fides gothica* a la ortodoxia nicena: inicio de la teología política visigótica. *Antigüedad y Cristianismo* 3: 117-144.

Goodenough, E. R.
1953   *Jewish Symbols in the Greco-Roman Period.* Princeton: Princeton University Press. [Abridged edition J. Neusner (ed.), Bollinger Series, Princeton University Press 1992].

Götze, A.
1907   *Götische Schnallen.* (Germanische Funde aus der Völkerwanderungszeit). Berlin: Ernst Wasmuth A.G.

Härke, H.
1992   Changing symbols in changing society: the Anglo-Saxon weapon burial rite in the seventh century. In *The age of Sutton Hoo.* M. O. H. Carver (ed.), pp. 149-165. Woodbridge: The Boydell Press.

Hübener, W.
1975   Goldblattkreuze auf der Iberischen Halbinsel. In *Die Goldblattkreuze des frühen Mittelalters.* W. Hübener (ed.), pp. 85-90. Bühl/Baden: Koncordia.

James, E.
1977   *The Merovingian Archaeology of South-West Gaul.* (British Archaeological Reports, 25). Oxford: BAR.
1980   Septimania and its frontier: an Archaeological Approach. In *Visigothic Spain: New approaches.* E. James (ed.), pp. 223-242. Oxford: Clarendon Press.

Jiménez Garnica, A. M.
1985   El origen de la legislación civil visigoda sobre la prohibición de matrimonios entre romanos y godos: Un problema de fundamento religioso. *Anuario de Historia del Derecho Español.* Pp. 735-747.
1995   La mujer en el mundo visigodo. In *Comportamientos antagónicos de la mujer en el mundo antiguo.* M. D. Verdejo Sánchez (ed.), pp. 127-160. (Col. Atenea, Estudios sobre la mujer). Málaga: Universidad de Málaga.

Jung, C. G.
1967   *Man and his Symbols.* London: Aldus Books Ltd.

Krause, C.
1991   Der fränkische Grabstein von Niederdollendorf. In *Spätantike und frühes Mittelalter. Ausgewählte Denkmäler im Rheinischen Landesmuseum Bonn.* J. Engemann & C. D. Rüger (eds.), pp. 140-149, figs. 86-91. Bonn: Rheinland Verlag.

Liebeschuetz, J. H. W. G.
1992   Alaric's Goths: nation or army? In *Fifth-century Gaul: a Crisis of identity?* J. Drinkwater & H. Elton (eds.), pp. 75-83. Cambridge: Cambridge University Press.

Lorren, C.
1976   *Fibules et plaques-boucles de Normandie. Contribution à l'étude du peuplement, des échanges et des influences de la fin du Ve au début du VIIIe siècle.* Thèse de troisième cycle, dactylographiée, preparée sous la direction de M. le Doyen de Boüard, Centre de Recherches Archéologiques Médiévales, 2 vols., Caen.

Marrou, H.-I.
1977   *Décadence romaine ou antiquité tardive? IIIe-VIe siècle.* Paris: Éditions du Seuil.

Palol, P. de
1950   *Bronces hispanovisigodos de origen mediterráneo. I., Jarritos y patenas litúrgicas.* Barcelona: Consejo Superior de Investigaciones Cientificas.
1956   Esencia del arte hispánico de época visigoda: romanismo y germanismo. In *I Goti in Occidente: problemi.* Pp. 3-64. (Settimane di studio del Centro Italiano di Studi sull'Alto Medioevo, IV). Spoleto: C.I.S.A.M.
1991   Arte y Arqueología. In *Historia de España Menéndez Pidal. III. 2, España visigoda.* J. M. Jover Zamora (ed.), pp. 269-428. Madrid: Ed. Espasa Calpe.
1995   Les reunions d'Arqueologia Cristiana Hispànica. *IV Reunió d'Arqueologia Cristiana Hispànica, Lisboa 1992.* Pp. 9-13. (Monografies de la Secció Històrico-Arqueológica, IV). Barcelona: Institut d'Estudis Catalans.

Palol, P. de, & G. Ripoll
1988   *Los godos en el occidente europeo. Ostrogodos y visigodos en los siglos V-VIII.* Madrid: Ediciones Encuentro.

Pérez-Prendes, J. M., & J. de Azcarraga
1990   *Lecciones de Historia del Derecho español.* Madrid: Universidad Complutense de Madrid.

Reinhart, W.
1945   Sobre el asentamiento de los visigodos en la Península. *Archivo Español de Arqueología* 18: 124-139.

Reydellet, M.
1981   *La royauté dans la littérature latine de Sidoine Apollinaire à Isidore de Séville.* (Bibliothèque des Écoles Françaises d'Athènes et de Rome, 243). Rome: Bibliothèque des Écoles Françaises d'Athènes et de Rome.

Richards, J. D.
1995   An Archaeology of Anglo-Saxon England. *After Empire. Towards an Ethnology of Europe's Barbarians.* G. Ausenda (ed.), pp. 51-74. Woodbridge: The Boydell Press.

Ripoll, G.
1985   *La necrópolis visigoda de El Carpio de Tajo (Toledo).* (Excavaciones Arqueológicas en España, 142). Madrid: Ministerio de Cultura.
1989   Características generales del poblamiento y la arqueología funeraria visigoda de *Hispania. Espacio, Tiempo y Forma* 1 (2): 389-418.
1991a   La ocupación visigoda a través de sus necrópolis (Hispania). Doctoral Thesis Barcelona, Thesis Microfiche 912. Universitat de Barcelona. Barcelona.

Ripoll, G. (*cont.*)
1991b   Materiales funerarios de la Hispania visigoda: problemas de cronología y tipología. *Actes des VIIe Journées Internationales d'Archéologie Mérovingienne. Gallo-Romains, Wisigoths et Francs en Aquitaine, Septimanie et Espagne, Toulouse, 1986*. P. Périn (ed.), pp. 111-132, 13 figs. Rouen: Association Française d'Archéologie Mérovingienne.

1993a   L'archéologie funéraire de Bétique d'aprés la collection visigothique du Römisch-Germanisches Zentralmuseum de Mayence. Doctoral Thesis Sorbonne-Paris IV. Thesis Microfiche 0741.15226/93. Université de Lille, Lille.

1993b   The formation of Visigothic Spain. *The Art of Medieval Spain, A.D. 500-1200*. Pp. 41-69. New York, NY: The Metropolitan Museum of Art.

1993-1994   La necrópolis de El Carpio de Tajo. Una nueva lectura a partir de la topocronología y los adornos personales. *Bulletí de la Reial Acadèmia Catalana de Belles Arts de Sant Jordi* 7-8: 187-250.

1995   Broche de cinturón bizantino con una escena del Fisiólogo, conservado en The Metropolitan Museum of Art de Nueva York. In *Verdolay. Homenaje a la Profesora A. Mª Muñoz Amilibia*. [Per. of the University of Murcia] 1995: 385-389.

1998a   The arrival of the Visigoths in Hispania: population problems and the process of acculturation. In *Transformation of the Roman World. Vol. 2, Strategies of distinction: the construction of ethnic communities, 300-800*. W. Pohl & H. Reimitz (eds.), pp. 153-187, 8 pl. Leiden: Brill.

1998b   *Toréutica de la Bética (siglos VI-VII d.C.)*. Barcelona: Reial Acadèmia de Bones Lletres.

Ripoll, G., & I. Velázquez
1995   *La Hispania visigoda. Del rey Ataúlfo a Don Rodrigo. Historia de España*, 6. Madrid: Historia 16 - Temas de Hoy.

Saitta, B.
1979   La rivolta di Ermenegildo. *Quaderni Catanesi di Studi Classici e Medievali* 1: 81-134.

1987   *Società e potere nella Spagna visigotica*. (Studi e ricerche dei 'Quaderni Catanesi', 9). Catania: Tringale.

Teillet, S.
1984   *Des Goths à la Nation Gothique. Les origines de l'idée de nation en Occident du Ve au VIIe siècle*. (Collection des Études Anciennes). Paris: Les Belles Lettres.

Velázquez Soriano, I.
1989   *Las pizarras visigodas. Edición, crítica y estudio*. (Antigüedad y Cristianismo, 6). Murcia: Universidad de Murcia.

Werner, J.
1946   Las excavaciones del Seminario de Historia Primitiva del Hombre en 1941, en el cementerio visigodo de Castiltierra. *Cuadernos de Historia Primitiva*. 1: 46-50.

1988   Eine goldene byzantinische Gürtelschnalle in der Prähistorischen Staatssammlung München. Motive des Physiologus auf byzantinischen Schnallen des 6.-7. Jahrhunderts. *Bayerische Vorgeschichtsblätter* 53: 301-308, pl. 51-52.

Wolfram, H.
1983   *Die Goten. Von den Anfängen bis zur Mitte des sechsten Jahrhunderts*. Munich: C. H. Beck.

1992   Das spanische Westgotenreich (507/68-711/25): Die erste Nation Europas. In *Das Reich und die Germanen zwischen Antike und Mittelalter*. H. Wolfram (ed.), pp. 365-388. Berlin: Siedler Verlag.

1993   *Origo et religio*. Ethnische Traditionen und Literatur in frühmittelalterlichen Quellen. In *Mittelalter*. W. Hartmann (ed.), pp. 27-39. (Schriftenreihe der Universität Regensburg, N.F., 19). Regensburg: Universität Regensburg.

Yáñez, G. I., *et al.*
1994   Excavaciones en el conjunto funerario de época visigoda de La Cabeza (La Cabrera, Madrid). *Pyrenae* 25: 259-287.

Zanker, P.
1987   *Augustus und die Macht der Bilder*. Munich: C. H. Beck. [Spanish edition, *Augusto y el poder de las imágenes*, Madrid: Alianza Editorial, 1992].

Zeiss, H.
1934   *Die Grabfunde aus dem spanischen Westgotenreich*. Berlin-Leipzig: Walter de Gruyter.

Discussion

DÍAZ: There was a change from original Gothic symbolism to Romano-Byzantine motifs. In fact, I am not sure if the artefacts where we can notice the symbolic elements are for durable use. If we are going to distinguish elements which were used for 100 years or elaborated and then used for a short time. I think that perhaps the Goths no longer produced artefacts with Gothic elements after they arrived in the Empire. This is an idea. Maybe they had been using these artefacts when they arrived into the Empire, but they no longer produced them afterwards.

SCHWARCZ: I don't think you can assert that.

DÍAZ: No, this is a question.

RIPOLL: It is a question referring to whether it is a production achieved after the entry of the Goths into the Empire. I do not believe that one may state the origin of craftsmen and their places of production. There is a clear evolution between the productions made in the Crimea and those in the Iberian Peninsula. What is certain is that, while there is a certain similarity between such distant areas, there is at the same time a great difference.

DÍAZ: With the same symbols?

RIPOLL: I don't believe that they are the same symbols. On the contrary, there ia an evolutionary process. Furthermore, there is the great problem of the total knowledge of the productions in Aquitania, keeping in mind that archaeology has not brought out any data on the cemetery complexes and on Visigothic personal adornments in that region.

SCHWARCZ: I have a question on this, because your example of that is the slates, the earliest were of the second half of the fifth century and in the *barbaricum*, so you cannot expect this at the beginning of the fifth in Aquitaine, you have to explain why the style originating in the *barbaricum* is so strong in sixth-century Spain. It is completely different from the Cherniakhov culture.

RIPOLL: Anyway, the debate continues and the doubts subsist considering that one doesn't know how to identify the Visigoths in Aquitania. Only literary sources allow us to talk about the Visigothic presence in Aquitania. Archaeology is absolutely silent in that area.

HEATHER: Yes, but the Aquitanian question, in English would call it a 'red herring'. In other words, I think it is quite misleading for the reasons that Edward James (1991) explained, mainly there has been very little archaeological excavation in Aquitaine. There have been more graves dug up in the Pas-de Calais than in the whole of Aquitaine. People mean that you don't get 'Reihengräber' cemeteries in Aquitaine. No one has any idea of whether if you look around for other things you will find people buried with odd foreign-looking material or not. It's simply an argument from silence. It's a problem, but on the other hand it is not the case that people have dug up the whole of Aquitaine and cannot find Goths. The fact is that they haven't dug in Aquitaine. So there still could be anything to find.

SCHWARCZ: Well, I wouldn't accept that. We know what happened in general south of the Danube immediately in the last quarter of the fourth century because new studies are done by, for instance Ludmil Vagalinski. He showed at the Caputh Conference in 1995 (unpublished) that there are traces of Cherniakhov in pottery but it changes visibly and rapidly under the influence of the local production. So, from this example two generations after the changes in the Balkans, you would expect that you cannot distinguish the Goths from other inhabitants of the cities.

But let's get on a bit because we must discuss the concrete points in the paper and I've got already two questions concerning the first page in your paper.

AUSENDA: I have a general remark. I am very happy that you want to call ancient Spain *Hispania*, provided you write it in italics. Don't call the people of *Hispania*, 'Hispanics', because that is a disparaging term, as it is also used by the U.S. Immigration and Naturalization Service to refer to people from the Caribbean and Central America.

RIPOLL: What, then, do you propose?

AUSENDA: I don't know. You propose it. You may call them *Hispanici*.

WOOD: *Hispani* is a better term.

RIPOLL: We should obviously adopt the Latin terminology.

GREEN: I have a question about what I think goes too far as a generalization on symbolism. At the end of the second paragraph on page 403, you say "symbolism is never logical". I question that. I think it would be more correct to say "Symbolism is never only logical", symbolism can be metalogical, but the metalogical does not exclude always the logical. That's the only point I wish to make there.

RIPOLL: Perhaps, beginning with the great theoreticians we should think about what is the logic of symbolism.

GREEN: And similarly in the line before that, you stick your neck out too by saying "Symbols never reflect a logical relationship". Both instances go too far I think.

RIPOLL: I would agree with your thought taking, however, into account the ideas of the great theoreticians in the final publication.

SCHWARCZ: OK, let's put this one on page 405 and go on there still with Dennis [Green] about national culture acquired under Ulfila. This is a question I would like listening to myself because I am sceptical about what is national culture by this time and I think we are both sceptical.

GREEN: On page 405, you imply an antithesis between a national Gothic culture acquired under Wulfila, on the one hand, and an adoption of a Latin-based Christian culture on the other. For me, in that contrast you are putting Wulfila precisely on the wrong side of the historic divide in Gothic history. Wulfila's Christianity is essentially Latin- and Greek-based. As I said in the last paragraph of my own paper, "Wulfila incorporates for Gothic culture Greek or Latin tradition, Christianity, and also a writing system based on a Mediterranean script". He is the turning point, he is on this side of the divide, not on the other side. This doesn't stop him being national or incorporating a national culture, but it is a national culture which has taken a radically new direction with him.

SCHWARCZ: I agree with this and my question has a slightly different turn, because I can't imagine what the loss of the national culture is. And I thought that might have been something that happened in translation, so I would like you to expound a bit on the point why you think that the national culture was lost.

RIPOLL: I agree with the thinking of Professor Green. Perhaps one should reformulate the phrase in a different way.

SCHWARCZ: OK.

DE JONG: On the identification of *Gothia* and *Romania*, it is to be sure that I understand you: it's about page 405. As far as I can see you envisage a Gothic identity and a Roman identity entirely bound up with faith, right? With the question of *fides Gothica-Romana*, the Latin says it. And on page 420 you seem to see no point in differentiating any longer between Goths and Romans after the third Council of Toledo. Do you take that as the watershed?

RIPOLL: The problem was brought up in other discussions of this session, especially when one talked about the problem of a mixed society and the new populations, and the differences for the existence of a *Romania* and a *Gothia*. Undoubtedly, I believe that one can perceive some archaeological differences between the two large population groups. These pertain especially to the first half of the sixth century, but not later. It is probable that the words used by Orosius to distinguish the Roman concept of 'Gothic' continue until the fight between Hermenegild and his father Liuvigild. I believe that it is an interesting problem to be discussed as one finds it at the bottom of many discussions. This means that the differences between population groups, or the definition of a mixed society are concepts which are surfacing during these days, and which one meets whenever one attempts any possible approaches concerning *Hispania* during that period.

I believe that there are several ways to talk about signs of identity which address many questions. Are religion, law, language or fashion signs of identity? Or do we only have a few funerary objects which can be interpreted as signs of identity? I believe that we are faced with a question having a very difficult and risky answer. I hereby address the problem to all of you.

WOOD: They are all signs of identity.

HEATHER: It depends on whether your evidence suggests they are.

RIPOLL: Therefore, I believe that it is of primary importance to know how we define, also from the present viewpoint, what identity is.

HEATHER: Yes, in some contexts, in and around this period, non-Nicene religion does function to some extent as a mark of identity. I mean these things are not a totality; you will always find Catholic Goths as much as there was an occasional Arian Roman. That does not mean that they are not nonetheless working as symbols for substantial numbers of people. And I think that this is so both for Vandal Africa and Ostrogoth Italy, although in the Goths' case there's no or only rarely a violent confrontation. You do have sufficient evidence to say that people would have thought, "Well, most Goths are Arian".

DE JONG: Wouldn't you think that this particular conflict was something that was above all of political élites that fought for power and their identity could be with either faith. It doesn't seem to involve a mass movement.

HEATHER: Well, that's where the destruction performed after Toledo III is a real problem. Because you don't have things like the papyrus from the Arian cathedral in Ravenna listing the clergy, you don't have any Gothic books or texts from Visigothic Spain. You might import what you find in Ostrogothic Italy if you think that's appropriate; perhaps it is. But, it is a perhaps, because you don't have anything from the Visigothic world.

SCHWARCZ: And, also conflicts in different places, about assigning a church to the Arians or the Catholics. You probably could have noticed it in the streets.

HEATHER: Yes, in Ravenna there is a separate Arian cathedral and baptistry, as I am sure you are aware. It is extremely clear, but I don't know any reference—this is my ignorance, I am sure—as to whether there are separate Arian churches in Mérida. Is there one? Yes. That's surely implied but not actually said.

WOOD: And presumably some churches are going to be Arian. Your point about it sometimes being a mark of identity and sometimes not, can be illustrated very simply for Liuvigild's reign when in Mérida after all there is a question of the king trying to use Arianism, not necessarily for national reasons or for ethnic reasons, but certainly to create a national image. But then Hermenegild, by converting to Catholicism, actually breaks the possibility of associating Arianism with Gothicness, because as soon as Hermenegild opts for Catholicism, then Catholicism is potentially as potently Gothic as Arianism.

HEATHER: Yes, and I'm sure what you have in Toledo III is at the end of a process. You could not swing Toledo III if the majority of the Goths were thoroughly attached to Arianism. Toledo III must stand at the end of the feeling that, "Well, we are all really the same, anyway". Which is essentially what Liuvigild was trying to do, by going back to an old kind of compromise position in accepting the full divinity of the Son and the partial divinity of the Holy Spirit: Macedonianism. But, that's a compromise in theological terms between Arianism and Catholicism. You either have to assume that the man was a raving nutcase or that there was an awful lot of common ground which he was trying to exploit there. And Liuvigild's other activity doesn't suggest that he was incompetent.

SCHWARCZ: A short remark, about the settlement of the Visigoths in Spain and a question of the complicated discussion about land or tax since Goffart's book (1980).

RIPOLL: I don't believe it is necessary to think about this problem in this context.

HEATHER: Yes, you don't have to discuss it [laughter].

RIPOLL: I only mentioned in the bibliography what I thought necessary for the discussion.

GREEN: On page 406, concerning the Visigoths' language in *Hispania*, at the end of the third paragraph in the context of saying that there is nothing to suggest that the Visigoths still used their language on arriving in *Hispania*, you say, "all that has really survived of this language are a number of lexical items and personal names". My comment there is that what has survived cannot simply be identified with what there was. I think you are making a bold deduction there from what is merely negative or nearly negative evidence.

SCHWARCZ: But I think that Giorgio's question concerns the same point.

AUSENDA: Yes on page 406 you say that "there is nothing to suggest that the Visigoths still used their language on arrival in *Hispania*". We already had a discussion on this question concerning the Franks and came to the conclusion that wide strata of that population, especially in the countryside, still spoke their tongue during the ninth century, as witnessed by the proceedings of a Council of Tours in which the assembled prelates requested that they be translated into the *linguam theotiscam* better to be understood by the faithful.

Field experience shows that languages persist for a long time even in areas with a different dominant language. In eastern Sudan, conquered by Arabic-speaking Egyptians in 1840, the women of Hadendowa agro-pastoralists in the bush still only speak To Bedawie, a Cushitic language not related to Arabic, because they are not allowed by custom to go to market, and so do many men, even though the language of the market is mostly Arabic. Even Arabic merchants with a Hadendowa clientèle speak To Bedawie with them.

Mixed marriages are a powerful factor of language change, because the language spoken at home is that spoken by the woman. However, mixed marriages are more frequent in the cities than in the countryside where segregated villages are easier to maintain. It stands to reason that the population in the cities is acculturated to a much greater extent than the population in the countryside.

When one bears in mind that marriages within tribal groups are considered alliances and are decided by the kinship group at large, not by the individuals involved, one can easily see that 'Romans' would not be motivated to give their daughters or sisters to 'barbarians' unless these barbarians had achieved status and power. At the same time, the 'barbarians' in positions of power would not be motivated to make alliances with Romans as it was more important for them to ally themselves to other clans, hence marrying women belonging to their own ethnic group. This means that inter-marriage developed very slowly.

SCHWARCZ: Well, I can give you an example which points completely to the contrary, the marriage of Theudis, the vice-king of the Visigoths, to a rich woman of Spanish origin, which enabled him to form a large retinue, and to become king over the Visigoths. He greatly enhanced his position by marrying a Spanish landowner whose fortune helped him to finance two thousand warriors.

AUSENDA: On the contrary, your example fits perfectly the pattern I described. I said that marriages are considered alliances (see above) especially among individuals in high positions, which is exactly the pattern you mentioned. These alliances are most frequent in the cities, hence language is a persistent phenomenon especially in the countryside. As far as the level of acculturation is concerned, this is true also among Hadendowa, where school teachers, government officials, etc. are completely arabicized while still speaking their native language. However, they represent less than 5 percent of the Hadendowa population, in addition to the fact that the Hadendowa in villages and cities are less than 30 percent of total Hadendowa population.

I would surmise that, even if Visigoths in the cities spoke vulgar Latin, they still maintained a knowledge of their language as a symbol of tradition which strengthened their 'right' to lead their own 'ethnic' group, the sole basis of their power; those in the countryside, still spoke prevalently Gothic. Of course it will be difficult to find traces of this because it was entirely oral, as all legal intercourse was in Latin. I do not know whether there are proofs of this grass-roots persistence of Gothic as there are in the minutes of the ninth-century Council of Tours for Frankish.

GREEN: I don't know of any proof for that in Visigothic Spain. I know we have evidence for it amongst the Franks, because of evidence for the same Germanic word coming across into Gallo-Roman as a loanword on two separate occasions. One can see that the occasions are different, because Frankish has undergone a sound change, which we can approximately date indicating a gap in time between these two loan processes, during which Frankish was still being spoken. What I don't know is whether the same situation applies to Visigothic Spain.

DÍAZ: The only reference we have in Visigothic Spain to the use of other languages than Latin, is a reference in the proceedings of the Council of Toledo III, in which the king speaks about the conversion meaning the end of the *plurimae linguae*, but perhaps the question is as you say about the liturgy. Probably the Arian liturgy was in Gothic, and when the *plurimae linguae* ended, they were going to have Latin only.

HEATHER: If the Arian liturgy was indeed Gothic, as it may well have been, that actually provided a fixed point and a reason why some Gothic would remain. So if you remove that fixed point, then it wouldn't last too much longer after that.

GREEN: Can I come in with one point which just occurred to me. It concerns not Visigothic, but at least another East Germanic language, namely the language of the Vandals, who passed through Spain over into North Africa. Well, there is evidence that the Vandals in North Africa used as a battle cry the words in Vandalic, which are very recognizable, as they are almost the same as Gothic, of *Kyrie eleyson*. This indicates that in traditionalized form the vernacular was still being used at some stage in the Vandals' passage through Spain. And what was possible with the Vandals may well have been possible with the Visigoths.

HEATHER: Euric is still speaking Gothic in the 470s; we know they come into Spain not very long after that.

DE JONG: But the question Gisela [Ripoll] is asking herself is whether this really remains an important sign of identity, of group coherence. I share your hesitation about the boldness of the statement, but I also share Gisela's hesitation and that accepting Gothic memories as....

HEATHER: Well, I think the problem is the book burning in Toledo III. I think if we think that the Visigothic Arian Church is using Gothic liturgy or Gothic books then to some extent Gothic would have survived.

AUSENDA: I'm sorry, more modestly, I would be much happier if people would just say "We don't know. It is still open to investigation. It might have been a public symbol or it may have not. We don't know".

HEATHER: Well, it is worth saying why we don't know.

DE JONG: This is the one thing we know something about.

SCHWARCZ: I would be rather careful and hesitate to say that in multilingual societies language is a defining sign of nationality. One of my colleagues Max Peyfuss, who is a specialist on the Balkans in the eighteenth and nineteenth centuries used to point out that peasants spoke four or five languages, for instance Romanian, Albanian, Serbian, Greek, Bulgarian and Turkish, because they were mixed. Only townspeople knew to which extraction they belonged. Those peasants would have never understood the question of nationality, if you would have asked them. And if this is the nineteenth century I don't see why speaking one language or the other in *Hispania* in the sixth century in the rural areas should be the defining sign of a gentile identity, especially with Gothic, which by all reports, especially Procopius of Caesarea (*Bell. Goth.* I. 1. 3.; III. 2. 1.; *Bell. Vand.* I. 2. 2; 1. 3. 1.), according to whom Gothic in the fifth and sixth centuries was a language used by more than one people.

HEATHER: Yes, but if they were talking Gothic, then we've got Goths in the middle of Romans, and that's why symbols function in a given context, the same thing will not be symbolic in different contexts.

SCHWARCZ: The point I want to get at is, the combination of Arian denomination and talking Gothic is significant, but not the speaking of Gothic alone.

HEATHER: I get your point, sure. I agree.

VELÁZQUEZ: On page 406, about Gothic loanwords into Latin, I would like to introduce a linguistic point of view in the sense, that when the Visigoths came into Spain they spoke Latin, but I want to make reference to the terms which Latin allows of common lexical background. For example, yesterday I mentioned *guaranèn*, *blavus* and other terms which make reference to colours or animals. There are few of them, personal and place-names. In fact, I think that in the sixth and seventh centuries the use of personal names of Gothic origin or Roman origin is completely mixed. It is wrong to believe that in the eighth century a Roman name, was related to a person of Roman language and viceversa. I think, about the names of the *iudices* on a slate with the *condiciones sacramentorum* and the names of the *iudex* and *vicarius* the text says *condiciones sacramentorum ad quas debeant iurare solus...ex ordinatione Ranimiri, Uiderichi, iudicibus, Archivindi vicariis*. Perhaps these were Gothic persons, but I'm not sure, because I think that in the seventh century it was a mixed society and there are things as fashions which are very important. Perhaps they were a symbol of prestige; perhaps some people used Roman names without being Roman.

GREEN: One has to take into account what I can best call onomastic fashion through the centuries. Celtic names were adopted as a fashion by *Germani*, especially leaders; Roman names were adopted by them. Frankish names were adopted by Gallo-Romans. The fact that a name is of a particular language group, does not indicate that the person bearing that name spoke that language.

SCHWARCZ: Of course, this is so especially in the seventh and eighth centuries.

HEATHER: Are your slates sixth-century?

VELÁZQUEZ: Sixth century and seventh century, yes. Dr. Green, I would like to ask your opinion about the strange language in the *Codex Salmasianus* (in the *Anthologia Latina*), the poems of the Vandals. Do you know them?

GREEN: No, I don't.

VELÁZQUEZ: Perhaps it was a very strange source of Gothic language.

GREEN: I'm afraid I don't know it.

VELÁZQUEZ: It is in the *Anthologia Latina* with only one manuscript which is preserved in the National Library in Paris; this *Anthologia* contains many poems of Vandals in Latin. It is called the *Codex Salmasianus* and it was published by Teubner (Shackleton Bailey 1982). It is a very important *Anthologia Latina*. The first poem is in a strange language which I don't understand.

GREEN: How long is it?

VELÁZQUEZ: It's only four or five lines. Very strange but a mix of languages that I don't know. I am translating the poems of the *Codex Salmasianus* into Spanish, but this poem is beyond my comprehension.

RETAMERO: On page 408 concerning 'unknown rural settlements'. I have two simple questions, on your project. About the cemetery of El Carpio de Tajo, are you interested in finding the unknown settlements attached to the cemetery?

RIPOLL: The excavations we completed on the ground did not yield satisfactory results. However, who knows whether we might find something if we should return to the area? Probably, yes.

RETAMERO: Is it a formal invitation? [Laughter].

RIPOLL: I have studied the topographical and aerial photographic documentation. I have investigated the area and I have tried to obtain information from those who know the area, but we didn't obtain any positive results.

RETAMERO: Such a big cemetery and the absence of remains of buildings is striking.

RIPOLL: In the case of El Carpio de Tajo, the problem lies in the agrarian changes and the construction of an important irrigation canal flowing from the Tage.

HEATHER: When did they change the river?

RIPOLL: I believe that it was during the 1950s.

HEATHER: On page 409 about graves without goods. In the El Carpio de Tajo cemetery, are the graves that have goods and the graves that don't completely mixed?

RIPOLL: Yes.

HEATHER: They are competely mixed, you don't find blocks of some with goods? This is a straight request for information.

RIPOLL: Yes. I believe it was addressed in my paper.

HEATHER: Yes, I couldn't remember the page [laughter].

DE JONG: On page 409-10 about kinship giving way to conjugal family. I wonder if on the basis of the archaeology you could be a bit more specific about chronology, as a result of passing of time gradually giving way and I started to wonder where it was, how and when, or am I asking the impossible now?

RIPOLL: I believe you are asking me for something extremely difficult, due to the fact that one cannot offer absolute chronologies.

DE JONG: Not the absolute. I am not asking you for precise years. I mean, obviously you have worked on this a lot, you have written about it. I have not seen that. You summarize it here very briefly. So you are talking about which period?

RIPOLL: I believe that we are talking about the two first generations of Visigoths installed on the Castilian Meseta. It depends on how many years we consider the length of a generation, 30 or 40 years, then we would reach only the first half of the sixth century. We are confronted with a very gradual transformation, during which apparently 'ethnic' differences were becoming imperceptible beginning with the second half of the sixth century.

DE JONG: And that is time and again the crucial divide in your chronology. That is what I'm trying to pin down. The middle of the sixth century.

RIPOLL: The chronological problem is difficult and probably not susceptible of being reliably dated; the problems are increased and the solutions are weaker.

DE JONG: On page 414, on the concept of social groups.

RIPOLL: Do you want a definition of what the social groups are, the concept per se?

DE JONG: Are you referring to something like élite, freemen, slaves or what? How large is the social group?

RIPOLL: I am referring to quite extensive social groups. I believe that the individual has a sign of identity with the group. In any case, I do not believe that this sign of identity should be confused with race, nation or ethnicity: far from my intention. I believe that we are closer to a personal identity in a social group.

GREEN: In the last paragraph of page 417, you say that something may or may not be a representation of Christ or of Wodan. I'm hesitant about even admitting the possibility of Wodan for two reasons. First because this god is a relatively late addition to the Germanic pantheon; secondly, and much more important, there is no clear cut evidence that the Goths worshipped this particular god.

SCHWARCZ: I would say it still more strongly than you do. I could actually deny the possibility of there being anything like a sign of Wodan in Gothic things and if it is a griffin, it is very clear that a griffin comes from Byzantium and it cannot be anything but within the *Physiologus*.

RIPOLL: Maybe we should discuss this with Dr. Claude Lorren, whose proposition I have referred to in a footnote. Personally I believe that this is an image of Christ as a symbol, or a picture of the owner of the piece.

HEATHER: It looked a lot like Christ on the picture [laughter].

SCHWARCZ: Anyway the question of the griffin has long been discussed with the archaeologists, and what is striking about that is that it is not specially Arian, but wherever it is, it comes from Byzantine production.

RIPOLL: So, this is why I have written in my paper "Personal adornment and laws for changing signs of identity". I think it is another Peter Stadler. Do you have recent bibliography about griffins?

SCHWARCZ: Peter Stadler. Just ask him.

RIPOLL: I have his works.

WOOD: On page 417 about Burgundian iconography, my question is simply that, given Burgundian 'Daniel iconography', can any emphasis be based on Daniel iconography as being Visigothic, or is it just sub-Roman?

RIPOLL: I don't know, but I think it is Roman.

WOOD: Yes, I think it is Roman as well.

RIPOLL: As far as the manufacture of the pieces is concerned, they are made according to a clear tradition of bronze-making both Roman as well as from other traditions. The iconography is known from Antiquity and frequently utilized and there are even clear examples in the Burgundian world.

WOOD: Can you define what you mean by production centre? Are you just saying basically that the finds come from a certain area and so you guess that they are made there, or has there been a particular discovery of, say, a workshop?

RIPOLL: Archaeologically one hasn't identified any production centre nor any workshop. The only thing we know, thanks to textual documentation, is how the *officinae* of late Antiquity worked. However, we don't know whether the Visigothic workshops functioned the same way. From the standpoint of archaeology, the only thing we recognized—if we make maps of the distribution of objects—are areas of material accumulation, from which we can infer that there was a distribution and hence few production centres. For example, the materials found in the south of *Hispania* in the *Baetica* represent almost 70 percent of the objects of the seventh century in the whole region of Toledo. We can presume this inasmuch as in this area there must have been one or more workshops with high levels of productivity and distribution. In any case, it is also quite possible that here were a few itinerant *officinae* or workshops, i.e. they travelled the same as traders of old objects from one place to another where they had customers. This working hypothesis is strictly tied to the problem of the supply of metals during the sixth and seventh centuries. The great gold and silver mines were shut. It looks as if the objects produced with precious metals were obtained by reclaiming other existing objects, and it is quite possible that the same happened with bronze.

HEATHER: It's a related question. I'm not interested so much in where in *Hispania* the ornaments might be physically made, what I'm interested in is, has the technical work been done as it has, for instance, with Anglo-Saxon materials to show how many individual workshops there might be, or are we looking at a few concentrated centres? The question I'm asking, in a sense, is particularly in the case of the earlier sixth-century remains, do they make their own Visigothic brooch, or is it distributed from a centre? Obviously that has strong implications as to how we might see any signs of ethnic identity working if we can make such a statement.

AUSENDA: Did someone say that, while ceramics can be easily produced on the spot, metallurgy is usually sedentary. At least it is always sedentary in Eritrea, Sudan and all these places. In other words it is located in a large market town. Because they cannot move around with all their dies, patterns and tools.

RIPOLL: It seems clear that there were itinerant craftsmen, seeing that there were finds of metal hoards as, for example, the trove in El Collet de Sant Antoni (Calonge, Gerona). This means that craftsmen recovered different objects and utensils to recast them to obtain new objects of personal adornment. On the other hand, metallographic analysis, which has been applied to various objects, has shown that the preparation of alloys destined for the casting comprised quite variable components without keeping to a fixed rule. Furthermore, one should note that those same studies show that in many cases the pieces were re-heated, which leads one to think that, in some cases, there were two stages in the preparation, a first stage to obtain the piece itself and the next dedicated to its decoration. In any case, all these suggestions are not enough to solve the exact parameters of production and its ensuing distribution. It is quite possible that the most ancient objects, the belt brooches and *fibulae* of the first decades of the sixth century correspond to productions which arrive with Visigothic craftsmen native to the peninsula. With reference to this problem, there comes up also that of the geographical distribution of those first objects limited to the Castilian Meseta, which lead us to believe in a very limited number of production centres in that area.

HEATHER: Yes, we mentioned before that there are strong hints that there were annual donatives given out. And you start to wonder if distributing this kind of item is part and parcel of what is going on. Has the manufacture not been very carefully studied yet? Has the technical stuff not been done on these finds?

RIPOLL: The hypothesis of the limited number of craftsmen and workshops on the Meseta is supported by the appearance of pieces morphologically equal in different and relatively distant cemeteries as, for example, elements which appear at El Carpio de Tajo are also found at Tiermes or Duratón. Visually they are exactly the same, which means that they could issue from similar or equal moulds, which does not mean that they are made up of the same alloys, a fact which will only emerge from metallographic analysis.

AUSENDA: You can see whether the moulds are the same. Because, to make the mould they use dies.

HEATHER: That's what they have done, I think, with the Northumbrian stuff.

RIPOLL: The moulds are important, however, we do not know them archaeologically. In any case, the key to the solution of the problem lies in the metallographic analyses.

HEATHER: And also the types of glues used to stick the garnets on.

SCHWARCZ: And you cannot make a complete analysis of the metallurgical composition without destroying the thing, and in Berlin they have got a new electrical method of measuring the exact composition.

AUSENDA: Yes, but they cannot do it because it is recovered material.

RIPOLL: The analyses which were carried out on the pieces of El Carpio de Tajo were based on two techniques: on one hand a metallographic analysis, on the other a spectrographic non-destructive analysis based on X-ray fluorescence. The results show quite heterogeneous alloys: Cu-Pb-Sn, Cu-Pb-Sn-Zn, Cu-Zn and Cu-Zn-Pb. The results were published by S. Rovira and M. S. Sanz (1985).

SCHWARCZ: Yes, it doesn't matter whether it's pure or not. You can measure the exact percentage of the different metals which are in it.

RIPOLL: The same analyses of El Carpio de Tajo prove that the different parts of the same belt brooch were obtained from castings of different melts based on the fact that the alloys were always different.

DÍAZ: I think that the question of the chronology cannot be solved. In fact, if we accept that Gothic symbolic artefacts are elaborated before they arrived in *Hispania* or in the Empire, perhaps we have the possibility of finding a chronology. We could associate the assimilation of new symbolic elements to the process of integration, with the 'evolution' of the Visigoths, with the assimilation of the new concept of monarchy, administration, etc. etc. I believe it is not possible to solve this question otherwise.

RIPOLL: I do not know to what extent there are symbolic barriers throughout the objects of personal adornment and if those are really part of a symbolic system, i.e. whether they are really carrying a symbolic message.

DÍAZ: A very concrete question about the use of metal. We have clues about the importance of the old artefacts, because they must be placed in a safe place in order to re-use the metal, because it is not possible to find new metal.

AUSENDA: On page 414, you noted that conversion to the Catholic faith may "have implied an abandonment of the old Visgothic traditions of dress and...the adoption of dress in fashion at that moment." The question of dress is important and one should consider also how much Visigothic dress, or 'barbarian' dress in general influenced the fashions of the time. In other words perhaps the change of dress among Visigoths was less than the change of dress among Romans.

DÍAZ: About the use of the Codes. We have references in the *Codex Theodosianus*, to the use of barbarian clothes. But in the Visigothic period, it may not have been possible to distinguish a Goth from a Roman by their clothes, probably.

SCHWARCZ: It is a scandal in the fifth century and Sidonius Apollinaris specially mentions Roman senators who go to the Visigothic court dressed as

Visigoths and he deplores the fact. He is not very enthusiastic about this. But you have other times and other places, for instance, the beginning or turn of the sixth to the seventh century where usually iron arm rings are worn as a sign of belonging to the Burgundian people.

AUSENDA: Sorry, you didn't understand my question; it was that I got the impression that you thought that the Visigoths were adapting to Roman dress and I think that it was more likely that Romans were adapting to Visigothic dress.

JIMÉNEZ: No, no, no.

AUSENDA: Today we dress in clothes which are more similar to what barbarians wore than to what Romans wore, and it must have begun some time ago [laughter].

RIPOLL: There are different fashions and different ways of dressing depending on their Roman or Visigothic origin.

SCHWARCZ: You see, they changed to pantaloons already at the turn of the fourth to the fifth century generally.

RIPOLL: It seems that in the sixth century shirt and pants were already in use, and a long mantle over the shoulders.

JIMÉNEZ: I thought it was a special kind of dress which disappeared after the seventh century.

HEATHER: They didn't necessarily wear it during the day. This is what they were buried with.

SCHWARCZ: There are other rituals for burial.

AUSENDA: Well, there is no consensus of opinion.

HEATHER: Yes, we think they dressed in a Mediterranean *koiné*, but after 580.

AUSENDA: I am still on page 414 where you talk about the "abandonment of cemeteries". Does this mean that the related settlements were abandoned or that the Visigoths abandoned their own cemeteries to have their dead buried close to the Church together with non-Visigoths?

RIPOLL: The problem of the abandonment of cemeteries on the Castilian Meseta is quite complex. On the one hand we know these cemeteries, but we don't know the settlements; therefore, making a parallel with chronological indices of occupancy is impossible. On the other hand, the great cemetery complexes are quite scarce, they can be counted on the fingers of one or two hands, a fact which does not allow us to know the great evolutionary trends. It seems that the materials found in the tombs of the largest cemeteries do not go beyond the beginning of the seventh century. This leads one to believe that the period of maximum occupation is centred in the middle of the sixth century, with a decline ending at the beginning of the seventh. In any case, the interpretation is uncertain and risky, therefore, it should be kept as a hypothesis which, however, must be amply reworked.

JIMÉNEZ: I think this question is linked to mine concerning page 420. Is it possible that the grave goods disappeared when other forms of public ostentation appeared such as landed property?

RIPOLL: I don't know.

SCHWARCZ: I think that the legislation of Theoderic in Italy expressly forbade grave-goods. So, Christianization was a decisive factor for losing that tradition.

And generally, throughout the Christian world, when people became Christianized they first restricted grave-goods and then you have practically none.

RIPOLL: So, this is a good reason.

WOOD: I disagree with you entirely. Since bishops in sixth-century Gaul were buried with grave-goods, they cannot be a mark of paganism.

SCHWARCZ: But in the sixth century we speak of grave-goods because they disappear gradually, and gradually from the sixth to the seventh and eighth you have at least the normal burials in which ostentation decreases. This is a generally accepted fact in seventh-century archaeology.

WOOD: But it is not; it has been heavily debated. Christianity has largely been dismissed within north European archaeology as being a reason for the abandonment of grave-goods. It may well be that Christianity caused the abandonment of very specific grave-goods. But there is nothing in Christianity that causes the abandonment of grave-goods as a category.

DE JONG: About the observation by Ana [Jiménez] that there is some kind of ostentation in the foundation of new cult places. I am sure that this may be taken as an alternative for the ostentation of grave-goods. But I'm no expert, I just sit there and listen to all these archaeological interpretations.

SCHWARCZ: I think that you are more right in implying it is closer to what happened than in comparison to what is up in the North, because the North gets Christianized around the turn of the millennium.

WOOD: I mean *Francia* and England.

SCHWARCZ: There is a new study by Horst Wolfgang Böhme, of so-called 'Adelsgräber' in Merovingian and Burgundian times, showing how in the seventh century the nobility went over to church burials.

WOOD: That's not a new idea, it is an old one.

SCHWARCZ: I think that he has made the most complete study of graves which has been published to date.

RIPOLL: I think the problem is completely different because there are differences in the burials.

WOOD: You have to separate all these questions out.

RIPOLL & JIMÉNEZ: Yes, the problem is completely different.

SCHWARCZ: Weapons are a sign of ostentation. In the ninth century you find Slavs buried with a gold leaf cross on their breast, but this is not what people are buried with in the fifth century.

WOOD: On page 423, I just want to know whether you would give the transept capitals at S. Pedro de la Nave a date or not. Do you think that they can be dated, or not?

RIPOLL: This is one of the great problems of architecture and sculpture considered up to now to be Visigothic. At present, researchers who work on the Iberian Peninsula and on this type of production are addressing the problem of how far the traditionally established chronologies may be wrong.

WOOD: I would be happy with that because it could be compared with a Merovingian case.

RIPOLL: It is quite possible that even the origins and traditions of all this art should be placed in relation to Roman production in late Antiquity, even though they are evidently later, even later than the Visigothic monarchy of Toledo.

WOOD: I'm very happy with that, because there is a late Merovingian text which talks about capitals, which it describes as *figurata*, and which seems to be rather good evidence that there were capitals with figures sculpted on them, which could have been of humans. Are similar carvings known from Visigothic churches?

RIPOLL: The problem is very difficult. The question posed, whether it is Mozarabe, Visigothic, pre-Romanesque, Ummayyad or Caliphal are difficult to solve at the moment, especially since we do not know exactly the Roman manifestations in late Antiquity in *Hispania*. Personally I think that the analysis sbould be conducted with minute care, taking into account the before and after of what we have supposed all these productions to have been. What is really clear is that the arguments for the classification as Visigothic are, so far, quite weak.

References in the discussion

Textual sources:

Codex Salmasianus: see Shackleton Bailey (ed.) 1982.
Codex Theodosianus: see Mommsen *et al.* (eds.) 1904-1905.
Physiologus: see Sbordone (ed.) 1936.
Procopius of Caesarea
         Wars: see Veh (ed. & trans.) 1966 & 1971.

Bibliography:

Böhme, H. W.
    1995   Adelsgräber in Frankenreich. Archäologische Zeugnisse zur Heraus-bildung einer Herreschicht unter den merowingischen Königen. *Jahrbücher [1993] des Römisch-Germanischen Zentralmuseums Mainz 40 (2): 397-534*

Goffart, W.
    1980   *Barbarians and Romans, AD 418-584.* Princeton: Princeton University Press.

James, E.
    1977   *The Merovingian Archaeology of South-West Gaul.* (British Archaeo-logical Reports, 25). Oxford: B.A.R.

Mommsen, T., P. Krüger & P. Meyer (eds.)
    1904-05   *Codex Theodosianus*, I-II. Hildesheim: Weidmann. [Repr. 1990].

Rovira, S., & M. S. Sanz.
    1985   Análisis metalúrgico de los materiales de la necrópolis de El Carpio de Tajo (Toledo). In *La necrópolis visigoda de El Carpio de Tajo (Toledo).* G. Ripoll (ed.), pp. 227-254. (Excavaciones Arqueológicas en España, 142). Madrid: Ministerio de Cultura.

Sbordone, F. (ed.)
    1936   *Physiologus.* (In aedibus societatis D. Alighieri). Milano/Genova/Roma: Albrighi Segati & Co.

Shackleton Bailey, D. R. (ed.)
    1982   Carmina Codicis Salmasiani. In *Anthologia Latina*, I. 1. Stuttgart:
                    Teubner.
Stadler, P.
    1995   Einsetzmöglichkeiten von EDV in der Archäologie heute. Versuch der
                    Darstellung des "State of the art". *Archäologie Österreichs* 6 (1): 86-98.
Veh, O. (ed. & trans.)
    1966   *Prokop. Werke (vol. 2). Gotenkriege.* Munich: E. Heinemann Verlag.
    1971   *Prokop. Werke (vol. 4). Vandalenkriege.* Munich: E. Heinemann Verlag.

CULT AND RELIGION AMONG THE TERVINGI AND THE VISIGOTHS AND THEIR CONVERSION TO CHRISTIANITY

ANDREAS SCHWARCZ

Institut für Österreichische Geschichtsforschung, Dr. Karl Lueger-Ring 1, A-1010 Wien

Cult and religion are central aspects of collective and individual identity in a tribal society. Cult dominates the customs of the tribe, the way in which everyone's daily life is led. From the cradle to the grave, worship of the holy is linked to tribal tradition, tribal self-identification preserved and formed in the tribe's origin myths. These founding traditions often lead back to a mythical primeval founder or ancestor, of divine origin or at least acting under the guidance and protection of a god or goddess, and worship of these gods is part of tribal identity. Who denies sacrifice and worship to the tribal deities may exclude him- or herself from the tribal community.

However, cult and religion are not static elements of society. They develop and change under external influence or innovations in the inner life of their bearer communities. Changes may be due to changing political conditions or to new contacts in a new environment. If we are lucky, we find traces of these developments in material culture or in our written sources. Without these, we can only speculate.

For the first centuries of the history of the Goths we have little evidence of their religious beliefs in the written sources. Tacitus and Pliny do not give us any information whatsoever about the gods and goddesses the *Gutoni* or *Gotones* worshipped. More is known today by archaeological means, especially concerning their burial rites (esp. Bierbrauer 1994:51-171). As far as nowadays ethnic identification in archaeology is accepted at all, the results of Polish, Russian, Ucrainian, Moldavian and Romanian research show that we must seek the *Gothi* of the first two centuries AD within the Wielbark culture, autochthonously developed out of the Oksywie culture and existing well into the fourth century (Kokowski 1995:26-31), and in the Cherniakhov-Sîntana de Mureş culture which developed organically out of Wielbark in the third century. According to Völker Bierbrauer, typical burial features for both Wielbark and Cherniakhov are bi-ritualism, i.e. both inhumation and cremation with a slight preponderance of the latter, female burials with a costume with one to three fibulae, prismatic bone amulets ('Donaramulette'), pieces with runic inscriptions and weaponless male burials in contrast to all neighbouring contemporary cultures in the Baltic Sea region, especially to the Przeworsk culture and to funerary practice in contemporary Scandinavia (Bierbrauer 1994:54-7, 67-75; de Vries 1956-1:147). As far as we may interpret the absence of iron weapons in male graves, contrary to all their neighbours, the Goths seem not to have thought of the realm of the dead as a place to which a dead Gothic warrior had to bring his own weapons. This central

447

difference makes a cult community with the neighbouring Lugian confederation or with Scandinavia extremely unlikely (otherwise, but noting the difference, Wolfram 1990:50-1).

But customs change with geographical displacement and with new contacts in other surroundings. Contrary to the Wielbark culture, human heads in Cherniakhov inhumations are not exclusively oriented to the north, there is also a noticeable proportion of east-to-west oriented burials (Heather & Matthews 1991:62). Cultural interchange and intermarriage with Daco-Getans and Sarmatians led to a process of acculturation to the peoples of the steppes and the Carpathians evident in material culture, especially in funerary practice. From the Sarmatians the people of the Cherniakhov-Sîntana de Mureş culture took over the practice ot making niches in graves or even building funerary chambers, and the use of metallic mirrors (Kazanski 1991:55-7).

Striking is a change in the burial ritual made at the beginning of the fourth century in the area of the so-called Masłomęc group recently excavated and thoroughly reseached by Andrzej Kokowski: following the example set by their Dacian neighbours, the Masłomęc people gave up almost completely the practice of inhumation and took to cremation. In a special area of their cemetery a rectangular space of about 3m x 2m was marked with wooden posts and probably spanned with textile material, forming a temple tent. A circle having a diameter of 15 m was drawn around this and the place used to scatter the ashen remains of the cremations which formed a layer of about 15 cm (Kokowski 1995:97).

In these cultural surroundings, especially in the Sîntana de Mureş part of the Cherniakhov culture , we must seek the *Tervingi*, first mentioned in a panegyric for Maximianus Augustus in the spring of 291 (*XII Panegyrici Latini* XI (III), 17. 1; cf. Wolfram 1990:34). That they called themselves also *Visi* is shown by the creation of two *Auxilia palatina* with the names of both *Tervingi* and *Visi*, probably organized by Theodosius I out of the retinue of Athanaric after his death in Constantinople in 381 (*Notitia dignitatum or.* 5. 61, 6. 61; cf. Wolfram 1990:84; see also Schwarcz 1984:47; Hoffman 1969-1:169, 241, 278, 467).[1] If we seek to enlarge our knowledge of their cult and religion by turning to the evidence of our written sources, we shall find them scanty and thin. The best analysis is still to be found in Herwig Wolfram's masterly study (1990:114-121) revising much of the speculations of the older literature and relying mainly on the evidence of Wulfila's Bible and hagiographic literature.

According to this we must assume that cult regulated village life and was, on the other hand, modified by the oligarchic structure of Tervingian society. Eunapius notes that each *phyle*, which must be equalled to the *kuni*, the tribal unit under the leadership of the *reiks*, a *regulus*, had its own object of worship accompanied by priests and priestesses when they crossed the Danube in 376 (Eunapius fr. 2; Thompson 1966:56-7). In these statues or wooden posts they may have worshiped the ancestors of their leaders, called *Anses* according to Jordanes. Eunapius can be

---

[1]   Hoffman thinks that they were formed out of the followers of Fritigern after 382.

correlated to a notice by Sozomenos that Athanaric ordered an object called *xoanon* to be driven around on a cart and worshipped during his persecution of Christians after 369. Of course this may not have been a single object for the whole tribe, but would have applied to each *kuni* separately. Anyway this episode proves both the use of 'Kultwagen' (ceremonial waggons) and wooden idols (Jordanes, *Getica* 78; Sozomenos *Historia ecclesiastica* VI. 37. 13; Thompson 1966:59-61; de Vries 1956-1:385; Wolfram 1990:114). In his report of the battle of *ad Salices* in 376, Ammianus Marcellinus notes that the Goths began fighting by shouting the *laudes* of their ancestors (Ammianus Marcellinus, *Res gestae* 31. 7. 11). Eunapius specially stresses the tribal character of this cult by the strict silence which its followers had to keep about it to all outsiders. If we can believe a letter written by St Ambrose to the three *Augusti* with accusations against his Arian opponent Julian Valens of Poetovio, who is described as having presented himself in this accoutrement before a Roman army, its priests were adorned with arms rings and necklaces. In Wulfila's language the priest is *gudja* or *gudblostreis*, stressing his role in sacrifice. However, they seem to have existed only in connection with the cult maintained by the rulers of the *kuni* or their ancestors or patron god, not in the villages (*Gesta concilii Aquileiensis ep. 2 (10)*; Schwarcz 1984:43; Thompson 1966:58; de Vries 1956-1:390, 398; Wolfram 1990:115).[2] All authors, to varying degrees, also assume shamanistic rituals among the *Tervingi*, taken over from their Sarmatian, Finnish and Dacian neighbours, but the amount of this cannot be ascertained (Wolfram 1990:115-6). Jordanes' account of the *haliurunnae*, witches whom King Filimer drove away and who became the ancestresses of the Huns, seems to indicate that Gothic society knew sometimes at least about witchcraft and necromantic rituals, practiced but not officially acknowledged, maybe sometimes even actively persecuted by tribal leaders (Jordanes, *Getica* 121; cf. de Vries 1956-1:323).

The keeper of the cult was the whole village community. The time of the full moon seems to have been the ordained time for sacrifice and feasts, possibly called *dulths*, during which the sacrifices were eaten by the whole community, as indicated by a significant change introduced by Wulfila in his translation of the letters of St Paul. The etymology of '*dulths*' seems to imply a connection with the Germanic feast of spring (de Vries 1956-1:470).

The second name of *Naubaimbair* (a derivation from Latin), the month of November, *fruma jiuleis*, first month of Yule, in a surviving fragment of the Gothic Church calendar, shows that the winter solstice was also celebrated with a feast (Thompson 1966:62-3; Wolfram 1990:120). If the Goths celebrated the feast of midwinter, as it seems, they probably also celebrated midsummer and the autumn harvest (cf. de Vries 1956-1:445-8), but there is no actual evidence for it in the sources. The sacrifices were prepared and made by the speakers of the community,

---

[2] However, Jan de Vries remark (1956-1:398) on the priests being from the social stratum of the *pilleati*, the same as the kings, must be taken with a grain of salt, because Jordanes (*Getica*, 40) whom de Vries cites for this, in his turn cites Dio Cassius on the *Getae*, not on the Goths.

not by priests, and then the whole village joined them in the sacrificial meal. The village assembly decided to offer St Saba unblessed meat, a way out of martyrdom which the saint declined (*Passio sancti Sabae*, III. 1 ff.; Wolfram 1990:113). One of the more gruesome customs the Goths seem to have shared with other barbarian peoples was the habit of killing off their aged relatives, if we may trust a remark in a sermon wrongly attributed to John Chrysostomos (Migne 1859; cf. de Vries 1956-1:188).

Nearly nothing is known about the gods the *Tervingi* worshiped. The long contacts with the Mediterranean world must have led to syncretism in this aspect. According to Jordanes, like the Goths in general, the *Tervingi* may have worshiped their ancestors considering them *Anses*, nobles and demigods (Jordanes, *Getica* 78; cf. de Vries 1956-2:7). It seems reasonably certain that, like all other people of Scythia, the Goths also worshiped the god of warfare, possibly called **Teiws-tius* in Gothic, whose epiphany was the sword, and may be equated with Tiwaz-Tyr. By the fourth century the names of Ares and Mars may already have supplanted the original tribal name (Wolfram 1990:117-8). Jordanes at least, tells us that the Goths used to worship Mars with awful ceremonies, implying human sacrifices (de Vries 1956-2:10; Wolfram 1990:117-8).[3]

Speculation about a special worship of Jupiter evaporated with modern reassessments of the ring of Pietroassa, now dated to the fifth century, and its inscription. A recent study done by Hermann Reichert with a thorough scrutiny of the original in Bucarest in 1992 gives as the most plausible reading of this runic inscription "*gutane jer weih hailag*", a blessing for a fruitful and prosperous year (Reichert 1991-93:235-47).[4] St Augustine reports that Radagaisus offered daily sacrifices to Jupiter (Aurelius Augustinus, *Sermo* 105.10; cf Wolfram 1990:118), but he was not a Tervingian Goth and he and his followers escaped from Hunnic domination a generation after the end of the transdanubian *Tervingi*, and mostly were former Greuthungians who had coalesced as a result of Hunnic domination. So this may not tell us anything about Tervingian tribal religion.

Special worship might be assumed for the rivers. They played an important role in the spread of settlements in the Cherniakhov culture. According to R. Shishkin, who at a conference in Caputh in 1995 (unpublished) presented a study of 599 Cherniakhov settlements in the Ukraine, the settlements followed the rivers and were concentrated along the smaller ones. St Saba found his martyrdom in the river Musaeus-Buzau (*Passio sancti Sabae*, VII). This may be interpreted as a sacrifice to the river god. One the other hand, the worship of the Danube implied by Claudian may only be a literary reference to the Dacians (Claudian, *De bello Gothico*, vv. 81 ff.; cf. Wolfram 1990:399 n 72).

Of course the most decisive external religious influence on the *Tervingi* was the process of transformation of the Roman world by Christianity. It had already

---

[3] "*...Martem Gothi semper asperrima placavere cultura* (Jordanes, *Getica* 41).

[4] Jan de Vries (1956-1:337) declined to speculate about the traditional reading "*gutaniowihailag*".

reached the Goths before they split into *Tervingi* and *Greutungi*, because there were Christians among the prisoners they took during their raids in the middle of the third century. Wulfila's ancestors came by this route from Cappadocia, and the blossoming mission Church of the fourth century among the Goths maintained close relations especially with the Church of this province of Asia Minor. Basilius of Caesarea tells us of the transfer of relics from *Gothia* north of the Danube, and thanks to him we also know of the activities of Eutyches, who spread the Christian faith in this region according to the Nicaean creed, at the latest probably under Constantius II.[5]

We find a Theophilos, bishop of *Gothia*, whom Socrates calls the teacher of Wulfila (*Patrum Nicaenorum nominum LXIV*; Socrates, *Historia ecclesiastica* 2. 41. 23), already in the lists of this first oecumenical council (Nicaea 325). Because Philostorgios called Wulfila the first bishop of the Goths (Philostorgios, *Historia ecclesiastica* 2. 5), this has been a point of discussion for a long time, which led Jacques Zeiller and Ludwig Schmidt to suppose that the see of Theophilos was in the Crimea, near Bosphoros and Chersonesos, a choice lately favoured also by Peter Heather (Zeiller 1918:409-14; followed by Schmidt 1941:233; and by Heather 1991:93). The traditional view, shared by Wolfram, was recently emphasized once again by Knut Schäferdiek, who also pointed out that, bearing in mind developments after 325, Theophilos' theological point of view may not have been radically different from Wulfila's. He surmises that Theophilos may have belonged to the broad so-called 'middle party' around Eusebius of Nicomedia, finally sharing the christological convictions of the second Antiochene formula of 341 (Delehaye 1912:284; Schäferdiek 1990:37, 49; Wolfram 1990:87). Schäferdiek's view is supported by contemporary archaeology, which finds the first signs of permanent Gothic settlement in the Crimea only in the last quarter of the fourth century and a second wave of Goths after the end of Attila's reign (von der Lohe 1995). The localization of Theophilos in Tomi, once again brought into discussion by Evangelos Chrysos, was already rejected by Schmidt, and is firmly and finally done so by Schäferdiek (Chrysos 1972:85-8; Schäferdiek 1990:233; Schmidt 1941:233).

Personally, while sharing in the main the view of Wolfram and Schäferdiek, I think that Theophilos was a predecessor of Wulfila, that there might have been a difference in their mandate. Both were *episcopi intra gentes*, but Wulfila was clearly designed for the federated Goths under treaty with the Empire, i.e. the *Tervingi*, whereas Theophilos' *Gothia*, not so strictly connected with imperial policy, may also have included the southern regions of the *Greutungi*, where Christian beginnings from the same roots, i.e. prisoners, and from the *poleis* on the

---

[5]   Concerning prisoners: Philostorgios, *Historia ecclesiastica*, 2. 5; Syncellus, *Chronicon*; Zosimus, *Historia nea* 1. 28. Concerning conversion through prisoners: Philostorgios, *Historia ecclesiastica*, 2.5; Sozomenos, *Historia ecclesiastica* 2. 6. 2. See also Basilius, *Epistulae* 155, 164; Schäferdiek 1978:502; 1990:39 (dates Eutyches around 300 AD); Schwarcz 1987:107; Thompson 1966:82; Wolfram 1990:87).

Black Sea coast are also possible. This difference may explain Philostorgios' remark. Anyway, Christianity among the Goths before Wulfila is also attested by St Athanasius, who counted the Goths among the peoples whom the word of the Gospel had already reached (Athanasius, *De incarnatione* 51. 2; Schäferdiek 1978:498; Schwarcz 1987:107).

As for the second quarter of the fourth century, one should also mention the efforts of the old schismatic Audius of Mesopotamia among the Goths. Exiled to the province of *Scythia minor* by Constantius II at the end of the emperor's reign, he crossed the Danube to evangelize the *Tervingi*. He is said to have been so successful that he even consecrated a bishop named Silvanus as his successor from among his pupils there. We only know another of his followers by name, Uranius. His community must have come to an end with the second wave of persecutions organized by Athanaric after 369, because it is no longer heard of afterwards (Epiphanius, *Panarium adv. LXXX haereses* 70; Hieronymus, *Chronicon s.a.* 341; Theodoret, *Historia ecclesiastica* 4.9; Schäferdiek 1990:49; Zeiller 1918:419).

In the beginning, especially under the Tetrarchy and under the reign of Licinius, we have to suppose that Christianity was at best tolerated among the Goths, if not persecuted as in the Empire. This might have changed after the heavy defeats suffered by the Goths at the hands of Constantine and his son of the same name in 324 and 332. We have to reckon with a determined and coordinated policy of gaining influence among the Goths by the Church of the Empire under his guidance, maybe already after Constantine's victory over the *regalis Alica* near Chrysopolis in 324, surely in the thirties of the fourth century. We have sure evidence of the political assessment of the victory of 332 and indications of the grown dominance of the Empire north of the Danube in gold *solidi* of Constantine and his son Constantius coined at Trier with a defeated *Gothia* on the reverse with the inscription "*debellatori gentium barbarum*", bronze medallions of Constantine coined in Rome with the message "*victoria Gothica*", and Constantine's claim to have restored Dacia to the Empire in the form of a *Gothia Romania*, satirically commented upon by Julian. It seems that also the *ludi Gothici*, celebrated in Constantinople between 4th and 9th February, were institutionalized then, and the inscription of a victory statue of Constantine tells us of the "*Fortuna restituta*" because of the victory over the Goths (Julian, *Caesares* 30. II. 2; Bruun 1966:215 nr.531 & nr.534, 283, 333 nr.306; Chrysos 1973:52-64; Fiebiger & Schmidt 1917:86 nr.164; Wolfram 1990:71).

Growing missionary efforts among the Goths and imperial protection for the Christians among them may well have been part of this policy, which Constantius II, especially honoured in the Gothic calendar, continued after the death of his father. According to Thompson and Schäferdiek there must have existed an ecclesiastical organization in at least a rudimentary form already before the consecration of Wulfila as bishop because of his rank as *anagnostes*, reader, at this point. His participation in Gothic embassies to the imperial court and his consecration by Eusebius of Nicomedia, under Constantius II transferred to the see of Constantinople, clearly show the political weight given to the emerging Church of *Gothia* by both the Empire and its Gothic federates.

Against Schäferdiek's dating of this consecration to 336 I still prefer, the same as Peter Heather, the traditional date of 341. It is not only more in accordance with the account given by Auxentius of Durostorum, but we would otherwise have to date the eviction of the Gothic bishop and his followers to 343, for which there are no indications whatsoever. Furthermore, the canons of the second oecumenical council of Constantinople in 381 and of Chalcedon in 451 stress that the Church of Constantinople continued to be responsible for the *ecclesia in gentibus et in barbaricis*, a clear indication that the see of the New Rome was so also in 341, and that Eusebius acted in his official capacity as bishop of Constantinople.[6]

The persecution which led to the flight of Wulfila must be dated to 348, a date for which we also have clear evidence. Libanius in his panegyric for the emperor given in 348/349 mentions raids across the Danube during the winter and praises Constantius II for maintaining peace with the Scythians during the war against Persia. As already noticed by Schmidt and by Thompson, this indicates a modification of the terms of the *deditio* of 332, and the tacit acceptance of the persecution of Christian Goths by the Tervingian *iudex* Aoric, who may have seen them not only as a disturbing factor against tribal cult, breaking the holy bond between the *Tervingi* and their ancestral gods and heroes, but also as a dangerous Roman "fifth column" north of the Danube. After his bloody defeat at Singara in 348, Constantius needed fresh recruits against the Persians and a quiet Danube frontier (Libanius, *Oratio* 59. 89-83; Schmidt 1941:229; Schwarcz 1987:108-9; Thompson 1966:16-7; Wolfram 1990:72-3).[7]

The "*grandis populus confessorum*" of Wulfila's followers under the leadership of their bishop, whom Constantius II is said to have called a "second Moses", was "*honorifice susceptus*", a technical term indicating a rather good reception into the Empire without the loss of personal freedom and dissolution of group identity, and were settled around Nicopolis ad Istrum, where Jordanes in the sixth century still called their descendants a "*populus immensus*" (*Maximini episcopi dissertatio*, 35-38; Jordanes, *Getica* 267; Schwarcz 1987:109; Wolfram 1990:73). There Wulfila led and taught his people until his death in Constantinople in 383, actively taking part in the religious life of the imperial Church as a member of the ecclesiastical faction dominant at court, with the exception of the short duration of Julian's reign, until the death of Valens.

Not all Gothic Christians left the *Tervingi* with Wulfila, and there are clear signs of a continuation of ecclesiastical life north of the Danube in the second half of the fourth century, as is shown especially by the *passiones* connected to the persecution launched by Athanaric between 369 and 372. There seem to have been

---

6   Canon 2 of 381 states that everything shall remain as before, canons 1 and 28 of 451 repeat this and especially stress Constantinople's responsibility *in barbaricis* (Hefele & Leclerque 1908:770-2; Heather & Matthews 1991:142-3; Schäferdiek 1990:39-40; Schwarcz 1987:108, 110; Wolfram 1990:66-7, 94).

7   Peter Heather (1996:61) suggested 347/348 as the date of Wulfila's reception into the Empire.

both Orthodox Christians preserving the traditional links to Cappadocia, and Homoean followers of Wulfila. The martyrs Inna, Rhina and Pinna, the presbyters Guththika and Sansalas, and St Saba, whose *passio* gives very important and useful information about the inner structure of the *Tervingi* and their village life, seem to have been orthodox Christians. Bishop Vetranio of Tomi and the *dux* Soranus, who organized the transfer of the bones of St Saba, both came from Cappadocia. However, there are also Homoean martyrs, 26 of whom were burned in a wooden church on the orders of the *reiks* Wingurich (Schäferdiek 1978:501-5; Thompson 1966:95-102; Wolfram 1990:78-80, 91-3).

The outbreak of this persecution was of course linked to the end of the war of 367 to 369 between the Empire and the *Tervingi*. The *pax* between Valens and Athanaric in the middle of the Danube meant not only the end of Roman *annonae* for the Goths and of Gothic federated troops for the Romans. It also meant a strengthening of the role of Athanaric as *iudex Tervingorum*, whose function traditionally included sacral elements, as is shown by his refusal to leave the tribal territory while exercising his office. This enabled him to purge the Christians as possible partisans of the Romans; he had nothing to fear from the latter. The Romans' precarious situation on the Persian frontier had forced them to conclude a peace on the Danube, a necessary precondition for the transfer of the eastern praesental army under the *magister militum* Arintheus, a Christian Goth in the service of the Empire, to the eastern frontier. Only after the successes against the Persians of 371 could the Empire once again intervene in the affairs of the *Tervingi* (Schwarcz 1987:111; Seeck 1921-5:444-6; Stein 1959-1:187; Wolfram 1990:501-5).

A perennial point of discussion is the date of the conversion of Fritigern and his followers, with which I shall conclude my paper, not because it marks the end of the process of conversion, rather the beginning of its final stage, but because it is crucial for the discussion of the end of the *Tervingi-Visi* and the beginning of the ethnogenesis which would lead to the Visigoths of the fifth century. Peter Heather has made a strong case for a conversion of Fritigern in 376 (1986:289-318). The main difficulty in this interpretation lies in the necessity of devaluing the evidence of Socrates. However, in line with Schäferdiek, of all the garbled accounts of this affair given by Socrates, Sozomenos and Theodoret, I still think that Socrates' report is by far the clearest among them (Socrates, *Historia ecclesiastica* 4. 33; Sozomenos *Historia ecclesiastica* 6. 37; Theodoret, *Historia ecclesiastica* 4. 27; see Schäferdiek 1978:504; 1990:46; Schwarcz 1987:111). According to this, there was a rebellion against Athanaric, and Fritigern, who was losing, turned for help to the emperor who gave orders to his *dux* in Thrace to support him. Out of gratitude for this, Fritigern is said to have converted to Christianity. As this must have been a small local affair not involving the court or the central army units, the silence of Ammianus Marcellinus may be easily explained. All are agreed that any conflict between Fritigern and Athanaric must have taken place before 376 north of the Danube (Cf. Heather & Matthews 1991:106 n6). A strong argument for the possible involvement of Wulfila and his pupils in the conversion of this group is the fact, recently stressed by Schäferdiek, that Demophilus, bishop of

Constantinople between 370 and 380, responsible for the mission, had previously been the bishop of Beroia-Stara Zagora in Thrace, and surely had close contacts with Wulfila (Schäferdiek 1990:47). Anyway, the imperial help was not designed to depose Athanaric, but only to prevent the destruction of Fritigern's group, and it is clear that during Athanaric's fight against the Huns, Fritigern's followers and other unnamed *reiks* and *optimates Gothorum* kept themselves apart. These others need not necessarily also have been Christians. Probably not even Alaviv, who seems to have been the most prominent leader of the group which crossed the Danube with Fritigern, and, judging by his name, possibly belonging to the family of the *iudices Gothorum*, was a Christian. However, the fact that Fritigern was one already and was a federate of the Empire before crossing gained them admission into the Empire. After all, even Eunapius, clearly hostile to Christians, admitted that there were already priests, bishops, and monks among those crossing the Danube. Hence Fritigern, who resembles more a medieval ruler rather than a late antique tribal chieftain in this respect, on 8th August of 378, on the eve of the battle of Hadrianople, sent to Valens a priest as his personal messenger to whom he could entrust a secret message (Eunapius frg. 2; Ammianus Marcellinus, *Res gestae* 31. 12. 8 ff.; see Schäferdiek 1990:47; Schwarcz 1987:111-2; Wolfram 1990:133). Twenty years later, Alaric's followers were at least as thoroughly Christianized as the rest of the population of the Balkan provinces. Their new tribal religion was the Homoean variant of Christianity, an important fact also for the question of continuity between the *Tervingi* and the Visigoths.

References

Textual sources:

Ammianus Marcellinus
     Rerum gestarum libri: see Rolfe (ed.) 1935.
Athanasius
     De incarnatione: see Kannengiesser (ed. & trans.) 1973.
Aurelius Augustinus
     Sermones: see Migne (ed.) 1865a & 1865b.
Basilius Magnus Caesareae
     Epistulae: see Migne (ed.) 1886: col. 219 - col. 1111.
Claudian
     De bello Getico: see Platnauer (ed. & trans.) 1922.
Epiphanius
     Panarium sive Arcula, adversus LXXX haereses: see Holle & Dammer (eds.) 1980.
Eunapius
     Historiae: see Blockley (ed. & trans.) 1983.
Gesta concili Aquileiensis: see Zelzer (ed.) 1982:313-368.
Hieronymus
     Chronicon: see Helm (ed.) 1984.

Ioannes Chrysostomus
  Homiliae: see Migne (ed.) 1859:455-532.
Jordanes
  Getica: see Mommsen (ed.) 1882.
Julian
  Caesares: see Lacombrade (ed. & trans.) 1964:32-71; Rochefort (ed.) 1963.
Libanius
  Orationes: see Foerster (ed.) 1903.
Maximini contra Ambrosium dissertatio: see Hamman (ed.) 1958: col. 693 - col. 728.
Notitia dignitatum orientalium: see Seeck (ed.)
XII Panegyrici Latini: see Mynors (ed.) 1964.
Passio sancti Sabae: see Delehaye (ed.) 1912: esp. 216-221.
Patrum Nicaenorum nominum LXIV: see Gelzer, Hilgenfeld & Cuntz (eds.) 1898.
Philostorgios
  Historia ecclesiastica: see Bidez (ed.) 1913.
Socrates
  Historia ecclesiastica: see Hansen (ed.) 1995.
Sozomenos
  Historia ecclesiastica: see Bidez (ed.) 1995.
Syncellus
  Ecloga chronographica: see Mosshammer (ed.) 1984.
Theodoretus
  Historia ecclesiastica: see Parmentier (ed.) 1954.
Zosimus
  Historia nova: see Paschoud (ed.) 1971-81.

Bibliography:

Bidez, J. (ed.)
  1913   *Philostorgius Kirchengeschichte*. Leipzig: J. C. Hinrichs.
  1995   *Sozomenos Kirchengeschichte*. (G. C. S., N.F., vol. 4). Berlin: Akademie
          Verlag.
Bierbrauer, V.
  1994   Archäologie und Geschichte der Goten vom 1.-7. Jahrhundert. Versuch
          einer Bilanz. *Frühmittelalterliche Studien* 28: 51-171.
Blockley, R. C. (ed. & trans.)
  1983   *The Fragmentary Classicising Historians of the Later Roman Empire:
          Eunapius, Olympiodorus, Priscus and Malchus*, vol.2. Liverpool: Francis
          Cairns.
Bruun, P. M.
  1966   *Roman Imperial Coinage*, 7. London: Spirk & Son.
Chrysos, E. K.
  1972   *To Byzantion kai hoi Gotthoi*. Thessalonike: Etairèia Makedonikòn
          Epoudòn.
  1973   Gothia Romana. Zur Rechtslage des Föderatenlandes der Westgoten in
          4. Jahrhundert. *Dacoromania* 1: 52-64.
Delehaye, H.
  1912   Saints de Thrace et de Mésie. *Analecta Bollandiana* 31: 161-300.
Fiebiger, O., & L. Schmidt
  1917   *Inschriftensammlung zur Geschichte der Ostgermanen*. (Denkschriften
          der kaiserlichen Akademie der Wissenschaften in Wien. Philosophie-
          historische Klasse 60/3, 86 no. 164). Vienna: Hölder - Pickler - Tempsky.

Foerster, R. (ed.)
 1903   *Libanii Opera.* (3 vols.) Leipzig: Teubner.
Gelzer, H., H. Hilgenfeld & O. Cuntz (eds.)
 1898   *Patrum Nicaenorum Nomina.* Leipzig: Teubner.
Hamman, A. (ed.)
 1958   *Supplementum, Vol. I. Patrologiae Latinae Supplementum I.* Paris:
             Éditions Garnier Frères, 6 rue des Saints-Pères.
Hansen, G. C. (ed.)
 1995   *Sokrates Kirchengeschichte.* (G. C. S., N.F., vol. 1). Berlin: Akademie
             Verlag.
Heather, P.
 1986   The crossing of the Danube and the Gothic conversion. *Greek, Roman
             and Byzantine Studies* 27: 289-318.
 1991   *Goths and Romans.* Oxford/Malden, MA: Oxford University Press.
 1996   *The Goths.* Oxford/Cambridge, MA: Blackwell Publishers.
Heather, P., & J. Matthews
 1991   *The Goths in the Fourth Century.* (Translated texts for Historians, 11).
             Liverpool: Liverpool University Press.
Hefele, J., & H. Leclerque
 1908   *Histoire des concils d'après les documents originaux,* 2. Paris: Letouzey
             & Ané.
Helm, R. W. O. (ed.)
 1984   *Die Chronik des Hieronymus.* (3rd ed.) (G. C. S.). Berlin: Akademie
             Verlag.
Hoffman, D.
 1969   *Das spätrömische Bewegungsheer und die Notitia dignitatum,* 2 vols.
             (Epigraphische Studien, 7). Düsseldorf: Rheinland Verlag.
Holl, K., & J. Dammer (eds.)
 1980   *Epiphanios Panarium.* (2nd rev. ed.) (G. C. S., 25, 31, 37). Berlin:
             Akademie Verlag.
Kannengiesser, C. (ed. & trans.)
 1973   *De incarnatione.* (Sources Chrétiennes, 199). Paris: Les Éditions du Cerf.
Kazanski, M.
 1991   *Les Goths (Ier-VIIe siècles après J.-C).* Paris: Éd. Errance.
Kokowski, A.
 1995   *Schätze der Ostgoten.* Stuttgart: Theiss.
Lacombrade, C. (ed. & trans.)
 1964   *L'empereur Julien. Oeuvres complètes.* Tome II, 2ème partie. Discours de
             Julien empereur (Les Césars - Sur Hélios-ros - Le Misopagon). Paris:
             Société d'Édition "Les Belles-lettres", 95 blvd. Raspail.
Migne, J.-P. (ed.)
 1859   *S.P.N. Ioannis Chrysostomi Archiepiscopi Constantinopolitani opera
             omnia quae extant vel quae eius nomine circumferentur,* vol. 3, *pars
             posterior. Patrologiae Graecae tomus III.* J.-P. Migne (ed.). Paris:
             J.-P. Migne in rue Thibaud, once rue d'Amboise. [Repr. Turnhout:
             Brepols].
 1865a   *Sancti Aurelii Augustini Hipponensis episcopi Opera omnia, etc.
             Sermonum classes quatuor, necnon sermones dubii. Classis prima:
             Sermones de Scripturis. Classis II: Sermones de Tempore. Classis III;
             Sermones de Sanctis. Patrologiae Latinae Tomus XXXVIII.* J.-P. Migne
             (ed.). Paris: J.-P. Migne in rue Thibaud, once rue d'Amboise. [Repr.
             Turnhout: Brepols].

Migne, J.-P. (ed.) (*cont.*)
1865b   *Sancti Aurelii Augustini Hipponensis episcopi Opera omnia, etc.*
           Sermonum classis IV: Sermones de diversis. Patrologiae Latinae Tomus
           XXXIX. J.-P. Migne (ed.). Paris: J.-P. Migne in rue Thibaud, once rue
           d'Amboise. [Repr. Turnhout: Brepols].
1886   *Sancti Patris Nostri Basilii, Caesareae Cappadociae Archiepiscopi Opera*
           omnia quae extant, etc. Patrologiae Graecae Tomus XXXII. J.-P Migne
           (ed.). Paris: Garnier Frères & J.-P Migne Succs. [Repr. Turnhout: Brepols].
Mommsen, T. (ed.)
1882   *Iordanis Romana et Getica. Monumenta Germaniae Historica. Auctores*
           antiquissimi, 5, 1. Hannover: Hahn.
Mosshammer, A. A. (ed.)
1984   *Ecloga Chronographica.* Leipzig: Teubner.
Mynors, R. B. (ed.)
1964   *XII Panegyrici Latini.* Oxford: Oxford University Press.
Parmentier, L. (ed.)
1954   *Theodoret. Historia Ecclesiastica.* (G. C. S.) Berlin: Akademie Verlag.
Paschoud, F. (ed.)
1971-86   *Zosime, Histoire Nouvelle*, 3 tomes. Paris: Les Belles Lettres.
Platnauer, M.
1922   *Claudian, Poems.* 2 vols. (Loeb Classical Library). London:
           W. Heinemann Ltd. [Repr. Cambridge, MA: Harvard University Press].
Reichert, H.
1991-93   Gutani ? Wi Hailag. *Die Sprache* 35: 235-247.
Rochefort, G. (ed.)
1963   *L'empereur Julien. Oeuvres complètes.* Paris: Budé.
Rolfe, J. C.
1935-9   *Ammianus Marcellinus.* 3 Vols. (Loeb Classical Library). London:
           W. Heinemann Ltd.
Schäferdiek, K.
1978   'Germanenmission'. *Reallexikon für Antike und Christentum*, 10,
           pp. 492-548. Stuttgart: Hiersemann Verlags-GmbH.
1990   Gotien. Eine Kirche in Vorfeld des frühbyzantinischen Reiches. *Jahrbuch*
           für Antike und Christentum 33: 36-52.
1996   Germanenmission. *Reallexikon der germanischen Altertumskunde* Vol.
           10: 492-582. Berlin: W. de Gruyter.
Schmidt, L.
1941   *Die Ostgermanen. Geschichte der deutschen Stämme bis zum Ausgang*
           der Völkerwanderung, 2. München: Beck.
Schwarcz, A.
1984   Reichsangehörige personen gotischer Herkunft. Prosopographische
           Studien. Phil. Dissertation. Universität Wien.
1987   Die Anfänge des Christentums bei den Goten. *Miscellanea Bulgarica*
           5: 107-118.
Seeck, O.
1876   *Notitia Dignitatum.* Berlin: Weidmann.
1921   *Geschichte des Untergangs der antiken Welt*, 6 vols. Stuttgart:
           Siemenroth und Troschel.
Stein, E.
1959   *Histoire du Bas-Empire*, 2 vols. J.-R. Palanque (ed. & trans. for vol. 1),
           E. Stein (trans. for vol. 2). Paris/Brussels/Amsterdam: Desclée de
           Breuwer.

Thompson, E. A.
 1966   *The Visigoths in the Time of Ulfila.* Oxford: Oxford University Press.
de Vries, J.
 1956   *Altgermanische Religionsgeschichte*, 2 vols. (Grundriss der gemanischen
             Philologie, 12). Berlin: de Gruyter. [Repr. 1970].
Wolfram, H.
 1990   *Die Goten. Von den Anfängen bis zur Mitte des 6. Jahrhunderts. Versuch
             einer historischen Ethnographie.* [3rd edition]. Munich: Beck.
Zeiller, J.
 1918   *Les origines chrétiennes dans les provinces danubiennes de l'empire
             romain.* Paris: E. de Boccard.
Zelzer, M. (ed.)
 1982   *Sancti Ambrosi Opera. Pars decima. Epistularum liber decimus. Epistula
             extra collectionem. Gesta concilii Aquileiensis. Corpus Scriptorum
             Ecclesiasticorum Latinorum, Vol. LXXXII.* Vienna: Hoelder-Pichler-
             Tempsky.

Discussion

WOOD: A general question: I wonder, given that you talk about Orthodox Christians among the Goths, whether before 376 the Christians among the Goths would have seen themselves as belonging to different Christian groups or whether the distinction really only came after 381.

SCHWARCZ: Well I think that this depends on the whole development of the Christological strife in the fourth century. What seems clear to us today was not at all clear to all that the participants in the theological debate in the Empire. No one thought in the beginning that they finally were going to develop into different Christian denominations. So, it is a different answer to your question for the first part of the century when, for instance, the followers of Arius probably thought they were the only right thinking ones and all the others were not orthodox. And slowly this kind of distinction developed in the second half of the century and especially, I think, the turning point is here about 380. And specially when in the quarrels between rival theological factions, the party of those now called Arians but who were theologically rather 'Homoeans' were driven from the cities in the middle of the realm of Valentinian II. They seem mostly to have gone to the settlements of the Goths and there tried to influence those who were already Christians to side with them.

DE JONG: On page 447, concerning religion and tribal identity, the first paragraph and, Andreas [Schwarcz], some reflections to see whether I can get you to agree with me [laughter].

SCHWARCZ: I will see what I can do.

AUSENDA: You have a right to disagree once only [laughter].

DE JONG: This is about your opening paragraph, where you discuss cult and religion as central aspects of collective and individual identity in tribal society. In the rest of this paragraph I substituted the expression 'tribal society' by any post-

Roman Christian society or early medieval *gens*, and it actually works quite well. Your statement that "whoever denies sacrifice and worship to the tribal deities may exclude him- or herself from the tribal community", this could also go for the various post-Roman polities where the *gens* was defined in terms of a New Israel: the community of the Goths, the Franks, etc. What I'm getting at is: how different are these 'tribal communities' you are conjuring up from any other situation in which religious unity sustained political identity?

SCHWARCZ: I say this is a question which cannot be answered generally. Of course there the question of collective identity which is generated in tribal societies by the common worship of the gods of the tribe and in the Roman Empire by the state. But subsequently there is the question of tolerance expressed, for instance, for the Jews. There the situation is quite different, for instance, their situation was still better during the Carolingian reign in east *Francia*, than it was in contemporary Spain. There they took over the line of the anti-Jewish laws of Byzantium of the time of Justinian, and the situation of the Jews in Spain changed for the worse in the course of the seventh century. There is also the question of tolerance that the Islamic law extended to Christians.

But, on the whole, I would say about the question of identity for Christian society and for Islamic society, it was not so different from what I said about tribal societies.

DE JONG: Yes, this is, I think, what we were discussing this morning with regard to Peter [Heather]'s remark about the universality of Christianity. I then maintained that early medieval Christianity often was exclusive, in that one had to profess oneself a Christian in order to belong to the Visigothic political community. For this very reason the Jews could not be part of the Visigothic *populus*.

SCHWARCZ: Of course, excommunication and other legal pressures like banishment mean that people were expelled from society.

DE JONG: I hesitate to say this, for I'd rather keep the tribes out of it, but, according to your definition, early medieval Christianity would have a tribal element.

SCHWARCZ: This is what I would say.

GREEN: Why not keep the word 'tribal' there then?

DE JONG: Andreas [Schwarcz] is talking about pre-Christian tribes, and I am wondering whether what he says makes any sense for Christian post-Roman communities who defined themselves as *gentes*—and if not, why not?

SCHWARCZ: Yes, I agree to that.

DE JONG: Yes, of course, for certain emperors.

HEATHER: There are more than a few hints in different contexts that there is some kind of expectation that political victory and domination will be followed by the implanting of the victors' religious cult, not to the exclusion of the cult of the losers maybe, but in addition to it. I think of some seventh century examples in Anglo-Saxon England as recorded by Bede, where Christianity seems to be spread with the overlordship and so on. And there are one or two instances, I think, in the pattern of *Tervingi* and Roman relations where Constantine's victory has Christianizing overtones and then a change in the political dimension precedes the expulsion of Ulfila.

WOOD: In England the model you are suggesting is associated with Christian overlords much more than with pagan ones.

HEATHER: Yes they couldn't be more aggressive.

AUSENDA: Could I suggest that Christianity is more powerful than tribal religion?

HEATHER: Yes, but I think you also have to have a model which includes the effects of pagans being exposed to aggressive Christianity. Medieval Lithuania is a classic example, where aggressive Christinanization produces a pagan religion which is much more like Christianity in terms of its power and self projection. And it does seem to me in the Anglo-Saxon context that these Saxons who had taken over from Christian Britons, their religion was going to be changed by that conflict. Anglo-Saxon religion in 600 is not going to be the same as it was in 400.

WOOD: That's why I wouldn't want to call it traditional religion; it's actually a rather new paganism.

HEATHER: Yet it's changing and, for the Goths, for instance, like Masłomęc evidence suggests something very different in the burial practice about beliefs in the afterlife.

SCHWARCZ: Yes, that is a point I want to make about archaeology because especially Bierbrauer very much stresses the continuity of the Goths in the different archaeological cultures which are attributed to them, whereas we must also consider the question of in what way the Goths were accepted as part of these cultures. I also wanted to point out that not everything is continuous there, but that the new environment certainly shows acculturation and dependence on the new surroundings and, of course, a corresponding change of customs.

GREEN: I think the other point which can be made is to stress the essential difference between a polytheistic and a monotheistic religion, in that the former is ready to add a new God to its pantheon, even if it were a Christian god, whereas of course with Christianity that's excluded.

SCHWARCZ: But not completely so, because just the process of Christianization shows that Christianity picks up a lot of traditional religion.

GREEN: Yes, yes. Not officially acknowledged.

SCHWARCZ: By the way it cannot be the other way around, that's the difference.

GREEN: On page 447-8 concerning the Wielbark culture, runic inscriptions and *Lugii*. I have three points there. Just a small one first, Andreas: in English we normally have the Polish spelling for Oksywie with a ks not an x.

SCHWARCZ: Yes, I took the Polish spelling.

GREEN: Yes, then there should be a ks; it isn't there, not x.

SCHWARCZ: The Polish publication I have shows x. The Germans write it Oxhöft.

GREEN: The question I had to ask about this is: how do you see the Wielbark culture developing approximately out of the Oksywie one?

SCHWARCZ: Well there is, of course, a lot of archaeological discussion going on. But possibly we may take the most modern version of this that the Oksywie culture was the primary stage of Wielbark.

GREEN: So, essentially, you see them as one but in a different time continuuum.

SCHWARCZ: Yes it's the first stage ever around 200 BC.

HEATHER: The basic difference between the stages is that they stop burying with weapons. Which means that something funny has happened to their belief structures, whatever it is.

SCHWARCZ: One of the most significant things is where and when you notice any change.

GREEN: My second point then concerns runic inscriptions. I would like you to specify these because one is struck above all by the paucity of Gothic runic inscriptions. Have you or someone else come up with new runic inscriptions in Gothic?

SCHWARCZ: There are some new examples usually on pottery and combs and household ware, but there are just signs, no words.

GREEN: Just odd signs, but nothing one could interpret linguistically.

SCHWARCZ: Nothing that one can interpret linguistically except for the known ones.

GREEN: And, thirdly, at the end of the first long paragraph you say "it is unlikely that there was a cult community with the neighbouring Lugian confederation". Would you be ready to accept that there was a kind of community with the Lugian confederation, even though it was not a cult community with them?

SCHWARCZ: Well, there you have to make a comparison of the written sources and of archaeology, which I didn't go to great lengths with here, to work this out. The answer is clear if you read the historical sources for the first century AD. By comparing those notices of Tacitus (*Germania* 44. 1) and the elder Plinius (*Historia naturalis* 4. 99 & 37. 35) with the texts before, especially what changed from Pytheas of Marseille to his citations by Pliny (see above) about the mention of *Gotones*, to the one by Tacitus, you get an approximate dating for the formation of the *Gotones*. I took a close look at the foundations of the assumption of a cult community. It is simply an assumption by the fact that the *Tervingi* are named once beside the *Lugii* and another time beside the Vandals in both this sense and in both items there is not a word about a cult community. And so you cannot infer it really from the written sources, and the archaeology shows that the burial rites are totally different. So this is one of the things I wouldn't hesitate to call a speculation.

HEATHER: On page 449 concerning entirely local cults. I was quite surprised that you were so confident that there cannot have been a single object for the whole tribe, that each *kuni* had its own separate cult object.

SCHWARCZ: On this I just follow Thompson (1966) and Wolfram (1990) not because I'm totally convinced that it couldn't be possible, but there is the logistic argument that these objects must be taken around; there would have been a lot of difficulty to drive one object around the whole territory.

HEATHER: Yes, what I had in mind was what we have been talking about a minute ago, the effect of Roman Christianity on Gothic paganism, making it more coherent and aggressive. I take your point about logistics, and it may be not have been done by driving around, but it surely wouldn't be very surprising if there was some kind of communal cult in addition to whatever other local ones existed.

SCHWARCZ: Yes, I agree to taking into account the growing political role of Athanaric after 369, so I wouldn't completely exclude it. So I am less positive about this than you. There is a basic difficulty that having doubts that there was, we are going against the sources. And the source says there is one object.

GREEN: On page 449 concerning shamanism. I don't wish to deny in principle the possibility of an influence of shamanism on the Goths, but I do strongly express doubts about the kind of argument which has been put forward by Scardigli.

SCHWARCZ: Yes, I know it.

GREEN: He takes a number of words in Gothic for which no known Indo-European etymology has been established and says "These are obviously signs of non-Indo-European influence from the steppes in the sphere of shamanism". I think that is completely unproven. It may be that some of the words in fact are expressive of shamanism, but you cannot establish it by that kind of negative argumentation. But the possibility exists, I don't call that into question. One word which cropped up in my paper might point in that direction—although even here one has to be careful—the word for 'hemp' or *cannabis*, that could point in that direction, but not necessarily; in fact Herodotus, for example, says expressly of the Scythians that they were acquainted with *cannabis*, but did not use it to induce any form of ecstasy in them.

SCHWARCZ: Well, I agree and that's why I was so careful not to be too specific about shamanism because I don't agree that there is a written source which can prove it and I am a bit sceptical about this, but also about the signs of shamanism assumed by archaeological science. But there are at least in the archaeological material some indications that it might be so.

DIAZ: On page 450, concerning sacrifices to the river god and possible memory in Alaric's funeral ceremony, what do you think about the relation between the sacrifice to the river god and its possible memory in the burial ceremony of Alaric?

SCHWARCZ: I think mainly of the combination that in the one case it is sacrifice, in the other case it's assuring the protection of the river god for the dead, even if Alaric should have been and certainly was a Christian.

DIAZ: Well, it is curious that it occurs in the burial ceremony of Alaric.

SCHWARCZ: I am sceptical about the whole burial ceremony because it seems to me that the account parallels what is said about Attila. So, I would not completely exclude that this is a ritual, but we can call it either way. That's what made me suspect. And, you see, Jordanes knew what was said about Attila and it seems to be a doublet.

WOOD: Javier Arce thinks that the description of Attila's funeral may be derived from the descriptions of Roman funerals.

SCHWARCZ: Yes, so I don't want to find the grave in the Busento because I'm not quite sure that it ever was there.

HEATHER: I have another question on page 450, because there are a lot of reasons why you might live by a river, logistic, economic, and other, and we have bog people executions as well without river gods. Do we have any other kind of reference to river gods?

SCHWARCZ: Not so many, but I mention it only as a possibility. But the thing about this that there must have been something about hydronymics because they keep the old names while the settlements change.

WOOD: You would do better in that first sentence of that first paragraph on page 450 to say "A special worship 'might' be assumed", because that is rather more positive.

SCHWARCZ: 'Might' is better.

AUSENDA: Well the river god was quite popular also among the Goths in Ravenna. Do you remember the river god in the central mosaic of the baptism of Christ in the Arian baptistry?

WOOD: It's the Jordan and it's in both the Arian and the Catholic tradition.

SCHWARCZ: And one has to have settlements by the river. I was struck by the enormous amount of settlements that they had. At the Caputh conference on the Cherniakhov culture there was a lecture in Cherniakhov settlements and there were at least 7,000 of them in the Ukraine. They were distributed according to the size of the rivers.

HEATHER: Will that be published?

SCHWARCZ: I hope so.

GREEN: On page 450 Ares and Mars, then Pietroassa. At the end of your first paragraph where you say that the name of the Gothic god of war *Teiws*, may have been replaced by the name Ares and/or Mars. Here you are following Wolfram and it's a point where I find it difficult to agree with him. The only ground for his belief I can possibly imagine is the fact that there are a number of Christian loan-words of Greek origin in Bavarian, especially in the names of days of the week for which Gothic transmission is likely to be the explanation. And the Bavarian word for Tuesday, Ertag would go back then to a Gothic *Arjaus dags* which would be the equivalent of Greek *Areos hemera*, the day of Ares, Tuesday therefore. The trouble with that is this: one has to place this argument in a much wider context, the context of naming of the days of the week in Europe at large, where the Western Church follows a different model from the Eastern Church. The Western Church was unprepared or unable to avoid making use of the names of the planetary divinities in the names of the days of the week from Sunday, Monday, Tuesday, Wednesday and so on, whilst the Eastern Church for the most part avoided that by using either specifically Christian words such as Sabbath (post-Sabbath pro-Sabbath also occur) or making use of numbered days of the week. There are, of course, reflections of both these methods in various vernaculars. On the Western side we have it in Germanic, Celtic and Romance, and on the Eastern side we have it in Greek, but also in Hungarian, in some cases, in Slavonic and in Gothic insofar as Gothic can be reconstructed from the few examples which we have in Wulfila plus these examples from Bavaria. Now, if that is the case, the Eastern Church and these vernacular reflections of Eastern terminology go out of their way to avoid making reference to pagan divinities, which makes it philologically much more likely that, if the Goths took over a word such as *Arjaus dags* from Greek *Areos hemera*, they were taking it over merely as the name of a day of the week and not as the name of a deity which they worshipped in place of their Germanic deity. Precisely the fact that eastern Europe exercises this Christian censorship on such naming makes it highly unlikely that the Goths took over this word as an explicitly pagan term.

SCHWARCZ: Well, I wondered too over the possibility that taking over the worship of the war god meant, as you claim, that they actually took over the name of the god of their Iranian neighbours. But it must hold water.

GREEN: I'm prepared to accept it as a possibility of syncretism, but I don't think you can prove it along that line.

SCHWARCZ: This is why I didn't take in the Iranian possibility. It's only a thought, but I think if one takes a look at mass movements, one must take the idea that they took over with their movement in new areas also the worship of the gods they found there, not only the Roman and Greek ones.

HEATHER: But having conquered the Ukraine, were they likely to abandon their own name for the war god and take on the river gods of those they conquered?

SCHWARCZ: That is a question of who they thought was important at the moment. This is the trouble with tribal relations where they are so open, they can take in any new god that appears.

GREEN: Yes, but under these conditions, I think you are much more likely to be willing to take in rather than to drop, especially when the god in question has proved a success.

SCHWARCZ: But, you see, to say something new on the gods, we should have new material for these names possibly. But we haven't got anything new. Even with the new reading of the ring of Pietroassa we cannot prove anything.

GREEN: Yes, but the counter-argument there is that the god Tius is attested in other Germanic dialects and you would need to come up with a very strong argument to say that something so widespread in *Germania* is not to be found in Gothic.

SCHWARCZ: Well, exactly the difficulty I have with Tius is that all the others are burying their warriors with weapons and the Goths don't. So I'm not so convinced they called the god of war Tius even when they were in Poland.

GREEN: Yes, but in that case that argument applies just as strongly against their using the names Ares or Mars as it does against their using the vernacular Tius.

DE JONG: Also what you said about the openness of the tribal religion contradicts your first paragraph about the people's, the Goths' identity.

SCHWARCZ: But the myth certainly changes even if it is very rigid at the moment, but it may change within a century.

DE JONG: OK, yes.

SCHWARCZ: And I didn't mention a few other things which happened in the changeover from Wielbark to Cherniakhov which are also rather interesting points, for instance, there is horse burial in Cherniakhov.

DE JONG: Horse burial?

SCHWARCZ: Of course there was horse burial within Cherniakhov, sometimes even half a horse, I think, taken over from their Sarmatian neighbours so there must have been religiously a lot of syncretism going on in the third century and so I said openly the only thing which prevented me from omitting the thing about Ares and Mars was that at least for this one there was some sort of argument or else I would not have written that you can say nearly nothing about the high gods.

GREEN: I have got a second point on that page, if I may, on the inscription on the ring of Pietroassa. I must confess, I haven't read the article by Hermann Reichert. But I would add though that I, too, in the sixties spent a week working on that ring in the vaults of the State Bank in Bucharest with a couple of Romanian police standing around me all the time. The trouble with interpreting this inscription is that the ring, as you know, is broken in half, and it's broken at precisely the point which gives rise to the difficulty of interpretation. There are two readings possible at this break and the trouble is that the runic sign in question for each of the two possibilities is so close that it is difficult to make a distinction between them, especially if you bear in mind that the break in the ring runs vertically through the middle of the character in question. Either reading is possible: either a long o or a j. The peculiarity about runic signs is that they are not just letters of an alphabet, they are also symbolic characters standing for a concept and, therefore, a magic wish for fulfillment of that concept. In Germanic the long *o* stands for *oi°al*, meaning 'landed property', 'landed wealth' and the sign *j* stands for *jer*, meaning not 'year' but 'prosperous year, a good harvest'. Now, I don't intend to dismiss Reichert's interpretation in terms of *j*, but I wish merely to keep both possibilities open. It is, as far as I can see, impossible to read that break in the ring clearly enough to say that it is one character rather than another. I think one must keep one's mind open as regards both possibilities.

SCHWARCZ: Well, what I want to say about this is that they even made a clay of this with these new materials where you get very exact impressions and they went on to make photogrammetric pictures with special equipment at an institute for these studies. There are some scratches which used to be taken as an indication of the upper part of a letter. Now it seems that these are really only scratches whereas the lower part of this letter is very clearly incised. So they threw out the o and it is pretty sure that it is a j.

GREEN: The trouble is, of course, that the ring was snapped by a thief in the nineteenth century, it was snapped with some form of pliers and the metal is abrased to a degree. But I would still wish to plead strongly for keeping an open mind on this.

SCHWARCZ: I'll send you a copy of the paper on this. Reichert is pretty sure and he only got this by the other part of the letter.

HEATHER: On page 451, on Theophilos. You make a perfectly fair point about how the Cherniakhov relates to later Goths in the Crimea. But Theophilos signs Nicaea near the Pontic bishops which is what led me to take that point of view.

SCHWARCZ: Ah, well one argument I didn't put in was the lecture of Alexander Popa (unpublished) last year who seems to have indications that in the southern part of the Cherniakhov culture near the Pontic coast there are a lot of stone buildings some of which could be interpreted possibly as churches but he hasn't got any further proof, it is just a suspicion. That's why I strongly suspect that the *Gothia* of Theophilos is not totally identical with the one of Wulfila. It may be that the whole space north and west of the Black Sea coast was under the influence of the imperial Church at the beginning of the fourth century and not exclusively the Tervingian region but it is also quite sure from the reports of the archaeologists from the Ukraine at the Caputh conference of 1995 (unpublished) who occupied themselves with the Cherniakhov culture, and from the lecture of Bierbrauer's pupil Karl von der Lohe about the Crimean Goths, that we must exclude an early dating of the Crimean bishopric. Karl von der Lohe spent six months in the Ukraine and returned with special results on the Crimea.

I think it is quite clear that the first indications of anything of Cherniakhov culture in the Crimea are from the last quarter of the fourth century.

HEATHER: I am happy to withdraw. A Bishop Theophilos signs the acts of Nicaea and no one knows where he comes from, it's just that he signs near the Pontic bishops.

SCHWARCZ: With the list of the approving bishops?

HEATHER: That's right. Had they done any more work—it wouldn't be the Ukrainians, it would be the Romanians, and I wouldn't know it they were at the conference—on when you start getting the Cherniakhov material between the Carpathians and the Danube? The Roman Empire cleared the *Carpi* out of that region up to the early fourth century and Goths moved in behind them, it's quite a tight time frame to get Theophilos in there already by 325.

SCHWARCZ: I think that this is another point to take. I would say that it is impossible to get the Goths into the Danube region that early. So it must be further north much nearer to the coast. There are all indications that it's rather later in the third century that they began to move into the Carpathian region, and before they reached the Danube there is still a great time gap because that is in the second part of the fourth century.

GREEN: On page 452 concerning Constantius II. You say quite rightly that Constantius II was especially honoured in the Gothic calendar. I merely add that he is also especially honoured by the Gothic term for the supreme ruler *thiudans*. I think both go together.

SCHWARCZ: Of course yes.

HEATHER: But is *thiudans* more than just the translation of emperor?

GREEN: Well it is in Gothic terms normally a term for the king, but then here it is applied.... But also the interesting thing is that, as late as the Old Saxon Heliand, middle of the ninth century, the corresponding word in Old Saxon, *ceodon*, is about Christ but also for the Roman emperor.

HEATHER: Do we have no other Gothic reference to what they call the emperor?

VOICES: No.

GREEN: Except the name *kaisar* is used not as a name but to indicate an emperor. And there is naturally no native Gothic term for it.

SCHWARCZ: And what was their expression for the other imperial title in Greek, *basileus* = *rex*?

GREEN: The word *reiks* is used by Wulfila also, I mentioned it this morning, as a negative term, in the sense of tyranny, used as the devil's tyranny over men in enslaving them. I suspect that he has in mind there the wide excessive authority, not of Rome, because Rome for him is already a Christian Rome, I suspect the authority exercised by someone like Ermanaric. But that's a hypothesis.

JIMENEZ: On page 454, concerning Fritigern's conversion from pagan religion to Christianity. What I fail to understand is why could Fritigern move so quickly from traditional religion to Christianity?

SCHWARCZ: Well he could because it is in the century of the Christian conversion of the Goths and it is the turning point of Christianity with the Goths. And he is not the only one. If you take a look at all those *Passiones* and *Vitae* we have a special reference to Gothic aristocracy. It is quite clear that in a lot of these cases the debate about religion went on all the time among the class of the *reguli*, and that people are converted individually. And some of them stayed behind after the arrival of the Huns, for instance the widow of the Gothic prince Arimir, Gaatha and her daughter Dulcilla. Up to the eighties of the fourth century, the people north of the Danube were still Christian there and they had no need to become converted by going over the river into the Empire, they were converted north of the Danube. So, I think it is much more plausible that an already christianized part of the *Tervingi* had arrived at the Danube in 376 and were let in just because of this, because there already was a precedent, and Romans liked to act upon precedent, there was the precedent of the reception of Wulfila in 348-49. So this could have established a precedent according to which the followers of Fritigern were treated. To suppose that Fritigern and his followers were converted after crossing the Danube brings another difficulty: the fourth century had many precedents on what happened if a foreign group got converted. That would have implied a grand ceremony at Constantinople with the emperor officially sponsoring the baptism. And this is just what was not done in this case, but immediately before the battle of Hadrianople, Fritigern sent a special envoy, a presbiter, to Valens and that means that it was someone he completely trusted, so much that he gave him messages he might not even have discussed with his closest warriors.

GREEN: May I come in here? Andreas [Schwarcz], I find fascinating what you said (these are your words, I think) about "individually converted". Can you tell us what the evidence is for that?

SCHWARCZ: Well, there is the evidence of the *passiones* collected by Hippolyte Delehaye in *Analecta Bollandiana*, especially the *Passio sancti Sabae*. It is Saba who gets killed as a martyr and....

HEATHER: And an unnamed one.

SCHWARCZ: So we must presume that like in the Empire before 313 there had been many individual conversions.

HEATHER: Otherwise Athanaric's persecution of Christians does not make any sense. There wouldn't have been anyone to persecute.

SCHWARCZ: This would assume that even after 349 there were many Christians among the *Tervingi*. If every Christian was driven out then why was it necessary to start another persecution after 369?

AUSENDA: And then there is the evidence of golden crosses in early Langobardic burials. They might have been individually converted before the mass conversion of 568.

SCHWARCZ: It is possible.

HEATHER: You always have to think of conversion as a process. And I don't think that there is any argument between anyone as to what the process of Gothic conversion is, nor over the time frame, or some of the different elements in Ulfila's time, the various other bishops who are mentioned as being active at different moments. There had clearly been a steady but certainly substantial conversion north of the Danube. And whether you place Fritigern's adherence to Christianity between 370 and 376, which Andreas [Schwarcz] would do following Socrates, or in 376 doesn't change the process.

SCHWARCZ: It doesn't change the general picture, but these are precedents and I'm quite sure that the conversion of Fritigern was before he asked for acceptance.

GREEN: How independent of that context?

SCHWARCZ: I think it must have been that much before that it was an accepted fact.

HEATHER: One can fight about this, but that's absolutely pointless. I think all I would want to do here is underline the issue. The issue is how you think Socrates lines up against Ammianus. Do you think Socrates' account of Fritigern's conversion, which takes place in the context of a conflict with Athanaric, is talking of a separate sequence of events from Ammianus's account of the break-up of the *Tervingi*, i.e. Alavivus and Fritigern leading part of the *Tervingi* south of the Danube in 376? If you think of those as two separate sets of events then you place Fritigern's conversion between 370 and 376. My own feeling is that Socrates is actually feeding you a confused version of what Ammianus says. Therefore, I place the conversion in 376. But this doesn't really change the process. Just one or two comments on Andreas [Schwarcz]'s additional verbal arguments. Valens was in Antioch in 376 and engaged in the Persian war and, for two years, he was not able to detach himself to come to the Balkans, and he could not detach any kind of army for one year. I am not sure, therefore, that the lack of a reception ceremony is terribly impressive evidence.

SCHWARCZ: But I think they would have made war for this. They were discussing the reception of the Goths in the imperial *consistorium* and, according to Ammianus, the emperor and his advisers were quite satisfied that they could take them.

A point which must be also taken into account is Eunapius' mention of barbarians taking bishops and monks over the Danube and hiding their wooden heathen symbols. Such a thing, I quite agree, cannot be attributed exclusively to the Goths, because he does not mention them in this case. But just in this period those which mostly arrived were Goths, Huns and Alans, and it certainly makes sense for the Goths.

AUSENDA: A general question which relates indirectly to Andreas [Schwarcz]'s paper. I understand that Goths were not Arian but Homoean, hence they were in line with the accepted creed during the fourth century.

HEATHER: Until 380.

AUSENDA: When did Catholic Christianity reject the Homoean version, was it during the Council of Constantinople of 381? How then were these Homoeans perceived by their contemporaries as Arians, witness Gregory of Tours who twice in his *Histories* refers to Arius as having being damned and having lost his bowels in the outhouse, and the same opinion in the *History* of Paul the Deacon, plus that labelling of churches and baptistries in Ravenna?

SCHWARCZ: Yes, that is a good question. You see, at the turn of the fourth to the fifth century the fate of Roman Arianism was decided in a way that practically everyone who held a middle position between Arians and Orthodox beliefs was labelled an 'Arian', and both these and the fully Arian bishops became a persecuted minority.

HEATHER: Their allies the Homoiousians as well.

SCHWARCZ: Yes and a lot of other people, and everyone who was not orthodox according to the established law. So all those who had a position near the Arian one got labeled in the fifth century as 'Arians' and this is why the Visigoths, Vandals, Ostrogoths and Burgundians were labelled 'Arian' by their Catholic contemporaries. This is a process like Christianization itself that the theological definition of them is different in the fourth century from that in the fifth and sixth, because by then this Homoean position came to be labelled simply as Arian. Yes, but as I said in the morning I am not sure that there was a change of doctrine, but we must take into account that those proponents of Roman Arianism took refuge with these Gothic and Germanic kings and they formulated for the Arians the official theory.

AUSENDA: What I don't understand is why were the Homoeans accepted up to a certain point and then condemned? Was the condemnation sanctioned by the Council of Constantinople?

HEATHER: Yes, Nicaea put forward a definition of faith based on *homoousios*, but that was not accepted by substantial chunks of the East. It looks very much as though Constantine and a few cronies pushed through that definition of faith by strong arm tactics and suddenly found that it was not really acceptable. It took a further 55 years of argument and some redefinition of what *homoousios* meant for it to become something that achieved a critical mass support and could, therefore, be enforced.

SCHWARCZ: I think you must also take into account the Council of Aquileia and the position of Ambrose in Milan. He was able to dominate the last emperor who was Arian. This was Valentinian II and especially his mother Justina who was reigning for him. This middle realm which existed after the usurpation of Maximus and the death of Gratian in the Italian prefecture was, theologically, the last resort of the Arians, where they were able to hold some bishoprics in *Illyria* and even there the Catholics defeated them by the force of Ambrose and in spite of the fact that they were in part protected by the court of Milan.

AUSENDA: There was a theological debate within the Empire which brought to some kind of shift. Is this the position which emerged at the Council of Constantinople in 381?

SCHWARCZ: For the East it is the Council of Constantinople and then it's a question concerning where were bishops able to hold on, who did not subscribe to Constantinople. This is after Theodosius came to the rescue of Justina and Valentinian II. And then it was reduced to the tolerance for barbarians who still had this formula which was confirmed by the Council of Constantinople in 381 and still, concerning some points, by the Council of Chalcedon in 451, because Arianism became the religion of the barbarian soldiers who were necessary to the Empire. And one of the points of conflict of the Vandals especially with the Eastern Empire was that Arians were not tolerated by the Theodosian Code. There were measures against Catholics in the Vandal kingdom. So from a theological discussion between different groups of the same population, a theological discussion developed between a group which gradually became ethnically labelled within the Empire and its mainstream population. And the development of the Christological question in the Empire in the fifth century is dominated by other questions.

WOOD: Well, I think you have to remember that this religious argumentation does not just depend on straightforward intellectual debate; it also depends on linking your enemies with the names of previously condemned groups. By doing that you can put a group which has not yet been condemned, or which is rather more difficult to condemn, in with a group of people who are already defined as being outside orthodoxy.

VOICES: Yes.

HEATHER: That is the problem with the Homoaeans because they are seen as not definitely ruling out Arius. Another interesting element, I think, is also justified by accidental facts, that Constantine chose *homoousios* at Nicaea; he had a weight of conciliar tradition building up. And, once you've defined Nicaea as the great ecumenical council of imperial Christianity, it is very hard, in a long term, to throw out this theological definition to get to the other one, because the change has tremendous implications.

References

Textual sources:

Gregory of Tours
> *Libri historiarum X*: see Krusch & Levison (eds.) 1937-51.
Paul the Deacon
> *Historia Langobardorum*: see Waitz *et al.* (eds.) 1878.
Pytheas of Marseille
> *Fragmenta*: see Stichtenoth 1959:90.
Pliny the elder
> *Historia naturalis libri XXXVII*: see Rackham (ed.) 1975.
Tacitus, Gaius Cornelius
> *Germania*: see Winterbottom (ed.) 1975.

Bibliography:

Bierbrauer, V.
> 1994   See References at end of paper.
Delehaye, H.
> 1912   See References at end of paper.
Krusch B., & W. Levison (eds.)
> 1937-51   *Gregorii Turonensis Opera.* Teil 1. *Libri historiarum X. Monumenta Germaniae Historica. Scriptores rerum Merovingicarum,* 1. Hannover: Hahn.
Rackham, H. (ed.)
> 1949-52   *Pliny the Elder. Historia Naturalis Libri XXXVII.* Cambridge, MA: Harvard University Press.
Reichert, H.
> 1991-93   See References at end of paper.
Scardigli, P.
> 1964   *Lingua e storia dei Goti.* Florence: Sansoni editore.
Stichtenoth, D.
> 1959   *Pytheas von Marseille, über das Weltmeer. Die Fragmente übersetzt und erläutert von D. Stichtenoth.* Köln/Graz: Böhlau.
Thompson, E. A.
> 1966   *The Visigoths in the Time of Ulfilas.* Oxford: Oxford University Press.
Waitz, G. *et al.* (eds.)
> 1878   *Scriptores rerum Langobardicarum et Italicarum saec. VI-IX. Monumenta Germaniae Historica.* Hannover: Hahn.
Winterbottom, M. (ed.)
> 1975   *Tacitus. Germania.* Oxford: Oxford University Press.
Wolfram, H.
> 1990   See References at end of paper.

Location of Visigoths in space and in time

Heather opened the session by referring to the mention made during the preceding discussions of a 'first shuffling process' which had presumably taken place in the Balkans.

Green noted that the Balkan area was a lacuna in the preceding discussion since both Schwarcz and Heather had accounted for the Goths down to the north Pontic region and the participants "moved with an enormous jump to Aquitaine and Spain" leaving out the Balkans in what appeared to him as an "obvious lacuna", although he admitted that his "disciplinary point of view" (linguistics) would have had little to contribute to that. He had mentioned "one clear Gothic term" which could be located in the Balkans, while others "had been bedevilled by linguistic chauvinism", so that his contribution was at best "very much open to question".

Schwarcz seconded Green's remarks adding that the continuity of the *Tervingi* involved not only Aquitaine and Spain but also countries in between, such as the Balkans in the fifth and sixth centuries and even Italy. Furthermore, archaeology was still to be called into question as to how long the Cherniakhov culture lasted and where.

Heather agreed that the Cherniakhov culture should be a primary factor on the agenda. He asserted that there was "an awful lot of work going on" and there even was a "race in publishing the results" so that the question of the "further transformation of Gothic culture from 373/5 onwards" could very well be more thoroughly discussed at the first meeting.

Schwarcz cautioned the audience to the fact that there still was disagreement "on the points of interest". In fact, some archaeologists, such as V. Bierbrauer were "against a long continuity" of Cherniakhov people, especially those of the Crimea

---

[1] As this chapter is aimed at listing ideas to be researched for a future meeting on the subject, it behooves the series editor to make such comments as may help orient said research. While acknowledging the unconditional enthusiasm of some participants to this meeting for the idea that the Visigoths and Hispano-Romans had achieved a 'mixed society', without specifying the proportion of the 'mixture', as it might be represented by a point on a continuum ranging between 0 and 100%, I am nevertheless bound to the aim of the series which is to find "a new approach to the recovery of the customs and beliefs of the populations which settled in Europe at the close of the Western Roman Empire" (Ausenda 1995:1); in other words focussing on a post-Classical rather than a pre-modern approach, I hope that I will be forgiven if, in the subsequent comments and for the interest of further research along the guidelines which introduced the series, I will focus more on the differences rather than on the similarities, in an effort to motivate future researchers to thoroughly canvass the evidence, both historical and archaeological, for clues to the characteristics of those societies. The ensuing comments were contributed by the series editor when they pertained to anthropological examples and details, and by Pablo C. Diaz, who was present throughout the concluding discussion, when they pertained to historical examples and details.

and the Ukraine after 376, while others, such as Godłowski, thought of a continuation right into the first quarter ot the fifth century. Answering a question, he affirmed that, to his knowledge, dendrochronology had not been used, and that most of the evidence relied on the dating of pottery.

Heather and *Wood* agreed that for both north and south of the Danube both the literary evidence and archaeology left considerable problems and gaps.

Schwarcz added that there was so much "archaeologically disturbing" that since he had published his study shortly after Heather's book, which seemed to have been its direct parallel, he had only found *fibulae* south of the Danube, and since then he had become acquainted with the publications of Theodora Kowatcheva and Anna Haralambieva and her collection of *fibulae* throughout regional museums in Bulgaria, which could be attributed partly to Cherniakhov and partly to Migration type populations, which continued through the fifth and sixth centuries.

On *Jiménez'* question everyone agreed that one could not speak of Visigoths in the Balkans, but only of Goths.

Heather closed the discussion asserting that no one seemed too interested about Visigoths in Italy and that the particular period was well documented.

Visigoths in Gaul

Green reminded the participants that the topic had "come up for discussion at a number of points on this occasions", but there still was a lot of ground to be covered and that one should look at Gaul "with the idea of links between Goths and Franks and also between Goths and Burgundians". He mentioned Franks first because it was less difficult to "distinguish between Goths and Franks than...between Goths and Burgundians".

Wood remarked that considering Goths and Burgundians amounted to a comparative analysis, whereas the documentation for Frankish settlements was "totally different from the settlement of the Goths". He added that one got the same sort of literary evidence for the Goths in Toulouse and the Burgundians in the kingdom of Lyons-Geneva, the "same types of Latin descriptions reflecting the views of the Gallo-Roman aristocracy on the Germanic courts". The problem was not of making the Goths distinct, but to "look at the integration of barbarians into southern Gallic society" using further material than that already at hand, which was "a lot weaker than what [was available] for the...Burgundians after the 440s".

According to *Heather*, the Visigothic was not the only kingdom "carved out of the Western Empire, between 418 and 476", and the comparison of relations with the Roman state, still in existence, would be revealing.

For *Wood* the comparison between Burgundians and Visigoths would also help highlight the "oddities of the reign of Euric", because one would have there "two extremes, the Burgundians as the most pro-Roman of the successor groups", being even more eager than the Ostrogoths "to retain Roman titles and so on", which would also help to see the extent to which Euric was trying to make a break with Roman tradition.

Schwarcz agreed on the importance of the fifth century in relation to "the question of the transformation of the Roman world", in that Gaul was of central interest, and the Visigothic realm "was the breeding of an Arian realm on Roman territory". The gradual change in Visigothic policies accompanying the succession of kings and the "relations between the Visigoths and the senatorial aristocracy" in addition to the "absence of strife with the Church in that period, contrary to twohundred years later" would provoke fertile discussions.

Barbarians and people in the West

Ripoll considered the topic an 'unknown', not only in Aquitania, but also in *Hispania* in the fifth century.

Jiménez remarked that while in Aquitania there were a lot of ancient sources dealing with those relations, there were very few in *Hispania*.

Díaz agreed that the fifth century was a key century.

De Jong inquired about the information contained in the proceedings of the Councils, and *Jiménez* countered that there were none in the fifth century.

Díaz remarked that the first Toledo Council was in 400 and then there was a gap until 516.

Ripoll noted that "a lot of topics could be attached or discussed for the fifth century and going into the sixth" one of them was 'Mixed populations or new society?' and many others. Answering Heather's question, Ripoll explained that in archaeology there were not many materials, except for ceramics, and that there were sequences both in the numismatic record and in ceramics; in addition there was the possibility of studying rural settlements and their transformation "from the Roman world to Visigothic times". There also was some survey work going on and she cited a student of hers working with Helmut Roth on "The transformation of the Roman *villa* in late antique *Hispania*". It was also noteworthy to study how the "centres of power changed at the end of the fifth century and into the first part of the sixth". She also thought that the topic put forth by *Wood* on 'Originality and derivation of Visigothic sculpture' also came at the end of the fifth century and the beginning of the sixth. According to her "this would lead to understanding the new construction of the Visigothic kingdom in Spain".

Jiménez stressed the necessity of carefully defining the "political terms" relating to the 'kingdom of *Tolosa*' rather than to a 'kingdom of Toulouse' undefined in time. The problem was that of determining the time when a Visigothic king [chief] consciously assumed the role of 'king of *Tolosa*' and whether that kingdom "did really exist".

Heather thought the explanation lay in the fact that that was a "process, not an event". He thought he could safely assume that by the 460s one was dealing with an "independent entity" and in 475, by the time Euric had succeeded to the throne the 'independent entity' had become a kingdom in its own right.

On *Ausenda*'s request for 'directions for further research', *Heather* answered that it was impossible to suggest any directions for further research because of "the absence of an Aquitanian archaeology" which could very well mean that there was nothing. He added that he was interested in finding whether anyone was attempting to do it.

Ripoll ventured that in May of 1996 there was a 'Thèse d'état' on the 'transformation' of a *villa* from the Roman economy to the Visigothic one.

Jiménez asserted that the real problem was that French archaeologists were not interested in Visigothic, but in Gallo-Roman aristocratic remains and *Heather* concurred and mentioned Michel Rousse as an example.

Ripoll dissented mentioning Catherine Balmelle who had "looked for Visigoths in the Provence not only in the archaeological record but also in the textual sources"; on *Heather*'s request she admitted that she was the only one.

Jiménez considered it necessary not to confine the research to fifth-century Gaul but to extend it also to *Hispania* and consider "both realities together", because in the latter several "marginal" regions were contiguous with the *Narbonensis* and *Aquitania*.

Díaz aired the view that the relation of the Visigoths with the *Suebi* in the fifth century was of special importance because their conflict "was the starting point for the access to the South in Mérida, the first area where the Visigoths established a permanent town". At the same time their relations with the Romans continued. The resulting impression was of different relations with the *Tarraconensis*, with the Meseta, or with *Gallaecia*, which were going to define the future of the areas in question.

Heather agreed that the *Tarraconensis* remained more tightly linked longer to the Roman state.

Díaz pointed to the fact that in the fifth century "new local powers" arose in the Iberian Peninsula which were going to become important in subsequent centuries. He cited John of Biclar's chronicle describing "a process of reconstruction of power" regarding not only all the populations which were still part of the *respublica Romana*, but also the "new realities" which arose when there was no central power in the peninsula. Such an interesting topic could be approached through John of Biclar's chronicle.

Velázquez seconded by *Díaz* thought that the relations with Vandals at the frontiers, between *Hispania* and North Africa were quite important.

Ausenda asked whether there were any Tunisian archaeologists interested in the topic; *Ripoll* mentioned the name of Aisha ben Abed ben Qader, of the Institut National du Patrimoine in Tunis, who had worked in the area of the Roman villas in Carthage and on the excavations of a large church in the south of Carthage with Michel Fixot, a French archaeologist; she was also working in the town of Puput near Hammamet.

Velázquez brought up the "relations between the archaeological and the textual sources", meaning by those the "poems about *Gensericus rex*", quite interesting because they mention many buildings and constructions which might be located by archaeology.

Wood summarized the various contributions to the topic by noting that the participants, having "been forced to define what [they] would want to see in the fifth century", were "not just talking about the Visigoths" but "about comparison...or relations with other people". He added that in "the crucial period when the Visigothic *gens* was moving into *Hispania*, the real developments were going to come through comparative work" because the sort of evidence existing for seventh-century Spain, when one could "take Visigothic material on its own", was unavailable for the fifth.

Heather considered that "it was still a very international world" in which "frontiers were created...that did not exist"; this evoked a "realm of...diplomacy or international relations, creating a new world-order, the post-Roman, post-imperial world order". *Wood* agreed that the fifth was "the crucial century...where the major shifts" took place.

De Jong thought that the concept of 'nation' sounded anachronistic when applied to the fifth century.

Citing Suzanne Deillet as an example, *Ripoll* pointed out that many researchers spoke about 'nations' in the sixth century.

Wood countered that, even though anachronistic, the expression 'international relations' was "a good phrase to use for that period, because it made one think about it". He thought one might call it 'inter-gentile', but that the expression "might give the wrong connotation".

Díaz agreed to the number of questions and that the archaeology was limited adding that the *Chronica Caesaraugustana* was of little help, even though, as *Heather* remarked, it was useful in its own right.

Ripoll agreed that the problem was that "archaeology had never paid attention to the fourth, fifth, and sixth centuries; she suggested paying attention to the transformations during the fifth century in adjacent or related lands, and to Barkino in the fifth century; admittedly it was a difficult "exercise of the imagination". She offered the example of the basilica in which "all the persons in the Christian community" were identified as one piece of the puzzle. She thought that the transformations which had been implemented by Liuvigild had their roots earlier, even in Athaulf's time, and that one could try to identify them before the time of Liuvigild.

Heather pointed to "an obvious gap in the meeting" which had been highlighted by Schwarcz when, in the topics for discussion, he listed 'Relations between Visigoths and Ostrogoths'; he noted the use of the expression 'interval' in reference to the Ostrogothic involvement, remarking that "the word 'interval' didn't do justice to the importance of Theoderic's involvement in *Hispania*".

Schwarcz noted there was a lot to say about the relations between those people and of the domination in the Roman Empire in the fifth century (cf. Schwarcz n.d.); he was of the opinion that "the question of archaeology could not be settled without accounting for the reason why the material from the end of the fifth century had direct connections to the Danube and the Black Sea coast, not to Cherniakhov".

Answering *Ripoll*'s query about his question on *Visigothic cemeteries and non-Meseta cemeteries*, *Heather* ventured that "what seemed to [him] to be missing totally from the sixth-century material [was] some idea of what a cemetery not on the Meseta looked like; he noted that the participants only had a "context-less discussion of the Meseta", because "there was no sense of whether there was any difference with cemeteries in the rest of Spain; he was interested in finding out whether there was a 'non-Meseta' cemetery, and whether the cemetery of *Hispales* or any other running into the sixth century had ever been dug up or identified. The question seemed very important in the light of the finds of 'donaulandische pontische material' which had turned up in the Aquitaine; he added that he was not referring to the Visigoths as a people.

Ripoll explained that Spanish archaeology knew the "large cemeteries in the West" but not the rest. Several urban cemeteries were known from the beginning of the Christian tradition, such as those at *Tarraco*, or *Santa Maria*, and those related to the presence of a martyr, but they knew little or nothing about other types of urban or rural cemeteries. She went on to answer *Heather*'s query whether Visigothic-type *fibulae* or 'Fibeltracht', according to Völker Bierbrauer, were found also in the "martyrs' cemeteries" which continued into the sixth century, listing the few cemeteries which were known: those of martyrological origin, such as *Santa Maria* and *Tarraco*, plus two- or three-tomb cemeteries in four or five villas, and a little cemetery in Valencia near San Vicente; she concluded that that was "the silence of archaeology".

Retamero would rather call it 'the silence of society' in the sense that fifth-century society lacked "stillness and...stable organization", which meant a "thin evidence"; he suggested envisaging "a new archaeology" based on a different type of research; he remarked that in the light of the "overwhelming evidence left by Visigothic organizations", while the Roman state had vanished and the new one had not been established yet, it made little sense to talk about the "silence of archaeology", but one should rather find the key to the seeming "silence of society".

De Jong interjected that "even if their was no state, people still needed to build and to bury their dead".

Retamero agreed to a point, remarking that "the buildings and remains would not be comparable to Roman remains, or those left in Mérida in the sixth and seventh centuries"; *De Jong* countered that archaeology was not primarily looking for buildings.

Ripoll concluded that she only wanted to state that only three or four cemeteries were known from the fifth or sixth centuries, eliciting *Heather*'s remark that there was a "very interesting body of material from the Setif cemeteries" and that "one of the priorities was to make sense of it"; he insisted on the need for comparative evidence in *Hispania*. Based on which *Díaz* suggested studying the archaeological remains of the *Suebi* in the sixth century.

Schwarcz was of the opinion that dynastic changes could not be highlighted anyhow, and that there was no relation between the *Suebi* in *Suebia* and those in *Hispania*.

Ripoll insisted on the changes from the fifth century to the beginning of the sixth and on the possibility of introducing comparative studies between Aquitanian archaeology and *Hispania*, while *Heather* insisted on the importance of Ostrogothic-Visigothic relations.

Wood thought that studying the relations between sixth-century Visigoths and other peoples was not as useful as studying "the relations between the Visigoths and other peoples in the fifth century [which were] ...very useful and not just with the Ostrogoths"; he mentioned the Visigothic-Frankish relations and cited Jinty Nelson's article on queens in the Council of Toledo (1991), which really shed light on Visigothic queenship", as he was struck by the fact that the second signatory of the Council of Toledo III was the queen; he thought that one could "pursue the question of diplomatic relations" to further aspects of royal culture as emerged in the 560s and 570s.

Heather suggested discussing the topics the participants thought "should be covered in terms of the creation of the Visigothic kingdom in *Hispania* in the sixth century, and all the ensuing thrusts and mixed populations, the new kingdom and the dynamics of that".

De Jong admitted she was "struck...by the constant talk of an opposition between *Gothi* and *Romani*, parimarily based on sources like Orosius; she thought the agenda had been "dictated by the Goth-Roman opposition" and would like to hear more on such [presumed] diversity, if one could "get any".

For *Ripoll* the diversity of that society depended on chronology as in the fifth century one could already talk about all being 'Spaniards'. *De Jong* and *Heather* both observed that one had to take into account another kind of diversity, that within the peninsula.

Wood reminded the audience that Isidore made it clear he was dealing with Goths, Vandals and *Suebi*. He had been struck by the fact that Isidore had considered the Vandals worthy of his treatment; he thought the question could be investigated by someone to "approach the issue from a latinist point of view", by looking "at the whole question of *gens* and *lingua* in the prefaces of the Councils of Toledo" which, according to him, were an "absolute textbook set of discussions as to what the king and his bishops were trying to say about the *gentes* and their diverging languages".

Green suggested the name of Roger Wright.

Velázquez concurred on the necessity not to study texts "only with a historiographical criterium"; she thought it necessary to begin by studying the "literary unit" and then "examine the text with historiographical eyes"; she considered texts as grouped in units, for example the letters of bishops in the fifth and sixth centuries, e.g. the letters of Julian of Toledo and Hydatius which should be considered as texts relevant to the *Historia Wambae*. She also advocated a complete interdisciplinary revision, both philological and historical, of the *Etymologiae*.

De Jong was struck by the literarily stereotyped language of the lengthy pieces at the end of the Councils' proceedings, which were quite political because addressed to an "interesting audience".

Velázquez noted that, whereas for the Councils there were "very good critical editions", the same could not be said for many texts, such as, for instance, the large collection of *Patrologiae Latinae* by J.-P. Migne.

Comments on 'Location in space and time'

It is quite clear that more developed and detailed archaeological investigations are needed before one can map a settlement pattern of the Gothic immigration. Nevertheless, one should bear in mind that the demographic presence of the Goths was relatively small,[2] and that, especially during the initial period, the Goths probably utilized perishable materials for many of their dwellings.

During the discussion, the remark was made that deceased people must be buried. Indeed, in the case of other Germanic populations, e.g. the Langobards, several cemeteries have turned up and several more would have been availble for study if they had not been quickly obliterated because they stood in the way of major building programs. This situation will not be corrected unless more stringent laws are issued concerning respect for archaeological sites.

Dwellings and settlements

In Peter Heather's absence [he had to leave the meeting before the end for personal reasons], Dennis H. Green took over the task of chairing it, and asked *Ausenda* to introduce the topic he had listed:

Open and closed settlements, are there any courts in Aquitania and in Hispania?

Ausenda explained that the topic had been suggested to him by a sentence in *Jiménez Garnica*'s paper which stated that "those [Visigoths] who were from military life...were headquartered in cities", and later in the same paper she had stressed "the continuity of clustered and open dwellings" presumably without enclosures; he thought there must have been also rural settlements, as was common for other Germanic populations coming into western Europe. He referred to the Langobards whose many settlements in Lombardy and other regions of Italy were known, even in their own legislation, by the Latin term *curtis* (pl. *curtes*), and that there appeared to have been *curtes* also in Britain; he thought it would have been worthwhile to examine whether there were settlements similar to *curtes* in *Hispania* or *Aquitania*.

Green suggested coupling the suggested topic with the other, also suggested by Ausenda concerning *Rural dwellings of the Goths before crossing the Danube and*

---

[2] Concerning the strength of present-day agro-pastoralist tribes, bearing in mind that modern communications favour population increase, see Ausenda 1995:21.

in Aquitania and Hispania; his point was that both the Latin *curtis* and the Germanic *hof* had "both meanings, namely 'farmyard' or 'rural settlement' and also 'court', in the sense of the residence of the king or a potentate [one will note how the participants often mixed the two meanings, relating to one while the other was being discussed], *Green* thought "that it might help if one would take the two together and see how far they belong together and then separate them out if the need arises".

Schwarcz approved the suggestion to discuss the topic, as he thought it was one of the most complicated and badly explored subjects in the "...question of integration into the Roman Empire and the beginning of the kingdoms founded on the basis of the Roman Empire"; he thought one had to differentiate carefully between tribes and "political and chronological situations", bearing in mind that even during the first three centuries AD, and especially in the fourth, many Germanic groups had "been taken into the Empire and distributed in rural areas according to different legal bases, some as slaves, some as *coloni*, some as *gentiles* with military obligations, and some as regular soldiers with agrarian occupations in peacetime". He stressed the fact that, beginning in the fourth century, different treatments were meted out to "groups which were beaten and then left in place...as a rural population" with the obligation to supply soldiers, such as the Salian Franks by Julian, and others taken into the Empire and immediately taken into the Roman army, not to mention "the complicated question of the development from *dediticii* to *foederati*, and the fact that in the past the tendency was "to lump all together and to make one common picture" which didn't hold at all.

Green remembered having remarked during a previous discussion that for some French place-names containing the name of a tribe, e.g. *Taifali*, or *Alamanni*, or *Frisones*, it was impossible to tell "whether they were 'official settlements' sanctioned and carried through by the Romans when still in occupation of Gaul, and how far, on the contrary, they may have been tribal settlements after the crossing of the imperial frontier".

Jiménez thought that one should consider the difference between the Germanic and the Roman court, agreeing with *Heather* when he said that, bearing in mind the description by Sidonius how the description in the Code of Theoderic II fit better the court of a Roman nobleman than that of a Germanic one.

Schwarcz also noted a tendency by scholars to stress the aspects of *civilitas* neglecting the "Germanic tendencies which show that he [Theoderic II] was not quite romanized"; the king's "preoccupation with his Arian priests and bishops" seemed to confirm Sydonius' implication that "he didn't quite care for theological differences and might not have fully understood them, and the daily hour of piety [Sydonius] described seemed to be a clear diversion from the official model of the senatorial nobleman".

Jiménez recalled Priscus' description of Attila's court, according to her, a typical Germanic court where people ate and drank very much.

Ausenda tried to bring the discussion back to *curtes* as rural settlements; he mentioned Langobardic laws punishing individuals who violated enclosures by throwing arrows or spears across them, and asked Jiménez whether she meant that by 'clustered dwellings' in opposition to 'open dwellings'.

Jiménez asserted that by 'open dwellings' she meant those where a 'mixed population' was settled; she added that hers was not a "physical" but an "ideological" perception based on the fact that no remains of Visigothic settlements had been found either in *Aquitania* or in *Hispania*; her opinion was strenghtened by the fact that in the cemeteries which had been found to date the "Visigoths mixed with the Roman population", so if the "cemeteries were mixed, it was because in the 'physical dwellings' probably people were mixed as well".

Ausenda observed that if the case was as she described, the Visigoths were the only Germanic population which would have settled from the very beginning mixed with the local population, whereas Franks, Anglo-Saxons and Langobards had lived in separate settlements whether in rural areas or in cities; it seemed strange to him that the "Visigoths were the only ones" to have 'mixed'.

Green noted that "it hadn't been said that the Visigoths did not have their dwellings...[but] that there were no traces of them".

Schwarcz stressed the difference between Franks and Anglo-Saxons on the one hand, and Visigoths on the other, in that the Franks who had migrated piecemeal into Roman territory were "soundly beaten by the Roman army...and then left 'in peace' where they were", so that rural settlements were to be expected, whereas in the fourth century the Visigoths had "come in on a military basis and stayed a hundred years in Aquitaine on a military basis...and a Roman basis [added *Jiménez*]. *Schwarcz* continued noting that "in the written evidence there was not much to show that there was a great upheaval in land distribution" and that when the Visigoths had come into Spain, they had done so on military campaigns, leaving garrisons to secure their conquests "for the king who still had his court in Aquitaine"; he thought that a "stronger distribution of settlements" might have been possible in the late fifth century, but mostly in areas where also 'military people' were living who "were settled in the most fertile regions of Castilia". To support his view, he cited an analysis by Bierbrauer (1994) on the distribution of cemeteries showing that they were in "regions with enough water". In his opinion, since there was already a rural population and the Visigoths did not build new villages, they went to "villages which already existed" and lived in "military security with an agrarian occupation in peacetime", he concluded that there were no 'closed', meaning exclusively Visigothic, settlements as the region was "already well populated".

Ausenda was of the opinion that Schwarcz's convictions were not sufficient to rule out the need for more thorough archaeological investigations, as even in the case of an army settling in the huge expanses of *Hispania*, one could not exclude that there might be some detachments which might have settled on their own.

Green was conciliatory in suggesting that Schwarcz's argument did not necessarily exclude Ausenda's proposal. On the question of courts he asked whether in a future session if would be possible to discuss whether there was "any evidence for court offices or court-office holders amongst the Visigoths, as there certainly was amongst the Franks", he added that "if one was dealing with the question of courts, then the actual composition of a court might be of use".

Schwarcz was sure that for the king's court, "there was ample evidence of offices"; the other 'court' was the *curtis*, "the settlement of a peasant with his staff and family"; for this second 'court' there was considerable evidence in the laws, and he suggested comparing Visigothic law with the laws of the Frankish kingdom where there were ample excerpts of legislation for the situation of rural settlements. He asserted that his model did not hold that the Visigoths "didn't settle rurally, but only that one could not expect closed settlements but only mixed ones", a pattern which had to be investigated to understand how they could "function mixed up" in the sense that they "might have lived together" and how "the rural economy and the financing of the state" worked.

Green referred to the double function of a military group from wartime to peacetime when it was more settled around the ruler, which echoed the double function of the Germanic *comitatus*; he also recalled that the word *curtis* was a derivation from the Latin *cohors*, hinting to the fact that a 'court' in time of peace "emerged from the group of warriors when not on the battlefield".

Wood asserted that the problem was one "of identifying Germanic settlers on Roman sites" due mostly to the "difficulties with the archaeology". He concluded that, since there was no Visigothic archaeology in Aquitaine, the Visigoths should be "either in the cities or in the villas". He thought that even in the future one could not reach "clear conclusions" because "unless very different sorts of archaeological sites from those which [had] already been dug up were discovered", it would not be easy to distinguish Roman and Germanic settlers in villas or in villages in their preliminary stages. He allowed for the fact that further north, closer to *Francia*, the pattern changed; he also pointed out the fact that the Anglo-Saxons appeared to be building in styles closer to Brittonic usage than to Saxon buildings on the Continent; as far as using the laws for evidence, the problem was that "provincial Roman law provided a model for Germanic law, once the Germanic peoples were settled", for instance, the "famous farmers' law...which had been identified as being relevant to a Gothic community in Asia Minor, but now regarded as ordinary Byzantine law", was a document "dealing...with what an agrarian community looked like", but turned out to be a description of a late Roman or Byzantine community, not of a Gothic one; he thought that it was "something that could and should be analyzed", but he didn't think it was going to help with the question of highlighting whether Germanic or Roman, but would take one back to the question of describing what Jiménez called an open society, i.e ways of "defining a mixed or open society, not ways of defining what was Germanic".

Schwarcz recalled that in his dissertation he had described the integration [in the Gothic contingent] in 376, which combined groups of Goths, *Alamanni*, Vandals, and Franks "even from the inner parts of the Empire", that one had to "imagine the population of the provinces of the Roman Empire as a mixture with regional spots of concentration of a group or another before the crisis of 376"; this was already a mixed society and he had a "strong suspicion that everyday Roman common law of late Antiquity, showed a great deal of Germanic influence", the same as the 'practices' of the late Roman army in the fourth century when Ammianus Marcellinus, "Julian's very fine army officer", described what his soldiers had taken over from 'barbarian armies', "the way of fighting, of shouting insults at the opponents, of singing songs praising their ancestors before...[a] fight, the necklaces worn by the men which would be worn on the winners' shields"; he always got the impression, when looking at the sources, that "there might not have been all the difference that [one] made out, between the 'normal' population of the Roman Empire and the people just ouside its borders".

Green expressed the idea that in the case of the so-called 'barbarization of the Roman army' it was "not really a case of the Roman army taking over Germanic practices, but that the Roman army was largely composed of Germanic warriors anyhow". "Since Diocletian and Constantine" concluded *Schwarcz*.

De Jong agreed on the composition of the Roman army, but thought it necessary to explain "how great the impact of the army was on the rest of the population".

Schwarcz pointed to the pre-existing mixture in the rural population due to the fact that, because of the "constant manpower shortage" during the last centuries of the Roman Empire so many people were "taken in, distributed in the countryside and given to landowners on a basis which reminds one of the half-free status of medieval times" which coincided with the development of the 'Kolonat'; hence, when entire 'tribes' were settled within the Empire, they "didn't meet an exclusively Roman population" but one "already mixed since centuries" with "greater groups of Germanic people in between", which explained "why acculturation made progress quickly"[3] because there were not two "totally different models which clashed, but only different levels of acculturation which grew together".

On *Ausenda*'s query as to directions of future research on the topic, *Schwarcz* ventured that while the "sources gave a general picture" they did not show how it happened regionally, which still had to be shown.

De Jong agreed adding that the [general] perspective allowed for regional variations, whereas if one maintained that there was a separation between Germanic and Roman social groups and that "they always met the same way", one was "forced to apply the perspective one obtained from Langobardic law to all other situations" which could not be done.

Green summarized Schwarcz's model saying that it did not contemplate separate Germanic and Roman worlds, but "a Germanic world which was already romanized clashing with a Roman world which was already germanized".

De Jong remarked that this was what she "liked so much of Andreas' perspective.

Green reminded the audience that a further topic had been proposed concerning "not only the rural dwellings of Goths in *Hispania*, but also before crossing the Danube and in Aquitaine".

---

[3] Dr. Schwarcz's assertion that "acculturation made progress quickly" is just as much in need of demonstration as the assertion that the Hispano-Romans and the Visigoths were a 'mixed society' as early as the sixth century.

Schwarcz insisted that "there had not been one development to be looked into" because it was "a long phase contact between Germanic peoples and the Roman Empire beginning about the time of Caesar" and going on for centuries producing many "different situations, and the gradual acculturation of both".

Asked by *Green* to say something about the 'Aquitanian problem', *Jiménez* repeated that archaeologists had never seen a Visigothic settlement in Aquitanian remains; she thought they had to approach the situation from another point of view; she noted that the ancient excavations had been made "from the Germanic point of view exclusively" and that all that work had to be revised.

Retamero concurred adding that the problem was why "those people had only left cemeteries as an archaeogically significant remain". According to *Jiménez* the reason why there were no remains was that they built in timber.

Schwarcz observed that timber buildings also left traces such as post holes; *Jiménez* recalled someone having stated in the course of a preceding discussion that, while the cemeteries were 'fixed' on top of hills, the settlements were 'moving around them', which meant that one should widen the area to be surveyed, and *Retamero* commented that one "had to change one's concepts of settlements".

Jiménez cited the cemetery of El Carpio de Tajo, once considered a "Germanic cemetery" (because up to now archaeologists always saw "a Germanic population in the cemeteries") but now thought of as containing a 'mixed population'; she explained "why the point of view had changed completely" because the settlements had been studied "from the point of view of the law, contrasting the date of those settlements with the date of the law of Liuvigild" concerning "mixed marriages".

Velázquez asserted that the texts spoke about a mixed society and one had "to look for the way to combine archaeology with documents" and she pointed to El Carpio de Tajo as a good example.

On the topic of 'courts' *Jiménez* related that the origin of the ninth-century church of Santa Maria del Naranjo, in the Asturian kingdom, had been probably built as a 'court', i.e. a palace "just for the meetings of the king, i.e. an *aula regia*"; this showed that "historiographical tradition in the Asturian kingdom wanted to revise the ancient Visigothic tradition".

Size of the population in Hispania before and after the Gothic immigration

Ausenda recalled the need, when tackling any historical subject, of having a quantitative, even if vague, idea of the numbers interacting; he dissented from the scepticism of some participants by expressing his feeling that one could "make approximations based on several related parameters: surface, carrying capacity, population density", etc.; he recalled that "a high density for the population of a modern Fourth World country was about 10 individuals per square kilometre and he surmised that, at the end of the Western Empire, the various regions were more or less at the level of Fourth World countries, towns could be accounted for by adding an average population of about 10,000 for each town.

Schwarcz thought it was a useful idea and he contributed a "solution according to a count made for North Africa at the time of the Vandals" when some 500 bishoprics were counted according to the "lists of the regional and ecumenical councils".

Green cautioned that "then one would want to know what exactly was meant by a bishop".

Schwarcz asserted that "a bishop was the head of a city" and that during the fifth century there was a "subdivision of the *termina*"; he noted that at one time the main opinion was that there was a bishop for a whole province, but that that "didn't hold water any longer"; because the general picture was that a bishop was responsible for a city, [taking the multiplier suggested by Ausenda of 10,000 inhabitants on average per town] that would add up to 3 to 5 million souls for the population of North Africa including the Berber tribes and the populations all the way to the Sahara; as far as the Vandals were concerned, the estimate of the number of ships needed to carry them over to Africa pointed to a total number of about 80,000; he concluded by admitting "to the difficulty of numbers in late Roman sources".

De Jong, *Jiménez* and *Retamero* expressed their disbelief in the veracity of the numbers in the sources, followed by *Ausenda* who, however, added that one had to try "and gradually reach better approximations".

Retamero concurred that that might be possible for large areas and that it "would be interesting to calculate the size of so-far unknown settlements".

Schwarcz was of the opinion that it could be done very well by surveying cemeteries as one "could be sure that no one lived in a rural settlement who was not buried"; however, "outside the Empire and in a military settlement it would be difficult because...soldiers die away from their villages", he thought this difficulty might be overcome by physical anthropology which could perform genetic analysis even on ashes and calculate by "the ratios between males and females...what proportion of the male population [was] missing"; indeed in some cemeteries there were only 20% of males "which told something about the balance and the way of life of a society".

Wood asserted that "a lot of work had been done on population figures, and most regional histories of the Roman Empire...suggested population figures, and most studies of individual tribal groups suggested population numbers"; he thought "it was a point that one should always keep in mind".

Schwarcz seconded Wood's opinion recalling that "the physical anthropological analysis of cemeteries had just started", but that there was still a lot to be done as there was a "lot of material to be sifted".

Wood thought that at the "regional level it could be done on remains, however, at the provincial and imperial level the question should be kept in mind...because the way it was answered would affect one's view of how the integration of barbarian groups could take place".

Green reminded the meeting that, "in addition to trying to calculate the size of the Roman population area by area", one "also had to try to calculate the size of the Germanic groups that moved in, and that was much more difficult"; he stressed the problem "when any number was quoted in the... sources, the size of a Germanic army...what degree of credibility could one attach to that?" "Not very much" thought *Schwarcz*, "just probability".

Wood noted that even in the eleventh century, "when one had extremely good evidence for the figures...from a complete register of more or less the whole country, the different figures vary by a matter of form, which one has to treat with considerable caution".

Referring once more to the population in North Africa, *Schwarcz* noted how it was "much more fertile in the fifth century because it had to support its own population and the city of Rome, since all the grain eaten in Rome came from North Africa"; or, as *Green* put it, "it was the granary of the Empire".

De Jong, convinced that "numbers were vague and varied widely", asked Green "how many people were needed to bring about linguistic change, and did it have to do with the position they had in society when the minority imposed its own language".

Green replied that the question was so complicated that he could not give an answer, as the outcome varied "according to the language, the period and the linguistic change one [was] talking about", he strongly doubted that one "could make any extrapolation from linguistic change to numbers of speakers involved"; he referred to an example given earlier recalling that "there were about 30 Germanic loan words into the Latin of the early period of the Empire, before 400; of those, most are attested only once or with one Roman author only, so that knowledge of this linguistic intrusion into Latin depended on the minutest fragment of evidence possible"; and "in most cases one could trace the cause or the occasion of the entry of the word, but it was easy to imagine that one cause may not have been recorded in the historical evidence before it vanished".

Comments on population size

In future, better parameters will be discovered allowing one to obtain better approximations for ancient population numbers. However, certain upper limits can be set by looking at the populations of present-day Fourth-World countries, in all likelihood quite similar in population strength to barbarian successor kingdoms. A population density of between 7 and 10 per square kilometre, calculating only non-desertic areas, seems to be the upper limit for such pre-industrial economies. In fact, one should bear in mind that in ancient times plagues, famines and other natural calamities were much more frequent than nowadays and they affected periodically the populations keeping them at a low ebb. In particular, concerning the population of North Africa, the decrease from Roman (fourth century) to Byzantine times (second half of the sixth and first half of the seventh century) is dramatically evident. Whoever visited Tunisia will remember how subsequent Byzantine settlements occupied only a fraction of the area of the preceding Roman towns, the major agricultural production for export having changed from wheat for Rome to oil for Byzantium and reduced in consequence.

Kinship and marriage

Kinship and religion, is there a connection?

The topic was listed by *Mayke de Jong* who introduced it by referring to the change from "traditional German archaeology" to "the modern type of archaeology" as practiced by Gisela [Ripoll], a change which had not been applied as yet to the "thinking about the family and about kinship" nor had it been applied "to [one's] thinking about religion"; she recalled that in the scholarly tradition there was the idea of a "typical Germanic kind of kinship intimately bound up with religion, however, when the social structure changed, religion could also change, and with christianization the structure of the family would change accordingly "in the direction of individualization and of the conjugal family"; she considered this outlook increasingly problematic, primarily for the reasons outlined by *Schwarcz*, that there had been a long period "of acculturation in which the two types of religion could no longer be separated, perhaps"; she wondered "how different were 'paganism' and 'Christianity' when practiced for a long time next to each other in the same village?" She cited the instance of grave-goods which were not fobidden by Christianity even though they were not a "Christian practice". So that, in "christianized society the practice of putting grave-goods in graves went on for quite a long time without opposition from Christianity".

Wood concurred asserting that while there was opposition to "grave feasts" there was none to grave-goods.

De Jong came to her point that she wanted to look at the problem in an alternate way, i.e. to investigate, keeping religion out of the picture, how the social structure might have changed; i.e. that the presence of the conjugal family did not necessarily mean Christianity or descent, nor the presence of Christianity meant necesarily the conjugal family and descent.

Jiménez disagreed; she thought that when the Visigoths, or Germanic people in general, migrated into the Roman Empire "they preserved their 'private' life", and it was the aspect where the Church insisted most in destroying the traditional pattern "of Germanic family" and susbstitute it with another one, so that "the Christian family was completely different from the traditional one"; for Jiménez the family was the "first step" to be followed by other "steps" culminating with the institution of the state.

De Jong observed that her opinion was completely at odds with Jiménez' and suggested that perhaps "it could help if [one] could realize...that there [was] not one Christianity" even though "we think...of Christianity as something that does not change"; she challenged Jiménez' opinion about Christianity destroying "private 'Germanic' values", by asking her, "How do you know?", she also pointed out the fact that "in medieval society" there were "extensive networks of kinship which survived...[and] flourished within Christian contexts", in other words Christianity did not always "battle traditional patterns".

Jiménez agreed to the last assertion, maintaining, however, that Christianity had only "caught" the aspects which were at odds with the Christian ones.

Green commented that the process of christianization had changed; as Schwarcz had suggested previously, "in the pre-Constantinian period, christianization was an individual matter from the bottom up", thereafter it become "more and more a matter of christianization from the top down, certainly in western and northern *Germania*"; taking into account "that difference in the process of christianization" one should also consider the possibility that the "two processes involved different attitudes towards kinship and its relation to the new religion".

De Jong agreed that the aspects of private conviction were much more important during the individual conversions of the pre-Constaninian phase than in a later one; she thought it would be wrong to put the two "on a par", for example she didn't think that the "Frankish Church in the seventh century had the ambition to change peoples' private lives, it was a religion which asked for "ritual compliance...a public condition".

Green cautioned that in addition to "a degree of public dimension that it shared with Germanic 'pagan' religion,...it did contain a kernel of individual conviction", and one should look for "how far that kernel established its strength and [began] to operate at first under the surface of a public religiosity and slowly changed". Most "illustrative in this respect was the fact that words like 'to believe' in English, *galaubian* in Gothic, 'glauben' in German, have a religious function and are found only in Christianity", while "this was not a religious concept before the coming of Christianity".

De Jong conceded having been "a little blunt" for the contrary opinion.

Green concluded that "beneath public religion", be it pagan or Christian, "there was a kernel of novelty in the Christian function, and its fermentation was a slow process which one [should not] lose sight of".

De Jong agreed but lamented that there was a "tendency to only focus on that one kernel and forget all the rest".

Díaz focussed on a different aspect of the relation between kinship and religion and he mentioned "the cosmological concepts of the Christian conception of Germanic people"; he thought that concerning "the conception of the Christian cosmological order, the idea of the relation between religion and special groups [should] be rejected". However, in the evolution of Christianity "it was very common in the medieval tradition to associate a group, sometimes a family, with a perception of self identity, e.g. aristocratic values", even to this day. Furthermore, there are aspects of special worship within local communities; for example "it is very common in Spanish villages to associate a personal conception of religion...on a building" by calling it by different names: many villages have a special identification with "Santa Maria de l'arbol", "Santa Maria of the spring", "Santa Maria of the rock", a particularizing sense of "the universal idea of the...complex of Christianity". Perhaps, even if there is no evidence to hand, there is a continuity of association between kinship and some particular aspects of religion in Christianity; in any case in dealing with these aspects one should reject individual interpretations in the conception of Christianity: heresies must be rejected, while particularities are not easily ascertained.

Wood summarized the discussion: "My point, I think, relates to almost everything we have been discussing over the last few days, which is that the real problem rests in the assumptions that we bring to the study of the period, most of which have to do with the Germanic-Roman opposition, and I would like to get rid of those assumptions. All told, we don't have evidence to define what is 'Germanic', certainly not in anything wich applies specifically to individual groups. If archaeology will not take us that far, there are not enough texts that will. We might also try to define 'Roman', the one group of people for whom we do have enough evidence, but we are not asking the sort of anthropological questions that we could ask. What we could do is to define the material of a particular region, of a particular period and explore it on its own terms trying to throw out a lot of these assumptions. I think that coincides with what Mayke [de Jong] is arguing. Having done that we can make comparisons, i.e. explore the material on its own terms, do the sort of thing Isabel [Velázquez] is doing with individual texts, we ought to grapple with the texts about aspects of religion, and about aspects of kinship on their own terms to make certain that we understand them and why they have been written, whether they tell us about a particular group or whether they tell us only about the author or the author's motivations. Once we have done that, we can begin to make comparisons with other regions and other periods. It seems also that if we are going to embark on anything like that, as anthropologists who need to live among the people and be 'surprised' by them, we've got to do it this way, we have to throw out an enormous number of assumptions; and what we will then define is some social aspect of the period and the place with enough detail to be able to get beneath the general social picture, to define a very specific element of a particular group, when we notice that we only end up being able to describe one particular group, the nobility, while we will have no idea of what is going on with other groups. This is a plea for an even more extreme starting point".

Ausenda agreed on the necessity of focussing on the relations with neighbours of the Visigoths, such as the *Suebi*, Vandals, etc., but no one mentioned the preceding Iberian populations, as there must have been several which were different from Hispano-Romans, such as the Basques, and probably other 'different' populations.

Schwarcz wondered whether with Wood's directions one could define *Romanitas* "as a general picture for the Empire" as account should be taken of each population and its process of romanization, as *Romanitas* might just refer to "an imperial élite which might be called an international aristocracy with possessions all around the Empire and fundamentally homogeneous", which in no sense entailed that "the different regions of the Empire were alike"; he referred to the "long process of establishing *civitates* with an urban kernel and a rural territory in the regions of the Empire" where it took "two to threehundred years to establish such *civitates*, for example in the Balkans' and there was always the question of "how deep they went"; he was reminded of the similarities and differences between modern nations, Romania, Bulgaria and Greece in that region, which were quite different in language and customs even though they might "go back to a Thracian layer which was taken over by all". Prompted by *Green*, *Schwarcz* called the pre-existing pattern a *pre-Romanitas*.

Díaz distinguished between two different questions, on the one hand one "didn't really know whether the Germanic migrants arrived with one unified reality"; as for the local populations "one had references for central, north, and north-west Spain, but the problem extended beyond the sixth and seventh centuries; he said he thought of "an anecdotic situation concerning the level of self identification in northern Spain, where the religious experience was quite different" at distances as low as 20 km; there was no unified concept of Catholic orthodoxy, because it was not only a question of abstract religion, but of the ritual which developed in each community and of the mechanisms regulating relations between groups. He thought "it was not only a historical question, but probably a question about the meaning of religion in each community".

Wood accepted Díaz's point about the regionalization of the Roman Empire; he would, therefore, suggest that such regionalism "also be dealt with by the same methodology referring to material belonging to a particular place at a particular time"; he did not consider "the 'Romans' a sort of cosmic model".

Comments on 'Kinship and marriage'

The present difference of opinion concerning the 'closeness' of marriage in pre-industrial society, in particular among Germanic populations, will be solved by the increasing sophistication of DNA research showing considerable closeness between individuals buried in the same cemetery, hence belonging to the same village (Arrhenius n.d.).

Furthermore, research in the sources should prove that special treatment was accorded to the Anglo-Saxons, and comparisons between Roman law and the laws of successor kingdoms should show that increasing attention to 'incest' coincided with the conversion to Catholicism of the Germanic populations. For instance, while Euric's law on 'incest' forbade marriage with relatives within the third degree (Zeumer 1974:28), which is just one degree removed from what is recognized as incest in almost all human societies, i.e. fornication between brother and sister, incest was extended to the sixth degree by Reccared's (586-601) *LV* III, 5, 1. This might also be a clue to the fact that the Arian hierarchy was more lenient with 'incest' than the Catholic one.

While awaiting the vindication afforded by DNA studies to the contention that in simple societies marriage was between close kin, one can resort to graphics showing the complete network of kinship relations forbidden by the *Leges Visigothorum* IV, 1. 1 to IV, 1. 7 to draw some visual conclusions.

A brief explanation of the diagram is necessary for a better understanding. The centre of the diagram is Ego, whose degree (*gradus*) of distance is obviously 0. All the forbidden kinship relations listed in the above mentioned laws are schematically shown in the diagram with a ▽ for males and a ○ for females. Their

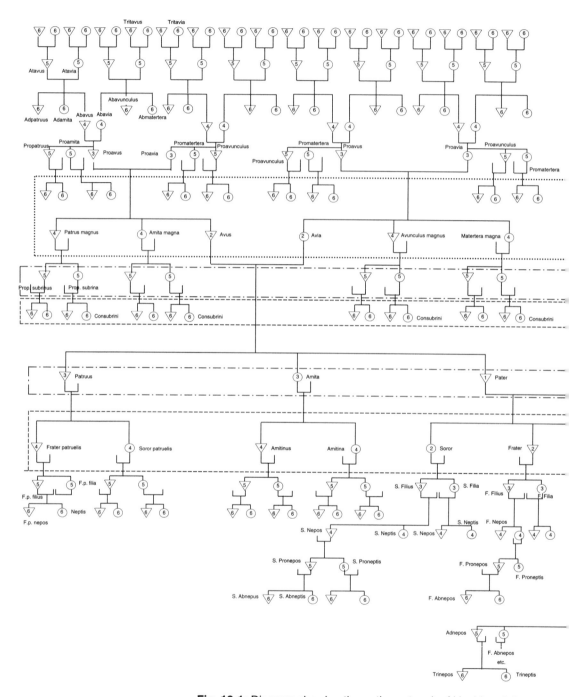

Fig. 13-1: Diagram showing the entire network of kinship relations

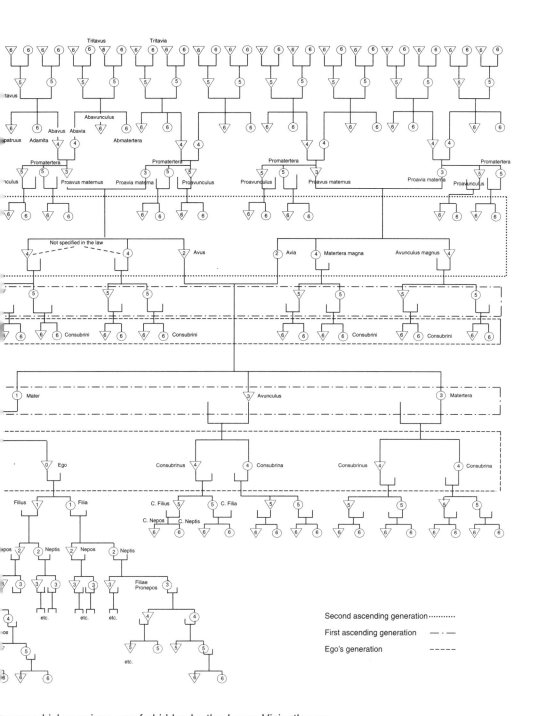

ween which marriage was forbidden by the *Leges Visigothorum.*

degree of distance from Ego is shown by numbers from 1 to 6 printed inside the triangles or circles that indicate them.

Vertical lines connect generations, horizontal lines connect siblings of the same genitors. Rising vertical lines with neither triangles nor circles at the top mark the presence of married affines that are not mentioned in the laws, but are necessary to explain the genesis of the next generation.

The calculation of the number of forbidden kin in the diagram was extended only to three generations, considered to be those generally present in a simple society where life expectancy is relatively short. To make the task of counting forbidden kin in those three generations easier, the positions belonging to each generation were enclosed by different lines: a hyphenated line for Ego's generation, a line of hyphens and dots for the first ascending generation, and a dotted line for the second ascending generation (see fig. 13-1).

Due to the considerable number of kinship relations at these three levels it was difficult to bring those belonging to the same generational level to the same level on the graph, as the jumble of vertical and horizontal lines would have made the diagram unreadable, so the same generational levels are found at different levels on the diagram, but may be recognized as they are enclosed by the same kind of lines.

One will notice that kin belonging to the same generational levels are all characterized either by even or by odd numbers of degrees of distance from Ego. The even-numbered ones range between 0 and 6, while the odd-numbered ones range between 1 and 5, as the 7th degree is not forbidden.

With these clarifications one can start discussing the diagram and its relation to the *Leges Visigothorum* referring to forbidden kinship relations. One will note that the brother and sister of Ego's MF are neither named nor described in the *Leges*, specifically IV, 1. 4, *De quarti gradus consanguinitate*. This might be a clue to the lesser importance of the maternal line, keeping in mind, however, that the relations may have been influenced by Roman ones.

Another clue to the lesser importance of the female line is the fact that the laws in question were obviously made for male Ego. This is shown beyond any reasonable doubt by the legislator's preoccupation of making sure that the same incest prohibition applied to the *consubrini qui ex duobus sororibus nascuntur* (*LV* IV, 1. 4). This clarification would not have been necessary if Ego had been female or unisex.

The most important result of this graphic exercise is to show the numbers of forbidden kin comprised in three generations only, i.e.

in Ego's generation	42
in the first ascending generation	20
in the second ascending generation	<u>24</u>
Total	86

This is a considerable number even if based only on two children per couple, whereas censuses in simple societies show that the average number of children is 3. Since the spouses of the agnates in the diagram were neither named nor counted, this means that one should add some 28 more to the 86 shown above, i.e. one third of the first total, bringing the total up to 114.

One can readily see that in a settlement of the early Middle Ages, in which the number of inhabitants hovered around 200 souls, the forbidden kin were more than one half of the population in the village. This shows that, not only was it quite probable that early Germanic populations practiced close kin marriage, but that they almost had to, to avoid the efforts and difficulties involved in marrying outside their own settlement. Awareness of the problems arising from the unexpectedly great number of people belonging to forbidden kin relations may have been the motivation for deacon Theodore of Pavia to write to Pope Zacharias asking for some flexibility, which was not granted (see page 172, this vol.)

Social relations: gender, age, class, ethnicity among Goths and between Goths and Romans in *Hispania*

Ausenda introduced the topic expressing the opinion that it was a very important one, and that a lot of helpful traces could be found in the laws; he thought that by going over the laws with attention for detail one could find many aspects related to the topic; he also thought that clues could be found in different texts and histories. The topic was also relevant to intermarriage, because the degree of intermarriage was an indication of the speed of both vertical 'miscegenation' between classes and horizontal 'mixing' towards a '*mixed society*', a related topic listed by other participants.

Wood remarked that "a lot along those lines had been done by David King in a book, but he also thought that the issue was that one could not talk about the Visigoths on their own", since the only evidence at hand was that of the laws, so that one had to "talk about the population for whom the laws existed", or as *Green* added, "a mixed population".

Wood repeated the term and stated he was "sure that within that [mixed society] it was possible to ask more anthropological questions than David King did; his work being in the school of Walter Ullman, i.e. very textual, he was sure that more anthropological insights could be added".

Importance of slaves among the Visigoths

De Jong, seconded by other participants, opened the discussion on the topic by telling how she had been "struck in the Visigothic laws by the enormous importance of slaves in that society".

Velázquez, *Jiménez*, and *Retamero* listed the following aspects concerning the topic: what was the difference between the status of slaves and that of the Roman population, and the real difference between dependents, e.g. peasants, and slaves, and their economic condition; what was a slave in Visigothic society; and, finally, what was a *servus*.

According to *De Jong*, a slave was "someone on which people very much depended; indeed, one of the ways to really get at the Jews, was to forbid them to own Christian slaves", she wondered whether they were 'agricultural slaves' and mentioned the fact that there was a deep divide between a *servus* and a free individual, attested by the terrible punishments for intermarrriage between a *servus* and a free woman.

Jiménez reminded the meeting that one of the most important points concerning marriage was that this was prohibited between persons belonging to different social groups. For *De Jong* that meant a "very rigid social stratification", while *Jiménez* insisted that it was a Christian concept or, in any case, brought about by Christianity.

Velázquez noted the importance of such relations in the process of acculturation, she said her interest was for the "real difference between the status of *servus* and that of free", where probably one of the main differences was in the harshness of punishment.

Ausenda recalled from his experience in the field that there were numerous misconceptions about slavery and the harshness of their treatment, because slaves had to be taken care of by their patrons, whereas free men had to fend for themselves, so that in some cases slaves had a better life than free men. One of the main differences between a slave and a free person was that slaves did not have genealogies so that to be married they needed the agreement of their patrons; he concluded that one had "to be careful about the misconceptions concerning slavery, such as those in *Uncle Tom's Cabin*, and that one should look without prejudices at every situation".

Jiménez observed that among the Visigoths there could be temporary slaves who in their former status had genealogies.

Retamero thought that the difference was "between what the sources call *servi fiscales*", and that "behind the term *servus* there was a wide range of levels"; he advocated the necessity to "distinguish these *servi* from the slaves of bishops or *comites*".

Jiménez' question as to whether *servi fiscales* were the same as *servi* was answered negatively by a few participants.

Schwarcz held that one could show that in late antique society a *servus* was a very "precious and expensive" asset, for instance after 405, on account of the many prisoners taken, the prices of slaves fell to one *solidus*, i.e. to about one third of the yearly stipend of a soldier as they made between two and five *solidi* a year; he had been struck by the fact that slaves among the Visigoths were not "punished" when their master died, because Roman law established that when a master died, all the slaves in the household should be killed to make sure that other slaves would not rebel; such leniency meant to him that even in Visigothic society *servi* must have been quite expensive.

Wood noted that that meant that they were not guilty for their master's death. *Schwarcz* replied that the law assumed that if the master died, "they must have been guilty"; one should, furthermore, bear in mind that "in late Antiquity, slavery was not the mainstay of the Roman economy", research in fact showing that "semi-dependent persons" were the majority in the Empire already in classical

Antiquity, means that the slave-worked "domain economy", taken over by the senatorial aristocracy from the Carthaginian example, never was a dominant factor in the Roman Empire (even though slavery was widespread in other sectors); one should "presume that in the...law many semi-dependent persons were subsumed under diverse very broad categories", he noted the question present from the fourth century onwards about the status of a "free person" when one sees that a Roman law made "free peasants bound to their land"; even the position of a *liberus* in some 'barbarian' laws was somewhat hazy, in that one got the impression that a *liberus* could be equated with a *homo liber*, a man free enough not to have to ask the king or the duke for permission to make decisions concerning his social group, i.e. "free [to the extent] that he could be equated with a nobleman".

Concerning slavery, *Ausenda* observed that, in Antiquity, changing territory on one's own was a hazardous undertaking for individuals without 'intertribal' connections, and going to another 'country' with no citizen's rights might even entail being killed impunely; hence, slavery was a way by which one could 'emigrate' and be protected by a 'patron'; this was the status of foreigners in Athens, and to the present day of foreigners in Saudi Arabia, where the Arabic word for 'patron', *kafíl*, has been euphemistically translated into English as 'sponsor'.

Green said that, while Germanic languages could throw light on the concept of 'free', they could not, for reasons he could not fathom, on the "idea of slavery"; he added that there were various words associated with the idea of 'slavery', but no "one Germanic word which one could load with this connotation".

De Jong called the meeting's attention to *"Lex Visigothorum* VI, 5. 12 ascribed to Chindaswinth...[which mandated] that masters should not kill their *servi* without due process of law, so the power of the masters on their *servi* [was] being curtailed"; and a further interesting proviso in the case of a master inciting his *servus* to kill someone, according to which the *servus* would get the "normal dishonorable punishment", *decalvatio*, 200 lashes, etc., while his master would "get the death penalty"; this aspect paralleled what Schwarcz has said about the value of *servi*.

Wood thought that one should "treat slavery in as new a way as possible"; he seconded Ausenda's cautioning about the 'traditional' American view of slavery, because even there, in the South, the treatment of slaves could be very good, while in the North the opposite opinion prevailed; both patterns were present in the early Middle Ages, where one could find both "individuals who were absolutely horrendous, and others who were very good in their treatment ot slaves"; this entailed looking "both at the laws and at anecdotes in documents to make distinctions between not just particular groups, but also particular individuals".

De Jong remarked that, in fact, there was an example of *servi* being outraged when they found out that their "lord was not a real lord", which suggested a pair off; *Retamero* observed that perhaps those *servi* were not slaves in that they were "shared by their leaders".

As a topic for future research *Velázquez* suggested "a lexical study of various categories of *servi*, e.g. *buccellarii fiscales, privati, ecclesiastici*; there were also *servi ecclesiae*, probably "a mixture of students and *servi*".

Retamero asked Wood whether in Frankish sources there was a difference between *servi fiscales* and *servi privati*; the answer was that "there was nothing clear before the Carolingians" and *servi* were much less common in the Frankish state than in *Hispania*.

Retamero asked how peasants were considered by the polyptycs, and *De Jong* answered that in the polyptycs "there was a clear distinction between *servi* and *coloni*", and disputes about "masters trying to push *coloni* down to the rank of *servi*, which is what eventually happened"; nevertheless the distinction "was still there in the ninth century", but there was no difference within a group of *servi* who were peasants.

Green asked Wood if he knew "whether the Carolingian sources used the word *slavus* or *sclavus* in the sense of 'slave'; he thought it came "obviously from Slavonic prisoners of war who were enslaved" but not "when it came first".

Schwarcz suggested that the usual term for 'slave' was *mancipium*.

Ausenda suggested that the term *sclavus* might have come via the Venetians, since they were constantly dealing with Slavonic populations; *Green* thought that was one possibility, but that the word might have come in from the North as well.

Wood considered it "fairly clear that there was already a slave trade in Slavs in the seventh century, but he could not remember any linguistic change taking place that early"; he thought it had taken place in the tenth century.

De Jong drew "the conclusion...that Visigothic law differentiated much more within...the group of *servi* than one knew from Frankish experience".

Díaz remarked that any claim to understanding the different categories should be accompanied by a clear appraisal of the references, because there were wide differences between the notarial documents, normally very primitive, the laws, and the private—or not so private—letters; one had to "contextualize the sources where one [read] the term, and also think about the implications and differences between the legal text and the real situations that one [was] able to understand"; he noted that the expressions *coloni* or *colonica* appeared only two or three times in Visigothic sources, where the latter, "the possessions of the *colonus*, the land he [was] working, [were to be] understood in the context of late antique fiscality...not in the context of a personal situation", he concluded that one was not "only reading the sources" but, what was more complicated, also "reading the different interpretations".

Velázquez added a further variable, i.e. "the evolution of classical to late Latin in the Visigothic period; she mentioned a hypothesis, the distinction between *mancipium* and *sclavus* was difficult, and one should study the way in which these terms evolved to late Latin and into the Visigothic period; she thought that "the terms made reference to different categories of men". She added that one should be careful in giving meanings to terms like *sclavus, mancipium, liber, conlibertus* and so on; however, in any case, the laws were "points of departure" to be studied, after which one should "study the application of the concept in real society".

Díaz dissented in that it was "not only a question of many categories of people...but that the same individual could be ascribed to different categories in different contexts: it could just mean a lower status person in the context of one source, who could be a *mancipium* in a legal context, or a slave in a fiscal context, or even a *servus* in relation to his patron"; the problem was that one was not faced with "a clear group of categories, but that the same individual could belong to many categories at the same time".

Schwarcz approved of the point made by Velázquez about the terminology of the law, a question to be closely looked into; he recalled there having been a study of legal terms by Gabriele von Olberg (1983), a pupil of Ruth Schmidt-Wiegand.

The aristocracy: its social and financial foundations, relation with the monarchy

Wood brought up the topic because he was aware that "in the majority of modern historiography on the Visigoths" the analysis of the political structure of the kingdom did not go as far as it could if it were possible to separate "what the aristocracy was". He was aware that there was little narrative evidence, and the little available focussed on "crucial moments such as kings' supposed murders of a large number of aristocracy", and for the most part they concerned episodes in war; he thought that one way forward was to follow the point made by De Jong earlier in the discussions of previous days, i.e. the "need to avoid seeing the episcopate as separate from the aristocratic classes", which caused him to think that there was a way of defining "more closely the aristocracy by using information [one] had on the episcopate and the most senior monastic figures"; this approach would not take one as far as one could get, as with the Frankish material concerning the seventh-century nobility "where the range of saints' lives was so much more useful"; he was aware "of the sort of questions that Frankish historians [asked] about the aristocracy and...[could not] be asked about the aristocracy in the Visigothic kingdom, because of the problems of documentation", and he was, therefore, trying to "formulate a way of getting a better hold on the [Visigothic] aristocracy".

Ausenda remarked that "whereas in Frankish histories one had a lot of bishops with Germanic names, in Visigothic history there were very few; *Green* replied that "name giving was subject to fashion, and there was no reason why a fashion should be popular in one country if it was popular in another".

Díaz admitted that in Visigothic society one could not "speak about aristocrats and sometimes one did not make a difference between Roman and Gothic [aristocracy]"; perhaps one should consider that "in some way they had the same interests" concerning the monarchy and the power structure, but did not have the same consideration; he thought that one of the main problems was the lack of uniformity in the "terminology": Hydatius' chronicle used different names for Roman aristocrats, and not always the same terms, a further difficulty that had to be taken into consideration.

De Jong talked about having read Julian's *Historia Wambae,* "as a document attempting to define the common aristocratic ideology, and it [was] not important whether it [was] bishops or lay aristocrats, whether it was Goths or Romans...that was largely irrelevant to what they were doing, to what Julian [she thought] [tried] to do; it [was] relevant to define what Isabel [*Velázquez*] thought very important, i.e. the 'new society' in the Visigothic kingdom". After this *De Jong* felt like introducing "the two points that Ana [*Jiménez*] entered and be done with it, that [was], she thought where Biblical notions came in, Old Testament connotations, as a common denominator, not for the entire aristocracy, but for something like the Carolingian inner circle with access to the king, the *aula regis,* and that it did not matter whether one [was] a bishop or a lay aristocrat".

Velázquez agreed, she thought Isidore's importance was not due to the fact that he was a bishop, but the member of an aristocratic family; and *De Jong* was satisfied that "in that way the Visigothic story fit in with a number of medieval stories in which high birth...gave one a special channel to the sacred..."; and on *Schwarcz*'s prodding she agreed that what was needed most was a prosopography of bishops, and she cited Stroheker.

Schwarcz declared that there was Heinzelmann (1982) for *Gallia,* while Stroheker had not covered the bishops when he had written a prosopography of the Visigothic kingdom (Stroheker 1948).

Ausenda referred to Gregory of Tours' list of remaining bishops in Aquitaine, noting that even after the Visigoths had been chased away they all had Germanic names.

Wood admitted that there might be a point in that if "one looked at the Council of Toledo, there were a lot of Germanic names, but of course they were primarily those who had been Arian and converted...[which was] perhaps the reason why Germanic names within the episcopal tradition [were] not terribly popular in *Hispania*".

Green insisted on refusing any kind of inference from the 'ethnic background' of names, saying that "the evidence from *Francia* showed that Germanic names could be taken over by non-Germanic speaking people, so that from the linguistic origin of a name it [was] unsafe to draw explicit conclusions".

Ausenda maintained that it was not so in that period; and *Wood* countered that there was a "classic example, in that Gregory of Tours' uncle, who was quite clearly completely Gallo-Roman, had a name Gundulf".[4] "And that was not isolated", added *Green*.

Schwarcz explained that the problem was that in "Heinzelmann's survey one saw that in Gaul the bishops usually were from the leading noble families of the cities, and one should assume that, in the beginning, that meant in *Hispania* the same sort of thing" and that was why "it was so important to make a real

---

[4]   One cannot exclude that Gundulf was one of the Catholic Burgundian aristocrats, who might have married within the local Gallo-Roman aristocracy.

prosopographic survey of both names of the aristocracy which one had, and the names of whichever bishops, saints and of the lists of the various Councils of Toledo and monasterial tradition to seek connections".

De Jong added the "complicating factor that after the phase in which bishops were recruited from the city aristocracy, one got a phase in which they were recruited *via* monasteries often having been brought up there and because of their oblation they would be renamed"; she thought the phenomenon had already started in the seventh century; *Green* added that it did not have to be confined to oblation monasteries, but could also be extended to conversion and entry into the monastic rule.

Comments on 'Social relations'

Mixed society

The historian's contribution was that *LV* III, 1. 1 (*Antiqua*) was a law [issued] by Liuvigild which authorized mixed marriages between Goths and Romans, superseding a law of the *Codex Theodosianus* III, 13. 1 which forbade marriage between Romans and *Germani*. Liuvigild's law must be understood in a context of integration [of the population], issued by a king who had planned a religious unification subsequently supplemented by his son Reccared with his conversion to Catholicism. It is probable that by this move one also solved some de facto situations; already at the beginning of the sixth century we have a mention of a Gothic nobleman who married a wealthy Hispano-Roman landowner; obviously it was the aristocracy which was interested in the legalization of the situation. Did this entail a massive population mixing? Did the Goths keep the tendency to plan their marriages solely within Gothic families? Documentation is scarce, as it is also difficult to find in the seventh century elements that could be identified as Germanic. In any case, I believe that the Gothic group remained 'endogamic' for a long time and that full social and cultural integration took place especially among the nobility [on both sides], an acculturation process which, in the long run, would bring complete mixing. However, the only way to grapple with the problem of the survival of Gothic peasant groups would be through a medieval epic which is confused and ideologically manipulated (the idea of the Reconquista was built on the legitimacy of the Goths who had taken refuge on the mountains in the North, and were attempting to recover the territories which the Moslem had seized; however this argumentation was invented by the Christian kingdoms, by the Asturian-Leon monarchy in order to annex the territories which it was conquering), or through toponymy; place-names (very few are really Germanic, if we compare them with the great wealth of place-names in the Iberian peninsula). At one time, the great quantity of Germanic names appearing in the Christian documents of the ninth and tenth centuries was taken as a proof. In some cases the percentage of Germanic names compared to the Latin ones is 80% vs 20%; however, here too there are many problems, on the one hand many of these documents were from Galicia, a region where Visigothic presence was quite low. Furthermore, we know that the percentage of Goths over total population was probably less than 5%, and there is a tendency to consider that the number of Germanic place-names during the Reconquista was a 'fashion', a way of claiming the ancient right of conquest, a fashion which was parallel to the ideological elaboration of the Reconquista, as a right of Christians, as heirs of the kingdom of Toledo, over the Moslem [comment by P. C. Diaz].

In the words of the anthropologist, both field experience and history show that the acculturation processes in general are quite slow, and that a quick genesis of a mixed group does not correspond to anthropological reality. During field work in Sudan, the writer witnessed that populations, such as the Hausa, who had sojourned in the region for more than 200 years still retained their customs, language and religious leanings, and that intermarriage was nil. The same was true of the Rashaida Bedouin from northern Arabia, who had immigrated beginning in the 1850s, who kept their own customs, dress, ornaments, religious leanings, Arabic dialect, etc. and did not intermarry, but kept to themselves in segregated villages, as any one who might come to the area may find out for himself.

Usually 'mixing' follows pretty quickly when the way is open to mixed marriages. In fact, one should bear in mind that the different customs of the spouses in an interethnic marital union can be quite unnerving. Mixed marriage can be very awkward when customs are different, as they impinge on the education of the children, on food habits, sleeping habits, the circle of friends and relatives, etc. These differences can be overcome in two situations, the earlier one is when the status of the women of a given group is considerably lower than that of the men belonging to the other group (this was not the case of the Romans nor of the Goths in *Hispania*), or when the differences have abated to the point that they are no longer irking, a process which takes a considerable length of time. As long as mixed marriages do not take place in significant numbers, it is highly unlikely that the different groups will live in the same surroundings, because even the rules of 'privacy' change from one ethnic group to another. Both towns and villages in eastern Sudan are segregated with rather sharp borders; this is true not only in eastern Sudan, but in modern cities, such as New York, where there are Jewish enclaves, Italian, Chinese, Puertorican, Dominican, Haitian, and nowadays even Russian, where people continue speaking their own language, eating their traditional foods, playing in the streets and mingling among themselves; and furthermore in the Sudan—and presumably in sixth-century Spain—there was a lack of that modern instrument of equalization represented by public schooling for the whole population, which is the main and most powerful instrument towards a mixed society in North America.

All these ethnic realities induce one to think that it was highly unlikely that the Romano-Visigothic reality of the sixth century, and even of the seventh, was so 'mixed' as claimed by some. One may object that already Liuvigild (568-586) (Heather 1996:280) had issued a law (*LV* III, 1. 1) allowing mixed marriages; however, even Leovigild's law, so often cited, was by no means without restraints, as it states that such marriages required approval "*premissa petitione*", so that one cannot imagine a rush to a mixed society right after Liuvigild. Furthermore, one should note that the law applied only to free men and with the *"consensu comite"*. This is in line with both historical and anthropological experience in that among stratified societies, as both the Roman and the Gothic ones were, mixed marriages generally started for alliance purposes between members of the upper strata.

Jural relations and conflict

Velázquez thought that also the fundamental problem of the origin of Visigothic legislation could be approached by looking at the texts not only in juridical but also in philological terms. She cited a student of hers who had begun working on a lexicon of the *Codex Theodosianus* as reflected in the *Lex Romana Visigothorum*; in this case a list of names was insufficient since also a complete study of the concepts was necessary.

Heather agreed on the importance of critical texts for the various laws and in "situating the patterns of legislative activity in the Visigothic kingdom in relation to late Roman", not on "individual rulings but on the patterns of how and why laws are given and...why codification takes place as and when it does"; he also thought there were "interesting points concerning the relationship between the *Lex Romana Visigothorum* and the tradition it started with".

Velázquez suggested an important topic, the different *Leges* of the various Germanic peoples and the different versions of laws from Chindaswinth to Erwig and Wamba; the additions and the changes in the laws, and why Erwig changed Chindaswinth's laws.

Traces of Gothic customary law concerning blood money, individual property and its disposal, property of kin group, etc.

Ausenda thought it was a very important topic as it could be approached directly by searching in the laws.

Díaz highlighted the problem inherent in searching through the laws, noting that the Visigothic laws did not dwell on questions concerning blood money between Gothic families, and that laws concerning property were in the Roman tradition; however, when one left aside the legal sources and went through the "historical accounts about the evolution of the monarchy" it appeared that the conflicts between members of the aristocracy to seize the kingdom, the rulership, "seemed to be conflicts between old enemies". Even in the nineteenth century "a quasi-artificial scheme" was built on two or three families, two or three groups of aristocrats who were constantly fighting to seize the rulership; he thought that perhaps "some elements could be used to understand some of these conflicts". As for the property of kin groups, the only extant references were not in relation to the Goths but to "more primitive traditions in northwest Spain; there were "splendid references about this question in the monastic rules".

De Jong suggested the *Regula communis*.

Velázquez thought that Visigothic law should be studied "in general", and that after studying, one could conclude whether there were some Gothic antecedents; admitting never having concealed her 'romanism', she cited an example of when she was studying the laws concerning inheritance and the evolution of the *Codex Eurici* into the *Lex Visigothorum*, she had found that a widowed father could dispose of 1/3 of the *bona materna* if his children had come of age, however, he could dispose of 1/2 of those *bona materna* if his children were married; she didn't know whether the 1/2 ratio belonged to the Gothic tradition, but she thought it did not belong to the Roman one, which was always 1/3.

De Jong declared having found enlightening the idea expressed during a previous discussion "that there must have been a romanization of Gothic customary law and a Gothicization of Roman provincial law", concluding that, after that discussion in San Marino, trying to establish a distinction was a futile exercise.

Ausenda disagreed and held that there was enough blood money compensation in Visigothic law to warrant a more careful analysis, whereas there was none in Roman law.

Wood maintained that "there was very little feuding".

Ausenda insisted that there were feuds and blood money compensation for wounds which came "straight from Germanic customary law", prompting *Wood* to maintain that "it did not come straight from Germanic customary law because there was no written law for Germanic populations before they came into the Roman Empire". With *De Jong*'s approval, he held that "it was more important to study the documentation that one had...and come to grips with that, and if, as a result of that, one [decided] that certain things had come from a non-Roman culture, then fine", but he thought that one "actually had to begin from the texts themselves, without coming with an agenda which [said] that [one had to] divide things one way or the other"; he supported the point made by *Schwarcz* in a previous discussion and just reiterated by *De Jong* that, "if the Goths or other barbarians had influenced Roman tradition before the migration, and the Romans had influenced barbarian tradition before the migration" then the expressions 'Germanic customary law' and 'Roman law', were meaningless and using them was not helpful, but if in the end one had to use them, before doing so one should "actually view the texts as they [stood]" before sentencing that an aspect belonged to the Germanic tradition; he suspected that "the places where one would be forced in that direction would be places where there [was] linguistic evidence, i.e. a specific Germanic loanword in the code" concluding that one had to begin with the texts rather than with one's concepts.

Green "wholeheartedly supported what Ian [Wood] had just said, even though that might be driving him to abandon his opinions: if on the linguistic side one had learnt anything in the last fifty years or so, it [was] to recognize that Germanic tribes were trying to establish what *Germania* was in its pristine purity, the Germanic tribes about whom [one] knew most were precisely those which had already been influenced by Rome, and because of that, an approach to what was Germanic was bedeviled by that fact".

Schwarcz said he kept an open mind about Ausenda's question and tried to check whether there was any evidence for it, and admitted that "to Romans, the idea of wergeld was a Germanic one, and he didn't think there was a trace of it in Roman law". The same was not true for feuds, even though the oldest legislation in which one could trace a development of feuds was the Icelandic one, and there it seemed that feuds "came stronger in more recent laws than in older ones" as the older ones had wergeld, while the most recent ones did not; he was not so sure that one could say that "there was a tradition of feud in Roman law".[5]

Wood thought that Schwarcz had just supported his position in pointing out a place where there was a Germanic term because Roman law did not have it; he believed he could go further in specifying that there was "nothing specifically Germanic about feud, as the first apparently feud story in Gregory of Tours [had] nothing to do with Franks, but revolved around Gregory's own family and the murder of his brother Peter", he concluded "that feud in itself was neither Roman nor Germanic" which led him to believe that the point Schwarcz was making coincided with his own, which was that one had to work on the assumption that one could not decide either way, and that it did not matter either way, excepting those cases which were positively linked to Roman law by "an exact comparison with the *Codex Theodosianus*, or by something which had to be Germanic because of the loanword involved".

Green cited the work of Schmidt-Wiegand (1979) on the *Leges barbarorum*, which followed that very type of approach.

Biblical influence in law-making in various post-Roman societies

De Jong illustrated the topic saying that she was interested in studying it as a "symbol of a new identity, acceptable to many groups, and therefore it could act as a catalyst in the acculturation process"; she thought it had to be studied in a comparative way, comparing law codes or different material, because "the speed at which the Old Testament [was] integrated into law codes as a source was very different; with the Visigoths it appeared relatively late...only with Erwig when [one got]...a reference to the Old Testament to support the nobility, while anointing was much earlier"; in conclusion, a whole field to be studied.

Jiménez remarked that two notions were implied: that of the Visigoths as a chosen people, so that it was not surprising if they took many ideas from the Old Testament, and the persecution against the Jews; notions which were hard to reconcile.

De Jong admitted it was very difficult to reconcile them, except for the "persecutors who always managed to reconcile this perfectly by the mechanism of the scapegoat", and the argument that the Jews crucified Christ; she thought that

---

[5] There are several mentions of *faida*, the word for feud, in Rothari's edict of 643 to state that after a given material or moral compensation the feud should cease: *cessante faida*, plus 13 .other laws among those issued by Rothari and Liutprand mentioned the word *faida*.

one had to start with the notion of competition between the two groups, as "that was what is was all about"; only "some sophisticated Carolingian theologian like Hrabanus Maurus may have entertained the notion that Christ was a Jew…and [one would have found] an exception on that".

Schwarcz cited "Justinian, who was personally interested in the Jews and tried to convert them"; so it was not only competitiveness between two ideologies, but also the Jews losing their position because they did not follow Christ.

Díaz thought that the serious answer was that "the chosen people were the Christians, not the Jews".

De Jong observed that there were "lots of people in the early Middle Ages, possibly false prophets, who 'projected' themselves as the new Israel", and were concerned with the idea of purification of the people; and possibly excepting Byzantium, there was "only one society which enforced the legislation that the Visigoths did in the seventh century".

Schwarcz noted that there was "a lot of radical legislation concerning Catholics".

De Jong thought they all fit into the role of scapegoats and said she was trying to understand how it fit with the audience's idea of 'state'; "did it mean an extremely weak state trying to acquire strength by creating imaginary enemies, or a fairly efficient state working so well that it could persecute?"

Ausenda thought that persecution was resorted to when a state was in a crisis; but *De Jong* recalled that in the twentieth century, persecution was practiced "precisely because a state had such incredible power of persecuting", so it worked both ways.

Schwarcz pointed to the "geography of the early Middle Ages recalling that, before the Arab expansion, Byzantium occupied not only the Near East, but the Balkans, North Africa and most of Italy and, adding the Visigothic kingdom in *Hispania,* one ended up with the better part of the Mediterranean world", excepting the area occupied by Islam, as the persecuting one, the Carolingian example was the exception rather than the rule.

De Jong noted that in fact persecution in *Hispania* stopped in 711; *Schwarcz* agreed suggesting that "that was one point why the Islamic conquest was successful".

Velázquez agreed on the importance of the topic proposed by Mayke [*De Jong*], "because [one] could see the Biblical influence not only in the law, but also in the Visigothic formula, and in the whole literature; the influence was so great that it was enough to give a Biblical reference without bothering to give an answer, since everyone knew it"; furthermore scholarly education was based on the Bible, especially on the Psalms and the Sapientials; and that was also a sign of identity; to which *Jiménez* interjected asking "when the new sign of identity began"; *Velázquez* continued asserting that she thought it had begun, for the Catholic world, at the [III] Council of Toledo, "but the Hispano-Roman society was Christian from the third century"; she remarked that the authors of the *Vitas* continually used Biblical references without even bothering to qualify them.

Schwarcz mentioned the parallel of Wulfila's biographers who "made his *Vita* important by comparing him to Moses".

De Jong accepted Green's observation that the topic had been discussed at length previously and declared she was satisfied.

War and the army - Where did the Visigoths in Hispania wage war

Díaz observed that, when dealing with 'barbarians', the Roman state, from the Republican period onward, "always faced warriors, first as enemies, later as *foederati* or mercenaries", so much so that in the last years of the Western Empire, "the only army of the Empire was an army of barbarians"; with the decline of the Empire these armies gave birth to new kingdoms, for which "war continued to be a very important aspect". Díaz pointed to how interesting it would be "to contrast" various aspects of war: the concept of war, the tactics, the concept of the warrior, the relation between war and the population, between warriors and the people, and the continuity of the Germanic tradition with the acceptance of the Roman elements, and to follow the evolutions of those concepts. He thought the parallel topic on 'Where did the Visigoths from *Hispania* wage war?' could be discussed together with the previous one. He thought it was difficult to talk about a "Visigothic army...perhaps one could only talk about private armies which joined together", or according to the expression used by Ammianus Marcellinus "*conspirantes in unum*"; he thought it was a very complicated question because one had to consider "all the history of the Visigothic tradition...and accommodate every stage to the historical situation of the moment".

Green said he was both fascinated and disappointed by the topic, the disappointment being due to "the fact that the Gothic language [died] out and that...as a consequence of that, [one] could not do with Gothic what [one could] do with Frankish and OHG" when considering the two words for a people, "which originally meant also 'army', namely the word 'Volk' and the word *here* in OHG"; in the development of OHG the two words "differentiated in complementary directions in that 'Volk' moved away from the idea of army to the idea of people..., and *here* moved away from the idea of people...towards a purely military concept of an army. He thought the differentiation was a consequence of a political differentiation, which however was a point of discussion, which could be followed on the OHG side and the OE side, but unfortunately not with Gothic.

De Jong referred to a book by Roger Collins on early medieval Spain in which he maintained that "the essential problem of Visigothic kingship was the fact that every new king needed to prove himself in war", and she asked Díaz to comment on it.

Díaz did not think "it was the situation in every case", because there were kings who "reached the royal dignity with enormous military prestige" but this was not always the case; he conceded that the warrior ideology was important in the Visigothic tradition and also in the ideology of the kingdom, but it was difficult to generalize on that; he thought that "normally the integration of the kingdom [started] with a war, against the *Cantabri*, or the *Vascones* or another group, as an indication of the strength of the new king", however, sometimes the new king's strength, as in the case of Erwig, was directed against the "inside enemies, the aristocrats"; he thought the theory had come through Menendez Vidal in his *History of the Goths*, and before him from a book by Pujol in 1892 about the social institutions of the Visigothic kingdom.

Ausenda commented on his contribution to the title in discussion by noting that trade and war were complementary, and the fact that they had few worthy enemies to wage war against might explain that they did not have very much trade either, which may have been one of the reasons for their decline.

Schwarcz agreed pointing out that "war as an economic necessity [was] greater in a tribal society than in a post-Roman society."

Wood saw "more than one type of power being exercised" at the moment when one got together an army; it was not only a matter of getting booty but also "of bringing together the whole of the aristocracy at regular intervals...so that the campaigns against the Basques may have [had] more than a simple economic aim".

Ausenda observed that it was difficult to "take men away from their land and homes without targeting something" that could reward their efforts.

Schwarcz stressed that in time of peace cities were stocked with goods so that they didn't have to be brought in [by force], he thought that "as long as they had a regular income, post-Roman society [did] not have to provide opportunities to obtain booty" which was needed in "tribal societies, because there was not enough surplus" among them.

Wood thought that the issue "raised by Roger Collins was rather more complicated...than he made out" because he hadn't solved the problem of the identity of the *Vascones* in Frankish sources, whether they coincided with the Basques, or whether it was a term referring in general to Aquitanian groups; and a further issue concerned the extension of the involvement, i.e. "not just the Basques against the Visigoths, but...a whole frontier zone from the Garonne down across the Pyrenees". Prompted by *De Jong*, *Wood* explained that the Merovingian sources were not clear whether they "consistently meant Basques or *Vascones*", as it often meant "the Aquitanian aristocracy who [were] not bothering to come to the court when asked to"; he thought that the term was "consistently used as a term of abuse".

De Jong observed that in the *Historia Wambae* there was a clear distinction in that "he made war on the Basques before going into *Gallia*".

Jiménez objected that what was meant by *Gallia* was the Visigothic province of *Gallia*; and *De Jong* agreed that it referred to the *Narbonensis*.

Wood disclaimed "lumping the two campaigns of Wamba together", all he wanted to imply was that "by taking the Frankish and Visigothic evidence for campaigns on either side of the Pyrenees, [one] might be able to re-define the problem of that war in a way that Roger Collins did not in his book on the Basques".

Jiménez pointed out that a Spanish archaeologist had found in Navarre two places with "the same buckles which were used in the Aquitanian region...so it [was] probable that...the *Vascones* were the same people who lived in Aquitaine as well"; *De Jong* thought that that made sense.

Comments on 'Jural relations and conflict'

The historian's comment was that in the beginning the Visigoths used Roman law adapted to their circumstances. This is the prevailing opinion in the present state of the research. Alaric's Breviary (*Lex Romana Visigothorum*) was Roman, and also the *Codex Euricianus* was essentially a text of vulgar Roman law, in its fragments it is impossible to find Germanic customs, nor is there any Germanic word in the surviving text, and this despite the fact that the consensus of opinion is that it derived from King Euric's entourage. If we consider the laws issued by the court of Toledo, it is especially difficult to identify Germanic customs, and the *Leges Visigothorum* are a wide collection of regulations issued subsequently during a span of about 100 years, when it is almost impossible to detect either formal or legal procedures alien to Roman [legal] tradition, with norms concerning property and family which are genuinely Roman. In concomitance with this idea, the opinion is gaining ground with some scholars that Visigothic written law was only applied in concrete circumstances and that a non-written Visigothic customary law was applied in parallel, of which a few clues appear in the written codes such as the *morgengabe* or the ordeals. In order to prove it, they cite the forms that local law took in Spain during the era of the Reconquista. This interpretation which counted many supporters until the first half of the twentieth century is presently denied by the majority, who consider that these laws proceeded from the vulgarization of Roman law and local norms, and when Germanic forms are encountered, they proceed from Frankish law which arrived with the Cluny reform beginning in the eleventh century.

Rather than the above two extremes one should probably accept that some Germanic legal customs referring to property, to family law, and to disputes involving honor continued in use, although probably only to solve problems between Goths, while the 'official' law was used when conflicts concerned Goths and Romans. The prohibition to use other laws enforced by the *LV* surely referred to old codes, e.g. the *Codex Theodosianus* and the *Codex Euricianus*, from the very moment that [the government] claimed to have put together a law code for all (Goths and Romans), preceding codes were superseded. Such a simple explanation is probably closest to [what happened in] reality. In some notarial documents (*Formulae Visigothicae*) one can detect some of these Germanic customs, and in Visigothic law there are concrete prohibitions which allow one to infer that people used parallel law codes, however in certain occasions these might have referred to the laws of arbitration by elders, not necessarily to Germanic customary law. Such parallel codes may have also referred to the local laws of cities which were so important during the first centuries of the Roman Empire, which may have been recovered after the decentralization of the fourth to sixth centuries. In fact the use of local customs is also considered in *C.Th.* V, 20. 1 = *BA* V, 12. 1, with its *interpretatio*: "*longa consuetudo, quae utilitatibus publicis non impedit, pro lege servabitur*"; in *LV* I, 2. 4, one reads that laws must be written in agreement with the customs of each city and the needs of each period and place: "*Erit secundum naturam, secundum consuetudinem civitatis, loco temporique conveniens*", and that tolerance probably also was applied to Germanic customary law.

On the other hand one must keep in mind that the documentation coming from the Spanish North-East suggests that in rural surroundings one continued to judge according to legal forms which had no relation to Roman law nor to Germanic customary law, but probably to pre-Roman local indigenous customary laws [comment by P. C. Diaz].

The above contribution by the historian makes sense in that the same pattern was true in most colonial situations, i.e. that oral customary law continued being used among the natives, while written codes were applied by the colonial authorities in matters arising between the natives and the colonists, be they private or the public authority. In parallel with this consideration, one should bear in mind that customary law is based on what one may define as 'private law enforcement', through the mechanisms of the feud and blood money compensation, as against 'public law enforcement', through penalties meted out by the authorities involving death, corporal punishments, jail, fines, etc. One should also recognize the fact that oral customary law can only function over the kinship network involving clans, lineages and families in the maintenance of 'law and order', through fear of private retaliation and inter-group consensus. It stands to reason that, if such customary law can function using kinship as its supporting network, it must necessarily decline and finally disappear with the decline of the kinship network, until it will be completely superseded by 'public law', i.e. law based on 'public law enforcement'.

I believe that quite a few traces of customary law can be detected in the *LV*, a few examples of which, apart from the *morgengabe*, are the ordeal by boiling water (*examen caldarie*), the prohibition of seeking revenge in case of minor injuries by *alapa* (slap), *pugno* (punch), and *calce* (kicks) "*ne...lesio maior aut periculum ingeratur* (*LV* VI, 4. 3), and in the same law a full list of blood money compensations which could only have proceeded from customary law, as it seems quite doubtful that they may have been contemplated in pre-existing Roman law, whereas they can be found in most laws of the successor kingdoms. A careful analysis of surviving early medieval law should give plentiful clues of preceding oral and customary law, which could be usefully compared with similar survivals in other successor kingdom law codes and with preceding Roman law codes to find out their most likely precedents.

A final important aspect to be studied as far as Visigothic law is concerned is how far this 'final' law code intended for both ethnic groups or—if one prefers— for the mixed population, was effectivelly followed by all those to whom it was destined. Already at the time of Reccared (586-601) two laws were issued, *LV* II, 1. 10, and II, 1. 11, enforcing the use of the 'official' law code, and at the same time prohibiting the use of any other law code, whether foreign, "*alienis institutionibus*", or Roman, "*Romanis legibus, nolumus amplius convexari*". The judge who insisted in using such Roman or alien law, superseded by the *Lex Visigothorum*, was condemned to a fine of 30 lbs of gold, a huge sum even by modern standards. It appears that these draconian punishments were even increased during the last years of the seventh century in an attempt to bring about full obeisance to the 'unified' law code. However, the mere fact that the penalties for using a different law code were so high induces one to believe that many 'judges' or arbiters continued using the superseded codes.

As one can readily understand from the above quick survey, there is still quite a lot of work to be done if one wants to correctly and thoroughly understand the ancestry and implementation of the Visigothic law code.

Rural economy

Peasant work: foodstuffs, tool systems, vocabulary, other archaeological approaches

and

Pottery

Retamero introduced the topic reminding the meeting that one knew "very little about kings, about *comites*", about people in authority in general, but one knew something about the places where they exercised their roles, i.e. *basilicae*, palaces, and also about comparative terms in legislation; he observed that one knew very little about their material life, "the fact of eating every day", as it was taken for granted.

Jiménez suggested that information on the food system could be found in the monastic rules; *Díaz* asserted that one knew something also about the processes to produce them, while *Retamero* dissented alleging that "archaeology had not paid attention" to these details.

Schwarcz mentioned new work in this domain by Joachim Henning (1987) concerning tools used in agriculture.

Answering a question from *De Jong*, *Retamero* said he was interested in the whole process from production, to storage and eating, and in particular how the *granadas punicas*, 'pomegranates', were produced and that he was interested in the whole span of life.

Schwarcz volunteered that grave-goods might be helpful towards the clarification of the problem of foodstuffs, because of the offerings of food and drink made to the dead; he thought something could be said for production from the archaeology of the tools, and by gleaning in the literary sources, especially the hagiographic ones, and that "it deserved looking into".

Retamero went on to decry the fact that one knew nothing about "field systems"; *Jiménez* asked what one expected to discover when one knew that "Visigoths were so romanized?" *Díaz* made it clear that the research concerned not specifically Visigothic agricultural practices, but the agricultural practices of the period, as it was impossible to distinguish the differences between "Visigothic and Roman agriculture".

Retamero summarized the situation saying that there were settlements were food was produced by Visigoths or Romans not only for themselves, but also for other people, and that scholars specializing on that particular period "knew nothing about how this crucial production was carried out: they had no idea of the size and types of fields, about the tool systems, about storage systems and so on".

Schwarcz was of the opinion that pottery would not reveal much because recent "surveys of pottery south of the Danube in the regions settled by the Goths after 376 had shown that the pottery quickly changed to the local provincial types"; answering *Ausenda*'s remark about Retamero not being interested in the difference between Roman and Visigothic, but in the agricultural production systems during Visigothic times, *Schwarcz* stressed that archaeologists rely mainly on pottery.

Ausenda answered that pottery was not only important per se, but also because of the traces of pollens or seeds it contained, and *Retamero* confirmed that analyses had already been made.

De Jong having asked *Retamero* whether he thought he could obtain all the information he had set out to get, he answered that he thought *Ripoll* might be able to help him; which was dispelled by *Jiménez* on the strength of the fact that *Ripoll* "had nothing on pottery". *Díaz* repeated that it was impossible to identify pottery as a Gothic production and *De Jong* reminded them that the issue was not about Goths, but about "how much one would get to know about the life of ordinary people in the countryside", and *Retamero* concluded that he was after "the very organization of the peasant world, which not only could inform one about the processes of producing foodstuffs, corn, barley, 'granadas,' and so on", but also about the "fiscal processes set up by authorities to 'take into account' the agricultural production"; he thought that there was "a very close link between which staples and how they were produced and the fiscal process" which was based on them; to him this was "only a starting point, a hypothesis to start work on".

Green submitted a question concerning the adoption of certain eating habits "assumed by the Goths from the Romans in a far earlier period than the arrival of the Visigoths in Spain"; the point hinged on the fact that one of the early loan-words from Latin into Germanic was the word for 'wine', and the evidence showing that "the word itself reached the Goths by trade routes when the Goths were still in northern Poland...which was borne out archaeologically by the discovery in northern Poland and Meklemburg of Roman wine services in Gothic chieftains' graves", which hinted to the adoption of Roman meal habits and drinking practices. Another word bothered Green as he was not convinced that the habit it represented could have reached the Goths that early, but later when the "Goths came face-to-face with the Romans on the Danubian frontier...the idea or the word expressing the idea of the Roman eating habit of reclining on a couch as they ate"; he explained that "the word in Latin was *accumbere* or *recumbere*, because the word came into Gothic 'semi-Gothicized' as *anakumbian*, *ana*-corresponding to the *ad*- of the Latin compound, and *cumbere* simply taken over as *kumbian*"; he thought it difficult to believe that the habit of "eating their meals in the Roman manner" could have been taken over when still in the North: he thought there must have been a chronological 'distinction' between the taking over of those two terms.

Wood thought there was no problem in assuming that "the chieftains might feel it would be the approriate way to drink out of their Roman wine services, as it was to lounge around in the way they had heard Romans lounged around"; he answered *Green*'s query on how they could have known of that manner, by remarking that they could have been told by the tradesmen who brought the wine.

Green objected that the wine which reached northern Poland was not necessarily brought there by Roman traders, as it was just as feasible that "it was Germanic traders who brought it"; *Wood* replied that "the chances of a long chain of traders, each taking the wine 20 miles and so on, were very slight, so that there probably were only one or perhaps two middlemen taking the wine from the Elbe up to northern Poland"; *Green* admitted not seeing "the wine going in short stages, but more likely by boat traffic by the North Sea and the Baltic".

Schwarcz remarked that there was a "classical study by Mortimer Wheeler (1954) on Roman trade", and it "was...clear that there was long-distance trade which reached far in all directions"; he was sceptical about the spreading of Roman drinking habits: he thought "the 'barbarians' took over Roman habits if the time of contact was long enough. To this effect he cited a "wonderful find...for the *Marcomanni* in Bohemia at Mušov of a 'Fürstengrab' with very sophisticated Roman furnishings specially made for someone with a Germanic outlook, because one of the best pieces was a vase with four heads of men with the typical hairdo of a Suebian warrior"; to *Ausenda*'s remark that it "must have been made to order", *Schwarcz* replied that "at least it was made to the taste of the man who used it"; he added that "in royal company drinking had special social functions" for instance in the case of a "Germanic chieftain drinking in the company of his war band" and that "sooner or later they would all be drunk and not able to stand", but he could not imagine them, at that stage, just quietly sitting around the banquet table.

Green still considered the "idea of such extensive romanization so far north and so early a little hard to take".

Wood did not think the taking over of the particular trait needed "extensive romanization...but depended on how drinking was viewed; if only as a normal process, then [Green] might be right, but if it was a sort of 'celebratory' thing...one may actually take on more than simply glasses...but actually the [whole] drinking ritual".

Schwarcz wanted to continue the "debate on Visigothic drinking habits" to point out that they wouldn't have drunk very much wine "because mostly they would have drunk beer, because they produced it themselves".

Green announced that from the Gothic word for 'a glass' and material 'glass' "it was clear that what they did to the drinking container was the act of serving it, but this was a drinking horn, and it would be difficult to drink from a drinking horn in a reclining position".

De Jong thought that it only was necessary to have a holder so as to put down the drinking horn; *Green* said he had tried but had poured the liquid "all over himself"; *Wood* suggested that the same would have happened with a Roman goblet since it was "not a particularly satisfactory way of drinking"; *Schwarcz* said it was necessary to incline it if one wanted to reach the bottom, and *Green* observed that the "angle was much more acute than the drinking horn", and *Wood* confirmed that it was possible to hold it up at 90°, while *Schwarcz* related that "he had had the opportunity to try goblets two years before, because of the custom of drinking unfiltered wine whereby one had to raise the goblet, rather than inclining it; *Díaz* contributed his experience of drinking wine from a 'porrón', a traditional Spanish glass to drink wine, from one of two very narrow beaks from which one had to drink very slowly so that the wine should not spill out of the second one; thus the discussion on 'barbarian' drinking habits came to an end.

Comments on 'Rural economy'

One of the observations made during the discussion of items for future research on this topic was that it would be impossible to distinguish Gothic from Hispano-Roman agricultural practice. This was quite well founded as it corresponded entirely to what could be ascertained on an anthropological basis. Field experience in two widely different agricultural basins, the Gash Delta near Kassala, and the Baraka River Delta near Tokar in eastern Sudan, have shown that agricultural practice becomes quickly equalized among different ethnic groups, as it is obvious that, by simple inspection, it is possible by anyone to improve his tools so as to obtain better results and save energy, to the point that the recent introduction of tractor-drawn ploughs was quickly accepted by all ethnic groups involved.

On the other hand, there remain considerable differences in food habits which could be reflected in the remains of meals which can be found in pottery or in the garbage of settlements; hence special attention should be paid to these apparently secondary details.

Even eating habits could be different as, for instance, the majority of the population in Sudan, especially in the countryside, squatting on mats laid on the floor for the purpose, eat with their right-hand fingers from a common bowl placed on the same mat on the floor; only few people belonging to the higher calls of society eat with knife and fork. Thus, eating habits can be important in the characterization of higher classes.

Drinking habits are more contagious as, in general, they are reserved to men, who also prepare the beverages. In particular, the penchant of Germanic populations, especially higher class individuals who could afford the expense, for wine is well known from the literature which often portrays them indulging in wine and being frequently drunk. Again, the presence of drinking kits in the archaeological record could be an indication of social status.

Urban economy (trade, education, etc.)

Latin and Greek linguistic (and literary) influence on Gothic

Green protested about adding the word 'literary' as he could account for the linguistic influence, but had no knowledge of traces of a 'literary influence'; he continued stressing the importance of Latin influence on Gothic because it could be shown to "have spanned a number of centuries". He divided the influence of Roman and Byzantine languages into three stages. During the earliest stage "one had the influence of Latin trade words, words for objects used for containers, and of objects in trade reaching the Goths while they were still in northern Poland, at least a couple of centuries before direct contact was made in the South on the Danubian frontier. The next stage consisted of "the greater wave of Latin linguistic influence which came, of course, when the Goths got down to southeastern Europe, where it was mainly a further trade group of words and a military group of words". The later stage took place with "the Christianization of the Goths, and the wholesale importation of Latin loanwords to do with Christianity". It was "in the last sphere [of Christianization] that Greek linguistic influence came into play, in that a lot of Christian vocabulary of Gothic was of Greek origin". He went on to point out that "sometimes it could be shown, on internal linguistic evidence, that a Greek Christian word did not come into Gothic directly but *via* Latin" and "the overall differentiation he would make between Latin and Greek was to say that, whereas Latin linguistic influence [on Gothic] was both Christian and non-Christian, the influence of Greek seemed to be restricted entirely to the Christian vocabulary of Gothic". The only exception could be found by "looking at the linguistic form of a number of Greek place-names recorded in Wulfila's translation of the Bible: it is clear that they fall into two categories, a later category is one that [Green] would call 'learned written biblical loanwords', where the word was taken over and still retained the Greek flectional endings in the middle of a Gothic text, but in earlier cases the place-names come in and no longer have Greek flectional endings, or Greek spelling, or Greek pronunciation, but are Gothicized to indicate that they have been present in daily use in the Gothic language long before Wulfila's translation of the Bible. The interesting thing about the early layer of Greek place-names in Gothic is that [here he admitted being subject to correction] for the most part they tie up with places in Asia Minor and in the Aegean, where Gothic raids took place once they reached the Black Sea area, and so that these place-names probably tie up with places where the Goths, however temporarily, got to long before they made contact with the biblical place-names which Wulfila translated in much more learned bookish ways".

Linguistic romanization of the Goths

Green continued on the linguistic theme explaining that the new topic "carried on historically or chronologically what [he was] concerned with, which [was] not simply loan words into Gothic but something more drastic and wholesale, namely what evidence there may be for the gradual loss of the Gothic vernacular by the

Visigoths and the slow acquisition of a vulgar Latin speech"; he observed that the problem had come up from time to time during the meeting, but it was "a problem of such importance and difficulty of solution that [he thought] that it deserved a separate discussion if not one focussing on the total process of linguistic and non-linguistic romanization of the Goths"; romanization which "passed beyond merely the abandonment of Gothic and the adoption of a form of Romance speech, Roman law versus Visigothic law, Roman dress versus Gothic dress".

Schwarcz advised him that "there was a question he should bear in mind, that the first contacts between Goths and Romans went back to the time of the birth of Christ [or shortly after], so for a long time there was some influence from the Mediterranean world on the Goths; in general one thinks of the Danube border for such contacts forgetting that that border was there after 270, and before that the border of the Roman Empire was further north", in fact evidence of Roman goods is found even in northern Europe. According to *Schwarcz*, contact took place especially in the Carpathian region, and he was inclined to think that 'the trouble' started after the Marcomannian wars, and that there may have been an active recruitment of Goths and other Gothic groups inside the Empire at the time of Caracalla; the picture should be somewhat expanded following the expansion of the Goths, in fact, at the end of the third century, the area of Gothic influence covered Poland and Transylvania; "the spread of the Cherniakhov culture into Romania, Moldavia and the Ukraine, using the modern terms, during the third and fourth centuries implied also contact with the Greek cities on the Black Sea coast, e.g. Tomi, Bosphorus, Chersonesos".

Answering *Green*'s question whether he would include also Tanais, *Schwarcz* explained that "the Georgian region was still a blank", as even Ukrainian publications "stopped with the documentation of the Cherniakhov culture at the borders of Russia, and the southern republics of the former Soviet Union [were] a blank in this respect"; he had discussed the problem with some Georgian archaeologists who were more interested in late Roman military architecture especially concerning the Roman castles on the coast, rather than archaeological evidence of the Goths; even though the question still had to be studied, one should consider "a lot of traffic by raids or peaceable means from the North East and the northern Black Sea coast" into the territories of the Empire, this means that contacts with the Greek world were over a rather long period. Furthermore, third-century raids brought many Greek-speaking people from Asia Minor as prisoners into the Gothic area, a movement thought to constitute the antecedents of the Christianization of the Goths in the early fourth century, and the basis of the "first layer of Greek". Immediately afterwards one finds an interesting "second Latin layer", because the only remaining Arian sources are in Latin and thought to come from the Pannonian, Illyrian and Balkan dioceses as a result of the conflict between Ambrose and his Arian and Homoean opponents; at the beginning of the fifth century the few Arian bishops remaining in Italy fled to the Vandals and Geiseric in North Africa, showing that the period of post-Wulfila Latin theological contrasts was quite active. During the same time, about the 420s, Greek theological discussion continued among Arians in Constantinople, confirmed by the chronicles relating that the *magister militum*, Plintha, a Goth, succeeded in stopping the riots between warring Arian factions in the capital.

Prodded by *Green, Velázquez* expressed the opinion that future research should focus on "all questions of loanwords from Gothic into Latin" and viceversa; she thought that the examples cited by Green of *asellus* and *vinum* were very interesting, and she advocated interdisciplinary studies between historians and philologists; she thought "loan words were the reflection of the social contacts between the people". As an example she cited the loanwords from Greek to Latin in the first century BC which were medical terms and terms of trade, while somewhat later ones were rhetorical and philosophical terms reflecting the relations between Greece and Rome after the conquest; in a similar way, the linguistic contacts between Gothic and Latin may reflect the relations during the early period; she admitted being more interested in the loanwords from "lower Gothic into Latin", at the same time recognizing that the obverse was "very important too".

Green did not deny "the importance of traffic" from Gothic into Latin, observing, however, that, "for obvious cultural reasons, there was much more in the way of loanwords from Latin and Greek into Gothic, than the other way"; for which reason he thought that, without excluding the other, loan traffic from Latin and Greek into Gothic deserved more attention.

Wood remarked that there may have been a "chronological difference between the two flows", a significant [result] because the tendency to borrow words from a higher culture would manifest itself in a flow of loan words from Latin into Gothic, whereas the flow "from Germanic languages into Latin represented a rather different type of integration".

Green noted that the same could be shown "of the contact with Latin established by other Germanic languages", because "the same pattern repeated itself with German and English": "earlier contacts from Latin into Germanic vernaculars, later ones and on a different level, from Germanic into Latin as well".

Characteristics of urbanization: monasticism

Ausenda recalled the distinguishing qualities of urban sites, where forms of communication became the main activities: schools, lawmaking, the market, trade, manufacture; he wondered whether a description of a Visigothic town was available similar to that made by Gregory of Tours of the town of Dijon.

Schwarcz thought it difficult to follow education in the urban history of early Spain because, while 'classical' education was centred in cities, the medieval system of education was based on monasteries in the countryside; he thought that, whereas trade and economics could be described, the same could not be done with education.

Green suggested looking for someone like Riché who might have explored the question of education among the Visigoths.

De Jong said she had looked into the matter as it applied to the recruitment of monks and nuns, and her impression, based on the evidence in imperial councils and monastic rules, was that the seventh century was "absolutely crucial as a turning point" as both in the Frankish and Visigothic realm "monasteries had become much more important"; while bishops continued to train their own clergy, the emphasis [in education] "had shifted from the towns to the country, and the same [went] with scriptoria".

Wood countered that there were few Visigothic manuscripts, so that one could not work on Visigothic scriptoria the same as on Frankish ones.

De Jong admitted she was referring to Frankish scriptoria.

Wood referred to work done in Barcelona by Miguel Barceló, but his impression was that "the majority of the evidence [came] from the Islamic, rather than from the Visigothic period".

Jiménez thought that there was also earlier evidence, and she referred to water mills in Santa Maria de Melque, an ancient monastery were evidence was found of dikes to provide water.

Díaz asserted there were many early references to water uses, which were commonplace in the wills; e.g. references to water canals in the will of Vicente, bishop of Huesca in the north of Spain dated in the sixth century, and more reference in Visigothic formulae; he also cited a system of using water to drive a water hammer to work iron in northwest Spain, which could have originated either in the Roman or the Visigothic period.

Ausenda agreed on water being the "basic form of energy for driving machinery that could be connected to a water wheel: it could be used to mill wheat, to beat cloth in a fullery, and to hammer iron and steel".

Díaz went back to scriptoria asserting that there were both types, i.e. in monasteries and in towns; he cited Valencia, around an episcopal church rather than in a monastery in the countryside.

Velázquez wondered whether the relation between schools, *scriptoria*, and the rural economy had been studied.

De Jong did not know, adding that more work "needed to be done on all these topics, because to produce manuscripts one needed sheepskin, which was very expensive, but monasteries could afford the expense because they had become "central places with economic technology".

Green concurred that monasteries had become similar to small townships.

De Jong mentioned J. Wallace having asserted that "monasteries were the cities of the early Middle Ages"; she had no idea of their size and concentration of people, but she thought that there were some which held up to 600 monks.

Jiménez objected that while monasteries could control large areas, the buildings themselves were small.

Díaz said that it was difficult to know because there were no "clear remains"; the evidence came especially from the rule of Isidore which referred to the material organization of the monastery, which was quite similar to that of a Roman *villa*; in the northwestern rule, not in the common rule, but in the *Fructuosus* rule, there was described a "small rural settlement similar to a *vicus*, because the house of the *abbas* was described in relation to the refectory, etc."; he remembered having read some time before about the spatial organization of monasteries and their differences.

De Jong thought that, even if not large, they must have had three units: one for women, one for men and a place where the children were reared; she referred to the *Regula communis*, c. XVII.

Díaz agreed that there were indications implying this sort of arrangement, but that they were not very clear and needed to be discussed.

De Jong was fascinated by the idea that the "rule spoke about the entire family: father, mother and children, and even servants".

Political relations

The notion of the Visigothic state in the fifth to seventh centuries: crisis and demographic decline?

Jiménez introduced the subject recalling that until then [one] "had interpreted the Visigothic state as a 'poor' reality" because it was in a moment of change; she stressed the need "to differentiate between what happened in the fifth century, especially in the second half, in the sixth and in the seventh", bearing in mind that in the seventh there was a considerable decline in population which probably caused a crisis which in turn brought about the "great crisis of the seventh century which ended with the Visigothic kingdom in 711".

Ausenda manifested his appreciation noting that while "the day before everyone held that demographic decline did not herald a crisis", what Jiménez had just said validated his thesis.

Jiménez held to her idea, while *De Jong* asserted that the relations between demographic decline and a crisis were not clear to her and asked whether "there was any archaeological evidence that [suggested] that there was a decline in the population".

Jiménez held that the evidence was not forthcoming from archaeology but from the Visigothic councils and the law "because provisions against infanticide became stricter and stricter".

De Jong saw no causal relation between decline in population and those provisions.

Ausenda thought it was fairly logical that when the number of children decreased punishment became harsher.

De Jong rebutted that "Europe's population [must have been] in decline everywhere when there [was] legislation against infanticide, and that [was] all over the place from the sixth...up to the eighteenth century", but one could not say that because "there [was] legislation against infanticide, so there [was] a decline in population"; perhaps there was some other type of evidence, not only legislation against infanticide "because that [was] pretty standard".

Jiménez suggested that monasticism could be a further proof as, when it grew, the population should have decreased, and *Ausenda* thought that that made sense too.

Schwarcz suggested that the 'rush' to monasteries was "different at different times", and *De Jong* said that there was another theory holding that a "tremendous explosion of monasteries" was tied to a "tremendous explosion of people"; she specified that it was well documented for England in the twefth century, when there was a relation between the rise in monastic settlements and the rise in population.

Jiménez recalled that the settlement at El Carpio de Tajo had been abandoned in the seventh century, while *Schwarcz* objected that the time of its abandonment was not known, and *De Jong* commented that "that was an argument [she could] buy, but what if [Jiménez] had suggested that the whole of Carpio had become monks?"

Jiménez justified her reasoning with the idea that, because the entries into monasteries increased, the population decreased, while, according to *Wood*, exactly the opposite would happen "because when there [was] an increase of population, the land would not support them, and [they] would put their excess children into monasteries"; *Jiménez* pointed to the fact that that was what happened in seventeenth-century Spain, but *Wood* countered with the example, cited by De Jong, of twelfth-century England where "the massive rise in the number of monks and nuns...[went] exactly tied in with the rise in population" in that century, he admitted that it might have happened that "people going into monasteries caused a decline in population" but one could not "work symply from the evidence of an increase in monasticism to a statement for a decrease in population", since they could be related but not causally linked.

Schwarcz suggested that there was the possibility of finding clues to a population decline in the sources, such as notices of long periods of droughts and famine, or signs of catastrophic plagues that would indicate that there was a decrease in population, and doubted whether monasticism could be taken as an indication, since *De Jong*'s interpretation that the "surplus of families which could not be economically supported...was sent to monasteries" sounded more fitting.

Requested by *Green*, *Díaz* gave his point of view that "it was a very complicated question, one on which the Latin sources [gave] no information"; asked about the possibility of using archaeology and continuing in the vein of the discussion, he answered that it was "very difficult to define a relationship between an increasing or decreasing population with the phenomenon of monasticism", and as far as archaeology was concerned, in his university there was "a project of intensive archaeological revision of big areas which had come to a first conclusion...that during the last years of the seventh century or perhaps during the first years of the eighth century the agrarian landscape [was] changing", so that perhaps "the impression...of an increasing or decreasing population" was due to "a change in agrarian usage"; it was a moment when "some central places, some villages, were abandoned, and new marginal areas [were] put under exploitation": there now were "more buildings with clues of rural exploitation of small areas"; he thought that putting these changes in relation with monasticism "could be a street with no end".

Jiménez asked to come back to the original topic of '*The notion of the Visigothic state*' on which she asserted that the Visigothic kingdom in the second half of the fifth century was "a reality built on a politically very organized society, the Aquitanian one", but when [the Visigoths] came into Spain "they found a society which was used, up to the sixth century, to live in a sort of self government", a population used to be self-governed in small units living in small territories; hence during the sixth century Visigothic kings "tried to apply the pattern of imperial government on that reality...and they failed", so that in the seventh century they had to build a new form of state; in essence she wanted to point to the considerable differences between the Visigothic kingdoms in the fifth, sixth and seventh centuries.

On *Ausenda*'s request to give an indication of the direction the research should take and the sources to be consulted, *Jiménez* continued suggesting that one should "first of all have an idea of the conception of the Visigothic kingdom, secondly an idea of the 'mixed society', whether there were rules over Romans and over Visigoths, or over a new society", the option which she preferred.

De Jong referred to Jiménez' statement that "the Visigothic kings had failed [to impose the pattern of imperial government on the local society]" and asked about the chronology.

Jiménez thought that the 'point of inflection' had come in the second half of the sixth century "because in the first half of that century" they were trying to cope with a "situation of self-government", while Liuvigild had to "build a new conception of power", perhaps having in mind that he was facing a 'new society', and for this "he legislated over mixed marriages...and tried to unify the religion of all his subjects".

Wood added that it was necessary to use the comparative method "in terms of similarities and also in terms of highlighting dissimilarities between the Visigoths, the Franks and the Langobards...a useful way of breaking down the national traditions of scholarship which each group [had] become associated with"; the methodology could be usefully applied also to the question of the 'mixed' and the 'new' society. He cited as a parallel the historiographical debate over the extent to which Romans were killed in the years following the Lombard invasion of Italy.

Díaz seconded Wood's idea saying that it was "a splendid topic for a meeting" in which by a comparison between Franks, Langobards, and Visigoths in addition to *Suebi* and Vandals "one could find the solution to these questions".

Wood thought that the Anglo-Saxons "should be brought in" as this would give "a range of possibilities...as each group provided...areas where the evidence [was] better than in equivalent places for other groups"; it seemed to him that "comparison was arguably the easiest way forward on that topic".

Ausenda recalled having tried to use the comparative method for 'kinship' without much success, and *Wood* thought that the difference lay in the fact that he "was looking for contemporary parallels".

Church and State in the Visigothic kingdom

Schwarcz presented the topic linking it to the question of "the notion of the Visigothic state in the fifth, sixth and seventh centuries", connected with Julian's history on the development of the monarchy, because recent discussions had also touched on the question of the III Council of Toledo; the question was whether the councils were symptoms of a weak or a strong state, as they "took over so much legislation"; he thought that an analysis of Visigothic society could only be done by "working on the interrelations between the political and the ecclesiastical system and how...both operated.

Wood approved of the stance adding that close attention had to be paid to the Visigothic Church Councils, avoiding the tendency to lump them together with kingship, without paying enough attention to chronology. He conceded there having been a wide gap after the Third Council of Toledo before the Councils became "a consistent round of Church legislation". He suggested once more the "possibilities of comparison" pointing out how "people failed to notice the extent to which, up to the third decade of the seventh century, Merovingian kings [operated] together with Church Councils more often than Visigothic kings [did]. And one should be aware of the fact that, even though it came later, the Visigothic development, in some place, became much stronger and more dramatic, while the Visigoths "actually [were] not particularly radical in their use of Church Councils until the 630s".

De Jong shared his opinion adding that there was the "problem of Carolingian miopia" looking at which from the ninth century [back] made the Visigoths an "obvious precedent"; she also noted the tendency to forget the "intensity of some of the Merovingian conciliar activity, accompanied by the [coupled] notions of the realm and Israel".

Díaz agreed that "the Church-State relations in Visigothic Spain had to be studied in comparison with all other realities"; he noted that, "in order to justify the situation in the nineteenth and twentieth centuries" the Spanish historiographic tradition of Visigothic history "paid too much attention to the relations between Church and State". This provoked an excessive stress on the involvement of the Visigothic Church in politics. This interpretive tendency had been remarkable not only in the Spanish tradition, but also abroad, e.g. P. B. Dams in the nineteenth century, A. K. Ziegler in the 1920s and 30s, and K. Schäferdiek more recently. Díaz believed that "a less emotional, or partial, approach would bring about a more balanced judgement".

De Jong thought it would be useful not to consider the "topos between Church and State", but two entities within the State; and *Díaz* concluded recalling that Wallace Hadrill (1952) had written that one must "be careful about the Councils, and about Church and State relations in the modern sense".

More on Church and State: Bishops and Church

Díaz had listed the topic and he thought that they had been discussed under previous headings; he wanted to rectify the impression that, when speaking about

Church and State one was speaking about "two abstract concepts"; indeed, the Church represented a group of people working, who were "contextualized at different moments of the evolution of the kingdom", and one could see that aspect reflected in the Councils; the Church represented the people, the relation of the bishops, i.e. the aristocracy and its relations and property; many leads for a new start. The same was true of monasticism as it was, perhaps, the most interesting institution because it was a typical product of late Antiquity, where one could find "the old and the new" since monastic institutions were "the catalysts of a new order". He thought that the two topics listed were rife with new questions to be explored.

He wanted to conclude on a topic which referred to the preceding discussion and applied especially to Visigothic Spain, but possibly also to other successor kingdoms; he thought that since one based one's research not only on the sources, but also on scholarly writings on the different questions, that it would be interesting to highlight the historiographical traditions in Gothic historiography; he thought that this was useful not only concerning the Visigoths, but also the Anglo-Saxons, the Franks, and the Ostrogoths.

Velázquez added that one should also study the "misrepresentation of customs" and the distortion of history after 711 to fit it into the modern history of Spain, whereby from the first Asturian kings to sovereigns like Charles V, the Visigoths were used as a "symbol of the new identity".

De Jong agreed that it was a very interesting subject; while *Velázquez* concluded that it was especially congenial to modern scholarship.

Comments on 'Political relations'

A list of Visigothic kings is prefaced to the comment on this topic for two reasons, the first is that it constituted a calendar for the population at large in that individuals could associate events in their life with the reign of a given king; the

Table 13-1
List of Visigothic kings

Fifth century		Seventh century	
Alaric I	(395-410)	Liuwa II	(601-603)
Athaulf	(410-415)	Witteric	(603-610)
Sigeric	(415)	Gundemar	(610-612)
Valia	(415-419)	Sisebut	(612-621)
Theodered	(419-451)	Reccared II	(621)
Thurismund	(451-453)	Swinthila	(621-631)
Theoderic II	(453-466)	Sisenand	(631-636)
Euric	(466-485)	Chintila	(636-638)
Alaric II	(485-507)	Tulga	(639-642)
		Chindaswinth	(642-653)
Sixth century		Recceswinth	(649-672)
Gesalic	(507-511)	Wamba	(672-680)
Amalric	(507-531) with Theoderic's tutelage	Erwig	(680-687)
Theudis	(531-548)	Egica	(687-702)
Theudisclus	(548-549)		
Agila	(549-555)	*Eighth century*	
Athanagild	(551-567)	Witiza	(700-710)
Liuwa I	(567-571/2)	Roderic	(710-711)
Liuvigild	(568-586)		
Reccared	(586-601)		

second is that a glance at the pattern of succession can offer a clue to the stability of the system.

A cursory glance at the succession pattern shows a series of nine rulers in the fifth century, nine rulers in the sixth and 14 rulers in the seventh; an additional count of the variations in dynasties might be even more revealing. The fifth-century pattern shows a certain stability, and so does the sixth-century one, when the structure, however, was strengthened during the first quarter of that century by the tutelage of Theoderic, king of the Ostrogoths; a short period of instability at mid-century was overcome by Athanagild and his successors, probably with the help of some structural changes, among which the attempt at unifying the populations through the, however conditional, liberalization of mixed marriages, and the catholicization of the Visigoths; these were not sufficient to change the inherent instability which grew during the seventh century and culminated with the demise of the Visigothic kingdom.

The relative ease, with which the poorer northern kingdoms started the Reconquista after the millennium, goes to show that full population unification was reached before that time.

Symbolic life

Art: the 'originality' or derivation of Visigothic scultpure

Wood introduced the topic saying that there was "a wealth of questions to be asked about Visigothic sculpture, again in a comparative way", he mentioned "setting alongside the richness of Visigothic sculptural traditions against the apparent absence of a Frankish tradition...and the wealth of an Anglo-Saxon tradition", he thought that many of the problems arising from looking at each tradition separately "might be more easily solvable if [one] looked at the...traditions next to each other"; *Green* suggested also the Langobardic sculptural tradition mentioning Cividale, and *Wood* added the city of Rome where the popes in the eighth century were building the great basilicas.

Schwarcz recalled the strong influence of the Byzantine development after the tenth and eleventh centuries, however separate; he thought there was an interchange but "mostly dominated by Greek culture".

Wood agreed that it was a further point of comparison adding that he thought that both Greek and Roman culture went "back to late Roman antecedents", which could be found also in Visigothic Spain, while in Anglo-Saxon England there was a specific problem as to "whether [there was] a Roman continuum, or the re-use of Brittonic models, or whether the inspiration came from Rome".

Schwarcz wished to clarify what he had meant in his previous remark, saying he was referring to the newly found frescoes in Santa Maria Antiqua in Rome which "very clearly showed the Byzantine tradition in the eighth century"; he thought one could not "make a clear break between ornamental sculpture and other ways of expressing art...such as illuminations in books," and that one may not "have much Anglo-Saxon sculpture, but there was a lot of insular illumination of books".

Wood clarified that "there [was] more scupture in Anglo-Saxon England than anywhere else", and *Schwarcz* admitted having obtained the wrong impression, but citing Langobardic sculpture and illuminated manuscripts, he thought that there was "astounding evidence of ways of [artistic] expression" based especially on what was known as 'animal style', which seemed to form an "international culture which [was] loose in the *barbaricum*, and in the art and the ornaments of the late fifth century".

Wood held that when looking at Visigothic art, one had to "work with sculpture", because of a lack of illuminated manuscripts which could be "firmly assigned to Spain before 711"; he agreed on the idea that "there was a late Roman and Germanic animal style influencing the tradition", and that convinced him even more that, "setting the material [one] had throughout western Europe in juxtaposition", one could see development and its speed "more clearly than taking the evidence in itself"; *Schwarcz* agreed saying that the point he was making was to look at art in a broader context, and *Wood* concluded that they were both saying the same thing.

Díaz pointed to problems about the originality of Visigothic art in general; one was the present trend in Spain to revise Visigothic art chronology, e.g. the church of 'San Pedro de la Nave' was no longer considered Visigothic, but now ascribed to the ninth century; furthermore, the same 'revisionist' group was of the idea that "nothing [was] new" and that Visigothic art should be understood as deriving from Roman provincial art; probably this becomes more evident if we compare it, not with the great masterpieces, but with some late pieces of local manufacture.

Concerning chronology, *Wood* thought that it would be useful for Spanish scholars to look at some of the Anglo-Saxon pieces, as they were clearly dated by inscriptions and particular linguistic moments.

Díaz conceded that sometimes there were references to time, but in other cases scholars were looking for "the more difficult interpretation".

Jiménez noted that "if in Aquitaine Visigoths did not leave anything original" why should one look for originality in Spain?

Schwarcz thought it a good question in that it concerned the "development of what in the sixth century [was] called 'Visigothic'...and it was clear that in the first half of the sixth century" symbols were used in *Hispania* which were not there before and they constituted the "starting point for the development in the seventh and eighth centuries", which, however, could not be sought in Aquitaine, but rather in Ostrogothic Italy.

Jiménez agreed and asked why Spanish scholars tended to forget the Ostrogothic period, which was very important for the development of 'Gothicness', which surely had begun in *Hispania* with the Ostrogoths; both *De Jong* and *Schwarcz* shared her views.

Literary production and culture

Velázquez recalled having mentioned the topic during a preceding discussion, but she renewed her plea about the importance of "studying the literary production in order to obtain a complete vision of the culture in the Visigothic period", however not limited to the cultural élite, but also the culture of the population at large; she cited the poem *Versus in bibliotheca* by Isidore of Seville as a proof of the existence of a well furnished library in Seville. She thought it was also important to study the inscriptions of the Visigothic period, whether epitaphs or other, which informed one about the people, the bishop, the abbot, but also on 'rhetorical culture', because one found out that everyone who had a special position where he could speak to the people was generous and esteemed, and all bishops were generous, which was obviously a topos, such as that about the qualities of Masona and the epitaph of bishop Johannes of Tarragon; she referred to a paper on the subject (Velázquez 1994). *Wood* considered this a good point and cited in this respect the work of Martin Heinzelmann (1976) on bishops' epitaphs in Gaul.

Symbols of power

Jiménez who had listed the topic explained its meaning in that symbols of power would change with its conception, for instance "in the fifth century and the beginning of the sixth, personal ornaments were symbols of power, but in the seventh century architectural monuments became symbols of power", she cited San Juan de Baños as an example, a church built by Recceswinth with an inscription by the king, on which he declared having built the church, hence it was a symbol of power.

Religion

Arians and Catholics

For this topic *Wood* once more favoured the comparative method; he noted the difficulty of working on Germanic Arianism, because "in every case [one was] looking at the religion of a group that [failed]"; hence one should work not just "on the evidence of Visigothic Arianism...[but also] of Burgundian Arianism...of Ostrogothic Arianism" noting that "Arianism [was] still one of the great unknowns", as [one] "didn't know enough about the Arian Church...and about what it meant to convert from the Arian...to the Catholic Church".

Green stressed the fact that the term 'Arianism' was used as a shorthand, but its reality was much more complex.

Wood proceeded to analyse the different natures of Arianism among various 'barbarian' groups; he noted that in the Burgundian Arian Church there was "more or less complete cooperation about doctrine between Arian monarch and Catholic Church...an open discussion about doctrine which the Catholic bishops were fairly civil about...and no problem in the conversion from Arianism to Catholicism in

516", a model which was never "adequately compared with the evidence one had either for Spain or Italy".

Schwarcz recalled that in Italy "it [was] an Arian monarch who [was] also judging on the Laurentian schism in the Catholic Church...as the Catholic bishops took Theoderic to decide who [was] the right pope, and he was very reluctant to get drawn into the matter...and [eventually] he decided by majority"; in essence most of "the theological debate was done by the Catholic respondent, while the administrative position [was] held by the Arian king".

Ausenda remarked that it "would be interesting to compare the conversion dates and situations for the three populations"; *Wood* explained that the Burgundians converted officially from Arianism to Catholicism in 516, the *Suebi* [had begun] as Catholics, then went Arian, and later came back, their second conversion to Catholicism being later than the Burgundian one; the Burgundians began as Catholics in the early fifth century, while members of their ruling *gens* went Arian, and then they abandoned Arianism altogether in 516, so both their first and second conversions to Catholicism were earlier than the Suebian final conversions to Catholicism; he agreed that there was a need to look at the various conversions from Arianism to Catholicism.

Returning to Italy, *Schwarcz* recalled that "Theoderic, for most of his reign, opposed the politics of the Constantinopolitan Church, supporting the pope against the emperor, but there was a crisis at the end of the Acacian schism when the pope [returned] from a mission to the emperor, Theoderic imprisoned him because...he was not satisfied with the outcome of the mission". Even later "there was no sign of a break between [Thoderic's] successors and the Catholic bishops, and their Arianism was not a pretext for...Justinian to wage war against the Ostrogoths, as it started after the murder of Amalasuentha; furthermore, the "main theological controversy of the sixth century [was] not the one between Arians and Catholics...but between Monophysites and the followers of Chalcedon".

Wood brought up the historiographical problem of the Vandal persecution having become the "dominant element in the interpretation of Arian-Catholic relations", something that sixth-century sources used for propaganda purposes; he cited Gregory of Tours using the Vandal model to "create the impression of a crisis between Arianism and Catholicism", while in Gaul there was no evidence of anything similar.

Schwarcz recalled how Martin Heinzelmann had drawn his attention to "the fact that Bishop Eugene of Carthage, who had inspired Victor of Vita to write a history of the Vandalic persecution, was exiled to Gaul, and brought the text with him".

Wood confirmed the close association with Vandalic material and with the exile of Eugene of Carthage of the beginning of book II of Gregory of Tours' Histories; and *Schwarcz* noted "that there had to be a lot of persecution to extol the saintliness of Eugene", even though many people died, he referred to a passage "in which Victor of Vita [described] how people were confined in some sort of concentration camp".

References

Textual sources:

Hydatius

        Chronica: see Burgess (ed.) 1993.

Isidore

        Versus qui in biliotheca Sancti Isidori sunt: see Migne (ed.) 1850: col. 1107-1114.

John of Biclar

        Chronica: see Mommsen (ed.) 1994.

Julian of Toledo

        Historia Wambae: see Krusch & Levison 1910: 500-535.

Regula communis: see Campos Ruiz & Roca Melia (eds.) 1971.

Vitas sanctorum patrum Emeretensium: see Maya Sánchez (ed.)1992.

Bibliography:

Arrhenius, B.
   n.d.   Kinship and social relations in the early medieval period in Siealand. In *The Scandinavians from the Vendel Period to the Tenth Century: An Ethnographic Perspective.* Woodbridge: The Boydell Press.

Ausenda, G. (ed.)
   1995   Introduction. In *After Empire: Towards an Ethnology of Europe's Barbarians.* G. Ausenda (ed.), pp. 1-13. Woodbridge: The Boydell Press.

Bierbrauer, V.
   1994   Archäologie und Geschichte der Goten vom 1.-7. Jahrhundert. Versuch einer Bilanz. *Frühmittelalterliche Studien* 28: 166-171.

Burgess, R. W. (ed.)
   1993   *The Chronicle of Hydatius and the Consularia Constantinopolitana. Two contemporary accounts of the final years of the Roman Empire.* Oxford: Oxford University Press.

Campos Ruiz, J., & I. Roca Melia (eds.)
   1971   *San Leandro, San Isidoro, San Fructuoso. Reglas monasticas de la España visigoda.* Madrid: Bibliotheca de Autores Cristianos.

Collins, R.
   1995   *Early Medieval Spain. Unity in Diversity, 400-1000.* [2nd ed.]. Houndsmill/London: Macmillan Publishers.

Dams, P. B.
   1864-74   *Die Kirchengeschichte von Spanien*, Vol. 2, Teil 1 & 2. Regensburg: Georg Joseph Manz.

Heinzelmann, M.
   1976   *Bishofs Herrschaft in Gallien.* Munich: Artemis.
   1982   Gallische Prosopographie 260-527. *Francia* 10: 531-718.

Henning, J.
   1987   *Südosteuropa zwischen Antike und Mittelalter. Archäologische Beiträge zur Landwirtschaft des 1. Jahrtausends unserer Zeit.* (Schriften zur Ur- und Frühgeschichte, 42). Berlin: Akademie Verlag.

Koratcheva, T., & A. Haralambieva
   1992   Fibulae from the time of the great migrations of peoples in the Pleven Museum (Bulgaria). *Izvestija na Muzeite v severozapadna Bulgaria* 18: 45-55.

Krusch, B., & W. Levison. (eds.)
1910   *Passiones vitaeque sanctorum aevi Merovingici.* (III) *Monumenta Germaniae Historica. Scriptores rerum Merovingicarum,* 5. Hannover: Hahn.

Maya Sánchez, A. (ed.)
1992   *Vitas Sanctorum Patrum Emeretensium.* Corpus Christianorum Series Latina, CXVI. Turnhout: Brepols.

Menéndez Pidal, R. (ser. ed.)
1940   *Historia de España. III. España visigoda (414-711 de J.C.).* Madrid: Espasa Calpe S.A.

Migne, J.-P.
1850   *Sancti Isidori Hispalensis Episcopi opera omnia* - Tomus V. *Patrologiae cursus completus. Tomus LXXXIII.* Paris: Publisher in rue d'Amboise, près la barrière d'Enfer, ou Petit-Montrouge. [Repr. Turnhout: Brepols].

Nelson, J. L.
1991   À propos des femmes royales dans les rapports entre le monde wisigothique et le monde franc à l'époque de Reccared. In *Disciplina atque scientia de Toleto, XIV Centenario Concilio III de Toledo 589-1989.* Cartel anunciador del XIV Centenario del Concilio III de Toledo. Pp. 456-476. Madrid.

von Olberg, G.
1983   *Freie, Nachbarn und Gefolgsleute. Volkssprachliche Bezeichnungen aus dem sozialen Bereich in den frühmittelalterlichen Leges.* (Europäischen Hochschulschriften, Reihe 2, Rechtswissenschaften, Vol. 627). Frankfurt am Main/Berlin/New York: Lang.

Ortega, A.
1961   Los *Versus Isidori. Helmantica* 38: 261-299.

Pérez Pujol, E.
1896   *Historia de las Instituciones Sociales de la España Goda,* 4 Vols. Valencia: F. Vives Mora.

Riché, P.
1962   *Éducation et culture dans l'Occident barbare, VI-VIII siècles.* Paris: Éditions du Seuil.

1979   *Les écoles et l'enseignement dans l'Occident chrétien de la fin du Ve siècle au milieu du Xe siècle.* Paris: Auber Montaigne.

Schäferdiek, K.
1967   *Die Kirchen in den Reichen der Westgoten und Sueven bis zur Errichtung der westgotischen katholischen Staatskirche.* Berlin: Walter de Gruyter.

Schmidt-Wiegand, R.
1979   Die volksprachlichen Wörter der Leges barbarorum als Ausdruck sprachlicher Interferenz. *Frühmittelalterliche Studien* 13: 56-87.

Schwarcz, A.
n.d.   Beziehungen zwischen Ostrogothen und Visigothen. *Integration und Herrschaft im frühen Mittelalter.* M. Diesenberger & W. Pohl (eds.). (Denkschriften der ÖAW). Vienna: Verlag der Österreichische Akademie der Wissenschaften.

Stroheker, K. F.
1948   *Der senatorische Adel im spätantiken Gallien.* Tübingen: Alma Mater Verlag.

Velázquez, I.
1994   Ambitos y ambientes de la cultura escrita en Hispania (s. VI). De Martin de Braga a Leandro de Sevilla. *Studia Ephemeridis Augustinianum 46: 329-351.*

Wallace-Hadrill
    1952   *The Barbarian West 400-1000.* Oxford: Basil Blackwell.
Wheeler, M.
    1954   *Rome Beyond the Imperial Frontiers.* London: Bell.
Ziegler, A. K.
    1930   *Church and State in Visigothic Spain.* Washington: The Catholic
                    University of America.

INDEX

Abduction; composition for - 154; marriage by - 137; of widow 148

Acacian schism 527

Acclamatio 369

Acculturation(ed) 181, 405, 406, 408, 461, 485, 488, 502; barbarian groups 139; Roman military - 94; to people of steppes 448

Acilii 96

Adaeratio 316

Administered trade 282

Administration; French colonial - 284; late Roman - 123, 284; Roman titles in - 333; Visigothic - 37, 280 n17

Adornment(s); male - 410; personal - 407, 409-412, 414, 421, 431, 442

Adultery(ers) 163-165, 192; law of - 384

Aeschylus; ref. to Scythian path 28

Aestii 20, 21

Aetius 98, 101-103

Affinal(es) kin 138, 142, 143

Africa; Alaric's attempt to reach - 328; Vandals in - 103, 434

Africae; comes - 96

Agde; Council of - 334

Age; legitimate - 162

Agila 335

Agnate(s); *gafan* 143

Agnatic; marriage 172; heirs 159; kin 138, 150, 161, 396

Agrarian; economy 312, 313; landscape 520

Agri deserti 98

Agricultural 87; & herding estates 409; practices 514; production 512; slaves 496

Agriculturalists; difficult to control 178

Agriculture 40, 214; city lived by - 119

Agro-pastoralists 144, 153

Agustus; -' death 193; -' penance 203

Ahistulf; law of - 188

Aiolphus 108

Alamanni 34, 140, 158, 360, 481, 483

Alan(s) 12, 15, 16, 19, 25, 36, 40, 47, 52 n12, 52-55, 63 n28, 63-65, 81-83, 87, 96, 101, 102, 120; Gratian predilection for - troops 82; nomads 27, 28; peace with - 80

Alaric 45, 47, 50, 52, 54, 55, 57, 63-65, 73, 79, 82, 84-87, 94, 95, 118, 121, 263, 323, 330, 406; -'s advance on Italy 51; -'s attempt to reach Africa 328; -'s burial 328; -'s *foedus* w. Arcadius 327; -'s followers 455; -'s force 49n; -'s funeral 463; -'s invasion of Italy 49 n8; -'s revolt 48, 53, 77, 79; Balth 58; Christian 463; Goths of - 327; head of army 327; imitated Roman model 261; *iudex* 326; king(ship) 78, 119;

Alaric II 109, 213, 230, 263, 332, 333, 335; -'s *Breviarium* 226, 230, 236, 333, 509; -'s defeat at Vouillé 334

Alatheus 46, 47, 50, 52 n12, 54, 56, 81, 84

Alaviv 46, 79, 85, 324; across Danube w. Fritigern 455, 469

Alfonso III; 373 n1

Alliance(s); broke down in 680 in Toledo 374; bw lineages 150; forbidden - 147; legitimize - 139; marriage - 162, 435, 436; Theoderic the Great's - by marriage 185

Allies; Paul's Frankish - 381, 383; Visigothic - 378

Alliteration(s) 84, 85

Alloys; different - 441, 442

Amal(s) 45, 56, 86, 87, 323; dynasty 87; family 57; genealogy 13; Ostrogoth - 55; princess 87

Amalaric 66, 334, 335

Amalasuentha 86; murder of - 527

Amalfi 276; merchants 277

Amber; road 15, 26; trade 20

Ambrose; St - of Milan 81, 391

Ammianus Marcellinus 16, 43, 46, 47, 52 n12, 63 n28, 66 n31, 76, 82, 118, 324, 325, 356, 358, 360, 361, 397, 449, 454, 469, 470, 507; battles in - 361; Julian's army officer 484

Amphorae; North African - 276

Amulets; bone - 447

Anagrip; unchaste treatment of woman 154

Anaolsus 98

Ancestors; *anses* - of leaders 448, 450; cult of - of *kuni* 449; Goths shouted *laudes* to - 449

Ancestresses; witches - of Huns 449

Andalus; coins in al - 291

Angels; slates with mention of - 308

Anglo-Saxon(s); burial rite 421; examples by Bede 460; invasion 28; special treatment accorded to - 491

Anicii 96 n3, 105

Animal(s); designs 419; griffin type - 416; style 525; themes 421

Annonae 116

Anointing(ment) 368, 369, 376, 394, 400, 401, 505; Celts - 392; legitimacy to king 393; of Pippin 373; ritual(s) 393, 399; Wamba's - 379

Anses; ancestors 448, 450

Anthemius 108

Anti-Jewish; Justinian's - legislation 396

Antiochene; in 341 second - formula 451

Antiquus mos 381, 387, 399

Aoric 85

Apotropaic function 424

Appellation; last - king 268

Application; of law 221, 227; of Roman law 264

531

Jacket photo: *courtesy of Nukhet Targan Samaja showing base of Constantinople circus* spina *with haut-relief of Theodosius, his family and court being paid homage by eastern and western barbarians*
Maps: *P. De Orlando, I - Novate Milanese (MI)*
Page setting: *Alta Qualità sas, I - 20144 Milano*
Phototypesetting: *Fotoedit srl, Serravalle (RSM)*
Printers: *Studiostampa S.A., Serravalle (RSM)*